Impolite Learning

LIBRAI. de FRAN. L'HONO. LIBRAI. de JAQ. DESBOR.

Devant de la Bourse d'Amsterdam

IMPOLITE LEARNING

Conduct and Community in the Republic of Letters
1680–1750

ANNE GOLDGAR

Yale University Press
New Haven & London

Designed by Gillian Malpass
Set in Linotron Bembo by Best-set Typesetter Ltd., Hong Kong
Printed and bound at the Bath Press, Avon, Great Britain

Library of Congress Cataloging-in-Publication Data
Goldgar, Anne.
Impolite learning : conduct and community in the Republic of
Letters, 1680–1750/Anne Goldgar.
Includes bibliographical references (p.) and index.
ISBN 0-300-05359-2
1. Europe—Intellectual life—17th century.   2. Europe—
Intellectual life—18th century.   3. Learning and scholarship—
Europe—History—17th century.   4. Learning and scholarship—
Europe—History—18th century.   5. Enlightenment.   I. Title.
CB203.G64   1995
94-48269
001′.1′09409032-dc20
CIP

A catalogue record for this book is available from
The British Library

Frontispiece: The *libraires* of François l'Honoré and Jaques Desbordes
in Amsterdam. From J.P. Ricard, *Les loix et les coutumes*
du change des principales places de l'Europe
(Amsterdam, 1715)

For Professor J.P. Watson

CONTENTS

Je ne promets rien; il y a beaucoup de Sçavans, qui ne sont pas traitables, & qui ne sont pas portés à communiquer la moindre chose; mais je n'aime pas ces humeurs farouches.

Gisbert Cuper

J'avouë . . . que de la maniere dont la Litterature est mênée aujourd'huy par je ne sais combien de Gens peu dignes de s'en mêler en degoute presque absolum^t & feroit quasi regretter de savoir lire: mais c'est un Inconvenient qui a toûjours été & sera toûjours, & dans la Republique des Lettres comme dans la Republique Civile, il y aura toujours des fous & des furieux pour faire rire & pour tourmenter les autres.

Prosper Marchand

J'avouerai sans peine que leurs moeurs etoient grossières, leurs travaux quelquefois minutieux; que leur esprit noyé dans une érudition pédantesque commentoit ce qu'il falloit sentir, et compiloit au-lieu de raisonner. On étoit assés éclairé pour sentir l'utilité de leurs recherches, mais l'on n'étoit ni assés raisonable ni assés poli, pour connoître qu'elles auroient pû être guidées par le flambeau de la Philosophie.

Edward Gibbon

ACKNOWLEDGEMENTS

To be an academic writing about academia is a peculiar experience. Everything you do, and everything everyone else does, becomes charged with
special meaning and ripe for analysis. It is particularly strange to write the
acknowledgements for this book, given the way they could be construed as
a claim of a *commerce très bon*. All I can say is that my friends feel it necessary
to remind me constantly that we are not living in the ideal Republic of
Letters; that I have been the recipient of many kindnesses; and that I hope
here to be able to express my great *reconnoissance*.

The Republic of Letters is large, and it would have been impossible to
explore it without the generous financial help of a number of institutions. I
would like to thank the Krupp Foundation of Essen, Germany, and the
Center for European Studies, Harvard University, for a Krupp Fellowship in
1985–6; the Fulbright Commission and the Netherlands-America Commission for a Fulbright Grant to the Netherlands in 1986–7; the Josephine de
Kármán Memorial Foundation for a grant in 1988–9; New York University
for an Arts and Sciences Faculty Fellowship in 1989–91; and Clare Hall,
Cambridge, for a Research Fellowship in 1991–3. My parents have also
invested huge sums in this project; I am enormously grateful and only wish
I could pay a dividend.

The example and encouragement of my three great mentors gives me
hope for the existence of an ideal Republic of Letters. Natalie Davis, whom
I had the good fortune to encounter first as an undergraduate, has inspired
me both through her vision of the past and through her extraordinary
generosity to younger scholars. Simon Schama, who supervised the 1990
thesis on which this book is based, has kept me going with equal doses
of enthusiasm and entertainment; his imaginative approach to history constantly informs my own thinking. John Brewer has been enormously helpful,
challenging and refining my ideas even while giving me opportunities to

express them. I consider myself extremely fortunate to have had three such teachers.

The conversation and comments of a large number of scholars contributed to my thinking in this book. Some of them I spoke to only once or only briefly, but their ideas helped me to think about my material in different ways. I would particularly like to thank John Brewer, Elizabeth Eisenstein, Graham Gibbs, Bertrand Goldgar, Dena Goodman, Roland Greene, Michael Hunter, Jim Secord, and the Literary Culture Reading Group at NYU (Tom Bender, Alice Fahs, and Marc Aronson) for giving me comments on drafts of my work. I have profited from conversations with (among others) Christiane Berkvens-Stevelinck, Hans Bots, A.R. Braunmuller, Jack Censer, Cathy Crawford, Michèle Cohen, Robert Darnton, Frank van Deyk, Tom Ertman, Mordechai Feingold, David Feldman, Jeff Freedman, Graham Gibbs, Dena Goodman, Tony Grafton, Michael Harris, Steve Jaffe, Adrian Johns, Larry Klein, Dilwyn Knox, Joe Levine, Susan Pedersen, James Raven, Craig Rodine, Jerrold Seigel, Larry Stewart, Naomi Tadmor, Jay Tribby, Michael Treadwell, Tim Wales, Françoise Waquet, Valerie Worth, and Frouke Wieringa. My knowledge of the history of science benefited greatly from talking to Patricia Fara, Michael Hunter, Simon Schaffer, Jim Secord, and Joan Steigerwald. I am very grateful to Michèle Cohen, Lorraine Daston, Dena Goodman, Daniel Gordon, Adrian Johns, and Simon Schaffer for allowing me to read their unpublished work. Julia Walworth and David d'Avray went beyond the call of friendship in their help with emergency translation; Kelly Boyd and Lane Barrow were generous with their computer help.

Thanks are also due to the staffs of the many libraries and archives I used, for all their help and kindness. I would particularly like to thank the staff of the former Deutsche Staatsbibliothek's manuscript room for allowing me to read manuscripts during a closed week; the staff of the Dousakamer at the Universiteitsbibliotheek, Leiden, for accommodating my many requests and my computer; and the staff of the Bibliothèque Wallonne for offering to open on extra days for me. The North Library and Manuscript Room staff at the British Library constantly confirmed my love of that library; I mourn its passing.

My thanks also go to my editor, Gillian Malpass, for her kindness, patience, enthusiasm, and imagination.

I certainly could not have finished this book (a very lengthy process) if I had not had the moral support of my friends and colleagues. My thanks go to all my friends in the Harvard History Department, Dudley House, the NYU History Department, Clare Hall, and the Institute of Historical Research; I am indebted to all my colleagues at King's College London for providing me with such a congenial environment in which to finish a book.

I would particularly like to thank Carrie Alyea, Noëlle Arrangoiz, Lane Barrow, Lee Bliss, Kelly Boyd, A.R. Braunmuller, Arthur Burns, Tony Claydon, Michèle Cohen, Stefan Collini, Cathy Crawford, David Daniell, Lee Davison, Gordon DesBrisay, Nicola di Cosmo, Patricia Fara, David Feldman, Camilla Finn, Bob Frankel, Elizabeth Honig, Steve Jaffe, Jean Marsden, Steve Maughan, Rohan McWilliam, Jinty Nelson, Susan Pedersen, James Raven, Joan Steigerwald, Sarah Stockwell, Naomi Tadmor, Frouke Wieringa, Jo Udall, Amanda Vickery, Tim Wales, Julia Walworth, and Betsy Wieseman.

My parents have been immensely supportive in every way; I am lucky to have them, and cannot begin to express how grateful I am for their encouragement and help. They always believed in me, even when I did not. It has been particularly nice to have my father working in the North Library with me, where he would read me funny passages and look things up for me. When I think of this project I will always think of that. To the rest of my family—Ben, Marci, Sarah, and Leah—I send thanks for keeping me amused.

If Professor Watson doesn't know how much I owe him, then he hasn't been listening.

King's College London
November 1994

ABBREVIATIONS

AN	Archives Nationales, Paris
ARA	Algemeen Rijksarchief, The Hague
BCUL	Bibliothèque cantonale et universitaire, Lausanne
Bibl SHPF	Bibliothèque de la Société de l'Histoire du Protestantisme Français, Paris
BJK	Biblioteka Jagiellónska, Kraków
BL	British Library, London
BN	Bibliothèque Nationale, Paris
BVBBB	Bibliotheek van de Vereeniging tot de Bevordering van de Belangen des Boekhandels, Amsterdam
BW	Bibliothèque Wallonne, Amsterdam
DSB	The former Deutsche Staatsbibliothek (now Staatsbibliothek Preussischer Kulturbesitz, Haus 1), Berlin
GA Amst	Gemeentearchief, Amsterdam
GA Den Haag	Gemeentearchief, The Hague
GL	Guildhall Library, London
Gen BPU	Bibliothèque publique et universitaire, Geneva
KB	Koninklijke Bibliotheek, The Hague
NSLB	Niedersachsische Landesbibliothek, Hannover
Neu BPU	Bibliothèque publique et universitaire, Neuchâtel
SMHR	Société du Musée Historique de la Réformation, Geneva
SPK	Staatsbibliothek Preussischer Kulturbesitz, Haus 2, Berlin
UBA	Universiteitsbibliotheek, Amsterdam
UBL	Universiteitsbibliotheek, Leiden
ZAAWD	The former Zentrales-Archiv der Akademie der Wissenschaften der DDR, Berlin

TEXTUAL NOTE

Unless otherwise noted, or unless both writer and recipient were English, all quotations from letters in the text have been translated by me from French. For quotations from printed works, titles will reveal whether or not a quotation was originally in English. Quotations in the notes have been left in the original French. I have attempted to preserve as much as possible the original syntax and punctuation in order to retain the flavor of quotations.

Original dating of letters has been retained. Nearly all are New Style.

PROLOGUE

As he approached his thirties, Charles-Etienne Jordan was getting increasingly depressed. Born in 1700 in Berlin to a family of Huguenot refugees, and possessing perhaps more ambition than ability, he desperately wanted to be a scholar. Unfortunately, his merchant father, who sent Jordan's two brothers into trade, assumed that (as Jordan's obituarists complained) "when you say a man of Letters, you mean a Minister or a Theologian."[1] "Without consulting Jordan's inclinations or talents," these eulogies all say, his father destined him for a career in the church. In 1725 he had to leave his pleasant student life in Villeneuve, the Huguenot quarter of Berlin, to become minister of the French church in Potzlau.[2] During his time there and, from 1727, at the French church in Prenzlau, he apparently did his best, but his correspondence suggests his mind was more on scholarly contacts than religion.[3] The death of his young wife, Suzanne Perrault, in 1732 was the final straw, and, dispirited, Jordan finally gave up his ministry and returned to Berlin.

He did not, however, remain there. Hoping to orient his life more directly toward arts and letters, as well as to dispel his gloom, Jordan took the advice, and funding, of his merchant brothers and in 1733 went on a six-month holiday. Travelling through northern Europe, he made major stops in Halle, Leipzig, Paris, London, Oxford, Amsterdam, and Leiden. But as these place-names might suggest, this was no ordinary journey, no grand tour: it was quite consciously a *voyage littéraire*. Jordan clearly had certain ends in view, and when he returned he wrote a book about his trip.[4]

The *voyage littéraire* was a tradition for students and scholars, particularly in the seventeenth century, and such luminaries as Fabricius, Vossius, Mersenne, and Gronovius had made such *voyages* in their time. Gronovius, who travelled with two students from 1639–42, toured England, France, Italy, and Germany, buying books, transcribing manuscripts, visiting centers of erudition, and meeting as many leading scholars as he could.[5] Clearly this was one way of getting to know the scholarly world. Jordan's account recognizes a potential conflict between this method and one that concentrated on reading books in the privacy of one's study; but Jordan was all for travel. "Some will say that time is wasted which could be used more fruitfully in the Cabinet . . . but, a Man who travels, with the object of visiting Libraries, of knowing Savant Men, of seeing Cabinets of the Curious, of visiting the Studios of famous Artists, of observing the Debris of Antiquity . . . a Man, in a word, who, in travelling, observes everything, who pays attention to everything, can he fear wasting his time?"[6]

There were no guidebooks for the Republic of Letters, as Jordan and his fellows called the scholarly world. Jordan's book might be considered a sort of guide, but he had no such direction when he set out in 1733. Yet his account suggests that he knew quite well what he was looking for; he did not need to be told what the Republic of Letters was.

Obviously the scholarly world had certain formal institutions, ones which, in Jordan's time, were increasing in number. From the middle of the seventeenth century in northern Europe, princes, governments, or scholarly associations were forming academies and learned societies;[7] and smaller literary clubs, such as the Société Anonyme or the Société Amusante in Berlin, sprang up across the continent.[8] A participant in the Société Amusante told a prospective member that "the society . . . does not merit the name of Academy, It is just a Society of young Men, who assemble regularly every Wednesday at the home of one of the members, and who have as their goal instructing and diverting themselves at the same time."[9] In the same period literary journals began to proliferate—some of which, such as the *Bibliothèque germanique* and the *Journal littéraire*, were written by literary societies.[10] The news they provided bound the communal network still more tightly together. Jordan could participate in the Republic of Letters by meeting scholars, reading and discussing journals, visiting academies, libraries, bookshops, universities, cabinets of curiosities. But this collection of sites was not the Republic of Letters, merely a space within which the Republic could exist. Jordan knew quite well that the Republic of Letters was more than this.

For historians today, however, the Republic of Letters is not so easy to define. The term first appeared in its Latin form in the fifteenth century and was used increasingly in the sixteenth and seventeenth, so that by the end of that century it featured in the titles of several important literary journals.[11] But its definition can only be gleaned from usage, for it had no formal manifestation. Unlike an academy or literary society, it existed only in the minds of its members. Its regulations and even its membership were nebulous at best, and any contemporary definition tended to be articulated in protest at the violation of these unwritten rules, suggesting, among other things, that they were as well-defined as they were usually unexpressed.

Certain broad features can, however, be painted into the picture of the Republic of Letters. The existence of communal standards highlights the first of these: that the scholarly world considered itself to be in some ways separate from the rest of society.[12] Seventeenth- and eighteenth-century scholars felt that, at least in the academic realm, they were not subject to the norms and values of the wider society. Unlike their non-scholarly counterparts, they thought they lived in an essentially egalitarian community, in which all members had equal rights to criticize the work and conduct of others. In practice this egalitarian ideal was not so solid, but the hierarchical structure the community did take on was based on different standards from society at large. Moreover, the Republic of Letters in theory ignored distinctions of nationality and religion. The chronologist Alphonse des Vignoles said that, although he was a Protestant minister, he treated other scholars with justice, "be they Protestants, be they Catholics, without any regard to the difference of Religion."[13] The learned world was one world, international and nondenominational, rising above the petty concerns of church and state. Or so, at least, scholars claimed.

This does not mean that members of the Republic of Letters were not part of the larger society. Indeed, most had no choice when making their living, as writing as a profession was scarcely established in this period. Some savants taught at universities and academies or worked in aristocratic or institutional libraries. Many others were involved in the church, as ministers, priests, or monks. Educated young Protestant refugees often also found employment tutoring the children of the gentry and the aristocracy. In general we can say that the population of the community was bourgeois and professional, and, although its interests were catholic, they tended more to the humanities than the sciences.

But these distinctions do not help us in the problem of determining who might be a member of the community. As Robert Darnton has written: "what, after all, is a writer? Someone who has written a book, someone who depends on writing for a living, someone who claims the title, or someone on whom posterity has bestowed it?"[14] The difficulty is even greater for the Republic of Letters, in which people might participate without writing at all. It appears that—as Dena Goodman has also said of the Enlightenment community—someone became a man of letters simply through self-election.[15] Maarten Ultee believes that this participation had to consist of scholarly correspondence,[16] but, as Jordan found, personal contact could be an even better means of entering the community. A mental identification with the Republic of Letters might even result from simply following the *nouvelles littéraires* in the journals. Those who took an interest belonged to the community, but their status in that community did indeed depend on their contacts with other scholars.

We can see this by looking back at the *voyage littéraire*. Savants could travel
for many reasons, such as the collection of material for a book, as in the case
of the ecclesiastical historian Jacques Lenfant; or the purchase of books, the
object of the collector Zacharias Conrad von Uffenbach; or, most commonly, the viewing of antiquities, libraries, and cabinets of curiosities. But in
all cases, scholars went to see their fellows in foreign lands. Uffenbach, for
example, visited at least seventy-two learned men during his trip in 1710,
and, according to his *éloge*, even did research on their interests beforehand in
order to keep them talking. Failing such artifices, the *éloge* confides, "most of
the visits which even the most distinguished Savants receive, are the most
laborious & the most boring thing imaginable."[17] Jordan, despite the width of
his definition of such a *voyage*, was notably single-minded in his pursuit of his
goal. Sightseeing was for the frivolous; so that he wrote of his visit to
London, "I saw St. Paul's Church: I won't say anything about it, because my
Goal is only to speak about Books, and about Literature."[18] Like his predecessor Gronovius, who had hated monuments and tourism, and in his letters
barely mentioned exciting incidents like being attacked by pirates,[19] Jordan
wanted to see sites of scholarly interest. For both, these consisted of nothing
other than scholars themselves. This concentration was a subject of praise for
his obituarists.

> [H]e did not limit himself to seeing Palaces, to contemplating Edifices, to
> making himself the Spectator of various Ceremonies different from those
> of this country, the only fruit most Young People's frivolity & lack of
> discernment gather from their voyages. . . . He only fixed himself on
> knowing the great Men, whose great Wit, whose elevation of Genius and
> Erudition, make them the honor of their Country & their Century.[20]

For Jordan, the ambitious young scholar, these contacts would naturally be
useful. His teacher, Maturin Veyssière La Croze, made this plain enough in
a letter printed at the front of the *Histoire d'un voyage littéraire*. "I will not
speak to you here," he wrote, "of all the Illustrious Scholars whose Acquaintance you have procured. It is too vast a field. You alone are the one who
must cultivate it."[21] But even more important is the conception of the
Republic of Letters implied by all this. For Jordan and his colleagues, the
scholarly community was foremost a collection of people. This collection was
tied together by certain shared values which were created by the interactions
among its members. Thus, more than the people themselves, or their works,
or their specific connections, it is important for us to look at the interactions
of citizens of the Republic of Letters to understand what the community
really was.

Although it is true that intellectual history has always included an interest
in the interaction of literary figures, in the past this has generally confined

itself to a curiosity about the personal relationships of particular individuals and, potentially, the resulting effects on their ideas. The central issue—obviously important—has been to uncover meaning. Thus any interest in the interconnections of scholars has aimed at the discovery of intellectual influences rather than social patterns. Moreover, the content of an author's writings has usually been considered of much greater interest than the sociocultural context of his work. The text has been thought to contain all meaning, even if that meaning was not intentional. But the meaning, or the identity, of an intellectual community is not necessarily to be found only in its writings. To assume otherwise is to beg an important question, and to impose our own discourse about intellectual life on another era. We must read between the lines, and ask whether scholars' world view was really entirely structured around the subject matter they discussed. We must consider whether the establishment of meaning was in fact the dominant motivation for members of the Republic of Letters.

Examining the social rather than primarily the intellectual component of scholarly communities is, of course, not new. In recent years historians have become more interested in the structures of the literary world and the place of authors in society. Sociability, particularly in Enlightenment circles, has proven of particular interest to scholars such as Robert Darnton and Daniel Roche, whose valuable essays provide us with details of institutional and individual strategies within the Republic of Letters.[22] The earlier period, moreover, is beginning to be explored fruitfully by such scholars as Françoise Waquet and Hans Bots.[23] Their work has begun to paint a picture of what it was like to live in particular moments in the history of the literary world. These more specialized studies have been pursued further by Dena Goodman and Daniel Gordon, whose work has focussed on the importance of ideas of sociability to Enlightenment circles.[24] They concentrate overwhelmingly on the Enlightenment, however, and consequently on a period when an intellectual and political program of sorts was integral to the intellectual scene.[25] Basing their work on Habermas' notion of a public sphere and the importance of public opinion, they see civility and sociability as notions which provided social space for political discussion. These studies provide valuable insights into what the Republic of Letters turns into in the second part of the eighteenth century: the "seriousness of purpose" which Goodman describes in her work.[26] But the Enlightenment Republic of Letters was based on very different ideas about the purpose of scholarship than the Republic of Letters of the earlier century.

In some ways the older Republic of Letters, as Habermas suggests, did witness the elaboration of institutions which helped to breed what utimately became the public sphere. Eventually, from the world of learning, literature, and the press, we begin to see a discursive relationship developing between private individuals and the social and political fabric. But the transition was not easy, and it did not necessarily proceed as Habermas describes. Habermas characterizes this development as a process of bourgeois class formation, which was ultimately expressed in the French Revolution. This picture must be modified on several counts. First, as considerable recent work has suggested, the political discourse in eighteenth-century France, at least, cannot accurately be termed "bourgeois."[27] Even if it were, however, the *érudit* Republic of Letters would not have fallen into this category. Although we can identify the general social origins and milieu of most scholars as bourgeois, that does not mean that they were self-consciously members of a bourgeoisie, and indeed their whole ethos entailed a redefinition of status according to the norms of their own community. The older Republic of Letters also did not operate in the fashion of Habermas' public sphere. The "public" my scholars cared about was each other. Their work was not primarily directed at public utility, their ideal society was not intended for general emulation, and the political aspect of their lives was to be divorced absolutely from their scholarship. Moreover, and crucially, the discourse in Habermas' public sphere was increasingly to be judged not on the identities of the speakers, but rather on the quality of their arguments. But in many cases, I would suggest, the opposite proves true in the earlier Republic of Letters, where content sometimes proved too problematic for the spotlight of public scrutiny. The situation was quite different later; and both the fragmentary nature of our picture of the whole Republic of Letters and the differences between the Enlightenment and its predecessor invite further inquiry about what overriding values linked the earlier scholarly community.

*   *   *

This book tries to look at the Republic of Letters of the late seventeenth and early eighteenth centuries on the most fundamental level. Its goal is to explore the informal institutions of the community. For Jordan and his colleagues, the Republic of Letters was not located—for example—in the Société Royale des Sciences in Berlin, but in the relations among its members and among other scholars, the quarrels, gossip, dinners, lending of books and sharing of information. Most important, the Republic was located in the values and attitudes which shaped these interactions and formed the concept of the community in the minds of its members. These values articulated quite clearly what was right or wrong, what was correct procedure, who was behaving well or badly. Jordan held these values; they are for us to discover.

This book argues that, in the transitional period between the seventeenth century and the Enlightenment, the most important common concern of members of the Republic of Letters was their own conduct. In the conception of its own members, ideology, religion, political philosophy, scientific strategy, or any other intellectual or philosophical framework were not as important as their own identity as a community. When it was necessary to choose between the content of ideas and the formal construction of scholarly society, savants frequently chose the way of moderation, concentration on form. This was obviously not always the case; Huguenot refugees, for example, had clearly made major sacrifices for their ideas. But as we will see, even that sacrifice did not negate a necessity for scholarly cooperation and the ignoring of differences. Communal bonds were the focus of community; the Republic of Letters was a reflexive event.

Recent historical work, particularly in the history of science, has paid increasing attention to questions of form.[28] Steven Shapin, in particular, both in his contribution to *Leviathan and the Air-Pump*, jointly written with Simon Schaffer, and in his recent articles and new book, *A Social History of Truth*, has concentrated on the role of civility in science in the seventeenth century.[29] In this important work he locates civility in science within the debate over the experimental life, arguing that in order to show the validity of experiment, it was necessary to provide authority for experiment (both experiment in general, and experiments in particular). Because of the social values of the period, experiments had to be authenticated by those known to be of gentlemanly stock, and therefore of gentlemanly bearing. The conduct of gentlemen thus became a crucial component of seventeenth-century science.

This convincing argument locates civility within an argument about epistemology. It also locates it within a specific context: the particular scientific projects of the Boylean camp in the Royal Society. The question is whether, when thinking of the whole Republic of Letters, we can use this causality to explain the importance of conduct. Does the stress on behavior have to stem from meaning? The work of Shapin and Schaffer suggests a progression from the particular view of how knowledge was to be constructed to the way the community of knowledge ought to be constructed.

Outside the scientific community, however, the same period also saw a much wider concern in society about issues of civil conduct. Much recent work, springing from Norbert Elias' *The Civilizing Process*, has emphasized the way that changing social and economic conditions in the late medieval and early modern periods brought about a new refinement of manners and the development of elaborate codes of courtesy.[30] The concentration in all fields of scholarship on form rather than content, exchange rather than the thing exchanged, moderation rather than vituperation in argument, suggests that civility was of much more fundamental importance to the Republic of Letters than merely a demonstration of party affiliation. Methods of conducting research and even particular political, religious, or even intellectual moments may have been less important in the long run than a general focus

on civility as a mode of social cohesion. Thus when historians locate particular modes of sociability in the question of whether (for example) one was a
radical or a conservative in politics and religion, as Margaret Jacob does, the
lines of the community are drawn too narrowly.[31] My view of the people
Jacob labels as radical in *The Radical Enlightenment*, people who also in part
populate this book, is that they are in fact conservative. They are not
necessarily conservative in politics and religion, although it is clear that some
of Jacob's "radicals" were actually conservative in these areas,[32] but, rather, in
their conception of their own society. Members of the Republic of Letters
used social techniques to draw closer together, not necessarily out of innovation, but out of self-protection. The emphasis on behavior preceded and
underlay all their other activities.

This kind of ideology means that relationships between individuals on a
micro, day-to-day level would be the most important defining element of the
community to its own members. Thus although we can place various scholars
and scientists in different religious, political, or philosophical camps, I would
argue that individual citizens of the Republic of Letters in the late seventeenth and early eighteenth centuries identified much more strongly with the
concept of a community to be defended by behavioral rules than with these
subsets of that community. Consequently the place to look for communal
values is interactions among scholars.

This book thus concentrates at least in part on the mundane, the everyday
contacts of scholars in correspondence and in fact. It looks at the chance
encounters, the trivial errands, the offhand comments, by which scholars
revealed their own assumptions about the structure, function, and dynamics
of their own community. But the mundane is not everything; for of course
the harmony of the ideal was rarely achieved in reality.[33] Despite the reiter-
ation of the need for communal politeness, scholars were frequently rude,
one reason why civility was so often urged. Gilbert Burnet may have
eventually apologized to the French historian Le Grand, with whom he was
battling in print, but in 1689 he did not spare his opponent.

I perceive . . . that this hot Summer, and his extraordinary Application,
have so dryed his Brain, and given him such an overflowing of the Gall,
that all the answer I can bestow on him, is to wish his Friends to look to
him, and keep him from running about the Streets, for he is in a fair way
to that. They will do well to Bleed him over and over again, to give him
some inward Refrigeratives, and now and then a few Grains of *Laudanum*,
and to take a special care of him at New and Full Moons. Pen, Ink, and
Paper must be kept from him as poyson, for these things set his Head so
a going, that his Fits redouble upon him at every time that he gets them
in his hands. But, above all things, care must be taken not to name me, nor

the *Bibliotheque Universels* to him, for that will certainly bring on him a most violent Paroxisme; and he being Young, and so mightily in love with himself, good Air and good Keeping, may at last bring him out of this Raving Distemper. So to be sure I will have no more to do with a Man that writes like a Lunatick.[34]

Burnet censured Le Grand for writing "like a Lunatick," forgiving him only after receiving "a Civil Message" from him years later;[35] but his own expressions hardly demonstrated a balanced civility. Both facts are significant here. Since values tend to be revealed when they are challenged, a major portion of this book concerns examples of flagrant disregard for communal norms, the outrageous, egregious behavior so often displayed by scholars in all periods to the delighted disgust of their colleagues. Along the way we will encounter plagiarism, theft, impersonation, and a host of other problems within the community. These incidents point out to us both flaws in the system and the system itself; infuriated comments about the breaking of rules will introduce us to the concepts of propriety which bound the Republic of Letters together. The analysis is complicated even further by the belief in the usefulness of debate and the fact that ideas about conflict and consensus were continually in dialogue with each other.

To discuss these issues we will focus particularly on Huguenot refugees who were scholars or writers. These refugees, or their families, left France at the Revocation of the Edict of Nantes to resettle in Protestant countries, particularly England, Switzerland, the Netherlands, and Brandenburg-Prussia. The Huguenots make a good case study for a number of reasons. Their attitudes toward scholarship and the behavior of scholars seem to have been fairly typical of the period, so that their correspondence and literary activity can serve as a sample of the way savants thought about their world. Some Huguenots, moreover, had special roles within the Republic of Letters. They acted as intermediaries between scholars, kept the community informed about itself by writing literary journals, and popularized, translated, and generally shaped the canons of better-known figures. By examining these roles in some depth we are able to explore not only the everyday mechanics of both formal and informal institutions, but such fundamentals as attitudes toward reciprocal duties and obligations and the group's hierarchical structure. Finally, the Huguenots were in a special position to test the assumptions and roles of the Republic of Letters. Although as scholars and "citizens" of the Republic they were bound by an ethos of international and nonsectarian cooperation, as Protestants and exiles they often held an entirely different set of political and religious allegiances. The way they handled these competing demands is an illuminating commentary on the dynamics of the Republic of Letters.

The appearance of a far-flung community of Huguenots produced links which added to the cohesiveness of the Republic of Letters. An examination of their role adds to our understanding of the period of transition at the beginning of the eighteenth century. Despite the post-Hazard recognition that this period constitutes a "crise de conscience européenne," studies of scholarly communities have continued to concentrate either on the scientific world of the seventeenth century or the established Enlightenment society of the mid- to later eighteenth century. It is almost assumed (particularly by backdating the Enlightenment into the early part of the century) that the transition from one period to the other was smooth, indeed almost inevitable. But if we again look on a micro level, we can see the difficulty with which the scholarly world made this transition. Most studies of the period point to the institutionalization of scholarly activities, with the foundation of journals, academies, reading societies, all contributing to the professionalization of scholarship. And indeed, as I argue here particularly in relation to agency and communication, institutions *did* develop which crystallized certain relationships within the community. But the very fact that the Republic of Letters concentrated on the personal made it very difficult to abandon individual relationships for more institutional identifications. Consequently institutions became personalized, with academies, journals, even the Republic of Letters itself becoming "people" who were expected to behave according to certain rules. The emphasis on the personal was thus not simply a minor feature of the Republic of Letters. It helped to define the community itself and the way its institutions developed in this crucial intellectual moment. The battle between the Ancients and the Moderns, usually defined as an intellectual debate, was also a battle about personal style, about the nature of social interaction.[36]

To view the conduct of personal relationships as fundamental to the Republic of Letters lets us see its behaviors in a new light. It explains Uffenbach's preparatory research on his learned hosts. He did not visit other scholars to learn anything special; he did not visit them because he liked them; he fully expected to be bored. He visited them because establishing contact, making exchanges, was what scholars did. In the same spirit Jordan ventured off into the Republic of Letters to meet its members. He had no project, unless we can call it a project that he wanted, by talking about anything and everything, by gaining control of information, to see scholars and become one of them. We will hear more of him later, but for now we can assume that his enthusiasm was for scholars, not for scholarship. He is admittedly an extreme example—the nineteenth-century bibliographer Robert Watt called him "a person distinguished more by his connections than his Works"[37]—but his general attitude toward the Republic of Letters does echo a tendency in his colleagues. Gisbert Cuper perhaps summed up this attitude best in a letter to Maturin Veyssière La Croze in 1710. The goal for him, he said, was not to publish; rather, it was to know things and to have something to say to people when writing letters.[38] Communication, not the thing communicated, was his focus. The community, not any project, was the goal.

Charles-Etienne Jordan set off on his tour of the Republic of Letters glad to gather any information and gossip he could. His goals in researching and writing the *Histoire* were to present the Republic of Letters to his readers and to have an enjoyable journey. In the end, he wrote only a mediocre book, though it did cheer him up. In our own journey we will explore the same territory as Jordan. Let us hope it will better accomplish both of his goals.

1

PHILOSOPHICAL TRANSACTIONS

THE REPUBLIC OF LETTERS AS A COMMUNITY
OF OBLIGATION

Honor Me with your Commissions

Imagine a young minister living in 1715 in the Pays de Vaud. He enjoys his work and is delighted already to have his share of time in the pulpit. But in his spare time, his thoughts are on other things. He is translating a little Horace, and he takes a special interest in antiquities. One day a parishioner brings him a fascinating medal he has dug up in his garden. The minister has his conjectures about its origin and meaning—no doubt from one of the Roman incursions into the region—but it is hard to be sure about details. Still, he feels a piece on the medal would make an interesting contribution to a literary journal or even a book.

As a young man living away from a major town, he is faced with a number of barriers to his scholarship. He does not have enough books on the subject of medals to assist him with his new project. He lives too far from either Geneva or Lausanne to make consultation at the academies practicable in the near future. He has no personal acquaintance with any scholars who would have specialist knowledge of this subject; his friends in the ministry show interest but can be of little help, and his old professors know more about theology than antiquities. And even if he is able to make valid conclusions about the medal, he is unsure how to publish them. He reads the journals avidly when they come to his part of the world, but he is timid about sending a contribution to, say, the *libraire* in Amsterdam who publishes the *Histoire critique de la République des Lettres* if he does not even know the authors' names.

Feelings of isolation in the Republic of Letters were often acute. Our hypothetical minister no doubt felt that proximity to Lausanne and its academy would help his research. Yet in 1716 the jurist Jean Barbeyrac lamented living in Lausanne rather than Berlin, since he could not find a copy of Van der Meulen's edition of Grotius. "If I were in Berlin, I would have no trouble finding either this book nor many others I might need. I would have the Bibliothèque du Roi, that of M^r. de Spanheim, currently also the king's, & various other libraries of individuals; so that it would be quite unlikely that what I was looking for would not be in one or the other of them."[1] But for those living there, even Berlin was not sufficiently at the center of things. Maturin Veyssière La Croze, librarian of the Bibliothèque du Roi so vaunted by Barbeyrac, wrote the politician and scholar Gisbert Cuper in Deventer, "Without you, Monsieur, & without several other friends I would know virtually nothing about what goes on in the Republic of Letters. The erudition of this country is reduced almost entirely to the pretensions of Princes, to Genealogies, and to politics. It is, I assure you, a lamentable thing sometimes to hear the reasoning of people raised up here as men of letters, & even elevated to quite distinguished positions for their supposed learning."[2]

Lausanne had no good libraries, Berlin no good scholars: the complaints were similar for many places condemned by their residents as "infertile in Curiosities, & in curious people."[3] Scholars hungered for news from the greener grasses of other locales. As Lambert Douxfils wrote from Brussels in 1752, "far from being indifferent to *nouvelles littéraires*, they are my principal consolation in my ill-fortune."[4] Given the scattered residence of scholars, the unavailability of books, the difficulty of travel, and the sometimes mystifying nature of the book trade, it is no wonder that the fictitious minister in the Vaudois is bewildered over where to turn with his medal. Indeed, it is difficult to imagine how such a fragmented Republic of Letters could have conceived of itself as a community.

Yet ties did bind this disparate community together. Formal institutions, such as academies, literary societies, and journals, reinforced the strong sense of communal identity pervading the Republic of Letters. But an important, indeed crucial, link among members of the community was not so much an institution as an attitude. The key is in La Croze's words to Cuper, a scholar he never met. "Without you, Monsieur, & without several other friends," he said, he could not manage in the Republic of Letters. The scholarly community was a community of obligation: mutual assistance between members was a constant theme, and the phrase "honor me with your commissions" echoes continually through the correspondence of the period.[5] In this chapter we will examine the communal bonds forged through service and agency, and the new professionalism brought to these connections by the eighteenth century.

The practical function of such a system is apparent. Almost any scholar doing specialized work was bound to need materials he could not find at home. The hypothetical minister in the Vaudois is a good case in point. His problem is particularly vexing because he is almost completely isolated from books and from fellow scholars. However, the network of obligation in the Republic of Letters, once entered, could at least in theory make available ways of solving all his difficulties.

And in fact the probable course taken by such a young scholar would be to consult other people almost immediately. In the minister's case, his colleagues have no specific knowledge, but perhaps one of them makes the suggestion to write to one of his professors at the Genevan Academy. Although the professor might have only limited knowledge on the subject of Roman imperial medals and inscriptions, his wide correspondence in the learned world means that he is on good terms with a number of people who can help. These kinds of introductions were important in the Republic of Letters. In 1714, for example, Albert-Henri de Sallengre wrote to a cleric in Paris asking a favor for "M. Cunningham, a very learned jurist, an excellent critic, in a word a man of infinite merit." The favor was to collate the manuscripts of Horace in the cleric's library with some passages sent by Sallengre.[6]

If an author already knew of someone who could offer assistance on a particular project, he might write directly to that person. In 1719, at the age of 19, the Abbé Denis-François Camusat in Besançon wrote to Pierre Des Maizeaux in London about a project to write a history of literary journals. He felt he could do so because he had positive knowledge that Des Maizeaux would encourage such a project.

When recently reading the *Nouvelles de la République des Lettres* composed by Mr Bernard, I happened on a letter that you wrote in 1701 and that he inserted in his journal of the month of August to the month of September of the same year; you proposed there the plan of several works of literature, and among others of a history of the journals that have appeared since M[r] de Salo invented them in 1665, I had already conceived the design of such a book, and if I hesitated to execute it, it is because it seemed of such enormous proportions that I scarcely dared to undertake it. Ignorant as I am of the German and English tongues, I see it is impossible for me to talk about the journals which were written in either of these two languages; ill-instructed even about what concerns French journals, I feared I would not entirely satisfy a curious reader. I was thus practically resolved to renounce my project, when I read that you would furnish information [*mémoires*] to those who wanted to work on this subject, and I deliberated for a moment longer and then resolved to ask you for all the elucidation that it is so easy for you to give me. I do not doubt, Monsieur, that with your *lumières*, very assiduous study & with an exact research into all the facts which could embellish a work of this type, I will in the end do a passable job. What reassures me even more is that, thank heaven, I am not gripped by the frenzy to publish, and if I ever decide to publish anything, I will not allow it to appear without having polished it at great length and having submitted it to your examination and to the critique of several enlightened persons.[7]

Des Maizeaux responded favorably to this letter, and Camusat proceeded to consult him over the next several years about the plan of the work, where to start, whether to write the lives of journalists, and other details. He had the beginning of the work printed and sent it to Des Maizeaux for evaluation. Des Maizeaux provided advice, sent *mémoires* on English journals, and procured a copy of Juncker's history of journalism from an English bookseller. Camusat responded with gratitude and, in 1720, aided Des Maizeaux's own research by sending him information he needed about Fénelon.[8]

Scholars in correspondence with each other felt free to ask for assistance in research whenever it was necessary; indeed, one of the functions of the *commerce de lettres*, the purely literary correspondence, was to promote opportunities for research. It was generally believed that if someone was *sur les lieux*—on the spot—he was fair game for requests in that place. César de Missy, a Huguenot minister in London, for example, helped collate several manuscripts of the Greek New Testament in England for Jean-Jacques Wetstein, a theologian in Amsterdam. Wetstein used his acquaintance with Missy to gain more information about the manuscripts, both from Missy himself and through Missy's acquaintance with other scholars.[9]

The same thing occurred, on a spectacular scale, when Jacques Lenfant, one of the ministers of the French church in Berlin and chaplain to the king of Prussia, was conducting major research. Among other works, Lenfant produced the *Lettres choisies de Saint-Cyprien . . . avec des remarques . . .* in 1688, the *Histoire du concile de Constance* in 1714, the *Histoire du concile de Pise* in 1724, and the *Histoire de la guerre des Hussites et du concile de Basle* in 1731. All these works relied on the goodwill of Lenfant's scholarly contacts abroad. In a letter to the librarian of the Bibliothèque du Roi in Paris, asking for information for the *Histoire du concile de Basle*, Lenfant reported that "I already have a good stock of Material from Geneva, from Bâle itself, from Frankfurt-on-Main; from Nuremberg, from Wölffenbüttel, from Leipzig, from Breslau, from Vienna, from England, and from other places."[10] Lenfant asked for help in finding books or getting synopses of them, in discovering useful manuscripts and copying them, and in providing information to help clarify the issues he intended to discuss. In writing to Jean-Alphonse Turrettini, professor at the Academy in Geneva, Lenfant begged, "In a word, Monsr, I pray you, page through books, search, have others search everywhere you write for some hidden treasure, and be assured that these will not be *pearls cast before swine*."[11]

Lenfant's pleas did not go unheard. He found cooperation everywhere, remarking on a research trip to Leipzig that "the Professors here are talented and communicative with their ideas and their treasures, which makes me hope that in several days I will carry considerable booty away from here."[12] The material he accumulated through these kinds of contacts was enormous; Lenfant's histories of the councils were praised at the time for their completeness and exactitude.[13] In one letter alone he reported offers of copies of documents from the library of the University of Bâle, fruitful correspondence with a leading scholar there, manuscripts from Vienna, important pieces from the archives of several towns in Saxony, an original manuscript from the Bibliothèque de Saint-Paul in Leipzig, information about manuscripts of acts of the council in the *chambre des comptes* in Dijon, and several other manuscripts from Paris and other towns.[14] "I have never better experienced than at this hour the truth of what our Master says: *Seek and ye shall find*," he wrote. "Every day I discover something and sometimes without even looking."[15]

Jacques Lenfant needed help on a large and exceptional piece of research. But in the more everyday activities of scholarly life, the ethos of the community also required people "sur les lieux" to render assistance to those far away. The haphazard distribution of books and the concentration of scholarly publishers in a few locales meant that scholars hoping to buy or even borrow books sometimes had to look far afield. Louis Bourguet, later professor of philosophy in Neuchâtel, used his new *commerce de lettres* with Gisbert Cuper in the Netherlands as a way to obtain books about Chinese. Cuper helped him through yet another acquaintance. "I am very glad, that you find me capable of doing you some service in this Empire or in Batavia. I give you my word that I will do all that I can to procure for you the books that you speak of, such as the Grand Dictionnaire Chinois, the Annales de la Chine, and the works of Confucius; I will employ in this my great friend, M[r]. the Burgermeester Witzen, one of the Directors of the East India Company, who loves scholarship very much, and who is the most obliging man in the world."[16] Scholars going abroad would be plied with commissions by their friends; the doctor Pierre Silvestre seems to have spent much of his time on a trip to the Low Countries in 1699 looking for medical books for his colleague Hans Sloane.[17] A letter from the young proselyte François Bruys to Des Maizeaux throws light on the mechanics of some of these transactions. Bruys was sending Des Maizeaux a copy of a book he had translated. "I send you a copy of Tacitus, as I promised you in my last letter. Remember that it is *propter amicitiam*, and that this should not be placed on account with M[r]. Du Noyer."[18] Du Noyer was a bookseller in London; presumably Bruys obtained books from a bookseller in The Hague and sent them to Des Maizeaux, who could pay for them at Du Noyer's shop. Scholars also lent books to each other, sometimes over long distances; Gisbert Cuper, for example, lent a book by the Père Bonjour on the Coptic language to Maturin Veyssière La Croze, even though the distance between them was from Deventer to Berlin.[19]

Although scholars may have gone to great trouble to find books for their friends and acquaintances, the premise behind the requests for them was, again, convenience. If a bookseller did not have the books one needed, the services of friends abroad were a frank necessity. Convenience also motivated other types of errands, such as the delivery of letters and of gift copies of new books. Postage could be quite expensive and was usually paid by the recipient; to avoid saddling themselves or colleagues with charges, scholars would attempt to find alternate routes for letters. One method was to send them via a bookseller, since that business required frequent use of the post. This worked well if the *libraire* was friendly enough to allow letters to pass for free. Covens and Mortier in Amsterdam, however, seem to have charged for letters sent through their shop; letters from Switzerland to London cost 15 stuivers, from London to Switzerland 10 stuivers, and from Berlin to London 4 stuivers.[20] Another, cheaper method was to send a letter enclosed in a letter from someone else; sometimes the enclosed letter was not to the original recipient, requiring him to pass it on to someone else in his area.[21] A person receiving a gift copy of a book from an author also commonly received a number of copies. These he was to distribute to certain other people he was likely to see. Usually this was a simple process, but it could be burdensome; Barbeyrac expressed relief at the death of the queen of England because he was thus freed from "the trouble of looking, perhaps in vain, for a means of sending her the copy of his book that M^r. de Crousaz destined for her."[22]

Knowing people "sur les lieux" was also useful for scholars who, like Lambert Douxfils, could never get enough literary news. In August 1686, Pierre-Daniel Huet, then bishop of Soissons, took advantage of the Huguenot Etienne Morin's recent flight to the Netherlands to say that "I would be very obliged to you if you would instruct me about what new books are appearing in your vicinity." (Huet continued to take advantage of Morin's proximity to *libraires* and the press; his later letters, in the 1690s, consisted almost entirely of requests for favors.)[23] The importance placed by most scholars on finding out what was going on in the world of learning is evident from the immense popularity of literary journals. The numbers of journals did not begin to proliferate until the 1680s, however, and in 1710 there were still few to choose from. Moreover, most came out only quarterly, and their authors themselves had to rely on their own literary correspondence for the *nouvelles littéraires* which customarily appeared at the end of each issue.[24] In the face of this, scholars continued to arrange *commerces de lettres*—regular, arranged correspondence, sometimes between strangers—with colleagues elsewhere. Through a *commerce* they could find out what works were in progress, which in press, who was in controversy with whom, and what other people thought of new publications. To give literary news was considered a service to the recipient of the letter. Pierre Coste chided Pierre Des Maizeaux from Paris for failing to show his friendship in just this way.

> I have not written you at all for some time, *beau sire*, because I saw by the Letters that you sent me in Holland, that you choose to reserve your important news for people whom you love less than me; that you do not wish to take any trouble to find in your surroundings or in your Memory details which you could easily guess I would be very glad to know, since you recounted political news that everyone knew in London at the time that you wrote me, and news of Books, which you very happily shared with Mr. l'Abbé Bignon. . . . Mr. Preverau is much more obliging than you. He does not treat me so cavalierly. He writes me long Letters, full of things that he knows must interest me greatly. See if you can find it in yourself to change your method.[25]

Indeed, a *commerce* could be regarded as a contract, with strict conditions which had to be obeyed. In August 1695 Henri Basnage de Beauval, a lawyer in The Hague who was also author of the journal *Histoire des ouvrages des savans*, entered into a *commerce de lettres* with Hans Sloane in London. He noted that "I had already remarked to M. Reg[is] how much it would oblige me to enter into commerce with you. He could scarcely render me a more agreeable service. There is everything to gain for me, and I accept with pleasure the conditions that you have the goodness to propose to me."[26] When Sloane failed to write after all, Beauval said that although he understood the silence, Sloane having just married a rich wife, "it is time that I remind you that you have offered me a *commerce de lettres*, and that is a contract which I do not consider broken by the other responsibilities that you have just taken on. Thus have the goodness to carry out what you promised me, and look kindly on my soliciting it. I would like to pay you in advance for the *nouvelles littéraires* that I expect from you. But I fear I know but little your taste in these things."[27] Part of Beauval's impatience may have been owing to his use of literary news in the journal. But the "contract" between him and Sloane was not set up on that basis, and only after the arrangements had been made did Beauval mention that "at least, Monsieur, your trouble will not be entirely lost: because I will share with the public the most curious things you tell me."[28] Beauval instead objected to silence because a *commerce de lettres* implied a mutual exchange of news, and in fact he worried that he would fail in his own fulfillment of the terms "and not return to you news that will pay for the trouble that you offer to take for me."[29]

The conventions of the Republic of Letters, then, were a great convenience to scholars throughout Europe. Even cities which could in no sense be called isolated, such as Paris or Amsterdam, always lacked certain amenities of scholarship. Many books published in the Netherlands, for example, only found their way to Dutch presses because they were prohibited in France. Manuscripts necessary for research were often in libraries inaccessible to people in other towns. Literary journals usually could not provide enough information with sufficient rapidity to satisfy the needs of most scholars. The existence of an ethos of cooperation and service within the Republic of Letters thus meant that even scholars in "a country . . . where Idleness & Ignorance daily become more deeply rooted," as Barbeyrac described Lausanne, theoretically had access to scholarly discourse and resources.[30] Our hypothetical minister from the Vaudois, through the network of acquaintance beginning with his old professors, could find books and information, garner opinions, and receive advice on his subject.

Pouring Each Other's Wine

It is clear that this cooperative code was of considerable practical value to the Republic of Letters. Yet the function of this code was not merely pragmatic. If its purpose were merely to make sure that everyone's errands were run, it might not even exist. Why should the Republic, in fact, have fostered such an ethos? One reason is that aspects of this code, particularly its stress on reciprocity and gratitude, promoted its usefulness for the community as a whole. Not only did individuals find it easier to pursue their research, but their entrance into the network of scholars and the system of reciprocal service drew them into participation in the larger scholarly world. The ethic of cooperation strengthened the communal identity of the Republic of Letters.

The importance of gifts and services as a social tie has featured largely in twentieth-century anthropological literature.[31] In particular, Malinowski's studies of the kula, the exchange ceremony of the Trobriand Islanders, stressed the way exchange of useless objects could institutionalize cooperation and cohesiveness among members of a far-flung society. The work of numbers of other economic and social anthropologists, most importantly Marcel Mauss, has pointed to the permeation of the reciprocal ethos through most social systems, historical and modern. And although some of these anthropologists disagree on approach, they all tend to support Mauss' general stance that "the object of [exchange] is to produce an amicable sentiment between the two persons involved."[32]

This is the important point: that the purpose of this kind of exchange is not profit in the sense that we know it. Instead—whether or not this is a conscious intention—it serves to establish or strengthen social relations. Lévi-Strauss illustrates this with the example of two strangers at a restaurant table, each with a one-glass bottle of wine in front of him. One man pours his bottle into the glass of the other, an act which cannot be ignored. Either the other man will pour his own wine into the first man's glass, choosing to be polite, or he will refuse to do so, taking the hostile path. Lévi-Strauss points out that cooperating in the first exchange brings on a series of other social bonds. Accepting the wine, he writes, "sanctions another offer, for conversation. In this way a whole range of trivial social ties are established by a series of alternating oscillations, in which offering gives one a right, and receiving makes one obligated, and always beyond what has been given or accepted."[33]

These analyses extend to the present day, when etiquette dictates that courtesies must still be returned, as must invitations. The concept is also clearly appropriate to the early modern period. According to etiquette books of the time, the willingness to do services was one of the principal marks of a gentleman. At the beginning of the seventeenth century, Eustache du Refuge wrote that "Civility consists principally in two points. . . . One is a certain Decency, Goodwill, or good grace, to which one must conform oneself as much as one can: the other is an agreeable Affability which not only makes us accessible to all who want to approach us, but also makes our . . . conversation desirable."[34] Services, in fact, were not just desirable, but a requirement for a good man. According to the Abbé de Bellegarde in 1690, "It is the duty of an *honnête homme* to declare himself for his friends, to espouse their interests, to attach himself to their fortune, & to do for them all that honor, justice, and conscience do not prohibit: One must not refuse a friend any good office, when the thing can be done honestly," although, he added cautiously, "one must not have a blind devotion which has no limits."[35]

The literature of the *honnête homme* also stressed the reciprocal nature of these services. A basic eighteenth-century courtesy book assured the eager learner that "Politeness is a duty that civil Men owe reciprocally [*réciproquement*] to one another."[36] According to the *Encyclopédie*, an act of goodwill or charity "excites us strongly to render the same as soon as we can." Gratitude, the encyclopedists wrote, is in fact a sufficient return in itself: "there is scarcely a more beautiful excess in the world than that of *gratitude*. People find such a great satisfaction in it, that it can serve on its own as recompense." So strong was the reciprocal ideal, in fact, that both Bellegarde and the encyclopedists felt compelled to warn against using friendship merely as a means to personal gain. "One must not however turn friendship into a commerce of pure interest," Bellegarde warned; "it is very base only to associate with people, because they can do you service; & it is even more despicable to neglect them entirely when they become useless to you, & your good fortune enables you to have no more need of them, or the misfortune of their affairs reduces them to the necessity of imploring your help."[37]

Gentlemen and Scholars

Services and their return thus formed an ethic for polite society in the early modern period. Yet in the Republic of Letters this ethic was particularly strong, and it was the existence of the Republic itself which sanctioned its invocation. This is evident from the appeal frequently made by people requesting favors to their common membership in the learned community. Jacques-Georges de Chaufepié, who continued Bayle's *Dictionary*, wrote to Prosper Marchand, "Excuse, Monsieur, the liberty I am taking, but I am availing myself of the Privileges accorded in the Republic of Letters, which authorize one to seek out the help one needs."[38] Similarly, the philosopher Jean-Pierre de Crousaz, knowing how letters were sometimes thought an interruption, began his first to Pierre Coste, "Is it permitted for me to write you a very long Letter the first time I have the honor to write to you? I flatter myself, Monsieur, the Rep. of Letters has its rights, & what others would consider an impoliteness, I assure myself, Monsieur, you will interpret as a mark of trust."[39] People were asked for favors as scholars, not just as gentlemen, and their kindness was deliberately praised in advance as "an extraordinary politeness, & a great inclination to give pleasure to the whole World," and—significantly—"principally to men of Letters."[40]

Scholars could identify with each other in this way because of the underlying premise that they all worked toward a common goal. Workers on the same team—in this case, the team seeking knowledge and truth—had special rights to ask assistance in their labors. Daniel Dumaresque said he would do services "with Pleasure for any Man of Learning (tho not personally known to me) especially if I thought that the Publick would any ways be benefited thereby."[41] Pierre Allix also used these terms in inquiring about a previous request for help:

> It was more than two years ago that I did myself the honor of writing to you about the Edition of the Critique of the P. Pagy on the Annales of Baronius which was done in your city by your nephew. . . . *As my goal was to do a service to the public in asking you* to have it delivered in person to the man who helped the père Pagi, in order to see what had been suppressed in your Genevan Edition I would be very glad to know what success this letter had.[42]

Sometimes quite considerable services could be asked of scholars for the sake of the Republic of Letters. In 1733 the *libraires* Wetstein and Smith wrote to Sir Hans Sloane on behalf of Theodore Tronchin and Louis de Neufville, "Young Men who are not yet known in the Republick of Letters, but who are in the way of acquiring soon, esteem and reputation in it." The two young men were writing a *Lexicon Medicum* and needed a copy of Sloane's *Natural History of Jamaica*, which at five pounds they could not afford. "It is in your power Sir to facilitate the Purchase of it, Or to let them have the use of a Copy as long as may be necessary for the composing of their Lexicon." As if to emphasize the men's credit in the learned community, and therefore their right to ask favors, Smith added that "Mr de Neufville, one of those Authors, translates into French Mr Albertus Seba's Thesaurus Rerum Naturalium."[43]

In 1710 occurred a spectacular case of services asked for the sake of a common scholarly goal. The Cambridge classicist Peter Needham was reading Michel de la Roche's literary journal, *Memoirs of Literature*, which published reviews and news in English of scholarly works on the Continent. He saw in the literary news from Amsterdam that Jean Le Clerc was preparing an edition of the *Characters* of Theophrastus. Needham immediately took up his pen to write to Le Clerc. "I think myself obliged to acquaint you," he said, "that by the direction of the Lord Bishop of Ely (a singular favourer & promoter of Learning in this Nation, as you no doubt have heard), & by the encouragement of D^r. Bentley, I have undertaken the same thing, & hope very soon to put it into the Press." Needham recounted the new materials he was using for the notes, such as a volume of manuscript lectures on Theophrastus by a Cambridge Greek professor, a copy of Casaubon's edition with his own notes, observations by Bentley, and collations from manuscripts at Oxford. He then bluntly continued, "If those helps toward a New Edition are greater than those that you are possest of, I would not have our Editions interfere by being publisht together, but if you please to communicate your Notes, Collation, &c. to me, I shall be very thankfull, & will print them with all due respect & acknowledgement of so great a favor."[44] In other words, for the sake of learning and the learned public, Le Clerc was to give up all the work he had done on his own edition. What is more, Le Clerc, always suspicious of other scholars, readily agreed to this arrangement, even though Needham continued to refer to it as "my Edition."[45]

Simply giving assistance to another scholar, then, was a means of reinforcing the concept of the Republic of Letters as a community. When someone like Jacques Lenfant asked for help on a major piece of research, he appealed not simply to his friendship with other scholars, but to the importance to learned society that the research be accomplished. In requesting assistance from Turrettini on the *Histoire du concile de Basle*, Lenfant asked for help with "that which will facilitate this project." The project, not the individual author, was the focus. It is true that he pointed out his ties with Genevan scholars—"I hope that I will not be refused in Geneva what people have accorded me in other places where I am less well known"—but these ties simply served as credentials for his ability to turn out a valuable work. Such a work might be praised as "worthy of you" (a rather ambiguous phrase), but it was more likely to be hailed as "doing honor to the Republic of Letters."[46]

The basic logistics of activity within the Republic also directly strengthened communal bonds. In taking each other's interests to heart, scholars would not only seek out materials or do errands themselves, but—as we saw in the case of the minister from the Vaudois—would put acquaintances in touch with those also able to help. Whenever this occurred, the scholarly network of two people would expand. Jacques Lenfant's research again provides an apt example. His original request was "to implore your help, *and that of your friends*"; when his contacts could not provide all the help he needed, they went on to third parties. While in Leipzig Lenfant heard from a professor of theology that the university had several Bohemian manuscripts about the Hussites; "he does not understand Bohemian any better than I do, but at Dresden there is a Minister who preaches in the Slavonic tongue, who will explain them to me."[47] And when Lenfant wrote to Jean Barbeyrac in Lausanne for help, Barbeyrac in turn wrote to Turrettini in Geneva. "He asks me to look in this country for all the pieces, either Mss. or printed, which could be of some help to him; for the Council of Bâle should have been transferred to or continued in Lausanne. If you know of any you will oblige me by pointing them out. I will see if there is anything here in the Archives, and before that I will consult M^r. Ruchat, who has done some digging, with the design of writing the ecclesiastical history of the Païs de Vaud."[48] In 1714 Lenfant asked, among others, the English clergyman White Kennett for some help with the histories of the councils of Constance and Bâle. He did so by asking Pierre Des Maizeaux to ask another scholar, John Chamberlayne, for help on the project, and then sent the letter to Kennett through Chamberlayne.[49] These requests on multiple levels had the effect of maintaining relations among some scholars and establishing relations with others.

Other everyday services had similar effects. The practice of sending letters with travellers instead of through the post, for example, did more for the Republic of Letters than keep one man in touch with another. The bearer of the letter was also rewarded for his service to the sender by meeting the recipient. The author-*libraire* Elie Luzac was fully aware of this when sending a letter to Jean-Henri-Samuel Formey in Berlin. His bearer was the jurist Van der Mieden, burgemeester in Alkmaar, who was on his way to Prussia. Luzac expressed his satisfaction with this arrangement: "Even though Men of Letters are already mutually bound, & so to speak Fellow citizens of the

Republic which has been given this name, and although I am easily persuaded that the acquaintance of Monsieur Van der Mieden would not have
escaped you, still I am very agreeably flattered that in some manner I am
contributing to the liaison of two amiable Savants."⁵⁰

This means of establishing scholarly relations was a common one in the
learned world. One service a scholar could do for another was to write letters
of introduction for him to take on his travels. The recipient of such a letter
would be enjoined to show hospitality to the bearer, including introducing
him to other savants; thus one or two people in each location might serve as
nodes for an ever-expanding network of acquaintance. When one of the
Masson brothers travelled to Geneva, he asked the minister Antoine Achard
in Berlin for help in meeting scholars; Achard felt the best way to accomplish
this was to address him solely to Turrettini, who would do the rest.⁵¹ And
when Charles-Etienne Jordan set off on his *voyage littéraire*, he quickly felt the
need for recommendations. Three weeks into the trip, Jordan wrote to a
number of older scholars, including Louis Bourguet and Maturin Veyssière
La Croze, asking for various letters of recommendation, especially one to
Pierre Des Maizeaux.⁵² Versions of these letters received by Des Maizeaux
take care to stress Jordan's worthiness in the Republic of Letters; Bourguet
called him "a Learned Man, one of my Friends, & a great *Littérateur*. I hope,"
he added, "that as he will be delighted to have the honor of knowing you,
you will not find for your part, that Mr. Jordan is not a savant worthy of the
esteem of all who have a Taste for Belles-lettres."⁵³ La Croze's letter said that
Jordan was "one of my best friends, a man of letters, with a very good
commerce." The underlying theme was thus that Jordan had the qualities
necessary to make him a member of the learned community. This once
established, both asked Des Maizeaux to render his services to Jordan, and
Bourguet specifically requested that Des Maizeaux introduce him to Sir Hans
Sloane, "President of your Royal Academy of Sciences."⁵⁴ The ethic of the
Republic now required Des Maizeaux to show Jordan whatever hospitality
he could; the *Histoire d'un voyage littéraire* Jordan wrote on his return shows
he was received kindly nearly everywhere.⁵⁵

Letters of recommendation for travellers not only fostered ties between the
traveller and other members of the Republic of Letters. They also strengthened the bonds between writer and recipient by emphasizing their previous
relationship. La Croze's letter recommending Jordan began with such a
reference, pointing out that "the person who will have the honor of bringing
you this letter will be able to give you news of my health and the state of my
affairs. No one can do so better than he."⁵⁶ Indeed, all letters, particularly
those containing literary news, were not simply services to scholars needing
information, but ties within the community. Communication itself provided
a link between scholars; to be *lié en commerce* with someone was to share a

special bond. When Cuper stopped hearing from Fabricius it was cause for lamentation, "for my great pleasure is to have correspondence with Savants, and to lose one, who is a very great ornament to Learning, gives me much grief."[57] On a higher plane, moreover, the news which made up much of these letters gave their recipients the sense of belonging to a large and unified society. Not all scholars maintained a correspondence with each other, but the letters that *were* written delivered messages, described news from other letters, and reported on scholarly activities far afield.[58] We have already seen that these letters were useful, providing helpful information (which might not appear in journals) about books and projects in other places. But these reports also inevitably highlighted one's own participation in a larger enterprise, the whole Republic of Letters.

Thus in addition to feeling a common goal with other members of the group, scholars had plenty of opportunities in their daily existence to make contact with their colleagues, often in a way that fostered their sense of community. But it was not only the accident of logistics that made services a bond in the Republic. As with the Tlingit and the Maori, in the learned community gifts were given and services performed in at least the vague expectation of counter-gifts, counter-services, or at least a warmer relationship. As Marshall Sahlins puts it, "If friends make gifts, gifts make friends."[59] It was exactly that expectation of a return that kept the system in operation.

It is clear from the way men of letters asked for services that they knew a return was in order. When Barbeyrac, still on the hunt for editions of Grotius, agreed to accept Des Maizeaux's offer to get him two English versions, he lamented Lausanne's inability to provide any new book that could in turn be of use to Des Maizeaux. He offered the choice of any older book instead.[60] Similarly, a scholar in Minden who "went to the source" and asked Jean-Henri-Samuel Formey, among other authors, for copies of his works, made sure to inquire whether there were services he could provide in return.[61] And the Abbé Bignon sent Des Maizeaux a map of the Auvergne as a present, commenting that this mark of his attention "is only too deserved [deuë] for the trouble you take with my *commerce* with our English savants."[62]

Many examples of services we have already discussed, in fact, contain elements of this emphasis on reciprocity. Jean Le Clerc's sacrifice of his edition of Theophrastus was amazingly generous, particularly for Le Clerc. But he did not go entirely unrewarded. Peter Needham stressed repeatedly his intention to "publish . . . gratefull acknowledgements of the favor you have done me"; as the encyclopedists pointed out, *reconnoissance* was as good as a material return, and a public acknowledgement of his generosity could only enhance Le Clerc's reputation. Moreover, Le Clerc also asked for a number of copies of the Theophrastus when it was finished; Needham replied that "you may depend upon my taking care of that," adding that, if

Le Clerc did not have one of Needham's works, he would be glad to send it as well.[63] In the same way, Henri Basnage de Beauval's bantering *commerce de lettres* with Sloane was not simply a correspondence but was intended as a true exchange of news. When Sloane did not keep his half of the bargain Beauval chastised him, and the whole transaction was commercial in metaphor if not in fact. The two had a "contract" [*engagement*], and Beauval, his letters unanswered, said he would "pay in advance" with literary news until Sloane fulfilled his part of the deal. The *commerce* entailed other reciprocal exchanges. Sloane offered the *Philosophical Transactions* of the Royal Society, and Beauval asked for copies of a journal called *Miscellaneous Letters giving an Account of the Works of the Learned both at Home and Abroad*; in return he sent his own journal, the *Histoire des ouvrages des savans*, "not as a thing that might occupy you with pleasure; but as a mark of my gratitude [*reconnoissance*] for all your good offices."[64]

This exchange of service for service, book for book, friendship for friendship, thus made of the practical necessities of learned life a true bond between scholars. Not only would a person obtain the tools of scholarship, but in doing so he would forge ties of mutual assistance with other people in his position. These ties, moreover, could branch into an extensive network of connections available to provide information and help of all kinds. Thus the ideal of reciprocal service, alongside the logistical encounters and common ideology of scholars, lent greater reality for its citizens to the invisible institutions of the Republic of Letters.

The Little Services of a Voluntary Cadet

When we look more closely at the anthropological literature, however, we see that much exchange was not, in fact, between equals. Not every member of society had the same rights and opportunities. Neither Malinowski nor Mauss went very far in considering the role of status in exchange, although Mauss did note that in the potlatch, "to give is to show one's superiority. . . . To accept without returning or repaying more is to face subordination."[65] But in general Mauss' work assumed a broadly egalitarian social system.

In *Exchange and Power in Social Life*, however, Peter Blau posits a general theory about the relations of status and exchange.

Furnishing benefits to others may lead to the development of bonds of fellowship with them or to a position of superiority over them. A person who distributes gifts and services to others makes a claim to superior status. By reciprocating and, particularly, by making excessive returns that now obligate the first to them, others invalidate his claim and invite further transactions in expanding exchange relations of mutual trust between peers. Their failure to reciprocate, on the other hand, validates his claim to superiority, and so does their failure to accept this offer, unless their evident affluence proves that their rejection is not due to their inability to enter into egalitarian exchange relations with him but to their unwillingness to do so, in which case it is likely to produce hostility. A person can establish superiority over others by overwhelming them with benefits they cannot properly repay and thus subduing them with the weight of their obligations to him. But once superiority is firmly rooted in political and economic structures, it enables an individual to extract benefits in the form of tribute from subordinates without any peril to his continued superiority over them.[66]

As Blau makes clear, once a hierarchy is established, gifts may take on opposite meanings from previous ones; they no longer establish superiority over the recipient, since they act simply as "tribute" from a lesser- to a higher-ranking person. These kind of relations could occur in the Republic of Letters; indeed, "tribute" is the very word Pierre Des Maizeaux used to describe the comments he contributed to the illustrious Père Niceron's *Mémoires . . . des hommes illustres.* "It is a tribute that I owe you, and that I beg you to accept, such as it is. If you make any use of it, please have the goodness to correct the Style &c."[67] Such gifts and services reinforced the existing structure, so that César de Missy said of his collations for Jean-Jacques Wetstein, "You should feel no obligation for my little services. You can think of them as those of a voluntary Cadet, sensible of the vanity of being able to say that he has made a campaign under the premier Captain of his century."[68]

Moreover, as Blau points out, in an institutionalized power structure a superior can provide gifts or services to someone of lower rank without challenging his own status. That status, in fact, is only strengthened by the inability of the subordinate to repay in kind.[69] We can see this played out in the correspondence between Gisbert Cuper and Louis Bourguet. Cuper was a classical scholar and politician, a burgermeester of Deventer, but Bourguet, who longed to be a scholar and later became a professor, until 1717 was a partner in Louis & Jean Bourguet Frères, a silk-stocking business trading in Venice, Neuchâtel, and Berne.[70] After suitable notifications by other scholars, Bourguet wrote himself to ask Cuper's help in his work. He had meant to write earlier, he said, "but as I flatter myself, that you will wish to honor me with your protection, I feel somewhat better that the encumbrances of Business have prevented me from putting into effect my plan to tell you my thoughts on various subjects of Literature, to procure some part in your affection, & to receive the *lumières*, that a person so universally esteemed and

of such vast erudition as yours, could communicate to me."[71] Bourguet's idea
of the network of obligation and patronage was complex, but it is clear that
he both regarded Cuper as superior to him in status and saw himself as the
principal beneficiary of the arrangement. One factor did not negate the other.

In most cases, however, differences in station in the Republic of Letters
were not this apparent. Unlike the societies portrayed by Blau, Malinowski,
and Mauss, status in the Republic of Letters was not dependent on wealth,
and exchange was usually beneficent rather than economic. Indeed, ranking
in the Republic was more than a bit nebulous. Marshall Sahlins, citing Alvin
Gouldner, points out that many such societies exist, and in them rank is not
established, but rather achieved. Exchange plays its role in this process.
"[H]ere reciprocity is more or less engaged in the *formation* of rank itself, as
a 'starting mechanism.' The connection between reciprocity and rank is
brought to bear in the first case [i.e. established hierarchy] in the form, 'to be
noble is to be generous,' in the second case [i.e. nebulous hierarchy], 'to be
generous is to be noble.' "[72] Because ranking in the learned world did not
rely on established and repeated patterns of wealth or political power, it was
continually remade as new and different scholars came to the fore. Those
reaching the higher regions of the hierarchy did so for a number of reasons,
including quality of scholarship, professional position, and access to patronage. But one attribute which raised a scholar in the minds of his fellows was
his willingness to oblige others.[73] *Eloges* to the memory of deceased scholars,
which appeared frequently in literary journals, often listed generosity to
colleagues as an important feature of the idealized deceased.[74] We see the
same tributes to scholars who were still alive. The *Bibliothèque angloise*, which
reviewed English books for the information of the Continent, praised John
Chamberlayne, who was "known to a great number of Foreigners for the
obliging manner with which he has received them at his house. He still
continues to welcome kindly Savants who travel in *England*, & he is always
ready to do them all sorts of good offices."[75]

The ability to be of use to colleagues placed a scholar in a superior
position, not only because these services might not be reciprocable, but also
because such an ability implied the possession of power. An example of this
gone wrong occurred when Charles Ancillon, director of the French colony
in Berlin, invited Cuper on his own account to join the Berlin Academy,
even though such an invitation had to be voted on by the entire society. To
do so, and to appear to be the motivation for the academy's invitation, made
Ancillon seem falsely influential in the learned community. La Croze wrote
scornfully of this incident, "such is the manner of behavior of the personage
who was impudent enough to make the first proposals of his own accord: he
has already behaved in the same manner toward others, & it is in this way

that he claims to make himself estimable in the world, being unable to do so otherwise."[76]

Among the Trobriand Islanders, participants in the kula had a number of partners in exchange, a number which varied according to their social status: the higher the status, the more partners in exchange.[77] In the same way, members of the Republic of Letters regarded a wide network of scholarly associations as a claim to higher rank. In his letter of introduction for Jordan, La Croze pointed out Jordan's worth as a scholar by mentioning that he had "a very good *commerce*," and Cuper, in speaking to Bourguet of his own scholarly achievements, places among them the fact that "I have a hundred or so volumes of letters, with the responses of Scholars, who honor me with their friendship and correspondence."[78]

A wide *commerce de lettres* brought status in part because it proved a scholar was in the center of the community. Marshall Sahlins suggests that "the span of social distance between those who exchange conditions the mode of exchange." Since kinship is so important in primitive societies, he examines this issue in that realm, concluding that exchange is at its most altruistic when it involves those closely related, and at its most devious and goal-oriented when it involves those of different kin groups. But since members of the Republic of Letters felt a strong communal identity, this reasoning is also applicable to that "clan"; savants in some ways also felt that "'nonkin' . . . often . . . is the synonym for 'enemy' or 'stranger.' "[79] Scholars were more likely to cooperate with or do kindnesses for people they felt were legitimately part of their own community. The minister and chronologist Alphonse Des Vignoles reacted suspiciously when a Monsieur de Vèze, formerly *receveur des gabelles* in Montpellier, asked him for details on Huguenot refugees for a literary history of Languedoc. Des Vignoles' friend Jacob le Duchat wrote to a scholar in Paris for more information. "You know Monsieur des Vignoles, *homme de qualité*, who deserves to be obliged when possible," he began, stressing Des Vignoles' own membership in the Republic. Le Duchat explained the situation, adding that "Monsieur des Vignoles would like to know if this Mr. Vèze is accounted a savant in Paris, or a man who writes well; also whether he is an old Catholic or a *nouveau Réuni*," that is, a Protestant converted to Catholicism because of the requirements of the Edict of Fontainebleau.[80] Des Vignoles' caution sprang from his allegiance to both of his communities. He wanted to make sure, before obliging a stranger, that the man was a worthy member of the Republic of Letters, and he hoped to discern what religious line would result from research on a sensitive topic. In the same way, La Croze emphasized the scholarly abilities of Paul-Emile de Mauclerc, the 16-year-old future author of the *Bibliothèque germanique*, when he wrote to recommend him to the good offices of Gisbert Cuper. "I have scarcely ever had a pupil who has profited more than this one, both in Philosophy and in belles lettres. He has a lovely knowledge of Greek, & a great passion for Reading, and," he added, "what merits reflection, is that he is one of the richest Refugees in Berlin." La Croze dwelt on Mauclerc's wealth at a time when his own fortunes were at an all-time low; but it was his academic skill that was intended to persuade Cuper to introduce the boy to an influential Dutch scholar.[81] To receive the benefits of the community, then, one must be seen to belong. Knowing people—having a *commerce de lettres*—was evidence of membership; and the merchant Louis Bourguet's first letter to Cuper, in hopes of a response, took care to mention that he was already in correspondence with Leibniz, La Croze, and Jean-Baptiste Ott.[82]

The special relationship of a *commerce de lettres* gave its participants the status necessary to ask for services. But people outside these connections—further from Sahlins' theoretical center—would not have these opportunities. That the *commerce* was a necessary tie is evident from La Croze's reaction to a favor he was asked. He was in touch with Adrien Reland in Utrecht, but only through the letters he wrote to Cuper; Cuper passed messages back and forth between them. But when he was asked to request a service of Reland directly, he balked. La Croze reported to Cuper that Starck, who catalogued the Arabic manuscripts of the king of Prussia, wanted to dedicate a treatise on Mohammedan prayers to Reland, whom he did not know. Starck pressed La Croze to ask Reland to accept, but to La Croze his own relationship with Reland was evidently not close enough to request such a service; he asked Cuper to write to Reland instead.[83] If he *had* been *en commerce* with Reland, the matter would have been different, and someone too far from the center could turn to him to act as an intermediary in soliciting services. The wider the *commerce* of a scholar, the greater his status, both because he clearly had the respect of many colleagues, and because his extensive network of contacts allowed him to procure assistance for many "subordinates" in the community.

The Go-between

In many of the services we have already discussed, the role of intermediary was prominent. Scholars wrote on behalf of others asking for hospitality, books, and help in research. Often the involvement of an intermediary was, again, a matter of simple convenience. Paul-Emile de Mauclerc asked Jean-Henri-Samuel Formey to deliver some money to Isaac de Beausobre in Berlin merely because Mauclerc was in Stettin and Formey on the spot, and

"I do not doubt that you are often in the House of M. de Beausobre."[84] People relayed messages and information from one savant to another to save postage and trouble; in the face of expensive communications, a go-between often proved the method of greatest expediency.

However, the use of an intermediary frequently had underlying sociological meaning. A request ending in failure can be both embarrassing and demeaning; refusal to perform a service could mean that the solicited party prefers not to enter into a reciprocal relationship with someone of lower status. Firth points out that an intermediary could provide a partial solution. "The use of an intermediary when one wishes to make a request or an arrangement is a well-known process whereby one attempts to achieve one's ends while not assuming the full burden of responsibility and loss of status if one is unsuccessful."[85] This was clearly the case when Daniel de Superville was attempting to join the Royal Society. Superville wrote to Jacob Theodore Klein to ask him to solicit this honor on his behalf. When Klein's first efforts bore no fruit, Superville urged him to try again; this indirect method was obviously best. "I confess to you, Monsieur, that if I had believed, that perhaps this affair was liable to run into difficulties, I would not have taken the liberty to seek it, but since I have asked for it once I pray you most earnestly to write to England once more in my favor on this subject, so that I will not be the one who is refused it, which tactless interpreters ordinarily explain as an affront."[86] Klein himself was unfortunately tactless enough to quote this solicitation verbatim to Sloane, the president of the Royal Society.

But an intermediary did not merely bear the brunt of refusal; he also contributed to a transaction's success. As we have noted, the ability to use an intermediary indicated that a scholar had at least one contact in the Republic of Letters. This gave proof of his membership in the group, and the intermediary would usually attest to his positive scholarly qualities. In addition, the intermediary usually had wider contacts and consequently higher status within the community. He thus had more credit with the person being solicited for a favor than did the beneficiary of the request. This accounts for the usual form of such an address, which implied that the intercessor was asking for a favor for himself rather than another. David Martin expressed this gracefully in a letter to Cuper: "all my life I will have a very humble gratitude for all the obligations you heap upon me, and in particular the recommendations you are giving for M^r. Cordes, whom I regard as another myself [un autre moi-même]."[87] Requests for kindnesses commonly ended with words such as "if you have the occasion to do him some service, you will oblige *me* greatly by doing so."[88] Jean Gagnier's succinct metaphor summed up the situation: "Any services you do him can be put on my account."[89]

Finally, the use of an intermediary established a useful social distance between the supplicant and his potential helper. By requiring the assistance of an intercessor, he acknowledged his lower status in the community and reaffirmed his respect for the other scholar. Even when this status difference did not in fact exist, the suggestion that it did was a judicious compliment. When relations were of long standing, of course, an intermediary was not necessary, except perhaps for convenience. In 1730 Pierre Des Maizeaux asked Jacob le Duchat in Berlin for a copy of Etienne Chauvin's rare *Nouveau journal des savans*, probably mentioning that Le Duchat could send it to him through the agent Charles de la Motte. De la Motte later wrote, "The old fellow is beginning to feel the infirmities of old age. I don't know how he read your Letter, but he imagined that you were asking for M. Chauvin's journal for me, & he reproached me obligingly for using you to ask him for something."[90]

But in more tentative relations, intercession provoked benevolence. The refugee minister Pierre Jurieu, perhaps for political reasons, found himself in the unusual position of abasing himself before the scholar and politician Gisbert Cuper. Having finally sent Cuper his *Histoire critique des dogmes et des cultes*, he apologized for the lack of an intermediate agent between them. "If I had dared to hope that this book would please you as much as I see it has done, I would have sent you the earlier one. I had planned to do so, and if death had not deprived us of our excellent friend, Monsieur de Bleswik, I had resolved to ask him to offer you one on my behalf: but finding myself without patron and without mediator near you, I confess to you sincerely that in the consciousness of my weakness I did not dare present to so piercing and so critically penetrating eyes a work which was only an *essai* of my youth."[91] Although Jurieu probably did not mean most of this, his avowed need for an intermediary emphasized Cuper's superiority; the likely result was for Cuper to be inclined to warmer relations between them.

It is evident, then, that although status differences did exist in the Republic of Letters, such differences in fact strengthened rather than weakened the community. The ethos of service, combined with the advantage of gaining status by obliging others, meant that someone of higher ranking was moved to assist his subordinates. In doing so, he reinforced ties between himself and other scholars. By arranging help for a scholar, he forged or hardened links with the person served, while at the same time reinforcing his reciprocal ties with the final provider of the service. The community also benefited from the expansion of the networks that such transactions brought about. When acting as an intermediary, and particularly as a recommender, a scholar provided two acquaintances with a new contact, thereby drawing more people into the larger society. Indeed, such actions furthered the work of the Republic of Letters by assisting research and scholarship. As we have seen, the idea that this was so was in itself an effective binding agent. The social practices of scholars thus ultimately harked back to the ideals of the learned community.

*   *   *

The young minister from the Pays de Vaud, then, was not so isolated after all. The tools were all there for him to accomplish his goals. His professors could write to other scholars for help or write him a recommendation so he could visit them himself. Scholars thus contacted might lend him books, copy out passages, show him medals similar to his own, or even give him advice on drafts of his work. In many different ways, these contacts made him feel a part of the scholarly world. One thing was still missing, however: he had to publish his work. For this an intermediary was almost always considered vital.

To find the reason for this we must return to the notion of people "sur les lieux." Most authors, if they hoped for a satisfactory edition, were compelled to send their manuscripts away from home. The Abbé de Longuerue in Paris was disdainful of non-French publishing, writing in 1697 that "in Germany, they simply reprint our books, and badly. In Holland they are just silly, and books coming from there are so insipid and impertinent that I do not know how a man with a little taste can keep from vomiting when reading them. In England, from whence I often have news, everything arouses pity, and literature there is in a bad way." But a year later he was forced to admit that "good books daily become rarer here, because foreigners steal many of them and none of them is reprinted."[92] Longuerue correctly assessed that books were often counterfeited in other countries; many others were originally issued outside France. Manuscripts found their way to Holland in part because of harsh censorship in France, a censorship which was based more on the output of French presses than on foreign imports.[93] Authors unable or unlikely to earn the government's imprimatur would turn to the Dutch; Thémiseul de St.-Hyacinthe wrote to the *libraire* Charles Le Vier that "I have a work that I want to tell you about in a little while which I believe can only be printed in Holland, and which, if I am not mistaken, will cause some stir, because of the importance of the contents and the liberty which reigns throughout."[94] Although civic censorship was practiced in the Netherlands, sometimes at the urging of religious authorities, the press was still markedly freer than in France.[95]

Many other reasons encouraged authors to send their works to Holland for publication. A compelling one for many authors was the broad trade network of Dutch *marchands-libraires*. This was in sharp contrast to the situation in other countries. Residents around Europe reported that English books rarely travelled abroad without being expressly ordered; there was little French-language publishing in Berlin even at mid-century; and, according to Jean Barbeyrac, "M^r. de la Motte says, that a Book printed in Geneva is only half public, the *Libraires* of Holl. hardly wishing to trade at all with those of Geneva."[96] In addition, authors reduced the risk of counterfeit by publishing in the nation doing most of the counterfeiting. Jean-Pierre de Crousaz complained that "the Libraires of Geneva no sooner print a work than those of Holland counterfeit it"; although it was sometimes difficult to control Dutch *libraires* from a distance, "we are nevertheless reduced to preferring the Dutch because in Geneva one must fear counterfeiting."[97] Authors were also often happier with works printed in the Netherlands because costs there were lower, pay sometimes better, and the product more beautiful, an important factor for scholars interested in *belles éditions*. The satisfied Barbeyrac remarked that "there is scarcely any country whose publications do more honor and give more pleasure to an Author."[98]

As Crousaz pointed out, however, for many Holland was far away, and it was difficult to make any arrangements to have a work published. Scholars appeared to equate this situation with the problem of contacting colleagues they did not know. They needed to find someone "known to the Libraires of Holland," as Charles-Etienne Jordan put it, in order to act as intermediary in the transaction.[99] In October of 1707 Leibniz reported vaguely to La Croze that "I have had my *Esprit* put into fair copy: but I don't know when it will be printed, because I have no liaison with the *libraires* of Holland, where I wanted to send it." He eventually got to the point, telling La Croze in November that "I would have a new obligation to you, concerning this same work, if you would procure its publication."[100] The intermediary might have been on the spot—Etienne Morin's residence in Amsterdam was the factor subjecting him to Pierre-Daniel Huet's many requests for help in publishing—or might simply have had friendly dealings with *libraires* or *libraires'* connections in Holland.[101] Huet's appeals to Morin were based on his "confidence in our old friendship," and his requests were no more specific than to "sound out your *libraires*, to see if they would like to undertake the publication" and to receive the copy in case of acceptance.[102]

These transactions worked in just the same way as other favors in the Republic of Letters. Those involved were scholars, not literary agents, and the services they performed were merely incidental to their existence and position in the learned community. But in fact real agents did exist. Their numbers were small, but few were necessary in the small and inbred world of Dutch publishing. These men, closely involved professionally with the printers and booksellers of Amsterdam and The Hague, by proximity alone made ideal contacts for authors aspiring to publication. It is here that we can begin to see how in the eighteenth century roles in the Republic of Letters were becoming professionalized.

Literary Agents and the Professionalization of Letters

Charles de la Motte was a corrector of the press who lived in Amsterdam from at least the beginning of the eighteenth century until his death in 1751. Very little is known about him; when Des Maizeaux wanted to address a preface to him, he himself joked that "this will provide some future editor with the opportunity to make a footnote, but he will have quite a problem in digging up this La Motte, and he will be reduced in the end to saying simply *Astratus vixit*. Joking apart, you would do better to use a name that is better known."[103] If he had not spent more than a year living and working as a partner in the correcting business with the Abbé Prévost, he would have received almost no attention whatsoever, and as it is, interest in his life has been small. He was probably born in Montpellier, probably in the 1660s; he may have been educated in Geneva; since he was a Huguenot, he probably came to Amsterdam as a result of the Revocation of the Edict of Nantes.[104] He spent the last forty years of his life, from 1711 to 1751, in a house (at times with the mysterious "lady with whom I live") on the Groote Leidsedwarsstraat in Amsterdam, a location which distressed him by its distance from the bookstores, especially as he had gout and was rather overweight.[105] He was also extremely short: people who were unfriendly toward him—such as the Abbé Prévost, after ten months in the same house with him—referred to him as a "pygmy," a "little hack," a "Lilliputian," or even "that little figure of papier-mâché."[106] Despite the survival of some correspondence—almost entirely about editions—this is virtually all that is known of De la Motte.

Prosper Marchand in The Hague is somewhat better remembered, in part because of several books he published, such as the *Histoire de l'origine et des premiers progrès de l'imprimerie*, in part because of recent attention to his work.[107] His grandfather and father were musicians, the latter at the French court.[108] Marchand was born on March 11, 1678, at St.-Germain-en-Laye and in 1693 began a career in the book trade. He was admitted to the corporation of Paris *libraires* in 1698, following a four-year apprenticeship, and set up shop in the Rue St.-Jacques. After converting to Protestantism, however, he fled to Holland in 1709 with the engravers Bernard and Etienne Picart. Except for a brief sojourn in England in 1726—which was intended to be permanent—Marchand spent the rest of his life in Amsterdam, Rotterdam, and chiefly The Hague. In 1710 he was admitted fully to the booksellers' guild in The Hague, but, tiring of the trade, he elected around 1713 to make his living instead by correction of the press. This was his chief support until his death on June 14, 1756.[109]

Both Marchand and De la Motte were correctors, but in addition to—or, rather, bound up with—this work was their role as literary agents. They were an invaluable asset to scholars whose access to the Dutch book trade was not so easy. They placed manuscripts, negotiated terms, and provided a link between the *libraire* and the author. Their proximity to the publishing industry also meant that they were useful sources of information and help in a variety of transactions. No one knew better than they what was being printed, what stage it was at, and the quality of the edition; given their access to information and the volume of their correspondence, they were an excellent source of bibliographical news. Moreover, their convenient contact with booksellers and their central location in an entrepôt nation gave them the ability to run errands, send on letters cheaply, and deliver gift copies of books.[110]

Many of these services, including the placement of manuscripts, sound a great deal like those we have seen throughout the Republic of Letters. The question thus arises of whether De la Motte and Marchand can properly be called "literary agents" at all. Until now, no one has thought that agents even existed until the end of the nineteenth century. The only scholarly book on the subject, James Hepburn's *The Author's Empty Purse and the Rise of the Literary Agents*, describes A.P. Watt in the 1880s as the first literary agent in the world, although Hepburn calls the placing of books with publishers "a task that others had been doing as long as authors have had friends."[111] This reference to the Republic of Letters is telling, but not necessarily convincing. Virtually no interest has ever been shown in the actual mode of representing an author in the earlier period, an interest which would show that these services differed from those scholars did for each other. Even Christiane Berkvens-Stevelinck, who has described some of these activities in connection with Prosper Marchand, sees his work on behalf of authors as only that of a kind of super-friend.[112] Were literary agents simply superlative adherents to the ethos of the Republic of Letters, or did they represent an actual change in the operation of the community?

One hint that these men played a more professional role was that, when scholarly intermediaries helped their colleagues place manuscripts, they in turn would often get in touch *not* with a *libraire*, but with a literary agent. After Charles-Etienne Jordan returned from his *voyage littéraire*, for example, he gave the manuscript of his account of the trip to his mentor La Croze. The latter then wrote to Prosper Marchand on his behalf, asking for help in finding a publisher in The Hague.

> Monsieur Jordan, my dear friend, is very content with you and with the politeness with which you received him. You can count on his sincerity. Everyone who knows him swears that his is one of the best hearts in the world. He has composed a little relation of his travels in France, in England, and in Holland. He does not dwell on bagatelles. Everything revolves around the savants that he saw, & on the Libraries that he

carefully examined. He has communicated his Ms^t. to me and I have urged him strongly to make it public. To get him to do it, I sent him a few little things, and I addressed a letter to him that he wants to put at the head of his work, which he has sent to all our savants, who unanimously agree it should be published. . . . Someone has offered to print it in Amsterdam; but the bad conduct [*mauvaises manières*] of the French Libraires of that city does not permit him to address himself to them.[113]

Similarly, Jean Barbeyrac, solicited in 1719 by Jean-Pierre de Crousaz to place a manuscript, reported his failure and that of Jean Le Clerc. This failure was not surprising, he said, "after Mr de la Motte could do nothing with it, and that is saying a lot, because there is perhaps no one, in whom the Libraires have more trust; I have certainly relied on him to take care of all the dealings I have had with those people."[114] This trust or confidence was the important factor for every supplicant; it stood out in the mind of an author who asked the lukewarm Pierre Coste to use his own influence with De la Motte. Coste wrote:

After so many *commissions* that I heap on you on my own account, do I dare pester you on the part of M. Gaignier, Author of the Life of Mahomet? He gave me a note dated 25 October 1726, copied by M. Des Maizeaux, from a Letter that you had written to this Mr. Des Maizeaux, in which you complained of some disorder in this Piece. First of all, you say, there is the title of one Chapter, & all the rest is a continuous discourse. M. Gaignier responds to this, that it is a purely arbitrary thing, that the rest can also be divided into chapters, or the first division can be removed, & everything printed in the form of a *continuous Discourse*. As for the Chronological, critical, or Grammatical distinctions, they are, he assured me, in such small number that they do not cause any distaste to the Reader. As for the punctuation, to the best of my knowledge it goes beyond condemnation. But, he says, that is a small inconvenience that would be easy to remedy. He begged me strongly to recommend his interests to you, that is to use your credit with M. Wetstein so that he will publish his Work, which is, they say, very good of its kind. I promised him that I would write to you. It is up to you to see what you can do to oblige this savant who is a very good fellow, & *cujus virtutibus obstat res augusta domi*.[115]

Another special feature of agents was the availability of their services to strangers. Although De la Motte and Marchand were in long correspondence with some of the authors they assisted, others were simply scholars who had heard about their services from friends. Unusually, as we have seen, they sometimes wrote directly to the agents without employing an intermediary.

In 1723 César de Missy wrote his one and only letter to Marchand, saying that "without having the honor of knowing you," he wanted to ask if any of his poetry could be published. In the same way, Simon Pelloutier, author of a history of the Celts, wrote in 1735 saying that "I have often heard from Messieurs Lenfant and Lacroze, that you are happy to do services not only for your friends, but even for people who are strangers and unacquainted with you."[116] De la Motte himself stressed the pragmatic, rather than the benevolent, aspect of these transactions. He remarked in 1709 to Des Maizeaux, "I will tell you in passing that I have often done everything I could to have Works printed whose authors I did not esteem nearly as much as I do you, because all that is necessary to recommend a Book, is that it will sell (and all sorts of things will sell), and also that one be very glad to oblige the Author."[117]

The most important difference between arrangements made by scholars and by agents was one of tone. It was more difficult for a scholar not on the scene to consult a large number of libraires, often having ties with only one or two. The situation was entirely different for the agents, who knew nearly everyone connected with the Dutch book trade. Although they were not always successful in placing manuscripts, they had the resources to keep trying. In 1741 Marchand wrote to Jean-Henri-Samuel Formey, for example, "I will also make you happy by letting you know that I have finally made a deal with a Libraire about your Polish Mst., after having been refused by 12 or 15."[118] Marchand reported that "it is a much more difficult thing than you perhaps think from where you are, to persuade Libraires to accept Ms^{ts},"[119] and indeed De la Motte was often forced to look hard to place some of the works he was sent. "I greatly fear that our Libraires will not want to take on the Works of the P. Le Courayer, because the subject matter is not at all interesting for this country & for Germany, & these books can only get into France with a thousand difficulties, [&] especially [because] the P. le Courayer wanted to be paid as one might expect for his work. I will try all our best Libraires nonetheless, I will even write to The Hague about it, & will answer by next Tuesday at the latest."[120]

Not only was the agents' application to the task more thorough, but their efforts were more businesslike. When a savant tried to solicit the publication of a work, his efforts were usually vague. The negotiations almost always had to be carried on by mail, and the medium did not allow for much haggling. Agents, on the other hand, would not only find someone to publish a work, but would bargain for better terms. Among the issues often discussed were pay (usually in money per sheet, and copies of the book), style and age of typeface, and what items might be included in the work. The discussions over the printing of Des Maizeaux's *Vie de Bayle*, in the edition of Bayle's *Dictionary* published in 1729 in Amsterdam, are characteristic of this genre of negotiation. Here is De la Motte's letter to Des Maizeaux after the preliminary discussions:

> You will have seen, Monsieur, by my last letter that I received your Letter of 1 April on time. I also received your last of the 8th yesterday & I was very pleased to see in it that you have finally resolved to provide your Vie de Bayle to insert it in the Edit. of the Dictionary. I have just been at the Libraires' to conclude the deal. They want to reduce a bit the price that you ask, they say that Guineas are not legal currency in this country, but they offer you ten Dutch florins per sheet. The difference is very inconsiderable, and they pay scarcely as much in copies. They will print it in the type of Bayle's Dictionary itself, both for the text and for the notes. You can make it as long or as short as you consider à propos, these Messrs believe sincerely that you are only interested in the good of the Work. But if you think it proper to include the pieces you mention, Acts of the Consistory of Rotterd. &c. the Condemnation of the Crit. of Calv. by M. de la Reynie &c. they want very much to include them, but they do not want to pay for the copy. See if these conditions suit you.[121]

De la Motte would counsel the author on the proper response to the offers of the *libraires*, saying in 1712 of a promised six florins per sheet from Fritsch and Böhm, "it seems to me that this is a reasonable offer that you ought to accept as soon as possible, for fear that they will retract it. I am persuaded you would not get this from another Libraire."[122]

After discussions of this kind, De la Motte would make final demands to the *libraire* which would usually end in a written contract. In a letter to Des Maizeaux he quoted his demands to the Compagnie des Libraires about the same *Vie de Bayle*.

> Messrs. les Libraires are asked to prepare a little Paper concerning the terms that M. Des Maizeaux requires for his Life of M. Bayle. 1. He asks one Guinea per sheet, I have proposed 10# [i.e. florins] he makes a good remark about this, the difference of these two prices is a small thing in regard to a Compagnie des Libraires, & much more for a poor Author who had to use a Copyist on this occasion.
>
> He also asks a Dictionary at the Libraire's price [i.e. trade rate].
>
> In the case that the Dict. with his Life is reprinted, he would like to be given a Copy, supposing that he survives until a new Edition comes out. I can promise on his part that he will do his best to prolong his Life until then. It is likely that he will provide Additions to it [the new edition].
>
> He would strongly approve the engraving of the portrait of M. Bayle after the Genevan edition. [They will not do it because the Engraver is asking too much time for this.[123]]

1 Contract between a *libraire* and a literary agent on behalf of an author. (UBL March. 44:3, f.1*.)

The Pieces which must be added to the Life are very necessary. There is a Journal of the Life of M. Bayle done by himself & enriched with Notes. All these Pieces will not take up more than 2 sheets. He believes that the Life should be printed in a larger type than the Text. (This is what I wrote & this is what M. Smith added to it.[)]
Mr. La Motte
I have shown the Conditions above to Messrs. Brunel, Humbert, Chatelain & Wetstein, & they approve all the Requests of M. Des Maizeaux. Thus you only have to write to him this evening, & ask him to hurry with the Life of Bayle.   V.S.G. Smith[124]

The language of these documents, and many others like them, bespeaks a skilled and professional representation of the author's interests.

Profit and Gratitude

So literary agents were willing to assist authors whom they did not know, and they were willing to go to great lengths to find publishers, make terms, and even, on occasion, represent authors in written contracts.[125] Another indication that agents were different from the scholarly citizens of the Republic of Letters would of course be that, whereas scholars performed their services for free, agents got paid. But in fact this was not the case. In all the correspondence I have read between agents and authors, I have never seen references to payment for services rendered. In fact, in bills from agents to authors, the only items mentioned were books purchased for others from Dutch booksellers. Even the service of procuring these books was apparently free.[126]

Sometimes, it is true, the author would give a copy of the newly published work to the agent, or the agent might even take it on his own. The Père Le Courayer wrote De la Motte from London in 1731, "You did quite right to take a copy of my work for yourself. I intended one for you, and no one deserves one more. I'm merely ashamed that I have nothing better to give you for all your trouble, and that I can only pay you in simple gratitude."[127] Even this gift copy was sometimes not offered, or was refused, because if the agent also corrected the edition he was supposed to receive a copy from the *libraire* as "droit de correcteur."[128] Thus La Croze dispensed with giving Marchand a copy of his *Histoire du christianisme des Indes*; "I do not know that I might not have committed an error in not giving you a copy of my Book," he wrote. "What prevented me is that I believed that that was the responsibility of Monsieur Vaillant"—the *libraire*—"and not mine."[129]

Nevertheless, the "simple gratitude" with which the Père Le Courayer paid De la Motte seems in itself to have been a valued return. De la Motte, unable to persuade the *libraire* Pierre Mortier to print some posthumous pieces in a translation of the works of Chillingworth, bridled at the translator's annoyance after all his trouble over the rest of the edition. "I believe it would be better to attribute the refusal to print the posthumous Pieces of Chill. to Mortier rather than to me. The Translator ought to be obliged to me for having procured the Ed. of his Translation, which has stayed hidden in my study for more than two years [i.e. because no one would print it]."[130] The gift copy itself was in fact simply a sign of this gratitude rather than actual pay. Marchand objected to the silence of the minister Jean Des Champs since the publication of his book, "of which he owes me at least a small Thanks if not a Copy of the Work itself. The Libraire, who is more attentive, has not failed in this little mark of Gratitude."[131] Marchand grumbled elsewhere that "it is mortifying that the People for whom one acts respond so badly to what one does for them."[132]

If agents were not paid, why should they take on these sometimes quite heavy obligations? This question brings us back to the issue of reciprocity and exchange. It is not that agents would expect return favors, although that was occasionally the case, or even that they appreciated gratitude for their trouble. Instead, the important point is that agents would in fact receive material benefit in return for their services. The refusal of gift copies in favor of the "droit de correcteur" should be a clue here. Agents were willing to work on behalf of authors because, if they placed a manuscript, they were quite likely to be employed by the *libraire* on that book's publication. Admittedly this did not always happen, especially when the *libraire* was in another city. De la Motte tried to find a *libraire* in Amsterdam for Des Maizeaux's collection of Bayle's letters; when this failed he succeeded with Gaspard Fritsch and Michael Böhm in Rotterdam. It would have been preferable for both agent and editor for the work to be printed where it was convenient for De la Motte to correct it. But "I doubt very much that Mr. Fritsch will agree to print this Work here, because they have their own Printing-house in Rotterdam, & they always maintain a Compositor & a Printer, whether or not they are working. But this should not disturb you, there is a *galant homme* who corrects their Books & does so very well."[133] Yet it was common enough for *libraires* to hire agents as correctors for the books they had promoted for De la Motte to report, "I never read the Mss. I have in my hands when they are going to be printed, I always wait to do it when giving them to the Printer."[134] So literary agents such as Marchand and De la Motte, who made their livings working freelance[135] on editions, were happy to place manuscripts at least in part because they were likely to profit from their own services. They were drumming up business for themselves.

Agents, then, received their return from the *libraire* himself. Sometimes, it is true, De la Motte's source of income seems a bit mysterious; the few times it is mentioned in his correspondence it sounds too meager to support him. After making arrangements for Des Maizeaux, De la Motte sighed that "as for me, I often prefer to give in rather than fight. I have rectified more than 100 Articles in the Index that the person who made the Index had not found. . . . I have copied and put in their place the critical remarks &c. in nearly 3 vols. & they promised to pay me for all this, I only asked them for a Copy of the Traité de la Police, I do not have it yet & I do not know if I ever will, but I will not ask for it again."[136] But aside from his complaints, a few references make it plain that he was regularly paid for his correcting work.

> Since Wetstein could not attend [the meeting of the Compagnie des Libraires], he asked me to give your letter to one of his Confrères. I did not want to go there myself, I have a complaint with two Libraires of this Company, & I was afraid of getting too angry with them. This is what it's all about. M. Devaulx & I corrected this Book, one of those who had to sign the account (There are two who have to sign it, & the third one pays it) but this was not necessary, because the account had been examined & approved by the entire Company, although attacked very *mal à propos* by 2. However the Cashier did not want to pay it on the pretext that the account had not been properly signed by the 2 directors. One signed it right off, but the other did not want to do it, & it will be necessary to attend this month's meeting. The Cashier's real reason is that he has used the money he received in another way. Another petty thing they have done to us, is that they want to give us only one Copy between the two of us.[137]

Isabella van Eeghen reports that correctors in the first quarter of the eighteenth century were paid between 12 stuivers and 1 florin 4 stuivers a sheet; in the 1750s and 60s the *libraires* Luchtmans in Leiden paid correctors of scholarly works between 5 stuivers and fl. 3:10 a sheet. Percy Simpson's figures for eighteenth-century England fall between 7/6 and 10/6 per sheet for scholarly work.[138] A regular supply of sheets to correct—and De la Motte complained repeatedly of overwork—meant a steady income at this level.

Agents, Scholars, and the Despotic Tyranny of Booksellers

Was the agent thus simply a commercial figure, comparable to a travel agent who is paid by the airline rather than the customer? It has been suggested to me that literary agents were not agents for the author at all, but rather the *commissionnaires* of the booksellers.[139] Of the five definitions of *commissionnaire* given by Jacques Savary's *Le parfait négociant* (1675), none exactly suits the work done by someone like De la Motte. The closest, perhaps, is Savary's first definition: "The first sort or type of *Commissionnaires*, are Traders who live in Manufacturing areas, or in the Town where there is much commerce, who buy merchandise on the account of Traders living in other places, who entrust it to them [i.e. the *commissionnaires*]."[140] Yet most transactions involved not looking for manuscripts for *libraires*, but rather looking for *libraires* for manuscripts.[141] The agent was there to persuade the *libraire* to accept a work, whether or not the agent himself liked it; he might not be hopeful for its chances, but he would try all the same. De la Motte reported to Des Maizeaux in 1711 that "I hope that I will soon be able to bring Humbert & Bernard around to printing your life of St. Evremond. I believe I have convinced them that it is in their interest."[142] He might have to work hard to manage this, and he was held morally responsible for the decision. In 1730 Thémiseul de St.-Hyacinthe stopped sending the copy for a book; three months later De la Motte grumbled that "the Libraire is persecuting me, because it was at my solicitation that he began printing without having all the Copy, against his better judgment."[143]

The issue is not completely straightforward, however, because the agent sometimes felt a responsibility to both parties. Sentiment entered into the transaction. When De la Motte was trying to place the translation of Chillingworth by Durette, a work he considered flawed, he asked Des Maizeaux whether it should really be published. "It would be hard on Mr. Durette, who has taken the trouble to translate them, and who is expecting a recompense for his work, to see himself frustrated," De la Motte said. "But on the other hand, it would be a shame to engage a young *libraire* who has confidence in you and me in large expenses that he will not be able to recover."[144]

Once the agent was working for a *libraire* on an edition, he became his spokesman in correspondence with the author. Often, in the course of publication, he would convey messages to the author about when copy was needed, how to send material to Holland by a means cheaper for the *libraire*, when to send errata found on the second proofs, and so on. He appeared to identify with the *librairie*, often using "nous" to describe those working on the publication: "It was 8 days ago, Monsieur, that I sent you the 2 sheets of the Vie de Bayle, here are two more of them, & the sheets are being printed at the moment, they finish at page 48 of the Copy. As there is an extra Compositor & the Work is hoped to be finished this Month, it is desirable that we receive the next part as soon as possible."[145] Messages to be passed to the author from the *libraires* were almost always sent through the agent, and indeed De la Motte commented at one point that "I hope Messrs. Fritsch [and Böhm] will pay me the postage for your Letters, which concern them, neither you nor I is rich enough to afford these costs."[146]

This behavior was natural, given that after the contract stage De la Motte gave up his role as agent to take on that of corrector of the press. He was now the employee of the *libraire* and had no responsibility to the author. Yet, interestingly enough, once this change was effected his defense of the author's interests continued.

This was logistically possible because of his considerable control over the details of publication. Until now very little has been known about what I call the direction of editions: who was the intelligence behind decisions about format, whether there should be an index, who should write the preface, what the title page should look like, where the notes should be, how wording might be changed, and so on. In many cases it is clear that the freelance De la Motte was in fact this intelligence. His interest for us lies not merely in the availability of his letters, but also in the fact that he was known at the time as the premier corrector in Holland. Jean Barbeyrac wrote to Jean-Alphonse Turrettini in 1712, "you can count on M^r. de la Motte not to neglect anything he can do to have them [Turrettini's works] printed well. He will be the Corrector himself, & a more exact person could not be found. He has corrected everything I have published, & he corrects almost everything important that is printed in Amsterdam."[147] Again at the end of his career he was identified as having been the most important corrector of his time. Jean Des Champs, when in Amsterdam in 1747,

did not fail to visit the good Mr. *La Motte*, an old man in his eighties, and of very short stature, for I am taller than he is by half a head. You know that he has had the role of *Corrector* all his life. . . . Currently it is Mr. *Cartier de St Philip* author of the *Je ne sais quoi* [a journal] who is the principal *Corrector*, and after him Mr. *Massuet*.[148]

The high regard of printers and publishers for De la Motte's work meant that he often was given free rein over the details of publication. This meant that he was able, if he so desired, to arrange the book as best suited the author. As early as 1705, when the *libraire* Pierre Mortier showed signs of intransigence about a work, De la Motte took it out of his hands and warned the editor, "when you have something to be printed, just propose it to me, and I will try to find you a more accommodating *libraire*. There are several who leave everything entirely to me concerning the arrangement of their works, and if those are your *libraires* you can be sure that all your wishes will be followed."[149]

The attitudes of both the *libraires* and corrector were thus of considerable use to an author like Pierre Des Maizeaux.[150] They put the corrector in a position to be of both general and specific assistance. De la Motte would make use of his access to information about what was happening in the Dutch publishing world to encourage an author in his career, pointing out in

December of 1728, for example, that since the fourth edition of Bayle's *Dictionary* would probably not appear until March, Des Maizeaux had time to contribute the life of Bayle he had contemplated for over twenty years.[151] In the conduct of actual editions, he consulted closely with authors over minute details of format. This meant that authors could have far more say in the appearance of editions than has previously been thought. Pierre Coste thus felt free to write with instructions on the exact appearance of a title page,[152] and Pierre Des Maizeaux could get results when he asked that text be more easily distinguished from notes. De la Motte wrote him about his edition of Bayle's *Letters*:

> You will see by the sheets, that part of what you wanted has been done, the lines of text have been put in larger type than the Notes, but they [the *libraires*] felt that, besides the fact that the type of the Notes better suits that of the Text than a larger one, it will make the Volumes too large. They need to keep the book from being too expensive, at least by much. I have diminished the pages by one Line, put in little vignettes in front of each Letter, & put a title page at the beginning of the first sheet. I also made all the corrections that you sent me. It is not possible that there is even a capital Letter where you do not want one. The Copy is full of them, even the Notes written in your hand. In fact I have to pay particular attention to them, because I am accustomed to putting them in various places where you would not want them.[153]

Even more striking is that De la Motte would sometimes alter the very production of an edition for the sake of the author. Des Maizeaux was very anxious for a portrait of Bayle to appear in the 1729 edition of the *Dictionary*, but the engraver needed six months to do it. It seemed very unlikely to be finished by the time the book was to appear. So De la Motte promised Des Maizeaux to take so long in making the index that the book would still be in press when the portrait was done. All this, naturally, he did without saying anything to the *libraires*, who would certainly not have approved.[154] Similarly, in 1720 he defied the wishes of Mortier on a new edition of Boileau in duodecimo. Mortier did not want to add anything to the edition and even planned to remove the *Vie de Boileau* by Des Maizeaux. De la Motte told Des Maizeaux that he would use the latter's notes in any case, adding that "if you have any others that you would be very pleased to put in, I could certainly include them without saying anything to Mortier, even though I do not read all the Proofs."[155]

The most telling example of De la Motte's allegiance to authors over publishers comes from 1728. The Compagnie des Libraires was to publish Des Maizeaux's edition of Bayle's letters, having promised thirty copies to Des Maizeaux as part of the payment. But in November 1728, when the work was printed, they reneged on the promise of so many copies. De la Motte had earlier tried to make a written contract but could never get the whole group together at once. His only recourse in helping Des Maizeaux was to show them the letter he had written him, laying out the agreed conditions; he himself had thrown away Des Maizeaux's response. This required him to get the letter back from Des Maizeaux.

But I am afraid that you will not have kept it. If this is so, I would like you to send me another Letter dated either the end of the year 1726, or the beginning of 1727, where you write that you pray me to ask in your name 3 florins per sheet & 30 Copies for the copy, & point out that you are obliged to give a number of copies to the people who furnished you with the Letters, I will not have any scruple about saying several days after I have received it that I have found the Letter again. I mortally hate dissimulation and oblique methods, but in truth on this occasion I would be pardonable. In any case you must address this Letter to me directly, & you must not go to van der Hoeke's until you believe that I will have received this Letter, & you must then write me under cover of Wetstein [one of the *libraires* in question] that you were not in town when my Letter of Friday arrived, so that no one suspects that we have conspired together and that you have sent me such a Letter.[156]

De la Motte was thus willing to lie to his employers to uphold the interests of the author, his long-time "client" in his role as literary agent. He also showed considerable discomfort in his role as representative of the *libraire*. On one occasion he wrote a letter on behalf of the *libraire* Mortier, to be sent by the *libraire*, urging authorial diligence on an edition; the same day he wrote a private letter by another route, criticizing his employer. He did the same a week later, and it is clear whose interests he ultimately had at heart.

I wrote to you by the last post in Mr. Mortier's packet, but I wanted to write to you by another channel in order to be able to say *entre nous*, that I do not have enough power over the mind of M. Mortier to oblige him to do what you wished, & I doubt that there is anyone who can make him change his mind once he has made it up. . . . I spent all of 2 Sundays (the only day when he has some leisure) in persuading him to use the title *Mélanges curieux*. All the Letters that you have written me on this subject have passed through his hands, before coming to me he has read them, & he excused himself by saying that he had not noticed they were addressed to me. . . . All I can do is say that, if you have something else to publish, you must choose another Libraire, & I am sure that I will be in control.[157]

Like the scholars of the Republic of Letters, then, agents would promote manuscripts with *libraires* at least partly for the sake of reciprocity, and in the latter case the reward of the action was success in their own business of correction of the press. We have also seen that, even when the agent's role was transformed during the printing of a work, he would continue to identify more strongly with the interests of the author than with those of the *libraire*. Given that De la Motte's livelihood depended on the *libraires* of Amsterdam, why should he have been willing to trick them for the author's sake?

One reason is that the reciprocal relation between author and agent would not end with the placing of the manuscript. The agent not only mediated between the *libraire* and the author, and tried to carry out the author's wishes, but also profited from a continued good relation with him. When an author received good service from an agent, he would not only return to him the next time he had written something, as we have seen in the case of Jean Barbeyrac, but also mention him to his friends, as Barbeyrac did to Turrettini, and Lenfant and La Croze did to Pelloutier. Thus the cycle of exchange, service for business, could go on and on.

But another reason ties the agents once again into the Republic of Letters. For the fact was that agents identified with scholars because they felt more akin to them than to their employers, the *libraires*. From the sixteenth century on, proofreaders were often drawn from the ranks of the learned. This was more common in the early days of printing;[158] later on the profession became more specialized, but learned men continued to look to correction as a source of income in hard times. Bayle did occasional work as a corrector for Leers, for example, and indeed a job sometimes sought by educated Protestant refugees was as corrector of the press.[159] The professional corrector had to be an educated man; the job demanded it. According to Joseph Moxon in the 1680s,

> A *Correcter* should (besides the *English* Tongue) be well skilled in Languages, especially those that are used to be Printed with us, *viz.* the *Latin, Greek, Hebrew, Syriack, Caldae, French, Spanish, Italian, High Dutch, Saxon, Low Dutch, Welch, &c.* neither ought my innumerating only these be a stint to his skill in the number of them, for many times several other Languages may happen to be Printed, of which the Author has perhaps no more skill than the bare knowledge of the Words and their Pronunciations, so that the Orthography (if the *Correcter* have no knowledge of the Language) may not only be false to its Native Pronunciation, but the Words altered into other Words by a little wrong Spelling, and consequently the Sense made ridiculous, the purpose of it controvertible, and the meaning of the Author irretrievably lost to all that shall read it in After times.
>
> He ought to be very knowing in Derivations and Etymologies of Words, very sagacious in *Pointing*, skilful in the *Compositers* whole Task and Obligation, and endowed with a quick Eye to espy the smallest *Fault*.[160]

Both Marchand and De la Motte fell into the category of professional correctors who were educated, rather than educated men who did some correction. Correcting and editing for them was a full-time job and their source of financial support. Yet they did participate in the learned world. At the age of 15 Marchand was certified by the rector of the University of Paris as "adequate in the Latin language and ... he can read Greek."[161] After giving up the *librairie* to turn to correction, he also did some scholarship, particularly on the history of printing, and wrote for several literary journals. We know nothing about De la Motte's education, except that he spoke several languages, and he never published a work. He said that "although the work I do is not very taxing to the mind," he was glad that writing tired him, not wanting to "fatigue the public with my feeble productions, something which is even more to be feared since I am continually surrounded by manuscripts and books to be printed."[162] But despite his unwillingness to contribute to scholarship, he behaved very much like active scholars, socializing with them, commenting learnedly on the latest books, and acting as probably the best source in Europe for literary gossip.[163] When his eyesight began to fail in the 1730s, one of his correspondents, the Huguenot minister Armand de la Chapelle, commented that "this is afflicting news for people who admire you, and even for the Republic of Letters, to which you were so useful in so many ways."[164]

Moreover, as we have already observed, the agents' distaste for many *libraires* was marked. Marchand himself, a former member of the booksellers' guild, was incensed when in a literary quarrel Des Maizeaux referred to him as an *"Ex-Libraire."*[165] This was a common attitude among scholars, who believed that people involved in the book trade were more interested in money than in learning. In his book on the Plantin Press, Léon Voet points out that "a publishing printer is not a philanthropist. He decides what texts he can print on the basis of their potential sales."[166] But it was just this mode of thought which disturbed the scholars, since books that would sell were rarely those which would "do honor to the Republic of Letters." Godefroy Clermont wrote in 1716 that

> I see more and more with a terrible sadness the small interest *libraires* take in the edition of the best books. Present them with Satiric writings, books of fables and stories, in a word books which do more to corrupt the heart than solidly to instruct the spirit, the terms are soon made and the book on the press, but as for good books, either of erudition or of Theology, they have all kinds of excuses for slowing or refusing publication.[167]

The mercenary spirit of the book trade was thought to engender a dishonesty completely foreign to the ideals of the Republic of Letters. Jacques de Pérard, later an editor of the *Bibliothèque germanique*, returned from a trip to Holland with the report that "if you made a journey to Holland and you got to know yourself the *libraires*, the Correctors, and all the intrigues of these two professions you would be amazed to find so much duplicity and deceit among people who talk so much of probity and good faith."[168] And Jacques Bernard, professor of philosophy at Leiden, said in 1701 that he could write a fat book about all the tricks of which *libraires* were capable, later adding, however, that "several among them would set the Republic of Letters alight, and perhaps the *libraires* would ill-treat me."[169]

Scholars chafed at having to be subject to what Michel Mattaire called "the Despotique Tyranny of Booksellers."[170] *Libraires* may have shared their interest in books, but for the wrong reasons; they were not members of the Republic of Letters.[171] They ought to show respect to scholars instead of treating them shabbily. Antoine de la Barre de Beaumarchais complained in his literary journal that the authors of another journal, published by the Wetsteins, had used the word *chargé* when describing a *libraire*'s negotiations with a scholar. "A Libraire does not *order* a man such as Monsieur *Saurin* to do a work. He tries to engage him to do it, he prays him for it. Perhaps the good Monsieur *Wetstein* behaves less politely with these Messieurs?"[172] All in all the issue in most minds came down to Pierre Coste's assertion: "Books must not be for the Libraires, but for the Public."[173]

The agents participated in these views of their employers, thus implicitly identifying themselves with the Republic of Letters. De la Motte commented frequently on the crudity and avarice of *libraires*, calling the firm Covens and Mortier, for example, "the most defiant and the most impolite of the Bibliopolic type that I know, and that is saying a lot, because the Lord has blessed this species of animals." He even said of a *libraire* who was on his deathbed, "In my opinion he is better off in this world than he will be in the next."[174] Agents, like scholars, felt that *libraires* were only interested in selling books, whereas they were anxious for editions that would instruct and enlighten, works, again, that would "do honor to the Republic of Letters." Marchand, who was in constant professional and social contact with *libraires*, had no doubt that they would ruin editions if they thought it to their profit.

You will see new Proof of this in a little while in the *Histoire de Mr de Thou*, put into French in haste in Paris by various hired Writers, scrapping the 1st Vol. because they are going to use the one of Prévot-d'Exile[s] which will be better, revised or rather mangled by four or Five Wretches who are absolutely incapable of doing anything good with it & printed as hastily here as it has been botched in Paris. If You read the Lettres Juives, You will see in the New Edition which has just appeared, how people are talking here of this terrible Rhapsody. . . . A Book like this, & such a respectable one, doubtless deserved a better fate, but nothing is safe from the acquisitiveness of Libraires who only employ People as famished as they themselves are greedy.[175]

Libraires' desire to suit the popular taste was as serious as their indifference to scholarly standards. In 1743 Marchand returned a manuscript to Formey, having failed to place it with any *libraire*; here, he said, was "your Manuscript of the *Sources of Morality*, with which, despite all my trouble, I could do absolutely nothing. Considering the way our Libraires are fashioned, if this had been some freethinking, even dirty Treatise, of the *Pleasures of Vice*, I would have infallibly succeeded."[176]

The existence of even a few literary agents in the eighteenth century gives us clues to an important trend in the Republic of Letters. The literary community was becoming more professionalized.[177] Institutions—academies, journals, literary societies—took over some of the roles, duties, and activities of scholarship. Communication, for example, did not have to be from individual to individual; it could take place between academies, and pass thence to scholars, or be encapsulated in literary journals, to be diffused among the whole scholarly community. Literary agents, working for *libraires* but sharing the values of the learned community, demonstrate this professionalization on the most fundamental level. The roles they played represent the crystallization of scholarly ideals in a more professional connection.

We have seen that the Republic of Letters invoked an ethos of service whose existence strengthened its members' sense of community. This ethos itself rose out of communal operations; it was self-reinforcing. The assistance of others was of vital importance in accomplishing the goals of scholarship, and, knowing that cooperation was an unwritten rule of learned society, scholars relied on the "rights of the Republic of Letters" to ask the services they required. The increased contact engendered by this process expanded the networks of individual scholars and entangled them in more complex ties of indebtedness and obligation. It also drew them into the community by identifying their own interests with those of the wider scholarly world.

In these processes, the need for intermediaries was manifest. Status differences within the Republic, as well as the need to show respect, made the intervention of others a helpful expedient in getting things done. An agent or intercessor generally had more credit with the person asked for services than did the person profiting from the request. The action of an intermediary, moreover, would promote contact within the community, contributing to communication and a sense of scholarly enterprise.

Not surprisingly, savants tended to look for help where it could best be found. They naturally turned to people they knew, but in the case of specific services they would find the person most likely to achieve the desired result. Lenfant, for example, appealed to all his contacts for manuscript sources for the *Histoire du concile de Basle*, but his first recourse was to professors at the university of Bâle itself, who could provide the most important archival materials. The case of literary agents was similar. As scholarly publication in books and journals became more widespread, and the book trade expanded in the eighteenth century, scholars hoping to publish once again looked for a way to accomplish all of their goals. They usually felt they could not write on their own account, recalling the need for an intermediary for a satisfactory result in most transactions. And although scholars themselves contacted *libraires* for their colleagues, their lack of expertise in the trade meant that they could not deal in details, not to mention control the progress of the edition. In most cases, moreover, an individual scholar was not close enough to the book trade to be very persuasive. Maturin Veyssière La Croze, writing from Berlin, probably could not make much more specific deals with the *libraires* of Amsterdam than his friend Leibniz, for whom he acted.

Literary agents like De la Motte and Marchand were a valuable resource precisely because they stood halfway between the Republic of Letters and the "Despotique Tyranny of Booksellers." Their close involvement in the production of books and their wide acquaintance with the whole world of the Dutch book trade put them in good credit with just those people scholars hoped to influence. And, crucially, their identification with the goals of learning—their interest in new books, ability to correct scholarly footnotes, and disdain for the money-grubbing spirit of the *librairie*—meant that literary agents were not only able, but willing to serve the interests of scholars. Their influence over the details of production allowed them to carry out authors' wishes in detail; their identification with the scholarly community made them able to comprehend and approve of those wishes. By using agents who were neither mere scholars nor mere factors, the learned indeed found the most useful contacts for their needs.

The increasing density of the eighteenth-century learned world made activities possible which would foreshadow those of the "first" agent, A.P. Watt, in the late nineteenth century. Ever-increasing contact, and ever-increasing desire for contact, made the professionalization of that contact attractive for scholars in the Republic of Letters. The agent's wide correspondence and links with publishing made him, like his new country, an ideal entrepôt, in this case for messages, letters, and manuscripts. Like so many aspects of the learned world, this work added to the spiral toward a closer community. And in his mediating position between the scholars and the traders, the agent sowed the seeds for an even more complete institutionalization of the ideals of the Republic of Letters.

The future was already visible in this period. Indeed, one enterprising *commissionnaire* in Paris was offering his services for pay, doing for all Englishmen "Curious in Books, and other Matters in the Learned Way" the kinds of commissions normally performed by friends. For two guineas a year he would obtain books and manuscripts, send information about book publication and auctions, and transact any other scholarly business required of him. In fact, "the said Commissioner having a general Acquaintance with the Chief Learned in Paris, & several other Parts of Europe, if any of the Gentlemen Subscribers shou'd have occasion of Consulting any of them, either in regard to the Publishing any Learned Works, or any Affair of Literature, he can procure their Advice or Correspondence." At the time of advertisement, he claimed already to have fifty clients for the scheme.[178]

But Charles de la Motte, paid only obliquely for his favors, was a better representative of the eighteenth-century Republic of Letters than our anonymous *commissionnaire*. De la Motte did not make literary agency his only profession, and he did not make his living directly from it. The *commissionnaire* was a man of business; but the trading of information for money was, among scholars, beyond the pale. Marc Meibom, who reportedly "only wants to reveal . . . the Mysteries [of his work] for a large Sum of money," was described by the scholar Groddeck as "the most impertinent man in the world. . . . I remember having asked him something I can't remember now, and he said, if you give me two Ducats I'll tell you, otherwise I won't."[179] This was not scholarly reciprocity; it was commerce, and thus outside the Republic of Letters. The ethos of personal obligation remained; and in the next chapter we will see how the values of the Republic of Letters obstructed its own professionalization.

2

WRITING TO THE PAPERS

LEARNED JOURNALS AND THE REPUBLIC
IN TRANSITION

The End of the World

Pierre-Daniel Huet, Bishop of Soissons, was predicting doom. In the 1680s and 1690s he foresaw at least the decay of learning, if not the fall of civilization. The seeds had been planted first in the 1660s, but as he was writing, the malevolence was suddenly multiplying and spreading its evil tentacles to the corners of Europe. The culprit, for Huet, was the literary journal.

"You would be appalled," he wrote to a friend in 1698,

> if you knew what decadence letters have fallen into in France/ I received a letter two days ago from one of the principal Libraires of Paris/ He told me, that if you took a Latin book to be printed in the rue S^t. Jacques, people would laugh in your face/. . . . since I have been alive, I have seen the sciences declining continually/ I don't see that they are managing any better in Holland/ England is the place defending itself the best/ In the Preface of the little treatise I wrote, I could not help but speak against the barbarousness of this century, of which all these Abridgements of books people are publishing in Paris, in Rotterdam, in Leipzig, are the indubitable proofs/

He concluded dramatically, "When in Rome people made Abridgements of the great Latin works, & at Constantinople of the great Greek works, barbary followed close behind."[1]

Some people had been deluded by the journal, Huet said, even claiming it had benevolent effects. By synthesizing information and news, and speeding communications among scholars, journals were making scholarship easier and quicker; and to the hardworking this appeared to open the Republic of Letters to the *demi-savants*. Adrien Baillet pointed out early on that summaries and abridgements of books, a subset of which made up the bulk of the literary journals, accrued enemies primarily among "the Critics & generally all the studious" because they appeared to promote laziness and superficiality among scholars. "Many love & seek out these Abridgements," Baillet wrote, "because they are appropriate to their laziness, because they want to skim over the surface of things, & because they consider themselves skillful when they know the general definitions, the divisions & the terms of the Arts. But judicious persons believe rightly that it is better to be entirely ignorant of things than to know them badly."[2] Huet said that journals were for "those who do not want to give themselves the trouble of reading the entire books/ People believe they are attaining knowledge by these abridged methods & people are fooling themselves/People are rather attaining ignorance."[3]

When Pierre Bayle founded his *Nouvelles de la République des Lettres* in 1684, he had no real inkling of its future influence. His was not the first such journal, but its tremendous success prompted an explosion of literary periodicals which represented fundamental changes in the Republic of Letters. Noting in 1698 the refounding of his former journal, the appearance of new Latin periodicals in Lübeck and Frankfurt, and the possible continuation of Henri Basnage de Beauval's *Histoire des ouvrages des savans*, Bayle predicted that "all of Europe is going to fill up with *journaux des scavans*."[4]

In the justificatory prefaces which usually accompanied such journals, most made specific reference to Bayle's example.[5] The *Nouvelles* had been an instant success. As Elisabeth Labrousse points out, Bayle's provincial origins made him uniquely able to understand the type of material that would be of interest to his chosen public.[6] That fact, combined with his lively style, his use of French, the comparative freedom of the press in the Netherlands, and the good connections of both the Dutch book trade and the new Huguenot Réfuge made his journal so popular that it was immediately imitated. Many of these journals were by Huguenots and other French-speaking refugees, and, wherever they were written, most were published in Holland. The importance of this foreign press for the Francophone reading public is evident from figures calculated by Jean Sgard: of the 350 French-speaking journalists known between 1685 and 1789, 86 lived in Holland, 45 in England, 20 in Germany, and 30 in Switzerland.[7]

But the praise for Bayle was not just because he had done so well. By founding a journal he had also answered a crying need in the Republic of Letters. According to the *Bibliothèque raisonnée des ouvrages des savans de l'Europe*, newly formed in 1728, "It's not at all for the sake of multiplying books without necessity that we have formed the design of this Literary Journal. One must regard it less as a new Work, than as a Continuation of those, of the same type, which have appeared, in *French*, since 1684. in the *United Provinces*. On the example of Mr. *Bayle*, for more than 40. years, various authors there have set themselves up as Nouvellistes of the Republic of Letters."[8] The *Bibliothèque raisonnée*, in other words, simply performed the function whose necessity Bayle had proven to the Republic of Letters.

Journals did represent a new and different way of conducting business in the Republic of Letters. Like the printed book before them, journals intensified and multiplied the circulation of information; and since they consisted largely of book reviews (known as *extraits*), they increased enormously scholars' potential knowledge about what was going on in their own community. Just as manuscript *nouvelles à la main*, news-sheets, and eventually newspapers grew out of an increasingly voracious market for information, not to mention an increasingly organized business designed to supply it, literary journals stemmed from an institutionalization of previous contacts.[9] Humanist and *érudit* circles had sent their news by letter; now a more formalized and widespread communication was possible. By focussing the transmission of information about the Republic of Letters onto an institution, the journal, rather than onto individuals, the scholarly periodical gave shape to a sense of participation in the learned community. But by institutionalizing relations in the Republic of Letters the journal also had to confront scholars' values about communal relations. The results, as we shall see, were problematic.

Without the help of literary journals, scholars had to rely on personal connections, which were sometimes formalized in regular news-letters.[10] Gisbert Cuper may have had such an arrangement with Godefroy Clermont, to whom he wrote in 1715, "I have already seen and read the literary News, of which you are sending me six sheets, I will have them brought here by the Deventer messenger every week; they please me very much, and tell us various details, which are not disagreeable to read."[11] Although many people were not so regularly provided with information, correspondence still served to keep most people at least vaguely in touch with the rest of the Republic of Letters. This was usually not satisfactory to people insatiable for news, however, and since, as we saw in the previous chapter, literary news was one commodity of exchange for the Republic, it was important to everyone to have news to send as well as to receive. Camusat remarked in the 1720s on "the excessive desire to promote oneself through news [*de se faire valoir par des nouvelles*]," which in his view made many *nouvelles littéraires* unreliable.[12]

Although literary journals did not necessarily solve the problem of the need to exchange news, they greatly supplemented and indeed in some ways replaced the *commerce de lettres* as a means of disseminating information quickly. Scholarly letters and scholarly journals tended to discuss the same sorts of topics: what was being published, when, and where; what people thought of it; who was working on what; who was quarreling with whom and about what. The resemblance was apparent from the very beginning of the first journal, the *Journal des Sçavans*, which promised that until new books came out to review, the journal would talk about those which are "still . . .

the most usual subject of the conversations of Savants."[13] Literary journals simply codified and formalized such conversations and correspondences for wider distribution. Thus although Jean-Pierre de Crousaz might have written to Jean-Théophile Desaguliers in London to learn more about his scientific ideas, he mentioned in doing so that he had already read a great deal about Desaguliers and that, in fact, "I wish that the French Journals of Gr. Britain talked to us more often about you & about what you are doing."[14]

Françoise Waquet has argued that literary journals did not in fact replace the *commerce de lettres*. As she correctly points out, journals depended on letters for their own information. Moreover, the periodical press often failed to satisfy the scholarly desire for news. Its publication and sale were often too slow to satisfy readers, and its discussions of books and news could seem incomplete for such reasons as specialization, religious bias, or simple distortion.[15] Letters clearly remained desirable and useful. Yet it is certain that, from the time journals became a central feature of the Republic of Letters, many readers gained their news primarily from that source. So Jean Jallabert could write to Louis Bourguet from Geneva that "You ask me, Monsieur, for literary news, I do not know any which could be [new] for you, since you apparently receive the journals as quickly as we do."[16] In the same way, Cuper dispensed himself from informing Bignon of the books newly printed in Amsterdam, pointing out that "their titles & their contents are in the Journals, which no doubt are sent from here to Paris; thus I need not tell you about them"; and Paul-Emile de Mauclerc told his teacher La Croze that "the Journals will instruct you of the News I could tell you."[17] Cuper even made the connection between the growth of journals and the change in the *commerces*, telling Clermont that "the multitude of Journals assuredly means, that people do not speak of literary novelties very much in familiar letters."[18]

Moreover, literary news from the journals themselves actually became a subject of letters between scholars. A letter from Jean Barbeyrac to Jean-Alphonse Turrettini in 1710, for example, read in part, "I do not know if you have the 1st part of Vol XXI of the Bibliothèque Choisie yet in Geneva, which I just received. You will see there a new Letter from M[r]. Lenfant, on the subject of the N.T. of Mill, of which the critique that M[r]. Kuster made in the new Edition of this N.T. was the occasion of one of the previous remarks of M[r]. Lenfant. There are also Extraits of several English Treatises which are very virulent & very carried away against the Book about the *Droits de l'Eglise Chrétienne* &c." Such references to articles appearing in recent journals were a staple of eighteenth-century scholarly correspondence.[19]

But as Huet's example makes plain, not everyone was pleased with the effects journals were having on the community. When someone like the classicist Gisbert Cuper remarked, as he did in 1708, that "one could call this

Century, the Century of Journals," he was not necessarily enthusiastic. Cuper, like Huet and Baillet, pointed out that "many people content themselves with them [i.e. journals] & scarcely consult the originals, which assuredly is nothing else than touching superficially on their Studies."[20] And although by 1719 journals had become well-established as a means of scholarly communication and interchange, their first historian, the Abbé Denis-François Camusat, reported that for the same reasons "there still are pig-headed people prejudiced against this useful invention."[21]

Yet despite Cuper's objections to journals, he did adapt to their use. His correspondence makes it clear that he read the journals with interest. In 1708 his personal library contained copies of the popular Francophone periodicals by Le Clerc, Bernard, and Basnage de Beauval, as well as Van Gaveren's *Boekzaal der Geleerde Weereld*, Burkhard Struvius' *Acta Litteraria, Nova Literaria Germaniqe collecta Hamburgi, Bibliotheca Antiqua Jenae*, Jean-Jacques Scheuchzer's *Nova Literaria Helvetica*, and the *Bibliotheca Librorum Novorum* by Ludolph Kuster and later Henry Sikes. Cuper even wrote to the author of the *Nouvelles de la République des Lettres* that he took "great pleasure in reading" the journal, "and I see with pleasure that you make the Extraits very faithfully, and that you sometimes publish letters that one would perhaps not read without your care."[22] Moreover, as early as 1687 Cuper was sending in books for review, and he was happy to use periodicals such as the *Histoire critique de la République des Lettres* to carry out literary discussions and publicize his own works in progress. He published his answer to an anonymous correction of Callimachus in volume IV of the *Histoire critique*, and in 1715, after negotiation with the journalist Samuel Masson, the "Plan d'un nouvel Ouvrage que Mr. Gisb. Cuper a dessein de publier incessamment, sur les Medailles anciennes où l'on trouve des Elephans" appeared in volume X.[23]

Cuper's objections to the proliferation of journals were apparently not very strenuous. And, indeed, most scholars by this time would have agreed with the authors of the *Journal littéraire*, who in 1713 called journals "perhaps the most advantageous thing that talented men have ever invented for the Republic of Letters."[24] Thus when Leibniz sketched rough plans for a new royal academy at Berlin, one of his important points was that the academy should subscribe to all the European journals or "diaria eruditorum."[25] By 1731 the Academy's library owned some or all of the runs of twenty-nine Francophone periodicals.[26]

Cuper's position on this issue is instructive. He recognized the novelty of journals and was suspicious of their usefulness in the Republic of Letters. Yet he read them and was converted to their use. They provided him with information about books and news of other scholars that even his voluminous correspondence could not have accomplished. But as he became accustomed to journals as a tool, Cuper at the same time found it difficult to think of them as an institution. Contacts were still personalized in Cuper's reading of journals, even if he did not know the people concerned. He could not forbear communicating directly with the authors, managing the new instrument of the Republic just as he had managed the older ones.

Such behavior and such attitudes on the part of both readers and journalists are useful gauges of the state of mind of the learned community in this period. Both the way readers used journals and the way their editors organized their publication indicate the new formalization of relationships in the Republic of Letters. Indeed, the publication of some journals was so professionalized that appropriate relations among the authors were set down in writing. Yet the conception of the journal, from the viewpoint of both reader and author, was still complicated by conceptions of the importance of personal relationships, by the ethos of *honnêteté* and *politesse*. The world of the literary journal puts in focus the way these ideals were changing, and the problems of this difficult transition.

Talking to Themselves

The purpose of literary journals was essentially idealistic. Obviously considerations of power and economics promoted their establishment; journalists became important men in the community, and *libraires* would not have published journals that did not sell. But these very points suggested the importance journals gained in the community and the demand that they filled. Journalists would not have become important, or journals successful, if people did not read them. Conceptions of the Republic of Letters and its proper operations were bound to emerge in journals, so entwined were they with the communal and communicative image of the learned world.

This was particularly true because it appears that the audience, as well as the authorship, of literary journals was largely the Republic of Letters itself. The question of readership is not easy to address. As Elisabeth Labrousse has pointed out, the Republic of Letters consisted not only of its active, productive members, but also "a vast class of passive citizens, pure 'consumers' of books" whose desire for knowledge about such books would have remained unfulfilled without journals such as Bayle's *Nouvelles*.[27] As few journals used subscriptions and we lack subscription lists for nearly all of the others, this group is especially difficult to identify. In their work on the *Novelle Letterarie* of Florence from 1749 to 1769, Françoise and Jean-Claude Waquet found that of its overwhelmingly Italian readership, approximately 44 percent were ecclesiastics, especially regular clergy. Of the remaining lay population, constituting about 55 percent of the total readers, the majority (58.3 percent in 1749–53) were nobles, while a significant proportion (20.1

percent in the same period) were "dottori." Other occupations represented by about 5 percent of the total each were doctors, administrative personnel, lawyers, and professors.[28] However, as the Waquets point out, we cannot necessarily extrapolate this evidence to other journals, as it is in many ways specific both to Italy and to the particular journal in question. Much of the journal, for example, consisted of articles about the church, and most of the authors were themselves ecclesiastics (although not, in general, nobles).[29] Although similar conclusions might be reached about the readership of journals in Protestant countries, where it is certain that many of the authors were clergymen, the fact that most journals promised and at least attempted to keep religion out of their pages makes it difficult to compare the Waquets' findings with a hypothetical readership of northern European journals.

Daniel Mornet's famous study of 500 French sale catalogues is also both instructive and inconclusive. It shows that many of the journals we are interested in were popular in France, but the social breakdown of their popularity is unclear. The 500 private libraries Mornet studied belonged to the following social groups: 62 high nobility, 34 unspecified nobility, 45 ecclesiastics, 29 magistrates, 43 lawyers, 8 *notaires*, 14 doctors and apothecaries, 16 academicians, 2 officers, 1 merchant, 1 painter, 2 architects, 74 functionaries ("inspectors, secretaries, controllers, registrars, councillors, treasurers, commissaries, clerks, directors, pay-clerks, receivers, etc."), 63 unspecified occupations, and 106 anonymous persons.[30] At the time of sale, scholarly journals appeared in the 500 libraries with the following frequency:

Nouvelles de la République des Lettres	101
Le Clerc's various *Bibliothèques*	101
Journal des Savants	83
Histoire des ouvrages des savans	74
Mémoires de Trévoux	50
Journal litéraire	42
Bibliothèque germanique	40
Mémoires littéraires de la Grande Bretagne	40
Du Sauzet's *Mémoires littéraires*	30
Bibliothèque italique	30
Bibliothèque britannique	29
Histoire critique de la République des Lettres	29
Bibliothèque françoise	23
Bibliothèque raisonnée	26
Journal britannique	3[31]

It is interesting to see how popular certain journals were, particularly the *Nouvelles de la République des Lettres*, which, except for Desfontaines' popular journal, was the most widely owned of all the periodicals listed by Mornet.

This is particularly notable since the journal was prohibited in France. But Mornet's figures cannot be used to great effect in discerning either the general popularity of these journals or the makeup of their audience. Since his work only dealt with private libraries in France, any speculation on the meaning of these figures must take into account censorship, differences in taste between France and its neighbors, the operations of the book trade, and the large audience for Francophone periodicals outside France. And since Mornet did not break down the demand for these journals *in* France by social grouping, it is impossible to tell which of the 500 people were most interested in the *Histoire critique* rather than, say, the more popularly oriented *Mercure de France*. The most that can be derived from this study is the notion that more people than those designated purely "Académiciens" owned scholarly periodicals in France.

Another way to discern the intended audience of literary journals is by examining their texts. Casual remarks, language, and contents can all give clues to who might be interested in reading these works. On this basis, there is an indication that some journals, at least, were intended for a general readership, including women. Camusat relates that by calling his journal the *Journal des Sçavans*, Denis de Sallo denied himself readers "who, not believing themselves to have a very extensive erudition, believed that they were being told by this [title], that this work was beyond their understanding." This was still true by the time of the directorship of the Abbé de la Roque, which began in 1681: "At least we see that he was obliged to warn that although the frontispiece of his books seemed to require only Savants by profession, the *Erudite*, for Readers; nevertheless he could assure the uninstructed [*les ignorans*] that they will always find something to amuse themselves & that most of the things discussed there contained nothing which was above the most mediocre intelligence."[32]

In volume II of the *Nouvelles de la République des Lettres*, model for so many other journals, Bayle indicated that he too was taking a middle ground. He reported that some readers were pleased that he was not including "a lot of Chemical, Anatomical, Astronomical, Geometrical, &c. Remarks, nor the description of Monsters, & of unusual diseases." The reason was not that "these things are not very curious, very useful, & very important, but that one can find exactly these in all the Works similar to this which are published throughout Europe." Instead, he said, "it is to be wished that some Nouvelliste of the Republic of Letters attach himself uniquely to other subjects proper for everyone, not excepting Ladies, who presently are enjoying themselves very much in reading good books, provided that there is nothing in them that offends their modesty." Other readers disagreed, however, feeling that such matters—scientific reports and curiosities—ought to be discussed in the journal. In the same way, Bayle wrote, some readers wanted the text to be completely serious, while others appreciated the "little grains of salt" which served to spice up otherwise lengthy accounts. The latter group pointed out that "these Nouvelles are not so much for Doctors, & for Savants by profession, as for an infinite number of people in the world whose natural laziness, or the strains of a heavy job, prevents them from reading a great deal, although they would be very glad to learn." But Bayle refused to take sides in this debate, saying that "it is impossible to satisfy tastes so different; the best thing one can do is sometimes to satisfy one group, sometimes the other."[33]

Another hint that women may have formed part of the readership of journals is that very occasionally authors appear conscious of offending them with obscenity or blasphemy. Potentially offensive items might be translated into one of the learned languages unavailable to most women. The *Bibliothèque italique*, for example, translated into Latin an Italian piece on the voices of eunuchs, pointing out that "the nature of the subject demanded that one translate it into Latin rather than French." And the *Bibliothèque angloise* refused to translate an English passage by Dodwell on the inspiration of the prophets into French, charging that it was irreverent; instead the passage appeared in Latin.[34]

But on the whole such evasions were uncommon, and it appears that the major audience intended for the journals was both educated and male. The content of such journals alone suggests this, most consisting largely of works of classical, historical, and theological scholarship; and although the *Journal littéraire* is a major exception, for the most part journals made little or no attempt to appeal to readers of literature, of whom women made up a considerable proportion. Jean Cornand de la Crose made this quite clear when he asked for books to review in the *Works of the Learned*: "But that they may not lose their books, they [i.e. authors] must remember that this is the *Works of the Learned*, and that I cannot mention Plays, Satyrs, Romances and the like, which are fitter to corrupt men's morals, and to shake the grounds of Natural Religion, than to promote Learning and Piety."[35] Language, again, is an important clue to what was expected of readers. Most journals thought nothing of quoting in Latin, and some even in other languages; the *Bibliothèque italique* occasionally quoted in Italian without bothering to translate.[36] Readers were also supposed to be up on the latest literary news, and journals took care not to offend by presuming otherwise. The *Histoire critique* declined in 1713 to review a new edition of Samuel Bochart's *Opera Omnia*, remarking that "this excellent Work is too well known, for it to be necessary to discuss it with the Public. And it would show a bad opinion of the Reader, to detail what is contained in it."[37]

If we look at the attitudes of the authors of journals in times of strain, we see that the theme of being an educated man, a scholar, was fundamental to their own self-image and their image of their audience. This is evident, for example, in the bitter quarrels among journals competing in The Hague at the end of the 1720s. It must be remembered that to read a journal was in some ways to belong to a club, the club initiated with information provided by that journal. The insults thrown back and forth, usually but not exclusively in aid of a war between *libraires* Jean van Duren and the Wetsteins, suggest that the most fundamental qualification for membership in the group was erudition. Antoine de La Barre de Beaumarchais, author of the *Lettres sérieuses et badines*, felt he could count on the solidarity of his audience when ridiculing the *Bibliothèque raisonnée* on this score. Aiming at Jean Rousset de Missy, one of the authors of the *Bibliothèque raisonnée* who also wrote the *Gazette des savans*, Beaumarchais declared in 1729 that a friend was founding a *Gazette des ignorans*. As the "friend" reportedly wrote,

> MONSIEUR, up to now people have written diverse Relations of what Savants are doing, & they have been published under the Titles of *Diaria, Ephemerides, Acta, Transactions, Nouvelles, Ouvrages,* & *Gazettes des Savans.* But no one has done anything of the kind for the Ignorant. It is clear that this is a crying injustice. On the one hand, the multitude of the latter gives them a considerable rank in the Republic of Letters. *Defendit numerus junctaeque umbone phalanges.* On the other hand, they are the born Judges of the Works which Savants produce, & they make the final judgment on them, the witness of which is the Arrêts which the BIBLIOTHEQUE RAISONNEE pronounces four times a year. These reasons have determined me to put out on Tuesdays & Fridays a GAZETTE DES IGNORANS. I propose to praise therein their Works, & to give an air of wit to their idiocies.[38]

Similarly, Beaumarchais could count on his audience to snicker at his accounts of the *Bibliothèque raisonnée*'s errors of style and reasoning, and particularly his implication they were ignorant of Greek and Latin.[39] At the end of volume I, part 1, he provided a set of translations of the Latin tags in his journal, remarking that "As it has been learned that some of the Savants who work on the *Bibliothèque Raisonnée*, do not understand *Latin,* either because they have not learned it, or because they have forgotten it, it was felt necessary to give here a translation of the Passages written in that Language, which are found in this Work. It is expected not only that this mark of our attention will give them some pleasure, but that they will even be grateful to us for having relieved them of their ignorance on this point."[40] Once again, the implication is that every reader was in a position to scorn such ignorance.

The tone, language, and content of journals thus imply that journalists defined their audience as, essentially, the Republic of Letters: either those who took an active role by writing and instructing others, or those who

2　Frontispiece of the first volume of the *Bibliothèque raisonnée des ouvrages des savans de l'Europe* (Amsterdam: July–Sept. 1728).

contented themselves with reading books and following the debates in the journals. In either case, the audience was assumed to share the same values of erudition and scholarship as the journalists.

The ideals of the Republic of Letters as a community thus come out in journals, both in their own statements of purpose in prefaces and introductions, and in their actual contents. Just as one goal of a *commerce de lettres* was to inform two people, the goal of the journal was to inform many. In the literary journal we see the scholarly community turning, or trying to turn, from individual associations to communal ones.

Journalists and readers alike agreed that, as the *Journal littéraire* said, "the unique goal [of journals] is the utility of the Public & their particular instruction."[41] In the short run, this meant providing the learned community with information; the *Mémoires de Trévoux* promised to provide "generally everything which could contribute to satisfy the curiosity of men of letters," while the *Journal des Sçavans* promised "to make known whatever new is happening in the Republic of Letters."[42] Like letters, journals were to provide publishing information, opinions of new works, news of discoveries and works in progress, and literary gossip from across the map of Europe.

The most important of these functions was to keep the Republic of Letters fully informed about the books being published in other cities. In Charles de la Motte's view, that was virtually the only purpose. On sending Pierre Des Maizeaux the *Histoire des ouvrages des savans* in 1710, he remarked that "the public could, it seems to me, do without this journal, especially at the moment when so few New Books are being printed,"[43] suggesting that outside of its notification of such books' publication the journal was useless. One reason journals inspired such attention and impatience was that, short of consulting an exceptionally well-informed local bookseller or obtaining catalogues from book fairs such as those at Frankfurt, it was difficult to learn about the latest publications. Journals provided this much-needed information; according to Jacques Bernard, "there is scarcely a book printed in this Country worthy of your curiosity, which I don't mention in one manner or another in my Journal."[44]

The importance of this information to readers is apparent from the format of the periodicals. Nearly every journal continued as the *Journal des Sçavans* had begun, consisting almost entirely of "an exact Catalogue of the principal books which will be printed in Europe. And we will not content ourselves with giving the simple titles, as happens at present in most of the Bibliographies: but we will say further what they discuss, & how they can be useful."[45] Journals varied in the amount of information they chose to give about the books they reviewed. However, it became standard in many journals to mention the major points of the book, often quoting sections to illustrate these points, and frequently offering somewhat generalized praise or blame for the style or the content. Works were "ingenious," "curious," "useful," "savant," "eloquent," "solid," or perhaps (more rarely) full of errors or insults, judgments often backed up with examples. More meager treatment sometimes elicited complaint; François Bruys, who admittedly bore a grudge against Jean Rousset de Missy for their conflict over Jacques Saurin, chose in his *Mémoires historiques* to attack his method of writing *extraits*.

> He furnishes most of the Historical Articles to the *Bibliothèque Raisonnée*. To make the extrait of a Book, he copies the title, & marks, according to custom, the number of pages; he takes a few Items from the Preface; & taking on opening the volume the first things he sees, he judges on these scraps the merit of a Work, with as much assurance as if he had read it several times.[46]

Novelty was also an important factor for readers eager for the latest information, as well as a source of anxiety for journalists facing slow production time and uncommunicative *libraires*. Journals would lose their readership if they could not offer up-to-date news about what was being published and where it was available. Jacques Bernard complained about the *Mémoires de Trévoux* that they did not fulfill this important duty: "I know that these Messrs. could do better, if they wanted to give themselves the trouble. They do not take any trouble to distinguish the New Books from the Old. They do not know the Authors. Their Extraits are usually fairly skimpy. They seem to know very little about what is going on in the Republic of Letters, because they often give extremely detailed Extraits of Books, which the other Journals talked about very amply eight or 10 years ago."[47]

Journalists often circumvented this problem by giving news in the section called *nouvelles littéraires* of editions in press or even still being written. Soon after journals came into being, they began to mention as a matter of course the *libraire* who had published the book, as well as the work's size and length. This information was provided for the many readers who considered buying the books discussed in the journals. A similar motive was at least partially responsible for the increasing tendency to make judgments on the books themselves. As Camusat pointed out, for many readers the main point of reading a journal was to find out "what Books would be worth buying"; such prior information, said Jean Cornand de la Crose, "is a means to save both Time and Money."[48]

The saving of time, so decried by Huet and the authors summarized in Baillet, was of considerable importance to scholars who looked to the journals for summaries of books they would have no time to read. The *Journal litéraire* made this a point of pride, pointing out that "true Savants" would gain the most from their journal. "They have studied the subjects deeply, & a fairly exact Analysis of a new Book will allow them to understand at once the views of the Author. When one sets before them the most essential things he says, they guess almost all of the rest, & a good Extrait will allow them to see, so to speak, a whole Book at a glance."[49]

However, many journals aimed expressly at an audience which would never see the books they discussed. This was not because the readership was not sufficiently learned, but rather that, for one reason or another, the books proved unavailable to potential readers. Part of the problem was price; Camusat pointed out that an important function of journals was to "furnish to poor Scholars the means of studying at a low cost."[50] But another serious hindrance to scholarship was the limited availability of many works in the European market, particularly in languages which, unlike English, were comprehensible to the majority of scholars. The purpose of many periodicals—which are best represented by the national "bibliothèques" such as the *Bibliothèque italique*[51]—was not so much to provide a *catalogue raisonné* of books on sale as to provide needed information to the rest of the Republic of Letters. The implication of all such journals was that valuable work was being done even in obscure and inaccessible corners of the learned world, and that the dissemination of such work would aid the general progress of learning.

The worthiness of the work pursued in these various European regions was a matter of insistence by their publicists. Both the *Bibliothèque germanique* and the *Bibliothèque italique* began their runs with accounts of the type and value of scholarship in those countries. That such scholarship should—through the vicissitudes of the book trade or the obstructions of mountains, sea, and language—prove unavailable to the Republic was a serious matter. Michel de la Roche wrote at the beginning of the *Bibliothèque angloise* that "you could say in general that *English* books are scarcely known outside this Island & those that are translated from time to time into *French*, or of which the Journalists speak, do not suffice to give a just idea of the state of the Sciences here today, nor to satisfy the curiosity of the Public."[52] Such efforts were indeed appreciated by readers otherwise deprived of any knowledge of such books. After the appearance of the first volume of the *Bibliothèque italique*, Charles-Etienne Jordan wrote from Prenzlau to Louis Bourguet that "this project can be nothing other than very advantageous for the public, because through this it will find itself informed about books which appear in Italy: we know but little the books which are published in this country, or if we know them it is only by very imperfect means: I do not believe I have seen the *Giornali de Letterati* in our Bookshops."[53]

Moreover, as both La Roche's and Jordan's comments illustrate, discussions of these journals frequently appealed to sentiments of fellowship in

the Republic of Letters. Authors of journals appeared to make special efforts
to discuss books which, as the *Bibliothèque italique* said, "many Men of Letters
... perhaps will never possess."[54] If the books such journals discussed could
be read by all, the journals would be unnecessary, a fact acknowledged by the
journalists themselves. Translation was one factor here, and the *Journal
littéraire*, for instance, summarized Pope's preface to the *Iliad* and his essay on
Homer for the French reader precisely because "apparently he will never
have [them] in his own language."[55] Similarly, La Roche several times
declined to review works imminently to be translated into French in
Holland, both because such *extraits* were unnecessary for audiences soon able
to read the works for themselves, and because to summarize at length would
deny the work "the grace of novelty, when it appears in *French*." As he
remarked at one point, "if all the good books in *England* were translated into
French, I would not amuse myself by publishing this Journal."[56] Such sentiments could also work in reverse, and knowledge available to all was often
considered unnecessary in a journal. In discussing an English book on
gardening, La Roche simply summarized, saying that "in foreign Countries
[for which this journal was intended] there are a great number of works on
Gardening. Thus I imagine that a general idea of the matters contained in this
one, will suffice to satisfy the curiosity of Readers."[57] Thus whether the
decision was to include or exclude material, the point was to inform as well
as possible the Republic of Letters.

The provision of useful information to the learned community was also the
goal of the *nouvelles littéraires*, a section which in most journals followed the
extraits to conclude the volume. Generally such news was presented by
country and city, probably because the journalist received it in letters from
people across the Continent.[58] This meant that a journalist, to be well
respected, needed a formidable network of correspondence; thus Simon
Pelloutier predicted the demise of the *Bibliothèque germanique* in 1744 in part
because the new author did not have the "correspondances" of his predecessor.[59] Volume VIII of the *Histoire critique*, for example, printed "Nouvelles
de Littérature" from Oxford, London, Rouen, Paris, Geneva, Leipzig, Silesia,
Berlin, Utrecht, Rotterdam, Amsterdam, and Leiden.[60] The timeliness of
such news, moreover, was obviously crucial. For the *Bibliothèque germanique*
and the *Bibliothèque impartiale*, at least, the *libraires* arranged that it be sent in
by the authors and printed last, which accounts for its placement at the end
of the volume.[61] Because such news could not be obtained in any other way,
or at least not in such quantities, readers considered the *nouvelles littéraires* one
of the best features of literary journals. Louis Bourguet wrote in his preface
to the *Bibliothèque italique* that it was sufficient reason to undertake a journal
that people would be able "to learn many things that they would otherwise
never know, or that they would only have known very late."[62]

Although *extraits*, and occasionally *nouvelles littéraires*, could be quite substantial, many journals also presented opportunities to find out the ideas of working scholars at even greater length without having to wait for or purchase books. Most journals would usually contain a number of articles interspersed with the *extraits*. The first part of volume IV of the *Journal littéraire*, for example, besides reviewing six books on subjects ranging from an English *Historical Geography of the Old Testament* to volume two of the Abbé de St.-Pierre's *Projet pour rendre la paix perpetuelle en Europe*, provided three articles either contributed by regular authors or sent in from outside. One was a letter from the conservative minister Gabriel d'Artis, directed against articles in the *Histoire critique* suggesting an allegorical reading of the 110th psalm; another, from Nicolas Hartsoeker, discussed the movement of the planets, while a third, by the scientist and journalist G.S. 'sGravesande, gave "Remarques sur la Construction des Machines pneumatiques."[63] While most journals were not so scientific as the *Journal littéraire*, they did present material on a variety of subjects which tended not to be particularly specialized. The *Histoire critique* consisted almost entirely of such articles, often about subjects in classical philology or theology.

Such items otherwise might not have quickly (or ever) seen the light of day. According to Bayle, indeed, preserving ephemera was always one of the goals of *journaux des savants*.[64] Jean Cornand de la Crose pointed this out in his *Memoirs for the Ingenious* in 1693.

[N]othing can more contribute to the progress of Learning, than the speedy publishing of small papers, which contain new inventions or rare observations; for tho their Authors, should be glad to be taken for what they are, yet as the learned'st are ordinarily not the richest sort of men, so they are loth to appear on the public Stage, at the expences of their Purse, as well as of their Wit.

Besides there are but few, who have so much time to spare, as to write huge Volumes, and they know that flying Sheets and Sixpenny Books, are as soon lost as printed; which things being all put and considered together, it will not seem strange, if the Learned be thereby discouraged from publishing their Works.[65]

Through the provision of *extraits*, articles, and *nouvelles littéraires*, journals thus simplified life for savants. Finding out what works were in progress, what books one ought to buy, and so on, became less a matter of a voluminous correspondence with colleagues—although such correspondence continued—than of obtaining the appropriate journals. Scholars could profit from the reading, the letter-writing, and the contacts with *libraires* of *other* scholars across Europe, scholars whom they did not necessarily know and to whom there was no need to be introduced.

Authors, Libraires, *and the Structures of Power*

The operations of particular literary journals provide an image of the Republic of Letters in microcosm. Some journals were written by individuals; Pierre
Bayle, Jean Le Clerc, Henri Basnage de Beauval, Antoine de la Barre de
Beaumarchais, and François Bruys are all prime examples. But others were
written by groups, whose nature, like that of the Republic of Letters, was
inevitably social. Studying the arrangements authors made among themselves
and with their *libraires* to produce literary journals will serve a dual purpose
for the student of the scholarly community. Not only will we improve our
understanding of the technical background of these important periodicals, but
we can also observe the changing ideas of social relationships within the
Republic of Letters.

A journal could be founded on the initial suggestion of either an author or
a *libraire.* Sometimes authors made the first proposition; Jean-Henri-Samuel
Formey, an author of the *Bibliothèque germanique* and several other journals,
mentioned in 1743 that the *libraire* Neaulme had rejected his proposal of a
series of *Discours moraux,* a project later undertaken with the Leiden *libraire*
Elie Luzac.[66] According to Marianne Couperus, the *Glaneur* began at the
instigation of its author, J.-B. de la Varenne, and may even have been printed
at its author's expense.[67] Certain journals, such as the *Nouvelles de la
République des Lettres* or the *Histoire des ouvrages des savans*—ones written by a
known person or group—were commonly considered the "property," albeit
informally, of that person. When a society of scholars in London thought to
undertake a new journal about English savants, they wrote to Armand de la
Chapelle, formerly author of the *Bibliothèque angloise,* to make sure he had
really renounced the journal and left the field open for them.[68]

Many *libraires* would be disposed to take on such a project, since an
enterprise consisting so largely of book reviews was a likely source of profit.
Even if the journal itself did not sell widely, it could still help the bookselling
side of the business by publicizing which books a *libraire* had issued or which
he had in stock, or even by attacking the books of competing publishers.
Reinier Leers, *libraire* in the 1680s of the *Histoire des ouvrages des savans,* made
sure to point out in the journal that he carried all the books reviewed there.[69]
The author of a journal, in his turn, had the advantage of fame, of some
profit, and of a modicum of power in the Republic of Letters.

Arrangements for the enterprise were not left to chance or goodwill. The
more tangible advantages to an author were customarily set down in a
contract. Such contracts, when we can find them, are useful tools for
discovering what was important to an author about his association with a
journal. We can determine several different arrangements between authors
and *libraires* over payment. The first, when a journal was written by a single

author, was for the *libraire* to pay for the journal in the same way he would pay for a normal book: in money by the sheet, and in a certain number of copies of the book. In 1725 Michel de la Roche reported that he had been receiving six florins a sheet for his journal, the *Bibliothèque angloise*.[70] Similarly, when in 1749 Formey arranged with Luzac to produce the *Bibliothèque impartiale*, they agreed that Formey should receive seven florins per sheet and twenty copies postpaid. Since the journal came out four times a year, and each volume contained about eight sheets of Formey's composition, he received each year about what he made in 1751: 214 florins.[71]

The *Bibliothèque italique* is an example of a journal with multiple authors. This periodical, in the late 1720s and early 1730s, was written by five scholars in Lausanne and Neuchâtel and published by Marc-Michel Bousquet in Geneva. Louis Bourguet, professor of philosophy at the Academy of Neuchâtel, was the director of the journal, and for this duty he received 50 silver écus of Genevan money for each quarterly issue, or 200 écus per year; there is some evidence that by the end of his association with the journal, in 1734, he was making 300 écus a year. However, the other four authors, who in fact were the ones to negotiate this contract, received nothing but one copy of the journal apiece.[72]

We find a third way of organizing payment in the middle years of the *Bibliothèque germanique*. In the late 1730s the director, Paul-Emile de Mauclerc, contracted with the *libraire* Pierre Humbert to provide a quarterly volume of fifteen sheets, for which he would be paid either by 100 florins in money or by 115 florins' worth of books, in addition to thirty copies of the journal. But since Mauclerc did not want to write the journal on his own, he paid a subordinate author, Formey, to provide seven of the fifteen sheets of copy, or 112 pages for each issue. For this, his "contingent," as it was called, Formey received approximately 20 Reichsthalers, or about 40 florins, out of Mauclerc's pocket.[73] The profits of the *Bibliothèque germanique* were thus divided,[74] but in this case as well as that of the other journals studied here, other people who sent in articles were rarely paid anything for their contributions.[75]

However, contracts often dealt with more than payment. Just as authors of books were often anxious to specify the format and typeface of their works, journalists interested in both beauty and sales would make sure they agreed with the *libraires* on these and other details of production. When Formey and Luzac agreed to put out the *Bibliothèque impartiale*, among the stipulations of the contract were the frequency of publication, the format and character (which were to be the same as those of the *Bibliothèque raisonnée*), and the amount of authority the author would have over the content. The *libraire* promised that the author should have complete control, but pointed out the inconvenience of showing everything to Formey in advance, since Formey

was in Berlin and the press in Leiden.[76] Mauclerc's and Formey's contracts for
the *Bibliothèque germanique* made similar stipulations. The *libraire* agreed to
print at least four issues per year, and the journalist promised to provide
enough copy; the *libraire* had to pay the postage of all articles sent to him; and
the journalist had complete authority over what would go into the journal,
and where, "naturally understanding, of course," the contract said, "that he
will not put in anything which could do harm to the Libraire."[77] The
contract for the *Bibliothèque italique* required that the new journal look like
the *Bibliothèque germanique*.[78] These conditions show that authors did not
simply want to get paid, but also to ensure their own power, the aesthetic
quality of the journal, and the regularity of its publication.

Despite the image of certain periodicals belonging to their authors, and
despite the attempts of these authors to control the content, the copyright of
continental journals belonged to the *libraire*, and it was common for such a
libraire to make his own arrangements for authors to begin or continue a
literary journal.[79] One example is the *Nouvelles littéraires*, which was published
by and known as belonging to the *libraire* Henri du Sauzet. The journalist
Justus van Effen had promised the *libraire* in 1720 to furnish the principal
extraits, but instead abandoned the enterprise to tour Sweden and Paris with
Prince Charles of Hesse. Du Sauzet, "frustrated in his hopes, yet not wanting
to abandon his project entirely, addressed himself, in hope of better, to *Du
Limiers*, but required him to be sure not to call himself in any way the author
of the journal." The *libraire* was afraid for his sales, saying privately that Du
Limier's "erudition is in fact as small as they come"; he required the journalist
to keep strict anonymity because "his name alone would disgust an infinity
of people" and "would suffice to discredit any passable Book." When Du
Limiers failed to keep this promise, he was dismissed from the publication.[80]

The best example of a journal seeming to belong to its *libraire*—the
example anyone at the time would have cited—was the *Bibliothèque raisonnée*,
run from 1728 until 1741 by the Amsterdam firm of Rudolph Wetstein, his
son Jacob Wetstein, and his son-in-law William Smith.[81] The authors of the
Bibliothèque raisonnée were not even supposed to know each other's identity,
and, as Prosper Marchand, an author of the *Journal littéraire*, commented, "It
is not a single *Savant* who composes this Journal: there are seven or eight of
them, all very humble Slaves of their Libraire, only praising what pleases him,
and destroying with Fury and Bad Faith everything that does not suit him."[82]

But despite the *libraires'* possession of the copyright, authors felt quite free
to change *libraire* if they did not agree with his policy, terms, or execution.
They did so simply by changing the title of the journal. Thus the authors of
the *Bibliothèque germanique*, tiring of the slowness and intransigence of Pierre
Humbert in Amsterdam, moved their business to Isaac de Beauregard in The
Hague, changing the title to the "*Journal Littéraire d'Allemagne, de Suisse et du*

Nord by the authors of the *Bibliothèque Germanique.*" When Beauregard proved an even worse choice, the journal became the *Nouvelle Bibliothèque Germanique*, published in Amsterdam by Pierre Mortier. As a friend of the principal author remarked, "My colleague is very disposed to be lenient with his Libraire, but he will never give up his authority. Wetstein and du Sauzet can say *my journal* if they want—they are the despotic masters of theirs—but as for the *journal Littéraire d'allemagne*, if it has to change Libraire twenty times, it will never be of that class."[83]

In the conflicts between authors and *libraires* we can see the first problem with the formalization and commercialization of scholarly communications. For the *libraire* the journal was a commercial proposition of which he was the director. Authors, who also believed they were running the enterprise, cared less about commerce and more about their own vision of the content, mission, and audience of the periodical. These viewpoints were apt to collide, and, when the question of authority was mixed with contempt for the mercenary, conflicts were likely to be fierce. Nothing can demonstrate better scholars' view of the the specialness of the Republic of Letters than the battles which raged between journalists and their *libraires*. Some of the problems had to do with diligence, or lack thereof, but, as we can see from the remarks above, many concerned the issue of what type of person was really in charge. The fight for control of journals was thus a fight for the integrity of the Republic of Letters.[84]

The journalists not only fumed about this issue in private as they fought their battles behind the scenes, but they also made it clear that one function of journals was to expose the trickeries of *libraires* to their compatriots in the Republic. A friend of the authors of the *Journal litéraire*, Sebastian Högguer, was moved to comment on the strength of that journal's attacks on the book trade and suggested ironically that perhaps his friends should watch out for the consequences.[85] In 1714 the journal published a contribution which pointed out the "fourberie" of *libraires*' reissuing old books under new titles, which had recently occurred with Lenglet's *Méthode pour étudier l'histoire.*[86] Such a remark, appearing as it did in an article on the necessity of the public sending articles to journals, suggests at least some unity of purpose and identity between the journalists and their audience.

The extant contracts suggest that authors tried to maintain their authority over everything that went into the journals; but this was rarely successful. *Libraires* would often seek to advertise their own publications in their journals, a ploy which infuriated, for example, the authors of the *Bibliothèque italique.* They also tried to dictate content on the basis of what would sell, an issue not necessarily of paramount importance for the authors. In 1751 Pierre Mortier told Formey he wanted him "to put in our Journal as few extraits as possible of books on Theology published in Germany"; in 1751 he refused to inform the public about a project for a dictionary competing with his own, pointing out that "in my own journal I cannot prejudice myself." It was Humbert's putting on "little airs about the disposition and the content of the B.G.," as Mauclerc put it, that finally drove the authors to find a new *libraire*.[87] And Luzac, *libraire* of the *Bibliothèque impartiale*, assured Formey of the author's power over everything even as he took control, hired other authors, and threatened to close the journal to begin his own Dutch-language periodical.[88] Gabriel Seigneux de Correvon's furious outburst about the *libraire* of the *Bibliothèque italique* says it all:

> We are the ones who had the idea first, we are the ones expected to perfect it continually; we are the ones, in a word, who must fulfill the engagements we have contracted with the Public. This being so, it is not proper for us to be at the disposal of anyone; the direction must come only from us, and I will even go so far as to say that we should not receive any extrait that we have not read over and approved.[89]

Behind the Scenes at the Bibliothèque germanique

The process of publishing literary journals involved surprisingly formal arrangements. This formalization, significantly, involved not only relations between authors and their *libraires*, but also relations among the authors themselves. Especially since many authors were at some distance from their *libraires*, and sometimes from each other, procedures had to be developed to ensure that everything was actually done. These included ways of gathering material, dividing responsibilities, and delivering copy to the *libraire*. Such procedures may not have been dictated or official, but their existence can be discerned from the daily operations of the journalists and their means of dealing with each other. Journalists thus developed working relationships which did not necessarily revolve around scholarly courtesies.

Although there is evidence from a number of different literary journals concerning their mode of operation, we will concentrate here primarily on the *Bibliothèque germanique*, whose editorial discussions are well documented. This journal began in 1720 in Berlin. Its purpose, according to the plan published in the first volume, was to give the French-speaking world a better understanding of German academia, as yet largely unavailable to audiences unable or unwilling to learn about it from German or Latin sources. The authors, all Huguenot refugees, pointed out that although the renewal of letters in Europe was due to the Italians, the invention of printing occurred in Germany, which ought to get some of the glory. Moreover, natural law, mathematics, experimental science, and particularly history and antiquities were all studied there. So the *Bibliothèque germanique* planned especially to discuss or include academic treatises and dissertations, as well as *extraits* from German journals, concentrating on items about public and natural law, natural, sacred, and profane history, philosophy, and *belles lettres*. No discussion of religion or personal satires would be included. These points were similar to those in the prefaces of other national *bibliothèques*, such as the *Bibliothèque britannique*.[90]

The journal was the outgrowth of a small literary society, the Société Anonyme, which met every Monday night at the home of Jacques Lenfant, a French Protestant minister who shared the duties of chaplain to the Prussian king with another member of the society, Isaac de Beausobre. These two were the principal authors of the journal, although other members, such as the chronologist Alphonse des Vignoles, and the young minister, Paul-Emile de Mauclerc, also made contributions. As we have already noted, for the first twenty years of its existence the journal was published in Amsterdam by Pierre Humbert.[91]

As time went on, other authors became more prominent, culled from the rising young ministers in Berlin. Lenfant had died in 1728, and Beausobre was aging. Jean-Henri-Samuel Formey, a distinguished young minister, professor of philosophy at the Collège Français, and later Secretary of the Berlin Academy of Sciences, and Mauclerc, now French minister in Stettin, took over more of the writing in the 1730s. After Beausobre's death in 1738, Mauclerc became director of the journal, with Formey as second author in the arrangement previously described. In 1741 they switched *libraires* to Beauregard, changing the title. Mauclerc's fellow-minister in the French church at Stettin, Jacques de Pérard, took a lively interest in the progress of the journal, without writing anything of significance. But after Mauclerc's unexpected death in 1742, although Formey was to become director of the journal, Pérard, who was on the spot, stepped in to sort out the late director's papers and negotiate a settlement with the widowed Madame de Mauclerc. After the journal operated for a time with Pérard in the subordinate role, he began to take over control of its operations. In February of 1743 Formey, disgusted with the slowness of the *libraire*, ceded the direction of the journal to Pérard and reverted to the second position. They moved their business to Mortier in 1746 and once again changed titles. The authorial set-up lasted until 1749, when Pérard grew so overburdened with other responsibilities that Formey once again took over. He wrote the new journal nearly on his own until it finally ended in 1759.[92]

Since the journals usually consisted largely of *extraits*, a first necessity in their composition was to obtain books to review. It is difficult to make generalizations about just how this was accomplished. Jean Barbeyrac, one of the authors of the *Bibliothèque raisonnée*, stressed in negotiating with a new *libraire* in 1742 that he would not review anything that he did not want to buy and read himself or that he already owned, "because it was on that footing, & on no other, that I worked on the *Bibl. Raisonnée*. Ever since I started furnishing Extraits regularly, I declared this to Smith; & in the whole Journal there were only two Extraits of Books that I did not have in my study. . . . I recognized quite early how inconvenient it was when I did not always have available the books which I had to review."[93] This suggests that often authors had to obtain their own books, probably because of laxity by the *libraires*, and that Barbeyrac, who certainly knew his way around, was able to circumvent this problem.

However, in many cases, it seems that in one way or another the *libraire* was able to acquire the necessary books. In the 1680s, Reinier Leers wrote to the London bookseller Samuel Smith to ask him to send a copy of anything new he obtained or printed in English or Latin that he thought proper for (as he put it) "my journal."[94] And in fact, since an *extrait* in a widely-read journal was excellent advertising, it became common for *libraires*, and especially authors, to send a copy of a book to a journal as a matter of course. As this was also cheap for the journal, it was mutually beneficial, and in 1713 we find the *Histoire critique de la République des Lettres* asking "Authors & Libraires to send us the new Books they publish, if they want them to be talked about in this journal."[95] In letters to journalists we can often find friends and scholarly acquaintances sending books and asking meekly for a good review. Thus Emmerich de Vattel, who had been a schoolfriend of Formey's, wrote him in 1748, "You will no doubt already have been sent a copy of my new Edition from Dresden, in which you will have found two new pieces. If you think this little Work worthy of mentioning in the Bibliothèque Germanique, I will be charmed to see it announced by the pen of a Friend."[96] Such an action did not, of course, always guarantee good treatment. As Charles de la Motte reported to Pierre Des Maizeaux, "your Libraires have made a present of your S. Evremond to M. Le Clerc. They did not intend to do so at first, but I persuaded them to. Just between us, if one were to judge this debt by the Extrait that M. Le C. gave of it, I think the Libraires could have dispensed with this liberality."[97]

Naturally journalists could not always rely on other scholars to send the books they had in mind for review. To ensure the success of their journal, some *libraires* would lend their authors the necessary books. This was the case with the *Bibliothèque italique*, whose contract specified that Bousquet's publishing-house in Geneva would furnish all the books necessary for the *extraits*. These would be sent free to Lausanne and, after use, could be returned, also free of carriage, to Geneva. Bousquet also agreed to provide the literary news, an item which, because of postage, could be quite expensive.[98]

Although the evidence is incomplete, it appears that the *Bibliothèque germanique* operated at least partially on this system. After Formey had taken over sole authorship of the *Nouvelle Bibliothèque germanique*, the *libraire* several times sent books for him to review.[99] And certainly it was common during the directorships of Mauclerc and Pérard for the director to send Formey books which he was meant to return after writing his *extraits*. Since Formey, in Berlin, was much more at the center of things than either of the directors out in Stettin, it seems likely that the reason for this procedure was not convenience, but rather that the *libraire* in the Netherlands was sending books. Sometimes the book would be awaiting Formey at a particular bookseller's, but only rarely did Mauclerc ask Formey to find a book by looking around for it in Berlin.[100] Of course, Formey also reviewed many other works without any provision from the director of the journal.

One reason he could do this was that it was not always indicated to an author which books he should review. In most of the journals documented here, considerable leeway was left to the major authors to choose which books interested them. Although Mauclerc was director of the *Bibliothèque germanique*, Formey often wrote whatever he wished, so that in 1737, for example, Mauclerc asked him to "do me the pleasure of telling me approximately what articles you are planning for volume 41 of the B.G."[101] Mauclerc's main stipulation about the material, it seemed, was that it should "be as agreeable as possible for the public."[102]

What this seemed to mean in practice was a greater diversity of materials, a theme on which not only Mauclerc but other directors and *libraires* also harped. The journal had a responsibility to publish materials about Germany—Mauclerc said that, in choosing books, "German works will suit the best, because they are little known to foreigners"—but, as Pérard wrote Formey in 1743, "Although I have enough material, you'll oblige me in any case by sending me some when you have some tidbits saved up, so that we can intermingle the old and the new, & give some variety to the Journal." This issue became of considerable import in the 1750s, when Formey's *libraires* felt he was giving all the interesting material to his other journal, the *Bibliothèque impartiale*. Mortier's partner, Schreuder, pointed out early on that "Many people here [i.e. Leipzig] complain that there are so few interesting items in the Nouv. Bibl: Germ: & that it is entirely filled with trivial things: Some people in Amsterdam are not buying it any more, perhaps for the same reason."[103] But although the directors or *libraires* of these journals talked much of variety and interest, they often did not do much to inform an author about how to achieve these goals.

One way to improve this situation was to have a number of authors. This was useful in any case, since being a solitary journalist was hard work and intrinsically demanding. Camusat, formerly author of the *Bibliothèque françoise*, commented, perhaps a little idealistically, about the talents required of a journalist. "The occupation of Journalist demands a range of talents which are

rarely to be found in the same person." Among them, in his view, were the
scholarly languages, a perfect knowledge of the vernacular, and, if a journalist
wanted to give accounts of works published throughout Europe, a smattering
of the modern tongues. He also had to understand the subject matter of the
books, and since literary journals were rarely specialized in their material, "he
has to show himself to be a Mathematician, Astronomer, Natural Philosopher, Jurist, Theologian"; he must understand everything from antiquity to
the present day. Moreover, the journalist, "if he does not want to fall
constantly into ridiculous errors, or in problems even more to be feared . . .
must be consummate in Literary History, & especially in the Literary History
of his Century."[104] As Camusat observed, the problems of this demanding
occupation could be at least partially overcome by dividing the work among
a number of authors. "As each one only has to speak of the Science he
possesses perfectly, and only of Books in his area of competence . . . there is
no need to fear that lack of knowledge will bring about a precipitate & unfair
judgment."[105]

   In practice it was not so easy to divide up the material for review as
Camusat suggested. A journal might have only a few authors, or certainly not
enough to give one person all the medical books, one person all the historical
ones, and so on. And since individual scholars did not usually have firm
specialties, divisions among talents were even more difficult to make. There
was at least a vague belief that if someone did specialize he should pay
particular attention to a book in his own field. Thus in trying to get the
philosophy professor Formey to review the works of the philosopher
Christian Wolff, Mauclerc said coyly, "It's proper for a Professor of Philosophy to make them known to the public."[106] Jean Barbeyrac, who is well
known to scholars today for his work as a jurist, reviewed all sorts of books
for the *Bibliothèque raisonnée*, but when the Huguenot minister Armand de la
Chapelle chose to review in the same journal a legal work by Cornelius van
Bynkershoek, Barbeyrac complained that "M[r]. de la Ch.[apelle] stole from
me the Extrait of M[r]. de Bynck[ershoek]'s book, which belonged to me for
more than one reason."[107] In general, however, most learned men were
thought sufficiently well-educated to write accounts of works on theology,
history, grammar, antiquities, or travel; this was why people such as Bayle
and Le Clerc could legitimately write journals on their own. It was mainly in
the sciences that special help was considered necessary, and in both 1739 and
1743 Formey was asked whether, as Pérard put it, in Berlin "you have any
Doctors or Mathematicians up your sleeve."[108]

   The social relations of the principal authors of a journal, which were
affected by their sometimes distant geographical location, had an important
influence on the way responsibilities were divided. The various journals

whose records survive show considerable diversity in methods of discussing policy and in the distribution of power. The journals we will examine here vary from the egalitarian to the dictatorial; but as we will see, the more businesslike the journal, the less the *honnêtetés* of scholarship appeared to figure.

One way of planning a journal was for all its authors to meet together. This was obviously not practicable for many journals, but for some, especially those which grew out of literary societies, proximity made the journal a part of the authors' social routine. As we have seen, the early *Bibliothèque germanique* emanated from the Société Anonyme, when all its major authors were living in Berlin. But the best-documented journal of this type is undoubtedly the *Journal littéraire*. In the seventeen-teens, the authors of this journal met every Friday at a coffee-house in The Hague for a convivial evening of joking, drinking, conversation, and the reading of verses and amusing discourses written for the occasion.[109]

Margaret Jacob, in her book *The Radical Enlightenment*, wants to see in this group an early Masonic order with a highly developed ritual and symbolic system. As Graham Gibbs and Christiane Berkvens-Stevelinck have shown, this assessment misses the point.[110] The tone of the occasions was a *badinage* without ritualistic overtones, and the "Chevaliers de la Jubilation," as they called themselves in one document, also referred to themselves as the "Society of the Authors who compose the Journal Litéraire," a title more indicative of their priorities.[111] There should be little surprise that correspondents all over Europe "had somehow discovered this congenial literary and intellectual circle centred in The Hague," as Jacob puts it, given that the group was publishing a literary journal which, like many, specifically requested letters and pieces from its readers.[112] It is better to regard this society simply as it described itself in its letters: as "a troop of friends, who have known each other for ages," and among whom "union, something rare enough in a Society, reigned."[113]

The journalists offered the same arguments for operating as a society as Camusat would give later on. "It is very difficult, not to say impossible," they said, "for a single Author to labor with success on a Work whose worth depends on so many different and often opposing qualities."[114] The group acquired new members by election, not for Masonic reasons, but, as a letter announcing an election stated, "Because we need Members to help us work."[115] These elections and the surviving documents show the solidarity of the group; they always wrote in unison (always saying *nous*) to their correspondents and journeying fellow-editors.[116] According to the authors refounding the journal in 1729, some of whom had worked on the original work as well, in the first *Journal littéraire*

Each worked on his own, but the Extraits were brought to an Assembly, which took place every Week, of those of the Authors who were in The Hague, of whom the number was always big enough to make a severe Examination of everything that was read there.

Everyone worked only on the Books on which not only he felt himself capable of making an extrait, but about which the others made the same Judgment.

The Extraits were sent to the Examiners, to confront them with the Books; after which they were read in the Assembly, before they could be printed. In these Readings, people often added to the Extraits Remarks on the Works being discussed.[117]

The authors saw each other often in any case, and it was at least proposed that even travelling members must also provide materials for the journal.[118] These operations show that the journal had a strongly social and egalitarian element which was increased by its authors' geographical proximity to and warmth of feeling toward each other.

The *Bibliothèque italique* was written by graver men, including professors at the academies of Lausanne and Neuchâtel, but their organization in some ways resembled that of the *Journal littéraire*. The authors worked on terms of surprising equality—surprising since, as we have seen, only the director, Louis Bourguet, was paid. As he said to a fellow author, "the trouble you have given yourself, Monsieur, turns as much to my profit as to your glory."[119] This equality, like that of the society in The Hague, was perhaps due in part to the geographical arrangement of the authors. Except for Bourguet, who lived in Neuchâtel, all the principal authors lived in Lausanne, where they could confer together freely. Even before the foundation of the journal, one of those concerned, J. Bibaud du Lignon, was urging Bourguet to move to Lausanne, where he could not only have plenty of students, but also be able to "work on a Bibliothèque Italienne, which a Libraire of Geneva wants to publish." The need for Bourguet in Lausanne continued to be felt after the journal began; in 1727, for example, Du Lignon wrote telling him what the other authors were writing, but saying that "your presence is absolutely necessary here, even if it is only for two or three days. . . . You will see that in one or two conferences we can arrange matters so that we can decide on the content of two or three volumes, which will last until spring; if you refuse I am afraid that Bousquet [the *libraire*] will break his contract."[120]

Another reason for the comparative equality of the authors of the *Bibliothèque italique* may have been their inexperience as journalists. They knew enough to imitate other authors; one wrote of the proposed journal that "I think it ought to be in the taste of M^r le Clerc, while allowing less spirit of party."[121] But since all were beginning on the same footing, and were somewhat bashful about their accomplishments in the Republic of Letters— Bourguet, we will recall, had been a merchant before attaining his dream of becoming a professor of philosophy—they worked together to make the journal as proper and as plausible as possible. Du Lignon, for instance, thought it important to get straight just how an *extrait* should be written.

> It seems to me that to make an Extrait it is necessary to start by indicating the size of the Volume, the number of Pages, then one must start by speaking of the Author, of his nation and of several of his Works, then to say in how many books it is, speak of the Preface, then of the Method with which the author treats his material and give several places in the work to demonstrate this, you cannot always make extraits in the same taste, books being different, but it is necessary to be dogmatic [and] not chase after the places with the most marvels, one can make comments but with a modest air, especially a new Journalist, without showing a great deal of the spirit of party or religion.[122]

This consciousness of their newness in the business and indeed in the Republic of Letters returned when the authors began to bicker with the *libraire*. Bourguet wrote furiously to another author, Seigneux de Correvon, in 1729,

> The Libraire in Holland who prints the Bibl. Germ. has never treated the Authors of that journal in this way even though they are much further away from the place of publication. It is true that these Messieurs of Berlin have acquired a great Reputation by big works but nothing is standing in the way of the Authors of the Bibl. Ital. becoming famous. You have already given glorious marks of Erudition and discernment, especially in literature; Mons. de Bochat has shown very advantageously his taste for the Law, History, and Criticism; Mr Ruchat made a name long ago in the Rep. of Letters by various useful and interesting Works.

"And," he concluded somewhat lamely, "M^r Du Lignon is very Capable of making himself useful among Savants in many ways."[123]

Whatever the reason, the ostensible director of the journal was in no way its ruler. Bourguet asked advice on policy and consulted his fellow authors about which *extraits* he should write. When he wrote the preface to one volume, the prerogative of every director of a journal, he sent it to Lausanne, telling Du Lignon, "You can, Monsieur, along with Messieurs our Illustrious Friends, change it, reform it, add to it, or even get me to write another entirely different one, if you think it would be more suitable."[124] This was not simple courtesy on Bourguet's part, or at least his colleagues did not interpret it as such. When Bourguet made a list in 1734 of all the articles he had provided for the journal, he noted after several that another author had "retouched" them, adding that "in doing which he gave great luster to my extraits. Although occasionally I would have preferred that he had made fewer changes." The supposedly subordinate authors of the journal once sent back an article by Bourguet twice for revision, telling him that "we are obliged to do it for our own reputation[;] we are known as having a part in the Bibliothèque Italique thus we believe that one cannot work on it with too much care either for content or for style."[125]

We have already seen enough of the *Bibliothèque germanique* to suspect that it did not work in quite this fashion. In the 1730s and 1740s its authors lived a great distance from each other—Berlin and Stettin—and not only rarely saw one another but almost never discussed anything but the journal in their correspondence. Their relationship, distant though not uncordial, made itself felt in the conduct of the journal. The authors of the *Bibliothèque germanique* regulated their relations by written rules; although no copy is extant, we can infer them from their letters. We already know, of course, that the subordinate author had at least some say in what books he intended to discuss. But it was very often the case that Mauclerc or Pérard would simply instruct Formey to write a certain review, perhaps sending the book along with these instructions. The usual form of the request was, as on January 1, 1739, simply "Here is a little Work of M. *Zorn* of which I ask you to make the Extrait." In asking for a review of an edition of Pope, Mauclerc said he needed it immediately so "I address myself to you for this, my dear brother, knowing you as a man both very obliging and very expeditious." Mauclerc's tendency to tally up exactly how many pages Formey owed to the journal showed through at times in his attitude toward Formey's "contingent"; in telling him to review a new piece, he suggested Formey add it to another extrait which "you still owe to the Journal and to the public."[126] It is clear who was in control.

Besides telling his junior partner which books to review, Mauclerc would occasionally give instructions on what to say. Of the Pope edition he asked "that, without lacking in the duty of impartial Journalists, we speak of it honorably." But sometimes he was more specific. Mauclerc wrote of a treatise on natural law sent to him by the President of the Academy of St. Petersburg, "He seems to take a particular interest in it. And in any case the Material demands a great deal of attention, and an exact comparison with the ideas of Grotius, of Puffendorf, and of *Coccejus* senior, of F[rank]furt on the Principles of Natural Law. All this neither is nor ought to be foreign to you."[127]

The director of the *Bibliothèque germanique* not only had at least a partial say over which books should be reviewed for the journal, but he made the final decision over which articles would appear and in what order. We have already noted that Formey as subordinate author had a duty to send in 112 pages or seven sheets' worth of copy per issue, but he was not exact in this and, with the provision of articles from other sources, the journal sometimes ended up with a surplus of copy. It was thus not a given that Formey's articles would appear, and certainly not necessarily in the issue for which they were intended. Mauclerc would simply let Formey know which articles of his would be published, and it was clear that the decision lay solely with him. In a typical letter, he wrote that "I read with a true pleasure your two Letters on the étern[ité] des peines. The 1ˢᵗ will certainly go into the next Volume, and the other in the following. If you have a lot to do at the moment, you can put off working on the journal for a bit. I have enough to send off Vol. 45 and even over and above that."[128]

Significantly, however, although Mauclerc and later Pérard took charge of the *Bibliothèque germanique* and tried to operate it with a firm hand, Formey as second author demanded respect and recognition. In 1739 he made several complaints, among which was the seeming obscurity of his position as subordinate author. (When he took over as sole author in 1750, he innovatively put his name on the title page.) Mauclerc was anxious to avoid any accusations of domination.

I am ready, in order to show you how little I affect anything *exclusive* concerning my *Author of the BG*, to declare to the public, *the 1ˢᵗ time that there is a natural occasion to do so*, that you have worked on the Journal for many years; and I beg you to make sure that I recall it. In general, I stay far away from all chicanery; and I will enter with pleasure in all the arrangements which suit you; just as, on your side, I flatter myself that you will not propose anything which does not have as its basis *our Conventions*, which, having been made on both sides with good grace and good faith, will be, I hope, executed in the same fashion.[129]

Even before this time, Formey was consulted on which *extraits* or articles were most important or most pressing, the result of an earlier complaint; Mauclerc wrote in August of 1739 that "I want to keep my word to you exactly concerning the Extraits that you want to appear promptly."[130]

Even more telling than this dispute, instigated as it was by Formey, was Mauclerc's hesitance about criticizing the work of his junior. Mauclerc showed extreme uneasiness in making any editorial corrections, and his delicacy in handling Formey shows an apparent uncertainty about his right to do so. In 1742, for example, he wrote, "I am charmed, Monsieur my very dear and v[ery] h[onored] Brother, that you have consented to the suppression of all of *art. 6*, and that you are taking in good part what I took the liberty to say to you. . . . I assure you that I will always receive with gratitude and docility the Advice of my Friends, and yours in particular." And after correcting some factual errors in a review, he wrote, "Pardon me, in any case, these little signs of frankness and friendship, and prove that they do not displease you by showing the same to me."[131] So although it was agreed in writing that one figure should rule the journal, this was a situation which made even the director himself uncomfortable.

In the last type of authorial arrangement, there was no need for delicacy between editor and author; it avoided the editorial stage, and consequently the Republic of Letters, entirely. This was the case at the *Bibliothèque raisonnée*, where no author or scholar made any editorial decisions; these were all made in Amsterdam by the *libraires*, the Wetsteins and Smith. As we have already noted, it was known that this journal was under the *libraires'* strict control, and even that the authors did not know each other's identities. The Wetsteins wrote in the first issue that "The Authors, who work on our Journal, will never be disclosed by us. We will even do anything we can to keep this knowledge from all the earth, & to go even further, we can even assure that they are by no means known to each other, & that they are working without each other's knowledge."[132] This was in fact not strictly true, but it apparently *was* the case that the authors were not in regular communication with each other, at least about the contents of the journal. In 1742 Jean Barbeyrac wrote to the journal's corrector, Charles de la Motte, of a review in his own journal, "This Extrait is, in any case, pitiful, and if you except the Articles of Mess[rs]. Vernet, La Chapelle, & Wetstein, the others seemed to me as bad, both in taste & in style, as those in the II. p. of Vol. XXVII. I was surprised at what you told me, that M[r]. de la Chapelle had furnished Wetstein with the Extrait of *Middleton*."[133]

From the correspondence available between several of the principal authors of the *Bibliothèque raisonnée* and De la Motte, it appears that much of the time each author would choose his own subjects for review. Barbeyrac would simply announce to De la Motte what he was providing for the journal, and it was only in exceptional circumstances, his quarrels with his synod, that Armand de la Chapelle had to write of Smith "that if he wants me to work on the next part of the Bibl. Raiso. he will have to send me or indicate to me some Material; because in the retreat in which I've lived for 4 months, I am off the beaten track of the Librairie."[134] But some of the time the *libraires* did choose books for their reviewers, as, among other things, the accusations of slavishness we saw earlier indicate. The dealings between authors and *libraires* were filtered through the correspondence of the corrector, De la Motte, who urged authors to get in their *extraits* and literary news on time, who sometimes suggested new authors and made minor editorial decisions, and who took care of negotiations between all parties.[135]

But dictatorial *libraires*, lack of communication, and comparative isolation all proved a problem for this journal. When the Wetsteins themselves com-

municated with the authors, their rudeness was a matter for frequent comment. One submission of *nouvelles* by Des Maizeaux was greeted bluntly by
Jacob Wetstein, "they only consisted of entire subscription lists, and even
these too late to be placed [in the journal], we don't care to put subscriptions
in to fill the space which ought to be for short and succinct nouvelles
Litteraires of Books which are printed in England."[136] Armand de la
Chapelle, who it is true was often disagreeable himself, found much to
complain of in these arrangements. After the dissolution of the partnership
between Jacob Wetstein and William Smith, and Smith's death in 1741, La
Chapelle gave De la Motte his true feelings about journalism and the
Bibliothèque raisonnée.

> Out of consideration for the poor Deceased whom I esteemed & whom I
> liked, I certainly was disposed to agree to work on a new journal that he
> proposed to establish [at the end of the partnership], & I assure you that I
> was only doing it out of pure friendship. For this work never fails to have
> many unpleasant aspects, which more than once have disgusted me. Some-
> times by accident I made Extraits which had already been made by other
> people. Sometimes I did not have the books I needed, or I had to get ones
> that were not at all to my taste. Often I was sent ones that did not suit me
> in the least and which it was extremely boring for me to read. Often,
> again, being obliged to write Articles to order, I found myself incon-
> venienced. Most important, my secrets did not stay in Mr. Smith's hands,
> but passed, through correction or otherwise, to people who betrayed them
> to my enemies, & you know quite well whom I mean. So to speak frankly
> to you, I would not have been at all upset that the Bibliothèque Raisonnée
> had been suppressed, or, had it been continued, that it had excluded me.
> I would even have made this a subject of pleasure rather than chagrin.[137]

No matter how the authors of a journal arranged their working relationships, the copy would eventually have to be sent to the *libraire* for production. To examine this process, we will again look mainly at the
Bibliothèque germanique, although even in this case our information, especially
about the actual printing, is incomplete. We already know how the various
materials were supplied. Formey, in Berlin, would send his copy to the
director in Stettin by means of Naudé, a bookseller in Berlin who served as
their go-between. Once it had arrived, the director had a number of duties.
He did his best to read all the copy sent to him, mainly for the sake of
making the index, but also in part so that he could correct any errors and
prevent the wrong sort of remarks from going into the journal. However,
this was a duty about which he was at best uneasy; and when telling Formey
that he had sent off a piece without having time to read it, he said "in any
case this was not necessary, since this Volume has no index."[138] The copy

would presumably have been sent to the director in the format he wanted: each article in a separate notebook, with each page numbered. So before sending it to the *libraire*, the director would simply have to decide which pieces would go in, and in what order, and then ship them off, usually also via the bookseller Naudé. The copy did not necessarily go in all at once, and in fact if the *libraire* found that there was not enough, the journalists would have to provide more.[139]

The copy would usually be sent directly to the *libraire*, who would hand it over to his corrector. This man had a great deal of say over how the publication should proceed. For many of the journals of this period, it was the same person, Charles de la Motte, who corrected the *Bibliothèque germanique* for much of its run; when he became too old, he was replaced by Pierre Cartier de St. Philippe. Mortier left all the details of the production of the *Nouvelle Bibliothèque germanique* to Cartier, saying in 1751 "I abandon to him the care of arranging the different Materials that you send in." De la Motte's correspondence about the *Bibliothèque raisonnée*, which he also corrected, makes it clear that it was he who actually gave the copy to the printer and discussed with him the procedures of printing the journal. But the corrector would also sometimes edit the articles he dealt with and conducted much of the negotiations with the authors, even on a journal designed along the lines of the *Bibliothèque germanique*. Of course he also read the proof, which was not sent to the authors for correction, but which they did receive in the second half of each volume for the sake of the index. The corrector would also have to remind the authors to send the *nouvelles littéraires*, which, to be up to date, was always sent and printed last; it was up to the director to compile this section of the journal. The journals usually appeared every three months, and the process could take the entire time to complete.[140]

Sometimes the corrector would be called upon to serve in his double function of literary agent because the *libraire* did not always fulfill his obligations to the authors. The slowness of Humbert and Beauregard sent the authors of the *Bibliothèque germanique* into despair, and Mauclerc tried all expedients in an attempt to speed things up, from sending in the copy one or two issues ahead to advancing Beauregard 400 florins to encourage expedition.[141] In the end, the agents had to take over. De la Motte presented Mauclerc's ultimatum to Humbert, and, when the director's conditions were not met, took the accumulated copy out of the *libraire*'s hands. The agent Prosper Marchand transmitted it to the new *libraire*, Beauregard, with predictably bad results.[142]

Such problems did not always occur, of course, and if we look back on what has been covered, we can see that an issue of the *Bibliothèque germanique* has, essentially, been completed. The copy is all in, even down to the *nouvelles littéraires* and the index; the corrector has done his work with the printer and, with the help of various expedients, perhaps the issue has even come out on time.[143]

The Box under the Arsenal Clock

We have seen that there were a number of different ways of organizing the authors of a journal, with varying degrees of control over editorial decision and the provision of articles. The authors could work on terms of equality, be ruled by one director, or simply deliver their materials into the hands of the *libraire*. But the formal operations of the journals did not necessarily dictate their content. The journal's existence as an organ of the Republic of Letters, as an institutionalization of its values, complicated its nature. In the ideology of the scholarly community—if not in fact—the journal was to be a forum for all members of the Republic. Its contents thus did not necessarily consist of *extraits* and articles by the major authors. In fact, contributions to journals shaded from articles by the most official, contract-bound principal authors to anonymous submissions from obscure corners of literary Europe.

In the first place, many journals had secondary authors who would occasionally send in material, often in the form of articles whose subjects were not commissioned or suggested by anyone at the center of things. The operations of the *Bibliothèque germanique* are a good case in point. As Pérard wrote in 1740, before he had anything much to do with the journal, "Formey . . . is a journalist of the B.G. He is alone with M. De Mauclerc, but friends who want to work on it are welcomed & encouraged." Friends of the authors, such as Simon de Pelloutier, were occasionally assigned *extraits*, and others, such as the minister Jean Des Champs, frequently would send in material; Des Champs sent in 1748 "a Letter for your Journal as my ordinary contribution."[144]

An excellent example of a regular contributor of this type was Léonard Baulacre, a minister and librarian in Geneva. Baulacre sent in whatever he had on hand, which generally meant works of piety and theology. Among the items he sent to the *Bibliothèque germanique* in the late 1740s and early 1750s were articles on a tenth-century missal in the library in Geneva, explications of part of the Gospel of Matthew, and other such items, some of which, as he candidly confessed, he had dug up out of the bottom of a portfolio or had simply cut out of a copy of the *Journal helvétique*. Baulacre admitted that "items of Literature are better suited to your Journal than subjects of piety, but the latter are more suited to me, since I am in my declining years and must occupy myself with Religion more than anything else."[145]

In addition to having such regular contributors as Baulacre, most journals would also solicit materials. Sometimes authors of a journal would request a scholar to write an article or a review, courting him in terms of politeness and obligation. Mauclerc, for example, wrote several times in the 1720s and 1730s to the philosopher Jean-Pierre de Crousaz, inviting him to contribute to the *Bibliothèque germanique*. When Crousaz sent in one item, Mauclerc thanked him in flowery language, adding that "If you would like, when the occasion presents itself, and it will present itself when you think it à propos, to do us the same pleasure once again, and to send us pieces you have written, they will be, M^r., perfectly welcome, no matter what area of the Sciences they concern; For we are not ignorant of the fact that you have an abundance to choose from."[146]

Of course, one important section of the journals depended on outside help, and that was the *nouvelles littéraires*. Journalists who—in the case of the *Bibliothèque germanique*, for example—were located in one provincial town had to rely on their peers for the necessary information. This was not always easy to arrange, and third parties, such as Charles de la Motte or the *libraire* Jean-Louis de Lorme had to offer their assistance in finding correspondents. The authors of the *Journal litéraire* were forced to send out letters of inquiry all over Europe, asking in Paris, Hanover, and Lausanne, among other places, if people there could "let us know what is going on in the Republic of Letters."[147] Hans Bots, who has edited the correspondence of Henri Basnage de Beauval, counts 145 letters from France, 76 from England, 48 from Italy, 34 from Germany, and others from Portugal, Sweden, Switzerland, and the Spanish Netherlands. Similarly, Dieter Gembicki notes contacts in Belgium, Frankfurt, and Cologne who could provide Jean Rousset de Missy with information for his *Epilogueur moderne*.[148] Pierre Des Maizeaux became a mainstay of both the *Nouvelles de la République des Lettres* and the *Journal des Savants* by carrying on a literary correspondence with their editors, and he also contributed *nouvelles* to many other journals, including the *Bibliothèque raisonnée* and even the Jesuit *Mémoires de Trévoux*.[149] Des Maizeaux alone provided Jacques Bernard's *Nouvelles* with all its news from England; as Bernard said in 1701, "I owe to you the better part of the happy success of my Journal."[150]

However, the journals were open to more contributors than simply primary and secondary authors and their selected friends. In theory, at least, they were open to everyone. Although many journals made special arrangements to obtain *nouvelles littéraires*, anyone could send them in, and articles from the pens of readers were also welcomed. From the very beginning, journals would run short notices pointing out that, as the *Journal litéraire* put it, "Those who have curious Pieces of Literature, or those which concern the Arts & Sciences, which they wish to insert in this Journal, can address them to the Libraire, and should pay the postage."[151] The *Mémoires de Trévoux* even

3 Pierre Des Maizeaux's account with the *libraires* Weststein and Smith, Amsterdam. He is debited for books and journals purchased and credited with contributions to the *Bibliothèque raisonnée*. (BL Add. Ms. 4288, f. 269.)

provided, courtesy of the Duc de Maine, a box "in the Arsenal under the clock" so that potential contributors in Paris would have an easy way to speed their materials to the journal.[152] And the *Histoire critique* promised outright to publish "all that are sent to us on the subjects of *Criticism* and *Literature*. Such as everything that could concern the science of Medals; Inscriptions; Rites & Customs of Antiquity: & the Works of ancient Authors, both those of the Poets and of Authors of Prose."[153] When people began to get restive at the journal's failure to include everything as promised, the author, Samuel Masson, asked them "not to get impatient, if they do not see [the articles they wrote] appear; they will have their turn."[154]

Naturally the possibility of filling up some of their quota of copy with other people's work was an appealing one for journalists. But there was more to it than that. For both journalists and readers, journals were a community effort, an institution fashioned by those it was meant to serve. Many publications, for instance, not only invited provision of articles, but also criticism and correction of their own material. The *Mémoires de Trévoux* announced in its first issue that if anyone found its proposed plan for the journal "defective in some point, he will give pleasure by warning of it, & pointing out what he feels must be added to make it more perfect. Those who must execute it, intending only to make it as useful as it can be, are disposed to profit from the remarks people would like to give on this subject."[155] In this spirit, Pierre Des Maizeaux provided textual and factual corrections to the *Journal des Sçavans* in 1708 and 1709. Although the director, the Abbé Bignon, eventually took offense at this, pointing out a few errors of spelling and fact in Des Maizeaux's own letter, for the most part he expressed the gratitude of the journal, asking for more extensive remarks and promising that "I am very resolved to enter in all this, in all your views, and to profit greatly from your counsels."[156] Within limits—the limits of courtesy—the journal was for all learned people to modify.

This kind of openness was a result of a shared ethos about communication and information in the Republic of Letters. For journalists and authors alike, the point of literary journals was the profit of everyone in the community. Part of this profit, as we have seen, was access to information and opinions otherwise unavailable to scholars in widely scattered locales. Baulacre, for example, was conscious of the assistance his contributions might make to the scholarly community by providing information, as in his article on the new-found missal, or by disabusing the credulous public, as in a piece revealing lies in the works of the pyrrhonist Gregorio Leti.

Providing such information was a duty; of Leti's lies Baulacre said that "it is important to bring them to light when one has Mémoires for that purpose."[157] But it was also a privilege, since so often the items sent in to journals would bring renown for the author or, perhaps, allow him a forum to defend himself or his friends against opponents. When Jacques Bernard's continuation of the *Nouvelles de la République des Lettres* praised Jacob Gronovius' edition of Herodotus, in which Ludolph Kuster was disparaged, Kuster took on himself both the duty of informing the public and the privilege of his own defense. He asked Jean Le Clerc to insert in his journal a letter by the anonymous Abbé S★★★ defending Kuster against his opponent Gronovius and attacking the favorable judgment of Gronovius' book by Bernard. The letter read in part:

> What idea does Mr Bernard claim to give of the continuation of the Repu. des Lettres . . . since he begins with outrageous praises of the Edition of Herodotus by Mr Gronovius, an Edition generally distrusted by all distinguished persons of letters. He says among other things, *that the Edition of Herodotus of which Mr Gronovius has made a present to the public* is *worthy of him*; he is right so far, but we do not agree with the same ease with these words which he adds, and *of the savants, for whom he has destined it*[.] Never has an Edition been more worthy of a man like Mr Gronovius because it is full of gross and puerile blunders. . . . Permit me therefore to exhort you to warn the public against the false praises of the Author of the Republic of Letters. Again if mons. Gronovius had only given a bad Edition the evil could be repaired by a better one, but to give it more Prominence he attacks with impunity the most distinguished persons in a fashion which shows that he has Even less politeness than Erudition.[158]

Kuster's choice to use one journal to defend himself against comments in another was not uncommon. The *Histoire critique*, which seemed to encourage dispute, even advertised that it could provide "an easy help" to "Authors mistreated by one of their colleagues."[159] But more telling was the frequency that such a defense would appear in the same journal as had the attack to which it responded. Some journals made it quite explicit that they would accept such pieces, and even that giving both sides of an issue was part of their *raison d'être*. In his *Mémoires de littérature* Sallengre printed a letter concerning the fight over the proposed 1720 edition of Bayle's *Dictionary*, not, he said, because he took one side or another, but because it was his policy to discuss important issues in the learned world. "I am placing this Piece here just as it was sent to me without claiming to enter into this dispute in any manner," he wrote. "I am only following my Plan by inserting a Letter which concerns the edition of an important book, which the Dictionary of Bayle is. On the other hand I offer a place in these Mémoires, to responses people might make to this Piece."[160]

Similarly, when the *Bibliothèque raisonnée* began a multiple-part *extrait* of Allwoerde and Mosheim's *Historia Michaelis Serveti* with unpleasant remarks about Mosheim's ideas on Calvinism, the journal responded kindly to a letter from Mosheim explaining his real views. "[I]t is just to give satisfaction to this savant Professor. His letter, in the part which concerns the Author of these Extraits . . . is that of a perfectly *honnête homme*, & shows the character of the most estimable Christianity. He complains with an extreme sweetness, & yet with force that I had suspected him sometimes of blaming *Calvin* purely with the motive of hate for *Calvinism*."[161] Journalists would even write to scholars who were attacked by contributors in their pages, suggesting that a response would be gladly accepted. The authors of the *Journal litéraire* informed Christian Wolff well beforehand that the issue currently in press would contain an attack on him from England. "If you or one of your friends wants to respond to this piece, such as it will be, in our Journal," they wrote, the contribution would be welcome. As long as the author gave his name, it would be printed exactly as it was sent.[162]

The willingness to print both sides of a dispute was, of course, a commercially sound decision. Everyone was interested in arguments, and printing the statements of both parties would both sell journals and put the journalists in the position of neutrality dictated by the unwritten rules of the community. But it was more than simple pragmatism, especially as sales seemed to matter more to *libraires* than to journalists. By providing a forum where all could air their ideas—whether they were new discoveries, curiosities, or arguments about the failings of other scholars—journalists followed the fundamental rule of the Republic of Letters to instruct its members. The avowed goal of journals was to inform; and the opening of the journal's pages to public submissions, and to disputants often on both sides of an argument, suggests an at least partly disinterested attempt to maintain these standards.

Another indication that journalists had the profit of the public in mind was their effort to cooperate with each other. This effort began with the attempt to find a niche within the field of journals available to the public. Some of the better-known journals, it is true, aimed to cover the entire field of scholarly works; the *Histoire des ouvrages des savans* or the aptly-named *Bibliothèque universelle* are examples. But even these generally found it necessary to point out holes in their potential audience's provision of journals. The *Histoire critique*, for example, pointed out the difference in its contents, which were "more extensive, & even very different, in several points, from those of ordinary Journals."[163] And in 1713, the *Journal litéraire* remarked on the dearth of general periodicals now available in Holland.

I have noticed that for some time most of those who read or who buy books, are complaining that this Country lacks a good Journal, to instruct them about the state of the Sciences, & the occupations of Savants, since the *Histoire des Ouvrages des Savans*, & the *Nouvelles de la République des*

Lettres, have both ceased, by the death of the Author of the first, & by the occupations of the person who wrote the other.

The *Bibliothèque Choisie* of the Savant & judicious *M. le Clerc*, still continues, with all the reputation that such an excellent Work deserves; but the small extent of this Journal not permitting it to discuss much material, it appears that it does nothing but excite the curiosity of the public still further; so that it will not in the least prevent the good reception of another Journal, where a great quantity of subjects will be treated, & to a greater extent.[164]

Fifteen years later, the *Bibliothèque raisonnée* used the same argument to justify its appearance on the literary scene.[165]

While more general journals pointed to the lack of their type of periodical as a justification for their existence, more specific works, such as the national *bibliothèques*, simply remarked on the failure of the general periodicals to cover books from their particular province. The *Bibliothèque italique*, for example, needed only to remind its potential readers that "The Journals of Germany, of France & of Holland, speak of too small a number of Books from Italy, & they speak of them too late."[166] There was only need, or only room, for one journal of this type per country, so that the *Bibliothèque britannique* only began once Armand de la Chapelle had ceased to publish the *Bibliothèque angloise*. The new authors said they would only speak of books published since the end of the latter journal, "so that our Journal can serve as a continuation of it."[167]

This reasoning was not simply rhetoric, as is evident from its appearance in private correspondence about the fortunes of journals. When Formey had in mind the founding of a new periodical to be published by Etienne Neaulme, the agent Prosper Marchand counseled him in similar terms.

You believe, you say that M[r]. de M[aty] writes the *best* Part of the *Bibliothèque Britannique*. People attribute to him some extremely boring Extraits of Pedantries [*Rabbinage*], & several others of *Rableserie* [*sic* for Rabelaiserie], which are not more diverting. Thus, you see that the *best* is absolutely too much. This *Journal* will have trouble sustaining itself; and without various Extraits from here [The Hague], I believe that it would already have ceased to appear. That of the *Bibliotheq. Raisonnée* has absolutely failed since Messrs. Barbeyrac and de la Chapelle have renounced it, beaten down by the Incivilities of the Libraire. The *Nouvelle Bibliothèque*, having changed Libraires and Arrangement does not promise much to judge from the horribly incorrect first Trimester. And the *Journal d'Allemagne*, conducted with the Diligence which you know, is scarcely proper to keep up the Taste and the Eagerness of those Curious about these sorts of Works. All this will have to influence M^r. Neaulme to respond to your ideas.[168]

As with other editorial decisions we have considered, patriotic adherence to the laws of the Republic of Letters was not all that was at stake. Clearly it made good commercial sense not to compete directly with another journal for a small market, since Francophone readers interested in English books would be unlikely to read both a *Bibliothèque angloise* and a *Bibliothèque britannique*.[169] Moreover, cooperation among authors of various journals— depending on who they were—could make or break the success of a periodical. After the *Journal littéraire* printed some *nouvelles* attacking the powerful Jesuit Père Tournemine and his *Mémoires de Trévoux*, its authors learned that perhaps he was not the wisest person to offend. Albert-Henri de Sallengre, on a visit to Paris in 1714, reported back to his fellow-journalists that Tournemine "had been very surprised that both the Journal and his person had been attacked, without his having given the slightest occasion." When Sallengre apologized for the *Journal*'s having taken the offensive, explaining that they had printed the *nouvelles* exactly as they had been received from correspondents, Tournemine accepted this explanation. In- deed, after conversing with Sallengre he "finally concluded that if our society was willing not to attack their Journal, nor their Corps, he would do the Journal and the Society all imaginable Services, and he would make the journal known with praise all over France." This was a particularly satisfac- tory outcome, since Tournemine was quite capable of the opposite. In fact, he was willing to damn another journal in just the way that would be most beneficial to the *Journal littéraire*. Sallengre reported: "He also said to me that if Moetjens [the *libraire* who owned the copyright of the *Nouvelles de la République des Lettres*] gave the Republique des Lettres to Aÿmon, he would have it prohibited in France, which shows again that it is advantageous to the Journal to have peace with him and the Jesuits, because he being in great credit it would only cost him two words to prohibit this Journal in France, and if M^r. Johnson [*libraire* of the *Journal littéraire*] wishes it I can get him in touch with the P. Tournemine and with Ganeau who sells the Journal de Trévoux."[170] From being in danger of censorship themselves, the authors of the *Journal littéraire* ultimately saw the prospect of a rival being censored instead. Cooperation certainly had its commercial uses.

This story, of course, has yet another side. Behind the cooperation with the *Mémoires de Trévoux* lurks the gleeful hope of damaging the competing *Nouvelles de la République des Lettres*. And it is true that journals attacked each other, sometimes viciously, as we have already seen in the case of the *Lettres sérieuses et badines* and the *Bibliothèque raisonnée*. However, although some of this enmity was the result of personal conviction, much was the direct result of the commercial interests of the *libraire*. The *Lettres sérieuses et badines* appear to have been founded solely for the purpose of defending one book, François Janiçon's *Etat présent de la République des Provinces Unies*, which had been published by its *libraire* Jean van Duren. When the Wetsteins, Van Duren's enemies, apparently urged their authors to excoriate Janiçon's book in the pages of the *Bibliothèque raisonnée*, Van Duren retaliated by hiring Antoine de la Barre de Beaumarchais to write a journal, half of whose first issue consisted of a defense of Janiçon.[171]

Journals in some instances did see themselves as competing with each other, sometimes aiming to be the first to publish an *extrait* of a work. Mauclerc, for example, wrote to Jean-Paul de Crousaz in 1731 about the latter's *Examen de Pyrrhonisme*, asking, "When do you expect it will be finished printing. I would like our Journal to be the first to give an Extrait of it. Is there a way for the Sr de Hondt [the *libraire* publishing the book] to send me the first Volume as soon as it is finished?"[172] A journal with the earliest *extraits* might come to seem the most reliable or the most profitable to read.

Yet despite the commercial advantages of competition, it is notable how often the ethos of cooperation won out. The weight of evidence, in fact, is on this ethos rather than on the desire to thrash other journals in the race to review, a desire whose expression is rare in the available documents.[173] The prevailing view was that since the goal of journals was to instruct the public, if one periodical reviewed a book there was no need to discuss it in another. This attitude is expressed frequently in the texts of the journals. In a typical example, the *Histoire critique* declined to give an *extrait* of Ludolph Kuster's *Diatribe Antigronoviana*, writing instead that "for what concerns the latter Book by Mr. *Kuster*, we direct the Reader to those excellent *Masters*, Messrs. the *Journalists* of Paris, *March* 1713. where a both clear & well-reasoned Extrait is provided."[174] This attitude held whether the book had been newly reviewed or the *extraits* in other journals had been available for some time. In either case, the knowledge of the book normally offered by an *extrait* was already in the hands of the public. The *Histoire critique* thus took a similar view of a new edition of the *Voyages de Mr. le Chevalier Chardin en Perse*, originally published in French in 1686, as it had to Kuster's more recent book.

As soon as this Work had appeared, Mr. *Bayle* gave a quite ample extrait of it, in his months of *September* & of *October* of the year 1686. of the *Nouvelles de la Republique des Lettres*, in which he gave a very advantageous judgment of this Book. It would thus seem entirely useless to undertake to talk of these three first Volumes after what this famous Journalist has said about them.

The only conceivable reason to do so, in the view of the *Histoire critique*, was that since that time the author had made considerable additions "which certainly deserve that Journalists should stop a little, to instruct the Public of them. We will also be able to speak of several places which occur in the first Edition, & of which Mr. *Bayle* says nothing in his Extrait."[175] In other words, the only items worth discussing in the book were those of which the public had not yet been told.

This attitude is especially noticeable in the journals which covered a particular piece of territory in the learned world. The authors of such periodicals profited from their usually unique claim to that territory, and in general they stuck to their special task of informing their colleagues about, say, works published in England. In 1728 the authors of the *Bibliothèque italique* felt compelled to apologize for printing an article entitled "Sur une Observation des Anciens Chaldéens," an article neither about Italy nor by an Italian. "Although the Article about to be read is not by an *Italian* Author," the journalists wrote,

> We believed that our Readers would not disapprove of our going thus beyond our Plan, in order to give them little Works of the taste of the one here. We believed it necessary to forestall the censure of some Persons, who had condemned us before having read the Piece.

Their excuse for offering this article—and for welcoming contributions of this type in the journal, "despite its Title"—was that "Some distinguished Italian People of Letters, have let us know that they would view them with pleasure. We must do ourselves the pleasure, of marking this deference to their advice."[176] Thus the link to Italy, however tenuous, was maintained.

Remarks such as these—about the territory of a journal, or the abilities of learned journalistic colleagues—might appear suspect. Given their location in printed journals, their inclusion might seem to have the ring of flattery or of a desire to be seen playing the game. But the manuscript evidence available indicates that journalists actually were concerned to divide up the responsibilities of informing their audience, rather than competing for that audience. When Louis Bourguet wrote an *extrait* of a book by Viridet which had nothing to do with Italy, his colleague Du Lignon wrote him tartly, "I received . . . the extrait of the Book by Mr Viridet, which is not of the Jurisdiction of the Bibliotheque Italique, but of that of the Bibliotheque Germanique, thus you could have dispensed with writing this long extrait, if you want to limit yourself, to working for the Bibliotheque Italique you will see Monsieur that you will have energy and time to spare." Du Lignon sent the unusable *extrait* to Holland for the use of the *Bibliothèque germanique*.[177] Even after the *Bibliothèque italique* suggested in print that it was its policy to accept unrelated materials, if only to oblige Italian scholars, it was clear that in private its authors were none too happy to do so. In 1729 Bourguet fumed at the propensity of their Genevan *libraire*, Bousquet, to add articles unrelated to Italy, such as projects of two dictionaries to be published by his *librairie* and an *éloge* of Le Clerc, "a savant, it is true, but Protestant and Genevan." Such items, not being Italian, belonged elsewhere: "these two Dictionaries belonged in the Nouvelles and the Eloge fell within the competence of the Bibl: Germanique." As Bourguet rhetorically inquired, "What does this have in common with the Bibl: Italique[?]"[178]

Similar views reigned on the staffs of other periodicals. Jean Catuffe of the *Journal litéraire* wrote to his fellow-authors that although it was ill health that prevented him from writing an *extrait* of "*l'Histoire secrete &c.*," "perhaps I would not even have done this Extrait, if I could have; I believe that it would not be a bad idea to content ourselves with saying about this, that as we have been anticipated (by the Biblioth. raisonnée) we are not giving an Extrait of it, & that we are contenting ourselves with making the remarks that M. Marchand has written on the attached note."[179] And Jean Barbeyrac of the *Bibliothèque raisonnée* told Charles de la Motte that the *libraire* Humbert had suggested an extrait of the *Discours sur la nature du sort*, "because he did not think it had been spoken of in its day. He forgot, that there was a fairly long Extrait in the *Journal Litteraire*. M^r. Le Clerc talked about it also, but succinctly, in the *Bibl. Anc. & Moderne.*"[180]

The important point, then, is that journalists shared the notion that their purpose was mainly to give the public information to which it did not already have access. We have already seen that novelty was valued in the Republic of Letters; books which were to be translated were often not reviewed, and the provision of information from distant parts was particularly "useful." If books were old but inaccessible, such as many books from England, their inclusion was also acceptable, as Michel de la Roche found with his *Bibliothèque angloise*.[181] Camusat explained that "the goal of Journals, whatever they are, must be not only to inform about what things are going on in the Republic of Letters, & to give a faithful & exact relation of them, but also to accompany this with new things, or at least things which are unknown to the greatest part of the readers."[182] By cooperating with each other to bring this new information to the public, journalists—who, after all, were themselves members of the Republic of Letters—participated in the same ethos which prompted the formation of *commerces de lettres*. As with their provision of a forum for discussion, and their agreement that the learned community participated in the shaping of journals, the division of news and information-gathering among journalists is yet another sign that a group ideal underlay the institution of the literary periodical.

The Journal as Person

In acting out this public role in the Republic of Letters, journals became in a peculiar way a personification of the group as a whole. Attitudes of both journalists and readers suggest that a literary journal was regarded as in some sense an ideal member of the Republic of Letters, one who, on the basis of this status, had special rights in the community. When scholars wrote *éloges* of their colleagues, or wrote *extraits* of admirable books, they often praised qualities such as *politesse, honnêteté*, and *droiture*. Des Maizeaux reported that Bayle "disputed without heat, & without taking a dogmatic tone," while books such as Jacob Spon's *Histoire de Genève* or Jerôme à Costa's *Histoire de l'origine, & du progrés des Revenus Ecclesiastiques* were praised in journals for their own dissociation from "prejudices & Bigotry."[183] Journals were supposed to display to perfection these same good qualities, indeed to act as an example to the rest of the community of correct learned behavior.

Although these ideals were rarely achieved, it is evident from comments on both sides that the Republic of Letters set high standards for the conduct of its journals. Camusat's disparaging remarks about the *Histoire critique de la République des Lettres*, a journal often criticized by contemporaries, indicate in reverse the way such a periodical was expected to act.

> The *Historien Critique* uses haughty airs with everyone; He finds fault with & mistreats the most respectable deceased. He quarrels with the living, he makes of his Nouvelles Litteraires a field of invectives, a sort of entrench-ment from which he aims his blows at those who have the unhappiness to displease him. I have heard tell that in Holland, before having determined to have his *Histoire Critique* in Utrecht he addressed himself to *Fritsch & Böhm* Libraires of Rotterdam, & that to show them the merit of his Work he promised them *to crush the le Clercs & the other demi savants whose merit consisted in triumphing over good sense & pure & sound erudition*.[184]

The journalist Camusat's shocked tone implies that proper literary periodicals behaved with *honnêteté* toward their readers, honored the dead, and behaved fairly and kindly toward the living, including other journalists.

The *Journal littéraire* thus offered reciprocity for its criticisms, saying that "if we believe we have the right to criticize others, we are not so unjust to dispute with them the same privilege with regard to us"; the *Histoire des ouvrages des savans* asked for the "indulgence" of its readers; and Michel de la Roche broke off in the middle of an article in the *Bibliothèque angloise* to request information on a point of scholarship.[185] Such behavior even extended to offers of (or invitations for) services. The *Histoire critique* said that if encouragers of letters would favor the journal "with their help & with their good offices," it would in turn reciprocate by producing a volume of the journal. In fact, it was "entirely disposed to render to Persons of Letters & to true Savants all the little services of which we are capable"; for this reason it was willing to print all pieces readers sent in.[186] The journal was behaving like any good scholar, inviting exchange of information and goodwill for mutual benefit.

The issue of fairness and impartiality exercised the learned community for much of this period. As a good member of the Republic of Letters a journal was expected to deal fairly with its subject, an ethic clearly behind the desire to present both sides of an issue. The *Bibliothèque italique* pointed out "that justice, equity, & politeness, whose rules people of Letters must follow, more exactly than anyone, are so opposed to partiality, that an Author delivered over to this base passion is surely sullied in the spirit of *honnêtes* people of all Communions."[187] If scholars were required to behave better than the rest of society, then journals, as representatives of all learned people, had to behave best of all.

From the first, periodicals which did not observe the rules of impartiality were rebuked by readers, so that the *Journal des Sçavans*, whose *extraits* contained few comments compared to some later journals, was forced to apologize in 1666 for its lack of restraint. Bayle had the same problems with the *Nouvelles* in the 1680s, reporting that he "has been reliably warned that people do not like his taking sides in the matters of which he speaks, & that people would prefer that he confine himself in the limits of a disinterested Historian, who is sparing with his Reflections." He promised to profit from the warning.[188]

Journalists acknowledged these responsibilities, often vocally. Several were so insistent on the importance of impartiality and their incarnation of it that they made it the main selling-point of their work: thus the titles of Formey's *Bibliothèque impartiale* and François Bruys' *Critique désintéressée des journaux*. Others vied to make the most extravagant promises of neutrality, scolding each other for their failings in this regard. The authors of the *Bibliothèque italique*, for example, worried in their preface that the reader would not believe their assurances of impartiality. "All *Journalists*[,] he will say to them, have made the same promise, & almost all have violated it on some occasion. MM. of *Trevoux* promised on *oath* to observe it; they are accused, however, often enough, in the Journal of Venice, the most circumspect of all about them, of not having kept their word."[189] Michel de la Roche reported in the *Bibliothèque angloise* of 1718 that the *Journal des Savans* had made recommendations on how he should fulfill similar promises. The *Journal* reminded La Roche that true neutrality consists less in the choice of books than in the way they are discussed; he then pointed to his own past success in this area.[190]

The reason for all this insistence on the neutrality of a journal, was, again, at least partly one of *politesse*. A truly *honnête homme* was one who did not behave unfairly and did not allow personal considerations to enter into his academic judgments. Journals, as representatives of the rest of the community, were particularly responsible for maintaining this neutrality, especially as they provided information for the rest of the group. For this reason, Jacques Bernard refused to publish a satirical piece against the *Journal des Savans* in the *Nouvelles de la République des Lettres*; the piece ultimately appeared in the Dutch edition of the *Mémoires de Trévoux*. He commented to Delaissement that "I believe that it is a trait of an *honnête homme* not to want to make Enemies of his own free will, in the Career that I am in, Neutrality is always the surest course."[191] The expectations of literary journalism required him to behave, if not to think, like the most admirable of all scholars.

An example will show these values in practice. Jean Le Clerc became angry with an *extrait* in the *Journal des Savans* of Perizonius' *Quintus Curtius vindicatus* which appeared to take sides against Le Clerc in the literary quarrel between the two.[192] The journalists agreed that to do so would have been *malhonnête*, insisting that the failure to mention Le Clerc's response to Perizonius in the *extrait* was simply an error. The Abbé Bignon, director of the journal, wrote to Le Clerc that Pouchard, author of the *extrait*, "believed he was doing nothing else than reporting the thoughts and the expressions of M. Perisonius without either approving them or condemning them, leaving the freedom to the public to make whatever judgment it chose. In my opinion, I have always imagined, perhaps without much reason, that this was the true character of good journalists."[193] In the end one journalist, Joseph Saurin, admitted that Pouchard had "fallen I don't know how into the partiality with which he is reproached in the Letter," defending him only with his other good qualities: "he is otherwise a quite talented man, & fairly judicious; He is Professeur Royal in the Greek language."[194]

To be a good citizen of the Republic of Letters was to be an *honnête homme*, and to be an *honnête homme* was to judge impartially; since journals were representatives of the rest of their community, they must judge impartially too, and to do otherwise was either an error inspired by ignorance, as Bignon suggested, or, according to Saurin's interpretation, a reprehensible fault. In either case, the moral of the story is clear: journals, because of their position in the Republic of Letters, were expected to behave like the best of their fellow-citizens.

Because of this status, moreover, periodicals were in the position of influencing their readers in matters of conduct. Their pronouncements about the way they, and other members of the learned world, should behave at once reflected and reinforced these views. François Bruys, characteristically outspoken, appeared to feel that controlling behavior was one of the main functions of a journal, one which most journalists did not adequately fulfill. His journal, the *Critique désintéressée des journaux*, which reviewed the journals themselves, was intended to rectify this lack in the Republic of Letters. Here he complains of old books reissued under new titles.

When one examines things from close up, one easily recognizes that most new Books only are such [i.e. new] through a striking & lying title. Thus the Libraries of the Curious are insensibly filled with Works below the mediocre. Several other abuses have crept into the Republic of Letters which impunity authorizes & multiplies. It is true that the goal of Journalists seems to be to repress them: but do they truly work toward this goal? That is a Problem that will be decided clearly in this Work. Now, it suffices for us to say that the Public cannot be too grateful toward People of Letters who undertake sincerely to suppress disorders, which are infinitely prejudicial to the interests of Individuals.[195]

Other journals carried the same message, if more indirectly. We saw, for example, that the *Bibliothèque raisonnée* accepted Mosheim's complaints about an *extrait* because "his letter . . . is that of a perfectly *honnête homme*, & shows the character of the most estimable Christianity. He complains with an extreme sweetness."[196] Not only did this indicate the journal's willingness to listen to both sides of the issue, but it also subtly legislated the type of behavior it was willing to tolerate. The implication is that if Mosheim had not written his complaints politely and sweetly, the *Bibliothèque raisonnée* would not have listened to them. Other features of periodicals reflect the same tendency; journals both responded to the views of their audience and suggested how that very audience ought to behave. A number of journals promised to avoid "bitter & personal disputes," as the *Bibliothèque italique* expressed it, and asked their readers to be gentle toward others in their submissions to the journals. The *Journal littéraire* even said that if readers would not obey this important maxim, "Journalists who want to remain impartial, & as far as possible not to offend anyone, must be permitted to edit out these places." Pierre Bayle explained that in the *Nouvelles de la République des Lettres* "we are not claiming to establish a *bureau d'adresse of backbiting*, nor to use Articles whose only goal is to stain people's reputation. It is a license unworthy of an *honnête homme*, & nothing shocked us more in the *Mercure Sçavant*, than the tendency which reigns there of mistreating very illustrious Persons."[197]

Journalists sometimes cited instances of scholars acting either badly or well, drawing the appropriate conclusions. Both A.-F. Gori and A.-M. Salvini worked on a particular Roman monument without fighting, a source of admiration for the *Bibliothèque italique*, which pointed out that because of their cooperation, "the Public profits infinitely."[198] But of the dispute between Jacques Basnage and Maturin Veyssière La Croze, the *Journal littéraire* could only pronounce that it is a shame that a misunderstanding, after having given rise to a too bitter Censure on the part of the latter [i.e. La Croze], has thus sown discord between two People even more estimable by their merit than by their Erudition. This could take the place of a lesson of distrust to all Readers against the Critiques of many Books: in effect, if the secret motives of most of them were known, people would see with surprise, perhaps even with indignation, that they are made less against the deficiencies of the Works that they censure, than against their Authors.[199]

These periodicals clearly felt it was their role to pass judgment on the behavior of scholars, both proper and improper. By recommending that their readers learn a lesson—even a "lesson of distrust"—from these accounts, journalists set themselves up as moral guardians of the Republic of Letters.

As such a guardian, as an ideal scholar, the journal not only was in a position to dictate etiquette but to direct scholarship itself. Journals often functioned as a central node in a network of savants; their necessarily far-flung correspondence and wide span of readers made them in many ways an institutional equivalent of the scholarly intermediary. No collection of friends or colleagues could hope to equal the resources a journal could potentially tap. It was for this reason that scholars published "projects" of their work in progress in journals, hoping for whatever help might be forthcoming from possibly unknown colleagues; and the *nouvelles littéraires* frequently had the same results. Jean Cornand de la Crose, for example, informed readers of his *Memoirs for the Ingenious* in January 1693 that "an ingenious Gentleman having undertaken to write a *General History of Fountains*, he desires the Assistance of the Learned, in order to finish so useful a performance. And therefore if any have Advices, Experiments or Papers of the like Nature, to impart to him, he is intreated to send 'em to the Author of these *Memoirs*. . . . Or if any had the same Design, and had so far advanced it as to be ready for the Press, he is desired to give notice of it to the said Author, that his Friend may desist from a fruitless Undertaking."[200]

Who knows what exchange of information might be engendered by such an announcement? In the previous chapter we saw a number of examples of scholars with common interests locating each other through mention in journals. Denis-François Camusat was spurred to write his *Histoire critique des journaux* after reading an article by Pierre Des Maizeaux in the *Nouvelles de la République des Lettres,* and his subsequent correspondence with Des Maizeaux gave him valuable material and assistance. In the same way, Peter Needham's perusal of the *Memoirs of Literature*, which reported in English on the activities of Continental scholars, resulted in a correspondence with Jean Le Clerc and a collaboration of effort on Needham's Theophrastus. As the *Mémoires de Trévoux* explained, "by the means of these Memoires you can consult at once all the Savants of Europe, & in a short time receive all the elucidation you need. This correspondence of all men of Letters with one another, so easy to establish & to preserve, can serve infinitely toward the perfection of the Sciences."[201]

As a super-citizen in the Republic of Letters, then, one who not only provided a moral example but also an amplified ability to give scholarly assistance, the literary journal was in a position to dictate not only behavior but academic activity. Besides inviting scholars to assist each other by re-counting their projects in the *nouvelles littéraires*, a journalist might make his own suggestions about such projects. The *Histoire critique* announced to the world in 1715 that Maturin Veyssière La Croze had finished writing his Armenian dictionary; "it must be hoped, that he will decide soon to have it printed; as well as some other Pieces, which he has completely ready."[202] Mentioning a worthwhile piece of work might inspire others to undertake similar projects. Jean Cornand de la Crose noted the title of the sixth edition of Moréri's dictionary, edited by Le Clerc, which had just come out. He did so "not only to make this Book known to those that understand the *French* tongue; but chiefly to excite *English* Authors and Booksellers to undertake a work of that nature. For if Mr *Le Clerk* alone, has been able, and that in a short time, to bring this Dictionary to a great deal of perfection; how much more might it be improv'd, if several learned men would shake hands together, and make use of many Books and Libraries that we have here [London], and that neither *Morery* nor the learned Author of the *Universal Bibliotheque* could peruse."[203] As we have seen, some journalists were quite willing to assist in the prosecution of such projects, and Camusat praised the authors of the *Journal des Sçavans* for their efforts "sometimes to procure the necessary additions to imperfect works . . . often to encourage [contemporary authors] . . ., sometimes to eke out of them by gracious invitations & obliging solicitations Books which the Public would otherwise never have enjoyed."[204]

The personification of literary journals as ideal citizens of the Republic of Letters was thus in some ways a useful fiction. Placing the journals in this position gave the learned world a new institution to regulate its operations. Journals set standards of both scholarship and behavior, standards which, although they reflected ideals already governing the community, bolstered and codified such ideals through the force of print. As super-members of the Republic, moreover, periodicals both reinforced the ethos of scholarly coop-eration by suggesting that savants would benefit from assistance, and made efforts to provide such assistance themselves. The aim of any good scholar was to do what he could for his colleagues, all for the sake of the community as a whole. Journals performed the same function, with the same result; as the *Bibliothèque italique* said, "it must be agreed that the most imperfect of these

Works, have been universally regarded as of potentially great utility for the advancement of the Sciences."[205]

The Journal as Personality

Ironically, however, the very same view of journals which in some ways made them most useful in other ways undermined their usefulness. If periodicals were viewed as people, empowered through their authority to give publicity and assistance to scholarly efforts, they were also treated as people and expected to act like them. The identification of many journals with a single author, so that they became "Mr. de Beauval's journal" or "Mr. Le Clerc's journal," only magnified this tendency, although even journals with anonymous or multiple authors encountered the same attitudes, ones which to some degree these authors shared. The conflict such attitudes engendered was basic, for it was difficult for a journal which behaved like one of its readers to maintain its stature as an institution serving the entire community. The authors of such a journal could not in truth promise, as the *Bibliothèque britannique* did, to act as "faithful Reporters & . . . disinterested Historians."[206]

The very operations of the journals were shot through with this contradiction. The exchange relations so important to individual scholars were also integral to periodicals' editorial policy. The journal could not and did not escape from the fact that the world of scholarship revolved around services and favors, politenesses done to serve one's friends and colleagues. Its operations, even when hidden behind an authorless title page, could not be depersonalized. We have already seen that the rules of *politesse* appeared to conflict in Mauclerc's mind with his duty as editor of the *Bibliothèque germanique*. This duty required him to make what changes he deemed necessary in articles by his subordinate author; but the contradictory duties of *honnêteté* suggested that to do so was to take liberties with the work of a worthy colleague. In such a situation, it is not surprising that the smallest correction was followed by apologies and requests for reciprocal treatment.[207]

The openness of journalists to correspondence outside the journal was another symptom of this confusion of the personal and the institutional. With their extensive circle of contacts, journalists themselves were good people for a scholar to know. They were well-informed and often powerful, and many savants felt free to write to them as a way of extending their scholarly contacts and quickly prosecuting their business. When Isaac de Beausobre was doing research on Italian ecclesiastical history, he quite naturally wrote to Louis Bourguet for assistance in locating and obtaining books, "because I know that you work on the Bibliotheque Italique."[208] We have already observed Gisbert Cuper writing to the author of the *Nouvelles de la République des Lettres*, whom he did not know, to "chat" about a subject of interest to him (windows in old houses).[209] Others carried on long correspondences with journalists which mimicked personal correspondence between individuals. These exchanges entailed reciprocity, so that the authors of the *Journal littéraire*, for example, asked Christian Wolff "to let us know what would give you pleasure, and what utility we can be to you in this Country."[210] In 1714 Robert de Chelles, the author of the *Illustres françoises*, had a bantering exchange of letters with the authors of the *Journal littéraire* after his book was reviewed there. They had never met, and Chelles was not even aware of his correspondents' identities; but this did not stop the journalists from departing from an official tone. "We received last Friday the last letter that you did us the honor to write to us. It could not have arrived in a better way, because it found us all together. Your playfulness and several bottles of Champagne contributed no little to our passing the evening agreeably. We drank to your health, with pleasure, because you have the air of being a very *galant homme*, and because the wine was very good."[211] When a personal relationship was available between authors and readers, this suggested a carry-over of the relationship into the editing of the journal. And indeed the contents of journals were perceived on all sides to be affected by personal considerations.

This was in part a function of the nature of the enterprise. When an article or an *extrait* appeared in a journal, a number of people benefited. The author of the article, if he was not one of the principal journalists, found a means to disseminate his ideas and, perhaps, his name. If the article was an *extrait*, the author of the book reviewed and his *libraire* profited from the publicity afforded by the journal's circulation. The journalist, in turn, was often happy to receive contributions which might reduce the amount of space his contract required him to fill. This was one reason why journalists solicited materials from outside sources. To provide such materials might be as much a favor to the journalist as to the contributor.

Thus when Léonard Baulacre sent in articles to the *Bibliothèque germanique*, he considered not only the profit of the Republic of Letters, and of himself, but also that of the journal and journalists. During the journal's troubles with a *libraire*, Baulacre believed it had folded and sent several pieces instead to the *Bibliothèque raisonnée*, meanwhile asking for other, aging ones back from Stettin. This of course implies that the articles were not simply provided for the assistance of Formey and Pérard, but also for the information of the community—as in the revelation of the lies of Gregorio Leti—and for Baulacre's own record of publication. But when he learned of his error about the *Bibliothèque germanique*, he was all apologies, clearly viewing his action as a problem for the journal. "I recognize that I am your Debtor for the same quantity of pieces that you will have returned to me, and I contract myself to replace them with others which will be more in season, and which in consequence will figure better in your Journal when it gets under way."[212] Later, when Formey was laboring under the burden of both the entire *Bibliothèque germanique* and the *Bibliothèque impartiale*, Baulacre sent in three pieces, since "it is proper to help you a little in the dreadful task of producing two different Journals all at once."[213]

And just as Baulacre was doing the journalists a favor by providing them with copy, they did him the favor of printing his work. Indeed, even the use of material by principal authors could be viewed in this manner. Although Formey was officially involved in the *Bibliothèque germanique*, with a set amount of copy to provide per issue, he, like Baulacre or Des Champs, would benefit from the printing of his articles. Mauclerc bore this benefit in mind in 1740 when writing to tell Formey he had no room for one of his pieces: "I'll do what I can however," he wrote, "at the risk of annoying one of my other friends."[214] Apparently, one purpose of a journal was to oblige one's friends.

So in some sense it was a favor to Baulacre himself—and even to the professional Formey—to use his articles, and this is exactly the way it would have been perceived. Since the ability to prosecute scholarly discussions or quarrels in public was important to active scholars, the ability to use the forum provided by journals was prized. For Simon Pelloutier, the insertion of a letter in the *Bibliothèque françoise* was not a right, but a "politeness" resulting in an "obligation": "I have a great obligation to Monsieur de Bayer for the goodness he has shown in inserting my first letter in the Journal he directs. This is not the first politeness I have received on his part."[215]

The journalist—in this case Jean de Beyer—was the person able to grant such a favor, and although public submissions were requested, many scholars obtained space in journals in the same way as other favors: through an intermediary. Literary agents such as Charles de la Motte and Prosper Marchand knew the authors or worked themselves for many of the journals being published in Holland, and were thus in the position of influencing their contents. A typical example of an agent placing an article occurred during the fight between Pierre Des Maizeaux and Prosper Marchand over the 1714 edition of Bayle's letters. The war continued in the journals, and in 1714 Des Maizeaux asked De la Motte to find someone to publish a polemic he had written. De la Motte's response is indicative of the values underlying the placement of articles in periodicals.

I have received, Monsieur, your letter against Marchand, & I offered it to M. Le Clerc for his Biblioth. but he asks you to excuse him if he does not insert it, he does not want to get mixed up any more in this affair. . . . We will have to insert it in the Journal of M. Masson, he is tied up in this matter, and his older brother is one of your Friends. If you want, I will give it to M. Masson's Libraire, and I will correct it. . . . If you do not find it appropriate to use this Journal, I am assured that Waesberge would not refuse me in putting your Letter in the Journal des Savans, where you know that various Pieces which are not in the Paris Edition are inserted.[216]

Use of the article was clearly a service granted by the journalist or *libraire*, either to the agent or the author himself.

Significantly, the previous politeness Jean de Beyer had done to Simon Pelloutier was not to print one of his articles, but to give him a good review. In 1742 Beyer wrote a favorable *extrait* of Pelloutier's *Histoire des Celtes*; Pelloutier commented to Marchand that "I have reason to be very content with the Extrait of my Book in the *Bibliotheque françoise*. The Author of this Extrait, has certainly done me much more honor than I merit." And, he went on, "Since you know him Monsieur do me the grace of assuring him of all my gratitude."[217] A favorable *extrait* was no different from any other service in the Republic of Letters: it was a kindness, the proper response to which was gratitude or return. When Jean Le Clerc spoke well in the *Bibliothèque choisie* of one of Jean Barbeyrac's works, Barbeyrac thanked him, remarking on the "obligation I had to demonstrate myself my gratitude over it."[218] Scholars often wrote to journalists to show, as Ezechiel Spanheim put it, "a just and extreme gratitude for the equally savant, exact, and obliging manner, with which it has pleased you to describe [my last work] to the public."[219] A good *extrait* might even be cause for a return favor. Gally de Gaujac, a scholar in London, thanked Le Clerc for the kind review of his son's book, adding, "if we can do any service for you in this city . . . you have only to let us know it."[220]

This view of journals worked both ways. If a good review was a favor, a sign of goodwill, a bad *extrait* was on the contrary not an impersonal judgment, but a sign of malice.[221] Authors damned on the pages of literary periodicals sought personal motives for their damnation. When Basnage de Beauval, Le Clerc, and Bernard all attacked Maturin Veyssière La Croze in their journals, Leibniz wrote sympathetically, "I do not understand through what motive he [Beauval] is mistreating you and that he and M. le Clerc and M. Bernard, although otherwise scarcely friends, conspire against you? Is it that they are afraid, that in bringing you forward in the literary world, you could sometime *officere ipsorum luminibus*?"[222] Bad reviews appearing unprovoked baffled their recipients. Jacques Bernard, in a typical response, wrote to the *Journal littéraire*,

There appeared in the Journal of *Leipsich* [the *Acta Eruditorum*] an Extrait of my *Traité de la Repentance tardive*; this Extrait is completely unfaithful; it seems that the attempt was made to portray me as an Author who does not know how to reason, who says things for & against on the same subject, who contradicts himself grossly, & who, although very prolix, nevertheless omits the most important things. . . .

As I have never spoken of these Savant Journalists, neither in my Extraits, nor in my conversations, with anything but eulogy & with the marks of a perfect esteem, I cannot understand what caused them to treat me in a manner so unworthy & at the same time so unjust.[223]

Members of the Republic of Letters thus appeared to agree that journals did not operate independently of personal considerations. Authors sent their books to journalists with pleas to give them "a word of recommendation";[224] and if the author was a friend of the journalist, so much the better for him. Pelloutier counted on a good review in the *Bibliothèque germanique* because of his relationship with Mauclerc: "Since he is one of my Friends, it appears that he will have treated me with indulgence."[225] Such assumptions were well-founded. When Jean Des Champs found his work ridiculed by, among others, Voltaire, his friend Pérard asked his fellow-journalist Formey "is there not a means to pull poor Deschamps a little from the too great oppression where he is by giving a short and reserved article on his book."[226] This was, moreover, not simply an attitude for behind the scenes. After insulting one Haas in their "Reflexions sur la Poesie Hollandoise," the authors of the *Journal littéraire* frankly avowed in print that "if we had had the honor of knowing him, we would have spoken of his style with more consideration."[227]

Journalists even worried that the authors they reviewed would not be happy with the *extraits* of their books. Pérard was pleased to report to Formey in 1742 that "Prof. Kahle from whom we very recently received a letter . . . seemed to me content with the extrait which you gave of his work; he ardently wishes that the second part will appear soon, thus you could put it in T. III 1 ptie."[228] As this incident indicates, this was a matter of discussion between author and journalist; Mauclerc concernedly wrote to Jean-Pierre de Crousaz of two *extraits* of his *Examen du Pyrrhonisme*, "I hope, Monsieur, that both of them are honored with your approbation."[229] Indeed, it was a matter of conventional scholarly politeness, so that Jean de Beyer could write of an *extrait* of Formey in the *Bibliothèque françoise*, "Since the author of *la Belle Wolfienne* seems to be content with my reflections, I have good reason to congratulate myself for having made them. I thank him very much for his courtesy [*politesse*]."[230]

Such an *extrait* might be regarded, not as a professional judgment, but as a sign of friendship. Jean Bouhier, thanking Le Clerc for "the obliging manner, with which you had the goodness to speak of my Dissertation on the ancient Greek & Latin Letters in your Bibliothéque Choisie of last year," spoke of his desire to "try to merit a little a place in the friendship of a person, whose merit I have honored for so long." Bouhier expressed surprise and pleasure that he had received such treatment, "not having the honor of being known to you."[231]

Scholars thus acknowledged both in print and in private that journals were not in reality objective institutions of the whole community. They showed signs, however, of recognizing the conflict this represented between personal and professional values. This is apparent from the raised eyebrows prompted by examples of blatant favoritism, such as allowing authors to write *extraits* of their own books. This practice was in theory innocuous, for if journals always gave details of books without the customary remarks on quality, then it would not matter who wrote the *extrait*. Both Pérard and Mauclerc, for example, saw nothing odd in asking their colleague Formey if he wanted to write reviews of his own works.[232] The *Mémoires de Trévoux* actually invited authors to submit *extraits* of their works, remarking that "no one, ordinarily speaking, is more capable of doing the extrait of a book than the one who composed it."[233] But this was not usual, and indeed by 1712 the *Mémoires* had changed its policy.[234] Since every journal from the *Journal des Sçavans* on made comments on books, *extraits* written by authors could not fail to be suspect. Camusat, who often received such contributions unsolicited when he was writing the *Bibliothèque françoise*, was far from sympathetic to them.

> Another sort of people who flatter themselves without modesty, are those who construct an advantageous extrait of their works, & who send it completely finished to Journalists, or to the Libraire of a Journal. . . . I was subjected to plenty of abuse for having the impoliteness to refuse them. Here is a part of the roundabout means taken to acquire some trivial reputation by those whose lack of merit would, without this shameful trick, keep them eternally in obscurity. These acts at the same time show the small amount of confidence one should have in the praises living Authors distribute to each other. Often the Panegyrist & the Hero are one & the same person.[235]

Accusations of journalists praising their own works under cover of anonymity figured, among other places, in Beaumarchais' attacks on the *Bibliothèque raisonnée* and André Dacier's literary war with Jean Masson.[236] And Jacques Bernard was amused that, although Jacques Basnage was apparently the author of an *extrait* of his own anonymous book in his brother's journal, he cited another of his own books as "a *Learned Work*."[237]

This attitude made journalists and authors circumspect. Le Courayer, planning an *extrait* of his own book for the *Bibliothèque raisonnée*, told the corrector De la Motte that "although it is fashioned in a favorable way I have

pretended not to eulogize it, and I even inserted a few reflections in it, which
will make people think that it comes from another hand."[238] When Pérard
asked Marchand, who was in The Hague, to do the *extrait* of Marchand's
own *Histoire de l'imprimerie* for the *Bibliothèque germanique*, he was even more
careful. Pérard told Marchand to write the *extrait* as a letter dated from a
town in Germany, addressed to the authors of the journal. The journalists
would then copy it over so that the *libraire* Humbert would not recognize the
handwriting; thus no one could suspect that Marchand himself was responsible for it.[239] Clearly writing one's own *extrait* was not a matter of universal
approval.

The mixed opinions on this practice demonstrate in miniature the conflicts
in attitudes toward literary journals. In different circumstances—and sometimes circumstances which were the same—scholars acted as if friends or
close colleagues both should, and should not, receive preferential treatment in
journalistic matters. It was at once perfectly natural for the person best
informed about a book—its author—to give an account of it, and dubious
scholarly practice to allow authors to sing their own praises. The heart of the
difficulty lay in the view of the journal as ideal scholar. Such a journal was
expected to be two things: *honnête* and *utile*. But were these two virtues
necessarily compatible? Could a journal be both?

This confusing issue called into question the whole purpose of a journal.
As we have seen, one perceived aim of journals was to serve the community
as any *honnête* scholar was obliged to do. Yet we have also seen that, often
enough, authors viewed praise as a gift or favor, available particularly to those
with connections to journalists. All this of course fits in with the ideals about
the workings of the learned community we examined in the previous
chapter. But these ideals presented a problem. If one facet of *honnêteté* was
providing services for colleagues, the journal became a favor-granting institution. The question then arose of whether an institution devoted to civility
to others could serve the needs of the entire community. Those needs
demanded the impartial reporting of literary news, including reports on the
latest products of publishing-houses. If such reports were affected by personal
considerations, were they truly reliable?

The *Histoire critique de la République des Lettres* acknowledged this problem
in its *extrait* of a book by Barbeyrac, assuring the public that "My praises
cannot be suspect, because I do not have the honor of knowing him, as I am
also entirely unknown to him."[240] When, on the contrary, Formey introduced just this conflict into the *Bibliothèque impartiale*, he was chastised by Elie
Luzac, his *libraire*.

You praised Mr. Heerkens because Mr. Racine praised him & because his
poetry was presented & recommended to you by Mr. de Lohman. But are

these reasons for an Author of a Bibl. Imp[artiale]. Admit, Monsieur, that such determinants must do harm to a Journal. I hope that in the future, you will speak for yourself, & according to your own lights.[241]

A really *impartial* journal, a journal that is *utile* to all, would not speak well of a book simply because of favors. Yet a journal that is *poli* or *honnête* might well do so. This conflict lay behind much of the uneasiness about the role of journals in the community.

The view that a periodical must behave like a person in the community led to another, related problem. If the journal was just a person, or just a product of a person, it was not necessarily to be trusted. Indeed, its exalted position in the community could be a matter of outrage, given that its election was purely the result of self-choice and some negotiations with a *libraire*. Before Jean Le Clerc began his own journal, he expressed annoyance at Bayle, "the illustrious Author of the Repub. des Lettres who has set himself up as Universal judge of all the Books which will appear from now on."[242] Mathieu Marais wrote vividly in the same vein of Le Clerc himself. The *Bibliothèque choisie*, he said, was "filled with a presumptuousness so proud that I Believe Scaliger, the prince of letters, humble in comparison to this man, he imagines himself having been sent from on high to distribute the favors of Apollo to whomever he pleases. . . . I imagine Seeing him on his Fantastic Throne judging the Living & the Dead, and placing himself above all those he has judged."[243] By pronouncing himself a competent spokesman for the community, a journalist acquired power over his peers which was at times difficult to accept, since, as Camusat pointed out, one of the great rewards of being a journalist was "the pleasure of seeing oneself in some fashion the Arbiter of the reputation of Savants."[244]

That the journalist was a person, and his journal viewed as one, thus worked against him as well as for him. He and his journal might have been perceived as representatives of all that was good in the community, of enforcers of scholarly morality; but he was also an individual whose judgment, like everyone's, was fallible. This meant that the *utilité* of the journal—its provision of news and particularly of recommendations of books for purchase—was also called into question. And since the opinions of journals carried great weight, some scholars feared that vesting so much power in one person was risky for the Republic of Letters. Camusat pointed out that even journalists who did not ordinarily inspire confidence could have deleterious effects on the community when their judgments were picked up by other authors: "that is how errors multiply themselves."[245] Journalists themselves had doubts about their own powers—Bernard wrote to Des Maizeaux that "I am beginning to emancipate myself a bit in giving my opinion of books; but to tell you the truth I distrust my talents & my taste terribly"[246]—and they usually made motions toward agreement with readers who complained of partiality on these grounds. The *Journal des Sçavans* said that to judge books would be "to exercise a sort of tyranny in the empire of Letters"; Bayle wrote that to "claim an authority so sublime" would require "a ridiculous vanity"; and Jean Cornand de la Crose said that pointing out faults in books "is thought too great a Province for any one man to be trusted with."[247] Here again the personal side of journals went sour. People were not perfect; a journal was proportionally less *utile*.

Yet if the journal *did* represent the ideal scholar, and was not so *malhonnête* to suggest that a book was bad, scholars still found it lacking. For if the goal of periodicals was indeed *utilité* as well as *politesse*, what was the use of one which made no judgments? Camusat complained of the Abbé Gallois, the second author of the *Journal des Sçavans*, that he placed politeness over utility, rendering his journal pointless.

> [H]e pushes this politeness, or if you like this obligingness, so far, he sometimes praises authors so unpraiseworthy, that one can scarcely prevent oneself from wishing him a bit of harm. When for example, he says in speaking of the History of the Indies written in Latin by the P. Maffée Jesuit "that such a beautiful History would certainly merit being translated into French & that it could not be done by a person more capable than M. l'Abbé de Pure, well known by his other Works." Where is the reader, mediocrely informed, who is not revolted by such Eulogies? who does not know that this Abbé miserably maimed this beautiful Work, and that all his versions were generally scorned, despite the purity of language which Sorel praised in them. But must one take the word of a man so prodigal in pleasantries that he throws them in handfuls on all authors indifferently & who even applauds the versions of the Abbé de Marolles.[248]

Despite the desire for *honnêteté*, then, readers who looked for assistance in their choices of books were not necessarily satisfied with the kindness of universal praise. Even though the prefaces of journals reflected an outcry in favor of impartiality, scholars generally preferred "reflections" in their *extraits* for the sake of *utilité*. Indeed, journalists found it virtually impossible to avoid making judgments, and some of the periodicals, such as the *Bibliothèque angloise*, which were loudest in their protestations of impartiality, were the most inclined to give their opinions. When readers were looking for information, this was in general not a matter for complaint.

Journals which commented on quality were not only more useful, but also more interesting. The *Bibliothèque raisonnée*, arguing at its inception in 1728 for the right to make judgments, said that a journal without judgments would be "of all printed things, the most insipid & the hardest to sell. No one would want it." Generosity, *honnêteté*, were for the *Bibliothèque raisonnée* both impossible and out of place in a journalist.

> But, people might say, . . . is it absolutely necessary for a Journalist to decide on the value of Works? . . . Let him limit himself to giving faithful Extraits; let him tell us how many pages, Books, & Chapters are in the Volume; let him tell us generally the Plan, & the Goal of it. No one asks more from him & when he charges himself with the office of biasing the public, either for good or for bad, he leaves his Sphere, and arrogates to himself, in the Republic of Letters, a Despotism, which is insufferable. . . . Messieurs, when we dig up a Journalist of the sort you require, who can go through a boring Work without showing disgust, who never sees anything but good in Books, who pardons a thousand false reasonings in favor of one good thought, who reads the Writings of others with the eyes of the Author, who absolutely never gives in to his Preju- dices, & who can never fall into error, when, we say, we dig up such a Journalist, we promise to give him to you, however much he costs. In the meantime, content yourselves with those that we are giving you, in the persuasion that if we had been able to choose better we would not have failed to do so.[249]

Camusat suggested that, as time went on, the debate over impartiality subsided. As journals became well ensconced on the literary scene, he wrote, "people of Letters complained more rarely, although the Public knew well enough that they were given just & frequent occasions."[250] This may have been true; but Camusat's very statement suggests that the value of impartiality remained, and certainly the *Bibliothèque raisonnée*, and other journals like it, still felt at the time Camusat was writing that they had to defend their course of action. The problem was in part one of degree, for one could try to judge without unpleasantness. Jacques Lenfant pointed this out in 1687, when he wrote from Heidelberg to give Jean Le Clerc some journalistic advice. "I will only tell you in general that people find the extraits of your bibliotheque too dry, and that there is a middle ground between judging as M. Bayle does, and not judging as you do. It seems to me too that one can judge without taking sides. And people even believe that it will be impossible for you to keep this promise of not judging. . . . page 172 is full of a satiric tone which is more disobliging than a decisive judgment would be."[251] Yet, as Vigneul-Marville's criticisms of Denis de Sallo confirm, this balance was not easy to achieve. "As for method," he wrote in his *Mélanges*, "which one will you choose, Mon- sieur? Will you take that of the Critics who put everything on trial; or that of the Historians who only recount things, without getting involved either by reproving or by criticizing? This latter is assuredly the most natural and the most proper to your subject: but take care that it is not cold & dull. The former has more spice, it piques the Reader, & revives his attention; but perhaps it will wound the Authors, & excite murmurs & quarrels."[252]

The problem was encapsulated here: how not to offend, how to be *honnête*, without being dry, boring, and useless. It was a conflict that would continue to plague the Republic of Letters. The move toward a greater liberty of judgment, chronicled by Jacques Bernard in his own editing of the *Nouvelles*, represents at least in part an attempt to make journals into institutions useful for the whole Republic of Letters. But the operation of journals, their reading, and the interaction of their audience and their authors, suggest a tangled web of ideas about how such an institution ought to behave. Individual goals conflicted with group aspirations, and both clashed internally with themselves. At the most basic level, the difficulty lay in separating the professional from the personal, for the journal could not at the same time fulfill the demands of each. The growth of the journal, coinciding with other types of institutionalization in the Republic of Letters, met a reluctance to adapt to those changes on the part of everyone involved. Even its institutionalization was accomplished in terms of the individual, as the journal became supreme arbiter in the community on the basis of its "personal" attributes. Among such attributes was—as Camusat pointed out—a multitude of "indispensable obligations" to the Republic of Letters.[253] But it was difficult, in the intellectual climate of the early eighteenth century, to sort out those different obligations. And even to phrase the problem in those terms—the terms of obligation—was to bring home the confusion surrounding the journal's essential role.

3

HOW TO BECOME AN *HOMME ILLUSTRE*

THE FORMATION OF HIERARCHIES IN THE REPUBLIC OF LETTERS

In the early 1740s a lively correspondence passed between Voltaire and César de Missy, a whimsical Huguenot minister in London. Or perhaps lively is not the word; for it was lively only on one side. Although Voltaire was only nine years older than his correspondent, and not notably dignified, in this exchange of letters his manner differed markedly from Missy's. His letters, although polite, were usually terse and devoted mainly to business; but Missy wrote in his beautiful hand page on page of strained wit and eager verse. It was evidently not just the paucity of literary news in Brussels that made Voltaire remark, "if you really want to have a correspondence with me you will give more than you receive."[1] Voltaire was happy enough to deal with Missy while the minister was arranging for the publication in London of the *philosophe*'s play *Mahomet*, banned in Paris; but after the beginning of 1743 he maintained a silence which left Missy anxious and "grieved . . . to have served you ill."[2] The correspondence has the air of a charming but slightly annoying puppy frolicking hopefully around the feet of its distracted master.

Voltaire called his relation with Missy *amitié*.[3] Every aspect of it, however, suggests his implication of an equality between them was only *politesse*. Missy himself declared that his own place was in the Third Estate of the Republic of Letters, a mere *roturier*, and that it was only his correspondence with Voltaire which provided his *lettres de noblesse*.[4] Of course, this remark, no less than Voltaire's, was a matter of *politesse*. But it was also true.

Certainly this asymmetric exchange seems to belie the pronouncements sometimes made by scholars in the eighteenth century characterizing the Republic of Letters as a community of equals. Adrien Baillet wrote in his *Jugemens des savans* that "if the commerce of Letters is a true Republic, as its name says, it seems that its true character must be liberty. '*Populo libero sunto*

suffragia.' That is why Monsieur de Balzac was right to say that the field is
open to whoever wants to enter it, & that it is exposed to the pillage of the
first comer."[5] "Parnassus," according to Boileau, "is always a free country,"
and both he and others asserted that this freedom specifically allowed all
citizens of the Republic to judge the works of their fellows.[6] Whether this
right in fact encouraged an atmosphere of camaraderie is another matter.
Johann Burchard Mencke, ever cynical about his colleagues in scholarship,
thought not. "Here, Messieurs, is what they call the Liberty of the Republic
of Letters," he wrote: "complete Liberty, Liberty without limits, Liberty to
attack with impunity, & to insult whomever one likes, on the slightest
pretext."[7]

Significantly, the same Baillet who was so quick to mention the rights of
all to judge works was criticized for his audacity in doing so himself. Like
journalists who, unappointed, took it upon themselves to tell the rest of the
community what to read, Baillet appeared to some to be enjoying liberties no
one had granted him. Pierre-Daniel Huet disapprovingly called him "a young
man who has set himself up as a censor of all books/He has ripped up right
and left everything he has encountered/And he has attacked the ill-humored
people, who have judged him in his turn[.]" Everyone in Paris was talking
about it in 1686.[8]

No matter what scholars chose to believe about the "liberty" and "equality" of the Republic of Letters, their behavior in practice shows a clear
awareness of status differences in the community. The Republic was not a
monarchy, but it was not a democracy either. Certain people were acknowledged as "savants of the first order," while others were, as Missy said,
relegated to the *tiers état*; some had "Authority in the literary world," as
Malcolm Flemyng flattered Thomas Birch, while others had none.[9] As we
noted in Chapter 1, however, outside of some of the scholarly families,
whose very names helped to classify their members, the hierarchy of the
Republic of Letters was refashioned from generation to generation. Unlike
the nonacademic community, in other words, birth or family were usually
not features which marked a particular scholar for distinction. Mathieu Marais
wrote that it was pointless to think about a great scholar's background: "the
Heroes of Letters hold nobility by Their Knowledge," their scholarly names
sufficing to ennoble their own ancestors.[10] The makeup of the community
was thus unstable and theoretically anyone could rise to the top. And for this
reason the community had to have other standards by which to measure the
merit of its members.

In this chapter we will examine the nature of these standards and their role
in the ideology and practice of the Republic of Letters. To do so, we will
look in some depth at the dynamics of two interactions between scholars
clearly on vastly different levels of the hierarchy. The behavior of those on
the lower echelon toward their betters, alive or dead, and the communal

reaction to that behavior, point the way to eighteenth-century scholarly power.

Coste and Locke

Pierre Coste, born the son of a prominent merchant of woolen cloth in Uzès, was by 1690 a 22-year-old *bon esprit* enjoying life and trying to make a living in Amsterdam. Having finished school in Anduze and then studied theology at Geneva, he had visited the academies at Lausanne, Zurich, and Leiden before being received by the Walloon Synod in August 1690 as a *proposant*, or apprentice minister, in Amsterdam's Eglise française. Although he was still called "a young theologian, proposant, refugee" in a letter of 1695,[11] he appears to have been losing interest in an ecclesiastical career, apparently turning instead to literature and correction of the press.[12]

He seems to have inspired affection in many of his comrades. "That loveable Monsieur Coste," as Dr. Pieter Guenellon called him, was in Jean Le Clerc's words "a young man with a very sweet nature," "not only with very good sense, but with a sweet and compliant humor, besides having all the talents necessary for what he is undertaking [i.e. translation] and which he is in the position of acquiring all the time."[13] In Amsterdam Coste moved in the social circle of Charles de la Motte, who either shared lodgings with him at the home of Mlle. Prades "op de Lawrier gracht in de Goude Appel," or who moved in after Coste went to England.[14] Decades later De la Motte was still writing of him as his "best friend."[15]

Coste's charming correspondence with his friends in Amsterdam testifies to his youthful playfulness and involvement in an enjoyable community in the Netherlands.[16] The company may have been all a young man could hope for; he wrote to one of his friends that "coming to consider that I have good friends in this world, I say to myself, it is worth the pain of living in order to enjoy a pleasure so sweet."[17] But Coste must have found life difficult on the wages of a corrector, a profession in which, as he wryly said in 1699, "one can hardly get rich."[18] He began to look around for a new establishment, perhaps as a tutor in some noble household.

Coste had already published a *Discours sur la philosophie* in the Huguetans' edition of the philosophy of Pierre Sylvain Régis in 1691 and a *Histoire de Louis de Bourbon* in 1693 (with another edition in 1694). But his main literary work was as a translator, putting volume I of Gregorio Leti's Italian history of Cromwell into French, and Redi's observations and the fourth century of Ellie du Pin's *Bibliothèque des Auteurs Ecclésiastiques* into Latin. In the mid-1690s he was asked by the *libraire* Henri Schelte to translate John Locke's *Some Thoughts concerning Education* into French, a task Coste took on in part to improve his English.[19] This was the first translation of any of Locke's works into French, and on its appearance in 1695 it was very well received. Le Clerc reported to Locke in July of 1695 that "it is selling extremely well," and Coste said in his first letter to Locke that "the true mark that a Work is excellent, is that it pleases generally all those who can hear it; and that is just what has happened concerning your Treatise. It pleased in English, it also pleases in French."[20]

As this account will have suggested, the translation was made without Locke's knowledge or permission; indeed, Le Clerc told Locke that "I would not have failed to write you that it had been translated into French, and by whom, if I had thought that you would wish to know it."[21] Given the nature of the book trade, there was little thought on the part of a *libraire*, or even friends of the author, that Locke might want a say in the translation of his book. But although Coste was too shy to send a copy of his translation to Locke, saying that "nothing is more disagreeable for an author than to see his Work completely disfigured by a bad translation," once Locke received it from Guenellon the young translator asked for comments. He had already "consulted, or, to put it better, pestered Monsieur Le Clerc about the least difficulties which presented themselves to my mind."[22]

Locke was well pleased with the translation and kept up a correspondence with Coste, sending him a copy of the new English edition of the *Education* in the summer of 1695 which Coste could use for the next French edition. Coste was interested especially "whether by chance you had satisfied several small Objections that people had proposed to me concerning certain places in the first Edition. You have done it effectively in certain occasions, such as the place where you prove by examples, that there is no danger in bathing the feet of Children in cold water." He had been defending in conversation Locke's viewpoint on this subject, which "many people had found . . . a bit strange, without being able to say why."[23] Coste himself had a small objection to one passage, in which Locke said that a mother could teach Latin to her child without knowing it herself; but he posed the problem deferentially and even suggested that Locke knew a proper method for this: "I pray you to tell me what this is." Throughout Coste was eager and earnest, saying that Locke's approval would only make him more anxious to become worthy of it.[24]

Just as no one consulted Locke about this translation, however, no one asked him about who might translate his *Essay concerning Human Understanding*. Before Coste even received a copy of the *Essay* Locke sent him in the spring of 1696, he could report that "I have already contracted to translate this Work. It is with the same Libraire who printed your Treatise of Education in French." However, although Locke was left out of the decision-making process (and presumably the profits), Coste continued to show deference to Locke's opinion: "I will neglect nothing to bring me through this enterprise with honor. I greatly fear that it is above my abilities; but in the end I hope that this fear will make me more exact and more circumspect. In an extreme necessity I will profit from the liberty which you have so kindly [*honnêtement*] given me, to consult you; but this will only be after I have consulted Mr. le Clerc, which will spare you much bother."[25]

Yet the tone is double-edged. Along with Coste's deference, his fear of disturbing the great man, is the suggestion, perhaps unintended, that this work—the translation—was *Coste's* book. Thus it was truly a bother for Locke to help him, and truly a favor to Coste to be helped; the assumption is that Locke would not naturally take an interest in the edition because it was not his. This only had the effect of increasing Coste's veneration and respect; and in gratitude for Locke's attentions and the gift of the *Essay* he sent a copy of a "little English Book" he was translating called *The Reasonableness of Christianity*. Coste was unaware that Locke was also the author of that book;[26] perhaps for that reason he was frank in recounting criticisms of it. Even among those who agreed with the author, he said, were some who were amazed that he could not explain what is meant by the Messiah; and others were surprised not to see anything on the death of Jesus Christ and its role in remission of sin.[27] Although Coste was unsure of his views about *The Reasonableness of Christianity*, both the irony of his unwittingly expounding on the book to its own author and his assumptions about his proprietary role in the *Essai concernant l'entendement* point to his future behavior and attitude toward his editions of Locke.

The circumstances which brought Coste and Locke together on the translation of the *Essay* were not as planned as they have sometimes been portrayed.[28] Coste was looking for a tutorship in a gentleman's household, but not necessarily near Locke. Le Clerc asked Locke's help on his behalf in finding "an establishment in England," but this was simply a manifestation of the tradition of figures higher in the hierarchy helping those lower down to locate work.[29] At the same time he was negotiating with a friend in Wesel who proposed that Coste should "enter the household of a French Colonel, to raise two children there of 12 to 13 years on condition that I am given beyond Food and Lodging, one hundred écus per year."[30] And among the houses Locke was considering for Coste were ones no more convenient to him than Amsterdam, such as William Molyneux's home in Dublin.[31] Similarly, in the search for a tutor in the house where Locke lived, for Francis Masham, son of his friend Damaris Cudworth, Coste was not the first candidate to come to mind. In July of 1697 Locke was still negotiating with a tutor named De la Treille, who ultimately backed out of the arrangement.[32] It was only after this that Coste became the candidate for the Mashams, and he did not arrive at Oates until September of that year.[33] Thus, although Locke was willing to grant that "he is an ingenious man, and we like him very well for our purpose," it was not the philosopher's desire to have a say in the translation of his *magnum opus* which brought Coste to England.[34]

Coste lived with the Mashams and with Locke for the rest of Locke's life—a further seven years. Since he and Locke were now in the same place, little evidence remains of the dynamics of their relationship. Besides tutoring Francis Masham, Coste seems to have acted as an extra connection between Locke and the publishing world in Amsterdam; although Locke himself was a friend of Le Clerc's,[35] Coste also passed on valuable news about what was in press (including Locke's own works) which he had heard from him or from De la Motte.[36] It is usually said that Coste acted as Locke's secretary; certainly Coste did errands for Locke when he was in London, although in one of very few references to such errands Locke asked a friend to have Coste send a copy of a pamphlet which "I would be glad to have . . . by him or Sir Francis or any body."[37] In some letters, such as the letters to Limborch after October 1697, Coste translated passages into French and wrote these passages in his own hand.[38]

Most important, of course, Coste worked with Locke on the translation of the *Essay*. One of the few letters extant from Coste to Locke after his arrival in England contains detailed information about "the citations or references which I have added in several places in your Book."[39] These details suggest that Coste felt it necessary to consult Locke on the specifics of the translation; he called the subject the one "which concerns you the most closely," and said that "if I make other references, I will alert you to them immediately."[40] In the translation's first edition, Coste reported that Locke had "had the goodness to review my Translation," and that in the many places in which Coste had "tormented" himself over the meaning of a passage, Locke had quickly cleared things up.[41] Locke and Coste both mentioned that the whole edition had been read aloud to the philosopher and subject to his comments; Locke was full of praise.

The clarity of Mind & the knowledge of the French Language, of which Mr. *Coste* has already given such visible proofs to the Public, could be a good enough guarantee of the excellence of his work on my *Essay*, without it being necessary that you ask me my opinion of it. If I was capable of judging what was written properly & elegantly in French, I would feel myself obliged to send you a great eulogy of this Translation, which I have heard that several persons, more talented than I in the French Language, have assured could pass for an Original. But what I can say concerning the point on which you wished to know my opinion, is that Mr. Coste read me this Version from one end to the other before having sent it to you, & that all the places which I found to differ from my thoughts, have been brought back to the meaning of the Original, which was not easy in Notions as abstract as are some of those in my Essay, the two Languages not always having words & expressions which correspond so well one to the other that they completely fulfill Philosophic exactitude; but that Mr. Coste's justice of spirit & the suppleness of his Pen have allowed him to find the means to correct all these errors which I found as he was reading me what he had translated. So that I can say to the Reader that I presume he will find in this Work all the qualities that one could desire in a good Translation.[42]

Locke was thus consulted, and even the *libraire* now wanted his opinion; he had the "goodness" to help; and Coste's translation was so excellent that "it could pass for an Original." Coste was modest about his accomplishment, attributing errors in part to "the smallness of my genius," although he also suggested that both the subject of the work and the way it was written were very complex.[43] But the tone, again, shows hints of the future, when Coste perhaps felt his *génie* was not so *petit* after all.

So little is known of Coste's life at Oates that it is difficult to assess accurately his relationship with Locke at the time of the philosopher's death in 1704. But there seems to have been a problem. De la Motte, who as Coste's close friend was in a position to know, wrote much later that Coste had "been mistreated publicly in a Country where he is unknown . . . where this could have done him wrong & truly did so in the mind of many people." Two days before his death Locke had apparently even written Coste a letter—perhaps merely unpleasant, perhaps accusatory—which was to be given to Coste after he had died. "[Coste] only had to publish this Letter, & even the people who are the least friends to virtue, would agree that it is the act of a . . ." De la Motte would not finish the sentence.[44]

It is impossible to judge the nature of this mistreatment, as neither details of it nor the letter De la Motte mentioned seem to have survived. But one mark of strain between the two was taken to be Locke's failure to compensate Coste in his will. In 1705 Des Maizeaux was amazed by this, as was De la Motte, who wrote:

You are right to find it strange that Mr. Locke left nothing in his Will to M. Coste. There are few people who have as much esteem for this Great man as I. But I could not prevent myself from regarding his conduct in this matter as a stain on his Memory. There are in this city many *honnêtes gens* who knew & greatly esteemed Mr. Locke, but all were scandalized by his ingratitude. I am almost assured that if he could hear everything that people are saying about it, he would certainly repent having neglected Mr. Coste.[45]

It was primarily Coste's translation that deserved reward. In 1728, wearied with correcting feeble translations, De la Motte again grumbled that

> perhaps these mediocre works make me see the Translation by Mr. Coste, which is being printed at the same time[,] as a masterpiece, & I scarcely correct a sheet that I do not say that M. Locke was a *malhonnête* man for not having rewarded it as he could & had promised such a good Translation. He would have deserved as bad a Translator as the one who translated his Book into Latin, or the good M. Mazel, who translated the Gouvernement civil, which never sold even though the Subject was quite in fashion.[46]

Services by a subordinate to a superior, particularly literary services such as translation, apparently deserved monetary recompense after death. This was no doubt even more true because of the public nature of a legacy. Friends had the same reaction when, after Des Maizeaux had caused Anthony Collins' works to be translated and publicized, Collins failed to reward him adequately in his will. Jean Barbeyrac said that "M[r]. *Collins*, who was so rich, & who, I believe, leaves no children, could well have made a larger legacy to M[r]. des Maizeaux"; as for De la Motte, "I learned with pleasure that M. Collins left you 100 pieces, one more Zero & his Library instead of his Mss which he could leave to the Butter-makers, would have given me more pleasure."[47]

However Coste felt about Locke's treatment of him, his public reaction to the philosopher's death was one of admiration and grief. He wrote a lengthy "Character of Mr. Locke" which he sent to the *Nouvelles de la République des Lettres*, where it was published in February of 1705.[48] Locke, Coste said, "was born for the good of mankind," and his death was "a general loss" which "is lamented by all good men, and all sincere lovers of Truth, who were acquainted with his Character." Indeed, he said that "since Mr. LOCKE departed this life, I have hardly been able to think of any thing, but the loss of that great Man, whose Memory will always be dear to me."[49]

As the title of his *éloge* suggests, Coste did not concentrate on Locke's works. Their best "Elogium" is "the general esteem they have attained" and "the service they have been to England in particular, and universally to all that set themselves seriously to the search for Truth, and the study of Christianity." Instead, "without dwelling any longer upon considering Mr. LOCKE in the quality of an Author, which often serves only to disguise the real character of the Man, I haste to shew him to you in particulars much more amiable, and which will give you a higher notion of his Merit."[50] Coste then proceeded to discuss the particulars of Locke's manner and character, painting him as a wise and prudent man whose first thought was always for others. People at all levels of society were charmed with "his gentle and obliging Manners"; "they were charmed with this condescension, not very common among men of Letters; and which they so little expected from a person, whose great qualities raised him so very much above all other men." People who knew him only by his writings "were perfectly amazed to find him nothing but Affability, Good-humour, Humanity, Pleasantness, always ready to hear them, to talk with them of things which they best understood better than himself, than to make a show of his own Science." His whole conduct was informed by "the sincere desire he had of being serviceable to all mankind," and in this, as in all of his actions, "he instructed others by his own Conduct." Indeed, Coste said Locke was his own model of behavior: "happy, if, as I admired him for many years, that I was near him; I cou'd but imitate him in any one respect!"[51]

Locke "aspers'd and blacken'd"

When this "Character" was reprinted in 1720 in a volume of Locke's incidental writings,[52] however, it was preceded by an accusatory letter from "some of his [i.e. Locke's] friends" which intended to cast doubt on Coste's integrity.

> Mr. COSTE liv'd in the same Family with Mr. LOCKE, during the seven last years of that great Man's life; whereby he had all possible opportunity to know him.
>
> The *Letter* was written some time after Mr. LOCKE's Death; and appears to be the production of a man in raptures, and struck with the highest admiration of Mr. LOCKE's Virtue, Capacity, and of the excellency of his Writings; and under the deepest affliction for the loss of a per-son, to whom in his life-time he had paid the most profound respect, and for whom he had constantly express'd the greatest esteem and that even in writings, whereof Mr. LOCKE did not know him to be the Author.
>
> And therefore, Mr. LOCKE's Friends judge its publication necessary, not only, as they think it contains a just Character of Mr. LOCKE, as far as it goes; but, as it is a proper Vindication of him against the said Mr. COSTE, who in several Writings, and in his common Conversation throughout France, Holland, and England has aspers'd and blacken'd the Memory of Mr. LOCKE; in those very respects, wherein he was his Panegyrist before.
>
> For, they conceive, the Elogium contain'd in the following Letter, must stand good, till Mr. COSTE thinks fit, either to deny his own Experience; or to confess, that the same things, which he then thought praise-worthy, have since changed their Nature.[53]

This letter is mysterious, as Coste was issuing new and presumably improved editions of Locke's works, an activity which he continued until his death in 1747. Although we have seen that Coste might have had cause to complain of Locke, it is impossible to re-create his conversation and has appeared equally impossible to locate written attacks on the philosopher. The *DNB*, in considering this problem, merely states that "no public 'aspersion' is traceable."[54] However, manuscript sources indicate that it was at least in part these very "improved editions" of Locke's works that bothered the anonymous "friends of Mr. Locke."

Although Pierre Des Maizeaux was in part responsible for the collection in which this letter appeared—he signed the book's dedication—Anthony Collins also had a hand in the shaping of the edition.[55] It was Collins' idea to chastise Coste in the book. "[T]his much I owe to the memory of M[r]. Locke," he wrote in 1716, "as to think of some plan of vindication of him from the treatment of M[r]. Le Clerc & M[r]. Coste."[56] It is unclear who was ultimately responsible for the piece; an extant draft is in Collins' handwriting,[57] and Des Maizeaux, disclaiming responsibility, hinted that Collins was the author.[58] No matter who wrote it, however, the situation was the same: formerly good friends were squabbling about the reputation of a famous scholar. And Collins objected to Coste and Le Clerc because, as he said to Des Maizeaux, they

> both servily flatterd him during his life and made panegyricks upon him immediately after his death. M[r] Coste not only in his Travels thro France & Holland, but in republishing works, which he thought it a glory to translate, has acted the part of a calumniator both in the manner of attacking him, and in the attacks themselves which are the efforts of a man who has Persons & not things in view. I think that deserves to be calld senile flattery, which is said to a man in his life time, & contradicted afterwards.[59]

What was it in these works which so incensed Collins and Des Maizeaux? Since Locke's death, Coste had issued new editions of the *Education* (1708), the *Essai concernant l'entendement* (1714), and the *Christianisme raisonnable* (1715). The *Essai* differs little from the edition which Coste produced under Locke's aegis in 1700. But the translations of the other works provided evidence of a tendency which was to continue for the rest of Coste's life: an assertion of his intellectual independence.

The *Education* is the milder of the two. Although it contains more changes, they tend to support Locke's position. However, they do hint that Locke, and Locke's expressions, could be improved. Coste said in the preface that the additions Locke had made since the first French edition had caused the translator problems, problems he had tried to solve by editing.[60] "Because in general the additions with which at various times this Book was enlarged, have somewhat spoiled its economy, & introduced several useless repetitions to it, I have smoothed it out as much as I could to hide this double flaw."[61] Coste also took it on himself to divide the work into sections to make it easier to understand.[62]

In addition to improving the text, Coste sought to add to the contents by providing his own comments and information. This began in the preface, where, in praising the author's ideas on education, he "takes the liberty of adding" a remark of his own about the importance of perfecting the knowledge of one's mother tongue.[63] In the work itself, Coste made a few corrections of Locke's facts (how many soldiers were in Xerxes' army, for example).[64] But his chief alteration of the work was to support Locke's views by adding quotations or information from a number of authors in whom the translator was particularly interested: mainly Montaigne, but also Plutarch, Horace, Suetonius, La Rochefoucauld, and La Bruyère. Coste was involved in editions of three of these—Montaigne, Horace, and La Bruyère—during his life.[65] In the preface he wrote of these additions:

> In any case whatever liberty I have taken in this Translation, I have always remembered not to mix up my thoughts with those of the Author. But having found in *Montagne* many thoughts, which have a marvelous relation with those of Mr. *Locke*, I have done myself a pleasure in citing some of them. It is an embroidery which can agreeably refresh the Reader. The lively & original tone which is lacking in my Translation, he will always find in *Montagne*. If I did not fear augmenting this Volume too much, I would have adorned it with many other thoughts of this Author, completely identical with those of Mr. *Locke*; for there are few things concerning the Education of Children which *Montagne* did not touch on in his *Essays*. He holds this subject close to his heart; he comes back to it at every turn.[66]

Although Coste points out in his first citation of Montaigne that Locke himself had read the author "and thought a great deal of him,"[67] the tone of these notes not only suggested Coste's love of the essayist, but also that Montaigne had thought of many of Locke's points first. As Coste wrote, for example, of Locke's idea that children must get into the habit of going frequently to the toilet, "This is what *Montagne* had already perceived."[68] The impression of Locke as simply a latter-day exponent of Montaigne's ideas—an impression conveyed throughout Coste's notes—could not fail to detract from readers' views of the author.

Given the timing of Collins' complaints, it seems likely that the true provocation of "the friends of Mr. Locke" came from the 1715 translation of *The Reasonableness of Christianity*. Although the notes were much more sparse than in the *Education*, seven years after that edition Coste was taking a more adversarial tone.

> As for me I will take the liberty of declaring here, that I do not adopt all of Mr. Locke's lines of argument, although I have taken the trouble to put his Book into French. The proofs of this will be seen in one or two places in this new Edition. It would have been easy for me to increase the number of them, if I had wanted to criticize the two or three first Chapters of the First Volume, where, based on some fairly uncertain explications of some Passages of Scripture, Mr. Locke has engaged in arguments which do not appear to be very sound: but I have been quite happy to spare judicious Readers the annoyance of reading reflections which they will easily be able to make for themselves.[69]

We saw when Coste was first translating this book in 1696 that he had some doubts about its argument. He does indicate near the end of the new edition that in general he agrees with Locke (although "my function as Translator did not oblige me" to do so).[70] But without opposing Locke's reasoning, Coste felt free to enlighten the public by publishing a few of his own opinions in his footnotes. In Book I, for example, Locke states that since virtue and prosperity are rarely found together in one person, virtue rarely attracts many adherents. Coste responds by taking the argument to its furthest extent, that behavior lacking in virtue must be "the most advantageous in this World," and that if one forgets about heavenly rewards it is more profitable on earth to be "a knave than sincere." Coste cannot agree, saying that "I am persuaded that Vice is by itself less proper for making us happy, than Virtue. . . . I will abandon the opinion of Mr. *Locke* on this point to embrace that which *Horace* establishes with so much force in these beautiful verses"—and he quotes, first the Latin, and then the French translation of the Père Tarteron.[71] He questions Locke again on the same issue several pages later.[72]

The tendency to challenge Locke, or to add reflections to those the philosopher had provided, only increased as Coste went through life. He continued to produce editions of the works he had translated, adding more comments and citations as he did so. This is particularly noticeable in the *Essai concernant l'entendement*, which went through four editions before Coste's death in 1747. As we have seen, the 1700 and 1714 editions contained few real remarks, except for Coste's notation of occasions when the experience of his translation helped to reinforce Locke's own arguments on language.[73] In the 1735 edition, however, Coste took on new confidence. He added to his old "Avertissement du Traducteur" the suggestion that his

ESSAI
PHILOSOPHIQUE
CONCERNANT
L'ENTENDEMENT
HUMAIN,

*OU L'ON MONTRE QUELLE EST L'ETENDUE DE NOS
CONNOISSANCES CERTAINES, ET LA MANIERE
DONT NOUS Y PARVENONS.*

PAR M. LOCKE.

TRADUIT DE L'ANGLOIS

PAR M. COSTE.

Quatrième Edition, revûe, corrigée, & augmentée de quelques Additions importantes de l'Auteur qui n'ont paru qu'après sa mort, & de plusieurs Remarques du Traducteur, dont quelques-unes paroissent pour la premiére fois dans cette Edition.

*Quam bellum est velle confiteri potius nescire quod nescias, quàm
ista effutientem nauseare, atque ipsum sibi displicere!*
Cic. de Nat. Deor. Lib. I.

VIVITUR INGENIO.
CETERA MORTIS
ERUNT.

J. Naert fecit 1738.

A AMSTERDAM,

Chez *PIERRE MORTIER.*

M. DCC. XLII.

---

4 Title page of Coste's translation of Locke's *Essay concerning Human Understanding.* Note
the similarity in size of Coste's and Locke's names.

own comments to Locke had improved the book: "I can say . . . that my scruples obliged M. Locke to express many places in English, in a more precise & more distinct manner than he had done in the first three Editions of his Book."[74] Once again he criticizes the repetitious quality of Locke's style, saying that some people had suggested he edit out the extraneous material.

> Some people of very delicate taste have strongly solicited me to cut absolutely these sorts of repetitions which appear more proper to fatigue than to enlighten the Mind of the Reader: but I have not dared to try my luck. Because besides the fact that the enterprise seemed to me too laborious, I considered that when all is said and done most people would blame me for having taken this liberty, for the reason that in cutting these repetitions, I could easily have allowed some reflection or some argument of the Author to escape. I thus have limited myself entirely to retouching my style, & to rectifying all the Passages where I believed I had not expressed the thought of the Author with sufficient precision.[75]

The translator seems to have abandoned this idea with reluctance; the principle of cutting Locke's words in itself was not troublesome, only the fear that he might cut too much.

But the intensification of Coste's attitude toward Locke is most tangible in the notes. In the 1735 edition of the *Essai* he let himself go, objecting at length to particular sections of the argument. For example, on the question of whether animals have concepts, Coste insists in a series of heated notes that they do, citing Pliny, Montaigne on elephants, and a dog Coste knew which tricked other dogs to get a warm spot by the fire.[76] He challenges Locke on facts and on reasoning, sometimes in an acid tone: "I do not know why Mr. Locke mixes reasoning with thought here. This only serves to confuse the Issue."[77] The 1742 edition of the work added even more "rather important Remarks" on the subjects interesting Coste.[78] He expanded his remarks on ideas and animals, even adding a discourse called "RÉFLEXIONS sur la manière dont M. Locke introduit son opinion sur la cause du sentiment qu'on remarque dans les Bêtes"[79] in which he does not spare Locke in his language. "Here M. Locke confuses from the start two things which must be exactly distinguished. . . . M. Locke is mistaken again in imagining. . . ."[80]

Coste's intention in such notes was not to refute Locke. He simply viewed his translations as opportunities for further discussion of the issues. As he said of the question of animals' ideas, "I have considered this Question for a long time."[81] Indeed, he considered the editor's function to be, in part, a commentator or corrector of his subject's ideas. In a note to the 1744 edition of the *Education*, he recommended Barbeyrac's 1724 translation of Grotius' *De jure bellis ac pacis* precisely because Barbeyrac tried "not only to put the arguments of this great man in a new light, but also sometimes to correct them, or to confirm them by stronger & more direct evidence."[82] Once again, in other words, the implication was that Locke's books were not completely Locke's. In some ways they were now Coste's. They certainly provided Coste with a forum for publishing his own ideas on the matters Locke discussed. He also asked in 1739 for his name to be included on the title page of the *Christianisme raisonnable*, "since it is known in France, in Italy, in England, in Holland, &c." that he had translated it.[83] Even more telling, Coste began dedicating the books himself. Later editions of the *Education*, for example, carried an eloquent dedicatory epistle to De la Motte, who Coste said had given him some of the ideas for improving the translation; and in fact De la Motte reported in a letter of 1725 that the 1708 edition would have been dedicated to him if as the corrector he had not had the opportunity to suppress the dedication.[84] Similarly, the 1735 edition of the *Essai concernant l'entendement* was dedicated to Coste's 13-year-old pupil, the Duke of Buckingham.[85] And even if Coste did not view these works as his own, he certainly thought that they were now part of the public domain. He felt he had something to contribute to these debates, and so he did.[86]

As we have witnessed, of course, not everyone saw it this way. "The friends of Mr. Locke" criticized both Coste's writings and his conversation for the way they "aspers'd and blacken'd" Locke's name. Apparently challenging Locke's facts and reasoning, or suggesting that he was not the originator of his ideas, was a crime against the great man. There is some suggestion that personal motives prompted the whole controversy; De la Motte knew that Collins had quarreled with Coste, and theorized that Des Maizeaux had fallen out with him over the latter's dedication of an edition of Boileau, which Des Maizeaux had expected to write;[87] and of course Coste appeared to have a motive to criticize his scholarly patron after Locke's poor treatment of him at the end of his life. In trying to understand the motives for Coste's condemnation, this is not a side issue, since it is clear that conversations Coste must have been having about Locke were part of what upset his opponents.

The outline of the problems in this controversy is perhaps most easily understood by looking at De la Motte's defense of his friend. The corrector's letters to Des Maizeaux rarely contained much besides details of the presswork on the latter's editions. But he departed from his norm to chastise Des Maizeaux for his behavior toward Coste. His reasons were both the manner of Coste's treatment and the subject of complaint.

It was ridiculous, he said, to criticize Coste for his tone in the editions of Locke's works.

You know . . . that M. Coste has not said anything in his Writings against M. Locke that an Author who would not burst with self-love could not suffer someone to say of him, for there is not the least offensive personal remark [*personalité*], & it is not forbidden to think differently from M. Locke & to say so, as he did himself in regard to other Authors. As for what people claim M. Coste has said of M. Locke in conversation, it is very weak [*une grande pauvreté*] to print this, because nothing satisfactory can be said about it, I believed that the custom of citing conversations died with M. Jurieu.[88]

In addition, if Coste did say something bad about Locke, it was only to be expected, since everyone else said the same thing about him. In fact, both Des Maizeaux and Collins had done so.

If M. Coste said of M. Locke what it is claimed, wouldn't he have said what all *honnêtes gens* have said of him? Didn't you write to me in similar terms a little while after the death of M. Locke? Didn't M. Collins say it to me here in very good company? I perhaps pardon M. Collins who was an intimate friend of M. Locke, & who is English, two qualities which permit him to be impassioned, but I cannot say the same of you, who esteemed M. Locke along with everyone else as a talented man, but who did not have the same idea of his heart.[89]

It was this emphasis on Locke's heart, rather than his mind, which appears to have caused much of the controversy. Coste's conversations about Locke, and even his challenges to his ideas in writing, struck someone like Collins as an attack on Locke's character. De la Motte said that it would be fine if people had only complained of Coste's view of the works, but they should not have said that Coste had denigrated Locke as a man.

If people had only criticized the judgments that M.C. made of several places in the Works of M. Locke, I would not say anything; that is permitted & very often useful. M.C. himself says here that he would cut something he had put in the Traité de l'Ed. des Enf. because he no longer thought it well-founded, & he left me a Copy where this Note was removed, as well as various objections he had put in the Copy of l'Entendem. humain that he left me in going to England, & which he effaced in returning to France. . . . Nothing is more free than judgments on Books & nothing more inconstant than these judgments. . . . But this is very different from what concerns the person. Although few people have more reason to complain of someone than M.C. has to complain of M.L. as everyone knows.[90]

As De la Motte pointed out, Coste had in his possession proof of Locke's malign nature, in the form of the letter Locke had written him. All Coste would have to do is publish the letter, and everyone would agree with him about Locke. Yet Coste had not done so, and in De la Motte's view this was the proper choice. "I would blame M.C. for having done it, because this would destroy the good which the Works of M.L., full of good things, can do."[91] Precisely to protect Locke's reputation as a scholar and the force of his works, unfortunate details about his character should be suppressed.

Indeed, in De la Motte's admittedly biased view, it was Des Maizeaux who was most to blame, because of his treatment of Coste. It was not so much that they were all supposed to be friends, but that they were all scholars. Maybe Des Maizeaux was angry with Coste for other things, such as the dedication of the edition of Boileau. "Whatever the truth is, the fact is certain, that when you published the Letter you were not a friend of M.C. Otherwise you would never have resolved to publish such a Letter, I do not Say against a Friend, but against a man of Letters."[92] It was not proper to write against someone, because "Writings stay around, & that is why it is necessary to think more than once before publishing them when they concern someone's reputation. It is in this circumstance above all that one should consult friends, but entirely neutral ones."[93] Coste had behaved well by not deigning to answer such attacks.[94]

This controversy, then, revolved around a number of questions posed by the scholarly hierarchy. What made a great man? Was it his works, his benefit to society, his admirable nature? How should such a man—or his memory— be treated when a lesser scholar has reason to criticize both his heart and mind? How should all scholars behave toward each other? Why was this important? Before analyzing in depth all the questions raised by the arguments over Coste and Locke, however, let us first look at another situation which will throw even more light on these issues. It was a quarrel that was raging at the same time as Coste's difficulties over Locke, and it involved some of the same people. But instead of "the friends of Mr. Locke," here we find "les Amis de Mr. Bayle."[95]

Des Maizeaux and Bayle

We have already met Pierre Des Maizeaux, the Huguenot refugee in London whose extensive correspondence, now in the British Library, provides such a wealth of information about the eighteenth-century Republic of Letters. But we still have not heard much about him. Indeed, we would probably know or care little about him today—and Thomas Birch might not have bothered to buy his correspondence—if it had not been for his association with Pierre Bayle. Even though Des Maizeaux and Bayle spent less than two months in the same country, Des Maizeaux became Bayle's biographer and the protector of his image.

Like Pierre Coste, Pierre Des Maizeaux was much younger than the great man with whom his fortunes became linked. He was born in 1673 at Paillat in the Puy-de-Dôme, the only son of a French Protestant minister. In September of 1685 his father Louis was charged with sedition for a fairly moderate sermon relating to kingship and the plight of the Protestants. Soon after, the family emigrated to Avenches, a community in the Pays de Vaud containing about fifty refugees. Des Maizeaux went to school in Avenches for the next few years. Hoping to launch him in an ecclesiastical career, his family sent him first to the Lyceum in Bern in 1690, where he remained until May 1695, and then to the Academy in Geneva. But when Des Maizeaux left the Academy in 1699, he travelled to northern Europe, and on his travels he gradually abandoned his plans. In Holland he met Bayle, and although in two months he left for England, never to return, his contact with the philosopher became one of the central features of his life.[96]

Des Maizeaux apparently managed, in his short time in the Netherlands, to get into good scholarly company. The breadth of his correspondence suggests an ability to make contacts which was evidently well-developed by this time. Le Clerc, for one, befriended him, sending him to England with a letter of recommendation to Locke: he was "a *fort honnête homme* . . . of whom my friends in Geneva tell me all kinds of good things." Coste, who had heard from Le Clerc first, told Locke that Des Maizeaux was reputed to be "quite reasonable, and not at all a slave to the opinions of his masters."[97]

Des Maizeaux, although only recently a student and still lacking a profession, had the qualifications to be a welcome addition to the refugee scholarly communities in Amsterdam and Rotterdam. He was a man of some reading, with a good knowledge of the classics and French literature; he could read Hebrew, Italian, Spanish, and English. In the view of his biographer, J.H. Broome, it was the exposure to this community which probably persuaded him to abandon the ministry as a career.[98]

Bayle appears to have taken on Des Maizeaux rather hesitantly. Broome says that Des Maizeaux actually forced his way into his circle, although Bayle ultimately found Des Maizeaux's wide correspondence and talent for publicity a useful resource.[99] Once the young scholar had moved on to England in the fall of 1699, Bayle tried to beg off from having to correspond with him regularly; Des Maizeaux kept writing, however, and Bayle continued to reply.[100] According to Elisabeth Labrousse, although their relations remained "fairly stiff," Bayle "seems to have conceived a certain affection for his

London admirer," an affection which prompted him to present Des Maizeaux with some old books.[101] As Bayle's admirer set up in London as a tutor to aristocratic and gentry children and pursued a low-level literary career, he made further contacts of use both to himself and to Bayle. He quickly became familiar with the booksellers of London, and after meeting St.-Evremond and Shaftesbury, he became for a time the intermediary between those luminaries and Bayle.[102] Having a young, admiring contact in London was clearly convenient for Bayle. But when Bayle died in 1706, Des Maizeaux's involvement with him was just beginning.

In part through Bayle's assistance, Des Maizeaux had already begun activities as a biographer and editor, working on the beginnings of a collection of lives of scholars, and assisting St.-Evremond in collections of his works, both genuine and specious.[103] Having been told by De la Motte in 1701 that the *libraire* Pierre Mortier was planning a second edition of St.-Evremond's works, Des Maizeaux told him that he thought he could provide much more exact copy than in the previous edition. He did this without St.-Evremond's knowledge, and when the poet learned about the project he was not particularly happy about it. But in 1703 St.-Evremond changed his mind and, as Des Maizeaux put it, "did me the honor to choose me, to review his Manuscripts with him, & to put them in order." St.-Evremond told him which pieces to print; Des Maizeaux copied them out and sent them to the poet; then they read them together while Des Maizeaux gathered information about their composition.[104] He and the Huguenot physician, Pierre Silvestre, continued after St.-Evremond's death to carry out an editing project on works attributed to him. Broome comments that "it would be idle to pretend that his attentions to St. Evremond were disinterested. . . . The penniless adventurer obviously regarded the old man somewhat in the shape of a commercial proposition."[105] A similar view was expressed more kindly by Shaftesbury, who noted just after St.-Evremond's death that "the Mark he has plac'd on you of his Esteem & Friendship will I hope be of Advantage to you in helping to make you known & valued."[106] That Des Maizeaux should begin his literary career by latching onto yet another great man—and writing his life—is of telling interest for our study of hierarchy.

Almost immediately after Bayle's death in 1706, Des Maizeaux turned to the philosopher as a subject for a commemorative life, in any case a popular sort of work after the death of a famous man. He began collecting materials from Continental informants and friends of Bayle's. Bayle's executor, Jacques Basnage, approved of the project, although he did not know Des Maizeaux, feeling that "in forming your judgment on all these subjects you would defend [*feriez lapologie de*] M. Bayle."[107] "His letters, if you could collect them, would have more impact" than publishing a piece on Bayle attributed to Pelisson, Basnage counseled him; "and I do not doubt that people would be very glad to have them. Two days ago I looked to see if there were any from among those he wrote to me that could be sent to increase your collection, and I have got permission from the heir of his papers to send them to you."[108]

Des Maizeaux wrote off to France, Prussia, and Holland, asking for letters and any other materials. Charles de la Motte acted as a gleaner of information and conduit of materials in this effort. Des Maizeaux's idea of a life won approval from scholars. He and De la Motte wrote either directly or through other scholars to obtain letters Bayle had written to people such as Bignon, Terson, Buffier, Ancillon, Regis, Caze, Constant, Turrettini, Chouet, Minutoli, La Monnoye, and Le Clerc; the response was good when the letters had survived. When Des Maizeaux proved slow to publish—in 1708 he wrote a rough, anonymous version in English but failed to work on a more complete biography in French—people began to get impatient. Mathieu Marais virtually pleaded with Des Maizeaux to finish. "Pardon me Monsieur if I press you, & even if I persecute you about this promise to us which you must keep. You know how much all of us, his friends, & his partisans must have our Hearts set on this work. . . . We will not live as long as it does not appear. What obstacle is there? What prevents you? In the name of The Tenderness which he had for you I Beg you Monsieur, not to turn your eyes elsewhere & to finish what you have started."[109]

By 1710, still reluctant to write a final version of the life, Des Maizeaux began to consider printing a collection of Bayle's letters on their own. He later explained this decision by saying that since "there were several of them which would have had to be quoted in their entirety, to mark well certain traits of the Life, or the Character of Monsieur Bayle's mind, . . . it seemed more convenient to have them printed, because then all that would be necessary was to cite them in general. . . . Moreover, I did not doubt that the Public would be very happy to find in these letters a Portrait of the mind and the heart of Monsieur *Bayle*; an idea of the manner with which he wrote to his Friends; and a very large number of curious Facts, or anecdotes."[110] By May of 1711 Des Maizeaux had 101 letters from Bayle, contributed to the edition, as he explained to a potential donor, out of "Zeal for his Memory."[111] He got De la Motte to look for a publisher; and since they were already negotiating with the new firm of Gaspard Fritsch and Michael Böhm in Rotterdam for Des Maizeaux's collection of lives and for editorial work on several of Bayle's books, it was not overly difficult to persuade them to print the letters as well. There was some quarrel over Des Maizeaux's pay for the edition, but on September 20, 1712, Fritsch and Böhm wrote to say they had struck a deal with De la Motte for the letters, that the agent had already sent the ones he had on hand, and others had come and were still coming from elsewhere. They now hoped Des Maizeaux would finish the *Vie*, since the public was so impatient for it.[112]

Things seemed to be going well for Des Maizeaux's edition. But then trouble arrived in his life: trouble in the form of Prosper Marchand. Marchand at this time was working as a corrector of the press for Fritsch and Böhm, with whom he was good friends, and he was put to work on the edition of Bayle's letters. In London, away from the action, Des Maizeaux found the situation thereafter increasingly confusing. As was customary, Fritsch and Böhm had begun sending him copies of the proofs as they were printed, so that he could send them any corrections he thought necessary. On seeing the sheets he found that Marchand was in charge, and—he later said—taking charge in a most improper way. Several letters were missing, and wording was changed; Marchand had added his own notes to the notes Des Maizeaux himself was providing. Des Maizeaux had indeed already allowed the fact to pass that Marchand had virtually taken over the editions of Bayle's works on which he himself was supposed to be helping, and he later said there was not much to be done in that case either.[113] He wrote an obliging letter to Marchand, saying that "as my principal goal was to make this Collection agreeable to the Public, I am no less obliged for the trouble you have taken to suppress several of these letters, as for the Notes, both curious & instructive, with which you have enriched the others."[114]

This was on March 20, 1713; things got more and more bewildering for Des Maizeaux from then on. In the middle of May he received an anonymous letter dated from Aix-la-Chapelle from someone claiming to be the editor of the letters—a letter obviously from Marchand.[115] The letter's tone showed that Marchand felt he had considerable editorial control over the edition; he said that he had cut certain portions of the letters because "they did not seem to me worthy of such a talented man, & I believed that Equity did not permit the publication of such productions of youth, capable of damaging the memory of a man to whom one owes so much."[116] The letter was in a disguised hand (which slipped somewhat toward the end), but Des Maizeaux knew perfectly well who had written it. Marchand nevertheless mysteriously asked to remain anonymous, and Michael Böhm preserved this anonymity two weeks later by referring to him only as "the person who has agreed to take the trouble to add several necessary notes."[117]

The edition was quickly slipping away from Des Maizeaux, for from that moment on he heard nothing and received no more of the proof sheets being printed for the edition in Rotterdam. Six months of this put him in despair, and he went into action in December, writing to Marchand that

Although I have no reason to doubt that you are the Author of the notes on the Letters of Monsieur Bayle, however as you had *very particular reasons* not to be known as yet; I would not take the liberty to write to you today under your name, if I was not forced to by the surprising conduct of Messieurs Fritsch and Böhm toward me for some time: for they are no longer sending me the sheets of the Letters of Monsieur Bayle.[118]

He asked Marchand to use his influence to let them know that—as he put it—"this is not the way they ought to behave." Des Maizeaux then continued by saying ironically that he knew that *Marchand* could have no part in what was happening to him.

In effect, Monsieur, you could only have prevented them from continuing to send me the sheets of these Letters for one of these two reasons: the first, because you would like to publish them yourself & you are appropriating the edition; but that is what I could never attribute to you with the least verisimilitude; because besides the fact that you are not capable of committing a baseness and injustice such as this, it is also too well known to the Public that I collected these letters and I sent them to Messieurs Fritsch and Böhm, for anyone ever to be persuaded to the contrary. The other reason which might have made you act in this way, is that the Notes on the sheets which followed those that I have already received, must contain calumnious and defamatory things concerning the people to whom these Letters are addressed; you are afraid that if I saw them I would complain and have them suppressed: but please God I would never attribute to you such dishonest and abominable conduct as that.[119]

Des Maizeaux was remarkably accurate in his predictions about the edition, no matter how much he ironically disavowed them. For indeed Marchand *had* taken the edition away from him. When the *libraires* finally wrote to Des Maizeaux on April 13, 1714—after the volume had appeared— they said that the previous year "one of our Friends in London" had told them someone was translating the letters into English at just the same pace as they were sending Des Maizeaux the proof sheets. "As it is in our Interest that this Translation did not appear at the same time as the original, we did not think it appropriate to continue to send you the sheets. We do not want to discuss this information & you will be pleased to dispense us from naming the person who gave it to us. If it isn't true, so much the better for us."[120]

It seems unlikely that this was in fact true, especially as no such edition ever appeared; Des Maizeaux later argued that there would be no reason to try to re-sell the sheets, as no market existed for Bayle's letters in England.[121] And in fact, from a letter Fritsch had written to Marchand in November of 1713—before Des Maizeaux had even complained about the silence—it seems clear the *libraires* simply felt Des Maizeaux's name would be a liability on the edition.

I have never doubted for a moment that you were a more talented man than Monsieur Des Maizeaux, who has lost his reputation since he meddled with writing the life of Boileau, thus the commentary that you add to the Letters of Monsieur Bayle and the choice that you have made of them, will make the edition esteemed in a very different way than if we had produced it in the form that Monsieur Des Maizeaux submitted it to us; I personally have a much better opinion of it now than in the beginning.[122]

Marchand, in combination with the *libraires*, had stolen the entire edition.

Des Maizeaux lost money on this transaction, since Fritsch and Böhm decided to pay him only for the letters he had sent and not for the annotations, even though some of the notes published were in fact by Des Maizeaux. His fee was reduced by a full third to 141 florins.[123] But in fact the diminution of profits, or even the dishonesty of the proceeding, did not cause such an uproar as the actual content of the book. For Des Maizeaux was also right in predicting that Marchand would say unpleasant things about the people who had sent in the letters—and even about Bayle himself.

Burning the Temple of Ephesus

Marchand was never restrained in his language, and he vented his spleen in full both in his notes and his index, even when Bayle's own remarks failed to justify it. He called books which Bayle had not criticized "awful" and their authors unjustifiably and intolerably proud.[124] The Abbé de la Trape, for example, was described as "a Man as calculating as he was ambitious"; and Le Duchat's notes on Rabelais, which Bayle did not even cite, were mentioned only to point out that they "do not fulfill in any way the Hopes that had been placed in them . . . leaving. . . . this *Author* . . . as obscure as he ever was."[125] Marchand pointed out contradictions in Bayle's words and ridiculed his erudition, asking in several places "whether it was not a very surprising thing" that Bayle had never heard of a particular work.[126] He also cut out words, phrases, lines, and even entire letters, a proceeding he acknowledged in the preface.

I have taken care to reject not only all those which were too careless to be preserved, but also those which, although written with more care, nevertheless contained nothing which is worthy of the *Attention* of a *reasonable Reader*. I have done more; I have removed from all those that I have preserved a considerable quantity of *Compliments*, of *Commissions*, of *Thanks*, and I don't know how many other things of this Nature; in a word, everything which did not seem to me proper to instruct, or to delight the Reader.[127]

Marchand was pleased with his editorial skill, but many scholars did not agree with his assessment of his own powers.[128] Elie Benoît, for one, criticized the "impertinence" and "ignorant impudence" of "a certain garçon libraire."[129] The combination of suppressed letters, altered wording, and nasty remarks in the notes and the index made the edition seem not only unfair to Pierre Des Maizeaux, but dishonorable to the memory of Pierre Bayle. Indeed, it was said to dishonor the entire Republic of Letters.

It was on this basis that the collection sparked a propaganda war, waged largely in the Continental literary journals, which lasted for years. Scholars were not worried so much about the insults to Bayle or to themselves, although they were certainly not happy about them. But their concern about changes in the text turned to panic when they realized that Marchand was taking on the editing of other works of Bayle's. In the edition of the *Lettres* Marchand pointed out his responsibility for the new edition of the *Commentaire philosophique*, one of the works wrested by him from Des Maizeaux's grasp, saying the book was preferable to the first edition primarily because of "the Care I took to re-establish exactly the *Meaning* of the *Author*, in an infinite number of *Places* where *Typographical Errors*, and the *Inexactness* of the first Editor, had strangely disfigured them."[130] Such words were beginning to have an ominous ring, and some scholars worried what Marchand's ventures into textual editing might mean for the memory of Bayle. When the *Journal littéraire*, for which Marchand wrote, announced a project for a new edition of Bayle's *Dictionary*, things seemed to have gone too far. Bayle's greatest work was about to be desecrated.

Marchand had already announced that this edition was going to contain "an infinite number of Additions and Corrections, very essential to the *Dictionary* of Monsieur *Bayle*, and which will render it incomparably more agreeable and more useful than it previously was, [plus] the *Supplement* will contain a number of *New Articles*, very curious, very extensive, and extremely interesting."[131] Bayle himself had written a supplement to the dictionary, never published in his lifetime, but he wanted this supplement to be published separately from the rest of the work. But the project described in the *Journal littéraire* said the *libraires* could not do this, because if they instead incorporated the supplement in the rest of the dictionary, it would help protect them from the plans of the Genevan *libraires* Fabri and Barrillot to counterfeit the entire edition.[132] And the suspicion among scholars—a justified one, as it turned out—was that not only would new articles be interspersed with old, but extra articles, not written by Bayle, would also be inserted in the edition.

It was these alterations of Bayle's original text that disturbed his partisans in the scholarly world. Ougier, whose opinion Marchand asked, wrote as much to him in 1716.

Since you do me the honor, Monsieur, to ask me my opinion on your Project for the new edition of the Dictionary . . . I will take the liberty to say to you sincerely . . . that I believe, that you would do well not to change the order and the disposition of the Dictionary of Mr. Bayle; and not to alter his style and his expressions in the least, either in the Text or in the Remarks. That you should certainly not insert new articles in the supplement, which are not truly by this Author; nor change anything, or add to him marginal citations, not even his Spelling and punctuation; as that would possibly change the meaning of the Discourse . . . In a word, you must publish the Dictionary of Mr. Bayle just as he composed it, and as he had it printed himself, and follow his Manuscript for the Supplement exactly, so that one can be assured that this is this famous Author's own work.[133]

In a whole book of articles protesting this new edition, admittedly published by the competing *libraires* Fabri and Barrillot, "the friends of Monsieur Bayle," as they called themselves, complained that

one must not be surprised if before the Invention of Printing, when Original Manuscripts were either lost, or in the hands of a few people, there were Imposters who corrupted the copies that were made of them; because in our Century there are people capable of truncating and falsifying the Works published by the Authors themselves, and distributed everywhere. . . . That is what the person called *Prosper Marchand* has done in the edition of the *Commentaire Philosophique* . . . and what he proposes to do in the new Edition of the *Dictionnaire Critique*. . . . Since his only goal is to make people talk about him, he has chosen the writings of Monsieur *Bayle* as the object of his impostures, just like that Unfortunate man, who burned the Temple of Ephesus, to pull his name out of obscurity.[134]

These attacks went on for pages, and for years. The controversy did not end until a final outburst after Des Maizeaux published his own edition of the letters in 1729. But what was really behind the public outcry on this subject? Just what were the "friends of Bayle"—or, for that matter, "the friends of Locke"—so upset about?

The similarities between these two examples are striking. They both involve young French refugees—not just Coste and Des Maizeaux, but Marchand as well—who wanted to advance themselves from positions of relative obscurity in the Republic of Letters. Fairly early on in their lives and careers they came in contact with an acknowledged "great man," an *homme illustre*, and in dealing both with the man himself and his works, they tried to associate themselves with his glory. It was not just that they wanted fame for themselves, but that they wanted to add to the fame of their particular *illustre*, by translating, publicizing, defending—or even attacking. In so doing, they must have thought, they would add to their own status as well. And if they could *add* something to the debate on the issues, or to the collective knowledge of the Republic of Letters, then they could raise themselves even more, to stand high up on the shoulders of giants.

Tyrants over Texts

But if this behavior involved altering the works of such giants, many scholars could not approve. As E.J. Kenney points out, through the sixteenth and seventeenth centuries there had been a history of hesitancy about textual criticism,[135] so that a daring emender such as Richard Bentley came to many in the early eighteenth century as a rude shock. Although Bentley was better appreciated on the Continent—Graevius called him "that new and brilliant light of Britain"[136]—his enthusiasm for conjecture in editions of both classical and modern authors appeared to some in the literary world as a dangerous innovation. Shaftesbury told Le Clerc that Bentley's Horace "will be the most elaborate Monster that the Learn'd World ever saw produc'd. He has mangled him and torn him in pieces so as that the Author is scarce knowable in his own Text." His "horrible Corrections" had, even worse, "frankly displac'd the Readings of the Manuscripts," which was, to Shaftesbury's mind, "presumptiouse."[137] Similar views were expressed by Thomas Edwards, who attacked William Warburton's Shakespeare in a pamphlet of 1748, sardonically observing that "a Professed Critic" feels he has "a right to declare, that his Author wrote whatever he thinks he should have written," that "he has a right to alter any passage which he does not understand," and that "he may alter any word or phrase, which does not want amendment, or which *will do*, provided he can think of any thing, which he imagines *will do better*."[138]

Although critics like Bentley were better accepted by some on the Continent, the debate over textual emendation also raged there as a sort of sideshow to the quarrel of the ancients and the moderns. Anne Dacier's disgust at the "corruption of taste" displayed by Antoine Houdar de la Motte's modernist edition of the *Iliad* captured the attention of the entire Francophone literary audience. La Motte cheerfully reported his excision of whole books, his rearrangement of what was left, and his invention of new material, an avowal met by Dacier with an anger the *Journal littéraire* likened to "Theological zeal."[139] In the 1690s she had already defended Terence against the depredations of a critic who had wanted to make great alterations, a successful defense according to an *extrait* in Jean Cornand de la Crose's

History of Learning.[140] In her view, the important thing in translating was to retain the sense of the author, something which could not be done in translations into verse, which necessarily entailed changes, cuts, or additions.[141] Thus of La Motte's verse translation of Homer, in which he reduced the poem from 16,000 lines to only about 4,600,[142] she could only moan:

> I hope that after the success which this new endeavor of M. de la M. has had the Modern Wits will disabuse themselves, & that they will discard the insane hope of ruining the reputation of these Works which every age has honored, respected, and consecrated, & that they will finally see that the only way that they have to correct their completely corrupt taste, is to follow the way that they have abandoned, & to form their judgment on these excellent Originals to make it just.[143]

One of the strongest objections to this new sort of editing was a sort of arrogance which was perceived to accompany it. As Baillet remarked, "it is a Pedantry to want to make us think that Livy, Terence, Aristotle, &c. did not know their own language, & . . . to give Grammar lessons to the Ancients who have taught us their language & who wrote in the time when it was spoken the best."[144] Yet these editors did not hesitate to stress their power over the text. Lewis Theobald, who edited Shakespeare by collating his plays with old copies and sources before making any conjectures based on common sense or Shakespearean parallels,[145] wrote in 1726 that it was not productive to respect such works as unalterable. He did not feel, he said, "that the Writings of SHAKSPEARE are so *venerable*, as that we should be excommunicated from good Sense, for daring to *innovate properly*; or that we ought to be as cautious of altering *their* Text, as we would That of the *sacred Writings*."[146] And Bentley's tone was enough to put off the most open-minded reader. Francis Hare, Bishop of St. Asaph, remarked pointedly that Bentley, "as if he had obtained, sole and alone, the highest place in Criticism, denied that laws applied to him, and does not suffer himself to be restrained by any rules; he recognizes no limit to the power of his criticism; by virtue of his arbitrary authority he riots with impunity in the writings of the ancients; and allows whatever pleases."[147]

This sort of arrogance was in opposition to many scholars' concepts of community. If an editor was to make corrections or conjectures, they must be careful and modest, for they affect the general understanding. Theobald, opposing Pope's wild emendations, made the communal objection explicit.

> Certainly, what Physician would be reckon'd a very unserviceable Member in the Republick, as well as a bad Friend to himself, who would not venture to prescribe to a Patient, because not absolutely sure to cure his

Distemper; As, on the other hand, he would be accounted a Man of very
indifferent Morals, if he rashly tamper'd with the Health and Constitution
of his Fellow-Creature, and was bold to try Conclusions only for private
Information. The same Thing may be said with regard to *Attempts* upon
Books: We should shew very little Honesty, or Wisdom, to play the Tyrant
with any Author's Text; to raze, alter, innovate, and overturn, at all
Adventures, and to the utter Detriment of his Sense and Meaning.[148]

Moreover—and this is most important for our purposes—to "play the Tyrant" this way over a renowned author was upsetting to a community
protective of the reputation of a few great men. Who was someone like La
Motte to slash at the words of Homer? As the *Journal littéraire* (perhaps
sarcastically) remarked, "it was morally impossible that an audacity of this
nature should rest unpunished."[149] In pulling down the reputation of an
author by pointing out his errors, critics seemed to be thinking not of the
community, but only of their own reputations.

> When Dulness, smiling—"Thus revive the Wits!
> But murder first, and mince them all to bits;
> As erst Medea (cruel, so to save!)
> A new Edition of old Æson gave,
> Let standard-Authors, thus, like trophies born,
> Appear more glorious as more hack'd and torn,
> And you, my Critics! in the chequer'd shade,
> Admire new light, thro' holes yourself have made.
> "Leave not a foot of verse, a foot of stone,
> A Page, a Grave, that they can call their own;
> But spread, my sons, your glory thin or thick,
> On passive pages, or on solid brick.
> So by each Bard an Alderman shall sit,
> A heavy Lord shall hang at ev'ry Wit,
> And while on Fame's triumphal Car they ride,
> Some Slave of mine be pinion'd to their side.[150]

These were just the kind of complaints Bayle's defenders made about
Marchand. The idea that a mere corrector, a former *libraire*, should place
himself on Bayle's level was a shocking one. An article in Sallengre's *Mémoires
de littérature*, quoting Marchand's view that " 'it is an insufferable
temerity . . . to have put at the end of an entirely Latin citation, *initio*, instead
of *in the first pages*,' " added that "without doubt it is an *insufferable temerity* in
a man like Marchand, to claim to correct M. Bayle, in making him say things
that he did not say, & that he did not want to say."[151] Such changes in the
author's text were unconscionable. As the article stressed, "You know that

the expressions of an Author are sacred, & that it is not permitted to alter them."[152] The types of textual alterations Marchand made only worsened the crime. "Instead of always expressing himself as a great man, as a Writer of the first order, Marchand has him speak and express himself like a journeyman bookseller, or like a compiler of Catalogues of Books."[153] Bayle seemed suddenly more like Marchand, that corrector and former *libraire*, than like himself. And at the same time, like the Dunces in the *Dunciad*, both Marchand and Coste seemed to be making their names through their depredations on the works of great men. Far from preserving their subjects' memory, Marchand and Coste were ruining their reputations for posterity.

The Primacy of Reputation

This posthumous reputation was of great moment to scholars like the "amis de M. Bayle" or the "friends of Mr. Locke": of more importance, in fact, than the purpose of their works. They preferred to see an authentic version of the *Dictionary* rather than one which was made more useful by contributions from other scholars. This was the case even though Bayle himself had said his *libraire* was allowed to insert any articles which seemed suitable, without consulting him first.[154] Marchand at times seemed uncertain of his right to correct or add to Bayle, saying, for example, that some of the changes he had made in his *Projet* for the *Dictionary* were only copyist's errors,[155] and saying the sample article (AMBOISE) contained no outside material.[156] But he did not deny that new information would be included in the work, only that it would not be intermingled with the words of Bayle.[157] And indeed those whose main concern was the utility of Bayle's enterprise, rather than the preservation of his memory, would have no objection to this proceeding.[158] An edition of *A General Dictionary*, based on Bayle's, which was published in London from 1734 to 1741, took this point of view. Its authors asked for benevolence both for "our Endeavours to give an accurate Version of his excellent Work, and to supply such considerable Articles as were omitted by him, especially those relating to our own Nation."[159] In the same way, Pierre Coste's argumentative footnotes in his editions of Locke were intended to provoke further thinking on the issues Locke had raised. When he was planning a new edition of the *Christianisme raisonnable*, Coste wrote to De la Motte, "I do not want to forget to ask you to let Mr. Barbeyrac know that if he is of my opinion on the long Note where I criticize M. Locke, I would be very obliged if he would like to strengthen it by more solid & elaborate reflections when announcing this new Edition in a little Article in the *Bibliothèque raisonnée*. It would be easy for him to do this, & the Public would profit from it."[160] But the argument for public profit did not prevent either him or Marchand from being accused of both audacity and defamation. The goal of increasing knowledge and understanding could conflict severely with that of honoring the illustrious dead.

This conflict extended to differing attitudes toward the proper curiosity about great men. Jean de Beyer, who was always pestering Marchand for details about his old associates, and who published his uncle's letters for the benefit of the scholarly community, confessed in 1742 that he had "a weakness concerning Men of Letters; the least details of their lives interest me."[161] This view was common. The *Journal littéraire* pointed out that when great men die, "everything that concerns them is precious. The reputation that they merited extends to the tiniest circumstances of their Life, it seems to communicate grandeur to them, and make them interesting: the exact knowledge of their character, of what they have done, of what they have written, seems to introduce us in some measure into familiar friendship with these rare men."[162] These attitudes explain the tremendous popularity of the works known as *Ana*—books of table talk such as the *Naudaeana, Patiniana, Scaligerana, Sorberiana, Furetieriana,* and so on. Such books were compilations of remarks, marginal notes, and general gossip by famous scholars. They sold remarkably well; the report from Amsterdam in 1704 was that the *Chevraeana* was selling much better than Chevreau's collected works, and Nicaise referred to them as the "drugs of this age."[163] They had just the appeal cited by the *Journal littéraire*; Des Maizeaux said in his edition of the *Scaligerana* and other *Ana* that "besides the utility that can be had from these domestic conversations, there is also the pleasure of seeing that these Savants show themselves *dans leur naturel*. They tell us what they think about all sorts of subjects: it seems as if they hear us speak, that we live with them, & that we are in their confidence."[164]

Yet the *Ana* were often amazingly trivial in character. The *Naudaeana* consisted of accounts of such matters as where the Vatican is, whether scorpions in Italy are poisonous, and whether there has ever been a perfect hermaphrodite. The first page of the *Pithoeana* read, "MONSIEUR DE THOU is not savant, outside of Poetry & good speech. MR. HERAUD is very savant. MR. RIGAULT is not savant, but very brazen. My brother was jealous because Monsieur CUJAS named me in his will. MR. CUJAS was susceptible to drunkenness. I gave the Pére SIRMOND all the most difficult places in Ennodius." And the *Furetieriana* included prodigies (a baby born laughing), gossip from court, stray facts (that the Athenians spent more on spectacles than on war), and miscellaneous thoughts and anecdotes, mostly not about scholars.[165] Small wonder that by 1803 and the appearance of the *Addisoniana*, the editor should remark that "ostentation and display of reading [are] highly unbecoming in the compiler of an *Ana*," or that the *Elite des bons mots* of 1704, which called itself a collection of *ana*, is less a compilation of learned *dicta* than a simple joke book.[166]

As we have seen, however, the respect which motivated the curiosity which produced such books could also prompt a protectiveness about the reputation of the great, a protectiveness running directly counter to the spirit of the *Ana*. Obviously the publication of such inanities could do nothing to enhance someone's reputation as a great scholar, no matter how much it made the reader feel like his intimate friend. One reason to write the lives of the dead, or to republish their works, was to honor them and their memories—as Jacques de Pérard put it, "to throw flowers on [their] grave."[167] It was no coincidence that the lives of authors published by academies and literary journals were not customarily called *vies*, but rather *éloges*. This being the case, those wanting to commemorate the dead would not want to disseminate unworthy writings or information, even if they were authentic or true.

This in fact was Marchand's stated reasoning when he chose to improve the antiquated style of the letters he published. Publishing works of little value was, he said, "to do Authors, otherwise *illustrious* and with a *distinguished Name* in the *Republic of Letters*, the most crying *Injustice* that one could ever do to them."[168] Given Marchand's harsh attitude toward Bayle in the footnotes and index of this edition, this statement should perhaps be taken with a grain of salt. But it is notable that Des Maizeaux and other partisans of Bayle held much the same view. Although Des Maizeaux begged at least one of his contributors to provide Bayle's letters "cut[ting] . . . as little as you can, & nothing if it is possible," and to "give the proper Names in full,"[169] his own inclination, and especially that of his fellows, was to cut out material dishonorable to Bayle. Des Maizeaux said that to include every little detail, even those which authors such as Scaliger and Perron "would have disavowed," was the result of an "ill-considered zeal" on the part of the "Disciples of these great men."[170] Some people criticized the editors of the *Scaligerana* because (as Gilles Ménage noted) "they were so prejudiced in [Scaliger's] favor that, taking everything he said as an oracle, they believed (to say nothing of trifles, bagatelles, and lies . . .) that they should not omit the insults, unworthy of an *honnête homme*, & the obscenities he let fly."[171] Scholars such as Mathieu Marais, Jean-Alphonse Turrettini, and Théodore Huet all suggested that some of Bayle's letters were written, as Huet said, "with too much negligence, to do him honor," or even that they showed a bad side of Bayle: "one must not immortalize these hatreds & these malignities."[172] Thus letters, at least, might be altered; and trivial details gathered for a biography, such as Jacques Lenfant's story of Bayle falling into a canal, might deserve suppression for the sake of dignity.[173] Sometimes the great needed protection. And anything which reflected badly on Bayle might—as Marais feared—"destroy the temple we are building to him."[174]

In writing Bayle's life, Des Maizeaux was concerned more than anything else with one issue: whether Bayle had actually written the *Avis important aux refugiez sur leur prochain retour en France*. This work, published anonymously in 1690 and now generally ascribed to Bayle,[175] was written from the point of view of a liberal Catholic convert; it ridiculed the abandonment of absolutist political theory by extremist Huguenot refugees in favor of an opportunistic Whiggism and support for William of Orange. If the Huguenots really wanted to return to France, the *Avis* said, their antimonarchical writings and their own intolerant behavior were far from the way to accomplish that goal. Bayle may have hoped to spark rebuttals representing his true beliefs; but the idea that he might have written the *Avis* horrified those, such as his enemy Pierre Jurieu, who believed that it must represent his true sentiments.[176] Marchand took it as a given that Bayle was the author of the *Avis*, even though Bayle denied it consistently during his life; in the 1714 *Lettres* Marchand mentions his authorship repeatedly.[177] Des Maizeaux, however, refused to assert that Bayle could have written the work, and even after the most exhaustive inquiries in Holland, down to the very man who had corrected the proofs and recognized Bayle's handwriting, he was reluctant to acknowledge authorship in his editions of Bayle's life.[178] He even said that Jacques Basnage, who in fact eventually decided Bayle had written the piece, had remained convinced that Daniel Larroque had written the *Avis*.[179]

But although Basnage had actually decided on Bayle's guilt, he shared with Des Maizeaux a belief that it should not be made public. He was particularly distressed that Bayle had known Jurieu was not only right, but had proof positive of Bayle's role. "I am confiding this secret to you," he wrote to Des Maizeaux in 1714, "which I beg you to guard also, because I believe that you must handle this affair carefully, and rather leave the public in some kind of doubt, than let it see that such a great man had the weakness to deny publicly a thing which his enemy could prove."[180] Basnage felt as De la Motte had about Coste's decision not to publish the letter revealing Locke's ungracious nature. Rather than destroy a great man's fame with the truth, these men preferred to preserve his reputation with half-truths and falsehoods. And even though in the affair of Bayle's letters Des Maizeaux wanted as many details as possible printed for the sake of the curious audience, in this case he agreed to suppress the damaging information.[181]

Indeed, Des Maizeaux was not above lying for the sake of Bayle's reputation. Richard Popkin has revealed that one of the letters in Des Maizeaux's own edition, in 1729, was not in fact by Bayle at all, but rather inserted by Des Maizeaux to defend a position of Bayle's. In his article on Spinoza in the *Dictionary*, Bayle had said that Spinoza and the Prince de Condé had met, a detail Spinoza's followers denied because it appeared traitorous on his part. In the 1729 *Lettres* Des Maizeaux presented several pages from an *extrait* of a life of Spinoza as a "letter" from Bayle in 1706, adding notes with information from members of the editor's acquaintance who had known Spinoza and could testify that Spinoza and Condé had met.[182] After this, all of Des Maizeaux's protests over alterations to Bayle's text must be seen in a different light. Like many, he surely felt that authors' works were "sacred"; but their image was more so, and when they conflicted it was the image that won.

It was not just Bayle, however, but also the Republic of Letters which needed protection. For all their concern about Bayle's image, a healthy note of self-preservation also characterized his partisans' worries about the letters. Complete openness might bring down the entire edifice of the learned world. Marais balked at the inclusion of letters *to* Bayle, given their potential for laying bare real relationships in the community. "If there are Letters written to M^r. Bayle it would be a strange infidelity to publish them," Marais wrote. "[T]here are a thousand secrets in these letters which concern both individuals and entire families, there is enough there even to make people scorn some men of Letters, who make humilating requests & if this should come about, it would be necessary to renounce forever writing to Strangers, that is, to take all the sweetness out of life, for me most of all."[183] One of the major objections to Marchand's edition of the letters was the way all the names, and consequently the hatreds, of scholars were spelled out, and even obligingly provided in case of the letter-writer's own discretion. The minister Théodore Huet was cynical about this. "I am pretty much in agreement with Everyone on this subject; that is, that there are certain People, and certain things, which should not have been so largely revealed. But, Monsieur, you must wonder at the malignity of the human heart; for the very people who think in this fashion (except those actually concerned) are pleased enough that this fault has been committed, and I do not doubt that this will increase [the letters'] sales."[184] Both the prurience of readers and their own condemnation of Marchand suggest a sense, conflicted as it was, of concern for the integrity of the community.

This leads us to the reasons why people like Marais and Des Maizeaux were so anxious to preserve a great man's image. We have already seen that it served an individual function for friends of the deceased, who for their own sake wanted to "throw flowers on his grave." It even served a commercial function, for in this case the publishing war between Fritsch and Böhm in Rotterdam and Fabri and Barrillot in Geneva took the form of a battle over Bayle's reputation and works. But more generally, and more importantly, the image of a great man served a communal function.

Learned Lives, Learned Icons

In the first place, the telling of the story of learned lives helped to create a sense of a communal history for members of the Republic of Letters. Pierre

Des Maizeaux, as a biographer and editor, was perfectly aware of this. In the introduction to the edition of the *Letters* in 1729, he wrote that "Literary History has as an object all the people who cultivate Letters, the Arts, and the Sciences. They form an Estate distributed in every Estate, a Republic, in which each Member, in a perfect independence, recognizes only the Laws which he has prescribed for himself. One takes an interest in it to clarify the details of the Life of Scholars, of their Writings, and of their Disputes. Since the Republic of Letters provides Historians to all sorts of estates & conditions, why shouldn't it have its own Historians?"[185] Thus the *éloges* printed in journals and the publications of academies provided not only praise for the illustrious deceased, but an exact detail of his life, insofar as it pertained to the Republic of Letters.

In 1755, the Earl of Macclesfield, a Fellow of the Royal Society, described in a letter about the late Martin Folkes what kinds of things ought to enter into such an *éloge*. There should be

> for instance, some account of the family he came from; the time and place of his Birth; where he was educated, the time of his going to the University; which of the Universitys, and what College there he went to; how long he continued there; the time of his being elected Fellow of the Royal Society; what papers he delivered, and when, as also what services or good offices he did to the Society; what learned men (now deceased) he was intimately or chiefly acquainted with at home, from the time of his leaving the University; the time he went abroad; how long time he employed in his travels; what places he visited; what learned foreigners he then became acquainted with at those several places; with which of them he chiefly kept up a correspondence after his return home; when chosen President of the Royal Society; . . . what parts of Science he chiefly applied himself to, and was best acquainted with; what book or books he has published, or was concerned in writing, and at what time he wrote them; some acct of his . . . valuable collection of English Coins; &c.[186]

This sort of account, familiar to any of us accustomed to reading obituaries, formed an important subject of reading for scholars. *Eloges*—and even more so the many collections of scholarly lives, such as Niceron's *Mémoires pour servir à l'histoire des hommes illustres*—fed a passion for facts about scholars which in turn provided a history and a legitimacy for the community of the learned. Not everyone merited an *éloge*; Niceron said that one problem with the Germans was that everybody got one—"they push . . . things to excess"[187]—and Camusat noted approvingly that Cousin's *éloges* in the *Journal des sçavans* "were not these insipid Eloges which equally fit the Savants of all Countries & all Centuries."[188] The *Bibliothèque britannique* promised *éloges* "when death has taken from us a person distinguished by his knowledge, or by his love for Letters."[189] These articles were not written merely for the entertainment of their audience. Niceron wrote that he undertook his work on savants' lives both "for the glory of Scholars, and for the instruction of those who want to know them."[190]

As Niceron suggested, such accounts provided not only history but object lessons for their readers. For they all, explicitly or implicitly, described the qualities of a great man. Such qualities may or may not have actually belonged to the people to whom they were attributed. That ultimately did not matter. But by describing the institutional affiliations of each man, and, even more important, by ending each life with the *illustre*'s character, commemorative writing drilled into readers of literary journals just what they might have to do, or have to be, to become figures themselves in the scholarly pantheon.[191]

This is, of course, in the nature of biography. Most writers on biography recognize that a major function—perhaps *the* major function—of biographical literature from the Middle Ages into the eighteenth century was instruction for the reader. Biographies might preserve the memory of the dead, but for the living they were also much like saints' lives. They provided ideal members of society, ones whose lives should not only be remembered but, as far as possible, emulated.[192] Charles Paul writes that the *éloges* of the Paris Academy of Sciences were in some sense a public relations effort for its members in the outside world.[193] The point is well taken; but the members themselves needed these efforts, for, as Diderot wrote, "the éloge is an encouragement to virtue."[194] Thus the editors of the augmented English edition of Bayle's *Dictionary* (which was in the form of a collection of lives) dedicated the work to Hans Sloane and the Royal Society, saying that as "the subject of it is the Lives of eminent Men, many of whom bear so near a resemblance to Your Selves," the dedicatees might profit. After all, "the bare Names of NEWTON and of BOYLE raise the most exalted Ideas, and image to us something more than human."[195] Apologists for the art of literary biography in the eighteenth century thus continually referred to utility as the standard for judging their efforts. Charles Ancillon said that "no one can doubt that the Lives of savant men are of a great utility"; François Bruys said that in his *Mémoires historiques* he would not describe the countries he had visited because "it is more useful to get to know [about] great men: their example inspires emulation."[196] So it is not surprising that Des Maizeaux should use this idea as an appeal in his edition of Bayle's letters. "Literary History is useful to those who devote themselves to Letters, because of the example that it offers, and the emulation that it inspires."[197] Bayle's letters, and his life, were not only for those who wanted to remember him. They were intended to serve as an example and an inspiration for all scholars.[198]

Becoming an Homme illustre

The premise behind all this, of course, was that the Republic of Letters was an open community. As we have already seen, some scholars, accurately or not, believed that the Republic of Letters "is always a free country," one in which "each Member, in a perfect independence, recognizes only the Laws which he has prescribed for himself." It was a recognition of the inaccuracy of such images of equality, according to Robert Darnton, which so embittered some late eighteenth-century writers who manifestly were not of the highest rank.[199] Although in the earlier period we do not see such protests against the academic establishment, the potential equality of members was at least tacitly recognized. The idea that the emulation of the great should be in any way efficacious suggests that social mobility was an easy matter—or at least a different matter from such mobility in the outside world. For the assumption in the scholarly community was that its status system differed— or was supposed to differ—from that of the rest of society. Even though almost every savant divided his life between duties to scholarship and to the outside world, to pastoral responsibilities, teaching, or legal work, in the scholarly realm they apparently felt judged primarily by another sort of standard.

Thus Vigneul-Marville intended to amuse the audience of his *Mélanges* at the ridiculousness of the woman in one of his anecdotes who refused to admit to her husband's philosophy lectures anyone "who did not have an air of quality, persuaded that it was necessary to have this air to deserve to listen to her Husband. The good man practically killed himself in telling her that fortune does not always give Philosophers fancy clothes; she wanted to see velvet, and wouldn't give up on it."[200] Colletet, the translator of Sainte-Marthe's *Eloges des hommes illustres, qui depuis un siecle ont fleury en France dans la profession des lettres*, used the same sort of image in 1644 to explain his author's intentions to the French public. "The intention of my Author was to show that it is not just great birth, nor great wealth, great titles, nor great offices which make people illustrious, but particular or public Knowledge, and manifest or hidden virtue. In short, that a Palace, and a shanty, the purple, and the homespun, do not distinguish men in this august Temple of Honor, and that in the reasonable world all that is necessary to attract praise is to do praiseworthy things."[201]

The *éloges* of deceased scholars provide numerous examples of people who became famous in the learned world despite artisanal or mercantile origins; the *Bibliothèque italique*'s account of the life of Antonio Magliabecchi, for example, noted that "although destined by his Relations to the profession of Goldsmith, he soon raised himself by his talents above such a slender destiny."[202] Of course, the fact that this was remarkable—that Louis Bourguet's career in business required excuses from learned patrons such as Leibniz—

tells us something about how much normal societal values actually penetrated the world of learning. La Croze, for example, told Cuper that Bourguet's "profession of Merchant should not put you off, I assure you he is a learned man."[203] But the image, at least, was one of possible advancement, as some of César de Missy's terrible verses to Voltaire testify:

> *Moi qui suis paresseux, je suis fort ignorant:*
> *Mais tant qu'on vit on étudie:*
> *Qui sçait? petit poisson pourra devenir grand*
> *Pourvu que Dieu lui prête vie.*[204]

What was necessary to become one of Missy's big fish? When scholars judged who was valuable in their community, obviously great works and evidence of genius were major factors. But it is interesting how quickly this intellectual greatness gave way in the Republic of Letters to a more social one. As we have seen, books useful to scholarly society were hailed as "doing honor to the Republic of Letters," and savants frequently urged each other to write particular works for the use of the rest of the community. The *éloges* frequently praised virtues which seem initially private, but which in fact resulted in works which graced the shelves and footnotes of fellow-scholars. Thus talents such as a prodigious memory or a proficiency at languages were admirable in part because of their ability to increase the knowledge of others. The spartan lives led by some scholars were of particular interest. One literary journal praised a professor of law at Frankfurt-on-the-Oder for devoting "very little time to sleep, and for several years even [abstaining] from dining, in order to be able to study more freely"; and Niceron was fond of explaining the domestic arrangements of people like Tanneguy le Fèvre, who "ate little, & practically always worked while eating. . . . In his youth he went to bed late, and often sat up; but since then he changed his method."[205] The asceticism of a literary saint who sacrificed himself to the god of learning was a powerful image for a community anxious for integration.

The social aspect of literary greatness did not limit itself to the study or the work-table. As Des Maizeaux wrote in the dedication of his life of Boileau, "it is very common for the admiration that one has for the Writings of an Author, to give birth to advantageous opinions of his person, and for one to wish to be instructed about his Background, his Behavior, and his Fortune."[206] This, of course, is the sentiment which prompted the popularity of the *Ana* and other literary biography. It is evident from the content of *éloges* that it was only the community that counted; other details were not important. Bayle said in the *Nouvelles de la République des Lettres* that there was no point in paying attention to things like wives and children, since "among Authors one thinks of oneself not so much as husbands, or as fathers, but as making books. The Republic of Letters does not enter into marriages, nor into births, these are things which do not serve it in any way."[207] And

Niceron decided in writing his books that "as it is principally the knowledge of Works which I have in view, I will only report of the life of each Author, what can make him known in the quality of Savant, neglecting all which is foreign to this quality." Some details were important for the community, however; so Niceron added to this statement, "except however in certain things which can better discover his character, & make it easier to judge his Works."[208]

But as Des Maizeaux's words suggest, for many it was the understanding of the author rather than his works which was at issue. Paul-Emile de Mauclerc was delighted with his correspondent Crousaz's anecdotes of Bionens because "these sorts of things give one more ability to judge the character of an author than one can achieve through a repeated reading of his Works."[209] If the author were in fact alive, this social impulse often found an outlet in letter-writing. The *commerce de lettres* commonly began with an avowal of this sort. "For a long time," the journalist Mathieu Maty wrote to Formey, "I have wished to know you in another way than by your works"; Gisbert Cuper began a *commerce* with Montfaucon by saying that "for a long time I have wished to conduct a friendship and a scholarly correspondence with you, because of your great knowledge, of which your excellent books are incontestable witnesses."[210] The reason for this transferral of communication from the printed page to the manuscript letter was that members of the Republic of Letters thought of their world as not only an intellectual, but also a social community.

Indeed, if we look at some of those acknowledged in *éloges*, we see that great works were not necessarily the only criterion for those deemed illustrious. Although the *Mémoires de Trévoux* announced its intention to record the deaths of "persons distinguished by their science, if they have published something,"[211] other authors indicated that a large output was not important. In its review of volume XIX of Ellies Du Pin's *Nouvelle Bibliothèque des Auteurs Ecclesiastiques*, the *Journal littéraire* remarked on his inclusion of people who had written little: "One must not always decide on the merit of an Author by the multitude of his Works; such a one sometimes will produce only one which is better in its genre, than someone else who has included in his all the sciences."[212] In fact, it was not merely a matter of one great work as opposed to many mediocre ones. Scholars could even achieve renown without writing at all. We have already seen that Magliabecchi achieved renown in the Republic of Letters despite his origins in trade. But that renown was apparently not the result of his brilliant scholarship either. In its *éloge* of Magliabecchi, which referred to him as "an Oracle in the sciences," the *Bibliothèque italique* remarked that "although it would have been very easy to enrich Savants with his Works, he never composed any, at least which came to the knowledge of the Public. He seemed to be limited to enlightening himself without respite, or in enlightening others in a way that would bring him the least fame."[213]

The emphasis on acts rather than works is evident in much of the community's eulogistic literature. One compliment to the "savants of the first order" was to say they had been "born for the good of the Republic of Letters," not necessarily because of their scholarship, but because they were so helpful to their colleagues. The *Bibliothèque angloise*, for example, hailed Montfaucon in this way in his lifetime because of his generosity in collecting manuscripts for the work of John Porter, Bishop of Oxford; and the *éloge* of Perizonius in the *Histoire critique de la République des Lettres* ended its biographical account, "Such was the life of a Man, born for the good of Letters, who spared neither late nights, nor work, who consumed all his strength in the noble & ardent desire to be useful to the Public."[214] A non-publishing teacher like Jean-Robert Chouet of the Genevan Academy deserved perhaps more credit than a solitary scholar devoted to publication. According to the *éloge* in the *Bibliothèque italique*, "Although Monsieur CHOUET passed the best part of his life in Civil Employments, & he is not known by any work in the Republic of Letters; his name nevertheless deserves to be conserved with honor, as one of those who have contributed the most to the flourishing of good Philosophy in the past century. He did more than be an Author; He was one of these great Masters who form others into them."[215] Johann Joachim Ewald paid the same compliment to Formey, who was both professor of philosophy at the Collège Français in Berlin and a journalist who performed a teaching function for his public. "Occupied as You are Monsieur in perfecting so many others who call You the author of all their *lumières*," he wrote in 1748, "You merit more than any other, to be for a long time a subject of esteem and admiration."[216]

We have already seen in our first chapter that the Republic of Letters functioned through networks of exchange and mutual assistance. But an examination of the various biographies and *éloges* indicates that such cooperation was not only the basis for scholarly relations, but also an acknowledged ideal of the community. As we have just observed, for a community avowedly dedicated to scholarship, the primacy in its value system of social interaction rather than scholarly output is remarkable. Even its literary output was of course a form of social communication and help, and it was recognized as such in the *éloges*. But many of the other virtues described in such literature directly addressed the issue of functioning within the community. If we look back at Macclesfield's description of what should go into an ideal *éloge*, we can see how many of the details he suggested referred specifically to a scholar's place in learned society. True, he mentioned what books Folkes had published, not to mention his "valuable Collection of English coins," but these visible scholarly achievements took up little space and came at the very end of a list made off the top of his head. The list instead emphasized indications that Folkes was accepted by his fellow scholars and participated fully in the activities of the group. For example, it stressed his membership in certain scholarly institutions, a membership which not only labelled him as a recognized member of the community but also hinted that he had entered into the collective aspect of scholarship. The *éloge*, he said, should mention which university Folkes had attended, and which college, when he was elected a Fellow of the Royal Society, and—significantly—"what services he did to the Society." Even more important was the inordinate amount of space Macclesfield gave to a man's contact with other scholars; it was crucial to mention both which learned men the scholar had known well, both at home and abroad, and which he kept in touch with later. It is no coincidence that Des Maizeaux's life of Bayle ends with a list of his friends in every country.

The importance of this lies in the fact that such obituaries were not merely accounts of the lives of scholars, but *éloges*, eulogies, which were intended to praise as well as to inform. So details of contact with other scholars did not simply provide facts for the reader, but reasons to think highly of the subject. The good qualities mentioned in connection with the deceased may not have been real, but they did represent an idealized view of just what comprises the character of the illustrious. Many of the virtues cited directly addressed the issue of functioning within the community. These included openness with information, the willingness to lend books, assistance in other people's research, instructive conversation, anxiousness to be of service, gentleness with opponents, and even assisting indigent men of letters. Thus Des Maizeaux's portrayal of Bayle was not intended to justify his position in various controversies. He boasted instead that the reader would find "a faithful Portrait of his Manners: humble, modest; a constant, obliging, disinterested Friend."[217] To be a truly great scholar, apparently, meant to be generous and cooperative with other scholars.

These virtues were naturally useful ones for all members of the community. But some even assisted in forming the idea of a community in the first place. For other praiseworthy features were simple correspondence with other scholars and membership in learned societies. To conduct a *commerce de lettres* or to participate in the proceedings of the Academy of St. Petersburg was to acknowledge the importance of community, an acknowledgement which had to be made for the sake of communal survival.

Beyond the Pale

If they failed or refused to recognize these fundamentals, great scholars were therefore not so great after all. Admittedly, such a savant could still be a

"savant of the first order," but his fame might come largely from his unpleasantness rather than his works. When 1716 saw the death of a number of
famous men, the *nouvelles littéraires* of the *Journal littéraire* had a special note
about each.

> It seems that the end of this year was fatal to savants of the first Order. The
> celebrated M. de *Leibnitz*, who recently died at Hanover, was certainly one
> of the greatest ornaments of the Republic of Letters; and these Provinces
> recently lost the savant M. *Cuper* (Gisbertus Cuperus) Burgermeester of
> Deventer, well known in the savant world by his great knowledge of
> Antiquity: as well as M. *Gronovius* learned Professor at Leiden, well known
> for his quarrels with almost all the other Savants: He did not have the
> satisfaction before his death to learn of that of his greatest Antagonist M.
> *Kuster*, which happened at Paris a little while before that of M. *Gronovius*
> in Leiden.[218]

As this passage suggests, Gronovius' main feature in the minds of his fellows
was his disobliging character; far from promoting the idea of community, he
disregarded it. Mencke said that Gronovius, like all critics, imagined that if
another author were praised, then his own reputation was in some way
damaged: "where, I say, is the talented Writer of this Century, whom
Gronovius has not persecuted to excess? . . . [U]nhappy, and three times unhappy is the man, who has in the least clashed with the Sentiments of
Gronovius, Gronovius will hate him, will pursue him, will make him suffer the
pain of his temerity."[219] A well-known figure might receive no *éloge* at all if
his behavior was not worthy of the honor. A latter-day devotee of the
minister Pierre Jurieu, the corrector Pierre Cartier de St.-Philippe, complained in 1750 that Jurieu had never received an *éloge* anywhere,[220] a result
doubtless of his violent attacks on the politics and religion of most of his
associates.

The behavior of such figures as Gronovius and Jurieu was disagreeable in
part because of their deliberate disregard for the demands of community.
While personal antagonism naturally played a significant role in their activities, they also demonstrated an interest in different priorities from those of
their colleagues. They placed other matters—the quality of scholarship and
the purity of religious and political conviction—above the ideals of generosity
and cooperation. Yet in large part it was the way a scholar behaved in the
community, his acknowledgement of its nature *as* a community, which was
an important means of judging his worthiness in the hierarchy. When Hans
Sloane was elected to the Académie Royale des Sciences, the president,
Bignon, said the whole group was particularly struck by his letter of thanks.

> It has just achieved what your Works and your reputation had begun, and
> it has completely convinced us that you possess to the sovereign degree all

the qualities of a true Academician. We already knew that you were infinitely estimable through your merit; but now we feel that you are no less amiable through your modesty, and that to a profound knowledge, you join an extreme politeness, and all the virtues which bring pleasure to society.[221]

It was really not enough, in other words, to be a brilliant scholar. The Academy was echoing a frequent compliment in the Republic of Letters, which stressed the importance of the heart over the mind, of politeness over intellect. Barbeyrac told Le Clerc that "the qualities of your Heart [are] a thousand times more estimable than all the talents & all the erudition which have secured you such an elevated rank in the Republic of Letters"; an early recommendation for La Croze said that "his Heart has qualities even more excellent than his Mind however beautiful the latter might be."[222] To be "a true Academician" required personal and social qualities which acknowledged and contributed to the whole community.

The issue of elections to academies highlights what has been evident throughout this discussion: that the ranking of scholars within the hierarchy was a matter of judgment by their fellows. It was not possible to become a great scholar on one's own. This point is illustrated by a bizarre incident which took place in 1731. A man called Pingré, who claimed in conversation to be a botanist of the first order, became annoyed when an Amsterdam doctor, Garcin, failed in talking to him to recognize him as a botanist at all. This prompted a propaganda war in the journals in which Garcin claimed that Pingré had never written about or discussed botany, and that in fact when he found out that Garcin himself *was* a botanist, he refused to talk about botany any more. Both men said that the other was simply pretending to be a "savant" botanist. Garcin's satiric attack on Pingré in the *Bibliothèque italique* shows that there were particular ways—besides studying botany—that one became a great botanist in the Republic of Letters. "It is amazing," Garcin wrote,

> that Mr. Pingré shows such a bad humor toward a man who only said after a conversation he had with him, that he did not recognize him as a botanist. I believed that modesty and integrity were appropriate to a learned man, and that they always did him honor. But Mr. Pingré has not used them in his Writings against his Adversaries; probably because he judged that these qualities were not appropriate to a genius of his order, who wanted to acquire reputation. . . . He believes that there is more grandeur of soul in hiding his knowledge in his conversation with Doctors and Botanists, than in the families which give him practice for the exercise of his Profession. He seems in all this to be taking a very different route from other Savants in order to acquire renown. He does not want to

communicate with these Savants. He conceals his knowledge from them. He finds it better to argue individually with people who do not understand the profession he has embraced. . . . The Botanists of Europe, who all know each other, because there is only a small number of them, are surprised never to have heard of a Botanist who is named Mr. Pingré. They are even more surprised that such a talented man as he is in the knowledge of Plants, never had a commerce de Lettres with any Botanist, as they all do among themselves, and finally that he has never been mentioned in the Nouvelles Littéraires, nor in any individual's Letter, as is usual among Botanists.[223]

Garcin naturally meant to intimate that Pingré was not a botanist at all. But the interesting point is that he could not have been a botanist—much less, as he claimed, a botanist of the first order—if he did not participate in the community of botanists. As Garcin suggested, it was communication, interchange, and assistance—participating in the community—which provided the usual route of scholars toward reputation and renown.

Garcin's own botanical credentials, meanwhile, were simply that Jussieu, Boerhaave, Commelin, Sloane, Sherard, and Rand all knew him and knew that he was a botanist.[224] In a social community, the mere fact of knowing another scholar was enough to provide status. These values are evident in the *éloges*, where scholars are praised for the size of their acquaintance. For example, when Formey and Pérard were planning the *éloge* of Mauclerc, their late journalistic and ministerial colleague, Pérard told Formey that although Mauclerc had never written anything besides the *Bibliothèque germanique*, "his Reputation, his Materials for the history of Brandenburg, & the great *Commerce* he had with all the men of Letters will be able to make up for the formal quality of Author which he lacked."[225] Similarly, the *Bibliothèque italique*'s *éloge* of J.-J. Zanichelli, an unusually learned pharmacist, reported that "he was in *commerce Littéraire* with various Savants, both in Venice and elsewhere. . . . Mr. CRISTIN MARTINELLI Noble Venetian, Mr. JACQUES DIEZ, & Mr. the Doctor ODDONI, delighted much in his conversation. And the following received his Letters with pleasure; Messrs. *Morgagni, Vallisnieri, Macoppe, Poleni, Monti, Marsili, Micheli, Giorgi, Lancisi, Bonanni, Langio, Bourguet, & Negrisoli.*"[226] Niceron wrote of Etienne Baluze that he was "connected during his whole life with all the men of Letters in France, & in Foreign Countries," while Jacques Rhenferd, professor of theology and philosophy at the University of Franeker, was distinguished by "universal applause, & the great crowd which appeared right away at his Lessons and his Classes, & which he always kept . . . all this made him shine, not only in the University of *Franeker*, but also in all the Republic of Letters in general."[227]

This emphasis on the role of colleagues in the determination of status will explain the revulsion of most of the Republic of Letters against those, like Pingré, who tried to bypass the acknowledgement of the community in their quest for greatness. John Toland appears particularly negatively by making false claims on the subject: "After having spent some time in Holland, M. Toland went back to England, where he bragged of having merited the esteem & the friendship of several savant Men of the United Provinces; but [of] M. *Limborch* & M. *le Clerc*, whom he named in particular, the first declared that he had never seen him, & the other declared that he had only seen him twice, & that far from applauding his new opinions, he had opposed them."[228] The verb *s'ériger*—to set oneself up—was often tossed off in disgust to describe someone who took it into his head to exercise power in the Republic when he had acquired that power from no one but himself. As we observed in our discussion of journalism, one objection to the existence of journalists was that they had been chosen by nobody, yet acted as if they could judge books for the rest of the Republic of Letters. Thus Jean Le Clerc said that Bayle had "set himself up [*s'est érigé*] as universal judge of all the Books which will appear from now on"; Huet accused Baillet's *Jugemens des Savans* of the same crime. The same could hold true for other professions; Mencke criticized all grammarians of arrogance for occupying themselves with trivial issues yet "setting themselves up [*s'érigent*] as Sovereigns of the Republic of Letters."[229]

Knowing One's Place

Despite what Mencke said about grammarians (such as Gronovius), the problem was not that these activities were not worthwhile. It was simply not accepted to accord oneself status or to acknowledge too freely the status that one had. This is why most scholars considered it improper to write the *extrait* of one's own book; others could praise you, but you should not praise yourself. Perhaps the most consistent theme in the *éloges* and other literature about the behavior of scholars was the necessity for modesty. The Abbé du Pons, defending Antoine Houdar de la Motte in the *Journal littéraire*, wrote that "the sovereign *éloge* of M. *de la Motte* is that of having known how to ally the most eminent talents, with the most modest opinion of himself."[230] And if a savant failed to display the requisite modesty, his colleagues would be quick to notice. Thus when Barnaud discussed the fall from favor of Christian Wolff, which actually stemmed from the disagreement of his ideas with Pietism, he neglected almost entirely anything but Wolff's character. "We had already learned of the disgrace of Mr. Wolfius. . . . They say that he showed a too good opinion of himself, & that he had been accustomed to speak of others with too much scorn. Such a way of behaving is not proper for making Friends. I know at least one man of wit, who saw him at Halle, & who was very little content with him on this score. I can only speak of it historically. As for his Metaphysics, I don't know anything about it at all."[231]

As this example indicates, it did not matter if a scholar was talented; he still was required to be modest. The literature is full of references to able men who were imperfect citizens of the Republic of Letters; as Jean Cornand de la Crose wrote of Gaspar Scioppus, he "was one of the best Grammarians of this Age, but he knew it too well, for he quotes himself on almost every page."[232] Indeed, Maturin Veyssière La Croze said that he had more admiration for the modest of low station than for talented men overcome by vanity. In a not entirely atypical letter, he wrote to Gisbert Cuper in 1716:

> I am very edified by what you tell me, Monsieur, of the esteem that you have in general for all the men of letters, even for those who can only pass as demi-savants. It is certain that the greatest or the smallest literature should not be the rule of our esteem, that we should properly speak only of piety and virtue. All the knowledge of men is a very little thing in itself. However it often has the unhappiness to produce ill effects, among others pride, and the injurious scorn of others. . . . As for me I will always esteem more highly a shoemaker or a tailor who is a decent humble man than a proud man of letters, be he more savant than all the Scaligers & all the Saumaises.[233]

Pride was a sin no matter who committed it. But even in La Croze's eyes it was worse for those who had no claim to it. Mixed in with his edifying words above is another sentiment: disgust with untalented scholars with no perspective on their own abilities. "How many examples are there in our time of people whose knowledge is much below mediocrity, who nevertheless imagine themselves to be Heroes, and who insult left and right all those they encounter on their way? One must love these people as men & as Christians; but it seems to me that it is very difficult not to scorn them as men of letters."[234] The problem, again, was the self-assignment of glory, as Jacques Bernard told Delaissement in a similar passage: "I pardon ignorance easily, when it is accompanied with modesty; but I cannot suffer an ignorant person, who wants to be esteemed by the whole Human Race, and made everywhere the Master and the doctor."[235] Thus the "Titulomanie" so hilariously criticized by Mencke in his *Charlatanerie des savans* focussed primarily on the failure of scholars to deserve the titles which they had given themselves.

> [A]re you not amazed along with me at the unmeasured ambition of our Fathers, who dared to transport into the Academy Titles reserved for

Roman Senators, & crowned Heads. See, I pray you, this Man, unknown
even in the suburbs of his City, arrogantly give himself the Title of *Very-
Renowned*? See this one, who has himself called the *Magnificent*, despite the
frightful Misery to which he is reduced? Would you believe that this
limited Genius, without judgment, without experience, vaunts himself as a
great Personage, consummate in affairs, in a position to give the best
Counsels in the world: And that this other, whom a Schoolboy of two
days could teach, qualifies himself as *Very-Excellent*, even though this Title,
joined to that of *Very-Admirable*, is the only Praise that the Emperor
Charlemagne won for his Treatise of Images against the Greeks? However
today, O Tyranny of Usage, there is no little Doctor with a simple tonsure
who does not have the right to appropriate it, & who is even treated as an
imbecile if, at the example of M. *Bouillaud*, he refused the Title of
Excellency. But what am I saying, Excellency? Since the beginning of the
Restoration of the Sciences, has not this fury for Titles, & if I dare to speak
so, this *Titlemania*, been carried as far as giving a simple Jurist [Bartole] the
Title of *Invincible monarch of the Empire of Letters*. Do not expect that I speak
to you here, Messieurs, of these Scholastic Doctors, Doctors [who are]
Angelic, Seraphic, Illuminated, Subtle, Admirable, Universal, well-
founded, very-resolute; nor of this Visionary, who according to the report
of several people worthy of belief, had his Portrait engraved on a steel plate
underneath a Crucifix, to which he inquired laconically, *Lord Jesus, do you
love me?* And the Saviour responded to him emphatically, *Yes, very-
illustrious, very-excellent, & very-learned Lord* Segerus, *Crowned poet of his
Imperial Majesty, & very-worthy Rector of the University of Wittenberg, Yes, I
love you.*[236]

Pride, then, was a particular evil in those who did not deserve it. Everyone
in the Republic of Letters should be modest, but it was especially important
for those lower on the hierarchy to understand their place in that hierarchy.
If a scholar was young, obscure, unheralded by journals, or had no regular
correspondence with well-known figures, he would have to take care in his
relations with those more acknowledged by the community. Demonstrations
that he was not aware of (or defied being placed in) his lowly position might
be greeted by outrage at his temerity. One reason for this was that those of
higher merit or higher rank in the community were thought to deserve
better treatment. The author of an article in the *Histoire critique de la
République des Lettres* arguing over Pliny with the Abbé Sevin protested that
"I am persuaded that my reflections on this subject cannot shock
him. . . . [T]hey will be within the proper limits, which are demanded by the
esteem & the consideration of which his merit renders him worthy."[237] Once
an author had established his position, through public recognition, office,

reviews, or otherwise, it was often his books which were judged by his rank, rather than his rank by his books. Thus the *Histoire critique de la République des Lettres* said the second volume of Perizonius' *Origines Babylonicae & Aegyptiacae* was "to be recommended by the merit of the Author, who for a long time has been among the number of those Savants who make the glory and the delights of the Republic of Letters."[238] Similarly, the *Bibliothèque raisonnée* reviewed Jean Le Clerc's *Histoire des Provinces-Unies* by saying that "MR. LE CLERC has been so celebrated for such a long time, by a great number of Works of different sorts, & he holds such a considerable rank in the Republic of Letters, that it is almost enough to see his name at the head of a Book, to know what one must expect in it."[239] This sort of judgment could work both ways, for if a book by a famous author was bound to be good, a book by an unknown one was bound to be bad. Antoine de la Barre de Beaumarchais, in explaining the anonymity of his *Lettres sérieuses et badines*, said that "I was afraid, in the first place, that if people knew who I am, they would be predisposed by the luster or by the obscurity of my name and would judge my Work by that."[240] It was obscurity rather than luster which Beaumarchais feared.

The unwritten rules thus demanded that those high in the scholarly hierarchy deserved especially respectful treatment. A model for relations with the great might be found in the letters of the young Jean Barbeyrac to John Locke. When Barbeyrac first wrote to Locke in 1702, he was a 28–year-old teacher at the Collège Français in Berlin and had not yet acquired his later reputation as a jurist.[241] He had never met Locke, but conveniently had a connection with him through Coste, with whom Barbeyrac had a *commerce de lettres*; thus when Barbeyrac sent his friend a few remarks on the style of Coste's French translation of the *Essay*, his name came to Locke's attention. When Coste reported Locke's goodwill toward the young author, based partly, it turned out, on his acquaintance with his late uncle, this authorized Barbeyrac to write directly to him: "Although I do not have the honor of being known to you, I take the liberty to write to you, without fearing to appear too brash. . . . Even if I were not reassured by what public renown says of your affability toward everyone, I would find a more than sufficient reason for confidence in the kindnesses which you have just shown me through the intervention of M. Coste."[242] Barbeyrac thanked Locke for his favor while abasing himself before the great doctor:

Accept then Monsieur, that I demonstrate myself my gratitude for it . . . at least as much as the feebleness of my wit permits me; for I avow, to my great regret, that I do not know how to find strong enough expressions, to let you know how sensible I am to such a great and such an unexpected honor. Who would have said, in effect, when I went to throw onto paper,

without design, and for my own use, a few Remarks, concerning the Style
of the French Translation of the Incomparable *Essay*, or rather the accomplished work, on the *Human Understanding*, that these minutiae would
procure me the glorious advantage of seeing my name come as far as the
ears of the Excellent author of this Book, and that they would even attract
authentic testimonies of his goodwill?[243]

Barbeyrac was particularly bowled over by Locke's inquiry about his
opinion of the work itself, and not just the translation. To ask someone's
opinion of a work was always flattering, for it suggested that both people
were on equal terms. Pierre Daval, a refugee friend of Des Maizeaux's in
England, said after the appearance of the latter's life of St.-Evremond, "I
regard as a pure Compliment what you ask me about The Style of M^r. de S^t.
Evremond. I am far from having such a good opinion of myself as to believe
myself capable of noting how this style is blamable or excusable."[244]
Barbeyrac took a similar tone with Locke. "I assure you, Monsieur, that if the
opinion of my incapacity did not keep me continually on guard against the
surprises of conceit, there would be something in that which would flatter
my vanity extremely. . . . As for me, who only regard myself, and with good
reason, as a Schoolboy, I would have to be very rash to dare to make a
Judgment on a Work as profound and as well thought-out as your *Essay*."[245]
Barbeyrac continued in this vein for some time, saying that if he had found
a few small difficulties in the piece, "all that I can conclude from that, is that
I do not have enough penetration to enter into your thought, or to understand the reasons you had for expressing yourself in a certain manner." He
had proposed one objection to Coste, and now asked Locke to let him know
via his secretary "in what way I am wrong."[246]

Barbeyrac appeared to understand very well the proprieties of his position.
He could only correspond with the great man at all because of his personal
connections with him, his late uncle and Coste, and because Locke had first
expressed an interest in him. If it had not been for that, Barbeyrac would
probably have restricted his correspondence to his *commerce* with Coste. His
letter to Locke was extremely flattering; every line emphasized his own
unimportance in relation to the philosopher and his modesty about his own
talents. It was up to Locke to forge past these protests and, in essence, raise
Barbeyrac in station by encouraging him to express his opinion on Locke's
book. Barbeyrac recognized this; his second letter said that Locke's praise of
him in his response to the first was "an obliging and ingenious turn, which
you are using, to encourage a person in whom you believe you can perceive
some disposition to look sincerely for Truth, and to follow its lights."[247] In
this second letter, although he remained respectful and self-deprecating, he
felt more free to mention his thoughts and his own work and to ask Locke

for his comments. Locke's benevolence extended not only to encouragement, but even to the gift of an English bible and a dictionary to help
Barbeyrac learn English.[248]

Barbeyrac was grateful, but he had evidently hoped for more. In his first
letter he had presumed on his new contact with Locke to mention his
"inclination for England, which I regard as the Center of the Sciences," and
to hint broadly at his desire to live there if "Providence" would ever furnish
him with employment.[249] The English books were the result. Yet it was not
surprising that Barbeyrac should have tried such a ploy, since, as we have
seen, it was standard for important figures in the scholarly community to act
as patrons for the more obscure. Samuel Masson was even more blatant in his
appeal to Gisbert Cuper in 1713; he first addressed an article in his literary
journal to the antiquary, whom he did not know, and then leapt on the
chance he had created to correspond with him directly. "It is infinitely
glorious to me, Monsieur, that a person like you, of the most elevated rank
in the *Republic of Letters*, deigns to approve the Liberty that I took in
addressing to him the little & unworthy *Piece* which makes up the I. Article
of the *Fourth* Volume of the *Hist^re. Critique*. . . . For alas! young as I am,
destitute of so much of the help necessary for Letters, a fugitive, a poor
escapee from the most bloody Persecution which ever was, I cannot be
considered more than a Novice in the Learned World!"[250] Masson must have
hoped to take advantage of Cuper's well-known sympathy for the Huguenot
refugees in procuring himself a better position.

Reflected Glory

Yet jobs and the stature of office were only the more tangible aspects of the
usefulness of associating with highly-ranked scholars. The fact that a young
and unimportant man such as Barbeyrac had a great philosopher's encouragement would be duly noted by the Republic of Letters; and César de Missy
was right to tell Voltaire that his *lettres de noblesse* came precisely from the
philosophe's willingness to correspond with him. For in a society which so
emphatically endorsed the importance of social relations and judged the
actions and productions of those acknowledged great by their authors rather
than themselves, the obscure could rise to prominence through their connections. It was thus self-serving of the *frères* Masson to publish praises of their
own works in the *Histoire critique*, despite the apparent modesty of the
proceeding; Jean Masson published a "Lettre de Mr. *J. Masson* à Mr. *de
Valincour*" remarking slyly that "I avow, that when even the flattering letters
of several Savants among my friends would have given me a good opinion of
my *Vie d'Horace*; never, however, would I have imagined, that a person

distinguished, as you are, by so many things, & with a such an enlightened
and delicate taste, would have deigned to encourage an unknown by compliments like those with which you have honored me."[251] His apparent
flattery of Valincour was actually an advertisement for the praise he himself
had received, just as his brother Samuel's addresses to Cuper in the same
journal were not only an appeal to Cuper himself, but also an attempt to
associate his name with that of the great statesman and antiquary.

The idea that who you know is as important as what you know was taken
to extremes by a former French monk characterized by the bishop of London
as "this great Cheat Gabillon."[252] During a trip to England in 1707 Frédéric-
Auguste Gabillon, who had already acquired numerous enemies in France
and the Netherlands,[253] outraged many with his tricks and presumptuous
behavior. Gabillon had earlier attempted to be ordained as a Protestant
minister in the Netherlands, but was rejected by the Walloon Synod.[254] In
various works he professed his Protestant orthodoxy; in particular he wrote
a virulent attack on the Remonstrant Le Clerc, with whom he had had an
argument in a bookshop, claiming that he was both a Socinian and an
ignoramus.[255] He attempted to dedicate this work to various famous people,
but no one was willing to accept it; in the end an unsuspecting English
aristocrat lent his name to Gabillon's campaign.

Gabillon's antics in England were various. John Chamberlayne told Jean Le
Clerc, "S[r]. I could tell you how he cheated a Bookseller of a large Sum of
money; how he behaved himself at Baron Schuts house the Hannover
Envoy, and many other of his pranks, but you will hear them from other
hands."[256] Among other things, Gabillon claimed to have great influence with
powerful figures. He told both the bishop of London and the queen that he
was commissioned by the States of Holland to write an account of the present
state of England, and asked their financial assistance; this request "appeared so
foolish" to the queen that she put him off, while the bishop doubted its
entire veracity.[257] Gabillon told one minister that he could sway the Duke of
Ormonde to provide him with a better benefice, and cheated another,
Cigala, of nearly all his money in return for presenting him to the bishop of
London. According to Chamberlayne, Gabillon,

> with an unspeakable impudence, and with an air of great familiarity,
> desired him (as his Lordship himself told me) to give him some good
> Benefice as soon as it shou'd be in his power, assuring his Lo[rdshi]p that
> he was a very honest man and his particular friend: whereupon the B[p]. in
> great indignation said to him, thou confident fellow, I have known this
> honest man (meaning M[r]. Cigala) near 20 years, and I have not known
> thee so many weeks, and yet thou hast the impudence to make him
> believe that thy recommendations have weight with me, get thee out of
> my doors and let me never see thee more.[258]

These false claims to have powerful friends were similar to Toland's boasts about the esteem of people he did not even know. But Gabillon went one step further in his claims. On a number of occasions while travelling in Essex, he pretended actually to *be* Jean Le Clerc. One French refugee, d'Origny Delaloge, found the false Le Clerc (wearing "a very blond wig, a black suit, short with a Damask vest, a clerical collar, and the rose on his hat, which made me take him for a minister") walking at nine o'clock in the morning outside his house. Gabillon addressed him in English, asking if this was "the house of M . . ."[259] When Delaloge had told him the householder was out and had called the servant and told him to introduce Gabillon to the master, Gabillon addressed him in French.

> [A]ccosting me, he asked me in French, if I did not know him; having answered him, that I did not believe I had ever seen him before, He replied, do you know Monsieur Le Clerc you who come from Holland? I answered that I Knew his famous name by his works, esteemed and honored his person and his merit infinitely, but that I had never seen him. At which this Monsieur said to me, eh bien M^r. I myself am M^r. Le Clerc. I immediately showed him that I felt an extreme joy to see a man to whom savants have so many obligations, & that for myself, there was not one of his books which I had not read.[260]

Gabillon told Delaloge that he had come incognito to England to take a chair of oriental languages at Cambridge, that he had his Latin inaugural address in his pocket at that moment, but that he was keeping things secret in case something should go wrong at the last minute. He was fed and invited to stay to dinner. Meanwhile he talked much of literature and tried to wrest from Delaloge's grasp a manuscript of French verse and prose the refugee had written "Saying that he would have them printed and insert them in his biblioteque choisie"; Delaloge managed to prevent this. Eventually his bizarre behavior—walking away when Delaloge stopped a coach for him, not to mention some of his talk—made Delaloge suspect this was not the real Le Clerc.[261]

But Gabillon managed to play the same trick on other ministers, and, as Chamberlayne said, "rambled from one Ministers house to another and received abundance of Caresses and good entertainment from them all." In the end he invited them to "a Splendid Dinner" at an inn in Romford, Essex, after which he slipped off "and left them in pawn for the reckoning."[262] According to the pro-Le Clerc propaganda, Le Clerc's reaction "was only to laugh, since he knew the impudence of this personage."[263] In fact all this occasioned much distress to Le Clerc, who in any case was concerned for his reputation in England, and the theologian and his friends spent much energy collecting information about the imposture.[264] Gabillon was trying to do Le Clerc harm; but he had also discovered that the codes of hospitality in the Republic of Letters, which garnered scholars good treatment if they came recommended by the great, presented even brighter prospects if they *were* the great.[265] He had taken the principle to its logical extreme.

Connections to those of high status, then, could bring stature in the community through a number of different avenues. The giving of gifts and information and the performance of services could put others in one's debt, raising one's status in relation to them. Deference to powerful scholars might incur their goodwill and perhaps the exercise of their patronage; better employment and higher prominence might result. Finally, simple association with the famous gave one an aura of respectability, since the judgment of well-known figures was to be relied upon. This connection, moreover, could even be extended to the editing of an author's works or to writing his biography, so that a lowly writer, a James Boswell or a Pierre Des Maizeaux, could be dragged into posterity by hanging on to the coattails of the great.

This analysis did not escape contemporaries. Charles Perrault pointed out in his collection of lives of the famous that most eulogies which showed the slightest eloquence "were more the affair of the Preacher than of the Deceased, and if the reputation of the person speaking often received a considerable boost, that of the Dead almost always stayed in the same condition as before."[266] Baillet made the same point about translators and editors, remarking that most people who had put out editions of or commentaries on ancient authors over the last two centuries had failed to be objective, instead having "covered them with glory, in the hope that this glory would reflect on back on themselves."[267] The matter was of singular importance for those milling, as it were, around the coffins of the late Locke and Bayle. Despite Coste's other works, which included French translations of Shaftesbury, Xenophon, Plautus, and others, as well as his many editions of Montaigne, Coste's status in the Republic of Letters was based largely on his relationship with Locke (and, through Locke, Shaftesbury). Not only is this his only claim to fame today, but in a contemporary account of his life it is these connections rather than his works which are stressed.[268] And when in 1729 Charles de la Motte tried to persuade Des Maizeaux finally to finish his biography of Bayle, he pointed out that if he did, "your name will always be linked with that of M. Bayle."[269] This was apparently a good incentive, since the new edition of the *Dictionary* to appear in 1730 finally saw the completion of Des Maizeaux's *Vie de Bayle* after stalling for twenty-three years. Certainly Des Maizeaux himself acknowledged this in 1734 in the second English edition of the *Dictionary*, where he first flattered Walpole by linking him with Bayle and into the bargain threw himself and his connections with both. "Permit me only to say, that as this great and applauded Work is like to last, Posterity (for Posterity will judge without anger or envy) will not think it unnatural to see the name of SIR ROBERT WALPOLE prefixed to the GRAND

DICTIONARY of MR BAYLE; and if by this way (this only way) I can purchase permanence to my own humble name, it is an Ambition which I hope merits pardon."[270]

The Preservation of Community

Des Maizeaux demonstrates the proper humility here, abasing himself before both a potential political patron and, more importantly, the memory of his subject. But others tried to profit from literary connections to exalt themselves in a more negative way. We have already seen that the reputations of great men were considered particularly important to preserve. Once a man was deemed of high rank, his name alone was sufficient testimony to the quality of his future works. And if such works were of poor quality, or the man himself showed *faiblesses*, in the interests of the community's self-image it was best to keep that quiet. Consequently, if scholars of lower rank ignored their position and were critical of the great, this was not only reprehensible, but destructive to the community.

Admittedly, it was permitted to correct famous men if it were done politely and modestly. Even well-known scholars owed this politeness to each other. Charles-Louis de Beausobre reported that his father's posthumous supplement to Jacques Lenfant's work on the Hussite war was "a Work in which my Father repairs the errors of this great man; but with the consideration and the respect which are due to the memory of Mr. Lenfant."[271] Similarly, Camusat ridiculed Denis de Sallo for protesting in the *Journal des sçavans* that Spanheim's work on medals was the work "of a man who affected to correct the Scaligers & other heroes of Literature on minutiae, & this in order to establish his reputation on theirs. No one could have been less capable of this manoeuvre than M. Spanheim: he corrected with politeness the errors which had slipped from these great men, because the subject required it of him. . . . But he did it modestly."[272]

Camusat insisted that this was the right of all authors, although he was quick to say that even if it belonged only to the great, "the profound erudition of M. Spanheim authorized him to use it."[273] But if this was so, humility was an even greater duty for those of a lower station, for the structure of the Republic of Letters had to be preserved. Barbeyrac provides a good example of the way unknown scholars ought to behave. As we saw, he did not cease scraping and bowing before Locke as he questioned one point in the *Essay*. Four years later, after having published his remarks on Pufendorf, he still had the same view of the proper relations to the great. Des Maizeaux praised his notes favorably in relation to the text, to which Barbeyrac responded:

I am delighted that what you have read of my Remarks on *Pufendorf* did not displease you: but I do not accept & I do not believe I can accept the too advantageous judgment, by which you say the Notes are worth more than the Text. Even independently of all comparison, I do not know if one should scorn *Pufendorf* so much. . . . I am not afraid to say . . . that we do not have such a good Work in this genre. . . . It seems to me that *Pufendorf* has taken the right direction in explaining Nat. Law & that one can only build on his principles. Now, short of saying many things which are new, it is necessary to leave an Author in peaceable possession of the glory which he acquired in writing on a subject: & it would be a particular temerity in a person with no name in the world, to give people reason to believe that he wants to raise himself up on the ruins of a famous Writer.[274]

The *Journal littéraire* praised Barbeyrac in 1720 for behaving in the same way toward Grotius: remarking on his errors but doing so "modestly, without dishonoring this great man, whose erudition, wit, judgment, & other good qualities he esteems more than anyone."[275]

Many other authors echoed the same view: that for the obscure to correct or attack the great smacked of both vanity and presumption. As Beaumarchais expressed it, "When you attack Writers who are well-esteemed, if you do not have a great name in the world yourself, you run the risk of making people see you as brazen, & it is very rare that you can persuade anyone otherwise."[276] So when the ultimate *demi-savant*, a Prussian cavalry officer named Christoph Heinrich Oelven, disabled by poorly-applied mercury treatments for venereal disease, began writing a satirical paper against Maturin Veyssière La Croze, the learned community in Berlin was particularly shocked. Oelven had originally asked La Croze to visit him, thinking he was Jean Cornand de la Crose of the *Bibliothèque choisie*; "I went to his house," La Croze reported, "& I found a man who only talked to me of Anagrams & the philosopher's stone." But he continued his visits and even lent Oelven books; thus he was surprised in 1708 when the *Monatliche Praesenten* began appearing, as it did for two years, full of insults against him.[277] Oelven was, in fact, a member of the Berlin Academy, which was at this point still not well-established;[278] Charles-Etienne Jordan nevertheless wrote of him that he "was among men of Letters, what *Momus* was among the *Gods*."[279] Certainly his scholarship seemed to be lacking; La Croze and Cuper had a good laugh over Oelven's printed explication of a medal in which he transcribed "Scymnus de Chio" as "Hymnus de Chiv."[280]

As a *demi-savant* who did not understand his place, Oelven was not to be dealt with or included in scholarly society. Henri Basnage de Beauval had been the means for Oelven to get the letter of approbation from Bignon which he so proudly printed with his article; and La Croze said that "M^r. de Beauval should be ashamed to prostitute men of the rank of M^r. l'Abbé Bignon, & to make them write letters to such persons. Everyone is mocking it here, & even those who do not like me at all are annoyed about it. Should M^r. Oelven write a dozen works against me, I would never respond to them."[281] Leibniz had urged La Croze to this view, saying, according to Jordan, that he should "not respond to a man who was completely ignorant of the proprieties one observes in a dispute."[282] Spanheim, to whom Oelven had written twice in London against La Croze, also "did not judge him worthy of response."[283]

Such men were not even in the Republic of Letters, since they would not obey its rules. Oelven perhaps had the excuse of his disease and its treatment; in April of 1710 he went "insane & furious," a condition from which the doctors predicted he would never recover.[284] But, fairly or not, Des Maizeaux used the same logic about Marchand. De la Motte had already praised him for not being responsible for the greatest excesses of their dispute.[285] In the apophatic early lines of an unfinished pamphlet of 1729, Des Maizeaux said that he would not respond to Marchand's new *libelle* on the occasion of the 1729 edition of the letters because Marchand was beneath his notice. "It is in vain, Monsieur, that you press me to respond to the Libelle of the S^r. Marchand. Ha! Who would want to throw one's lot in with a man who invents & raves brazenly whatever his Malignity suggests to him, & whom the most vulgar insults cost nothing? Consequently, the dispute is over: an *honnête homme* does not measure himself against a rogue."[286]

Both Oelven and Marchand, then, were accused of presuming to attack those above their station, an accusation based in part on their apparent ignorance of the etiquette of the Republic of Letters.[287] To refuse to debate with them, like La Croze, or to pretend to, like Des Maizeaux, was to drive home their presumption at including themselves in the learned community. If they were aware of the rules of literary society, they would know that it was not done to insult the great; their opponents, in La Croze's case at least, did not respond because such behavior suggested that there was no reason to include them in the social network of the Republic. To do so, as La Croze said, would be to "prostitute" oneself.

For it was the perceived failure to understand their station, or how to improve that station, which was behind the protests about Coste and Marchand. To "the friends of Mr. Locke," and particularly "les amis de Mr. Bayle," editions of famous authors' works which included corrections, textual alterations, and additions, were apparently an attempt to build a reputation on a connection with, and even a triumph over, the late philosophers. Not only were they critical, but they were not modest and humble in their criticism. The attacks on Marchand after his editions of Bayle's works accused him of that crime so inimical to the Republic of Letters: vanity. Des Maizeaux said that Marchand had only put out the *Lettres* in order to "figure among the Savants";[288] he was one of those scholars so complained of by contemporaries, who attacked their superiors just to make their names known. "It is apparent," said the *Mémoires de littérature*, "that he imagined that through all these changes he would, so to speak, appropriate this Dictionary, and in some manner make himself the Author of it."[289] To aspire to Bayle's status was presumption itself; yet that was just what Marchand—and, indeed, Des Maizeaux—did. We have already remarked that a major purpose of biography in this period was to inspire emulation, and the lives of the famous served as a pattern for other men's drive toward greatness. As the *Mémoires* suggests, the workers in the Bayle industry not only wanted to publicize Bayle, they wanted to *be* Bayle.[290] Both Marchand and Des Maizeaux tried to write biographical collections similar to Bayle's great *Dictionary*. Des Maizeaux's was never completed, but the lives he published of people like Boileau, Saint-Evremond, Chillingworth, Hales, and even Bayle himself were intended for it. Marchand owned a large collection of biographies, and he prepared, in minuscule handwriting on tiny scraps of paper, articles for a dictionary which was ultimately published posthumously by his friend Allamand.[291] These attempts to re-do the *Dictionary* were the extreme manifestations of the anxiety to emulate the great.

Both men wanted to move up in the hierarchy, a process which, as we have seen, was theoretically possible. After all, if a stocking-merchant like Bourguet or a pharmacist like Zannichelli could acquire status in the Republic of Letters, why not a refugee tutor or corrector of the press? The ideal of the community was that it was open. But it was not completely open, because, of course, to rise in it required the signs of refinement, education, and generosity so stressed in the *éloges*. Both of the principals in the controversy over Bayle's letters were accused of not having the qualities appropriate to real men of letters. Marchand said in a letter that Des Maizeaux "was much less upset about the reputation of M. Bayle, than about the money that he expected from his *Letters*," a fact Marchand said he could understand because "the loss of a few Guineas . . . must have been extremely upsetting for a Man of his character," one who, he said, was so dishonest that he was "a Spy for both the Whigs and the Tories, whom he betrayed one to the other."[292] But it was Marchand who really took the brunt of the mutual beating, for in the eyes of his critics he simply did not fit in.

In the first place, in 1714 Marchand seemed to be more of a *libraire* than a scholar, and his opponents made the distinction abundantly clear. Their writings usually referred to him as "Sieur," the title given to booksellers, and his identification with that trade was constantly held against him. Barbeyrac wrote disdainfully to Des Maizeaux that "if Mess[rs]. Fritsch & Bohm understand their interests, they will not give so much liberty to the director of their press, who can otherwise be very useful to them, if he keeps himself within the limits of his Job."[293] And the published polemics against Marchand made equal play of his pedestrian employment. "You must know, Monsieur," wrote one critic, "that this poor Garçon Libraire took it into his head to make himself an Author; & the violent passion that he has to write, sustained by considerable impudence & confidence, persuaded him very strongly that he had all the qualities necessary to succeed at it."[294] Clearly, his opponents implied, he did not have such qualities; Barbeyrac commented that "the knowledge he has of the title of Books, in his quality of Libraire, makes him believe himself a very talented man; although he has very little knowledge of anything."[295] In fact, he was not even a good *libraire*. The *Mémoires de littérature* said he showed "a crass and shameful ignorance, not only in literary history (which effectively is not his profession), but even in the Book Trade; that is, what concerns the *true Title* of Books, their format, the year of their printing, their different editions, etc.; details known by every Bookseller who is a little talented in his Profession, but unknown to the Sieur Marchand, who from Bookseller has set up as an Author."[296] The fact that such an ignorant person—*a libraire*—could be so arrogant as to correct the famous Bayle infuriated many scholars, because, as one article growled, "of all the species of Animals there is none more odious nor more intolerable than an Ignoramus who claims to be capable and talented."[297] The combination of vanity and obscurity was too much for his opponents to bear.

It was not just that Marchand had been a bookseller and still worked in publishing, although that was a weak spot of which his enemies were pleased to take advantage. There were plenty of *éloges* in the journals for great men who had started in a lowly position in the world. It was rather that Marchand, like Pingré, Oelven, and Gabillon, was walking the wrong route toward greatness. As our many examples have shown, the status system of the Republic of Letters, though nebulous at best, involved fundamental rules about how to acquire reputation. Besides the demonstration of talent and *lumières*, scholars had to become involved in the community. They had to enter into a network of scholars, perform services for others, and behave with the proper deference toward those of already high status. In essence, they had to be acknowledged by the community for behavior which contributed to the cohesion and achievement of the rest of the community. As scholars accrued reputation though a combination of useful works and appropriate behavior, their stature was reinforced by deference from people lower on the scale, whose humble demeanor, in correspondence and in general social communication, showed they recognized the difference of status between them. The process of rising in the community, if correctly followed, was thus self-reinforcing.

But if, on the contrary, an aspiring scholar confused fame with infamy, he might have great difficulties in the Republic of Letters. Marchand's behavior was objectionable because, far from reaffirming the structures of the community, he was attacking them. His decision to attack Bayle and the other well-known figures insulted in the notes and index upset all those to whom rank was an important feature of the learned world. One of his main faults, in their view, was his failure to respect the community's distinctions of status. Some of the people he attacked were not so well known, but, as one critic complained, "Do not think, Monsieur, that if these Writers had been of a superior Order, he would have treated them in another manner: you can count on his speaking no differently, even if they were to hold the premier rank in the Republic of Letters. This appears by what he says of several Persons of a very distinguished merit."[298] Indeed, as another author wrote, the top ranks should be the most concerned by "the Outrage committed against Mr. *Bayle* . . . because there is not one of them who does not have reason to fear (if one suffers that such Impostures become established) that one day their Works will be treated, as those of Mr. *Bayle* have been."[299]

Such shameless vanity overturned the established structure of the community. And by observing no proprieties, it exposed weak spots in scholarly society which many savants felt should be covered up. In the first place, attacks on great men suggested their fallibility, which put the whole power-structure into question. After reading Marchand's edition of the *Lettres*, Le Clerc said it deserved the harsh treatment Des Maizeaux had given it "for having offended so many *honnêtes* people, without cause. What is peculiar is that he says more ill of M^r. *Bayle* himself, than of anyone, for he passes him off as an absolute knave, which is not proper at all in recommending his Letters."[300] Not only did Marchand damage the image of Bayle, the perfect ascetic, independent, generous philosopher, he also exposed problems within the community at large. His policy of spelling out names in the letters and publishing material insulting to living scholars made relations shakier than before. Barbeyrac observed in 1714:

I have . . . received the *Lettres* of M^r. *Bayle*. It is certain that M^r. *Le Clerc* has it in for M^r. *Lenfant*: & I remember having heard the latter talk of a Letter from M^r. *Bayle*, where there were shocking things about M^r. *Le Clerc*, which fell into the hands of M^r. *Le Clerc* himself. This should have obliged M^r. Lenfant not to publish this letter, nor any other similar one, without knowing if M^r. Le Clerc, whose friend he has claimed to be for ages, would not be angry about it. One can see that he had only put the initial letters *P.* & *S.* to mark the P. Simon: but, even if M^r. *Marchand* had not explained these letters in his notes, people would have easily recognized who was concerned. For the rest, if I were in the place of

M^r. Le Clerc, I would be very glad that these sorts of letters are published. You can see by that that for a long time M^r. Bayle did not like him at all, & you can easily guess why.[301]

Instead of reaffirming the community, Marchand's behavior only weakened it. It is small wonder that many considered it so reprehensible.

These stories of cabals, of posses out to protect the integrity of the great, of false botanists, pretended theologians, and insane pamphleteers, show us how fragile in many ways the structure of the Republic of Letters was. They also point to the fact that not only community relations, but also the community's ideals about itself, were structured around the need to preserve that community. The ideal was that all members of the community were equal, or at least that everyone had an equal chance for advancement. But the same ideal dictated that one must advance on the community's terms. Harmony was the goal, however unattainable; so that even though the hierarchy tended to be continually restructured because of its largely non-hereditary basis, it still needed to pattern itself on something and work by special rules. That pattern was provided by the "great" of their era. Since their greatness stemmed in large part from their communal service, to use them as a model—accurate or not—was to promote the cohesion of the Republic. To shatter that model, as Marchand appeared to do, was thus to disassemble the structure of learned society. No one could become *illustre* that way; so that Barbeyrac could write as late as 1740, "I have not seen Marchand's *Histoire de l'Imprimerie*. But it is really true that in the *Nouvelle Bibliothèque* they gave the Author, and several times, too, the title of *Illustrious*. That really made me laugh, and you can bet that Mr. Des Maizeaux will not think that a very appropriate term."[302]

4

OF TWO MINDS

RELIGION, POLITICS, AND THE COMPETITION
OF VALUES

Historians today know of Jean Aymon because of his very useful collection, *Tous les Synodes nationaux des Eglises réformées de France*, a publication serving equally well the Huguenot cause and our studies of it. Aymon, who lived in The Hague, was an ordained minister in the Walloon church but supported his family with the help of a pension from the States-General and by teaching mathematics.[1] Jacques Basnage said that although he led "an obscure life in The Hague, [he] is nevertheless a good Mathematician, according to what the connoisseurs say."[2] Aymon also did some work on the possible reunion of the Catholic and Protestant churches, publishing a *Lettre du sieur Aymon* on the topic in about 1704.[3] In the spring of 1706 he disappeared.

Aymon had received a passport from the States-General that winter to travel to Constantinople to do research on the beliefs of the Greek church.[4] But he never arrived, a fact which would not have surprised his compatriots had they been intercepting his correspondence of the previous autumn. Aymon had written at the end of November to Nicolas Clément, librarian of the Bibliothèque du Roi in Paris, offering him a wonderful deal. He had purchased the huge herbarium—forty volumes containing 5,147 pressed plants—compiled by the late Hermannus of Leiden, and he was offering it to the library at cost.[5] The price of 3,200 florins (the cost of the book, of the auction, and of his stay in Leiden) was very cheap, and a German prince and two English lords had already offered 100 pistoles above this;[6] later he said it was "the one named de Beauval who writes the Ouvrages des Savans here at The Hague" who had proposed to buy the book for this sum.[7] "[B]ut as I did not do it for this purpose & because this work in the hands of a great lord or in the Cabinet of a Prince could be worth twenty-five or thirty thousand Livres, I rejected all the propositions which were made to me. . . . I would only have the pleasure of adding it to his [the king's] Library without demanding anything else above what I have spent or must spend."[8]

This generous offer, which held little interest for Clément, was evidently not all. Aymon seemed to want the pleasure of *literally* adding the herbarium to the Bibliothèque du Roi, for buried on the third page of his letter was the request that Clément let him know by what route it should be sent and what passports were needed; the two countries were, of course, at war. If the king wanted the book, Aymon needed this information

> without delay please so that I can make arrangements about several other things which depend on this & which are of great consequences for me who would also like to have a Passport from his Majesty to take me somewhere where I can give him more effective & more considerable marks of certain good designs which I could not put into effect in the service of his Majesty in the situation where I am. True Christianity, good conscience, & the fidelity which I owe to the Powers under whose Protection I live & even the pension which they give me are motives which will always engage me neither to say nor do anything which could prejudice them, but that should not prevent me from looking for another Asylum & under more advantageous conditions if my conscience is not involved.[9]

Aymon suggested Clément talk to the Abbé Bidal, the man whose correspondence about the reunion of religions had formed the basis of Aymon's published *Lettre*. After that he could explain himself more fully about the confused thoughts rolling in his mind "which are much more important than everything concerning the work of Botany," a work he offered "only with the idea of opening by this means a way of escaping from a certain state of persecution to which I have been reduced by my own confrères because of my sincerity & my good faith & because I do not disguise their erroneous opinions & their irregular conduct not to say abominations which I see everywhere among the Refugees who do not deserve the name of Reformed if they do not change their lives at least those whom I know."[10]

Aymon's apparent disgust with his Huguenot colleagues and desire to return to his homeland were perhaps explicable when one thought of his past. According to his own account, he had been born to a Catholic family in the Dauphiné in 1661 and studied belles-lettres and mathematics at Grenoble, theology at Turin, and civil and canon law in Rome. Through the intervention of Hercule de Berzet, bishop of Maurienne in Savoy, the pope granted Aymon a dispensation so that he could be ordained as a priest at an age even younger than that allowed by the Council of Trent. Subsequently he became chaplain and almoner to Berzet. After seven years as a curate, during which he became involved in various internecine struggles in the church hierarchy, he went to Rome to continue his education. Unfortunately (as he expressed it in his account to the Parisians), the in-depth study of "the most thorny matters of Religion, the refinements of Politics, and the maxims of different nations . . . carried him on the one hand to a practically universal pyrrhonism on the subject of the Sciences, filled with impenetrable difficulties, and on the other to live as a Stoic" because of the uncertainties of religion. Looking for spiritual consolation in the most simple parts of the Gospel, ignoring the mysteries, he came to realize that the Calvinists had taken the same path. His queries to the Cardinal about doctrinal and ritual-istic problems got no response. As Aymon decided the Cardinal's silence was the result of the very insolubility of these problems, he took the next logical step: he became a Calvinist. He also got married.[11]

Not only, then, was Aymon a former priest, but his reasons for converting were apparently not of the best. Nor did he seem happy in his new lot. As his correspondence with Clément continued, he began to complain more and more about his Calvinist environment. "[M]y Confrères . . . in calling them-selves Ministers of the holy Gospel cannot stand for one to say how things are among them & . . . persecute to the utmost Neophytes who embrace their Religion." That, he said, was why he had begun his correspondence with the Abbé Bidal.[12] At the end of December he amplified his vague complaints.

You are right Monsr. to say that the people to whom you have commu-nicated my Letters, found that what I insinuated, was not clear enough to be able to put any stock in it, I did not intend to push things that far, but simply to let you see that I was in a situation which did not permit me to communicate to you several important things which I had on my mind, & which did not concern my own interests so much as those of his Majesty, for whose service I find myself in a position to do many things of consequence, which no one could imagine could be executed by a person of my character. I can, thank God, live quite well in these Provinces where everyone enjoys all sorts of Liberty & where nothing lacks for me if it is not a sort of repose of conscience, which cannot be found among the Refugees, who destroy each other, & who moreover have no Religion, nor discipline, nor *honnêteté*, & who by their republican spirit, & their aversion for all those who conserve in some manner the French humor & maxims, or inclinations, make them entirely insupportable: not to mention that each Minister who calls himself Evangelical, preaches a different doctrine, & mocks with impunity all those who do not have the same opinions as he does[;] one part among them who left France[,] and the best writers[,] only aim to throw everyone into Pyrrhonism on matters of Religion. Among them I know Atheists, Deists, Latitudinarians, Socinians & a thousand different opinions which only agree in preaching against a certain so-called Antichristianity of the Papacy, of which they raise phan-toms in order to fight them.[13]

Aymon complained later that the refugee ministers

had no certitude nor sincere persuasion of what they teach or profess to believe . . . ; that ignorance reigns among some, and Fanaticism among the others: . . . and that all this comes from the fact that each is entirely of his own opinion, instead of submitting himself to the authority of the Universal Church, which the said Aymon recognizes to be an absolute necessity, to allow union among the Faithful of all Christianity. He moreover recognized by a fatal experience, that the Calvinists and Protestants are prone to vary continually in their dogma, and that their Morals are so corrupted, that one can find among them neither good faith, nor piety, nor zeal, nor virtue, but on the contrary every sort of vice and dissolution. Those who call themselves Refugees for the cause of Religion, are involved no less than the others in all the disorders of a scandalous libertinage, which produces an infinity of ills, to which the Ministers ordinarily add everything that corruption, spitefulness, roguery and impiety suggest to them to defend their worst causes, and to palliate the greatest crimes and the most enormous outrages, when it is a question of their temporal interests.

Aymon intended to write a book on the subject.[14]

Such a book might well be of use to the French, since his complaints about his compeers echoed so accurately the arguments made by Catholics against the Huguenots in printed religious debates of the period. The charge of varying in their dogma, for example, was one made by both groups against each other. In the later seventeenth century Jean Claude had conducted a spirited debate with the Jansenist Antoine Arnauld over the issue of transubstantiation, which Claude claimed had not been a doctrine of the early church. Arnauld defended himself in his book *La Perpetuité de la foy de l'Eglise Catholique*, using, among other proofs, evidence that the Greek Orthodox Church also held this doctrine. A new edition had been issued only the previous year.[15] To provide proof that the Protestants themselves varied infinitely in their doctrine would be a useful weapon for the Catholic establishment. In his letter of December 31, Aymon said he had enough material on the subject to write a "Manifesto full of such authentic proofs & in such quantity, that if I published it as I have projected, not only would it be proper for diverting those who are thinking of leaving the Roman Church, but even for making all those abandon the party of the Reform who are not blinded by their passions & as obstinate as are most of those whom I know & who are at bottom more ignorant than one could imagine, if one has not been at close quarters with them as I am every day."[16]

Not surprisingly, as this correspondence continued, the botanical volumes got less and less play. Clément in fact told Aymon that he could not obtain an agreement that the work should be acquired by the library. The minister did not seem to mind, simply remarking again that when he got to France he would be able to communicate to him or to high-ranking persons near to the king "several affairs of importance which can be worth or save several Millions to his Majesty, & which I cannot put on this paper."[17] These vague promises began to sound better and better to the French. Aymon helped them along in their decision by informing Clément on February 4, 1706, that he had obtained a passport from the States-General to travel with some merchandise as far as Louvain, where he would wait until he was sent the proper documents to get himself into France.[18] The merchandise, it turned out, "is contraband in this country, especially in time of war & can serve several of your friends & principally the Captain of the Royal Regiment who is engaged in furnishing to the subaltern engineers everything they need to help the enterprise of the great lord against the tartars."[19] His evident enthusiasm for the cloak and dagger appealed to one part of the government's interest; on the other side was his promise of "docility," if nothing further, in religious matters.[20] But the passport still did not come through, and by the end of February Aymon was starting to get nervous. He wrote a letter about himself in the third person ("the friend I told you about, he will not fail to come to see your beautiful Library"), signing it only "the secretary [who is] voluntarily exiled from his Country because of Religion."[21] By April he was in Paris.[22]

Once there, Aymon set about putting his proposals in motion. Barthélemy Hauréau recounts that Clément introduced Aymon to Pontchartrain, to whom he promised political and religious *mémoires* of considerable use to the king, and to the Cardinal de Noailles, archbishop of Paris, who asked Clément to let Aymon use the library to write these reports and *libelles*.[23] Aymon, who promised to do all he could to combat the Protestants, also asked Noailles if he could be placed in the seminary of the Missions Etrangères, according to the superior, De Brisacie, "to instruct himself and prepare himself to abjure heresy."[24] During his time there, De Brisacie reported, he went to mass nearly every day, participated in religious discussions with another member of the seminary, and asked several times to be allowed to abjure, take the sacraments, and say mass. The seminarians, however, felt that he was too occupied with his political work to turn his attention properly to his reconversion.[25] In other efforts to support himself, Aymon asked for a pension from the king, having abandoned his job at the Collège de Mathématiques in The Hague, which had brought him about 400 écus per year.[26] He still had not got one in September, when he pleaded, in a letter endorsed in Clément's hand with the words "this letter must be read with attention," for the means to support his wife and bring her to France and save her soul.[27]

Perhaps one reason for his failure to get a pension was the uselessness of the information he provided for the French church and government. His initial critique of the doctrines and lives of the Huguenots was not much more expansive than his letters had been,[28] and Clément later described his political *mémoire* as "so contemptible, that no one paid it the least attention."[29] It consisted mainly of exposing the plans of the Dutch to fight the French through such means as attacking their horses using triangular darts in their flanks, as well as small and easily-hidden globe-shaped grenades filled with iron filings, and a bombardment of grenades hidden in crates of oranges. Other than some general information, mostly from hearsay, about the plans of the Camisards, Aymon had little else to offer.[30]

Nevertheless, Aymon continued to work in the Bibliothèque du Roi and became a familiar face there. Clément later said that he felt sorry for him. "I regarded him . . . with the eyes of Christian charity, seeing him return with intentions which seemed to me so right and so sincere. I saw a man without protection, without acquaintance, come to give himself up to us without any other precaution than the word which had been given to him."[31] Clément got so used to seeing him there "that I willingly let him go into the rooms of the Library. He passed whole hours there by himself, under the pretext of looking for the Books which were proper for him for the plans of which he had spoken."[32] This industriousness on behalf of church and state could only be estimable in an erstwhile Huguenot refugee. But Clément was forced to add that in those days "I was far from thinking that I was introducing into my place, a serpent, who one day would pierce my heart by the most enormous of all treacheries."[33] For one day Aymon, as was his wont, disappeared again.[34] And with him disappeared some of the Bibliothèque du Roi's most important manuscripts.

Although the States-General had revoked Aymon's pension when he disappeared, he was apparently able to convince them to give it back after producing what he had taken.[35] After all, his passport to Constantinople was granted for the purpose of studying Greek religion, a topic, as we have seen, of considerable importance in the eucharistic controversy. And what had he stolen from the Bibliothèque du Roi? Among a number of manuscripts useful to the Protestants[36] was the famous *Concile de Jérusalem*, a declaration by Dosithée, patriarch of the Greek Orthodox Church, concerning his church's beliefs; indeed, it was the very manuscript used by Antoine Arnauld to write *La perpetuité de la foy*.[37] Now it could be published by the Huguenots, who could rectify all the errors and falsifications Arnauld had no doubt inserted into his version. Far from going to Paris to reconvert to Catholicism, then, Aymon had come away with a prize for the Protestant cause. The *libraire* Reinier Leers told Clément that although Aymon "is not capable of translating [the manuscripts], it doesn't matter, everyone will help him if it is true that in them one can discover lies used by those who wrote against Monsieur Claude on the subject of the Eucharist."[38]

Clément was as upset as any librarian would be once he realized the thefts had been committed. Unfortunately for him, recovering the manuscripts would prove difficult. Aymon claimed not to have stolen anything, saying that the *Concile de Jérusalem*, for example, had been given to him by a monk of St.-Germain-des-Prés sympathetic to the reform of the Catholic church and that in any case it was much too large for anyone to be able to steal.[39] Officials at the Abbey swore that the manuscript had never been kept there,[40] but as it had accidentally never been stamped with the seal of the Bibliothèque du Roi or inscribed in its registers, there was nothing to indicate its real provenance.[41] Moreover, as the French and Dutch were at war, it seemed unlikely that much cooperation could be expected from the Dutch government in recovering the stolen goods, even if anyone believed Clément's claims. Things looked bleak for the librarian.

While Aymon and his supporters crowed over the new acquisition for the Huguenots, however, Clément took a quite different line of argument. The question, he said, was not one of politics or religion at all. It was an issue of the Republic of Letters. When one is talking about the world of scholarship, after all, petty differences must be forgotten for the sake of learning. "This has nothing to do with the affairs of peace or war," he wrote to Leers;[42] and again, "after all the issue is not to know whether this MS. can or cannot serve to favor the opinion of the Protestants."[43] In a letter evidently meant for publication, Clément called on officials in The Hague to require the return of the manuscripts because the theft "concerned the men of Letters of all Nations."[44] Higher rules therefore applied: "judges [who are] disinterested and without passion" would recognize that this was even an issue of a violation of "the laws of mankind [*le droit des gens*] and those of the community of Christian nations," one which must be redressed "even during an open War."[45] For the etiquette of the Republic of Letters, an entity apart from European and Christian power relations, had been violated when Aymon "abused the confidence which had been placed in him."[46]

The argument was a clever one, especially given the reasons Aymon had been brought to France in the first place. It pitted one sort of allegiance, the allegiance of scholars to the Republic of Letters, against their allegiance to church and polity. Yet Clément, who told Leers that if the manuscripts were not returned "the men of letters of your country will not be allowed into or have any relation with the Bibliotheq. du Roy,"[47] no doubt believed in his arguments, and so did many in the scholarly community.

Reactions to the theft varied. Aymon was said to have powerful protectors who were pleased to see the *Concile* in Protestant hands,[48] and some of the literary journals made ironic little remarks about the provenance of the manuscript without actually stating that Aymon had stolen it. Jacques Bernard's *Nouvelles de la République des Lettres*, for example, said that "all [Reformed] Ministers must give very humble thanks to Mr. *Aymon* who has thus taken their part & their cause in hand," and the *Journal littéraire*, reviewing another of Aymon's productions, remarked that he was "already known to the Public by the care which he has taken to share with it what he found most worthy of his attention in several Libraries of France."[49]

But other Protestants, while perhaps pleased to have the manuscripts, also were uneasy at the way they were obtained. Practicing what he preached, Clément turned from using the Catholic *libraire* Guillaume de Voys to the more effective and better-connected Protestant Reinier Leers as an agent to solicit the manuscripts' return. Leers, perhaps wiser than most in the clashes between religious and scholarly values, initially found the naïveté of the librarian hard to credit. "As the affair of the S: Aymon seems just like something you would read in a novel," he wrote to Clément, "do me the favor of telling me in detail about all the principal facts contained in the Letter [i.e. Aymon's printed pamphlet]. Where you are do you really give a Passport to a defrocked and married Monk, who is passing in France under the name of a protestant Minister? Does a Benedictine Monk really give a Protestant pieces to prove the obliquities of the Roman Church? . . . Can one really steal a bulky in-folio, and an important one, from the Bibliotheque du Roy?"[50] But Leers was glad to assist in recovering the manuscripts. Admittedly, he was a businessman who was anxious to preserve a clientele which included Catholics as well as Protestants; his fellow-*libraire* Jean-Louis de Lorme refused to publish the stolen *Concile* "in order not to shock certain persons in France."[51] As a *libraire* he was in the business of putting aside religion and politics in favor of learning and profit. But it is telling that the journalist Henri Basnage de Beauval and especially his brother, the prominent Huguenot minister Jacques Basnage, were also active in assisting Clément.

Basnage, called by his friend and biographer Charles Le Vier "the soul of the Synods, which often chose him as President or as Secretary, especially when there were delicate matters to be discussed,"[52] used his influence to help the Catholics in this dispute. He kept Clément informed of what he might need to convince the Dutch government to force the return of the manuscripts and spoke to friends in high positions about the affair. It seemed of little consequence to him that the documents might help his party; "I could only hear with chagrin that your Generosity had been abused. If your satisfaction had depended on me and my advice you would have had everything [back] long ago. I have talked about it to all my friends in the state and I have let them know that equity alone demands that this affair be examined more promptly and that justice be done to you."[53] But to hold such views Basnage had to be circumspect. He begged his French correspondents not to tell anyone that they were in communication about the affair, for although he merely hoped for justice, other people might think he had a more sinister political motive.[54] One French friend warned Clément that "it appears that both M. de Beauval and his brother are suspected, and it is very proper to take care of them because they are good fellows who do all the service they can to those of their nation, and who have done, and do every day, great good of this sort."[55]

Perhaps it was this circumspection which made Basnage more lukewarm in his correspondence with Protestant scholars. While helping Clément retrieve the Concile, he also told Gisbert Cuper, who was fascinated by the affair, that "it is to be wished that they are diligent about printing [the manuscript] before the court case is more amply informed about it."[56] Or perhaps this was more ambivalence than circumspection. If he had ambivalent feelings, other Protestant scholars shared them. Cuper called the accusations against Aymon "atrocious" but seemed more interested in the actual issue of whether the Greeks believed in transubstantiation than in the violation of the sanctity of the Bibliothèque du Roi.[57] He even expressed pleasure at the publication of the manuscript the next year.[58] But Cuper also reported that Aymon was often reproached for his conduct, and he was inclined to listen to reports from Paris that Aymon's book was full "of ignorance, and even more of bad faith."[59]

The Dutch government, as it turned out, had little interest in this apparent triumph for Protestantism. With a war on, the acquisition of a manuscript to make some obscure point in a theological controversy evidently was not of as great moment to politicians as it was to the public.[60] Nor was the publication of the manuscript of particular use to Aymon's party, although that was evidently due to his own incompetence. Basnage reported that, far from restoring lost passages to the published Concile, "it appears that [Aymon] has retrenched a third of his edition which makes it imperfect and there is not a single word in this one from The Hague which is not found in the one printed in Paris. I have compared the one with the other very exactly and you can count on what I am telling you."[61] In March of 1709, a year after the publication of Aymon's Monumens authentiques de la Religion des Grecs, the Gecommitteerde Raden of Holland and West Friesland ordered Aymon to turn the manuscript of the Concile over to the Chevalier de Croissy.[62] The last of the other stolen items was not recovered until 1729, when Robert Harley returned thirty-four pages of the Epistles of St. Paul.[63]

"Here," Cuper wrote to La Croze, "is a nice tidbit for Ecclesiastical History."[64] But it is also a tasty morsel for the history of the Republic of Letters. Despite the anticlimactic ending and the evident lack of interest the controversy held for the authorities, Protestant scholars were clearly torn by Aymon's actions between two different and competing worlds. One was the world of politics and religion, a world in which Huguenots at the turn of the eighteenth century had a considerable stake. A theological victory, had one resulted from Aymon's theft, would have provided new hope and new confidence for the beleaguered Huguenot community. But the other world was the Republic of Letters, and its rules—of cooperation, of non-sectarianism, of internationalism—prescribed quite different behavior.

Aymon said that he could not be blamed for his actions "without injustice among the Papists & without an excess of ingratitude among us" for "bringing back in time of War, booty from the Camp of the Enemies."[65] But although other scholars had some feelings of this kind, they could not help but consider his actions slimy. Aymon was—according to Clément—"decried not only in France among the Catholics, but even in the United Provinces among the Protestants,"[66] and certainly those interested in the controversy tried constantly to raise it above the level of politics and religion. It was the rules of the Republic of Letters that Aymon had broken, by abusing Clément's "confidence" and "generosity" and by advancing himself through an act of scholarly turpitude. Clément said that Aymon, whom he called "ignorant" and "obscure," was actually "without faith and without religion"; the argument that the manuscripts were stolen for the sake of Protestantism "is a tack taken by the S^r. Aymon to authorize himself to possess these manuscripts, to give himself a name."[67] The issue was not religion at all, but scholarly hierarchy. Basnage was inclined to agree. "I have only seen him twice, I found him a very small Wit with a very great Pride, which he hides under an apparent humility, and in a very somber life. He has only been praised to me in the subject of Mathematics."[68]

Whether or not this was the reason for Aymon's behavior, it was a convenient excuse. The ambivalence visible in Protestant scholars like Basnage and Cuper is evidence of an attempt to reconcile perhaps irreconcilable values. Maturin Veyssière La Croze, a dedicated and conservative Huguenot, was sorry Aymon had published his book, not because he did not believe in religious controversy, but because "the Roman Catholics believe they have triumphed over us when they have defeated some author of no consequence, & although this does not damage the rest of us at all, it considerably prevents them from knowing the truth."[69] But religious controversy aside, he could not condone Aymon's behavior as a scholar. "I do not think M^r. Aimon is a very *honnête homme*. As a savant he assuredly is not."[70]

As a Man and as a Savant

On one side, then, was behavior as a man; on the other, behavior as a scholar. These ambivalences and ambiguities about roles reflected the division scholars made in their minds between the Republic of Letters and the rest of society. We have already seen that citizens of the Republic acknowledged a hierarchy of membership which differed from that in the republics and monarchies of the outside world. In the same way, concerns of political and ecclesiastical power were supposed to fall outside the academic realm. This might find expression in a condemnation of political censorship, as in the *Journal littéraire*'s *extrait* of a Jansenist work: "The Parlement of Paris condemned this Book by an Arrêt of February 21 1715: but, as no sovereign Authority is recognized in the Republic of Letters, & because a Book, although condemned by Arrêt, can be good, we will make an Extrait of this one."[71] Or it might be a brash assertion, like that of the *Bibliothèque raisonnée*, of the right to say what one pleases: "Except for the respect due to God, to good Morals, & to the Magistracy, we know no human considerations, which should prevent an *honnête homme* from pronouncing boldly on Books, of whatever order they are, & from whatever Pen they come."[72] Or a letter might turn from political to scholarly news by saying, as Henri Justel did in 1684, "I will leave the news of the world to come to those of the Republic of Letters."[73] Indeed, in Des Maizeaux's view it was a "failing" to be concerned about worldly things (such as national sentiment) at all; Bayle, he said, loved his country, which "I call . . . a Failing, because so thorow a Philosopher as he ought to have had larger Thoughts."[74]

Scholarly correspondence and literary journals were replete with suggestions that issues of politics, and especially religion, did not belong in the Republic of Letters. Although theology, for example, was a major preoccupation of scholars, the organs of the whole community claimed that religion and religious controversies had nothing to do with the activities of the group. When Bayle reported his plans to write *éloges* of famous scholars in the *Nouvelles de la République des Lettres*, he said that "We will not pay any attention to what Religion they were . . . ; it is enough that they were Famous for their learning. . . . What concerns us here is not Religion: what concerns us is Learning."[75] Similarly, when the controversy between André Dacier and Jean Masson over Horace extended to religious slurs of the refugee minister by the *nouveau converti*, the *Histoire critique de la République des Lettres* (written, it is true, by Masson's brother Samuel) asked, "What relation does the character of *Minister* have to the subject Mr. *Dacier* was supposed to be discussing? What is the Religion of Mr. *Masson* doing in a Work which has to do with a Pagan Poet? Where there is no issue except of Literature &c.[?]"[76] Even more telling is the appearance of these sentiments in the private correspondence of the journalists. Albert-Henri de Sallengre wrote to the other authors of the *Journal littéraire* that people of good judgment said they should not discuss in the journal a theological controversy "which has nothing whatever to do with the Republic of Letters."[77] In just the same way, journals claimed they would stay away from political books and political controversy; Jean Cornand de La Crose said that when the authors of political pamphlets tried to get him to mention their works, "I was sharp and short upon the whole matter, that I might be troubled no more with such trifles."[78]

We have already noted the readiness of most literary journals to protest their utmost impartiality in pronouncements on literary productions. This impartiality was in part an attempt to treat all scholars in the same way—an attempt, as we saw, fraught with difficulty in a community based on personal interaction—but its particular focus was the avoidance of political and religious subjectivity. Nearly all the journals made a special point in their first issue to emphasize their avoidance of these issues. The *Bibliothèque angloise*, for example, said it would "observe an exact neutrality concerning all the Parties which reign in this Island," and the *Bibliothèque britannique* promised that "If some Dispute on Topics of Religion or Philosophy is raised in these Islands, we will render an exact account of it, without ever swaying the Public, either for, or against."[79]

As the separation of the Republic of Letters from politics and religion might suggest, these avowals sometimes took the form of a promise not even to mention such disputes. The *Bibliothèque italique* promised that "Books of Controversy on the Dogmas which unhappily divide the Christians of today, will not enter into [the journal] . . . at least unless the principles which could serve to decide these Controversies, are not Facts of holy or Ecclesiastical History, which it is important for all Communions to know exactly."[80] Only the Jesuit *Journal de Trévoux* refused to make such promises.

> In the arguments which often arise between men of Letters in subjects of Learning, the Authors of the Memoires will never take sides, & they will only write a simple exposition of what is written on both sides, removing, however, whatever is nasty & injurious in these writings. They will also observe the same neutrality in all the rest, except when it concerns Religion, good morals, or the State: in which it is not permitted to be neutral.[81]

Even this argument, however, acknowledges the separation between the world and the Republic of Letters. For some journalists that separation meant that religion and politics should not be discussed, while for the journalists of Trévoux it simply meant that on those subjects the Republic's rules of impartiality, for once, should not apply.

The view that religious and political differences should not enter the Republic of Letters was not merely a rhetorical device of authors. As the Aymon case should indicate, it also extended to scholarly behavior and practice. The history of the Republic of Letters is in many ways a history of joint ventures between people of different nations and different communions. *Commerces de lettres* flourished between Protestant and Catholic scholars, and news of the academic endeavors of ecclesiastics was eagerly received by churchmen of other sects. A favorite correspondent of Basnage's, for example, was Passionei, the Archbishop of Ephesus, whom he referred to as "mon ami Passionei," and the correspondence of another Huguenot minister, David Durand, contained letters from cardinals as well as abbés.[82]

Huguenot refugees seem to have been even more involved than most in such friendships, and their experience of exile from Catholic friends may well have strengthened the nonsectarian character of the international Republic of Letters. While still in France, those who lived in Paris or in towns, like Caen or Rouen, which emulated Parisian values, found the highest intellectual circles (if not those lower down) open to their participation.[83] So when Henri Justel, for example, left his position as secretary to Louis XIV in 1681 and emigrated to England, he maintained friendships with eminent French Catholics like Richard Simon and Nicolas Toinard.[84] "Although I am outside my country I still have sincere friends there, full of affection, who are Catholics," he wrote in 1684. "Religion does not make honnêtes gens[;] one must be born with good inclinations and have a natural and essential probity."[85] We have already discussed the continuing relation of the Huguenot orientalist Etienne Morin with Pierre-Daniel Huet, the bishop of Soissons and later Avranches, after Morin's flight to the Netherlands. Morin and Huet were both from Caen, and despite the responsibility borne by his own church for Morin's exile, the bishop wrote two months after the Revocation of "the regret I had over your departure" and his hopes that the States of Holland and the Curators of the Academy at Leiden would not "leave a man of your merit without occupation for long."[86]

Religious differences were clearly on the minds of such scholars, but they chose to ignore them. Maturin Veyssière La Croze, who, although he did not leave France for religious reasons,[87] nevertheless became a devout Protestant, said as much in praising his old friend Dom Bernard de Montfaucon. "I do not think there is a better heart and a more honnête homme in the world than he is," La Croze frequently said, and "if he were a Jew or a Mohammedan, I nevertheless would give him the same testimonial."[88] As Huet ended a letter to Morin in 1692, "Wherever divine providence establishes me/I will conserve dearly the memory of our old friendship/and the title of exile, that you give to yourself will not diminish in the least the faithfulness with which I will be as long as I live, Monsieur, your very humble & very obedient servant."[89]

An "old friendship" might be one reason for cooperation between communions, but scholars who had no ties of friendship or even acquaintance also endorsed these values with their conduct. Although travel in Catholic countries was difficult for Protestants, those who could manage it generally received a warm welcome from savants. Charles-Etienne Jordan encountered this with some surprise. "There is no Place in the World, so far as I know," he wrote, "where it is so easy for a Foreigner to see Savants, as in Paris. If you are a Foreigner, you are received everywhere: if you are a Minister, if you are a Protestant, no one is troubled about it in the least."[90] Thus when Godefroy Clermont was named pastor to the Dutch embassy in Paris in 1714, the Parisian learned such as Bignon, Galland, and Huet took care of him and offered him friendship,[91] and Pierre Coste, who travelled all over Europe as tutor to a series of English aristocrats, reported similar treatment. "Paris is large, I have many acquaintances there," he wrote in 1713; "the days there pass with an inconceivable rapidity, one is always occupied with visits or in being visited."[92] He spent the following winter in Montpellier, where the bishop (brother to Colbert de Torcy) visited him, had him to dinner, and offered him the use of his library.[93]

Not everyone understood such sojourns, since they reflected a special ethos of the Republic of Letters. The wider Huguenot community in both Holland and England had trouble understanding Coste's travels, and he returned from one trip to France, "where I passed the time very agreeably for nearly two years, esteemed, caressed by persons of great merit," to find that "our good Refugees" had spread rumors in London that "I had become a monk."[94] Similarly, the French government was uneasy about Coste's presence in the country, despite his acceptance by scholars. Although the bishop of Montpellier paid him many civilities, the intendant was initially hesitant to allow Coste to stay in the province.[95] Indeed, in 1711 Colbert de Torcy refused to grant Coste a passport at all, stating that "the quality of French Protestant was an invincible obstacle." It is good evidence that the Republic of Letters shared a different view that De la Motte could quote a letter from the Abbé Bignon on the subject. "I am very mortified by this refusal, adds the Ab. Bignon, & *even more for the reason which was given for making it*. This passage charms me," De la Motte said.[96]

The welcoming attitude in the Republic of Letters, so different from the nonscholarly world, is reflected in the numerous learned projects which were cooperative efforts across national and religious boundaries. As Lorraine Daston points out, the large scientific investigations of the truth of Newtonianism, such as the expedition to test the shape of the Earth and the study of the transits of Venus, all involved major international collaboration.[97] The very existence of literary journals, which throve on news and contributions from all over Europe, is an important example of this phenomenon. Even the most frankly partisan journals, such as the *Histoire critique de la République des Lettres* or the *Journal de Trévoux*, included submissions by people of the opposite camp, not to mention *nouvelles littéraires* which vaunted the triumph of a competing viewpoint.[98] We have already noted the importance of cooperation even in the prosecution of individual scholarly projects, and these too profited from international and interfaith support. The

Jesuit Claude Buffier, for example, asked Des Maizeaux's services in writing a new French grammar, and French Catholic assistance on Basnage's project to republish the *Spicilegium* extended not only to research by monks but even advice on how to avoid the depredations of French censors.[99]

Such advice, like Clément's pleas for the integrity of his library, demonstrates the sense of separateness from the concerns of nation and church which scholars liked to cultivate. This is perhaps best demonstrated by the way that comparative indifference was regarded as the proper attitude toward war. As Maarten Ultee has pointed out, war could prove quite inconvenient for scholarly interchange.[100] War obstructed the circulation of books and delivery of letters, which in turn slowed the production of literary journals.[101] It was thus a commonplace among the learned that, as the *Journal littéraire* put it, war was the "enemy of belles Lettres."[102] "The Pagans placed Minerva among the warrior Divinities," declared Gisbert Cuper; "but nevertheless she does not get along with Mars & Bellona; & the Muses love peace, & not the blare of Trumpets."[103]

The fact that complaints about the effects of war were made in letters between scholars in two warring countries is compelling evidence for their attempts to ignore the meaning of warfare. Indeed, Etienne-François Geoffroy wrote Hans Sloane in 1709 that "scholars [would] scarcely notice these annoying times, if it were not for the problem of commerce with talented men in foreign countries."[104] Political differences simply made life more difficult. Instead of obeying governmental orders against interchange with foreign countries, or paying heed to the rulings of censors, scholars found alternate routes. When Bayle wanted to send Nicaise a copy of his *Dictionary*, Nicaise had to ask Reinier Leers in Rotterdam to send it to Jean Le Clerc in Amsterdam, who could send it to Le Clerc's brother in Geneva, who in turn could send it to Nicaise in Paris.[105] Similarly, Bernard in The Hague planned to continue his correspondence with Delaissement in Paris by way of Geneva after a proposed moratorium on commerce with France; and Bignon offered to use a pseudonym if his correspondence with Des Maizeaux was likely to cause trouble.[106] These attempts to maintain blissful ignorance of the political situation were all part of the strictures of another polity, the Republic of Letters, which stated, in Bignon's words, that scholars should show "much Zeal and union for the sciences in general despite the divisions of States and of individual opinions."[107]

Chevalier's Cabinet and the Intrusion of Opinion

If you happened to walk into Nicolas Chevalier's cabinet of curiosities in Amsterdam—and large numbers of scholars and *virtuosi* in the 1690s did just that—you would have been confronted by a jumble of natural wonders, exotica, and antiquities.[108] Chevalier's cabinet was a subject of intense pride, and he wrote several descriptions of it. Immediately on entering you would have found a library of books on "medals, antiquities, meteors and other curious matters," above which were two shelves of busts, instruments of sacrifice, a nude statue found in the foundations of Nijmegen, Roman seals, knives, keys, and some real Roman statues, including "a figure by which was represented the shameful parts of man and of woman and which one wore around the neck." Elsewhere in the cabinet were a microscope, a little Chinese boat used to pick up pieces of ships broken in storms, the horn of a rhinoceros, an elephant's trunk, the mummified hand of a monkey, armadilloes, a chameleon, a flying fish, the horn of a unicorn, an eight-foot crocodile, a monstrous serpent fifty feet long and four feet wide, a Brazilian lizard, ivory and glass pyramids, and other similar items. On one cornice alone were fifteen busts of emperors and philosophers—the largest one of William the Silent—as well two bottles, one containing a whole crocodile and the other a basilisk.[109]

Chevalier, formerly a student at Sedan, fled to the Netherlands after the Revocation of the Edict of Nantes; there he was known to scholars as an able antiquary, as well as a talented engraver and *libraire*.[110] He wrote a number of works on various antiquities and other curiosities, and sent Gisbert Cuper, among others, descriptions and engravings of statues and other antiquities in his itinerant cabinet.[111] Communicating about such collections and showing them to scholars was a customary courtesy of the period; Cuper sent Chevalier information from ancient authors about his statues and showed Chevalier his own library and curiosities, while when Bruzen La Martinière visited London in the 1730s he received the benefit of seeing Hans Sloane's "marvellous cabinet, worthy object of public admiration."[112] Among the scholars who signed Chevalier's guest book from 1692 to 1706 were Cuper, the antiquary and burgermeester Nicolaus Witsen, the classicist Almeloveen, the Huguenot ministers and scholars Pierre Jurieu, Etienne Chauvin, Jacques Basnage, and Etienne Martin, the engraver Romeyn de Hooghe, Jacob Gronovius, Pierre Bayle, Isaac 'sGravesande, Adrian Reland, Frederick Spanheim, J.G. Graevius, Peter Burman, J.F. Cramer, Gregorio Leti, and other luminaries of the scholarly scene.[113]

The guest book included not only the names of visitors, but also comments praising the chamber's contents. "In Gratitude and Remembrance of the Many favours Received from Mr. Nicholas Chevalier I own that this Cabinet of Curiosities is one of the finest I ever Beheld Labour & Pains are not in vain/if thereby wee content Regain," apostrophized one visitor in English.[114] Such praise is to be expected, as is the expression of gratitude "while awaiting the occasion to render him some Service."[115] But it is significant that a number of such comments made reference not only to Chevalier's wonderful collection, but also to his being a Huguenot refugee. One scholar, for example, wrote that "The reputation which Monsieur Chevalier acquired long ago for his Curiosities caused me to see his Cabinet which is full of several rare and Curious pieces, Which is a mark of his spirit which is already so strongly distinguished by the firmness he showed in our Blessed Religion And which I heard long ago in Paris."[116] Chevalier's Protestantism—in all its religious and political manifestations—was part of his essence, and his learned visitors were not about to separate out his scholarship from his religion.

Chevalier himself was far from doing so. For the centerpiece of his chamber was not the fifty-foot serpent or the embalmed basilisk, but rather a large painted cabinet laboriously constructed by its owner in honor of his hero, the savior of Protestantism, William of Orange. Chevalier—or, rather, his dog—had encountered William in the 1680s on a trip from Sedan through Holland, England, and France. While strolling with some other Frenchmen, singing "la marche Des Mousqueterre," and walking "un dogue d'angleterre pour nous divertir," he met a man on the city walls and spoke briefly to him. As the dog, in pursuit of a crow, ran between the man's legs, the man hit him with his stick, infuriating the animal. Chevalier calmed down the dog, "which did not fail to bite me but very lightly," and the man was properly grateful for Chevalier's putting himself in danger on his account. When Chevalier heard that this man was the Prince of Orange he was quite embarrassed. He said the prince "should pardon a stranger who had never had the happiness to see him before that if I had had this honor that I would have spoken with all the respects and the honor that one should speak to a person of his quality and such a great Warrior who is such a debonair and such a Christian Prince as he is."[117] Even then, before Chevalier was forced to leave France for his religion, he revered William; in 1691, when he built his cabinet, his reverence had turned to adoration.

The curiosities decorating the "chambre de raretez" were studded with numerous items dedicated to the glory of the prince and his ancestors. Along with the bust of William the Silent, on the third wall was a cabinet of medals topped with busts of William and Mary and painted with the scene of the sciences and the arts occupied with making medals and monuments to the actions of famous men. The inside was painted with the escutcheons of the princes of Orange and a picture of Renown blowing his trumpet "to publish the deeds and heroic virtues" of William III. On the fourth wall was a picture of William as a hero conquering an evil giant who was James II, as well as statues of William and Mary and images of a gladiator preparing for combat and of Hercules to show that "his Majesty was dealing such terrible blows to the power of Louis XIV that it cannot fail to succumb." The

optima quaeque dies miseris
mortalibus æui
Prima fugit . . . .

J'ay bien uoulu mettre cette deuise dans
ce Liure pour temoigner a monsieur
cheualier l'estime que ie fais de sa per
Sonne, et des Soins qu'il prend pour
ramasser des curiosités. fait a Rotterdam
le 21 d'octobre 1694 — *Jurieu*. SS. th.
D.

5 Pierre Jurieu's entry in the guest book at Nicolas Chevalier's *chambre de raretez*.
(KB, Ms. 69 B 8, f. 58.)

Roman emperors, whose busts and statues featured elsewhere in the chamber, were depicted as transported with admiration and wonder "to see the heroic deeds and the glorious exploits of King William surpass by far all their most amazing actions."[118]

All this was a mere prelude to the grand cabinet itself, which Chevalier had built and painted, and which was clearly his favorite item in the chamber.[119] His manuscript account of its decoration took up much more space than the rest of his treasures, and he had Romeyn de Hooghe engrave four pictures of the cabinet alone. It had painted allegorical panels both on the outside and the inside, all in praise of the glorious Prince of Orange. The front depicted, among other figures, inconstant Fortune chained by Jupiter and distributing crowns, scepters, and riches to an equestrian William III in front of a backdrop of scenes of war. The king had had success at war, but "presently his Majesty has just achieved the defeat of [his enemies in Ireland, Scotland, and elsewhere], and put Peace back in its original tranquillity."[120]

But it was the inner cabinet which gave most precisely Chevalier's view both of William and his own role. When the outer doors were opened they displayed a small inner cabinet containing all the medals concerning the king from his birth to the present. In 1692 Chevalier published a book about these medals in order "to conserve for Posterity the beautiful and glorious actions of such a great King."[121] The front of the smaller cabinet was painted with the arms of the king and the four scepters of the realms Chevalier considered him to rule: England, Scotland, Ireland, and France. These were surrounded by laurels and palms, representing "the glory that this Illustrious Prince has acquired both in Peace and War." On one side was represented Poetry and History, and on the other the goddess of the Sciences, with the goddess of War and all the works of Mars, "who eternalize the glory of Illustrious men by means of the medals, which are struck to do them honor and to serve as perpetual monuments to them."[122] Once again all the great figures of antiquity stood in awe of William's achievement, and one of the cabinet doors portrayed Truth and the Science of Medals pulling a vase of medals from the earth to keep in mind and "publish everywhere on earth the glory and heroic actions of King William the third."[123]

Even the most iconographically obtuse would have had little trouble in deciphering the cabinet's import. More confusing, however, was its placement. What was such a politically biased object doing as the centerpiece of such a learned collection? Chevalier's visitors had no problem with this issue, and, as his decorative art makes plain, nor did he. Like the figures on the cabinet, numismatics, antiquarianism, poetry, history, and the sciences were all meant to "eternalize the glory" of a great figure like William, who not only was "the terror of his enemies" but also "the support of the weak, and the liberator of the oppressed"—oppressed like the Huguenot Chevalier.[124]

6 Engraving by Romeyn de Hooghe of Nicolas Chevalier's cabinet, closed.
([Nicolas Chevalier], *Description de la Chambre de Raretez de la Ville d'Utrecht*, 1707.)

Of course this sort of propaganda was not limited to the Huguenots. The iconography associated with Louis XIV made exactly the same point, only for the other side. The arts and sciences were all part of a politico-religious system; they supported the system, and the system (to a point) supported them. That partisan opinion should have intruded on scholarship should be no surprise. But the learned community was supposed to ignore these distinctions; and the unapologetic presentation of Chevalier's views poses questions for us about the cosmopolitanism of the Republic of Letters.

Prejudice and the Nature of Scholars

In the most general sense, it was difficult for scholars to escape the stereotypes commonly expressed about the character of other groups, even if such groups included members of the Republic of Letters. The theoretical international-ism of the learned world, for example, could not always compete with the idea that learning was broken down nationally,[125] as the existence of so many national journals, such as the *Bibliothèque angloise*, the *Bibliothèque germanique*, or the *Bibliothèque italique* should make plain. This analysis was extended to the type of scholarship pursued in each nation, and contemporary thought even assigned savants of different nations various intellectual and personal characteristics based on the Aristotelian view that the climate forms the mind. Baillet, in a section of his *Jugemens des savans* called "Préjugés des nations," commented on the ridiculousness of this view but still thought he should report it.

> Although we said above that the qualities of the mind of a man are personal, & that there is a sort of injustice to assigning to a climate, a territory, or a Province the vices & the virtues that one finds in Authors: Nevertheless rather than diverging from the greatest number of Critics, one must agree with them that Authors, being composed of corporeal matter as well as spiritual substance, participate at least by that means in the quality of the air they breathe, & the earth which nourishes them. And one can grant to them that the particular genius of places communicates itself to the mind, either by the sense organs, or by whatever other impression they please.[126]

Baillet went on to report on the comments of such scholars as Scaliger, Naudé, Bodin, and Casaubon on the particular idiosyncrasies of the Italians, Germans, Spanish, Dutch, and English. Italians, for example, were long-winded, poetic, and vain; the Spanish were grave, unsubtle, and too con-cerned with their national glory.[127] The Germans came off worst in this round-up of national characteristics. A well-known *mot* of the period by the

7   Engraving by Romeyn de Hooghe of Nicolas Chevalier's cabinet, open. ([Nicolas Chevalier], *Description de la Chambre de Raretez de la Ville d'Utrecht*, 1707.)

Père Dominique Bouhours asked whether a German could be a *bel esprit*,[128] and this set the tone for Baillet's discussion. Germans had originally been completely barbarian, brutal, and savage, but through work—rather than native talent—they became good at scholarship. Still, they had no aptitude for poetry, rhetoric, or history; instead they excelled at the type of erudition which requires a lot of reading, such as philology, philosophy, medicine, mathematics, jurisprudence, and theology. And since all the application in the world will not change the nature of man, "the Germans will always be Germans in their Writings. . . . [S]o much work & so much merit has not allowed them to acquire the qualities which nature has not thought it appropriate to minds she has enclosed in robust bodies, & surrounded with a cold & crude air. Thus one should not look in the Works of most Germans for gentility, subtlety, brilliance, vivacity, delicacy, politeness . . . & one should not require of them anything but solidity, exactness, judgment, & erudition."[129]

These sorts of stereotypes, collected by Baillet in the seventeenth century, appeared with some frequency in the journalism and correspondence of the eighteenth. Several journals made similar summations of the type of scholarship to be expected from each country,[130] and rude remarks about nearly every nationality were commonplace. Chevreau, for example, said that "the Muscovite is properly the man of Plato, who is called in Diogenes Laertius, *an Animal with two feet, without feathers, who lacks nothing to be a man, other than reason & cleanliness*."[131] The Germans continued to suffer from insults to their style and ideas, while Jacques Bernard said he rarely mentioned Dutch books in the *Nouvelles de la République des Lettres* because they were all so awful.[132] Most national journals thus felt it necessary to defend themselves in their prefaces against the prejudices levied against them in the learned world. The *Bibliothèque italique* of 1729 printed *nouvelles littéraires* from Scipio Maffei challenging such views: "*To the Republic of Men of Letters*. To make it known with what small reason Italy is mocked in an Ultramontane Journal, saying that we do not know how to do anything other than translate French Books, or copy Editions made on the other side of the mountains . . . I am currently undertaking a new edition of the Works of Cassiodorus."[133] Unsurprisingly, then, the stereotype of the French was that they had no respect for scholars of other nations; the Père Le Courayer, writing from England, said that a project by Prévost was thought "quite *French*, that is, boastful. For in this country *vain* and *French* are two synonyms used to honor our Nation."[134] But most scholars agreed that of all the nations in Europe the one with the most respect for learning was not France, but England.[135]

To view scholarly style and ability as somehow innate in particular national groups was to deal a considerable blow to international views of the learned community. A similar blow was struck by religious stereotypes, which were much more often expressed in this period of religious controversy. The concept of judging a man by his religious beliefs is so well-known of this era that it scarcely bears discussion. But it nevertheless should be noted that such ideas infiltrated the supposedly nonsectarian Republic of Letters.

This is especially evident in Protestant dealings with the Jesuits, whose presumed character was rarely forgotten and who were considered unlikely to put their religious beliefs aside in favor of learning. A *malhonnête extrait* of a book by Barbeyrac was thus "fait à la Jesuite," and Jean Cornand de La Crose said "the Character of a Jesuit . . . doth not well agree with that of a sincere Writer."[136] Isaac de Larrey was amazed that the Père Tournemine, chief editor of the *Journal de Trévoux*, complimented him on his history of England, and Le Clerc's initial judgment of the journal's authors—"passionate and ignorant Priests . . . who observe no rules of justice or equity"—was a general one in the Protestant world.[137] The interesting point about these comments is that the prejudice was precisely that the Jesuits were unwilling to abandon their own prejudices. This was considered, in turn, prejudicial to learning: "I see with sadness," wrote Charles-Etienne Jordan,

> [how] the authors of the Histoire Litteraire de France [are] afflicted and persecuted: it is without doubt the Loyolists [i.e. Jesuits] who have hatched all of this. This Society has never done so much good to the public as the Benedictines have. It is in my opinion an edifying thing, the House these Messieurs have in Paris; they are only occupied with studying, and the advancement of belles lettres, as opposed to the Jesuits, who only think of aggrandizing themselves.[138]

If Catholics would just occupy themselves with studying instead of Catholicism, in other words, the Republic of Letters would profit. But non-Jesuit Catholics were not excused from such stereotyping, and Protestants remarked on their passion for domination and the fact that "even the most talented and the most modern of the Roman Church are not exempt from a certain bad faith which comes from their prejudices."[139]

These prejudices about other people's prejudices illustrate the larger point: that the values of two different communities were constantly struggling with each other. Protestants blamed Catholics for behaving as they themselves behaved, and all with the view of the cohesion of the Republic of Letters. Yet neither group was willing to abandon religious partisanship entirely for the sake of the proper functioning of the scholarly world. Consequently, allegiances to each community inevitably conflicted with each other within the minds of their members. Gisbert Cuper might avoid speaking of the war to a French Catholic friend, or pontificate vaguely to him about the evils of its effects on learning, but to the Huguenot minister David Martin he crowed about the success of the Protestant allies.

God be praised for the blessing he gives to our arms, I hope that even
Freethinkers will attribute all the glory of it to His Divine Majesty alone,
& that they will recognize along with you & me, that this is the work of
his hand. Praised be our Savior Jesus Christ, that he punishes so visibly a
King, who has done infinite harm to his People, which one cannot
consider without horror; a King who with his armies has desolated so
many Countries, & forced an incredible number of Christians to perish. I
hope that God will finally make this Monarch see, as formerly Diocletian
& Maximilian did, the crimes of which he is held guilty; that he will
repent of them.[140]

Exiles in Action

For the Huguenots in exile, the problem of being pulled away from scholarly
impartiality was hard to ignore.[141] A high proportion of Huguenot scholars
were either ministers or former theological students, and most of those who
did not fall into these categories were also committed Protestants. Even if
they had been too young to have made the choice to flee—and many of the
people we have been discussing left France because of their parents' decision—they not only chose to stay in exile but appeared to approve of the
choice which had been made. Jean Masson, for example, defended himself
against the Catholic proselyte André Dacier by saying, "The insult, by the
way, that this devout Convert believes he is making me here about my
Religion, honors me more than he realizes. When I left my Country, I was
scarcely old enough to know more Theology than my Catechism. I nevertheless was sufficiently educated, to follow very willingly a Father who was
sovereignly respected & beloved by all those who knew him, both Roman
Catholics & Reformed, by the sanctity of his values, & by the greatness of his
charity, which so many people felt without distinction of Party."[142] Louis
Bourguet made the same point in a private letter to Georges Seigneux de
Correvon.[143] The Huguenots' existence in diaspora, particularly in the earliest
decades after the Revocation of the Edict of Nantes, made taking sides in
religious and political disputes not only virtually unavoidable, but for many
a practical necessity.

It is well known that the Huguenot church itself took what action it could
on its own behalf. For many years its members had been participating in
controversies in print with the Catholics, and these naturally intensified after
the Revocation. The controversial materials, on intertwining issues of religion, history, and political theory, varied widely in their radicalism and their
goals. Writers like Jurieu and Benoît attacked the absolutist government of
France and its right to deny the Huguenots their rights, while other authors,

such as Bayle and Basnage, were more moderate in their criticisms, while still protesting their treatment by the French and asserting the right of the Huguenots to religious toleration.[144] Although there has been some debate over which group was more influential, it is important here to note that even the most moderate of the refugees still had an axe to grind against the French government and the Catholic church and felt it important to pursue their goals in writing.

Huguenots opposed their enemies in action as well as on paper. Collectively and individually, they took political sides, doing what they could to promote the success of the Protestant allies in the wars of the late seventeenth and early eighteenth centuries. Both on their own account and at the instigation of provincial and municipal governments, for example, the Walloon churches in the Netherlands prayed publicly for Allied and Protestant victory.[145] Numerous Huguenot soldiers fought in Allied regiments, including the scholar David Durand, who as pastor to a regiment of Protestant Languedocian cavalry was captured in Spain in 1707, imprisoned in a pigsty, and briefly condemned to be burned alive.[146] The Allied governments received Huguenots' proposals for a variety of offensives against the French, including projects to stir up Huguenots in the Cévennes and to land troops at various points on the west coast of France.[147] The famous minister and controversialist Pierre Jurieu carried through on such projects (unbeknownst to his ministerial and scholarly colleagues in the Netherlands)[148] by running, along with the Huguenot merchant Etienne Caillaud, a long-term espionage ring in France. Jurieu's spies, whose activity had begun by at least 1689, worked to encourage insurrection in Poitou and the Vaudois and assisted in the Camisard revolt. After 1692 the English government commissioned Jurieu's group to provide information about the plans and preparations of the French army and especially the navy. Although the ring suffered some setbacks—all its spies operating in France were arrested in 1696, and others were captured and executed later—it was able to renew itself and continued in operation until about 1712. Caillaud remained on the English payroll until 1722.[149]

Jurieu's action, as usual, went beyond the efforts of his fellow-Huguenots. But refugees of both the radical and moderate camps did pursue what diplomatic channels they could in securing the future of their party. Huguenots not only wanted immediate support, in the form of jobs and financial help, for refugees in the various Protestant countries, but they were even more anxious for measures to provide assistance to Huguenots still in France and especially to force France to tolerate their religion. Leaders of the Huguenot party, especially in the Netherlands, spent considerable effort over a long period in attempting to persuade the Allies to insist on a clause on their behalf in any peace treaties concluded with France. In 1694 the

Walloon synod first responded to the requests of several churches that "in
case peace negotiations come about, the Powers should be urged in the name
of God, & by the Compassions of *Jesus Christ*, to do whatever they can to
obtain the Re-establishment of the EDICT OF NANTES, &c. & the liberty of
our Brothers who are in the galleys & in the prisons." All ministers were
urged to take up the matter with the magistrates of their towns.[150] The same
issue came up in later synods as the treaty of Rijswijk and the negotiations to
end the War of the Spanish Succession came and went.[151] Huguenot leaders
such as Pierre Jurieu, Jacques Basnage, Elie Benoît, David Martin, and Daniel
de Superville were among those attempting to impress upon the representatives of all the Protestant allies both the need and the responsibility to help
their church. In deputations to the negotiations in Utrecht and The Hague,
letters to the duke of Marlborough, and, in Basnage's case, close involvement
in the final negotations themselves, these leaders stressed the importance of
this issue as best as they could.[152] But the issue of Huguenot refugees got very
little attention at the peace conferences, and in the end none of the treaties
mentioned them at all.[153]

The Huguenots put great effort into these campaigns, no matter what their
ultimate success. And, significantly, among those at the fore of such attempts
were people otherwise identified with the Republic of Letters. David
Durand, who had left his family's refuge in Switzerland "to look in Holland
for the Sciences & for Books," studied with Perizonius at the academy in
Leiden, and later wrote a *Vie de Vanini* and works on French grammar,
joined up with allied troops and, as he put it, "exposed my Life & lost in
Spain all that I had in the service of my Nation."[154] Henri Basnage de
Beauval, author of the *Histoire des ouvrages des savans*, who admitted in his first
issue that he was a Protestant but would try "to speak without any partiality
which could shock, or even afflict the other parties," asked the Walloon
synod in 1691 for funds to print a work of religious controversy.[155] Jacques
Basnage, a respected theologian and historian, was intimately involved with
efforts to promote Huguenot diplomatic interests, as well as writing numerous works of religious controversy; others involved in this effort, such as
Superville, Martin, and Benoît, were also scholars. And the list continues.
Savants did not allow the disinterestedness required of them by the Republic
of Letters to stifle their political or religious activities.

This is evident in one area of scholarship of which Huguenots appeared
particularly fond: the writing of contemporary history. As Graham Gibbs has
pointed out, the histories, collections of documents, and political journalism
written by Huguenots formed the opinions of the rest of Europe about the
Dutch Republic;[156] but the same might be said of other countries. Rapin, for
example, was the most highly respected historian of England of his era,
largely because of his oft-praised impartiality, and his history was constantly

cited by Whig and Tory alike.[157] But Rapin was unusual in this impartiality, despite the constant claims made for it by the historians themselves. Abel Boyer, historian of the reigns of William III and Anne, was no less partisan than his cabinet-making counterpart Chevalier.[158]

Political partisanship was sometimes connected to political work. Jacques Basnage, as official historiographer to the States-General, promised that his title would not divert him from "the impartiality necessary to a historian"; he was horrified by the partiality demonstrated by Abraham Wicquefort, whose unpublished history, biased in the wrong political direction, formed the basis for his new version. But Basnage's dedicatory epistle to the States of Holland and West Friesland stated that one reason for writing such a history was the neglect that partisan foreign historians had shown for "the Glory which the Republic is due," and he used an "impartial" account of past errors to illuminate the brilliance of the current administration.[159] No doubt some of this was a result of his close involvement in political and diplomatic affairs as a sort of assistant to Heinsius during the period of writing the history.[160]

The case of Jean Du Mont was much more blatant. Du Mont, a political journalist and historian who wrote for the *Lettres historiques contenant ce qui se passe de plus important en Europe* and published in 1699 the *Mémoires politiques pour servir à la parfaite intelligence de la paix de Riswick*, in 1700 hoped for employment as the States-General's historiographer. As he wrote to Heinsius, he was a French refugee under the protection of the States-General and was married to a Dutch woman whose father had worked for the government for more than fifty years; better yet, "living in The Hague . . . has given him the means to see and to know a great number of foreign Diplomats, and to cultivate by the same means the Study of modern History." He wanted "to transmit to Posterity the memory of the great things which the King [i.e. William III] [and] their H.H.P.P. [*Hautes Puissances*] had done in our days, in favor of the persecuted Church, and for a Europe about to fall into Slavery." It was important, he thought, for the States-General to have a historian who is "well-instructed, well-intentioned and who is not engaged in the Interests of any other Prince."[161] Heinsius took one look at these qualifications and focussed on his acquaintance with foreign diplomats. Du Mont was set to spy on Francisco Bernardo de Quiros, the Spanish ambassador to the peace negotiations, to whom he had dedicated his *Mémoires politiques* of the previous year. Instead of writing a history of the Netherlands, he wrote frequent reports on his conversations with De Quiros, providing Heinsius with access to the ambassador's state of mind and a conduit for putting ideas into his head.[162] Perhaps it was not that different from writing a history. Both, in Du Mont's view, were a service to the state, as his later productions as historiographer to the Emperor make plain.[163]

The demands of political allegiance, of religious conviction, and of personal interest thus provided strong competition for the ideals of the learned world. Elisabeth Israels Perry has suggested that after the Revocation some Huguenots "fled into a kind of cosmopolitanism, becoming citizens of the 'Republic of Letters.' They did not withdraw from the fray, but changed their techniques: their writings became more moderate, scholarly and philosophical."[164] While it is true that some of the men we are considering were moderate on religious issues, others were not, and, as we have seen, a lack of partisanship over the religious and the political situation does not seem necessarily to be correlated with membership in the Republic of Letters. The learned world required the kind of cosmopolitanism Perry describes, but the competing values of church and state made equal claims on scholars. A sort of compartmentalization had to take place, in which one person might have had to juggle two different systems of values.

Internationalisms

One way to distinguish among conflicting challenges, a way endorsed by scholarly ideology, might have been to give the broader community priority over narrow regional or sectarian concerns. But the international character of the Republic of Letters was not necessarily an effective counterweight to the demands of Protestant and political partisanship. Huguenots might have felt that in one sphere of their lives they could put differences aside for the sake of a stronger community, but the same ethos reigned within Protestantism itself. This movement was also international, but the union it sought was not one which always corresponded with the goals of scholarly unity. Scholars who belonged to both communities consequently faced further tensions in their loyalties.

The internationalism of the Protestant world was clearly felt by the refugees streaming out of France after the Edict of Fontainebleau. The character of the movement to force toleration down Louis' throat—ministers talking to political figures both in their own country and abroad—suggests the pervading sense that any Protestant nation could now be a home for a refugee. By virtue of their Protestantism, Queen Anne, Anthonie Heinsius, and the Elector of Brandenburg alike were expected to assist in settling their religious compatriots. Although many refugees continued to feel French, and others remained in and assimilated into their new countries, behavior toward the sovereigns of Protestant nations—such as the dedication of books to them[165]—shows how refugee scholars might at least initially direct their allegiance to a comfortingly large number of entities.[166]

The search for appropriate employment in any available location demonstrates the same belief. If someone was not happy in one Protestant country, others appeared to beckon. Barbeyrac, writing a recommendation for a young Swiss student in the Netherlands, told Des Maizeaux that

> he had come here, thinking to find some employment, which could help him study at this University [Groningen]: but nothing having presented itself, he has resolved to pass into England, where he will make his fortune. I believe that this is very casual: the people of that country imagine that all they have to do is to come here or to England, to find something, & they don't realize that, barring some great luck, it requires a great deal of time & expense to find some appropriate post.[167]

Barbeyrac himself had moved from Berlin to Lausanne to Groningen, and other scholars expected the same opportunities. Isaac de Beausobre considered leaving Berlin for London—Jacob le Duchat said that "as he believes he has reason not to be content with our court, it is said here that he is soliciting a place as Chaplain of your Queen"[168]—and La Croze's proposed solution to his own employment problems was "to go look for bread in England."[169] The experience of exile was of course in many ways disorienting, provoking a sense of rootlessness which in itself contributed to these migrations. But the particular nature of this exile also gave a sense, however misplaced, of a wider field of support, so that refugees searching for a feeling of community could find it at least in part in the community of international Protestantism.

These feelings were surely reinforced by the efforts at internationalism pursued by the Protestant churches. Charity toward other churches was one important field of international endeavor. Not only did the Walloon church in the Netherlands collect money for the Huguenot galley-slaves in France, but the Dutch Reformed Church did the same; when some were released, the Walloon synod thanked the Dutch synod of Zuid-Holland, saying that they were one of the chief instruments used by God to help sustain and encourage the poor *galériens*. "With what fraternal compassion have you not taken part in their sufferings? With what great care have you not looked for means to ease them?" These actions did honor to "the holy Religion which we all profess."[170] The Walloon church also supported churches in the Palatinate, the Pays de Vaud, and the valleys of Piedmont, and other Protestant churches pursued a similar course. One Huguenot minister in London, Claude Groteste de la Mothe, wrote a book called *Charitas Anglicana* to show how charitably disposed the Anglican church was to foreign Reformed churches, presumably to encourage the continuation of this disposition.[171]

Protestant churches also cooperated in everyday matters, passing information back and forth, and the reformed churches made attempts at uniformity in their service. The Walloon synod ruled that it was legitimate for its members to take communion in Dutch Reformed churches,[172] and when new liturgical formulations were devised it was considered advisable by some that they be introduced in all the Reformed churches. The lengthy debate over whether or not a new translation of the psalms by Conrart should be adopted in the Walloon church is a good example. The Genevan church had decided to use this translation in 1698 and thought it should be used elsewhere as well. The Genevan Academy, with Louis Tronchin at its head, wrote to the Walloon synod in 1700 about the utility of the venture,[173] and the churches of Brandenburg had printed a version of the new psalms by the summer of 1701.[174] In the event, the Walloon synod, annoyed at the presumption of the Genevans at making such a change without consulting them, initially refused to adopt the psalms, and the debate (led at first by Jurieu) lasted so long that some churches did not have the psalters until 1730.[175]

At first this will hardly seem an example of Protestant unity. Yet the debate itself indicates how much unity was assumed to be the desirable thing. The Genevans, having profited from the new psalter, thought all the other reformed churches should use it. The Walloon church also thought unity—although unity in orthodoxy—important, and it was the Genevan failure to acknowledge that unity by taking independent action which annoyed Jurieu and his followers. Both sides turned their debate into an international effort, writing to Brandenburg, for example, to urge conformity with its position. Both in England and in Brandenburg Jurieu's side received little support. Gilbert Burnet wrote that "If I did not know Mon[r] Jurieu so well as I do I should be amazed at the noise he had raised and the opposition he still gives to the new version of the Psalmes. . . . He is not like to find any among us on whom his ill humour will have any ill effects"; Lenfant in Berlin said "Messrs Jurieu and Benoît have filled this country with seditious letters both to the Churches and to individuals of some importance. . . . He [Jurieu] wrote a Latin letter to one of the Ministers of our court in the Style of a Monk of the tenth century, or of a Schoolboy of the third who writes his theme without a dictionary, and with the reasoning of an old man."[176] Although the Walloon synod was intransigent, other Protestant churches felt that unity was crucial.

Self-protection was an important reason for these views. The Protestants felt they had to stay on the defensive, for any weakening in their bloc would merely serve the Catholics. Both sides in the debate over the psalms took this line. Jacques Lenfant said of a letter to the churches of Brandenburg from the Synod of Rotterdam, "Without exaggeration this letter is conceived no differently, than if instead of the Psalms of Conrart you wanted to sing the Mass"; the letter was accompanied by a "feeble" *mémoire* by Jacques Bernard in which "most of the reasons they give for preventing the introduction of this new Revision, are exactly those which oblige them to do it, among others *the fear of rendering us ridiculous to our enemies.*"[177] As J.-F. Osterwald also pointed out, "What a subject of triumph for our adversaries, to see us tearing at each other, and that our Churches can agree on nothing!"[178] The church constantly strove to maintain at least an image of unified internationalism. This defensive posture was strengthened, moreover, by the more positive efforts to reunite the Protestant churches—advocated, among others, by scholar-churchmen such as Leibniz, Turrettini, Jaquelot, and Le Clerc—which were gaining momentum in this period. The international interchange of information, assistance, and goodwill among people of different Protestant communions at times rivalled that of the ideal Republic of Letters.

The Juggling Huguenots

The sense of breadth and unity, both actual and desired, among the Reformed churches and the Protestant powers meant that the learned community could not necessarily supersede political and religious values simply by virtue of its own internationalism. The combination of religious conviction and a perceived union in essentials made the Protestant movement strong enough that it was not always easy to appeal to a higher or broader cause when the issue was scholarship rather than religion. This was an issue of particular moment because, despite the commonality of their membership, the values of the two communities could differ so widely. We have already noted the conflict in attitudes toward partisanship, which was to be avoided in scholarly work yet was necessary, or at least unavoidable, in striving for victory for the "common cause." The same sorts of difficulties arose in other areas seemingly under the purview of both the church and the Republic of Letters.

The stream of manuscripts flowing to the "fertile crescent" outside of France is indicative of the views of the Republic of Letters about censorship. If works could not be published in France, French people were happy to send them elsewhere, and as we saw in the case of the bishop of Avranches, official rank seemed to make no difference to these views. For Bayle, the freedom of the press in the Netherlands was "an advantage which is not found in any other Countries":

> they accord the Printers such an extended liberty, that people address themselves to them from all parts of Europe, when they find themselves disheartened by the difficulties of obtaining a Privilege. Assuredly if Milton had lived in these Provinces, he would not have thought to write a Book called *de Typographia liberanda*, for he would not have felt that things there

were in servitude in that regard. Our presses are the refuge of Catholics as well as Reformed, & the Arguments of Messieurs of the Communion of Rome are feared so little, that all their books are allowed to be sold publicly, far from acting as in the Countries of Inquisition, where according to the report of the Chevalier Sandis, even Catholic Controversialists are not allowed to be put on sale, so much are they afraid of the objections of the Protestants, which appear in the Works of Controversy. . . . This *honnête* liberty of the Press is without doubt a very favorable advantage, to the plan to write a Scholarly Journal, & that is what has made me even more amazed that no one has undertaken such a work in this Country.[179]

Bayle quickly took care of the lapse on the part of his scholarly peers, and when other learned journals came to be written they were nearly all published in the Netherlands. While journalists and other authors did feel some need to control the *quality* of publications in the Republic of Letters,[180] the consensus was that freedom to express one's opinion was essential to the Republic's operations.

Related to this issue is that of disputation. Impartiality was important in books and literary journals because the goal was truth, rather than opinion. But scholars increasingly acknowledged that any individual member of their community might not have a monopoly on the truth.[181] Consequently, all sides of an issue had to be heard before any judgment could be made. There was nothing wrong with disagreement *per se*, and the *Journal littéraire* ridiculed "Authors . . . who are angry with us, because we have not thought as they do on the subjects they have discussed. Wouldn't one say, to hear them, that it is not permitted to be of different opinions without being declared enemies?"[182] Journalists had to remain impartial precisely so that everyone's differing views could be presented, and, as we have seen, those attacked in one issue might be invited to respond in another. Jacques Bernard, a later author of the *Nouvelles de la République des Lettres*, said of his journal that "as I permit everyone to follow his own views, I also wish to be allowed the liberty of following my own."[183]

Although these standards were frequently not achieved, the necessity for discussion remained an ideal for most members of the Republic of Letters. Quarrels were thus commended for their usefulness; Bayle said that "the contestations which arise between learned men are good because they contribute much to the clarifying of several dogmas on which people have only confused ideas," and Willem Jacob s'Gravesande thought discussions among those of different opinions were "the best means of advancing the sciences."[184] What might cause problems was style, for the fierceness of argument was detrimental to the Republic of Letters. According to Bignon, "the disputes of men of Letters can be very useful. It is only to be desired, that in their quarrels, they are seeking only the interests of the truth, and that in combatting opinions, they respect Persons."[185] To bring in gratituitous insults about religious choices was unscholarly of Dacier and Masson; to quarrel over Horace, however, might well be of value.

Nothing could be further from the views of the Walloon church. As in the Republic of Letters, union was desirable; the articles of the Walloon synod are full of appeals to the ministers to treat each other politely in their writings.[186] But the reaction to disobedience was to forbid any writing at all. When Pierre Jurieu and Elie Saurin got into a protracted printed quarrel, the synod in 1695 forbade them "expressly to write anything more against each other, in whatever manner, under pain of treating them in future with all the rigor of the Discipline, & even the suspension of Holy Communion, & of the Holy Ministry of those who violate this order."[187]

The way to gain peace was to avoid discussion. The synod printed in its articles an order of the States of Holland and West Friesland, which declared that "all Doctors, be they Professors, or Readers in Theology, or Ministers of the Reformed Churches of Holland, & of West Friesland, will conform in their Writings, Sermons, Catechizations, Lessons, & Disputes both Public, & Private, to the ordinary Formularies of the Reformed Churches, contained in the Catechisms, Confessions, & Canons of the National Synod of Dordrecht; & will take great care not to teach, nor write, anything which is contrary to it." Such an order, if obeyed, could only have a salutary effect. "[S]ince after this there will be no essential reason for dispute, they will live together in fraternal charity, peace, & union."[188] The concurrence of the Walloon synod with this analysis is evident. Its lengthy examination of the doctrine of Elie de Joncourt in 1707 concluded with the declaration that on the subject of the interpretation of the scriptures it would "never suffer in its bosom, neither sowing of division, nor shadow of partiality."[189] To disagree with the ruling of the synod was to destroy both unity and its own vision of objectivity.

It is one of the peculiarities of the Huguenot church that, although it was in the vanguard of struggles for religious toleration in Europe, it was itself relatively intolerant.[190] Although it argued for Catholic tolerance of the Protestant church, sectarian divisions within Protestantism were a serious concern in the early part of the eighteenth century. The Walloon synod, in particular, spent considerable time examining the beliefs of its members for fear of an infiltration of Arminianism, Cocceianism, Socinianism, or Amyrauldism, and it was a matter of some comment that, as Jacques Saurin wrote, "in the country of the world where tolerance is carried as far as the most unbridled license, the walloon Churches adopt some of the maxims of the inquisition."[191] One visitor from Geneva in 1711 summed up the situation in the Netherlands thus:

You ask me what disposition of spirit this country is in. People are still
very rigid here. The story of Mr Durant cited at the Synod for several light
suspicions of Arminianism shows how heated people still are about these
sorts of things. Messrs the ministers of Amsterdam are the most zealous and
the most prompt to accuse of heresy those who by their talent overshadow
them in some way. Several years ago, animated by these motives (according to what they say) they started a big trial of Mr Vignier, a refugee
minister, about his having said in one of his sermons that one cannot be
justified without doing good works. They recently complained of a sermon which Mr Chion made to them, for the same reason. Here [Leiden]
Messieurs the French Ministers are more moderate. You know the opinions of Mr Bernard on this matter. . . . He nevertheless does not fail at the
same time to be very reserved, so as not to say anything which could cause
scandal.[192]

Although the French church in the Netherlands was notably fierce on
these issues, it was not alone in its pursuit of orthodoxy. Just as theological
students in the Netherlands had to sign a *confession de foi* and the Synod of
Dordrecht, in Prussia ministers and students had to sign an act of orthodoxy,
and in Switzerland the *consensus helveticus* was in several periods enforced with
great rigor. The peregrinations of certain scholars bear testimony to the
international character of this intolerance.

Jean Barbeyrac's experience with the church in Berlin, for example, which
diverted his career from the ministry into jurisprudence, suggests the strict-
ness with which that consistory could deal with its own members. In April
of 1699, when Barbeyrac was to be examined to see if he could function as
ministre extraordinaire, the consistory—including Jacques Lenfant, David
Ancillon, Isaac de Beausobre, and other ministers—brought up "a proposition which I had made two months earlier, & which they said they had
heard contained heterodox opinions." The company also censured him for an
incomplete catechism he had been writing because of omissions it contained;
one minister, Bancelin, stated in justification that at Charenton Charles Le
Cène had been condemned for a single omission in the explication of a text.
The result, as Barbeyrac bitterly reported, was that "I was decried throughout
the town as a Socinian."[193]

This incident surely contributed to Barbeyrac's strong opposition to the
enforcement of the *consensus* in Lausanne, where he went in 1711 to teach
civil law. Although Barbeyrac signed a modified version of the *consensus*,[194]
"several Ecclesiastics, Enemies of Peace," sought to strengthen it, and after
Barbeyrac's departure for Groningen in 1717 the academy tightened its
requirements. This caused problems for Jean-Pierre de Crousaz, and, while
Barbeyrac thanked Providence "that it brought me here before the storm in

your country, in which I would have been enveloped," he did what he could for his friend, writing to the authorities and editing anonymously a collection of pieces on the subject.[195] He also tried to find Crousaz a job at Groningen, but the issue came up again: would Crousaz have to sign the Synod of Dordrecht?

> As you would come here in the quality of Professor of *Pphie* [philosophy] & Math. and not as a Minister, I believe that you would not have trouble in signing as *Pphe* & Mathematician, & like the professors of the other Faculties, outside of Theology: As for me, I only signed on that footing, not knowing, when we had to sign at our installation, if it was the Synod of Dordrecht I was signing, because they only read us a Formulary, where all that was mentioned was union, peace, concord & it was to union, to concord, to peace that I signed, resolved that, if I was asked for any explanation, I would declare that I did not concern myself with the disputes of Theologians on unimportant matters.[196]

While the resistance of scholars such as Barbeyrac, de Crousaz, Jean Le Clerc, and César de Missy to these acts of orthodoxy is certainly important, it is equally significant that the bodies enforcing such acts also contained scholars. Jacques Lenfant and Isaac de Beasobre, savants we have encountered before, were among those confronting Barbeyrac in Berlin; the academies themselves in Lausanne and Groningen required signatures of their professors; and the Walloon synod was made up of numerous scholars, including Jacques Basnage, called, as we have seen, "the soul of the Synods."[197] Scholars as a species did not divorce themselves from the orthodox passions of religious institutions.

The same point can be made about another focus of religious activity which conflicted with scholarly values: censorship. Freedom of the press was inimical to the church, as the Walloon Synod of Kampen made plain: "As the freedom of printing books which contain impieties & profanities is growing with impunity, the Synod recommends to the Churches to be as diligent as possible to stop their course, & in these cases to address the Sovereigns in its name."[198] All writings which had to do with theological matters had to be submitted to the "Eglises examinatrices," which would pronounce on the purity of their doctrine before the books could go to press. Jacques Saurin complained of these requirements in 1727:

> I have to submit my manuscripts to two Eglises examinatrices, who often name me to be examined by people some of whom do not understand our language, and most of whom have no common sense. Add to this the motives which animate some of those of our robe. The excess goes so far that even reasonable expressions are censured, so that I am obliged to

substitute for them ones which are not [reasonable] at all. I said, I don't know where, that the dogma of the Trinity *étoit l'écueil de la raison humaine*. There were very lively conferences about this word in the consistory of Rotterdam, where it was concluded that I would put, instead of this word *écueil*, that of *aheurtement*. Judge the whole by this sample.[199]

The discussion of books and reports of the *églises examinatrices* was a regular feature of the Walloon synods, and Charles de la Motte reported in 1711 that, particularly since the French refugees had taken over the Walloon church "it is certain that there is less liberty."[200] The synod even extended its deliberations to the frontispieces of books.[201] In 1704 its members were forced to acknowledge that "Books of Criticism, & of Literature, are not those that the Writers of our Corps are obliged to have examined, these sorts of examinations properly regarding only Books of Theology & of Morals";[202] but it continued to hanker after other sorts of productions, and the Dutch Reformed Synod of Zuid-Holland gave it its chance in a letter of 1719 which suggested the censorship of literary journals.

> P.S. The Christian Synod has found it à propos, that the Bibliothèques which are published each month, should be examined, in so far as they treat matters of Theology, in order to prevent any inconveniences, & especially the introduction of bad opinions. And since there are several French Journals and Bibliothèques, which are published, & from which one might fear the same results: the Christian Synod asks you very immediately, if you will have the goodness to join yourself to us, & to have such Journals examined, which treat matters of Theology, before they are printed.[203]

Again, these attitudes seem completely out of keeping for members of the Republic of Letters. Many scholars certainly cried out against the strictures of censorship, suggesting, as the *Bibliothèque italique* did of Italian censorship, that "the Sciences will suffer from it. They will never make progress without a little more liberty."[204] But once again it is not difficult to find scholars who, on matters of religion, agreed with the censors. Putting aside all those in the synod itself, we find Jean-Henri-Samuel Formey arguing with Elie Luzac as late as 1749 that *libraires* ought not to accept manuscripts which attack the doctrines of the faith.[205] Louis Bourguet said that although he would not persecute an atheist, much less burn him, "if it was possible for me I would prevent him from infatuating others with his impious principles."[206] And Gisbert Cuper complained of "excessive tolerance," which "saps the foundations of our Holy Religion":

> The liberty of a People is an admirable thing, & one without price, but perhaps, *nos nimia libertate laboramus*; in allowing all sorts of Books to be published without any discrimination. . . . I wish with all my heart, that a

way could be found to prevent the publication of these Books which are contrary to our Holy Religion, to faith & good morals, & in which are spread love stories & gallant adventures of the fair sex & among others of Monks, for they corrupt youth more than can be stated.[207]

It is difficult, then, to generalize about the feelings of Protestant scholars when confronted with issues of orthodoxy and censorship. Some may even have hidden their views, like Jacques Bernard, scorned by J.-F. Osterwald as "one of the number of the Orthodoxo-politici, or Politico-orthodoxi, a type which, *entre nous*, displeases me; I think more highly of a man who is in error and who speaks according to his conscience, than of these people who skew and disguise their true sentiments."[208] Bernard himself said that he had "signed the Consensus although in Silence; but I never would have wanted to sign it, if they had tried to oblige the French Ministers to promise that they would teach in conformity."[209] But in his literary journal, the *Nouvelles de la République des Lettres*, he would not allow items which were "shocking against Religion" because "one does not speak thus against sacred Authors in Holland" and because he did not want "to ruin myself entirely, along with a large family to whom I must devote myself."[210] Certainly the Republic of Letters provides examples—Barbeyrac, Crouzas, Le Clerc, Missy—of scholars who resisted the strictures of the religious community, and Charles de la Motte explained in 1711 that "to do justice to everyone, this unreasonable rigidity is only among the Ministers."[211] But many counter-examples must also be considered. Some historians of science have suggested that the flowering of English science, at least, must be attributed to the desire of scholars to find some topic which was not divisive.[212] This argument certainly has validity, and it is true that some regarded people carried away by religious passions as coming from a lower order of scholars.[213] It should be remembered, however, that participation in the Republic of Letters did not preclude strong religious—or political—sentiments. Many of the scholars we consider actually were ministers, many of them were fairly conservative, and most of them believed sufficiently in their religion to stay in exile because of it. The general trend of the Reformed church seemed to be intolerant and conservative. Consequently, anyone who believed in its tenets yet also wanted to participate in the Republic of Letters was faced with a problem. Many scholars who were religiously or politically partisan had cordial relations with ideological opponents. How was this possible?

The Refuge of Politeness

The solution seemed not to be abandoning either one's allegiance to the church or to scholarship, but performing a complicated juggling act with the two. This is a process most clearly evident in relations between Protestants and Catholics. Catholic writers, for example, sometimes found themselves in the uneasy position of wishing to praise their learned comrades who happened to be Protestant, an action which might look to their own church like some sort of endorsement of Protestantism. Nicolas Lenglet du Fresnoy's solution was to make a distinction between religion and scholarship. "[D]id anyone ever believe that the approbation of some personal quality one finds in a man includes the approbation of the vices he might have? . . . . Don't people praise the chaste moderation of Virgil every day. . . . [or] admire the gratitude of *Avicenna*, who did not fail, when he discovered a truth, to prostrate himself to render thanks to God, without claiming to authorize thereby, either the Paganism of the one, or the Mohammedanism of the other?"[214] Adrien Baillet also excused himself for doing this, saying that by lauding a Protestant scholar he was not denying the purity and truth of the Catholic faith, but he also felt it necessary to tell "those of the other communion" that "I never meant to disoblige them, much less to insult them, when I said something against one of their members."[215]

In communicating with scholars of another communion, an attempt was made to gloss over points which might disrupt scholarly relations. We have already seen something of this in Cuper's high-minded disparagement of war to a Catholic as damaging to learning while he was gloating over Allied victory to a Protestant. One reason to avoid controversy was to prevent books from being barred from countries with strict censorship. The Abbé de St.-Pierre complained that the *Journal litéraire*'s *nouvelles* from Paris were written in such "a satiric manner that they might forbid the Entry of their journal in france which would be a great loss for their libraire and all French men of letters"; Bignon had the same sort of worry about parts of Des Maizeaux's *Vie de St.-Evremond*.[216]

But trying not to give offense or cause problems with individual scholars was even more common. The way to get around this was to modify one's language.[217] Bayle said that "one writes differently according to the people with whom one corresponds. The P. Paul did not write in the same style to the Protestants, & to the good Roman Catholics," and Bernard, confronted with a "Journaliste de Trevoux" who wanted to correspond with him, said "my commerce consists in hardly more than responding to a few articles about the books he asks me about, and those when I judge it à propos to do it. . . . I am in a great reserve in regard to him."[218]

This did not mean that Protestants and Catholics could not be friends. Louis Bourguet, who spent much of his incarnation as a merchant in Italy, was eloquent on this subject. "When I spoke of distrust of my Friends in France, I only meant on that which concerns Religion. I had Friends in Italy with whom I was in commerce de Lettres for more than xx years. I never distrusted them I only was always very reserved on the subject of Religion."[219] But Bourguet, as a Protestant and a refugee who left France at the age of six, nonetheless had strong feelings, and guarding against their expression was all the more important. When two scholars asked him for a short *mémoire* on his life, he said it was too unimportant to write, and he was certainly not going to send it to France.

> I thus did not think I should give Memoires on my life to two Friends who were Protestants and Theologians. It would be even less suitable to send them to an Author of the R.[eligion] R.[omaine] because I could not pass over in silence what I know of the Dragonnade, remembering very well the voluntary exile which it produced in the whole family of my father. Would I be able to say nothing of a so-called miracle . . . of which I was a witness in the Tyrol and would I be quiet about the ridiculous issue of the Miracle-worker which happened at Venice, where I later learned it from C.[atholiques] R.[omains] who were ocular witnesses?. . . . Would I say nothing of the supposed Bowl from which the B. Virgin ate her soup, which I held in my hands . . . and the great surprise of the Priest who was showing it to me and who did not expect my action. And would I say nothing of what conclusions I drew from the examination I had just made of such a holy Relic? In short, Monsieur, I could not fail to say everything which I learned in Italy, which justifies the *Passe partout de l'Eglise Romaine* and other such Books. Thus I have too many things to say which are not honorable to this Religion to dare send it into France.[220]

When the bare details of his life were given, Bourguet said, they made too boring an account. But when scholars disagreed on religion, the best course was to keep silent.

Just as in the strictures of the Walloon synod to avoid quarrels, the goal here was to promote unity. Despite the pull of the orthodox tendencies of the church, the competing view that religion and politics were not part of the Republic of Letters meant that, especially if they were going to cause division, they should not be discussed. It was not so much that—as in the synod—everyone must have the same ideas, but that these ideas were not sufficiently important in the realm of scholarship to allow them to cause problems. As Barbeyrac planned to say if questioned on the Synod of Dordrecht, "I did not concern myself with the disputes of Theologians on unimportant matters."

At least in this sphere, unity was more important than religion. "We must set aside what divides men into different factions," declared Bayle, "& only consider where they come together, which is the quality of illustrious Man in the Republic of Letters. In that sense all Savants must regard themselves as brothers, or as if each is from as good a house as the other."[221] This did not mean that no discussion should take place, but that it should be carried out gently and fraternally. In this spirit, savants of different religions or political views would even send each other controversial works with the earnest hope that they were sufficiently moderate. Lenfant sent Bignon a book of sermons, hoping that "you do not find the partiality there which you believed you encountered in the Histoire du Concile de Constance. It was not my design neither in the one nor the other";[222] and Bignon in turn encouraged Le Clerc to feel comfortable sending him his history of the United Provinces. "Who does not know that each government in each country has its principles and its maxims, and that in Holland the manner of political thinking, is very different from that in other States. Do not let that reason stop you, I pray you, Monsieur, I will always be charmed to receive from You, whatever works, which with such success you continue to give to the public."[223]

Scholars had to moderate their discussions, or, if necessary, abandon them altogether for the sake of unity. This meant compartmentalizing one's mind. Religion, to most of these scholars, meant a firm opposition to the other communion; but scholarship meant cooperation which ignored religious and political distinctions. Religion, in the baldest sense, meant expressing the opinions of the institution; scholarship meant expressing one's own views. In order to deal with both worlds at the same time, scholars had to reserve particular views for particular sections of their lives. The juggling act was complex, but it seems to have been accomplished successfully by much of the learned world.

The process was potentially eased, however, by certain similarities between the church and the Republic of Letters. Both had concerns about the picture they presented to the outside world, and both, in varying fashions, approached this problem with a certain rigidity. Complete freedom of expression was not a feature of the idealized scholarly world. Discussion was to be controlled there, as it was in the church; and although there did exist a difference in degree, both the church and the Republic of Letters were anxious to maintain a unity which would smooth their own operations while making them look strong, and, more important, not ridiculous to outsiders. The Walloon church, faced with dissension, reacted by putting a complete prohibition on discussion of doctrinal matters; its structure, moreover, made it possible to enforce its own rules. This kind of control was not possible in the Republic of Letters, except through relatively weak institutions like journals and academies, which had little ability to do more than make recommendations. In some ways the Republic of Letters would not have endorsed the concept of institutional control over intellectual activity; arbitrary censorship, particularly from outside their community, was unwelcome, and the liberty to make judgments of others was, at least theoretically, fundamental to scholarly relations. But the strength of feeling surrounding the conduct of debate tells a different story. Expression of opinion was fine, if the opinion was worth something, and if it was expressed in a way suitable to a harmonious community. The censorial role of journals was only one example of the way the Republic of Letters could attempt to control its members' actions.[224] And just as the solution in the case of the Walloon church was to stifle debate altogether, in the Republic of Letters the answer differed from this largely in degree. A picture of unity, for the sake of one's own community and its image in society, was vital to survival: thus moderation, which downplayed debate, was always the goal. The concern for the display of moderation was so great that content became secondary to the conduct of the debate itself. Although control was still important, whereas for the church control could not compromise doctrine, here the subject of debate could recede in the face of quarrels. It was not only safer, but also more important, to think about form rather than content.

Moderation was the key, for if everyone was moderate then the community could continue to function happily. Indeed, this was even more necessary for scholars—who needed to cross normal boundaries—than for other people. According to Bignon, "the sort of Studies they apply themselves to, seem to impose on them the obligation to be more moderate and more polite, than the rest of men. All scholars agree on these Maxims."[225] But, again, this moderation was not so much moderation in opinion, but in behavior. Arguments seemed to concentrate more on the way the dispute was being carried out than on any actual difference of opinion. The quarrel between Anne Dacier and Antoine Houdar de la Motte, for example, was judged at least in part on their behavior rather than the issues. According to the *nouvelles littéraires* in the *Histoire critique*:

> the quarrel about Homer has started up again, with a great deal of vivacity. Madame *Dacier* has made a Critique of the Iliad of Mr. *de la Motte*, & of his Discourse on Homer. It has pleased this Lady to entitle her Work, *The Causes of the Corruption of Taste*, although she speaks about this very little, & after the 32nd page there is no longer any question of it. Her Best Friends have blamed this transport of anger against Mr. *de la Motte*, & the injurious things she says to him. Mr. *de la Motte* has responded with much moderation, & this moderation adds a new weight to his response.[226]

Individual learned bodies, such as academies, were always concerned about the subject of behavior. The project to combine the old and new scientific societies in Berlin is only one example. "The Society will take care exactly that, on the occasions when some members are of different opinions, they will use no term of scorn nor bitterness against each other, either in their discourse, or in their writings, and even when they combat the opinions of any savant at all, the society will exhort them only to speak with consideration."[227] Whether or not such exhortations were followed is another matter.

The sons of Nicolaas Hartsoeker protested about Fontenelle's *éloge* of their father because of its statement that he "had rudely qualified some specific thoughts of Mr. Leibniz." Most *éloges*, the sons said, were kinder, saying people had "an excess of naïveté & sincerity" which all societies would excuse. "And frankly," Hartsoeker's sons went on, ". . . if such Expressions, for which Monsieur Hartsoeker is so blamed, . . . were not permitted in the Republic of Letters, do you believe that an infinity of illustrious Savants, & even the most grave & the most moderate ones, would use them so familiarly & with such impunity?"[228] Hartsoeker's sons had a point. But it was nevertheless true that, attainable or not, a major goal of literary societies in specific and literary society in general was to maintain an edifying moderation and decorum.

The sentiment was just the same as that of religious groups, such as the Walloon synod, which spoke out against unpleasant language in the interests of harmony. Here, too, unity was at issue. But unlike at the synod, discussion was allowed, and when potentially divisive subjects came up in the Republic of Letters, special care was necessary. Indeed, without the guiding light of acts of orthodoxy, politeness became all the more critical for maintaining union.

Just as in quarrels over literary matters, then, quarrels about religion focussed on politeness rather than doctrine. For André Dacier to bring up Jean Masson's religious status "has been regarded as something so base, so dastardly, & so little worthy of a man who has his honor as recommendation," that reviewers who might have agreed with his views were justly upset.[229] Whether Dacier's or Masson's religious views were correct was not at issue. The *Journal de Trévoux*'s quarrel with Jean Le Clerc, who (outside their jurisdiction) edited the Dutch edition of the journal, is another good example. Although the actual issue was one of Protestant versus Catholic, neither party seemed to pay much attention to points of doctrine. Instead, the quarrel was all about manners.

Protestant Theologians will permit us to make a few more reflections on the reproach that M. le Clerc made to us, as if in their name, of not having enough moderation about them. If we treated them a little harshly in our Memoires would they have the least right to complain about it, they who for so many years have filled nearly all their Works & even their Journals, with invectives against the Roman Church in general, against the Pope, against the Bishops, against the secular & regular Clergy?. . . . As for us, we could complain on our side of [the injurious things] he said to us, we could easily bring up examples. He accuses us of ignorance: he accuses us of not knowing what Socinianism is, of not understanding the original of the Scripture, of not knowing how to read Hebrew or Greek, of not even understanding Latin; in all, of having little wit & equity, & of resembling the Censors of the Holy Office who, according to him, trust suspicions entirely, & who only try to defame those who have different opinions from theirs.[230]

The journalists promised always to do justice to the works of the Protestants, to praise their erudition and *politesse*, and only to talk about religion with moderation and restraint.[231] The *Bibliothèque italique* promised to ignore controversy because "justice, equity, & politeness, whose rules men of Letters must follow more exactly than anyone, are so opposed to partiality, that an Author given to that base passion is certainly branded in the eyes of *honnêtes gens* of all Communions."[232] Between Catholics and Protestants, both *politesse* and theology were at issue. In the end, it was *politesse* that took precedence.

The world of the Republic of Letters bore close similarities to some aspects of the religious and political world whose space, and some of whose members, it also shared. Both concerned themselves with language and behavior and union, worrying in their own way about the relationships among the three. Both vied for the attention of their adherents, and both had strong international organizations to whose ideals members in doubt could appeal. Yet despite the strength of religious and political sentiments, only augmented by the special situation of the Huguenot refugees, in the realm of scholarship other ideals reigned. For the sake, not of truth, but of unity, scholars glossed over religious quarrels, ignored political passions, pretended wars were not occurring. Even when tempers ran high and salvation itself seemed to be at stake, politeness, and consequently the integrity of the learned community, often seemed even more important. Moderation was the only way to maintain that integrity.

Nicolas Clément knew that his country was at war with the Protestant allies. He knew that he worked for the king of France and was confronted with dealing with the Dutch Republic. He knew that he was a Catholic, and that the manuscripts Aymon had stolen would help the Protestant cause. But he also knew he was a librarian. His appeals had nothing to do with party, nothing to do with religion or war. They were appeals from one scholar to another. Yet Clément nearly failed to get the manuscripts back. Some people supported Aymon for his treasure, it is true; but others merely disapproved, not of the religion or the politics, but of the *behavior* of the French Catholic side. As Basnage wrote to the Abbé de Beaumont, "M. L'Abbé Renaudot has written several letters here which are as proud as those of M. Clement appeared judicious and wise. He defies the Ministers, and compares M. Claude in Impudence with Aimon. He finds it strange that his good faith is being arbitrated with that of a minister who is nothing."[233] What good was it to argue that scholars should be above politics and religion, that the Republic of Letters should consist of brothers, if that unity was shattered by ill-humor and pride? Behavior was the true test; and Clément was lucky to see his manuscripts again.

5

TALKING ABOUT NOTHING

MANNERS OLD AND NEW

A Terrible Itch

When Charles-Etienne Jordan went on his *voyage littéraire* in 1733, his journey mapped in physical form an otherwise largely imaginary community.[1] Jordan did not merely wish to find the Republic of Letters: he wished to place himself in it. But to join the Republic of Letters required contacts. Indeed, to join the Republic of Letters essentially *meant* having contacts.

Jordan was clearly aware of this. For several years before he made his trip, he was already dipping his toes into scholarly waters. In the first place, in the mid-to-late 1720s he had begun *commerces de lettres* with a number of scholars in other places, such as the former traveller Uffenbach in Frankfurt, with whom he entertained a three-year correspondence between 1725 and 1728.[2] One of these *commerces* was with Louis Bourguet, whom Jordan began writing in 1728 because both were planning to publish collections about Leibniz. These books would of course link their names with his, even though, as Jordan frankly avowed, neither one of them was a "blind admirer" of Leibniz or his philosophy.[3] The natural thing was of course to get together on the project of the *Leibniziana*; but the added benefit of this for Jordan was to link his name not only with Leibniz, but also with the now-established Bourguet. Jordan himself said this in a letter to Bourguet in 1729. "Let us talk now about our project. I will begin by complaining of your excessive kindness. My name is of very small importance, little known: a young man who is only starting out, and who only has the desire to learn: while you, Monsieur, possess already everything I wish to acquire. Never could my name be better placed than next to yours; that would be a positive advantage to it. I will be your satellite, and you will be my Jupiter."[4]

Jordan had also already become known to some of the more important scholars in his hometown of Berlin, including Des Vignoles, the scholar of Rabelais Jacob le Duchat, and most particularly Maturin Veyssière La Croze.

La Croze was renowned for his learning, especially his command of languages; he was the author of dictionaries of Coptic, Armenian, Slavonic, and Syriac, as well as histories of Christianity in the Indies, Ethiopia, and Armenia. Jordan had studied with La Croze, who taught him out of friendship when he was in his early twenties, and later Jordan tended him in an illness which La Croze incorrectly thought was his last. The two also carried on a *commerce de lettres* while Jordan was in Prenzlau—one, however, in which, according to Jordan, the busy La Croze wrote letters which were "sometimes of a very great sterility," being merely a series of compliments.[5] These contacts promoted much affection between them, and, as we will see, Jordan exploited this connection for all it was worth.

He was first able to do this in his next venture in promoting his name, which was to write a collection called the *Recueil de littérature, de philosophie, et d'histoire*, which he managed to publish by asking Bourguet to help him find a publisher.[6] This book was an appallingly bad series of disjointed pieces and remarks in the mode of the *ana*, the collections of the table talk of the famous which were so much in vogue in the early part of the eighteenth century. The difference here was, of course, that Jordan was a total unknown, which meant that the usual justification for such works—that anything which drops from the pen of the great is worth reading—could not in this case apply.

Jordan used the *Recueil* to make claims for standing in the Republic of Letters in three ways. In the first place, he made himself into a provider of information, into the giver of a gift which would necessarily put him in a position of power. He printed documents which might not otherwise have been available to his readers (whether they wanted them or not), gave citations and remarks about old books, and even provided gossip in the form of the name of a bastard son of Leibniz. Secondly, he asserted his position by daring to make judgments about other scholars, all of whom, dead or alive, occupied a much higher standing than he. "Saumaise's book *de annis climacteris* is nothing much," he wrote. "After having read it you cannot say what the Author's intentions were."[7] "The style of *Gabriel Naudé* is affected, stilted: & in his *Mascurat* he flaunted a pedantic erudition."[8] But most importantly, Jordan made claims for himself by constant name-dropping. "M. Le Duchat had the goodness to communicate to me a Letter which contains an entirely new view on this subject," he wrote of one controversy. Monsieur Chauvin, the minister and journalist, gave him a secret for embalming animals. Monsieur Balthazar, professor of theology at Grypswalde, wrote him a letter.[9] But most conspicious was his constant reference to Maturin Veyssière La Croze, about whom he told constant stories and whose writings and letters were sprinkled liberally throughout this short and awful book.[10]

8 Portrait of Charles-Etienne Jordan by Antoine Pesne. (Witt Library, Courtauld Institute, London.)

Of course, when Jordan linked his name with the famous, that also meant their names were linked with his. This was not necessarily an appetizing prospect, and La Croze was not happy about it. After the book's publication in 1730 he wrote to Prosper Marchand:

> The Author of the Collection which you speak of is a young Minister of the French Colony of Prenzlau on the frontiers of Pomerania, a day and a half from here. His name is Monsieur Jordan. He was my pupil, very assiduous when he was with me, and did me great services in an illness from which I was on the point of death. You can conclude from this that I love him sincerely; and this friendship itself afflicts me because of the miserable work with which he has had the temerity to regale the public. He sent me this little book, and I let him know well enough what I thought of it. He was not exact in what he said about me in two or three places, where his memory deceived him. It would have been better if he had not cited me or named me. I reproached him about it: I don't know if that will have any effect; because he has a terrible itch to write.[11]

It was three years later, after the death of his wife and throwing over his career as a minister, that Jordan set off on his trip. As we saw in the Prologue, Jordan's book about his six-month journey through Germany, France, England, and the Netherlands, the *Histoire d'un voyage littéraire*, was ostensibly a sort of guidebook of the Republic of Letters which pointed out the major sights of that invisible community. But although this was a mapping of the scholarly community for both Jordan and his readers, it was also an attempt to change that map by placing Jordan firmly on it. Jordan used exactly the same techniques for promoting himself in that journey, and his published account of it, as he had in his one previous publication. At every turn the issue seemed to be one of power, of control, and of connections.

This is clear even from the very beginning of the trip, when, as is necessary on such travels, Jordan obtained the necessary letters of introduction. La Croze gave him recommendations for savants in Paris and London, and on May 15, 1733, when he had been on the road for three weeks, Jordan wrote from Strasbourg to Louis Bourguet for more, and particularly for a letter to Pierre Des Maizeaux in London.[12] Not only could La Croze and Bourguet vouch for him, but his large number of correspondents—his "very good *commerce*"—made him a worthy object of Des Maizeaux's attention. Once Jordan's worth was established, both La Croze and Bourguet asked Des Maizeaux to render him any services he could. Bourguet specified that one of these services was to widen his *commerce* by introducing him to Hans Sloane, "President of your Royal Academy of Sciences."[13] In other words, knowing Bourguet and La Croze increased Jordan's stature, and in fact would lead to a further increase in that stature, as his connections with them—and even with *their* connections—were used to expand his own personal net-work. At the same time Jordan served as an intermediary to tighten the bonds between Des Maizeaux and his two correspondents by tying them all into further relations of obligation to each other.

Jordan's book reflected these manuscript recommendations in its constant reliance for validation on contacts with others. Our traveller clearly vaunted his associations in Berlin when seeking to gain approbation from the many scholars he visited in Halle, Leipzig, Paris, London, and Amsterdam. His accounts of his conversations suggest that La Croze's name came up often, particularly with associates of La Croze such as Montfaucon and St. Gelais, but also, for example, with C.R. Dadichi—"he does Justice to Mr. La Croze, & believes him to be the most savant Man in Europe in the Knowledge of Oriental Languages,"[14] Jordan wrote. Praise of La Croze appears frequently in places where Jordan comments on conversations he has had about books and manuscripts: of one manuscript, whose false antiquity he discussed with Jean Masson in London, he remarked that the copy in Berlin "was purchased as a very old MS., but this false representation could not escape the clairvoyant Eyes of Mr. la Croze."[15] Jordan was clearly anxious to praise La Croze, but he also obviously hoped to appear worthy both to those he visited and to his reading public by his association with him.

But if Jordan was eager to point out his connections with the famous in Berlin, his entire journey was an effort to acquire further connections else-where. The *Histoire d'un voyage littéraire* is constructed almost completely around a series of visits Jordan made to scholars. Here is a typical paragraph from the book:

Mr. Böerner, Professor of Theology, who has published an augmented Edition of the *Bibliotheca Sacra* by le Long, gave us Coffee the next day. His Library, which is considerable, is very well chosen. He showed us a Greek New Testament, which formerly belonged to Rabelais, in which this learned Doctor wrote in his own hand. . . . I found an Edition of the New Testament of Robert Etienne from 1551, which is the first one where the Verses are distinguished. See on this edition Le Long *Bibliotheca Sacra* in Mr. Böerner's edition, page 488 vol. I. See Mattaire Hist[oria] Stephanorum pages 60 [to] 70. . . . This savant Theologian has a very considerable Collection of published Dissertations on Theological Matters, or on Passages of Scripture: he has arranged all this in a nice Order: it is to be wished, that we could have a list; [for] that would be very useful to those who apply themselves to the Study of Scripture, & of Sacred Criticism.[16]

This sort of account is repeated over and over as Jordan makes his way from bookshop to library to study. Many paragraphs of the book begin "I saw Mr.

so-and-so," with the name always italicized; one review of the book, in the *Bibliothèque raisonnée*, showed a clear understanding of Jordan's attitude by giving names of savants in block capitals; even town names did not get this kind of treatment, being merely in italics.[17] The *Bibliothèque germanique*, written by various friends of Jordan's, praised him for the way we can "promenade agreeably with him in the States of Europe where the Sciences are best cultivated" and for the way that, with him, we can "get to know Savants" and their character.[18]

Jordan took the opportunity to mention his kind reception by many of these scholars. Dartous de Mairan, for example, "received me with much Politeness," while others invited him to dine, showed him their libraries or collections, and talked to him of scholarship and of gossip. "Mr. Kapp showed me a Ms. he is going to print," he wrote of a professor in Leipzig; and "Mr. *Serces*, Author of the Work on Miracles, spoke much to me about the French Jansenists."[19] But although hospitality and generosity with information were part of the ethos of the Republic of Letters, praising savants for these qualities also reflected back on Jordan. The fact that he could say that the great names of learning, Fontenelle, Montfaucon, Du Bos, Réaumur, and so on, had received him and talked to him could only suggest to his audience that Jordan must in fact be worthy of their attention and their kindness. Jordan said of his afternoon with Fontenelle, "I will never forget the Pleasure I had of seeing this Great Man";[20] but we, his readers, are not to forget it either.

This picture is only reinforced by the way Jordan recounts his contacts with the famous. He did not simply go to pay his respects and leave; the visits included conversation, and conversation which could be reported, if only in summary. We have already seen that Jordan, like anyone in the Republic of Letters, was eager to impart information and to show that he was privy to it. The *Histoire* is filled with details about books he has seen, news about authors, such as the fact that Montesquieu was author of the *Lettres persanes*, statements such as "I learned two Things that day: one, that the best & most correct Maps made in England, are by Herman *Möll*: the other, that the Original of the *Magna Carta* was burned in the fire which destroyed several pieces in the Cottonian Library."[21] That the status gained from being the purveyor of news is the major purpose of the pieces of information provided in Jordan's published *Voyage littéraire* is more evident from the extreme diversity of material (as well as its often questionable interest). The fact that the earlier *Recueil* has a similar structure and ethos suggests that informing the public indiscriminately was not merely a result of circumstance, of the chronological reportage of a series of visits, but rather the product of a mind which considered the possession and transmission of information more important than its content.

To have information, then, was to have status. But to be able to say that that information was a gift of the great was, again, to enhance one's own position. Jordan was happy to pass on stray facts and information about books; but he was even prouder to be able to say that the Père de Montfaucon had told him the meaning of the word "abraxus," or that the Abbé Fourmont had said that you could trust what the late Monsieur Tournefort had had to say about Greece. Moreover, just as his connection with La Croze gave him access to documents which he had been able to print in his *Recueil*, making him both the recipient of a favor and the giver of one, here he acquired status both by being thought worthy to chat with, and by being himself the gracious donor of that information to the public. Jordan was obviously itching to gain control over some of the information he received. In one case, De Boze showed him a "key to the letters of Grotius," which he then gave to him, "seeing my eagerness to possess it." Jordan said in his book that "if I did not fear to give him some pain, I would have taken pleasure in printing this key here, which could only interest the Curious." But "it is for Mr. de Boze to do it, when he thinks it appropriate, or for him to permit."[22] In either case, whether De Boze merely spoke to him of the key or granted him rights to print it, Jordan's position would be enhanced by his contact with him; and despite his reservations he printed a three-page excerpt.

But this desire for control went further. Jordan edited his conversations like a text, adding citations, giving examples, referring the reader to sources in a way that showed Jordan's erudition to best advantage. Whenever he bought an old book, he was delighted to able to say if it did not appear in Michel Mattaire's magisterial work on early publishing, the *Annales Typographici*. These comments and criticisms, these attempts to assert control over his surroundings, extended to judgments of the scholars and the libraries Jordan saw; for he was not uniformly impressed.

> I saw the Abbé *Bonardi*: he is savant; but he is too much so in his Conversation. . . . I paid a visit to the illustrious Mr. *Rollin*, an Author whose Works the whole World esteems. He is a small Man, aged 75 years, not much to look at, who does not express himself as nobly as he writes. . . . I went to pay a visit to the Carmelites: I saw their Library, which is very awful, without taste, full of scholastics; I could not find a single Book, which was worth the trouble. I would not give 100 Ecus for this whole Library, although there are 4 or 5000 Volumes in it.[23]

The role of the judge in the Republic of Letters was always a troubled one, as we have seen in the case of literary journalists; although the ethos of the community was that anyone could judge anyone else's works, in fact a certain position in the Republic was thought necessary to make such judgments anything but audacity. By giving his opinions, in appreciation or in criticism, Jordan was asserting his right to speak his mind at all.

So Jordan went on his way, through Germany to Paris, to London, and then back through the Netherlands to Berlin. He published his book in 1735 with the help of Maturin Veyssière La Croze, who wrote to the agent Prosper Marchand to help find a publisher, and who used the book to attack one of his enemies, the Père Hardouin. The book was intended to make Jordan's name in the pre-Enlightenment Republic of Letters, to make him, through his contacts, his knowledge, and his ability to impart information, seem, even *be*, a worthy member of that community. And in fact Jordan did succeed in gaining status; but not at all in the way he probably expected.

The Arch Pirouette and the Ordure of the Universities

"How horribly difficult it is," wrote La Bruyère in his *Caractères*, "for a man who is without eulogists & without *cabale*, who is not involved in any *corps*, but who is alone, & who only has a great deal of merit for his entire recommendation, to come forth out of the obscurity he is in."[24] In the later seventeenth and early eighteenth centuries, scholars came to feel the need for a corporate spirit more strongly. Whereas Bacon could write in *The Advancement of Learning* about "the privateness or obscureness (as it may be in vulgar estimation accounted) of life of contemplative men,"[25] savants increasingly felt the need to participate in a larger community of learning. Off in every corner of Europe, they could, like Georges Guillaume Mousson in Danzig, be "always content with my state," but still feel that "one thing is missing from my satisfaction, that is to be informed about what is going on in the *monde savant*."[26]

The structures of the Republic of Letters, its modes of operation, in the main appear to be directed precisely to this end. Regular networks of communications such as *commerces de lettres* provided a means for information to travel through the community; *voyages littéraires* had the same effect while putting into action the ideals of the learned world. Mutual communication brought mutual assistance, and young or obscure scholars in contact with the rest of their society meant that they did not have only "a great deal of merit for their entire recommendation." The way the Republic of Letters operated in practice helped not only to maintain its integrity, but to strengthen its bonds.

The need for community both spurred, and was spurred by, the growth in this period of new scholarly institutions and structures. A new ease in communications, a rapid growth in the book trade, the establishment of academies for scholarly interchange, and the birth of the literary journal as a primary means of gaining information, all made contact among scholars easier than ever before. Indeed, it was contact itself which often seemed to be the goal. Jordan, on his *voyage littéraire*, was more anxious simply to be in the presence of other savants than necessarily to learn anything specific from them; and although learned projects also profited from joint ventures among various people, much of the communication in letters, in literary groups, and even in journals seemed to be more for the simple sake *of* communication than with any special intellectual goal in mind. The eclecticism of information provided in journals, for example, was certainly a sign of the unspecialized nature of scholarly activity in the period; but it also suggested that the drawing together of the community was in itself considered a worthy aim.

Ironically, however, the institutionalization of communal links tended not only to consolidate the community but also to alter its nature. The very institutions which canonized scholarly practice by professionalizing its operations also increased the impersonality of learned relations. Services to scholars, a fundamental bond in the community, began in at least a small way to be focussed on people best placed to perform them, such as the literary agents in the Netherlands. This was logistically useful, and agents helped to perform favors for other people, but in other ways this new system may have cancelled opportunities to create direct bonds between scholars.

That this behavioral ethos should be so prominently endorsed in all forms of learned communication only emphasizes the anxiety with which men of letters promoted the communal ideal. It is true that, just as the intellectual aims of the community could conflict with its behavioral norms, so could the stress on the personal conflict with the emphasis on community. Yet the sense that the individual relations of any set of scholars made up the whole of the community meant that a stress on etiquette was essential to the integrity of the Republic. The goal was to behave, as well as to write, in a way that would "do honor to the Republic of Letters."

Concentrating on behavior was, in a way, a means of avoiding potentially divisive ideological problems. As we saw in the last chapter, irreconcilable religious and political differences could be glossed over if scholars emphasized the *way* an argument was conducted, rather than the actual issues at stake. This was an effort which frequently failed, and religious insults were traded in quarrels which had nothing to do with theology. But the criticism of such quarrels on grounds of etiquette strongly suggests that politeness was the crowning rule of the Republic of Letters. Maintaining proper scholarly etiquette would protect the community, in the same way that idealizing the behavior of deceased scholars provided role models for proper behavior in the future.

But why should the primacy of community, of form over content, have been so important in this period? Why should European scholars have developed the concept of a utopian Republic of Letters, whose identity broadened in the period we have discussed?

The consolidation of the scholarly community can be, and has been, attributed to various positive sources. Scholars, according to these views, came together because of a sense of a task to be done and the need to develop tools to complete it. Historians of science have cited the rise of the new science in the seventeenth century and the conscious need for cooperation to develop its possibilities. Intellectual changes, moreover, could result in behavioral ones. Barbara Shapiro's seminal work on the development of the concept of uncertainty in various learned fields, such as natural science or history, has shown that seventeenth-century scholars had a new sense of the difficulty of resolving any problem. This meant that discussion was legitimate, impartiality a (sometimes unattainable) goal, and moderation the key to behavioral standards.[27] Moderation was encouraged by the ecumenical tendencies of some churches, such as the Remonstrants, and the desire of some religious figures to bring about the reunion of Protestantism or perhaps even of Christianity.[28]

Institutional development could also assist in the process of consolidation. Absolutism's new interest in the arts and sciences prompted the development of an intermediate level of communal organization in the new national academies in France, Prussia, Russia, and elsewhere. An increase in education and literacy produced a greater market for publishers and consequently more money for projects for the learned. And, as historians have long argued, the dispersal of Protestant savants from France at the Revocation widened scholarly networks. Not only did Huguenots maintain earlier friendships made at the Protestant academies, and develop new associations in their places of refuge, but the combination of new opportunity, a need for employment, and a sense of a new internationalism helped to connect other scholars through their literary journals.

These positive explanations of the development of the Republic of Letters are all valid and contribute much to the explanation of its consolidation. But our study of the values held by scholars, the way they behaved and the way they thought they *should* behave toward each other, suggests that another, more negative explanation could be added to these positive ones. Scholars may have joined together because of a sense of their mission and the need to overcome differences. But their community also developed out of a kind of conservatism, or even fear.

To savants of this period, the position of learning appeared in peril. Scholarly correspondence abounded in mutual commiseration about the state of scholarship, which, according to Simon Pelloutier in Berlin in 1745, was "truly in Agony."[29] Michel Mattaire in London had the same complaint at the same time: "How would it please me, before I die, to see . . . the revival of Letters!"[30] "People are complaining from all sides that the Republic of Letters is falling into decadence," wrote François Bruys in 1730, which for him was a reason to begin his literary journal, the *Critique désintéressée des journaux*.[31] Jean Le Clerc's *Parrhasiana* included a large section headed "Decadence in Belles-Lettres, where it comes from," remarking that for more than a generation there had been no one to equal the old critics of the past such as Scaliger, Lipsius, Casaubon, Saumaise, Grotius, and so on.[32] Pierre-Daniel Huet's comment in 1686 that "since I have been alive, I have seen the sciences declining continually"[33] shows how long these views had been circulating and how, in a period some historians have seen as one of the blossoming of science, scholars could still moan, as Gisbert Cuper did in 1710, "that here it is as it is elsewhere, little esteem for men of Letters."[34] Whether or not this was actually the case is not the issue; what is important is the perception that it was.

The problem was not so much that bad scholarship was being done—although that was also thought to be true[35]—but, as Cuper pointed out, there seemed to be "little esteem for men of Letters." Other priorities seemed to prevail; in England, as Obadiah Oddy wrote, "every Wheelbarrow is ready to run over a Man of letters. Money, Money is all yᵉ Cry: How go Stocks, & how stands yᵉ Bank."[36] These priorities took a number of tolls. In the first place, it seemed that no one was interested any longer in reading scholarly books. Complaints about the book trade centered not only on the tricks of the *libraires*, but on their mercenary pandering to the vile tastes of the public. Complaints about "méchants livres" were legion,[37] and their appearance was the fault of the industry: "the presses today are true factories of books, & made rather for commerce than for letters."[38] Earlier we heard Godefroy Clermont complain that *libraires* were only interested in "Satiric writings, books of fables and stories," and not "erudition or . . . Theology,"[39] as well as Marchand's predictions of success only for "some freethinking, even dirty Treatise, of the *Pleasures of Vice*."[40] Even a *libraire* such as Luzac held the same view, remarking of a manuscript by Emmerich Vattel that "it seems too good to me to hope for very good sales"; another, Henri du Sauzet, worried that his scholarly publications would not attract many buyers, since "that which suits Scholars does not always suit the *grand nombre*."[41] The erudition of the Republic of Letters was out of fashion, and a traditional scholar such as Maturin Veyssière La Croze despaired of ever finding a publisher for his works.

I have worked a great deal in the past and I am still working, without hope, however, of being able to communicate my works to the public.

Almost all my Manuscripts are written in Latin, and discuss subjects which no longer interest the public. I have thrown myself into the study of Oriental languages & Antiquities, where there are many discoveries to be made, and even important discoveries: but who is there today who cares about any of that? I am thus reduced to working for myself, and for my own edification.[42]

This new taste in the *librairie* appeared particularly threatening because, although it was rarely forthcoming,[43] a reliance on income from books seemed increasingly necessary. The type of patronage scholars—however unreasonably—had come to expect from the aristocracy appeared to be slacking off. It is a matter of some debate whether this was actually the case; patronage had always been confined to a small number of writers, and the desire of aristocrats to associate with authors actually increased in the eighteenth century.[44] But from the viewpoint of contemporaries, the golden age of aristocratic patronage was ending, and it was difficult for scholars in the early part of the century to be hopeful about the future. Paul Korshin describes the eighteenth century in England as a kind of "limbo between old-fashioned Renaissance munificence and the age of modern foundation and government grants."[45] In this limbo, savants formulating projects could only lament their inability to complete them. Bourguet, for example, despaired of the future of his work on the still-undeciphered Etruscan language: "it is quite apparent that, unless the liberality of some Aristocratic Maecenas puts me in a position to conclude my discovery, Savants will be guessing for a long time despite what I have already published."[46] He evidently did not expect such a Maecenas to appear.

The problem was, in part, the same as that in the book trade: the taste of the public for "trash." Either aristocrats and gentry were not interested in learning at all—as the antiquary Browne Willis wrote in 1715, "Learning is at a very Low Ebb amongst our Country Squires who are not very Conversable except ab[t] Horses & Doggs"[47]—or their tastes ran to *belles-lettres* rather than erudition. This was a division which scholars consciously made in the period; most journals did not include literature as a main focus, and modern literature in particular received virtually no attention. As we have noted, the major French journals made this distinction, with both the erudite *Journal des savants* and the literary *Mercure galant* receiving privileges from the king. These two journals were thought to have their own separate territories which ought to be respected; when scholars were attacked, the *Journal des savants* said, the *Mercure galant* had no right to offer their answers a place in its journal. "We will not prevent [the author of the *Mercure galant*] from getting into quarrels when he is attacked as he already has been; but as for other people he will accept that we would offer them another battleground which he has no right to present to them; & since we do not practice piracy on his Shores, we pray him not to come and make incursions in the Republic of Letters which is the hereditary country of [this] Journal."[48]

Around the turn of the century, then, the tastes of both scholars and aristocrats began to become specialized, and a division grew up between the erudite and *mondain* public.[49] Consequently, although the cliché that the status of authors as a group rose astronomically in the eighteenth century is essentially accurate, the authors who profited from this rise were belles-lettrists and writers of the Enlightenment. Voltaire's examples in the *Encyclopédie* of the changing stature of writers—the socially acceptable Balzac and Voiture—were *littérateurs*, not scholars.[50] Most members of the old Republic of Letters agreed that they were not part of this group, of which many did not approve; the Enlightenment "satires" rolling off the presses were condemned by *érudits* with different ideas about how to employ the printers. As late as 1763, Jean Deschamps ridiculed the idea of a figure of the Enlightenment getting mixed up in an institution of the old learned world.

> Will you then be having, as a new *Despot*, in your Academy [of Berlin], the Bel-Esprit à la mode, M^r. *Dalambert*? . . . A *President* who is a Bel-Esprit, in a *Germanic Academy*, what a risible Contrast! But the taste of the century formed by *Voltaire* has absolutely turned toward *Concetti*, *buffooneries*, and *impieties*. Happily *England* is still sticking to good sense and Reason, and hisses at all these frivolities.[51]

If private patrons were interested in supporting any authors, not to mention associating with them socially, it was the *littérateurs*, not the *érudits*. Scholars worried for financial reasons about the tastes of the *libraires* had just as much reason to worry about the tastes of the aristocratic public.

The trend of patronage in this period was also from private to public. The absolutist state's sponsorship of the arts and sciences, both by pensioning individuals and forming academies, is a well-known feature of the era. This appears to be a positive development, and certainly scholars expressed appreciation for states where "true science is on the throne."[52] When the Venetian government gave Maffei a hereditary title, for example, the *Bibliothèque italique* made the general point that

> it is so rare, that Men of Letters are recompensed for their labors, that we thought it our duty to mention this detail here, both to encourage those who destine their studies to the advantage of the public, and to show how much it is to be wished, that people should imitate the equally noble & praiseworthy example, which the Most Serene Republic of Venice had furnished on this occasion.[53]

The example of France and particularly Louis XIV's patronage of the arts and sciences animated even those who could not otherwise approve of the monarch's conduct. Although the purpose of such patronage was at least in part the pursuit of national glory, the nature of the Republic of Letters made it seem a more international act. The confirmation of the letters patent of the Académie des Inscriptions and the Académie des Sciences, the *Journal littéraire* commented, was royal "Protection from which all Savants receive such great fruits, that they cannot ignore them without ingratitude. . . . [T]hose whom particular reasons have forced to leave their Country, have found themselves obliged to recognize for their Benefactor, one whom they could not recognize as their King."[54]

Journalists, however, found it so important to acknowledge such patronage precisely because of its limited availability. As Alain Viala has pointed out, although from 1664 patronage in France became an official royal institution, it also became even more selective and continued to pay too little and to too few people. Moreover, after 1673 the war with the United Provinces took yet more money away from scholarly patronage, and from 1676 government sponsorship went into a clear decline.[55] In England, government subsidies of the arts had not yet become an important feature of the literary scene,[56] and in 1737 Sloane was forced to resort back to "our Nobility and people of consideration and of taste" to try to make up "the deficiency of the government of the royal or parliamentary purse."[57] And in Prussia the accession of an unsympathetic Frederick William I in 1713 saw an immediate withdrawal of patronage, to the consternation of scholars like La Croze, librarian of the king's library. La Croze temporarily lost his position, was forced into a series of onerous tutoring jobs (admittedly to royalty), and thought seriously of selling his books (the mark of true indigence in a scholar) and moving to England. Winning 4,000 florins in the Dutch lottery provided only a brief respite for him.[58] La Croze was far from unique. Barbeyrac said that "the n[ew] King of Prussia is signaling the beginning of his Reign by making himself odious to his subjects. Berlin is in a general consternation"; Berlin's entire entry in the *nouvelles littéraires* of the *Histoire critique* for 1713 concerned the fact that "the Muses, which had found an asylum here, which seemed to be assured, under the wings of the late King, are obliged to move & to leave this sojourn, however lovely it was."[59]

Moreover, even when state sponsorship was available, a patronage which took the form of a creation of academies was suspect to some scholars. Mordechai Feingold speaks of "a lingering distrust of government intervention in the private domain,"[60] and it was certainly true that such intervention was likely to rob savants of some of their autonomy. Despite the tradition of including foreign members, a tradition praised by the Marquis d'Argenson in a discourse to the Berlin Academy,[61] a goal of national academies was, unsurprisingly, to promote the glory of their particular country. This was in large part a tacit condition of funding. The Parisian Académie Royale des Sciences, for example, was from the start intended by Colbert to discover practical solutions to France's economic and military problems, as well as to give Louis XIV another reason to shine above his European peers.[62] Similarly, the reformed Berlin academy, whose "principal duty" was to "make the works it produces worthy to be offered to its august Chief," promised to cultivate "particularly the history of the Empire, and of the Estates of his Majesty, and at the same time to purify and polish the German language more and more."[63]

As Roger Hahn has said, an academician would have known that, to achieve his own goals, he "would be forced to abdicate considerable freedom of action by casting his lot with the king."[64] Although Frederick the Great tried to give autonomy to his newly reformed academy by, for example, giving it the right to grant its own pensions, the fact that it was he who conferred this right, who chose the *président perpetuel*, and who, with recommendations from his councillor von Schmettau, designed the membership, rules, and goals of the new society made it clearly subservient to royal power.[65] He himself admitted that (contrary to his wishes), the society was becoming less "a free assembly of men of knowledge & merit" than a department of state.[66] This knowledge did not prevent him from continuing to interfere in the operations of the academy, ruling in 1749 that because of the "small exactitude which some Academicians use in fulfilling their duty," all those who failed to produce one *mémoire* per year would lose their places and their pensions.[67] For all the pleasure expressed at royal sponsorship, royal patronage and particularly the creation of academies was in fact yet another example of absolutist governments co-opting corporate bodies and making their privileges suddenly conditional on service to the state.

The malaise scholars felt over patronage, moreover, may have stemmed in part from a difference in opinion over its point. This is evident in the example of academies. Alice Stroup points out that French academicians came to believe in the seventeenth century that pensions were theirs by right, providing the appropriate conditions for work, whereas government ministers considered them rewards, bonuses to normal income, or incentives for activity.[68] The government view was not one to encourage a comfortable sufficiency for scholars. And indeed, according to Priscilla and Terry Nichols Clark, this was always the condition of patronage; to prevent complacency, to maintain gratitude, objects of patronage had to be kept continually in debt, receiving patronage only in irregular spurts.[69]

To a scholar in the early eighteenth century, then, the future looked unfamiliar and not always uniformly bright. Caught between the apparent decline in aristocratic patronage and the supposedly frivolous tastes of the book market, subject to the mercenary ways of the *libraires*, dependent for money on royal power which proved capricious, domineering, and often simply uninterested, scholars perceived their position in decline. Learned privileges, already disappearing in the late Middle Ages,[70] seemed in the late seventeenth century to be losing out to the needs of the government. According to Gunter Grimm, in Germany privileges such as tax exemptions, freedom from billetting, the ability to postpone payment of creditors, the avoidance of debtor's prison, and the right to drive out noisy neighbors were increasingly difficult to enforce in practice. The scholar's sunken social status is evident in the rank-determination made in Hessen-Kassel in 1762, in which "doctors" were placed in the same class as valets and pastry-cooks.[71]

Paul Dibon has written of an "old" and a "new" Republic of Letters; the new, which developed in the late sixteenth and the seventeenth century, was more unified and more enlightened than the old. The scholars of the old community, he says, were people like Johannes Fredericus Gronovius, Joseph Scaliger, Hugo Grotius, or Claude Saumaise, as well as Mersenne, Descartes, Gassendi, and others, more interested in the ancients than the moderns. Certainly the spirit of the Republic of Letters changed in the seventeenth century, both in its interests and its operations. But the vicissitudes faced by savants at the turn of the eighteenth century, vicissitudes caused in part by the competition with a new taste for a *littérature mondaine*, suggest that the "old" Republic of Letters is more properly that of both Scaliger and of people like Barbeyrac or La Croze. The "new" Republic, instead, is the one which bears so little resemblance to the one we have discussed here: the Republic of Letters of the Enlightenment. The transition from the old to the new was difficult for more traditional scholars whose social and intellectual style was so different from that required by the aristocrats patronizing Enlightenment figures. Increasingly they were left behind, so that, although the social status of authors may have risen, that of scholars did not.

What could scholars do in the face of these changes? Their reaction was to band together and to promote their own society. One method was to dissociate themselves from what was going on. While consoling each other about the lack of esteem they commanded or support they received, they emphasized at the same time their deliberate lack of participation in the greater society. The Republic of Letters was supposed to have its own rules, its own hierarchies; and outside rules and hierarchies did not apply. According to Jean Le Clerc,

scholars must have the liberty to examine things in themselves in their studies, to think what they want about them and to talk among themselves in friendship, with an agreeable liberty, without getting angry with each other, if their thoughts do not conform, and without carrying their differences to a public theater. These are mysteries to which the People must not be admitted, because having neither the leisure nor the capacity to delve into and penetrate them, they cannot grasp them nor use them well.[72]

If scholars could do as they pleased, they need not worry, among other things, about the usual societal drive for money and status. This position is evident in the ambivalent attitude toward patronage at the beginning of the eighteenth century. We have seen that scholars were eager for support and extravagantly praised aristocrats or monarchs who provided it. In the seventeenth century it was a sign of success to be the object of patronage,[73] and at the beginning of the eighteenth century it was still considered by some to be shameful to have to live off one's writings. "It is notable that M. *Corneille* was anything but poverty-stricken," wrote the *Journal littéraire*; "it would have been very blameworthy of our century for a man of this merit to have had recourse to his literary and journalistic labours for his livelihood."[74] Yet many scholars faced the prospect of writing dedicatory epistles with repugnance; as Jordan said, "dedicatory epistles always suppose a view of interest which pains me."[75] Jordan's comment indicates a conflation of the distaste for patronage and that for a mercenary attitude toward literature. Charles Sorel wrote in 1671 of dedicatory epistles that "it is shameful that one should thus become accustomed to work for gain rather than for glory." Yet since patronage had declined so much, he said, there was usually little reason to think a book had been written for money; and "it is a great satisfaction to a Man to see himself above these things & even to have written several Volumes without having dedicated them. It shows him to be independent."[76]

Thus some scholars dedicated their works to their friends: "I have nothing else in mind," wrote Barbeyrac to Turrettini, "than to respond in some manner to the favorable sentiments you have in my regard, & to do myself the honor of your friendship. I prefer this to all the protection of the Great Nobles & other persons of credit"; he later said that "I am very disgusted, I swear to you, with Dedications addressed to Great Nobles."[77] This did not mean that they did not want patronage, however. Armand de la Chapelle was straightforward enough when he said that "a Dedicatory Epistle is always quite useless unless the patron pays for it," and Barbeyrac, who disavowed the need to court the great, was ecstatic when two dedications were rewarded by attentions and some silver basins from royalty.[78] The disgust with the process was in part a realization that "it is not a Gift, it is a Sale,"[79] but also a precaution in case the proceeds were not forthcoming. It was easier on one's pride and sometimes more useful to honor fellow scholars instead.

The same ambivalence is apparent in attitudes toward the court. To attend at court was demeaning, not fit for a free man like a scholar.

Marchand wrote to his friend the Marquis d'Argens, "I cannot be more astonished to see you so intoxicated with the fantastic *Honor of serving a great Prince* . . . the Grandeur of the Master usually only serves to make the Smallness of the Servant more easily felt . . . & I cannot prevent myself from laughing at the Emphasis with which you try to raise so high this imaginary Advantage."[80] The court was the home of bad morals, chicanery, and intrigue; Jacques de Pérard blamed it for Charles-Etienne Jordan's new relation toward him, which consisted of "cold and reserved politeness, reciprocal mistrust, that is the way things go in this world. It is very difficult not to change at the court."[81] Many scholars accepted court office when it was available, and Pérard himself lost touch with many of his scholarly friends when he had the good fortune to "enter into the *grand monde.*"[82] Again it appears that scorn of noble society and dependence upon it was in part a function of its unavailability.

One way for the Republic of Letters to deal with this was to assert equality with the nobles themselves. The claim not to participate in the normal social hierarchy meant that the learned could develop their own standards and assign nobility to them. Thus Abraham de Moivre could regard his election to the Académie Royale des Sciences as a conferment of nobility,[83] and various scholars with noble blood were described as "*more estimable by their love of Letters . . . than by their birth.*"[84] The *titulomanie* which so disgusted Mencke was clearly an effort to raise the stock of scholars, as were the rules of academies and literary societies, which generally avoided making social distinctions among members.[85] The implication was that all members were nobles. If scholars—most of whom came from bourgeois stock—could not succeed in the society of nobles, they could ennoble their own society.

These tendencies are reflected not only in the hierarchy of the Republic of Letters, but also in its rules of conduct. Scholars, in common with many other groups aspiring to favor during the later seventeenth century,[86] attempted to emulate gentlemanly conduct. Great stress was laid in the scholarly world upon the necessity for *politesse* and *honnêteté*. Savants were told that they must remember the requirements of "civil society & good manners," that quarrels must be moderate because—as the Abbé Bignon said of Masson and Dacier—"it was unworthy of an *honnête homme* to conduct himself like [a] lackey."[87] The insistence on polite behavior, which implicitly identified scholars with aristocrats, was one reason for the desire to protect the iconic great scholars of the past. When it came to the point, men of letters had to admit that their forebears had not always been so well-behaved. Their protests at the treachery of printing Scaliger's *grossièretés* in the *Scaligerana* indicated how painful it was to confess, as the editor Des Maizeaux did, that "in his time men of Letters did not express themselves with the same *politesse* as they do at present."[88] But to do so also pointed out the new-found *politesse* of the eighteenth-century Republic of Letters.

If scholars, then, were figurative nobles, they were no more than *nobles de robe*, for their civility was acquired rather than inborn. This would have suggested to any real aristocrat the falsity of their claims.[89] Indeed, they betrayed their bourgeois roots by their definition of *honnêteté*, which involved integrity, charity, goodness, and other moral virtues. The ethos of mutual help in learned society—an effect both of social class and the need for such help—is integral to their concept of the *honnête*. This chimes well with early conceptions of *honnêteté*, such as Faret's *Honnête homme* of the 1630s, in which the point of this behavior, at least at court, was not only for personal advancement and personal satisfaction, but also for communal purposes, the "*bien public.*" In Faret this is conceived in political terms; the courtier serves the prince, and the prince exists for the good of the state.[90] But in general the point of early seventeenth-century *honnêteté* is to create a harmonious society, even if that society is primarily conceived as that of one's peers.

Obviously a Republic of Letters which is international must by definition avoid specifically political goals. To constitute that realm, its citizens had to ignore at least to some degree the actual political structure in which they lived. However, the Republic of Letters *did* have a political identity in so far as it adopted basic premisses of civil society, such as the need for a code of practice to produce coherence and harmony among its members. This was necessary not only for the smooth functioning of the group, but also to protect group identity from the negative opinions of outsiders, on whom the community was forced to rely to some degree for material support.

Yet, as Maurice Magendie has shown, by the end of the seventeenth century the aristocracy had opted entirely for a different, *mondain* definition of *honnêteté*. Later behavior manuals for the same class, such as the Chevalier de Méré's *De la conversation* of the 1670s, became more exclusive in their definitions of what was acceptable. This included no emphasis on virtue, but rather exalted someone who shows *politesse, esprit*, grace, who excels in conversation and social intercourse with "the minimum of virtue indispensable to social relations. . . . Private life, the decency of morals, the intrinsic value of the soul, mattered little."[91] Much more emphasis was placed on style than on values; Méré and his contemporaries drained the stated goals of pleasing in society of their communitarian—not to mention their political—content.[92] The stress was on form alone, and that form was one which could not be learned, but rather was "a natural gift,"[93] a *je ne sais quoi*, something which could be grasped only by those already in the know. The new courtliness was specifically designed to exclude a bourgeoisie which threatened their own position from below—a bourgeoisie to which members of the Republic of Letters ultimately belonged. For the *mondains*, then, someone who was *honnête* was now someone who was a *bel esprit*.

This was a problem for scholars, who—no more than Germans—were not thought to be capable of being *beaux esprits*.[94] According to Bouhours' famous contemporary essay,

> The most happy birth requires a good education, & that usage of the world which refines the intelligence, & which makes good sense more subtle. From this comes the fact that professional savants are not ordinarily *beaux esprits*: as they are always buried in study, & they have little commerce with *honnêtes gens*, they do not have a certain *politesse* in their spirit.[95]

Scholars themselves were forced to admit that, as Sallengre wrote, "there are many people who . . . study long years, to become in the end pedants, and vain, and unsociable, and peremptory, and quibblers, & insupportable to all *honnêtes gens*."[96] Consequently, when someone with polished manners, such as Jacques Basnage, associated with aristocrats, his rarity was sufficient that "they were surprised to find a Savant, whose manners were more redolent of a man of the Court, than of a man of the Study."[97] Some theorists of *honnêteté* and *politesse*, such as Callières and Méré, specifically condemned learning as inconducive to *galanterie* and pressed the view that only the "science of the world" would "purge" a gentleman of the "ordure" of the universities.[98] "Among *personnes du monde*," Méré wrote, "anything to do with study is almost always ill-received. . . . One must distance oneself as much as one can from anything to do with study . . . I said to someone very savant . . . 'You would do much better to speak *en galant homme*; for however savant one might be, one must not say anything which is not understood by those who have *esprit*, & who know *le monde*.' "[99]

With these views in circulation, it would require aristocrats to change their minds about learning, and, even more so, for the Republic of Letters to change its own tone into something more *galant*, for the social status of scholars to rise. This in effect occurred, but only for the segment of the population which pursued the goals and the style of the Enlightenment. The new, more philosophical and literary turn—the "arch pirouette," as Norman Hampson has so eloquently expressed it[100]—seemed to entertain many aristocratic readers more than the philological mode of the *érudits*. In urban settings the *philosophe* was also able to play the man of the world, and, indeed, as contemporary writers pointed out, acquire the polish of the salons which would help him to advance in urbane favor.[101] According to Duclos, writing in 1751, the new connection of aristocrats and men of letters meant the latter had "perfected their taste, polished their wit, sweetened their manners, & acquired on several subjects enlightenment which they would not have gained from Books."[102] Obviously the connection had other benefits as well.

Garnier's *L'Homme de lettres* of 1764 complained that the charlatan, "supple, adroit, adept at seizing the occasion and the moment," tended to triumph in the competition for patronage over the true man of letters, who "does not know the art of applauding idiocies no matter where they come from."[103] And, as Garnier pointed out, when frivolity made reputations, should men of letters turn their backs on fortune?[104] Meanwhile, the rest of the "old" Republic of Letters, lacking this frivolity and appeal, could only attempt to promote its interests with a pretense to its own aristocracy.

Enlightenment writers behaved toward the conservative members of the Republic of Letters, who survived—in academies, universities, religious establishments, and other institutions—throughout the *philosophes'* success, much as the seventeenth-century aristocrats had behaved toward their *nouveaux riches* neighbors. The *érudits* did not have what it took to be *philosophes*—in the same way that some people did not have the style to be a true *homme du monde*—because their work did not require grace, finesse, and reasoning. The *Encyclopédie* said in its article on erudition that "there is no man who, with eyes, patience, & memory, cannot become very erudite merely by reading."[105] *Erudits* were seen as collectors and compilers, not philosophers; there was no point to their work.[106]

Such views highlighted an essential difference in tone between the *érudit* and *philosophe* Republics of Letters. The rhetoric of the Enlightenment made much of the wider implications of its productions, implications which were often evident from the width of their scope and the philosophical character of their approach. Enlightened authors claimed a role in a mission to change society—a change which frequently brought political engagement—expressed by Garnier as "bienfaisance universelle."[107] Humanitarian projects, such as the search for world peace, a universal language, and so on, featured regularly in Enlightenment literature, so that Mercier, writing in 1778, characterized men of letters as a substitute for the magistracy, forming the national spirit and directing national ideas.[108]

The situation in the old Republic of Letters was very different. The old Republic, although it hoped to appeal to an audience of patrons, was essentially directed inward. Its concerns were the concerns of scholarship, and its audience conceived largely as itself. Although the increase of knowledge was an avowed goal, its members could, like Charles-Etienne Jordan, be somewhat indiscriminate in the choice of that knowledge; and the benefit of the larger society was not a major concern.

Indeed, in striving to make its inner workings acceptable to the outside community, the Republic of Letters chose, like the aristocracy, to empty its internal relationships of content, choosing instead to concentrate on form. Despite the fact that disagreement was fundamental to academic existence, indeed considered valuable by many within the community, scholars tried—

though constantly failed—to gain society's approval by presenting a harmonious face to the world. The form of disputes—ideally moderate and
measured—was frequently the focus of attention, and arguments were often
judged on the politeness with which they were presented, rather than on
their intrinsic merit. Anything else might bring ridicule from a wider society
on whom the Republic depended for support.

Thus, for example, Beaumarchais criticized one book because it showed
"how hatred degrades men, how it makes them ridiculous & worthy of
scorn"; one should not be harsh in critical judgments, he said elsewhere,
because "would one expose one's Friends to public mockery?"[109] Peter
Needham of Cambridge was quite explicit on this point. "I am very sorry
that Learned Men cannot be content to follow their several studies &
Inclinations, without angry squabble, & uncharitable reflexions upon one
another, which, as you rightly judge, only expose Learning to the scorn of
ignorant Men, & make the Professors of good & usefull Literature appear
ridiculous to all about 'em."[110] Le Clerc begged his fellow scholars to "correct
themselves, & to gain the heart of the *honnêtes gens*, by completely opposite
manners," since faults in character, as perceived by others, had "defamed the
Sciences they cultivate . . . [and] ruined belles Lettres."[111] All this could have
serious consequences. The effect on funding, scholars warned, was palpable;
Le Clerc told the story of a rich man of authority who, on the advice of a
friend, tried to send his son to be educated in an academy, but, seeing all the
disputes there, concluded that "science . . . [was] pure charlatanry," and kept
his son away.[112] Unfortunately, however, if scholars were going to argue,
they often did not have the style now necessary to make these discussions
acceptable. Pierre Des Maizeaux attributed the "excesses of authors" to the
fact that

> they do not have enough experience of the Monde, & . . . that they think
> too highly of themselves; from that comes this pettiness of mind which
> means they do not have the courage to pardon their Adversaries, or at least
> to regard them as neutral parties [&] to treat them with the ordinary
> civility which is practiced among *honnêtes gens*. Authors only make them-
> selves ridiculous when they stray from the Manners of sensible & polite
> men of the World.[113]

Although some authors would end up doing well in the eighteenth
century, it was not easy to see that as the century began. Scholars as a
corporate group certainly had reason to band together out of pride, but the
problems facing them at this period forced them to develop that pride even
further as a sort of protective device. Thus although it is clear that new
institutions of learning in themselves brought the learned together, it also

appears that the vicissitudes of learned life helped unite a group which had only itself to rely on. When society scorned the activities of the learned, the reaction was to combine in an extensive publicity campaign (as in the *éloges* of the academies[114] or the praise of patrons) in which the value of scholarship and scholars was vaunted. Jean Barbeyrac, for example, gave a rectorial address at the Academy of Lausanne on the utility of letters and the sciences for the state,[115] while scholars gave each other extravagant praise (ridiculed by people like Mencke and Niceron) if none was forthcoming from elsewhere. The ethos of mutual service, moreover, was particularly helpful when people did not have wealthy patrons to assist them; scholars not only tried to find each other books but, when necessary, to find each other jobs. More importantly, this ethos gave a sense of community which was necessary at a period when their status appeared in decline. The efforts to protect the image of great scholars—scholars who had themselves helped their own community—show how anxiously men of letters worked to protect the integrity of the Republic of Letters.

The need to consolidate in the face of professional threats was not the only reason for the formalization of the community and the crystallization of its attitudes toward manners. Many other factors also made their contribution, including developments in education and literacy, the market and profession of print, the development of commercial institutions, and the rise of governments which wished to control cultural output. The Republic of Letters may have consolidated to some degree in this process, but its very nature as a community made this difficult to achieve. The problem with the institutionalization and professionalization of a community like the Republic of Letters was that its societal structure was based fundamentally on personal, one-to-one contacts. The increase in the interchange of information—only intensified by the Huguenot diaspora—contributed to the need to formalize some of these relations, especially in print. We can see this, for example, in the progression from letters to news-letters to newspapers. But this development did not successfully obliterate the conception of the community as a collection of personal contacts. The Republic of Letters operated on a system of favors and obligations, a system which a consolidated community, reigning supreme over its individual members, could not easily tolerate.

The conflict was, again, one of form versus content. If the relation of individual scholars with each other was the ultimate goal, the community was well served by its obligation-based social system. But if a higher aim—objective truth, for example—was instead of primary interest, favors and personal obligations were out of place. Literary journals clearly endorsed the theory of the Republic of Letters, both by donning the persona of super-scholar and dictating behavior to the community, and also by attempting to

cooperate with other journals in the task of informing their audience. Yet the
operations of the journals themselves show how difficult it was for their
authors to accept an impersonal role. Their view of the Republic of Letters
was still based on ideas of individual behavior; the community was a community in theory, and the importance of that community was paramount; but
in practice it was difficult to see it as separate from a multiplicity of one-on-
one contacts. It appears that, often enough, the ethos of personal obligation
was the view of the Republic which won out.

Consequently the conceptualization of the Republic of Letters was very
often a personification. Relationships between individuals and institutions
were visualized in the same intrinsic terms as relationships between individuals: in terms of obligation, *devoir*, honor, and reciprocity. Scholars perceived
both literary journals and academies in this personified, obligation-ridden
form. Even the Republic of Letters itself was conceived as a person to whom
gifts (such as publications) and duties were due. The relationship between the
scholar and the Republic of Letters altered depending on whether, in any
individual circumstance, the scholar conceived of himself as author or as
audience.

This does not mean that the Republic of Letters was some sort of chimera,
an ideal which personal contacts constantly negated. Rather, we should see
the emphasis on behavior—instead of truth, information, or scholarly objectivity—as an integral component of the learned community. The way the
community managed to consolidate was to create an ideology about itself
which in large part consisted of ideas about conduct. To belong to the
community, to be worthy in it, was to interact properly with its other
members: it was "horribly difficult" to "come forth out of obscurity" if you
were "without *cabale*." But the *cabale* was, inevitably, constructed out of sets
of individual connections.

This continuity of personal relationships as the primary vision for a community which tried to think communally was one major difference in self-
conception between the *érudit* Republic of Letters and the Enlightenment.
There has been considerable argument over the degree to which the Enlightenment community actually formed a community, and how coherent its
program ultimately was. But there is at least some consensus among historians
over the existence of certain basic areas of agreement among the *philosophes*
about areas to be studied, the approach to those areas, and the ultimate goals
of literary activity. In other words, more areas of communality, including
content rather than merely form, meant a greater potential for a profession of
letters and a community of letters than the *érudits* could muster. This, joined
with the inherent appeal of a more literary, light-hearted style and the growth
in a taste for philosophy among the public, made the *érudit* Republic of
Letters all the more in need of self-scrutiny and self-protection.

Trapped in the Temple of Taste

Of all the learned men Jordan visited on his trip, the Fontenelles, Montfaucons, Durands, Des Maizeaux, one seemed to capture his special attention, even though he did not seem to fit the mould. This was not a traditional scholar of history, languages, or classical literature, not an *érudit*, but rather a poet: for it was as a poet, rather than as a philosopher, that Voltaire was chiefly known in 1733. It is not clear how much contact Jordan actually had with Voltaire. He claimed in a letter to Bourguet from London that "Monsieur de Voltaire is one of those whom I frequented at Paris, we even formed a commerce littéraire together,"[116] but although a letter from Voltaire to Nicolas Claude Thierot in July of 1733 said he had tried to write to Jordan but lacked his address, no real evidence remains of this correspondence other than a mention in the book of a letter Voltaire wrote to him complaining about being ill-treated in print by Prévost. In the *Histoire* Jordan also quotes another letter from Voltaire "to one of his Friends" about government restrictions suppressing literary talent; Theodore Besterman, in his edition of Voltaire's correspondence, says that "it is of course to Jordan himself, though he does not say so,"[117] but given Jordan's penchant for name-dropping, I have a more skeptical attitude on the subject. In any case, Jordan's book makes it clear that he visited Voltaire at least twice in July and that Voltaire gave him a copy of the new edition of his *Henriade*. His account of the visits consisted mainly of a description of his manner and of what the public was saying about his *Temple du Gout*, with long quotations from a letter Jordan received on the subject, and two pages quoting Voltaire's poetry. Yet although this contact appears superficial, it is clear that Jordan admired Voltaire extravagantly. "I believe that this Poet can be regarded as the most distinguished Son of Apollo; &, that after his Death, one will not scruple to place him alongside the Corneilles & the Racines."[118] Jordan brought up the subject of Voltaire several times later in the book, particularly when he had visited people with something to do with the poet; when he visited De Boze's library, for example, he learned that the Abbé Rothelin, of whom Voltaire wrote kindly in the *Temple du Gout*, owned a particular manuscript: and Jordan went on to quote the lines from Voltaire's poem. Similarly, when in London he saw César de Missy, another admirer of Voltaire, and Prévost, a detractor, his account suggested that Voltaire's name had come up in conversation: "I found Mr. Demissy, who [is] content with the *Temple du Gout* of Mr. de Voltaire, [and] who showed me two small Pieces which he had written on this subject," pieces which Jordan then quotes. Voltaire's name does not dominate the book in the way that La Croze's does; but it is evident that after Jordan met him, Voltaire stayed firmly on his mind.

The sorts of visits Jordan paid on his journey, and the kind of talk he indulged in, clearly indicate that the kind of world in which he hoped to make his way was the world of La Croze, the world of the *érudit* rather than of the *philosophe*. Jordan endorsed the old scholarly world and his elderly mentor: yet in fact it was not Jordan's connection with La Croze that ultimately changed his status, but rather his meeting with Voltaire.

In September of 1736, a year after the publication of the *Histoire*, Jordan came to the attention of the young prince royal, Frederick, who in 1740 would become Frederick II, later called the Great. Frederick's obsession with Voltaire is well known, and in this period, when actual contact with the *philosophe* had just been made, the prince must have seen Jordan as a handy conduit to him. Certainly this is the view of the chaplain at Frederick's court, Jean Des Champs, who reported in his "Mémoires secrets" (unpublished until 1990) that

> what procured [Jordan] the happiness of approaching the Prince Royal, was principally the correspondence he had entertained with Voltaire, since his voyage to Paris. The Prince esteemed this Poet greatly, along with the inimitable Gresset . . . and he was charmed to have someone near to him who could instruct him about their works, and about their little adventures. He chose to this end Mr. Jordan, to whom he gave the post of his Secretary for his Literary correspondence.[119]

Des Champs admittedly had cause to dislike all three of the parties concerned; but it is certainly the case that Voltaire is a constant theme of the early correspondence between Jordan and his royal patron. Frederick repeatedly asked Jordan to convey messages to Voltaire and to send him the poet's works, and on several occasions he sent Jordan verses celebrating those works, in one of which he referred to Voltaire, tellingly, as "our hero."[120] When Frederick, by then king of Prussia, finally met Voltaire in 1740, he chose Jordan to confide his slight disappointment with his own performance: "I have seen this Voltaire whom I was so curious to know, but I saw him while I had my quartan fever, and my wits were as blunted as my body was weak. In the final analysis, with people of his type you cannot be ill; you even have to be very well indeed, and in fact better than usual if you can manage it."[121]

The connection to Voltaire could not help hallowing Jordan in Frederick's eyes. This was true in a prosaic sense; Jordan was useful in this connection and thus gained the king's favor, so that, for example, Frederick wrote to him in 1739, "My dear Jordan, you are the best boy in the world; every day you send me letters from Voltaire."[122] But it was true in a more metaphorical sense as well. When Voltaire was due back in Berlin in the autumn of 1743, Frederick sent Jordan a little verse about how he should lodge the *philosophe* in Jordan's capacious library. "That is all I have to say to you about the lodging of Voltaire," the king wrote.

What pleasure for a Jordan to possess at the same time the beautiful Horace bound in red morocco, and the valetudinarian Voltaire bound in a vest of cloth of gold! Messieurs Achard and Monsieur Boeriger [scholarly friends of Jordan's] will say: Ah! what a great man Jordan is; he has lodged at his house the most celebrated thing there is! An ode will be written for you as to the innkeeper of the Muses. What beautiful productions will be born! Jordan, divine Jordan, I touch you at the moment of your apotheosis, at this moment which I await with so much impatience, at this moment where all those titles of books learnt by heart, all this foul hodge-podge of literature will finally illustrate my knowledge.[123]

It is obvious from Frederick's bantering tone that Voltaire was not the only basis for his relationship with Jordan. They quickly became friends, and when Frederick came to the throne in 1740 he took care of Jordan's advancement, making him a privy councillor, whose responsibilities included, among other things, setting up new administrative boundaries for Berlin, devising new rules of policing the city, ridding the streets of beggars, and establishing workhouses. When both Jordan and the Baron von Keyserling, Frederick's beloved Césarion, died while Frederick was on campaign in the summer of 1745, the young king was devastated. "Think what unhappiness is mine to have lost, practically at the same time, my poor Jordan and my dear Keyserlingk," he wrote to Duhan de Jandun. "That was my family, and I think of myself at present widower, orphan, and in a more lugubrious and serious mourning of my heart than that of black livery."[124] I would be the last to deny the reality of this friendship. However, in thinking about how Jordan made his way in his short career, I think it is fair to say that the first steps were taken essentially because of a literary connection—his connection with Voltaire.

This is useful to us not just because it shows that connections were important to literary advancement, and that Jordan was fully aware of this. Rather, Jordan is interesting because he provides a concrete example of a moment of transition: the transition from the older Republic of Letters to the Enlightenment. For it seems to me that in his spectacular advancement Jordan was caught up in something which he did not understand, and of which he did not entirely approve.

Given the tenor of the *Histoire d'un voyage littéraire*, the types of people Jordan had as his early patrons, the types he chose to visit, and the sorts of subjects he chose to discuss with them, it is clear that he was a man of the old, *érudit* Republic of Letters. His praise for Voltaire's *Temple du Gout* seems to come from a misunderstanding of its major point; for in that piece, a sort

of French *Dunciad*, Voltaire was attacking everything people like Maturin
Veyssière La Croze stood for. This prose-poem—for it incorporates both
prose and verse—is an account of a trip to the Temple of Taste, a trip on
which Voltaire and a companion are obstructed by various obstacles. The first
of these was the sight of classical scholars, "the Daciers, the Saumaises, men
bristling with learned nonsense, their color yellow, their eyes red and dry,
their backs bent under a pile of Greek authors; all blackened with ink, and
coiffed with dust." In the poem Voltaire cried out to them from his carriage,
" 'Aren't you going to cleanse yourself in the Temple of Taste?' " to which
they replied, " 'Us, Messieurs? Not at all. Our studies aren't located there,
thanks be to Heaven; Taste is nothing. We are in the habit of editing
constantly, and exactly, what has been thought, but we don't think ourselves.' " The scholars then surrounded Voltaire's carriage "and wanted to
force us to read certain passages of Dictys of Crete, & of Metrodore of
Lampasque, which, according to them, Gronovius had maimed. We thanked
them for their courtesy, and continued on our way."[125] Voltaire wanted to
dissociate himself absolutely from such pedants, quibbling over dusty texts; he
was, in his view, on the side of both thought and wit. Yet the kind of
scholarship ridiculed by Voltaire was just the sort Jordan indulged in and
admired, and nearly everyone he visited on his *voyage littéraire* would have
fallen into the category of people denigrated by Voltaire, if not for their
learning, at least for their taste.

The feeling was, I hasten to say, mutual. Voltaire attracted the distaste of
many who held the values of the older Republic of Letters, including many
friends of Jordan. One of these, Simon Pelloutier, reported that Voltaire had
not made friends at the Prussian court, and that "I have not seen him and
even avoided him. In the event it appears that I did well. . . . Those who
have met him have caused everyone else to lose the desire to do so."[126]
Voltaire insulted another friend of Jordan's, Formey, in Jordan's own house,
by asking him whether he was one of those men paid to deceive the human
race (that is, a clergyman).[127] His learning was thought no better than his
manners; Jean de Beyer, a correspondent of Jordan's, wrote to another friend
a few years later that "Voltaire is . . . a sort of charlatan who spreads, with
great arrogance, all sorts of trash."[128] Far from doing Jordan good among his
compatriots in the Republic of Letters, his association with Voltaire was
thought by many to be detrimental to his reputation. Prosper Marchand said
as much in 1745: "When Mr. Jordan had his *Voyage* printed, I warned him
to be more reserved in his Effusiveness toward a Man whose Acquaintance
could be disadvantageous to him; but, he didn't listen to me, and maybe he
has repented of it since. All I know is, that this has been prejudiciable to him
in the Minds of many People."[129] This community even said the same thing

of Frederick himself: according to Elie Luzac, "This familiarity with Voltaire does him no honor."[130]

With names like Charles-Etienne Jordan and Prosper Marchand now buried in comparative obscurity, it is amusing for us to hear the latter remark that Voltaire will never arrive at Immortality as long as he runs after it with "giant's steps and seven-league boots."[131] But this was not just a conflict of one or two personalities, but a conflict of values about how the literary life should be conducted. Frederick, although quickly distracted by his military adventures in Silesia in the early 1740s, already had in mind a court which would include the *beaux-esprits* and *philosophes* of France, including, ultimately, Voltaire, d'Alembert, Maupertuis, and the Marquis d'Argens. This court would have a frivolous element, already evident in his court as prince royal at Rheinsberg, which sat ill with an atmosphere of serious scholarship. The traditional scholars, such as Pelloutier, author of a history of the Celts, looked on in distaste and disbelief; "with the exception of Mr. de Maupertuis," he wrote in 1750, "I don't see any of our beaux-esprits; and if I dare say so, I don't want to know anything about them."[132] The Enlightenment did not simply slide into cultural dominance without disenfranchising another, older Republic of Letters, left to function as best it could; and even a Prussian admirer of Voltaire's had to admit that, although if he had to choose between Homer and Voltaire, "I would prefer the French to the Greek poet; but I know . . . that the Savant Mr. La Croze [is] of an opinion very different from my own."[133]

Jordan was caught right in the middle of this transition. Although he participated in courtly life, his sympathies seem to have been considerably divided. In the first place, his works were mainly in the older tradition; besides the early collection and the history of his journey, he wrote a bland Latin treatise on Bruno (his first work) and a biography of Maturin Veyssière La Croze. He inherited La Croze's manuscripts after the latter's death in 1739 and might well have published them if he had not died himself in 1745, at the age of 44. What his later works might have been we of course cannot say; but it is notable that Frederick, far from encouraging Jordan's scholarship, became increasingly impatient with it. The truth was that hiding away in a study in Berlin was not suitable to the courtly life Frederick had in mind; and the king repeatedly wrote to Jordan berating him, in a bantering way, for caring more about scholarship than life at court in Rheinsberg, Charlottenburg, or Potsdam. In one verse letter headed in capitals "JORDANOMANIE"—Jordanomania—the king complained of "neglected Potsdam" and wondered when his "perfidious friend," as he put it, was ever going to "leave [his] library," as he was "always buried under a dusty pile of books" which no one else had ever heard of; and he added that

"I have renounced the desire which I had had of seeing you."[134] Another letter said Jordan was "only faithful to his library, he is dead for the living."[135] Although these letters were essentially playful, there is a sharp edge to them, as in a letter of November 17, 1743:

> Are you still in a dog's humor? Are you sad, somber, dreaming, crazier about your library than it is appropriate for you to be? So attached to your Boëriger, Achard, the wits of Villeneuve [the Huguenot quarter of Berlin], and to mannequins like Des Champs, that one can't even talk to you without seeing you overcome with impatience to rejoin them? If all this keeps up, I don't want to see you; but if you are wise, come to me on Tuesday after dinner, to accept my praises and my caresses.[136]

The problem of conflicting styles was compounded by the way Jordan was rewarded by the king; for this reward was to be called into government service by Frederick. As Betty Behrens has pointed out, under Frederick's reign literature and *littérateurs* assumed the reins of government, and Jordan's *éloge*, which may have been written by Frederick himself, asserts that "one should not say that the cultivation of the arts and the sciences makes men incapable of business."[137] According to this *éloge*, after Frederick ascended the throne Jordan was "reclothed"[138] in the guise of privy councillor; and this left him little time for scholarship: a fact celebrated by the eulogist, who said that "the wit, the merit, and especially the good character of M. Jordan, did not *permit* him to stay buried any longer in his study."[139] This meant that his worldly success, far from giving him leisure to talk to his scholarly companions about the origin of languages or the history of printed books, forced him to attend to orphanages, to hospitals, and to following his master on his campaign to conquer Silesia. His friends in the old Republic of Letters watched his rise to political power with some envy, but with some pity as well. In 1742 Pérard remarked of Jordan that "often he must sigh after the sweet Liberty which he enjoyed before his fortune,"[140] and during the Silesian campaign Jean de Beyer wrote to Prosper Marchand, "How happy we are, you and I, not to have to scamper off to Silesia in the train of the King of Prussia! I thank my Destiny for having kept me for 36 years far from the court of great nobles and their favorites, and I hope it will do me the same favor all the rest of my life. . . . I am very sorry for Mr. Jordan, and I wish with all my heart that he will have . . . more repose."[141] Certainly, according to his friend Pelloutier, Jordan's duties to the king prevented him from doing anything with La Croze's manuscripts;[142] and I think it is wishful thinking that made Jordan design a bookplate which quotes Virgil's "Deus nobis haec otia fecit."[143]

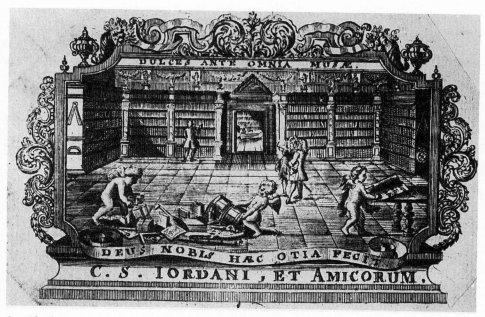

9   Charles–Etienne Jordan's bookplate. (From BJK, Ms. Berol. Gall. Qu. 26, frontispiece.)

So it seems that Jordan made his *voyage littéraire* at the wrong time. He mapped out for himself a literary community which was already fighting off an impending death from unfashionability; and nearly all his moves on that journey were intended to find himself a place in a world which was ultimately of no use to him. Jordan's encounter with Voltaire—made, in my view, largely without comprehending of the *philosophe*'s positions—was the one thing which gained him money and status. But it also lost him something more important; for he was not recognized as he might have wished in the community which really mattered to him, the world of the old Republic of Letters.

Perhaps the journey we should really have been looking at is the one made by Jordan's erstwhile friend, Jean Des Champs, the "little mannequin" of Frederick's complaints to Jordan (for he was very short). Des Champs, a royal chaplain and a committed disciple of the Leibnizian philosopher Christian Wolff, made the mistake of attacking Voltaire, an opponent of Wolff, in his abridgement of Wolffian philosophy; and for that crime he was ridiculed in a play written in part by Frederick himself. In this play, called *Le Singe de la Mode*, performed at court and in Berlin in the fall of 1743, a Molière-style ignorant nobleman wishes to furnish his empty library in a hurry and is offered whole shelves full of Des Champs' remaindered book. The resulting disgrace—compounded by a long coldness from the king—ultimately sent Des Champs packing to London, never to return.[144] Jordan, for fear of offending the king, refused to intervene for Des Champs; but the scandal was fuel to the flames of anti-Voltairian feelings among Jordan's scholarly associates. Jordan's *voyage littéraire* and his meeting with Voltaire brought him to the center of literary change, however little he desired it; Des Champs' encounter with the same *philosophe* caused him to flee from the same changing scene. Voltaire and the Enlightenment are at the heart of both journeys: but it is the flight of Des Champs, rather than Jordan's peculiar luck, which illustrates most vividly the fate of the old Republic of Letters in a changing world.

NOTES

PROLOGUE

1 "Eloge de Jordan" in *Nouvelle Bibliothèque Germanique* IV, pt. 2 (April–June 1748), 252. Also in "Eloge de M. Jordan," in Frederick II, *Oeuvres posthumes de Frédéric II, Roi de Prusse* (Berlin: Voss et fils and Decker et fils, 1788) IX, pp. 1–2.

2 Eugène and Emile Haag, *La France protestante*, 1st ed., VI (Paris: Joël Cherbuliez, 1856), p. 85. Jordan's early education was conducted by his uncle at a gymnasium in Magdeburg. In 1719 he was sent to the Academy in Geneva, but as he was suspended for three months for hitting another pupil in church, he decided to leave for Lausanne. By 1721 he was back in Berlin, where he continued his theological studies.

3 See chapter 5 below.

4 [Charles-Etienne Jordan], *Histoire d'un Voyage Littéraire, fait en MDCC. XXXIII. en France, en Angleterre, et en Hollande* (The Hague: Adrien Moetjens, 1735).

5 See Paul Dibon and Françoise Waquet, eds., *Johannes Fredericus Gronovius: Pèlerin de la République des Lettres: Recherches sur le voyage savant au XVIIe siècle* (Geneva: Librairie Droz, 1984).

6 Jordan, *Histoire d'un voyage littéraire*, p. 2.

7 See Daniel Roche, *Le Siècle des lumières en province: Académies et académiciens provinciaux, 1680–1789*, 2 vols. (Paris: Mouton, 1978); Roger Hahn, *Anatomy of a Scientific Institution: The Paris Academy of Sciences 1666–1803* (Berkeley and Los Angeles: University of California Press, 1971); Alice Stroup, *A Company of Scientists: Botany, Patronage, and Community at the Seventeenth-Century Parisian Royal Academy of Sciences* (Berkeley and Los Angeles: University of California Press, 1990); Richard van Dülmen, *The Society of the Enlightenment: The Rise of the Middle Class and Enlightenment Culture in Germany*, trans. Anthony Williams (Cambridge: Polity Press, 1992); Sebastian Neumeister and Conrad Wiedemann, eds., *Res Publica Litteraria: Die Institutionen der Gelehrsamkeit in der frühen Neuzeit*, 2 vols. (Wiesbaden: Otto Harrassowitz, 1987).

8 On some of these clubs see William I. Hull, *Benjamin Furly and Quakerism in Rotterdam*, Swarthmore College Monographs on Quaker History, no. 5 (Lancaster, PA: Lancaster Press, 1941), pp. 105ff; Margaret C. Jacob, *The Radical Enlightenment: Pantheists, Freemasons and Republicans* (London: George Allen and Unwin, 1981), chaps. 5 and 6; Margaret C. Jacob,

Living the Enlightenment: Freemasonry and Politics in Eighteenth-Century Europe (New York: Oxford University Press, 1991).

9 DSB, Nachlass Formey, A. de Campagne to Jean-Henri-Samuel Formey, f. 1ᵛ, Berlin, June 12, 1731.

10 See particularly the studies of Hans Bots and his students in *Studies van het Instituut voor Intellectuele Betrekkingen tussen de Westeuropese Landen in de Zeventiende Eeuw.* Jean Sgard has supervised two major projects, the *Dictionnaire des journalistes (1600–1789)* (Grenoble: Presses Universitaires de Grenoble, 1976), and the *Dictionnaire des journaux 1600–1789* (Paris: Universitas, and Oxford: Voltaire Foundation, 1991). A set of useful essays is *La Diffusion et la lecture des journaux de langue française sous l'Ancien Régime*, Actes du Colloque International, Nijmegen, 3–5 June 1987 (Amsterdam and Maarssen: APA-Holland University Press, 1988).

11 See Françoise Waquet, "Qu'est-ce que la République des Lettres? Essai de sémantique historique," *Bibliothèque de l'Ecole des chartes* 147 (1989) 473–502; Marc Fumaroli, "The Republic of Letters," *Diogenes* 143 (Fall 1988), 134–9; Paul Dibon, "Les échanges épistolaires dans l'Europe savante du XVIIe siècle," *Revue de synthèse* 3rd ser. 81–2 (May–June 1976), 32–3. Among the journals using this title were Bayle's famous *Nouvelles de la République des Lettres* (founded 1684) and the *Histoire critique de la République des Lettres* (founded 1712).

12 On this see also Hahn, *Anatomy of a Scientific Institution*, p. 39.

13 BN Ms. fr. 24469, f. 163, Alphonse des Vignoles to [Denis-François Camusat], Berlin, May 10, 1724.

14 Robert Darnton, "Reading, Writing, and Publishing," in *The Literary Underground of the Old Régime* (Cambridge, Mass.: Harvard University Press, 1982), p. 172.

15 Dena Goodman, "Pigalle's *Voltaire nu*: The Republic of Letters Represents itself to the World," *Representations* 16 (Fall 1986), 93–4.

16 Maarten Ultee, "The Republic of Letters: Learned Correspondence 1680–1720," *Seventeenth Century* II, no. 1 (Jan. 1987), 98.

17 Jean-Henri-Samuel Formey, *Eloges des académiciens de Berlin, et de divers autres savans* (Berlin: Etienne de Bourdeaux, 1757) I, pp. 315, 313.

18 Jordan, *Histoire*, p. 159.

19 Dibon and Waquet, *Gronovius*, pp. 2, 15, 17.

20 "Eloge de Jordan," *Nouvelle Bibliothèque Germanique* IV, pt. 2 (1748), 255–6.

21 Maturin Veyssière La Croze to Jordan, Berlin, May 1, 1734, printed in Jordan, *Histoire*, p. ii.

22 Darnton, *The Literary Underground*; Darnton, *The Business of Enlightenment: A Publishing History of the Encyclopédie 1775–1800* (Cambridge, Mass.: The Belknap Press, 1979); Darnton, *The Great Cat Massacre and Other Episodes in French Cultural History* (New York: Basic Books, 1984); Daniel Roche, *Les Républicains des lettres: Gens de culture et Lumières au XVIIIe siècle* (Paris: Librairie Arthème Fayard, 1988); Roche, *Le Siècle des lumières en province.*

23 Waquet's bibliography is voluminous; but see, especially, her excellent study *Le Modèle français et l'Italie savante: Conscience de soi et perception de l'autre dans la République des Lettres (1660–1750)* (Rome: Ecole Français de Rome, 1989). Waquet and Hans Bots have written a forthcoming book on the Republic of Letters; see also the studies of Hans Bots' Instituut voor Intellectuele Betrekkingen tussen de Westeuropese Landen in de Zeventiende Eeuw. All work on the earlier period is informed by Paul Dibon's essays on communication, "Communication in the Respublica literaria of the 17th century," *Respublica Litterarum* I (1978), 43–55, and "Les échanges épistolaires dans l'Europe savante du

XVIIe siècle," *Revue de synthèse* 3rd ser. 81–2 (Jan.–June 1976) 31–50.

24 Dena Goodman, *The Republic of Letters: A Cultural History of the French Enlightenment* (Ithaca, NY: Cornell University Press, 1994); Daniel Gordon, "The Idea of Sociability in Pre-Revolutionary France" (PhD dissertation, University of Chicago, 1990), forthcoming in print. I regret that Dena Goodman's book appeared too late for me to see it, but I am grateful to her for showing me the first chapter, and to Daniel Gordon for allowing me to read his thesis. See also Dena Goodman, "Story-Telling in the Republic of Letters: The Rhetorical Context of Diderot's *La Religieuse*," *Nouvelles de la République des Lettres* no. 1 (1986), 51–70; Goodman, "Pigalle's *Voltaire nu*," cited in note 15; Goodman, "Enlightenment Salons: The Convergence of Female and Philosophe Ambitions," in Lynn Hunt, ed., *The French Revolution in Culture*, special issue of *Eighteenth-Century Studies* 22 (Spring 1989), 329–50; Daniel Gordon, " 'Public Opinion' and the Civilizing Process in France: The Example of Morellet" in Hunt, ed., *The French Revolution in Culture*, pp. 302–28. Goodman and Gordon's work springs in part from the seminal work of Keith Baker; see Baker, "Politics and Public Opinion under the Old Régime: Some Reflections" in Jack R. Censer and Jeremy Popkin, eds., *Press and Politics in Pre-Revolutionary France* (Berkeley: University of California Press, 1987); Baker, ed., *The Political Culture of the Old Régime* (Oxford: Pergamon Press, 1987). See also Mona Ozouf, " 'Public Opinion' and the End of the Old Regime," *Journal of Modern History* 60 (Sept. 1988), 1–21; Sara Maza, "Le Tribunal de la nation: les mémoires judiciaires et l'opinion publique à la fin de l'Ancien Régime," *Annales ESC* (Jan.–Feb. 1987), 73–90.

25 In recent years the most influential works for historians have been Jürgen Habermas, *The Structural Transformation of the Public Sphere: An Inquiry into a Category of Bourgeois Society*, trans. Thomas Burger (Cambridge: Polity Press, 1989), and Reinhart Koselleck, *Critique and Crisis: Enlightenment and the Pathogenesis of Modern Society* (Oxford: Berg, 1988).

26 See Dena Goodman, "Seriousness of Purpose: Salonnières, Philosophes, and the Shaping of the Eighteenth-Century Salon," *Proceedings of the Annual Meeting of the Western Society for French History* 15 (1988), 111–18.

27 For a general overview, see William Doyle, *The Origins of the French Revolution* (Oxford: Oxford University Press, 1980).

28 There seems to be something of a *Zeitgeist* in historical thinking about the importance of civility to academia. The ideas for my 1990 thesis, on which this book is based, were developed in the archives, but some of them have been arrived at independently by other scholars, most particularly Steven Shapin, Mario Biagioli, and Paula Findlen.

29 Steven Shapin and Simon Schaffer, *Leviathan and the Air-Pump: Hobbes, Boyle, and the Experimental Life* (Princeton: Princeton University Press, 1985); Steven Shapin, "The House of Experiment in Seventeenth-Century England," *Isis* 79 (1988) 373–404; Steven Shapin, " 'A Scholar and a Gentleman': The Problematic Identity of the Scientific Practitioner in Early Modern England," *History of Science* 29, part 3, no. 85 (Sept. 1991) 279–327; Steven Shapin, *A Social History of Truth: Civility and Science in Seventeenth-Century England* (Chicago: University of Chicago Press, 1994). See also Mario Biagioli, "The Social Status of Italian Mathematicians, 1450–1600," *History of Science* 27 (1989), 69–75; Biagioli, "The Anthropology of Incommensurability," *Studies in History and Philosophy of Science* 21 (1990)

183–209; Biagioli, "Galileo the Emblem Maker," *Isis* 81 (1990) 230–58; Biagioli, "Galileo's System of Patronage," *History of Science* 28 (1990) 1–62; Biagioli, "Scientific Revolution, social bricolage, and etiquette," in Roy Porter and Mikuláš Teich, *The Scientific Revolution in National Context* (Cambridge: Cambridge University Press, 1992); Biagioli, *Galileo, Courtier: The Practice of Science in the Culture of Absolutism* (Chicago: University of Chicago Press, 1993); Paula Findlen, "The Economy of Scientific Exchange in Early Modern Italy," in Bruce T. Moran, *Patronage and Institutions: Science, Technology and Medicine at the European Court 1500–1700* (Woodbridge, Suffolk: Boydell Press, 1991), pp. 5–24.

30   Norbert Elias, *The History of Manners*, trans. Edmund Jephcott (New York: Pantheon Books, 1978; first publ. 1939); Elias, *Power and Civility*, trans. Jephcott (New York: Pantheon Books, 1982); Elias, *The Court Society*, trans. Jephcott (New York: Pantheon Books, 1983). The literature on this subject has been extensive. See especially Jacques Revel, "The Uses of Civility" in Roger Chartier, ed., *Passions of the Renaissance [A History of Private Life* vol. III] (Cambridge, Mass.: The Belknap Press, 1989), pp. 167–205; Marvin B. Becker, *Civility and Society in Western Europe, 1300–1600* (Bloomington: Indiana University Press, 1988); Roger Chartier, "From Text to Manners. A Concept and Its Books: *Civilité* between Aristocratic Distinction and Popular Appropriation," in *The Cultural Uses of Print in Early Modern France*, trans. Lydia Cochrane (Princeton: Princeton University Press, 1987), pp. 71–109. For a critique of Elias, see Roger Chartier, "Social Figuration and Habitus: Reading Elias," in Chartier, *Cultural History: Between Practices and Representations*, trans. Lydia Cochrane (Cambridge: Polity Press, 1988), pp.

71–94. For other sources on civility, *honnêteté*, and manners, see chapter 5 below.

31   Margaret C. Jacob, *The Radical Enlightenment: Pantheists, Freemasons and Republicans* (London: George Allen and Unwin, 1981).

32   The political and religious conservatism of members of this group has already been put forward by Simon Schaffer in "The Consuming Flame: Electrical Showmen and Tory Mystics in the World of Goods" in John Brewer and Roy Porter, eds., *Consumption and the World of Goods* (London: Routledge, 1993) pp. 489–526; and Jan Golinski, "The Secret Life of an Alchemist" in John Fauvel, Raymond Flood, Michael Shortland, and Robin Wilson, eds., *Let Newton Be!* (Oxford: Oxford University Press, 1988), pp. 147–67. There is plenty of evidence that many of the people Jacob labelled as radical because they were acquainted with radicals in fact did not share their acquaintances' ideas. Pierre Des Maizeaux, for example, protested vigorously at being attributed with Antony Collins' ideas merely because he was his friend—"Comme si les liens de l'Amitié auroient quelque droit sur les Opinions!" (BL Add. Ms. 4226, f. 318, draft article by Des Maizeaux, dated July 22, 1729).

33   For this point, see also J.A.H.G.M. Bots, *Republiek der Letteren: Ideaal en Werkelijkheid* (Amsterdam: APA-Holland Press, 1977) and Lorraine Daston, "The Ideal and Reality of the Republic of Letters in the Enlightenment," *Science in Context* 4, no. 2 (1991), 367–86.

34   Gilbert Burnet, *A Letter to Mr. Thevenot. Containing a Censure of Mr. Le Grand's History of King Henry the Eighth's Divorce* (London: for John Starkey and Richard Chiswell, 1689), postscript. Burnet apologizes in his *History of the Reformation of the Church of England*, part III (London: for J. Churchill, 1715), i. I am grateful to Tony Claydon for bringing

these passages to my attention.

35 Burnet, *History of the Reformation*, III, i.

36 On the Ancients and Moderns see especially Joseph M. Levine, *The Battle of the Books: History and Literature in the Augustan Age* (Ithaca: Cornell University Press, 1991).

37 Robert Watt, *Bibliotheca Britannica* (Edinburgh: Archibald Constable and Co., 1824) II, col. 555w.

38 KB 72 H 18, #42, Cuper to La Croze, Mar. 20, 1710.

1 PHILOSOPHICAL TRANSACTIONS

1 Gen. BPU, Ms. fr. 484, f. 198, Jean Barbeyrac to Jean-Alphonse Turrettini, Lausanne, Feb. 13, 1716.

2 KB, 72 H 19/I, #22, Maturin Veyssière La Croze to Gisbert Cuper, Berlin, Nov. 11, 1712.

3 KB, 72 H 25, ? to Cuper, Bern, April 16, 1707. Unsigned.

4 UBL, March. 2, L.J. Douxfils to Prosper Marchand, Brussels, Dec. 11, 1752.

5 See, for example, UBL, March. 2, Simon Pelloutier to Marchand, Berlin, Aug. 8, 1746; BL Add. Ms. 4281, f. 337ᵛ, François Bruys to Pierre Des Maizeaux, The Hague, Mar. 13, 1731. For another view of the relationship between reciprocity and scholarship, see Paula Findlen, "The Economy of Scientific Exchange in Early Modern Italy," in Bruce T. Moran, ed., *Science, Technology, and Medicine at the European Court 1500–1750* (Woodbridge, Suffolk: Boydell Press, 1991), pp. 5–24. Findlen stresses particularly the role of gifts in the determination of status.

6 KB, 72 D 37/12, Albert-Henri de Sallengre to [the Père] ?, The Hague, Aug. 30, 1714.

7 BL Add. Ms. 4282, f. 1. Denis-François Camusat to Des Maizeaux, Besançon, April 19, 1719.

8 BL Add. Ms. 4282, Camusat to Des Maizeaux, ff. 2–2ᵛ (Besançon, April

19, 1719), 3–4 (Paris, Oct. 8, 1719), 5 (Besançon, Jan. 28, 1720), 8 (Besançon, Mar. 17, 1720), 10–12 (Poligny, June 1, 1720).

9 UBA, A 158 a, César de Missy to Johannes Jacobus Wetstein, London, Dec. 29, 1746; UBA, Q 97 a, Missy to Wetstein, Marylebone, May 12, 1748; UBA, Q 97 b, Missy to Wetstein, Mar. 16 and 20, 1752 O.S.

10 BN Ms. fr. 22230, ff. 330–1, Jacques Lenfant to the Abbé Bignon, Berlin, Oct. 19, 1726.

11 Gen BPU, Ms. fr. 487, f. 365, Lenfant to Jean-Alphonse Turrettini, Berlin, Jan. 30, 1714.

12 Gen BPU, Ms. fr. 487, f. 367, Lenfant to Turrettini, Leipzig, July 24, 1714. Also printed inaccurately and misdated July 29 in E. de Budé, *Lettres inédites adressées de 1686 à 1737 à J.-A. Turrettini, théologien genevois* (Geneva: Imprimerie-Librairie Jules Carey, 1887), II, p. 192.

13 Eugène and Emile Haag, *La France Protestante*, 1st ed., VI (Paris: Joël Cherbuliez, 1856), pp. 550–1. They say of the *Histoire du concile de Constance*, "Au jugement de Nicéron, il est peu d'histoire aussi exacte et aussi sagement écrite que celle-ci, et selon Schröck, cet ouvrage suffirait pour rendre le nom de Lenfant immortel."

14 Gen BPU, Ms. fr. 487, ff. 371–371ᵇⁱˢ, Lenfant to Turrettini, April 13, 1715. Inaccurately reprinted in E. de Budé, *Lettres à Turrettini* II, pp. 195–7.

15 Gen BPU, Ms. fr. 487, f. 367ᵛ, Lenfant to Turrettini, Leipzig, July 24, 1714. Inaccurately reprinted and misdated July 29 in E. de Budé, *Lettres à Turrettini* II, 193.

16 BW, Ms. A 21, #3, Gisbert Cuper to Louis Bourguet, Deventer, April 25, 1713.

17 BL Sloane Ms. 4037, f. 239, Pierre Silvestre to Hans Sloane, Anvers, 20/30 March, 1699.

18 BL Add. Ms. 4281, f. 334ᵛ, François Bruys to Des Maizeaux, The Hague, Feb. 8, 1731. Bruys mentions on

f. 334 a number of books Des Maizeaux had asked him to find, for which he had written to Amsterdam and Rotterdam. Failing to get one of them, he gave Des Maizeaux his personal copy.

19 KB 72 H 18, #37, Cuper to La Croze, Zwolle, Dec. 31, 1709, draft. Prosper Marchand lent Jean de Beyer books frequently over a long period, although Marchand was in The Hague and Beyer in Nijmegen. See UBL, March. 2, Jean de Beyer to Marchand, *passim*. On gift copies, see Natalie Zemon Davis, "Beyond the Market: Books as Gifts in Sixteenth-Century France," *TRHS* 5th ser., XXXIII (1983), 69–88.

20 BL Add. Ms. 4283, f. 3, Covens and Mortier to Des Maizeaux, Amsterdam, Jan. 7, 1727. Cuper sent letters to Jacques Basnage in Rotterdam via the bookshop of Reinier Leers; see [Jean] de B[eyer], ed., *Lettres de critique, d'histoire, de littérature, &c. écrites à divers savans de l'Europe, par feu Monsieur Gisbert Cuper* (Amsterdam: Henri du Sauzet & Guillaume Smith, 1742), pp. 409, 411.

21 This could prove inconvenient for the sender; Jacob le Duchat wrote Marchand in 1722 that "Mrs Forneret et de la Roque vouloient vous écrire sous mon couvert, mais je m'en suis excusé." (UBL, March. 2, Le Duchat to Marchand, Berlin, Dec. 8, 1722). Examples of people delivering letters they were sent are numerous; see, e.g., ZAAWD,Nachlass Leibniz Nr. 3, f. 4ᵛ, Leibniz to La Croze, Hanover, Sept. 11, 1716, and SPK, Sammlung Darmstaedter K 1740 (1), f. 5, Marchand to Jean-Henri-Samuel Formey, Aug. 11, 1741.

22 Examples of the delivery of gift copies are found, among other places, in BL Add. Ms. 4313, f. 298, Mathieu Maty to Thomas Birch, Thriftstreet, London, Feb. 13, 1754, and KB 72 C 27b, f. 15, Cuper to Etienne Le Moyne, The Hague,

March 1687, draft. Barbeyrac's remark is in Bibl SHPF, Ms. 295, #79, Barbeyrac to Charles de la Motte, Groningen, Dec. 28, 1737.

23 UBA G 67 b, Pierre-Daniel Huet to Etienne Morin, Aunay, Aug. 8, 1686. For other letters from Huet to Morin, see entire G 67 series at the UBA.

24 For details on literary journals, see chapter 2 below.

25 BL Add. Ms. 4282, f. 269ᵛ, Pierre Coste to Des Maizeaux, Paris, April 30, 1713. Ellipsis in text.

26 BL Sloane Ms. 4036, ff. 215–16, Henri Basnage de Beauval to Sloane, The Hague, Aug. 1, 1695. Letter damaged.

27 BL Sloane Ms. 4036, f. 219, Basnage de Beauval to Sloane, The Hague, Nov. 10, 1695.

28 BL Sloane Ms. 4036, ff. 215–16, Basnage de Beauval to Sloane, The Hague, Aug. 1, 1695.

29 Ibid. Daniel Dumaresque, in St. Petersburg, used the same language when arranging a *commerce* with Thomas Birch in 1749. Governmental restrictions meant there was little he could communicate: "You see I deal fairly with you, and tell you, before-hand, how little you are to expect from me." BL Add. Ms. 4305, f. 63; Daniel Dumaresque to Thomas Birch, St. Petersburg, May 13, 1749.

30 Gen BPU, Ms. fr. 484, f. 204, Barbeyrac to Turrettini, Lausanne, Mar. 14, 1717.

31 I have relied particularly on Bronislaw Malinowski, *Argonauts of the Western Pacific* (New York: E.P. Dutton, 1950); Malinowski, "The Primitive Economics of the Trobriand Islanders," *Economic Journal* XXXI (1921) 1–16; Marcel Mauss, "Essai sur le don: Forme et raison de l'échange dans les sociétés archaïques," *L'Année sociologique*, nouv. sér. I (1923–4), which has been translated by Ian Cunnison as *The Gift* (New York: W.W. Norton, 1967), although this translation has

been criticized; Marshall Sahlins, *Stone Age Economics* (Chicago: Aldine-Atherton, 1972); Raymond Firth, "Themes in Economic Anthropology: A General Comment," in *Themes in Economic Anthropology* (London: Tavistock Publications, 1974); A.R. Radcliffe-Brown, "The Interpretation of Andaman Island Ceremonies," reprinted from *The Andaman Islands* (1922) in Adam Kuper, ed., *The Social Anthropology of Radcliffe-Brown* (London: Routledge & Kegan Paul, 1977); Claude Lévi-Strauss, *The Elementary Structures of Kinship*, trans. James Harle Bell et al. (Boston: Beacon Press, 1969; first publ. 1949); Lévi-Strauss, "Introduction à l'oeuvre de M. Mauss," in Mauss, *Sociologie et Anthropologie*, 3rd ed. (Paris: Presses Universitaires de France, 1966); Marshall Sahlins, "The Spirit of the Gift: *Une explication de Texte*," in Jean Pouillon and Pierre Maranda, eds., *Echanges et communications: Mélanges offerts à Claude Lévi-Strauss à l'occasion de son 60ème anniversaire* (The Hague: Mouton, 1970); Pierre Bourdieu, *Outline of a Theory of Practice*, trans. Richard Nice (Cambridge: Cambridge University Press, 1977); Michael Panoff, "Marcel Mauss's *The Gift* Revisited," *Man*, new ser. 5, no. 1 (March 1970), 60–70.

32 Mauss, "Essai sur le don," p. 62.

33 Lévi-Strauss, *The Elementary Structures of Kinship*, p. 59.

34 [Eustache du Refuge], *Traicté de la court* (Antwerp? 1615?), p. 6. Attribution and dating are the BL's.

35 Jean-Baptiste Morvan de Bellegarde, *Réfléxions sur ce qui peut plaire ou déplaire dans le commerce du monde* (Paris: Arnoul Seneuze, 1690), p. 44.

36 *Tablettes de l'homme du monde, ou Analise de sept qualitez essentielles à former le beau caractére d'homme du monde accompli* ("Cosmopoli, chez Auguste le Catholique, à l'Enseigne de l'Orthodoxie," 1715), p. 37.

37 D.J. in Denis Diderot et al.,

Encyclopédie (Neuchâtel: Samuel Faulche & Cie, 1765), XIII, p. 860, art. "Reconnoissance"; Bellegarde, *Plaire*, pp. 40–1.

38 UBL March. 2, Jacques-Georges de Chaufepié to Marchand, Amsterdam, Feb. 8, 1751. H. de Limiers wrote in similar vein to Des Maizeaux: "D'ailleurs l'interêt public pour lequel je sai, Monsieur que vous avez tant de zele me met en droit de vous suplier de concourir avec moi à son utilité." BL Add. Ms. 4284, ff. 247–8, H. de Limiers to Des Maizeaux, Amsterdam, July 6, 1716.

39 BCUL, Archives de Crousaz II/200, Jean-Pierre de Crousaz to Pierre Coste, [Lausanne, 1721], copy.

40 BL Add. Ms. 4281, f. 301, Bourguet to Des Maizeaux, Neuchâtel, Oct. 20, 1730.

41 BL Add. Ms. 4305, f. 60, Daniel Dumaresque to Thomas Birch, St. Petersburg, Aug. 19, 1748.

42 Gen BPU, Ms. fr. 484, f. 21, Pierre Allix to Turrettini, London, July 12, 1708. My emphasis.

43 BL Sloane Ms. 4053, f. 41, Jacob Wetstein and William Smith to Hans Sloane, Amsterdam, Sept. 8, 1733. Letter in English.

44 UBA, J 60 a, Peter Needham to Jean Le Clerc, St. John's College, Cambridge, May 4, 1710. Letter in English.

45 UBA, J 60 c, Needham to Le Clerc, St. John's College, Cambridge, Nov. 9, 1710 O.S. Letter in English.

46 Gen BPU, Ms. fr. 487, f. 365, Lenfant to Turrettini, Berlin, Jan. 30, 1714 (my emphasis); David Durand, among many others, uses this phrase ("une telle Edition feroit honneur à La Rep. des Lettres") in BL Add. Ms. 4283, f. 185, Durand to Des Maizeaux, London, Feb. 5, no year.

47 Gen. BPU Ms fr. 487, f. 365, Lenfant to Turrettini, Berlin, Jan. 30, 1714; Gen. BPU, Ms. fr. 487, f. 367^v, Lenfant to Turrettini, Leipzig, July 24, 1714.

48 Gen BPU, Ms. fr. 484, f. 152, Bar-

beyrac to Turrettini, Lausanne, Nov. 30, 1713.

49 BL Add. Ms. 4282, ff. 60–60^v, John Chamberlayne to Lenfant, Westminster, Aug. 10, 1714; BL Add. Ms. 4282, f. 61, Chamberlayne to Des Maizeaux, Petty France, Sept. 13, 1714.

50 DSB, Nachlass Formey, Elie Luzac to Jean-Henri-Samuel Formey, f. 69 (film), Leipzig, Oct. 20, 1750. [N.B. I use the designation "film" when using the microfilm of Luzac's letters to Formey because the pagination on the film differs from that of the DSB's manuscript.]

51 Antoine Achard to Turrettini, Berlin, Sept. 9, 1726, in E. de Budé, Lettres à Turrettini I, p. 10.

52 Neu BPU, Ms. 1274/4, f. 23, Charles-Etienne Jordan to Louis Bourguet, Strasbourg, May 15, 1733.

53 BL Add. Ms. 4281, ff. 305–305^v, Bourguet to Des Maizeaux, Neuchâtel, June 19, 1733.

54 Ibid.; BL Add. Ms. 4283, f. 34, La Croze to Des Maizeaux, Berlin, June 27, 1733.

55 Charles-Etienne Jordan, Histoire d'une voyage littéraire.

56 BL Add. Ms. 4283, f. 34, La Croze to Des Maizeaux, Berlin, June 27, 1733.

57 KB, 72 H 19/II, #23, Cuper to La Croze, Deventer, Aug. 13, 1716, draft.

58 See, e.g., Bibl SHPF Ms. 295, #85, Barbeyrac to Charles de la Motte, Groningen, Aug. 19, 1740, which gives a long account of the activities of Jean-Pierre de Crousaz drawn from a letter received from him. Virtually any letter between two literary figures will contain these sorts of details.

59 Marshall Sahlins, Stone Age Economics, p. 186.

60 BL Add. Ms. 4281, f. 32, Barbeyrac to Des Maizeaux, Lausanne, Sept. 11, 1716.

61 DSB, Nachlass Formey, J. d'Artenay to Formey, Minden, Jan. 4, 1742.

62 BL Add. Ms. 4281, f. 212, Jean-Paul

Bignon to Des Maizeaux, Paris, April 24, 1711.

63 UBA, J 60 b, Peter Needham to Jean Le Clerc, St. John's College, Cambridge, July 9, 1710 O.S. (letter in English); Encyclopédie XIII, p. 860, art. "Reconnoissance."

64 BL Sloane Ms. 4036, f. 219, Basnage de Beauval to Sloane, The Hague, Nov. 10, 1695; BL Sloane Ms. 4036, ff. 215–16, Beauval to Sloane, The Hague, Aug. 1, 1695.

65 Mauss, The Gift, p. 72.

66 Peter M. Blau, Exchange and Power in Social Life (New York: John Wiley, 1964), p. 113.

67 BN Ms. fr. nouv. acq. 14898, f. 122, Des Maizeaux to Jean-Pierre Niceron, London, Aug. 11, 1732.

68 UBA, A 158 c, César de Missy to Johannes Jacobus Wetstein, Marylebone, Mar. 10, 1752 O.S.

69 Blau, p. 110.

70 On Bourguet, see Haag, La France Protestante, ed. Henri Bordier, 2nd ed. III (Paris: Librairie Sandoz et Fischbacher, 1881), cols. 2–7. Bourguet's fluctuating addresses between 1702 and 1706 are evident from Neu BPU Ms. 1273/2, letters from J.J. Hottinger to Bourguet. The name of Bourguet's business is mentioned in KB 72 H 26/I, f. 101, Bourguet to Cuper, Venice, Feb. 2, 1713.

71 KB 72 H 26/I, f. 99, Bourguet to Cuper, Venice, Feb. 2, 1713.

72 Sahlins, Stone Age Economics, p. 207. For the concept "starting mechanism" Sahlins cites Alvin Gouldner, "The Norm of Reciprocity: A Preliminary Statement," American Sociological Review 25 (1960), 176–7.

73 For a fuller discussion of this subject, see chapter 3 below.

74 See, e.g., the éloge of Jacob Perizonius in the Histoire critique de la République des Lettres IX (1715), Art. XVI, pp. 413–14, which praises Perizonius for being "facile d'accès, d'un abord serain."

75 Bibliothèque angloise V, part 2 (1719), pp. 432–3.

76 KB 72 H 19/I, #8, La Croze to

Cuper, Berlin, March 8, 1711.

77 Malinowski, *Argonauts*, p. 91.

78 BL Add. Ms. 4283, f. 34, La Croze to Des Maizeaux, Berlin, June 27, 1733; BW Ms. A 21, #3, Cuper to Bourguet, Deventer, April 25, 1713.

79 Sahlins, *Stone Age Economics*, pp. 196–7.

80 UBL, March. 2, Jacob le Duchat to "Marchand," Berlin, Dec. 8, 1722. The UBL catalogues this letter as one to Prosper Marchand, but the text of this and surrounding letters shows that it could not have been directed to him. The recipient was living in Paris and had been to Berlin, neither of which was true of Marchand. My conjecture is that the letter is to Du Homel, an old colleague of Le Duchat's from Metz.

81 KB 72 H 19/II, #7, La Croze to Cuper, Berlin, June 30, 1714. La Croze, like many Huguenots with official appointments in Berlin, suffered economically from the change in régimes in 1713. Cuper responded favorably to his request; see KB 72 H 19/II, #10, Cuper to La Croze, Sept. 19, 1714, draft, which is also printed in Beyer, *Lettres de Cuper*, p. 158.

82 KB 72 H 26/I, f. 99, Bourguet to Cuper, Venice, Feb. 2, 1713.

83 These messages occur in KB 72 H 18, #29, La Croze to Cuper, Berlin, Sept. 14, 1709, and elsewhere in KB 72 H 18. The letter about Starck is KB 72 H 18, #15, La Croze to Cuper, Berlin, May 24, 1709.

84 DSB, Nachlass Formey, Paul-Emile de Mauclerc to Formey, f. 1ᵛ, Stettin, Oct. 28, 1737.

85 Raymond Firth, "Some Principles of Social Organization," in *Essays on Social Organization and Values*, London School of Economics Monographs on Social Anthropology (London: Athlone Press, 1969; 1st ed. 1964), p. 63.

86 Quoted in BL Sloane Ms. 4056, f. 247ᵛ, Jacob Theodore Klein to Hans Sloane, June 1, 1740.

87 KB 72 C 27g, David Martin to Cuper, Utrecht, April 13, 1686.

88 See, e.g., ZAAWD Nachlass Leibniz Nr. 3, f. 23, Leibniz to La Croze, Hanover, Mar. 24, 1715; BL Add. Ms. 4286, f. 271, De la Motte to Des Maizeaux, Amsterdam, June 26, 1725. My emphasis.

89 BL Sloane Ms. 4052, Jean Gagnier to Sloane, Oxford, Jan. 13, 1732. La Croze used the same metaphor in his recommendation for Jordan, BL Add. Ms. 4283, f. 34, La Croze to Des Maizeaux, Berlin, June 27, 1733.

90 BL Add. Ms. 4287, f. 105ᵛ, De la Motte to Des Maizeaux, Amsterdam, Sept. 26, 1730.

91 KB 72 G 33, Pierre Jurieu to Cuper, Rotterdam, May 20, 1704. Copy by Cuper.

92 Louis Dufour, abbé de Longuerue, to Turrettini, Paris, Aug. 30, 1697, in E. de Budé, ed., *Lettres à Turrettini* II, pp. 240–1; Longuerue to Turrettini, Paris, Oct. 27, 1698, ibid. II, p. 246.

93 Joseph Klaits, *Printed Propaganda under Louis XIV* (Princeton: Princeton University Press, 1976), pp. 37–8.

94 UBL March. 2, Thémiseul de St.-Hyacinthe to Charles Le Vier, June 9, no year. N.B. I use the term *libraire* rather than "publisher" or "bookseller" to avoid the confusion inevitably arising from the use of these terms to discuss the eighteenth century. The functions of publisher, distributor, and sometimes printer overlapped in the same people in this period. On this issue, see Philip Gaskell, *A New Introduction to Bibliography*, 2nd ed. (Oxford: Clarendon Press, 1974), pp. 179–80, and Michael Treadwell, "London Trade Publishers 1675–1750," *The Library* 6th ser. VI no. 2 (June 1982), 99–134.

95 See H.A. Enno van Gelder, *Getemperde Vrijheid* (Groningen: Wolters-Noordhoff, 1972), chap. 4, and I.H. van Eeghen, *De Amsterdamse Boekhandel* V¹ (Amsterdam: N. Israel,

1978), p. 21. Although Jacques Bernard mentioned in 1701 that "il est défendu en ce Pays de publier des Livres où il y aît des sentimens tendans au Socinianisme," in the same year he sent a *feuille volante* to a correspondent in Paris, boasting that "Vous verrez par là la liberté qu'ont nos libraires, puis que cette piece est directement contre l'Empereur le principal de nos Alliez." (BL Add. Ms. 4281, f. 100ᵛ, Jacques Bernard to Des Maizeaux, The Hague, Feb. 4, 1701; BN Ms. fr. 19211, f. 160, Bernard to [the Père Léonard de Ste.-Catherine de Sienne], The Hague, Nov. 4, 1701.) On French censorship see, *inter alia*, Albert Bachman, *Censorship in France from 1715 to 1750: Voltaire's Opposition* (New York: Publications of the Institute of French Studies, 1934); David T. Pottinger, *The French Book Trade in the Ancien Régime, 1500– 1791* (Cambridge, Mass.: Harvard University Press, 1958), chap. 4; Nicole Hermann-Mascard, *La Censure des livres à la fin de l'Ancien Régime (1750–1789)* (Paris: Presses Universitaires de France, 1968); J.-P. Belin, *Le Commerce des livres prohibés à Paris de 1750 à 1789* (Paris: Belin frères, 1913); Giles Barber, "French Royal Decrees concerning the Book Trade," *Australian Journal of French Studies* III (1966), 31–9; Anne Sauvy, *Livres saisis à Paris entre 1678 et 1701* (The Hague: Martinus Nijhoff, 1972); William Hanley, "The Policing of Thought: Censorship in Eighteenth-Century France," *Studies on Voltaire and the Eighteenth Century* 183 (1980), 265–95; Daniel Roche, "La censure," and "La police du livre," and Anne Sauvy, "Livres contrefaits et livres interdits," in Martin, ed., *Histoire de l'édition française* II, pp. 76–92, 104–19; Anne Goldgar, "The Absolutism of Taste: Journalists as Censors in 18th-century Paris," in Robin Myers and Michael Harris, eds., *Censorship and the Control of Print in England and*

France 1600–1910 (Winchester: St. Paul's Bibliographies, 1992), pp. 87– 110. On publishing outside France see Robert Darnton, "A Printing Shop Across the Border," in *The Literary Underground of the Old Regime* (Cambridge, Mass.: Harvard University Press, 1982), and, for the end of the century, *The Business of Enlightenment* (Cambridge, Mass.: Harvard University Press, 1979).

96   UBA, III D 24 #27, ff. 56–56ᵛ, Jean Le Clerc to Gilbert Burnet, Amsterdam, Sept. 14, 1703, draft; UBL March. 2, Simon Pelloutier to Marchand, Berlin, Aug. 2, 1752; Gen BPU, Ms. fr. 484, f. 129, Barbeyrac to Turrettini, Lausanne, July 28, 1712. Barbeyrac later reported that "on est fort prévenu en Holl. contre les Editions de Genéve: voilà le mal j'ai vû ici une Lettre écrite à Mʳˢ. Fabri & Barrillot [a *librairie*] par *Du Sauzet*, Libraire de la Haie, qui leur disoit tout franchement qu'on ne vouloit point de leurs Editions." (Gen. BPU, Ms. fr. 484, f. 198ᵛ, Barbeyrac to Turrettini, Lausanne, Feb. 13, 1716.)

97   BCUL, Archives de Crousaz II/21, J.-P. de Crousaz to Jean-Jacques Dartous de Mairan, Paris, Sept. 26, [1718], copy; BCUL, Archives de Crousaz II/173, Crousaz to François de la Pillonnière, [Lausanne, 1721], copy.

98   The cheapness of Dutch editions compared with French ones is pointed out by Christiane Berkvens-Stevelinck ("L'édition et le commerce du livre français en Europe," in Henri-Jean Martin and Roger Chartier, eds., *Histoire de l'édition française* [Paris: Promodis, 1984] II, p. 309), a fact partly due to the low taxes on foreign trade, which reduced the cost of paper (Van Eeghen, *De Amsterdamse Boekhandel* Vᴵ, pp. 22–3). Barbeyrac and Turrettini both commented on the higher payments available in the form of books and money in the Netherlands; see Gen BPU, Ms. fr.

481, f. 127, Turrettini to ?, Geneva, May 3, 1728, copy, and Gen BPU, Ms. fr. 484, f. 178, Barbeyrac to Turrettini, Lausanne, May 28, 1715. Barbeyrac's praise of Dutch printing appears in Gen BPU, Ms. fr. 484, f. 108ᵛ, Barbeyrac to Turrettini, Lausanne, Dec. 23, 1710.

99 Neu BPU, Ms. 1274/4, f. 4, Charles-Etienne Jordan to Bourguet, Prenzlau, Jan. 14, 1729. Jordan was asking Bourguet to intercede for him to get a collection of essays published.

100 ZAAWD, Nachlass Leibniz Nr. 3, f. 76, Leibniz to La Croze, Hanover, Oct. 14, 1707, draft; ZAAWD, Nachlass Leibniz Nr. 3, f. 70ᵛ, Leibniz to La Croze, Hanover, Nov. 5, 1707, draft (?).

101 UBA G 67 f, Huet to Morin, Bourbon, Oct. 3, 1695; UBA G 67 g, Huet to Morin, Paris, Jan. 11, 1697; UBA G 67 h, Huet to Morin, Paris, Mar. 28, 1697; UBA G 67 i, Huet to Morin, Paris, May 12, 1697; UBA G 67 j, Huet to Morin, Avranches, Jan. 28, 1698. A scholar in Lausanne offered to find a Dutch publisher for Bourguet because "Mʳ du Sauzet [a *libraire* and author] ... est fort en relation avec moi" (Neu BPU, Ms. 1270, f. 2, Du Lignon to Bourguet, Lausanne, Feb. 15, 1718). According to Otto Lankhorst, Pierre Bayle was subject to several such requests from his correspondents in France. See Otto S. Lankhorst, *Reinier Leers (1654–1714), Uitgever & Boekverkoper te Rotterdam: Een Europees "Libraire" en zijn Fonds* (Amsterdam: APA-Holland Universiteits Pers, 1983), pp. 52–4.

102 UBA G 67 f, Huet to Morin, Bourbon, Oct. 3, 1695. Barbeyrac was, unusually, rather more specific in his instructions to Turrettini, who helped him publish his *Discours sur la permission des loix* with Fabri and Barrillot in Geneva (Gen BPU Ms. fr. 484, ff. 180, 182, Barbeyrac to Turrettini, Lausanne, June 16 and July 21, 1715). He used Turrettini

to give instructions to the printers about the title page. This is the only time I have seen such detail in this type of transaction between scholars.

103 BL Add. Ms. 4287, f. 52, De la Motte to Des Maizeaux, Amsterdam, Feb. 22, 1729.

104 Jean Sgard, *Dictionnaire des Journalistes (1600–1789)* (Grenoble: Presses Universitaires de Grenoble, 1976), "La Motte," p. 220; BL Add. Ms. 4286–7 *passim*; for references to Geneva, see BL Add. Ms. 4287, ff. 6–6ᵛ, De la Motte to Des Maizeaux, Amsterdam, Sept. 5, 1727.

105 BL Add. Ms. 4286, f. 134ᵛ, De la Motte to Des Maizeaux, Amsterdam, Mar. 17, 1711; BL Add. Ms. 4286–7, *passim*.

106 UBL March. 2, Prévost to Marchand, April 3, 1736; UBL March. 2, Jacques de Pérard to Marchand, Grambzow, Nov. 4, 1738; UBL March. 2, Jacques de Pérard to Marchand, Sept. 27, 1738.

107 Christiane Berkvens-Stevelinck, *Prosper Marchand et l'histoire du livre: quelques aspects de l'érudition bibliographique dans la première moitié du XVIIIᵉ siècle, particulièrement en Hollande* (proefschrift published for the University of Amsterdam, 1978); Margaret Jacob, *The Radical Enlightenment: Pantheists, Freemasons and Republicans* (London: George Allen and Unwin, 1981); Elizabeth L. Eisenstein, *Print Culture and Enlightenment Thought*, The Sixth Hanes Lecture (Chapel Hill: University of North Carolina, 1986); Christiane Berkvens-Stevelinck, *Prosper Marchand: La vie et l'oeuvre (1678–1756)*, Studies over de Geschiedenis van de Leidse Universiteit IV (Leiden: E.J. Brill, 1987); Elizabeth Eisenstein, *Grub Street Abroad: Aspects of the French Cosmopolitan Press from the Age of Louis XIV to the French Revolution* (Oxford: Clarendon Press, 1992), chap. 3.

108 UBL, March. 2, "Stemma gentis Marchand." This family tree, in

Marchand's hand, was made in 1705, when he was 27.

109 Berkvens-Stevelinck, *Prosper March-and et l'histoire du livre*, pp. xxii ff.; ibid., "Prosper Marchand, 'Trait d'union' entre auteur et éditeur," p. 46; ibid., "La Cabale de l'Edition de 1720 du *Dictionnaire* de Bayle," p. 105. For other accounts of March-and, see Haag, *La France Protestante*, 1st ed., VII (Paris: Joël Cherbuliez, 1857), pp. 221–2, and E.F. Kossmann, *De Boekhandel te 's-Gravenhage tot het Eind van de 18de Eeuw* (The Hague: Martinus Nijhoff, 1937), pp. 251–3.

110 Numerous examples of these services appear in the correspondence. See UBL March. 2, *passim*, and BL Add. Mss. 4286 and 4287, *passim*.

111 James Hepburn, *The Author's Empty Purse and the Rise of the Literary Agent* (London: Oxford University Press, 1968), pp. 2, 22.

112 Berkvens-Stevelinck, " 'Trait d'Union,' " in *Prosper Marchand et l'histoire du livre*, pp. 44–78. This article was first published in *De Gulden Passer* 56 (1978), 65–99.

113 UBL, March. 2, La Croze to Marchand, Berlin, June 7, 1734.

114 BCUL, Archives de Crousaz XIV/8, Barbeyrac to Crousaz, Groningen, Aug. 5, 1719.

115 Bibl SHPF, Ms. 295, #15, Pierre Coste to Charles de la Motte, [London], Mar. 29, 1727 O.S.

116 UBL, March. 2, César de Missy to Marchand, Frankfurt, Aug. 7, 1723; UBL, March. 2, Simon Pelloutier to Marchand, Berlin, Aug. 18, 1736. Pelloutier's phrasing was of course an appeal to some kind of connection with Marchand, since he mentioned knowing two authors who had pre-viously corresponded with the agent. The same sort of appeal occurred in Jean-Henri-Samuel Formey's first letter to Marchand, in which, after mentioning the good things said about Marchand by Jordan, the late La Croze, and others, he asked if Marchand could help publish his

"Roman Philosophique," *La Belle Wolfienne* (UBL, March. 2, Formey to Marchand, Aug. 9, 1740).

117 BL Add. Ms. 4286, f. 74, De la Motte to Des Maizeaux, Amsterdam, Mar. 5, 1709.

118 DSB, Nachlass Formey, Marchand to Formey, f. 5, Feb. 6, 1741.

119 SPK, Sammlung Darmstaedter K 1740 (1), f. 4, Marchand to Formey, Aug. 11, 1741.

120 BL Add. Ms. 4287, ff. 43–43^v, De la Motte to Des Maizeaux, [Am-sterdam], Nov. 30, 1728.

121 BL Add. Ms. 4287, f. 59, De la Motte to Des Maizeaux, Amsterdam, April 26, 1729.

122 BL Add. Ms. 4286, f. 182, De la Motte to Des Maizeaux, Amsterdam, Aug. 9, 1712.

123 These brackets in text.

124 BL Add. Ms. 4287, ff. 61–61^v, De la Motte to Des Maizeaux, Amsterdam, May 31, 1729. William Smith, an Irish *libraire*, was a member of the Compagnie des Libraires (a publish-ing consortium) and was a partner in the *librairie* Wetstein and Smith, having married a Wetstein.

125 An example of such a contract is UBL March. 44:3, f. 1*, between the *libraire* Charles Le Vier in The Hague and "M. De la Motte agissant au nom et de la part de M. Pierre Coste."

126 BL Add. Ms. 4286, f. 145^v, Des Maizeaux's calculation of his account with De la Motte, on the back of De la Motte's letter of June 23, 1711; DSB, Nachlass Formey, Marchand to Formey, f. 18, "Au commencement de 1743," letter containing Formey's account with Marchand. The latter account begins with the money owed to Formey for sheets of Le Duchat's remarks on Villon (edited by Formey), and then subtracts the cost of a book, two bindings of the Villon in morocco and in calf, and postage of letters from Jean Des Champs to Formey "reçus p^r moi." Marchand refers to this as "notre petit Compte touchant Villon,"

suggesting that not only was he not paid for his services as agent but that he received the payment for the edition for the author and fronted money for the author's purchases in Holland.

127 Bibl SHPF, Ms. 295, #105, Le Courayer to De la Motte, London, Nov. 2, 1731.

128 DSB, Nachlass Formey, Marchand to Formey, f. 3, Dec. 20 [1740]; BL Add. Ms. 4286, f. 19ᵛ, De la Motte to Des Maizeaux, Amsterdam, June 5, 1705.

129 UBL, March. 2, La Croze to Marchand, Berlin, Dec. 21, 1723.

130 BL Add. Ms. 4287, f. 43ᵛ, De la Motte to Des Maizeaux, [Amsterdam], Nov. 30, 1728.

131 DSB, Nachlass Formey, Marchand to Formey, f. 22ᵛ, The Hague, April 19, 1743.

132 DSB, Nachlass Formey, Marchand to Formey, f. 1, The Hague, Nov. 15, 1736.

133 BL Add. Ms. 4286, f. 146, De la Motte to Des Maizeaux, Amsterdam, July 17, 1711. It was not customary for a *libraire* to maintain his own printing-house; *libraires* usually contracted with printers who maintained separate establishments. Fritsch and Böhm had purchased Reinier Leers' establishment in Rotterdam on May 2, 1709; unusually, it contained five printing presses and one copperplate press. See Otto Lankhorst, *Reinier Leers*, p. 130.

134 BL Add. Ms. 4287, f. 113, De la Motte to Des Maizeaux, Amsterdam, April 7, 1733.

135 It is usually said that correctors of the press worked for only one printing-house and actually worked at the press. See Pottinger, *French Book Trade*, p. 52; Marjorie Plant, *The English Book Trade: An Economic History of the Making and Sale of Books* (London: George Allen and Unwin, 1939), pp. 70–2; Léon Voet, *The Golden Compasses*, trans. Raymond H. Kaye (Amsterdam: Vangendt, 1972) II, pp. 174–5. Even contem-

porary sources, such as Moxon, suggest that the corrector worked in "some little Closet adjoyning the *Composing-room*" (Joseph Moxon, *Mechanick Exercises on the Whole Art of Printing*, ed. Herbert Davis and Harry Carter [London: Oxford University Press, 1958; first publ. 1683–4], p. 247). But De la Motte and Marchand worked for the *libraires*, not the printers, and the numbers of *libraires* who employed them make it clear that these correctors were freelance operators. De la Motte, for example, remarked of Pierre Mortier that "je n'aime point à travailler pour lui, parce qu'il y a beaucoup plus de peine à ses Ouvrages. La raison de cela est que ne payant assez les Imprimeurs, les bons compositeurs n'en veulent point" (BL Add. Ms. 4286, f. 35, De la Motte to Des Maizeaux, Amsterdam, Dec. 8, 1705). De la Motte worked at home and was sent proofs by courier (BL Add. Ms. 4287, f. 17, De la Motte to Des Maizeaux, Amsterdam, Mar. 9, 1728, and elsewhere). When De la Motte and Prévost went into a correcting partnership in 1734, they made a contract to live and work together, correcting whatever works they were given by *libraires* (UBL, March. 2, "J.B. le Prévost" to Marchand, Amsterdam, May 28, 1735). According to the accounts of the *libraires* Luchtmans in Leiden, the firm used four different correctors in an eight–month period (BVBBB, Archief Luchtmans, Personalia #7, "Cassaboek . . . 1753–1772," entries for 1760).

136 BL Add. Ms. 4287, f. 95, De la Motte to Des Maizeaux, Amsterdam, April 21, 1730.

137 BL Add. Ms. 4286, f. 278, De la Motte to Des Maizeaux, Amsterdam, Nov. 27, 1725. The confused language is in the original.

138 Van Eeghen, *Amsterdamse Boekhandel* V¹, p. 30; BVBBB, Archief Luchtmans, Personalia #7, "Cassaboek . . . 1753–1772"; Percy Simp-

son, *Proof-Reading in the Sixteenth, Seventeenth, and Eighteenth Centuries* (London: Oxford University Press, 1935), pp. 163–4 and Appendix I.

139 Conversation with Professor Robert Darnton, Oct. 30, 1987.

140 Jacques Savary, *Le parfait négociant*, ed. Philémon-Louis Savary (Paris: La veuve Estienne, 1736; 1st ed. 1675) II, p. 235. See also Ray Bert Westerfield, "Middlemen in English Business, Particularly between 1660 and 1760," *Transactions of the Connecticut Academy of Arts and Sciences* XIX, no. 2 (May 1915), 354–61.

141 Pierre Des Maizeaux, who appears to have acted as a literary agent in London, capitalizing on his connections with Dutch *libraires*, sometimes helped these *libraires* find manuscripts and helped negotiate the terms. This is particularly evident in his correspondence with the *libraire* Henri du Sauzet. See BL Add. Ms. 4288, ff. 13, 58–58ᵛ, 60, 61, 66–66ᵛ, 73–73ᵛ, Du Sauzet to Des Maizeaux, Amsterdam, June 10, 1718; April 3, 1722; May 8, 1722; July 28, 1722; Sept. 18, 1727; July 13, 1728.

142 BL Add. Ms. 4286, f. 149, De la Motte to Des Maizeaux, Amsterdam, Sept. 22, 1711.

143 BL Add. Ms. 4287, f. 99, De la Motte to Des Maizeaux, [Amsterdam], July 11, 1730.

144 BL Add. Ms. 4287, ff. 23–4, De la Motte to Des Maizeaux, Amsterdam, June 8, 1728.

145 BL Add. Ms. 4287, f. 80, De la Motte to Des Maizeaux, Amsterdam, Dec. 20, 1729.

146 BL Add. Ms. 4286, f. 186ᵛ, De la Motte to Des Maizeaux, Amsterdam, Sept. 13, 1712; see also Add. Ms. 4286, f. 146 (July 17, 1711) and Add. Ms. 4287, f. 50 (Feb. 8, 1729). The *libraires* also sometimes used agents' contacts with authors to obtain material for new editions or to make proposals to authors on works originating with the *libraire*. See, e.g., Bibl SHPF, Ms. 295, #18, Pierre Coste to De la Motte, [England],

Mar. 22, 1739.

147 Gen. BPU, Ms. fr. 484, f. 126, Barbeyrac to Turrettini, Lausanne, May 26, 1712.

148 DSB, Nachlass Formey, Jean Des Champs to Formey, f. 11, London, Dec. 26, 1747.

149 BL Add. Ms. 4286, f. 14, De la Motte to Des Maizeaux, Amsterdam, Mar. 31, 1705.

150 It should be noted that although most of my evidence comes from letters from De la Motte to Des Maizeaux, this has more to do with the survival of these letters than any special relationship between these men. The letters consist almost entirely of business. The letters to De la Motte, at the Bibliothèque de la Société de l'Histoire du Protestantisme Français, indicate a wide circle of "clients."

151 BL Add. Ms. 4287, f. 45ᵛ, De la Motte to Des Maizeaux, Amsterdam, Dec. 14, 1728.

152 Bibl SHPF, Ms. 295, #31, Pierre Coste to De la Motte, Nov. 19, 1743 O.S.

153 BL Add. Ms. 4287, f. 3–3ᵛ, De la Motte to Des Maizeaux, Amsterdam, July 4, 1727.

154 BL Add. Ms. 4287, f. 63ᵛ, De la Motte to Des Maizeaux, June 27, 1729.

155 BL Add. Ms. 4286, f. 240, De la Motte to Des Maizeaux, Amsterdam, Jan. 1, 1720.

156 BL Add. Ms. 4287, ff. 41–41ᵛ, De la Motte to Des Maizeaux, Amsterdam, Nov. 16, 1728; see also f. 39, Nov. 12, 1728. De la Motte clearly assumed that Wetstein was reading his post.

157 BL Add. Ms. 4286, ff. 14 and 15–15ᵛ, De la Motte to Des Maizeaux, Amsterdam, Mar. 31, 1705; and f. 13, Mar. 20, 1705.

158 Annie Parent, *Les métiers du livre à Paris au XVIᵉ siècle (1535–1560)* (Geneva: Librairie Droz, 1974), pp. 123, 125; Pottinger, *French Book Trade*, p. 49; Voet, *Golden Compasses* II, pp. 160, 191–2.

159 Lankhorst, *Reinier Leers*, p. 28; UBA J 82, Antoine Vattemare to Jean Le Clerc, London, Jan. 30, 1684[/5?]; BW Ms. A 21, #18, Gisbert Cuper to Louis Bourguet, Oxen, Sept. 8, 1715, postscript; KB 72 H 26/II, Bourguet to Cuper, no place or date [1715].

160 Moxon, *Mechanick Exercises*, pp. 246–7.

161 BN Ms. fr. 21586, f. 1652, quoted in Sgard, *Dictionnnaire des journalistes*, "Marchand," p. 258.

162 BL Add. Ms. 4286, f. 93, De la Motte to Des Maizeaux, Amsterdam, Nov. 15, 1709.

163 See, e.g., Gen BPU, Ms. fr. 484, f. 215ᵛ, Barbeyrac to Turrettini, Groningen, Oct. 16, 1717, where Barbeyrac mentions a dinner at De la Motte's which Le Clerc was also supposed to attend. Throughout his correspondence De la Motte provided information and opinions on new works, including the quality of their printing; in his role as corrector he was able to check citations in books from his own study. He also showed interest in reading new books which appeared off the presses.

164 Bibl SHPF, Ms. 295, #54, Armand de la Chapelle to De la Motte, The Hague, July 1, 1735.

165 BL Add. Ms. 4226, ff. 319–20, draft of journal article by Des Maizeaux.

166 Voet, *Golden Compasses* II, p. 283.

167 KB 72 H 13/I, Clermont to Cuper, Amsterdam, Aug. 7, 1716.

168 DSB, Nachlass Formey, Jacques de Pérard to Formey, f. 55, Dresden, Jan. 30, 1741.

169 BN Ms. fr. 19211, f. 137ᵛ, Jacques Bernard to [the Père Léonard de Ste.-Catherine de Sienne], The Hague, Jan. 1, 1701; BN Ms. fr. 19211, f. 151ᵛ, Bernard to Léonard, The Hague, June 2, 1701.

170 UBL March. 2, Michel Mattaire to Marchand, London, Jan. 29, 1742. In English.

171 Elizabeth Eisenstein has maintained that the role of literary patron she has described for the great humanist printers of the Renaissance continued into the eighteenth century. It is true that some *libraires* maintained friendly and sociable relations with scholars, and the bookshops were certainly good places to encounter colleagues. But savants tended to speak of their friends in the *librairie*, such as William Smith, as exceptions to the rule.

172 *Lettres sérieuses et badines* I, pt. 2 (1729; 2nd ed. 1740), 174, n. 1.

173 Bibl SHPF, Ms. 295, #16, Coste to De la Motte, [England], [Feb.?] 7, 1735.

174 BL Add. Ms. 4287, f. 113, De la Motte to Des Maizeaux, Amsterdam, April 7, 1733; BL Add. Ms. 4286, f. 130, De la Motte to Des Maizeaux, Amsterdam, Feb. 10, 1711.

175 BJK, Ms. Berol. Gall. Qu. 26, f. 479, Marchand to M.V. La Croze, July 28, 1738. Copy.

176 DSB, Nachlass Formey, Marchand to Formey, f. 22ᵛ, The Hague, April 19, 1743.

177 I should note that I use the term "professionalization" in its common, rather than specifically sociological, meaning.

178 BL Add. Ms. 4256, ff. 3–3ᵛ. "Proposals most humbly Offer'd to All Noblemen, Gentlemen, or Others who are Curious in Books, and other Matters in the Learned Way." N.d. Printed advertisement in the papers of Thomas Birch, thus presumably dating from before his death in 1766.

179 BJK, Ms. Berol. Gall. Qu. 26, f. 401. Groddeck to La Croze, Nov. 12, 1698. Copy.

2 WRITING TO THE PAPERS

1 UBA, G 67 j, Huet to Morin, Avranches, Jan. 28, 1698. The treatise Huet mentioned, "Commentarium de Navigationibus Salomonis," was published in John

Pearson, ed., *Criticorum Sacrorum* VIII (Utrecht: Van de Water, and Amsterdam: Boom, 1698). Baillet made a similar comparison to the abridgements of earlier times, referring in his summary of criticisms of such works to Constantine VII Porphyrogenitus (905–959), known for his sponsorship of encyclopedias which excerpted ancient and later authors. See Adrien Baillet, *Jugemens des Savans sur les principaux ouvrages des auteurs* (Paris: Charles Moette et al., 1722) I, 243.

2 Baillet, *Jugemens des Savans* I, 240, 249.

3 UBA, G 67 c, Pierre-Daniel Huet to Etienne Morin, Paris, Nov. 9, 1686.

4 BN Ms. fr. 9359, f. 362^v, Bayle to Nicaise, Nov. 27, 1698.

5 However, as Hans Bots has pointed out, Bayle modelled his journal on ones founded earlier, particularly the *Journal des sçavans* and the *Acta Eruditorum*. See Bots, "Un Journaliste sur les journaux de son temps: le cas de Pierre Bayle," in *Diffusion et lecture des journaux*, p. 203.

6 Elisabeth Labrousse, *Pierre Bayle* (The Hague: Martinus Nijhoff, 1963) I, pp. 189–90; Labrousse, "Les coulisses du journal de Bayle," in Paul Dibon, ed., *Pierre Bayle: Le philosophe de Rotterdam* (Amsterdam: Elsevier, 1959), pp. 98–100, 115. Among the later journals which paid homage to Bayle were the *Bibliothèque raisonnée* (I, 1728, v, "Avertissement des Libraires") and of course the *Histoire des ouvrages des savans* (Sept. 1687, preface), a continuation of the *Nouvelles de la République des Lettres* by Henri Basnage de Beauval.

7 Jean Sgard, "Journalistes français en Suisse (1685–1789)" in Jean-Daniel Candaux and Bernard Lescaze, eds., *Cinq siècles d'imprimerie genevoise* (Geneva: Société d'histoire et d'archéologie, 1981) II, p. 1.

8 *Bibliothèque raisonnée des ouvrages des savans de l'Europe* I (1728), (Amsterdam: Wetsteins and Smith, 1728) v–vi, "Avertissement des Libraires."

9 The history of newspapers and journals is now a major scholarly industry. For overviews of the Francophone press, see especially Jean Sgard, *Dictionnaire des Journalistes (1600–1789)* (Grenoble: Presses Universitaires de Grenoble, 1976), and Sgard, *Dictionnaire des journaux (1600–1789)* (Paris: Universitas, and Oxford: Voltaire Foundation, 1991), 2 vols. An excellent collection of essays on this topic is *La Diffusion et la lecture des journaux de langue française sous l'Ancien Régime*, Actes du Colloque International, Nijmegen, 3–5 June 1987 (Amsterdam and Maarssen: APA-Holland University Press, 1988). For information on the background of the first journal, see Georges Weill, *Le journal. Origines, évolution et rôle de la presse périodique* (Paris: La Renaissance du Livre, 1934); Howard M. Solomon, *Public Welfare, Science, and Propaganda in Seventeenth Century France: The Innovations of Théophraste Renaudot* (Princeton: Princeton University Press, 1972). On *nouvelles à la main*, see Roger Duchêne, "Lettres et gazettes au XVIIème siècle," *Revue d'histoire moderne et contemporaine* XVIII (Oct.–Dec. 1971), 491, 496–500; Joseph Klaits, *Printed Propaganda under Louis XIV: Absolute Monarchy and Public Opinion* (Princeton: Princeton University Press, 1976), pp. 39–40; Eugène Hatin, *Les Gazettes de Hollande et la presse clandestine aux XVIIe et XVIIIe siècles* (Paris: Librairie Richelieu, 1845), p. 22; Frantz Funck-Brentano, *Les Nouvellistes* (Paris: Librairie Hachette, 1905). On the first literary journal, the *Journal des sçavans* of 1665, see Betty Trebelle Morgan, *Histoire du Journal des Sçavans depuis 1665 jusqu'en 1701* (Paris: Presses Universitaires de France, 1928); Harcourt Brown, "History and the Learned Journal," *Journal of the History of Ideas* 33, no. 3 (July–Sept. 1972), 365–78; Raymond Birn, "Le

Journal des Savants sous l'Ancien Régime," *Journal des Savants* (Jan.–Mar. 1965), 15–35; Jean Ehrard and Jacques Roger, "Deux périodiques du 18e siècle: 'le Journal des Savants' et 'les Mémoires de Trévoux' " in François Furet et al., *Livre et société dans la France du XVIIIe siècle* (Paris: Mouton, 1965), I, 33–59; Cyril B. O'Keefe, *Contemporary Reactions to the Enlightenment (1728–1762): A Study of Three Critical Journals* (Paris: Librairie Honoré Champion, 1974). For imitations of the *Journal des sçavans*, see Hatin, *Gazettes*, p. 125; Hendrika Johanna Reesink, *L'Angleterre et la littérature anglaise dans les trois plus anciens périodiques français de Hollande de 1684 à 1709* (Paris: Librairie Ancienne Honoré Champion, 1931), p. 66; Jean-Michel Gardair, *Le "Giornale de' Letterati" de Rome (1668–1681)* (Florence: Leo S. Olschki, 1984), pp. 29–31, 294; Morgan, *Histoire*, Appendix I. On types of journals, see especially Claude Labrosse and Pierre Rétat, "Les périodiques de 1734: Essai de typologie," in Pierre Rétat and Jean Sgard, *Presse et histoire au XVIIIe siècle: L'année 1734* (Paris: Editions du CNRS, 1978); Marianne Couperus, "La terminologie appliquée aux périodiques et aux journalistes," in Couperus, ed., *L'étude des périodiques anciens: Colloque d'Utrecht* (Paris: Editions A.-G. Nizet, 1972), pp. 59–61. Recent works on individual journals include Hans Bots et al., *De "Bibliothèque universelle et historique" (1686–1693): En periodiek als trefpunt van geletterd Europa* (Amsterdam: APA Holland Press, 1981); Hans Bots, ed., *Henri Basnage de Beauval en de Histoire des Ouvrages des Savans 1687–1709: Verkenningen binnen de Republiek der Letteren aan de Vooravond van de Verlichting*, 2 vols. (Amsterdam: Holland University Press, 1976, 1984); Guus N.M. Wijngaards, *De "Bibliothèque choisie" van Jean Le Clerc: Een Amsterdams geleerdentijd-schrift uit de jaren 1703 tot 1713* (Amsterdam: APA Holland University Press, 1986); A.H. Laeven, *De "Acta Eruditorum" onder redactie van Otto Mencke: De Geschiedenis van een Internationaal Geleerdenperiodiek tussen 1682 en 1707* (Amsterdam and Maarssen: APA Holland University Press, 1986).

10 On newsletters, see Henry L. Snyder, "Newsletters in England, 1689–1715: With Special Reference to John Dyer—A Byway in the History of England," in Donovan H. Bond and W. Reynolds McLeod, eds., *Newsletters to Newspapers: Eighteenth-Century Journalism* (School of Journalism, West Virginia University, 1977), pp. 3–19.

11 KB, 72 H 13/I, Cuper to Clermont, Deventer, Feb. 26, 1715, draft.

12 Camusat, *Histoire critique des journaux* II, p. 112, n. 34.

13 *Journal des Sçavans* I (1665; new ed. 1723), 5, "L'Imprimeur au Lecteur."

14 BCUL, Archives de Crousaz II/137, Jean-Pierre de Crousaz to Jean-Théophile Desaguliers [Lausanne, 1721]. Copy.

15 Françoise Waquet, "De la lettre érudite au périodique savant: les faux semblants d'une mutation intellectuelle," *XVIIe siècle* XXXV, no. 3 (July–Sept. 1983), 347–59. Roger Duchêne makes similar points in his "Lettres and Gazettes." See also Paul Dibon, "Les échanges épistolaires dans l'Europe savante du XVIIᵉ siècle," *Revue de synthèse* 3rd ser. 81–2 (Jan.–June 1976), 31–50; René Taton, "Le role et l'importance des correspondances scientifiques aux XVIIᵉ et XVIIIᵉ siècles," *Revue de synthèse* 3rd ser. 81–2 (Jan.–June 1976), 7–22; Paul Dibon, "Communication in the Respublica literaria of the 17th Century," 43–55.

16 Neu BPU, Ms. 1273/7, f. 2, Jallabert to Bourguet, April 2, 1734.

17 Cuper to Bignon, Feb. 23, 1714, in Beyer, ed., *Lettres de Cuper*, p. 326; BJK Ms. Berol. Gall. Qu. 26, f. 497,

18 KB, 72 H 13/I, Cuper to Clermont, Deventer, Feb. 26, 1715, draft.

Mauclerc to La Croze, Dec. 1715. Duchêne gives examples of letters referring recipients to the gazettes for news, albeit gazettes enclosed in those letters. Duchêne, "Lettres et Gazettes," p. 499.

19 Gen. BPU, Ms. fr. 484, f. 103ᵛ, Barbeyrac to Turrettini, Lausanne, Jan. 5, 1710. Other examples of this phenomenon, from the Cuper correspondence, include KB, 72 G 17, f. 127ᵛ, Cuper to Le Clerc, Deventer, Jan. 25, 1711, draft; KB, 72 H 19/I, #11+, Cuper to Maturin Veyssière La Croze, May 25, 1711, draft, and KB, 72 H 19/I, #36, Cuper to La Croze, Nov. 22, 1713, draft. In the first instance Cuper discussed Jacques Bernard's fights with his colleagues, mentioned in the *Nouvelles de la République des Lettres*; in the second he mentioned the strange ideas of the Père Hardouin published in the *Mémoires de Trévoux*; in the third, he talked about the "Dissertation sur le Pseaume CX." in the *Histoire critique de la République des Lettres*.

20 Gisbert Cuper to the Abbé Bignon, Aug. 1, 1708, printed in Jean de Beyer, ed., *Lettres de Cuper*, p. 192.

21 BL Add. Ms. 4282, f. 1ᵛ, Denis-François Camusat to Pierre Des Maizeaux, Besançon, April 19, 1719.

22 KB, 72 C 27 p, f. 1, Cuper to the author of the *Nouvelles de la République des Lettres*, n.d. Draft. Although this letter is probably to Bayle, since there is no date it is not possible to tell whether it is instead to Jacques Bernard, who took over the *Nouvelles* in 1699.

23 Cuper to the Abbé Bignon, Sept. 25, 1708, in Beyer, ed., *Lettres de Cuper*, p. 201; KB, 72 D 58, f. 72, Jacques Basnage to Cuper, Rotterdam, Sept. 2, [1687]; KB, 72 D 58, f. 52, Henri Basnage de Beauval to Cuper, n.d. [1687]; Cuper to the Abbé Bignon, Dec. 16, 1713, in *Lettres de Cuper*, p. 315; KB, 72 H 25, Samuel Masson

to Cuper, Dordrecht, Oct. 30, no year [1714 or 1715]; *Histoire critique de la République des Lettres* X (1715), Art. IX. Some of the works Cuper referred to as "Journaux des Sçavans" in his list for Bignon might in fact appear to modern scholars more as single books; the fact that this distinction was not readily made in the beginning of the eighteenth century is evidence of the sometimes uneasy transition to a different *modus operandi* in the Republic of Letters. On this subject, see David A. Kronick, *A History of Scientific & Technical Periodicals: The Origins and Development of the Scientific and Technical Press 1665–1790*, 2nd ed. (Metuchen, NJ: Scarecrow Press, 1976), 15–31.

24 *Journal littéraire* I (May–June 1713), 2nd ed. (The Hague: Thomas Johnson, 1715), "Preface," vi.

25 ZAAWD, I-I-2, f. 6.

26 ZAAWD, I-XII-2, ff. 111, 114, G. Kirch, "Liste des Journaux François que nous avons dans notre Bibliothèque," Berlin, Aug. 18, 1731.

27 Elisabeth Labrousse, "Coulisses", pp. 102–3. My translation.

28 Françoise and Jean-Claude Waquet, "Presse et société: le public des 'Novelle Letterarie' de Florence (1749–1769)," *Revue française d'histoire du livre* n.s. 22 (Jan.–Mar. 1979), 54–7.

29 Ibid., 58–9.

30 Daniel Mornet, "Les Enseignements des bibliothèques privées (1750–1780)," *Revue d'Histoire littéraire de la France* XVII (1910), 453.

31 Ibid., p. 479.

32 Camusat, *Histoire critique des journaux* I, pp. 14–15.

33 *Nouvelles de la République des Lettres* II, 2nd ed. (1684), "Avertissement."

34 *Bibliothèque italique* VII (Jan.–April 1730), Art. VI, 121–2, prefatory note to "Lettre sur la voix des Eunuques"; *Bibliothèque angloise* I (1716; 2nd ed., 1729), 271. The latter example

might also have social implications.

35 *Works of the Learned* (August 1691), "To the Reader."

36 See, for example, *Bibliothèque italique* VI, 165–6, which quotes a letter in Italian from J.-J. Zannichelli. An example of Latin quotation is *Bibliothèque angloise* II, pt. 1 (1717), 81, 88.

37 *Histoire critique de la République des Lettres* III (1713), 280.

38 *Lettres sérieuses & badines* I, pt. 2 (1729; 2nd ed. 1740), 247–8.

39 Ibid. I, pt. 1 (1729; 2nd ed. 1740), xi, xiv ff., "A Messieurs les Auteurs de la Bibliothèque Raisonnée."

40 Ibid. I, pt. 1 (1729; 2nd ed. 1740), 262.

41 *Journal littéraire* I (May–June 1713), 2nd. ed. (1715), iv, "Avertissement du Libraire."

42 *Mémoires pour l'histoire des sciences et des beaux arts* I (Trévoux: De l'Imprimerie de S.A.S. [Prince Souverain de Dombes]), Jan.–Feb. 1701), Preface; *Journal des Sçavans* I (1665), new ed. [Paris: Pierre Witte, 1723], 3, "L'Imprimeur au Lecteur." The *Mémoires* were commonly known as the *Mémoires de Trévoux* or the *Journal de Trévoux*, which is how they will be designated here. The reason this journal was allowed to be published in France, despite the monopoly of the *Journal des Sçavans*, was the sovereignty of the Duc de Maine over the principality of Dombes. He invited the Parisian Jesuits to publish the journal in the capital of the principality, Trévoux, in 1682. See Alfred R. Desautels, *Les Mémoires de Trévoux et le mouvement des idées au XVIIIe siècle 1701–1734* (Rome: Institutum Historicum S.F., 1956), v–vi.

43 BL Add. Ms. 4286, f. 102, De la Motte to Des Maizeaux, Amsterdam, Feb. 20, 1710.

44 BL Add. Ms. 4281, f. 86, Jacques Bernard to Des Maizeaux, The Hague, May 20, 1700.

45 *Journal des Sçavans* I, 1665 (new ed.

1723), p. 3, "L'Imprimeur au Lecteur."

46 François Bruys, *Mémoires historiques, critiques, et littéraires* (Paris: Jean-Thomas Hérissant, 1751) I, p. 156.

47 BN Ms. fr. 19211, f. 159, Jacques Bernard to ? [Delaissement?], n.d. [1701], copy.

48 Camusat, *Histoire critique des journaux* II, p. 108; Jean Cornand de la Crose, *Works of the Learned* (August 1691), "To the Reader."

49 *Journal littéraire* I, pt. 1 (May–June 1713), 2nd ed., vi–vii.

50 Camusat, *Histoire critique des journaux* I, p. 18.

51 On the *Bibliothèque italique*, see Francesca Bianca Crucitti Ullrich, *La "Bibliothèque Italique": Cultura "Italianisante" e Giornalismo Letterario* (Milan: Riccardo Ricciardi, 1974).

52 *Bibliothèque angloise* I (1716), 2nd ed. (1729), "Avertissement."

53 Neu BPU, Ms. 1274/4, f. 5, Charles-Etienne Jordan to Louis Bourguet, Prenzlau, Mar. 30, 1729.

54 *Bibliothèque italique* X (Jan.–April 1731), 184, Art. VI. This was the second extrait of J.S. Asseman, *Bibliotheca Orientalis Clementino-Vaticana.*

55 *Journal littéraire* VIII, pt. 1 (1716), Art. I, 40. Other examples include the *Bibliothèque angloise*'s lengthy discussion of Milton's "Of Education," remarking that "Son *Traité de l'Education* n'est point connu dans les Païs étrangers. Nous croïons que les Lecteurs seront bien aises de savoir ce que cet habile Homme pensoit sur une matiere si importante." *Bibliothèque angloise* IV, pt. 2 (1718), Art. XI, 540.

56 *Bibliothèque angloise* II, pt. 1 (1717), Art. X, 280, concerning François de la Pillonnière's pamphlet, *An Answer to . . . Dr. Snape's Accusation*; *Bibliothèque angloise* I, pt. 2 (1717, 2nd ed. 1729), Art. XVII, p. 457.

57 *Bibliothèque angloise* II, pt. 1 (1717), Art. II, p. 17.

58 Claude Labrosse and Pierre Rétat

note that *nouvelles littéraires* were presented as they were in gazettes, and that the model of the letter comes from that genre. See Rétat and Labrosse in Sgard and Rétat, *Presse et histoire*, p. 50. However, in both types of periodical the information was actually gathered through letters, which explains both the form and its coincidence in each sort of publication.

59 UBL, March. 2, Simon Pelloutier to Marchand, Berlin, June 19, 1744.

60 *Histoire critique* VIII (1715), Art. XIII.

61 DSB, Nachlass Formey, Mortier to Formey, f. 9, Amsterdam, Nov. 21, 1749; DSB, Nachlass Formey, Luzac to Formey, f. 82 (film), Leiden, Feb. 1, 1751.

62 *Bibliothèque italique* I (1728), x, "Préface." See also Funck-Brentano, pp. 43, 46–7, and, on the importance of news, see Gardair, *Giornale*, p. 32.

63 See *Journal littéraire* IV, pt. 1 (May–June 1714), 155–73, 174–82, 182–208.

64 *Nouvelles de la République des Lettres* I (June 1684), 420–1.

65 Jean Cornand de La Crose, *Memoirs for the Ingenious* (Jan. 1693), Letter I, 2.

66 UBL, March. 2, J-H-S Formey to Prosper Marchand, Berlin, Nov. 29, 1743.

67 Marianne Constance Couperus, *Un Périodique français en Hollande: Le Glaneur historique (1731–1733)*, proefschrift Rijksuniversiteit te Utrecht (The Hague: Mouton, 1971), pp. 22–3. Couperus also suggests Prévost and Desfontaines as examples of journalists who proposed their journals to *libraires*; the *Journal littéraire* and *Bibliothèque angloise* are her example of journals begun by *libraires*. See "Les conditions matérielles de publication du *Glaneur*," in Couperus, ed., *L'Etude des périodiques anciens*, p. 64. In 1733 De la Motte reported a rumor that the *libraire* Pierre De Hondt "alloit entreprendre un nouveau Journal de Livres Anglois, & ce n'est point la suite de la Biblioth. Angloise." BL Add. Ms. 4287, f. 111, De la Motte to Des Maizeaux, Amsterdam, Feb. 17, 1733.

68 Bibl SHPF, Ms. 295, no. 53, Armand de la Chapelle to Charles de la Motte, The Hague, Feb. 19, 1733.

69 *Histoire des ouvrages des savans* I (Sept. 1687), Preface.

70 UBL, March. 2, Michel de la Roche to Marchand, London, Dec. 31, 1725. I am assuming that this is the journal he means when he refers to his "Journal Anglois"; although he customarily refers to the *Memoirs of Literature* this way rather than to his journal, the *Bibliothèque angloise*, in the manuscript the word "Anglois" is crossed out, and the word "François" added in a different pen, and perhaps a different hand. Further evidence is that he was paid in florins, which argues that he was not dealing with an English bookseller, and that he was negotiating with Marchand for Swart to continue this journal, which suggests that it was in French and published in Holland.

71 The conditions of the contract are discussed in DSB, Nachlass Formey, Elie Luzac to Formey, ff. 1ᵛ–2, Leiden, Feb. 11, 1749. The figure for 1751 appears in DSB, Nachlass Formey, Luzac to Formey, f. 110 (film), Leiden, Dec. 30, 1751. Numerous other references to payment occur throughout Luzac's letters to Formey; the salary increased to 8 florins by the mid-1750's (DSB, Nachlass Formey, Luzac to Formey, f. 211 [film], Leiden, Jan. 12, 1756). According to James G. Basker, the standard fee for reviews in English journals at mid-century was 2 guineas a sheet, so that theoretically the total payroll would have been about £12 6s. But on the *Critical Review* pay was lower than it could have been, and Smollett, a capital partner in the enterprise, may have forfeited his own share of pay to plough back into the journal. See James G.

Basker, *Tobias Smollett: Critic and Journalist* (Newark, Del.: University of Delaware Press, 1988), p. 49.

72 Details of this contract are in Neu BPU, Ms. 1270, ff. 83–4, Du Lignon to Louis Bourguet, Lausanne, Oct. 16, 1725. The figure of 300 écus is mentioned in Neu BPU, Ms. 1280/3, f. 73ᵛ, Gabriel Seigneux de Correvon to Bourguet, Lausanne, Jan. 19, 1734. Bourguet announced his decision to quit the journal in Neu BPU, Ms. 1262, Bourguet to Seigneux de Correvon, [Neuchâtel], Mar. 22, 1734.

73 A copy of Mauclerc's contract with Humbert (by Mortier, who wanted Formey to agree to the same conditions) is in DSB, Nachlass Formey, Pierre Mortier to Formey, f. 8. References to Formey's "contingent" appear, among other places, in DSB, Nachlass Formey, Mauclerc to Formey, f. 40ᵛ, Stettin, Aug. 21, 1739; Mauclerc to Formey, f. 47, Stettin, Feb. 5, 1740. Mauclerc sent payments in DSB, Nachlass Formey, Mauclerc to Formey, ff. 19ᵛ (Stettin, Aug. 29, 1738), 34ᵛ (Stettin, April 6, 1739), 38 (Stettin, July 6, 1739), 57 (Stettin, Nov. 4, 1740), 75 (Stettin, Dec. 15, 1741). My basis for this exchange rate is DSB, Nachlass Formey, J. Schreuder to Formey, f. 11, Leipzig, Oct. 13, 1753, in which Schreuder sends 105:20 Reichsthalers for two parts of the *Nouvelle Bibliothèque Germanique* (normally evaluated at fl. 200).

74 According to Raymond Birn, the authors of the eighteenth-century *Journal des Savants* received a lump sum negotiated by the director and then divided equally among the authors. In 1,729 this sum was 2,400 livres, or 400 per author; in 1735 it dropped to 1,800 livres, 300 per author. The total rose again to 2,400 in 1746 and to 4,800 in 1756. See Birn, "Journal des Savants," p. 30.

75 In 1711 Pierre Des Maizeaux expected, but did not receive, copies from Waesberge in payment for his

contributions and corrections to the Dutch edition of the *Journal des Savans* (BL Add. Ms. 4286, f. 126, Charles de la Motte to Des Maizeaux, Amsterdam, Jan. 9, 1711). He and other official contributors to the *Bibliothèque raisonnée* were paid (BL Add. Ms. 4287, f. 33, De la Motte to Des Maizeaux, Oct. 8, 1728). The *Bibliothèque raisonnée*, perhaps because of its commercial foundation, paid all its contributors, including those sending *nouvelles littéraires*. Pierre Des Maizeaux kept a running account with Wetstein and Smith, with *nouvelles* to his credit, and books (including copies of the *Bibliothèque raisonnée*) debited from his total. The journal (at 1 or 2 florins per quarter, coming to fl. 5 per year) cost Des Maizeaux approximately half of his usual earnings from the *nouvelles*. See BL Add. Ms. 4288, ff. 146 (William Smith to Des Maizeaux, Amsterdam, Aug. 12, 1738); f. 269, Jacob Wetstein to Des Maizeaux, Jan. 21, 1744.

76 DSB, Nachlass Formey, Elie Luzac to Formey, ff. 1ᵛ–2, Leiden, Feb. 11, 1749. This loophole proved problematical for Formey later on.

77 DSB, Nachlass Formey, Pierre Mortier to Formey, f. 8, "Copie du Contract entre Monsʳ Mauclerc et Mʳ Humbert au sujet de la Biblioth. germanique." On f. 11, enclosed in Mortier's letter of Nov. 21, 1749, is a virtually identical, unsigned contract between Mortier and Formey.

78 Neu BPU, Ms. 1270, ff. 83–4, Du Lignon to Bourguet, Lausanne, Oct. 16, 1725.

79 This way of managing things differed from England on the Continent. See Van Eeghen, *De Amsterdamse Boekhandel 1680–1725* Vⁱ (1978), p. 32. An example of a *libraire* buying the copyright occurred in 1728 with the *Journal littéraire*. De la Motte wrote to Des Maizeaux, "Un Libraire de Rotterdam a acheté l'Histoire litteraire de la Haye, & le va faire continuer, à ce qu'on m'a dit, par l'Auteur du *Je ne sai quoi* [a journal]." BL Add Ms.

4287, f. 25ᵛ, De la Motte to Des Maizeaux, Amsterdam, June 15, 1728. And at the death of Jacques Desbordes, De la Motte assumed that the copyright of the *Histoire critique* would be bought by another *libraire*: "Je ne sai qui se chargera du Journal de Mrs. Masson. Cela s'arrêtera pour quelque tems, jusqu'à ce qu'on ait vendu son fonds." BL Add. Ms. 4286, f. 213, De la Motte to Des Maizeaux, [Amsterdam], Feb. 22 [1718]. Discussions of *libraires* looking for new authors for their journals occur in Bibl SHPF, Ms. 295, no. 91, Barbeyrac to De la Motte, Groningen, Sept. 14, 1741; and Louis Saurin to Mlle. de St.-Véran, London, April 6, 1710, printed in J. Gaberel and E. Des Hours-Farel, *Jaques Saurin: Sa vie et sa correspondance* (Geneva: J. Cherbuliez, 1864), p. 167.

80 Gen BPU, Ms. fr. 484, f. 220ᵛ, Jean Barbeyrac to Jean-Alphonse Turrettini, Groningen, Jan. 13, 1720; BL Add. Ms. 4288, ff. 43–43ᵛ, Henri du Sauzet to Des Maizeaux, Amsterdam, Dec. 19, 1719; f. 36, same to same, Amsterdam, Jan. 9, 1720. See also f. 27ᵛ, same to same, June 16, 1719; ff. 29ᵛ–30, same to same, Aug. 4, 1719; f. 31, same to same, Aug. 22, 1719.

81 The journal was published "Chez les Wetsteins & Smith" until April–June 1734; from that time until April–June 1741 it was published "Chez J. Wetstein & G. Smith" or "Chez J. Wetstein." Smith and Jacob Wetstein dissolved their partnership in 1741 and Smith died the same year. On the Wetsteins, see I.H. van Eeghen, *De Amsterdamse Boekhandel 1680–1725* (Amsterdam: Scheltema & Holkema, 1967) IV, pp. 173–182, and M.M. Kleerkooper and W.P. van Stockum, Jr., *De Boekhandel te Amsterdam voornamelijk in de 17ᵉ Eeuw: Biographische en Geschiedkundige Aanteekeningen* (The Hague: Martinus Nijhoff, 1914–16) II, pp. 903–1001.

82 UBL, March. 2, Marchand to the Marquis d'Argens, no. 14b, "Remarques . . . sur les Lettres Juives," undated.

83 Hatin, *Gazettes*, pp. 218–19; DSB, Nachlass Formey, Paul-Emile de Mauclerc to Formey, f. 69, Stettin, July 31, 1741; UBL, March. 2, Jacques de Pérard to Marchand, Stettin, Feb. 2, 1742. Pérard was Mauclerc's "colleague" because they were the two ministers of the French church in Stettin.

84 Problems were no doubt exacerbated by the distance many continental journalists were from their *libraires*, both geographically and ideologically. A useful contrast is Tobias Smollett, who not only was in the same place as Hamilton, the *Critical Review*'s printer, but was involved, in cooperation with Hamilton, in most facets of publication. Basker states that Hamilton was "a kind of managing editor," though he did not write anything, evidence, Basker says, "of the unusual degree of editorial control that Smollett retained to himself." But in this respect the *Critical Review* also differed from another English paper, the *Monthly Review*, which was more subject to its bookseller. See Basker, *Smollett*, pp. 41–2.

85 UBL March. 2, Sebastian Högguer to Prosper Marchand, n.d. [1715?].

86 *Journal littéraire* V, pt. 2 (Nov.–Dec. 1714), Art. VII, 389.

87 Neu BPU, Ms. 1262, Bourguet to Seigneux de Correvon, Nov. 16, 1729, copy; DSB, Nachlass Formey, Mortier to Formey, f. 17, Amsterdam, May 21, 1750; DSB, Nachlass Formey, Mortier to Formey, f. 25ᵛ, Amsterdam, Jan. 13, 1751; DSB, Nachlass Formey, Mauclerc to Formey, f. 58, Stettin, Nov. 4, 1740. Pérard said in October of 1740, "M. de M.[auclerc] a eu bien des assauts avec m. Humbert au sujet de mon extrait, le dit sieur extrémement le fie depuis quelque tems & dégoute tellement mon

Collégue par ses difficultez, . . . qu'il a un autre Libraire tout pret, au cas que m. humbert ne se range pas a la raison. Je ne sai ce que vous avez eu autrefois ensemble, mais il a été piqué que vous ayez relevé la prémiere Edition de Mattaire ce qu'il n'est pas avantageux pour l'Editeur, il l'est avisé de critiquer tout mon extrait, il vouloit le supprimer, au moins ne lui pas donner la premiere place. tout cela est bien petit, Mon collegue a tenu bon, et n'est pas en gout de jamais se laisser gourmander par un Libraire, s'il en changeoit, il trouveroit le journal des conditions beaucoup plus avantageuses. Humbert vouloit trancher de Wetstein & que toutes les piéces étrangers fussent à son Bénéfice, mais la différence est grande les Wetsteins sont maitres de leur journal, c'est eux qui assemblent les piéces, qui dirigent le tout à leur fantaisie, il n'en est pas demême de humbert." UBL March. 2, Pérard to Marchand, Stettin, Oct. 12, 1740.

88 DSB, Nachlass Formey, Luzac to Formey, ff. 94 (Leiden, May 15, 1751), 102 (July 30, 1751), 110^v (Dec. 30, 1751), 121 (July 10, 1753), 181^v (May 10, 1754), 193 (July 11, 1759; *sic* for 1755), 194 (June 13, 1755), 205 (Nov. 23, 1756), 209^v–210 (Dec. 24, 1756), 226 (n.d. [1756]), etc. (film). Michael Harris notes similar signs of "self-interested censorship" in bookseller-owned English newspapers. See his *London Newspapers in the Age of Walpole* (London: Associated University Presses, 1987), p. 67.

89 Neu BPU, Ms. 1280/3, f. 7^v, Seigneux de Correvon to Bourguet, Nov. 10, 1729.

90 *Bibliothèque germanique* I (July–Sept. 1720), iv–viii, Preface. Cf. *Bibliothèque italique* I (1728), xiv–xix, Preface; *Bibliothèque angloise* I, pt. I (1717; 2nd ed. 1728), "Avertissement" dated 13/24 Nov. 1716; *Bibliothèque britannique* I, part 1 (April–June 1733), "Avertissement."

91 See J.-H.-S. Formey, *Eloges des Académiciens de Berlin* (Berlin: Etienne de Bourdeaux, 1757) II, p. 53 note (a), 120ff.; *Bibliothèque germanique* XLVIII (1738), pp. 68–81, "Mémoire Abrégé sur la Vie & les Ouvrages de Mr. de BEAUSOBRE"; Pierre Rétat in Jean Sgard, ed., *Dictionnaire des Journalistes*, "Beausobre," pp. 30–2, and "Lenfant," pp. 43–4; Hatin, *Gazettes*, pp. 218–19 (a very inaccurate account).

92 For Pérard's takeover, see DSB, Nachlass Formey, Pérard to Formey, f. 88^v, Stettin, Feb. 22, 1743, and UBL, March. 2, Formey to Marchand, Berlin, Mar. 16, 1743. For the everyday conduct of the journal and incidental changes, see DSB, Nachlass Formey, collections of letters to Formey from Mauclerc, Pérard, Mortier, and Cartier de St. Philippe, *passim*, and UBL, March. 2, Formey, Pérard, and Pelloutier to Marchand, *passim*. Simon Pelloutier remarked of Pérard's failure, "Pour la Bibliotheque Germanique il est fort à craindre qu'elle ne tombe, soit par la faute de Mr Beauregard, soit parce que Mr Perard n'a ni le tems necessaire pour vaquer à ce travail dont il demeure seul chargé, ni les correspondances qu'avoit Mr. Mauclerc" (UBL, March. 2, Simon Pelloutier to Marchand, Berlin, June 19, 1744). He added in 1747, "Quant à la Nouvelle Bibliotheque Germanique, je doute qu'elle continuë longtems, M^r. Formey etant trop occupé et M^r. Perard trop dissipé, pour vaquer à ce travail de la maniere qu'il le faudroit, pour mettre leur Journal en reputation" (UBL, March. 2, Pelloutier to Marchand, Berlin, June 30, 1747). According to Pelloutier, Pérard's problem was that he "a donné (entre nous) dans le grand monde" (UBL, March. 2, Pelloutier to Marchand, Berlin, April 4, 1750). See also UBL, March. 2, Pelloutier to Marchand, Berlin, Aug. 8, 1746.

93 Bibl SHPF, Ms. 295, no. 94, Jean Barbeyrac to Charles de la Motte, Groningen, May 29, 1742. De la Motte had made a proposal to Barbeyrac on behalf of the *libraire* Pierre de Hondt. See also Bibl SHPF, Ms. 295, no. 119, Charles Chais to De la Motte, The Hague, Nov. 20, 1746.

94 Reinier Leers to Samuel Smith, Rotterdam, Nov. 23, 1687, printed in Otto S. Lankhorst, *Reinier Leers (1654–1714) Uitgever & Boekverkoper te Rotterdam: Een Europees "Libraire" en zijn Fonds* (Amsterdam: APA-Holland Universiteits Pers, 1983), p. 229.

95 *Histoire critique* IV (1713), "Avis du Libraire."

96 SPK, Sammlung Darmstaedter, 2 h 1743 (2), Emmerich de Vattel to Formey, Neuchâtel, Jan. 19, 1748.

97 BL Add. Ms. 4286, f. 280ᵛ, Charles de la Motte to Pierre Des Maizeaux, Amsterdam, Oct. 25, 1726.

98 Neu BPU, Ms. 1270, f. 83, Du Lignon to Bourguet, Lausanne, Oct. 16, 1725.

99 DSB, Nachlass Formey, Pierre Mortier to Formey, Amsterdam, May 21, 1750. This also occurs elsewhere, e.g. DSB, Nachlass Formey, J. Schreuder to Formey, f. 42, Amsterdam, Sept. 16, 1756.

100 Among the times Formey was sent or promised books for review are DSB, Nachlass Formey, Mauclerc to Formey, ff. 4 (Stettin, Dec. 2, 1737), 5 (Stettin, Jan. 7, 1738), 9ᵛ (Stettin, Mar. 12, 1738), and DSB, Nachlass Formey, Pérard to Formey, ff. 101 (Stettin, Sept. 16, 1743), 117ᵛ (Stettin, Dec. 22, 1747), 118ᵛ (Stettin, Jan. 12, 1748). Formey was enjoined to return these books in DSB, Nachlass Formey, Mauclerc to Formey, ff. 4 (Stettin, Dec. 2, 1737), 7 (Stettin, Jan. 27, 1738), 14 (Stettin, June 16, 1738). Mauclerc suggested Formey find particular books in DSB, Nachlass Formey, Mauclerc to Formey, ff. 43ᵛ (Stettin, Nov. 9, 1739), 45 (Stettin, Dec. 14, 1739).

101 DSB, Nachlass Formey, Mauclerc to Formey, f. 3ᵛ, Stettin, Nov. 22, 1737.

102 DSB, Nachlass Formey, Mauclerc to Formey, ff. 24–24ᵛ, Stettin, Oct. 31, 1738.

103 DSB, Nachlass Formey, Mauclerc to Formey, f. 42, Stettin, Oct. 16, 1739; DSB, Nachlass Formey, Pérard to Formey, f. 94, Stettin, June 5, 1743; DSB, Nachlass Formey, J. Schreuder to Formey, ff. 6–6ᵛ, Leipzig, May 8, 1750. See also, for example, DSB, Nachlass Formey, Luzac to Formey, f. 63 (film), [Leiden, Aug. 1750]; DSB, Nachlass Formey, Mortier to Formey, f. 30, Amsterdam, Sept. 21, 1751, and elsewhere.

104 Denis-François Camusat, *Histoire critique des journaux* (Amsterdam: Jean-Frédéric Bernard, 1734) I, pp. 215–16.

105 Ibid., II, pp. 72–3.

106 DSB, Nachlass Formey, Mauclerc to Formey, f. 42, Stettin, Oct. 16, 1739.

107 Bibl SHPF, Ms. 295, no. 77, Barbeyrac to De la Motte, Groningen, Sept. 9, 1737.

108 DSB, Nachlass Formey, Mauclerc to Formey, f. 41ᵛ, Stettin, Oct. 16, 1739; DSB, Nachlass Formey, Pérard to Formey, f. 97, Stettin, June 21, 1743.

109 The papers of this literary society are in UBL, March. 1. Reference to meeting on Fridays is in UBL, March. 1, Varia, ff. 17–23, hand of Alexandre. On the contents of this journal, see Paul Hemprich, *Le journal littéraire de la Haye, 1713–1737* (Berlin: F. Hermann, 1915).

110 Margaret C. Jacob, *The Radical Enlightenment: Pantheists, Freemasons and Republicans* (London: George Allen and Unwin, 1981), pp. 182–5. Jacob's ideas are refuted by Graham Gibbs in a review of this book in *British Journal for the History of Science* XVIII (1984), 67–79, and in Christiane Berkvens-Stevelinck, "Les *Chevaliers de la Jubilation*: Maçonnerie

ou libertinage?" *Quaerendo* XIII, pt. 1 (Winter 1983), 50–73, and XIII, pt. 2 (Spring 1983), 124–48. Jacob answered Berkvens-Stevelinck in "The Knights of Jubilation— Masonic and Libertine—A Reply," *Quaerendo* XIV, pt. 1 (Winter 1984), 63–75.

111 The "Chevaliers" document is BL Add. Ms. 4295, ff. 18–19. For the name of the society, see UBL, March. 1, F. le Bachellé to the Society, Utrecht, Sept. 16, 1713.

112 Jacob, *Radical Enlightenment*, p. 185; *Journal littéraire* I, pt. 1 (May–June 1713), 2nd ed. (The Hague: Thomas Johnson, 1715), v, "Avertissement du Libraire."

113 UBL, March. 1, Authors of the *Journal littéraire* to the author of the *Illustres françoises* (i.e. Robert de Chelles), draft, Feb. 1, 1714; UBL, March. 1, Albert-Henri de Sallengre to the other authors of the *Journal littéraire*, Paris, April 16, 1714.

114 *Journal littéraire* I (May–June 1713), 2nd ed., xi, "Preface."

115 UBL, March. 1, Jacques Alexandre "au nom de tous" to Prosper Marchand, Dec. 8, 1713; on these elections see also UBL, March. 1, F. le Bachellé to the Society, Utrecht, Sept. 16, 1713, and Le Bachellé to the Society, Utrecht, Dec. 14, 1713.

116 See, e.g., UBL, March. 1, Correspondence with Robert de Chelles and A.-H. de Sallengre, *passim*.

117 *Journal littéraire* XIII, pt. 1 (1729), iii–iv, "Avertissement."

118 UBL, March. 1, Thémiseul de St.-Hyacinthe to the authors of the *Journal littéraire*; Sunday, May 7, no year or place; UBL, March. 1, Thomas Johnson to Humphry Ditton, n.d.; UBL, March. 1, Gabriel d'Artis to the authors of the *Journal littéraire*, Hanover, May 28, 1715; UBL, March. 1, Gabriel d'Artis to the authors of the *Journal littéraire*, Berlin, June 11, 1715; UBL, March. 2, Daniel de Superville to Marchand, Rotterdam, Nov. 6, 1730. This last letter concerns the revival of the

journal, but the editorial procedure seems to have been similar to that of the earlier version.

119 Neu BPU, Ms. 1262, Louis Bourguet to Gabriel Seigneux de Correvon, Feb. 16, 1729. Copy.

120 Neu BPU, Ms. 1270, f. 77, Du Lignon to Bourguet, Lausanne, Aug. 17, 1725; Neu BPU, Ms. 1270, f. 88, Du Lignon to Bourguet, Lausanne, June 13, 1727.

121 Neu BPU, Ms. 1270, f. 79, Du Lignon to Bourguet, Lausanne, Sept. 7, 1725.

122 Neu BPU, Ms. 1270, f. 81, Du Lignon to Bourguet, Lausanne, Sept. 21, 1725.

123 Neu BPU, Ms. 1262, Bourguet to Seigneux de Correvon, Nov. 16, 1729. Copy.

124 Neu BPU, Ms. 1262, Bourguet to Seigneux de Correvon, Feb. 16, 1729, copy; Neu BPU, Ms. 1262, Bourguet to Seigneux de Correvon, Sept. 4, 1734; Neu BPU, Ms. 1260, f. 182, Bourguet to Du Lignon, Neuchâtel, June 18, 1727.

125 Neu BPU, Ms. 1262, Bourguet to Seigneux de Correvon, Sept. 4, 1734; Neu BPU, Ms. 1270, f. 93, Du Lignon to Bourguet, Lausanne, Sept. 3, 1728.

126 DSB, Nachlass Formey, Mauclerc to Formey, f. 29, Stettin, Jan. 1, 1739; DSB, Nachlass Formey, Mauclerc to Formey, f. 6, Stettin, Jan. 10, 1738; DSB, Nachlass Formey, Mauclerc to Formey, f. 29, Stettin, Jan. 1, 1739. Mention of the authors' rules is in DSB, Nachlass Formey, Mauclerc to Formey, f. 44, Stettin, Nov. 9, 1739. Mauclerc was Formey's "brother" because they were both ministers.

127 DSB, Nachlass Formey, Mauclerc to Formey, f. 6, Stettin, Jan. 10, 1738; DSB, Nachlass Formey, Mauclerc to Formey, f. 48, Stettin, Mar. 10, 1740. See also, e.g., DSB, Nachlass Formey, Mauclerc to Formey, f. 30, Stettin, Jan. 23, 1739.

128 DSB, Nachlass Formey, Mauclerc to Formey, f. 30, Stettin, Jan. 23, 1739. See also, e.g., DSB, Nachlass For-

mey, Mauclerc to Formey, f. 41, Stettin, Oct. 16, 1739.

129 DSB, Nachlass Formey, Mauclerc to Formey, f. 44, Stettin, Nov. 9, 1739.

130 DSB, Nachlass Formey, Mauclerc to Formey, f. 40, Stettin, Aug. 21, 1739. See also DSB, Nachlass Formey, Mauclerc to Formey, ff. 31 (Stettin, Jan. 28, 1739) and 36 (Stettin, May 4, 1739).

131 DSB, Nachlass Formey, Mauclerc to Formey, f. 81, Stettin, Mar. 9, 1742; DSB, Nachlass Formey, Mauclerc to Formey, ff. 12–12ᵛ, Stettin, Mar. 30, 1738.

132 *Bibliothèque raisonnée des ouvrages des savans de l'Europe* I (July–Sept. 1728), (Amsterdam: Wetsteins and Smith, 1728), xii, "Avertissement des Libraires."

133 Bibl SHPF, Ms. 295, no. 94, Jean Barbeyrac to Charles de la Motte, Groningen, May 29, 1742.

134 Bibl SHPF, Ms. 295, no. 85, Barbeyrac to De la Motte, Groningen, Aug. 19, 1740; Bibl SHPF, Ms. 295, no. 98, Barbeyrac to De la Motte, Groningen, April 15, 1738; Bibl SHPF, Ms. 295, no. 116, Armand de la Chapelle to De la Motte, The Hague, Jan. 25, 1736.

135 De la Motte's activities as intermediary in the production of the *Bibliothèque raisonnée* are evident in his correspondence with Barbeyrac and La Chapelle in Bibl SHPF Ms. 295, and in his correspondence with Pierre Des Maizeaux, BL Add. Ms. 4287, *passim*. See especially BL Add. Ms. 4287, f. 33, De la Motte to Des Maizeaux, Oct. 8, 1728.

136 BL Add. Ms. 4288, f. 123, Wetstein to Des Maizeaux, Amsterdam, July 8, 1729. When the partnership dissolved and Smith proposed a new journal, De la Motte defected to Smith, who was well-liked by authors, and took a number of the *Bibliothèque raisonnée*'s journalists with him. See BL Add. Ms. 4288, f. 256ᵛ, Jacob Wetstein to Des Maizeaux, Amsterdam, Oct. 8, 1741.

137 Bibl SHPF, Ms. 295, no. 61, De la Chapelle to De la Motte, The Hague, Nov. 23, 1741. The lack of communication and faithfulness to the *Bibliothèque raisonnée* is evident from one example of double-reviewing, when both Barbeyrac and La Chapelle accidentally made *extraits* of the *Scaligerana*. Smith ultimately decided to publish Barbeyrac's, "ainsi l'Extrait du premier a deja paru dans la Nouvelle Bibliotheque du mois passé imprimée chez Mʳ Paupie à la Haye" (BL Add. Ms. 4288, f. 160ᵛ, William Smith to Des Maizeaux, Amsterdam, Nov. 22, 1740). Barbeyrac, who said that he had had "nulle pensée que je puisse me trouver là dessus en concurrance avec M.ʳ de la Chapp.," told de la Motte that "le Public n'y perdra rien, puis que l'Extrait de celui-ci paroîtra dans un autre Journal" (Bibl SHPF, Ms. 295 #86, Barbeyrac to De la Motte, Groningen, Oct. 15, 1740).

138 On Naudé as go-between, DSB, Nachlass Formey, Mauclerc to Formey, f. 8, Stettin, Mar. 17, 1738. On editing, DSB, Nachlass Formey, Mauclerc to Formey, f. 3, Stettin, Nov. 22, 1737, and ff. 12–12ᵛ, Stettin, Mar. 30, 1738. On the index, DSB, Nachlass Formey, Mauclerc to Formey, ff. 11–11ᵛ, Stettin, Mar. 30, 1738.

139 On arrangement, DSB, Nachlass Formey, Mauclerc to Formey, f. 38, Stettin, July 6, 1739. On Naudé as route to Holland, DSB, Nachlass Formey, Mauclerc to Formey, ff. 1ᵛ–2, Stettin, Oct. 28, 1737. On sending in copy, DSB, Nachlass Formey, Pérard to Formey, f. 98, Stettin, July 30, 1743. On provision of sufficient copy, DSB, Nachlass Formey, Mauclerc to Formey, f. 57, Stettin, Nov. 4, 1740, and DSB, Nachlass Formey, Pierre Mortier to Formey, ff. 14 (Amsterdam, Feb. 26, 1750), 15 (Amsterdam, Mar. 6, 1750), and 16 ([Amsterdam], April 10, 1750).

140 DSB, Nachlass Formey, Mortier to Formey, f. 25, Amsterdam, Jan. 13,

1751; BL Add. Ms. 4287, f. 64, De la Motte to Des Maizeaux, Amsterdam, July 1, 1729; BL Add. Ms. 4287, ff. 69–69ᵛ, De la Motte to Des Maizeaux, Amsterdam, Aug. 26, 1729; BL Add. Ms. 4287, f. 73, De la Motte to Des Maizeaux, Amsterdam, Sept. 20, 1729; DSB, Nachlass Formey, Mortier to Formey, f. 12, Amsterdam, Dec. 12, 1749; DSB, Nachlass Formey, Mortier to Formey, ff. 6ᵛ–7, Amsterdam, Sept. 19, 1749; DSB, Nachlass Formey, Luzac to Formey, f. 82 (film), Leiden, Feb. 1, 1751.

141 See, e.g., DSB, Nachlass Formey, Mauclerc to Formey, ff. 33–33ᵛ, March 16, 1739; DSB, Nachlass Formey, ff. 46–46ᵛ, Stettin, Jan. 15, 1740; DSB, Nachlass Formey, Pérard to Formey, f. 76ᵛ, Stettin, Oct. 16, 1742.

142 DSB, Nachlass Formey, Mauclerc to Formey, f. 65, Stettin, June 3, 1741; DSB, Nachlass Formey, Mauclerc to Formey, f. 69, Stettin, July 31, 1741; DSB, Nachlass Formey, Prosper Marchand to Formey, f. 21, March 22, 1743.

143 A lack of records makes it difficult to reconstruct what happened to journals after their completion. Some later ones were distributed by subscription, but this appears to have been rare for most we are considering; even subscriptions for books appeared much later on the Continent than in England. More evidence exists to suggest that the common way to obtain periodicals was either to order them from the *libraire* who published them, from another *libraire* who would order them himself, or to buy them directly in a bookshop. The second two methods were probably the most common. Uta Janssens-Knorsch cites a rare edition of the *Journal britannique* which lists 41 different *libraires* in Holland, England, Ireland, Scotland, Germany, the Spanish Netherlands, France, and Italy where the journal could be purchased. See Hans Bots,

"Deux périodiques hollandais," 56; Uta Janssens-Knorsch, *Matthieu Maty and the Journal Britannique 1750–55*, proefschrift, Katholieke Universiteit te Nijmegen (Amsterdam: Holland University Press, 1975), pp. 54–6; *Nouvelles de la République des Lettres* I (July 1684), 438; *Journal littéraire* V, pt. 2 (Nov.–Dec. 1714), 456, "Avertissement"; UBL, March. 2, Maichel to Levier [?], Tübingen, Dec. 1716 [?]; UBL, March. 2, La Croze to Marchand, Berlin, May 12, 1720.

144 UBL, March. 2, Pérard to Marchand, Stettin, June 3, 1740; DSB, Nachlass Formey, Jean Des Champs to Formey, London, June 22, [1748], N.S.

145 DSB, Nachlass Formey, Léonard Baulacre to Formey, f. 11, Geneva, Sept. 1, 1748; DSB, Nachlass Formey, Baulacre to Formey, f. 11ᵛ, Geneva, Sept. 1, 1748; DSB, Nachlass Formey, Baulacre to Formey, f. 26, Geneva, June 15, 1751; DSB, Nachlass Formey, Baulacre to Formey, f. 4ᵛ, Geneva, Sept. 22, 1746. Matthieu Maty had a set of occasional contributors to his *Journal britannique* who mostly belonged to a tea society of Huguenot refugees, mainly ministers. See Janssens-Knorsch, *Maty*, pp. 68, 71ff.

146 BCUL, Archives de Crousaz II/290–1, Mauclerc to J.-P. de Crousaz, n.d. [1723?]; see also BCUL, Archives de Crousaz XII/154–5, Mauclerc to Crousaz, Stettin, Dec. 11, 1733.

147 BL Add. Ms. 4286, f. 1, De la Motte to Des Maizeaux, Amsterdam, Feb. 1, 1700; Jean-Louis de Lorme to the Abbé Bignon, Amsterdam, April 5, 1708, printed in Van Eeghen, *De Amsterdamse Boekhandel* I, p. 140; Gen BPU, Ms. fr. 484, f. 150, Barbeyrac to Turrettini, Lausanne, Sept. 24, 1713; UBL, March. 1, authors of the *Journal littéraire* to Bocheron; UBL, March. 1, authors of the *Journal littéraire* to Eccard, Sept. 1714, draft.

148 Hans Bots, "Recueil des informations dans deux périodiques hol-

landais à la fin du XVIIème siècle," and Dieter Gembicki, "Le journalisme à sensation: 'L'Epilogueur moderne' (1750–54) de Rousset de Missy," in Pierre Rétat, ed., *Le Journalisme d'ancien régime: questions et propositions*, table ronde CNRS 12–13 June 1981 (Lyon: Presses Universitaires de Lyon, 1982), pp. 65, 246.

149 On Des Maizeaux and the *Mémoires de Trévoux*, see BL Add. Ms. 4289, ff. 1, 4, 12ᵛ, Ganeau to Des Maizeaux, Paris, Sept. 5, 1713; April 12, 1714; Mar. 23 [1714].

150 BL Add. Ms. 4281, f. 100, Jacques Bernard to Des Maizeaux, The Hague, Feb. 4, 1701. See also Bernard to Des Maizeaux in Add. Ms. 4281, ff. 86ᵛ (May 20, 1700), 88 (June 13, 1700), 98 (Dec. 15, 1700), and 100ᵛ (Feb. 4, 1701); and the Abbé Bignon to Des Maizeaux in BL Add. Ms. 4281, f. 201, Paris, Aug. 14, 1710, and after. On Des Maizeaux's contributions to continental journals, see Joseph Almagor, *Pierre des Maizeaux (1673–1745): Journalist and English Correspondent for Franco-Dutch Periodicals 1700–1720* (Amsterdam and Maarssen: APA-Holland University Press, 1989); Almagor, "Pierre Des Maizeaux and his Key-Role as English Correspondent for the Continent in the first half of the Eighteenth Century," in *The Role of Periodicals in the Eighteenth Century*, Werkgroep Engels-Nederlands Betrekkingen, Sir Thomas Browne Institute (Leiden, 1984), 41–7; and J.H. Broome, "An Agent in Anglo-French Relationships: Pierre Des Maizeaux, 1673–1745" (unpublished PhD dissertation, University of London, 1949), and Broome, "Pierre Desmaizeaux, Journaliste. Les nouvelles littéraires de Londres entre 1700 et 1740," *Revue de littérature comparée* XXIX no. 2 (April–June 1955), 184–205. Broome tends to overestimate the amount of material Des Maizeaux contributed to continental journals, assuming that

all information about England, of whatever slant, must have been craftily inserted in the journals for his own ends. Almagor's book is a detailed account of Des Maizeaux's relationships with Bernard's *Nouvelles de la République des Lettres*, the Massons' *Histoire Critique de la République des Lettres*, and Du Sauzet's *Nouvelles Littéraires*.

151 *Journal litéraire* I, pt. 1 (May–June 1713), 2nd ed., v, "Avertissement du Libraire." Similar notices ran in many other journals, including the *Journal des Sçavans* I (Jan. 5, 1665), "L'Imprimeur au Lecteur"; *Mémoires de Trévoux* I (Jan.–Feb. 1701), Preface; *Nouvelles de la République des Lettres* I (1684); *Histoire critique de la République des Lettres* I (1712); *Memoirs for the Ingenious* (Jan. 1693), "Advertisement"; *History of Learning* (1691), "Preface"; *Critique désintéressée des journaux* III (July–Sept. 1730), and elsewhere.

152 *Mémoires de Trévoux* I (Jan.–Feb. 1701), "Preface."

153 *Histoire critique de la République des Lettres* I (1712), "Avertissement."

154 *Histoire critique* VIII (1715), "Avis."

155 *Mémoires de Trévoux* I (Jan.–Feb. 1710), "Preface."

156 BL Add. Ms. 4281, f. 182ᵛ, Bignon to Des Maizeaux, Paris, Dec. 31, 1708; BL Add. Ms. 4281, ff. 194ᵛ–5, Bignon to Des Maizeaux, Paris, June 4, 1709.

157 DSB, Nachlass Formey, Baulacre to Formey, ff. 12–12ᵛ, Feb. 28, 1749.

158 UBA, C 73 b. Abbé S★★★ to Le Clerc, Paris, May 17, 1716, sent by Ludolph Kuster to Le Clerc.

159 *Histoire critique de la République des Lettres* I (1712), "Avertissement." In a similar spirit, Henri Basnage de Beauval wrote to Gisbert Cuper that he had heard the latter had been attacked over his *Harpocrates*: "Si mon iournal etoit propre oû à vous vanger, oû à prevenir l'attaque, vous ne devez pas douter que ie ne fisse gloire de tirer l'Epée pour vous." KB, 72 D 58, f. 55, Basnage de

Beauval to Cuper, Nov. 7, no year [attrib. 1688].

160 Sallengre, *Mémoires de littérature* II, pt. 2 (1717) 223, note. The letter was entitled "Lettre à Messieurs Le Clerc et Bernard, contenant des Eclaircissemens sur quelques endroits de leurs derniers Journaux, où il est parlé du Factum des Amis de M. Bayle, contre la nouvelle édition de son Dictionaire."

161 *Bibliothèque Raisonnée* II, pt. 1 (Jan.–Mar. 1729), 88–90.

162 UBL, March. 1, Authors of *Journal littéraire* to Christian Wolfius, Sept. 28, 1714, draft. Wolff had already been warned of the English article in an earlier letter. It attacked an article he had published in the volume for Nov.–Dec. 1713.

163 *Histoire critique de la République des Lettres* I (1712), "Avertissement."

164 *Journal littéraire* I, pt. 1 (May–June 1713; 2nd ed. 1715), iii–iv, "Avertissement du Libraire."

165 See note 2 above.

166 *Bibliothèque italique* I (Jan.–April 1728), xvii, "Preface."

167 *Bibliothèque britannique* I, pt. 1 (April–June 1733), "Avertissement."

168 DSB, Nachlass Formey, Marchand to Formey, ff. 22ᵛ–23, The Hague, April 19, 1743.

169 J.J.V.M. de Vet makes the excellent point that to review books already discussed in other journals would bore readers with "old news": a case of "idealism" not being "unlimited." See de Vet, "Echoes of the French press in Dutch periodicals in the age of the Ancien Régime," in *Diffusion et lecture des journaux*, p. 251.

170 UBL March. 1, A.-H. de Sallengre to other authors of the *Journal littéraire*, Paris, April 16, 1714.

171 See *Lettres sérieuses et badines* I, pt. 1 (1729).

172 BCUL, Archives de Crousaz XII/166, Mauclerc to Crousaz, Stettin, Feb. 9, 1731.

173 I have found only one other instance of this, and, significantly, it was expressed by a *libraire*. Elie Luzac

told Formey that in the case of the *Bibliothèque impartiale* "il faut à notre avis menager les livres dont d'autres ont parlé, parler avant & non pas aprés les autres Journalistes." (DSB, Nachlass Formey, Luzac to Formey, f. 38 [film], Leiden, Feb. 26, 1750.)

174 *Histoire critique de la République des Lettres* III (1713), 285.

175 Ibid. III (1713), 213.

176 *Bibliothèque italique* III (Sept.–Dec. 1728), Art. V, 102–3, asterisked note at beginning of article.

177 Neu BPU, Ms. 1270, f. 89, Du Lignon to Bourguet, Lausanne, June 27, 1727.

178 Neu BPU, Ms. 1262, Bourguet to Seigneux de Correvon, Nov. 16, 1729, copy.

179 UBL March. 2, Jean Catuffe to "Prosper Marchand," Amsterdam, Aug. 22, 1730. The UBL catalogues this letter as to Marchand, but both the quoted text and the salutation ("Messieurs") indicate that he was not the recipient.

180 Bibl SHPF, Ms. 295, no. 76, Barbeyrac to De la Motte, Groningen, June 25, 1737.

181 See *Bibliothèque angloise*. I, pt. 1 (1716; 2nd ed. 1728), "Avertissement," for La Roche's suggestion that since "les Journalistes n'ont rien dit jusques-ici" of these books, their discussion "ne sera pas desagréable, si je ne me trompe, aux Personnes qui aiment les belles Lettres."

182 Camusat, *Histoire critique des journaux* II, p. 139.

183 Des Maizeaux, "Vie de Bayle," in Bayle, *Dictionnaire*, 5th ed. in French (Amsterdam: P. Brunel, P. Humbert, J. Wetstein and G. Smith, et al., 1740), I, cx; *Nouvelles de la République des Lettres* I (April 1684), 207–8, and III (Jan. 1685), 32. See also *Histoire critique de la République des Lettres* III (1713), 262.

184 Camusat, *Histoire critique des journaux* II, pp. 164–5.

185 *Journal littéraire* I (May–June 1713;

2nd ed. 1715), xv, preface; *Histoire des ouvrages des savans* I (Sept. 1687), preface; *Bibliothèque angloise* II, pt. 1 (1717), 92.

186 *Histoire critique de la République des Lettres* I (1712), "Avertissement"; and ibid., III (1713), "Avis du Libraire."

187 *Bibliothèque italique* I (Jan.–April 1728), xxii–xxiii, "Preface."

188 *Journal des Sçavans* Monday, Jan. 4, 1666, "L'Imprimeur au Lecteur"; *Nouvelles de la République des Lettres* II (1685), "Avertissement." The issue of the *Journal* was the first written by a new author, the Abbé de Gallois.

189 *Bibliothèque italique* I (Jan.–April 1728), xx–xxi, "Preface."

190 *Bibliothèque angloise* IV, pt. 2 (1718), 334–5. The remark referred to appeared in the *Journal des Savans* of May 17, 1717.

191 BN Ms. 19211, f. 172, Jacques Bernard to Delaissement, The Hague, April 6, 1702.

192 UBA, C 41, Jean Le Clerc to the authors of the *Journal des Savans*, 1705, fragment of draft.

193 UBA, C 19 b, Bignon to Le Clerc, Paris, Feb. 27, 1705.

194 UBA, C 124, Joseph Saurin to Le Clerc, Paris, June 22, 1703.

195 *Critique désintéressée des journaux* I, [5–6], Preface.

196 *Bibliothèque raisonnée* II, pt. 1 (Jan.–Mar. 1729), 88–90.

197 *Bibliothèque italique* I (1728), xix, "Préface"; *Journal littéraire* II, pt. 2 (Nov.–Dec. 1713), 444–5; *Nouvelles de la République de Lettres* I (Mar. 1684), "Preface."

198 *Bibliothèque italique* VII (Jan.–April 1730), 2.

199 *Journal littéraire* VIII, pt. 1 (1716), 235.

200 *Memoirs for the Ingenious* (Jan. 1693), "Advertisement."

201 *Mémoires de Trévoux* I (Jan.–Feb. 1701), preface.

202 *Histoire critique de la République des Lettres* VIII (1715), 418–19, *nouvelles littéraires*, Berlin.

203 *Works of the Learned* (Sept. 1691), 60, Art. XVIII (II).

204 Camusat, *Histoire critique des journaux*

II, 82–3. Camusat cites a number of examples, including a book by Grimarest: "nous leur devons le Traité du *Récitatif*, puisque son Auteur, M. de Grimarest, avoüe dans la Préface de ce Livre, qu'il ne l'a composé qu'après y avoir été invité par *Messieurs* les Journalistes. Ils avoyent compris par quelques mots qui lui étoient échapez sur cette matiere, *qu'il en avoit penetré tous les recoins*, sur quoi ils l'exhortent avec beaucoup de politesse à ne pas envier au monde sçavant les réflexions qu'il avoit faites sur un sujet tout nouveau."

205 *Bibliothèque italique* I (1728), ix, "Préface."

206 *Bibliothèque britannique* I, pt. 1 (April–June 1733), "Avertissement."

207 See account above in section on operations of journals.

208 Neu BPU, Ms. 1266/8, f. 3, Isaac de Beausobre to Louis Bourguet, Berlin, Oct. 12, 1733.

209 KB, 72 C 27p, f. 1, Cuper to [Bayle?], n.d., draft.

210 UBL, March. 1, Authors of *Journal littéraire* to Christian Wolfius, May 18, 1714, draft.

211 UBL, March. 1, Authors of the *Journal littéraire* to the author of the *Illustres françoises*, i.e. Robert de Chelles, Feb. 1, 1714, draft.

212 DSB, Nachlass Formey, Baulacre to Formey, ff. 1ᵛ–2, Geneva, April 15, 1743; see also DSB, Nachlass Formey, Baulacre to Formey, ff. 4–4ᵛ, Geneva, Sept. 22, 1746, and DSB, Nachlass Formey, Jean Peschier to Formey, f. 16, Geneva, Dec. 24, 1745.

213 DSB, Nachlass Formey, Baulacre to Formey, f. 26, Geneva, June 15, 1751. Labrousse notes that Bayle regarded books sent for review, both by authors and *libraires*, "comme des 'présents' dont il doit remercier les donateurs." See Labrousse, "Coulisses," p. 107.

214 DSB, Nachlass Formey, Mauclerc to Formey, Stettin, Feb. 5, 1740.

215 UBL, March. 2, Simon Pelloutier to

Marchand, Berlin, May 1, 1745.

216 BL Add. Ms. 4286, f. 202, De la Motte to Des Maizeaux, Amsterdam, Nov. 27, 1714. Masson's journal was the *Histoire critique de la République des Lettres*; Waesberge was the Amsterdam *libraire* who pirated the *Journal des Savants* with additions. For this controversy, see chapter 3 below.

217 UBL, March. 2, Simon Pelloutier to Marchand, Berlin, June 26, 1742.

218 UBA, C 3, Barbeyrac to Le Clerc, Berlin, April 10, 1706.

219 UBA, C 130 b, Ezechiel Spanheim to Le Clerc, London, Feb. 11, 1707 O.S.

220 UBA, J 33, Gally de Gaujac to Le Clerc, London, May 4, 1726.

221 Jean-Pierre Vittu refers to three writers publishing angry responses to *extraits* of their works in the *Journal des savants*. See Vittu, "Diffusion et réception du *Journal des savants* de 1665 à 1714," in *Diffusion et lecture des journaux*, p. 170.

222 ZAAWD, Nachlass Leibniz Nr. 3, f. 59, Leibniz to La Croze, Hanover, May 1, 1708.

223 *Journal littéraire* III, pt. 2 (Mar.–April 1714), 413–14. For similar passages, see *Histoire critique de la République des Lettres* II (1713), 166, "Lettre de Mr. J. Masson à Mr. de Valincour," where Masson said of his *Vie de Horace* that he had seen "le violent Extrait, dont Mrs. les Journalistes de Paris avoient bien voulu regaler le Public, quoique je ne leur eusse jamais donné le moindre sujet de me maltraiter si cruellement"; also KB, 72 H 18, #43, La Croze to Cuper, May 12, 1710, and KB, 72 H 18, #46, Cuper to La Croze, June 28/July 1, 1710.

224 See, e.g., the report of Barbeyrac in Bibl SHPF, Ms. 295, no. 75, Barbeyrac to De la Motte, Groningen, May 28, 1737: "Je vous prie de remercier M^r. Bernard, de son présent de l'*Hist. des Yncas*. J'ai tant écrit aujourdhui, que je ne saurois, ni n'aurois pas le tems, de répondre à sa Lettre, où il me demande *un mot de*

recommandation pour son Livre. J'en donnerai avec plaisir un petit Article, & le recommenderai de mon mieux."

225 UBL, March. 2, Pelloutier to Marchand, Berlin, July 11, 1741.

226 DSB, Nachlass Formey, Pérard to Formey, ff. 92^v–93, Stettin, May 16, 1743. Voltaire had written a play, which was performed at the Prussian court, in which remaindered copies of Deschamps' book featured prominently in one scene. See Chapter 5 below.

227 *Journal littéraire* III, pt. 1 (Jan.–Feb. 1714), 179.

228 DSB, Nachlass Formey, Pérard to Formey, f. 73^v, Stettin, Sept. 25, 1742.

229 BCUL, Archives de Crousaz XII/153–4, Mauclerc to Crousaz, Stettin, Dec. 11, 1733.

230 UBL, March. 2, Jean de Beyer to Marchand, letter 24, Nijmegen, Nov. 18, 1741.

231 UBA, C 23 a, J. Bouhier to Le Clerc, Dijon, May 21, 1710.

232 See DSB, Nachlass Formey, Mauclerc to Formey, ff. 61–61^v, Stettin, Feb. 15, 1741; DSB, Nachlass Formey, Pérard to Formey, f. 15^v, Stettin, May 5, 1738; DSB, Nachlass Formey, Pérard to Formey, f. 120^v, Stettin, May 31, 1748. The first of these two letters from Pérard (f. 15^v) contained a message from Mauclerc on this subject.

233 *Mémoires de Trévoux* I (Jan.–Feb. 1701), preface. The *Bibliothèque universelle* made the same offer in 1686; see *Bibliothèque universelle* I (1686; 2nd ed. 1687), preface.

234 *Mémoires de Trévoux*, 1712, Avertissement, mentioned in "Notice abrégée des journaux littéraires" in *Table générale des matières contenues dans le Journal des Savans* X (Paris: Briasson, 1764), p. 669.

235 Camusat, *Histoire critique des journaux* I, p. 144.

236 See *Lettres sérieuses et badines* I, pt. 1 (1729; 2nd ed. 1740), xii, "A Messieurs les Auteurs de la Bibliothèque

Raisonnée": "Louez à votre aise vos propres ouvrages"; André Dacier, *Nouveaux Eclaircissemens sur les Oeuvres d'Horace, avec la Réponse à la Critique de M. Masson, Ministre refugié en Angleterre* (Paris: Pierre Cot, 1708), pp. 158–9.

237 BN, Ms. fr. 19211, f. 143ᵛ, Jacques Bernard to [the P. Léonard de Sainte-Cathérine de Sienne], The Hague, April 5, 1701.

238 Bibl SHPF, Ms. 295, no. 106, Le Courayer to De la Motte, n.d.

239 UBL, March. 2, Pérard to Marchand, Stettin, Nov. 2, 1739.

240 *Histoire critique de la République des Lettres* IV (1713), 318.

241 DSB, Nachlass Formey, Luzac to Formey, f. 112 (film), Leiden, Feb. 27, 1753. Jacques Marx, who has studied the extremely rare *Bibliothèque impartiale*, reports that it failed to live up to its name. See "Une Revue oubliée du XVIIIᵉ siècle: *La Bibliothèque impartiale*," *Romanische Forschungen* 80, Heft. 2/3, 289–90, and "La *Bibliothèque impartiale*: Etude de contenu (janvier 1750–juin 1754)," in Couperus, ed., *L'Etude des périodiques anciens*, pp. 89–106.

242 UBA, N 24 ae, Le Clerc to Robert Chouet, 1685, copy or draft.

243 BL Add. Ms. 4285, f. 54ᵛ, Mathieu Marais to Des Maizeaux, Paris, Nov. 15, 1706.

244 Camusat, *Histoire critique des journaux* II, p. 71.

245 Camusat, *Histoire critique des journaux* II, p. 25.

246 BL Add. Ms. 4281, f. 103, Jacques Bernard to Des Maizeaux, The Hague, April 5, 1701.

247 *Journal des Sçavans* II (1666; new ed. 1729), 6; *Nouvelles de la République des Lettres* I (Mar. 1684), preface; *Universal Historical Bibliotheque* (Jan. 1686), "The Preface to the Reader," in English.

248 Camusat, *Histoire critique des journaux* I, pp. 265–9. Bayle criticized the author of the *Journal des sçavans* because he "ne dit jamais rien de son

cru, ni ne juge d'un Livre" Bayle to Le Clerc, Rotterdam, June 18, 1684, in Bayle, *Lettres* (1729 ed.) I, 218.

249 *Bibliothèque raisonnée* I (1728), xiv–xvi, "Avertissment des Libraires."

250 Camusat, *Histoire critique des journaux* I, p. 49.

251 UBA, C 83 b, Jacques Lenfant to Le Clerc, Heidelberg, Jan. 4, 1687.

252 Vigneul-Marville (i.e. Noël Bonaventure d'Argonne), *Mélanges d'histoire et de littérature* (Rouen: Antoine Maurry, 1700) I, pp. 315–16.

253 Camusat, *Histoire critique des journaux* I, p. 249.

3 HOW TO BECOME AN *HOMME ILLUSTRE*

1 BN Ms. fr. 12933, f. 46, Voltaire to César de Missy, Brussels, July 18, 1741.

2 BN Ms. fr. 12933, f. 170, César de Missy to Voltaire, London, Oct. 21, 1745. This is the final letter from this correspondence in the volume. The other letters from this exchange are also in this manuscript volume.

3 BN Ms. fr. 12933, f. 53, Voltaire to César de Missy, Brussels, Oct. 29, 1741.

4 BN Ms. fr. 12933, f. 55, César de Missy to Voltaire, London, April 5, 1742. "Dans la République lettrée/ Mon Apollon vivoit sans nom & sans éclat:/A peine dans le Tiers-Etat/ Pouvoit il se vanter d'une place assurée:/Mais depuis que par le Courier/Il a vu dans ces lieux venir à mon adresse,/La lettre où de vos mains je reçois le Laurier/Qui croît sur les bords de Permesse,/Courage, m'a-t-il dit: *Si j'étois Roturier/Voila mes Lettres de Noblesse.*"

5 Baillet, *Jugemens des savans* I, p. 3.

6 Boileau, preface to first edition of his works, quoted in Des Maizeaux, *La Vie de Monsieur Boileau Despreaux* (Amsterdam: Henri Schelte, 1712), p. 38. Other assertions of this right to criticize appear, among other

places, in Baillet, *Jugemens des Savans* I, 5, and Sallengre's *Mémoires de Littérature* I, pt. 1 (1715), preface.

7   Johann Burchard Mencke, *De la Charlatanerie des Savans; par Monsieur Menken: avec des remarques critiques de differens Auteurs*, trans. from Latin by David Durand (The Hague: Jean van Duren, 1721), p. 95.

8   UBA, G 67 c, Pierre-Daniel Huet to Etienne Morin, Paris, Nov. 9, 1686.

9   BL Add. Ms. 4307, f. 91ᵛ, Malcolm Flemyng to Thomas Birch, Lincoln, April 20, 1763.

10   BL Add. Ms. 4285, f. 70ᵛ, Mathieu Marais to Pierre Des Maizeaux, Paris, Feb. 10, 1711.

11   Dr. Pieter Guenellon to John Locke, Amsterdam, July 12, 1695 N.S., in E.S. de Beer, ed., *The Correspondence of John Locke* (Oxford: Clarendon Press, 1976–82), V, p. 410.

12   For information about Coste's life, see Haag, *La France protestante*, 2nd ed., IV, cols. 730–3; De Beer, ed., *Correspondence of Locke* V, p. 395; Pierre Coste, *Histoire de Louis de Bourbon*, 3rd ed. (The Hague: Jean Neaulme, 1748), I, "Avertissement de l'Editeur"; *DNB* VII (1887), pp. 275–6; Gabriel Bonno, "Locke et son traducteur français Pierre Coste," *Revue de littérature comparée* XXXIII, no. 2 (1959), 161–79; Jan de Vet, "John Locke in de 'Histoire des Ouvrages des Savans,'" in Hans Bots, ed., *Henri Basnage de Beauval en de Histoire des Ouvrages des Savans* II, pp. 183–269. Coste was a theology student of good standing in Leiden in 1689; he became a *proposant* in August 1690. See *Livre synodal* [1688–1725], Synod of Vlissingen, Sept. 1689, Art. V; ibid., Synod of Heusden, April 1690, Art. XIII; ibid., Synod of Amsterdam, Aug. 1690, Art. XLII. The *DNB* erroneously states that Coste was received as a minister rather than a *proposant*; in fact, he was never ordained.

13   Dr. Pieter Guenellon to Locke, Amsterdam, October 19, 1697 N.S.; Jean Le Clerc to Locke, Amsterdam, Aug. 6, 1697 N.S., and Amsterdam, August 25, 1697 N.S., in De Beer, ed., *Correspondence of Locke* VI, pp. 223, 166, 178.

14   Pierre Coste to John Locke, Amsterdam, Sept. 13, 1695 N.S., postscript, and Coste to Locke, June 29, 1699 N.S., in De Beer, ed., *Correspondence of Locke* V, p. 435, and VI, p. 650.

15   See, e.g., BL Add. Ms. 4286, f. 242, De la Motte to Des Maizeaux, July 16, 1720.

16   Bibl SHPF, Ms. 295, nos. 1–12. Coste wrote to Suson Brun and her sisters soon after his departure for England: "Je m'adresse . . . à Mademoiselle Rouviére qui parlera pour moi, j'en suis sûr, & si fortement, que Mademoiselle Suson sera enfin obligée de rendre les armes. De qui parlez-vous-là, dira-t-elle? De ce nouvel Anglois qui voudroit peut-être bien être ici avec nous." Bibl SHPF, Ms. 295, #3, Coste to Suson Brun and her sisters Isabeau, Jeannette, Mme. Rouvière and Mme. Durand, no date.

17   Bibl SHPF, Ms. 295, no. 10, Pierre Coste to Suson Brun, n.d.

18   Coste to Locke, June 29, 1699, in De Beer, ed., *Correspondence of Locke* VI, p. 650.

19   Le Clerc told Locke that Coste, "qui est extrémement de mes amis," had taken on the translation "plûtôt pour apprendre la Langue, que pour se faire connoître par là." Le Clerc to Locke, Amsterdam, July 8, 1695 N.S., in De Beer, ed., *Correspondence of Locke* V, pp. 393–4.

20   Le Clerc to Locke, Amsterdam, July 8, 1695 N.S., in De Beer, *Correspondence of Locke* V, 394; Coste to Locke, Amsterdam, July 8, 1695 N.S., in De Beer V, p. 396.

21   Le Clerc to Locke, Amsterdam, July 8, 1695 N.S., in De Beer, *Correspondence of Locke* V, p. 393.

22   Coste to Locke, Amsterdam, July 8, 1695 N.S., in De Beer, *Correspondence of Locke* V, pp. 395–6.

23   Coste to Locke, Amsterdam, Sept. 13, 1695 N.S., in De Beer, *Corre-*

spondence of Locke V, p. 432.

24 Ibid., pp. 434–5.

25 Coste to Locke, Amsterdam, *c.* July 3, 1696 N.S., in De Beer, *Correspondence of Locke* V, pp. 661–2.

26 Bonno calls Coste's happening to translate this book without knowing Locke was its author a "détail assez piquant." "Locke et son traducteur français Pierre Coste," p. 166.

27 Coste to Locke, Amsterdam, *c.* July 3, 1696, in De Beer, *Correspondence of Locke* V, pp. 660–1.

28 See, for example, De Vet, "John Locke," in Bots, ed., *Henri Basnage de Beauval* II, p. 204; Rex A. Barrell, ed., *Anthony Ashley Cooper, Earl of Shaftesbury (1661–1713) and 'Le Refuge Français'—Correspondence* (Lewiston: Edwin Mellen Press, 1989), p. 101.

29 Le Clerc to Locke, Amsterdam, April 9, 1697 N.S., and Coste to Locke, Amsterdam, July 16, 1697 N.S., in De Beer, ed., *Correspondence of Locke* VI, pp. 72–3, 155–6.

30 Coste to Locke, Amsterdam, July 16, 1697 N.S., in De Beer, ed., *Correspondence of Locke* VI, p. 155.

31 Molyneux and Locke corresponded during the spring of 1697 about a tutor for Molyneux's son. Originally the discussion concerned Le Clerc, who was hoping for an ecclesiastical position in Ireland. Locke wrote to Molyneux on his behalf; Molyneux had to respond that Le Clerc's Arminian views would make it impossible for him to obtain preferment there. But Molyneux, not realizing that Le Clerc was not "a Single Man, and One of the Refugees in Holland, and wholy unprovided for," had the idea of "bringing him into my own family." Coste's name subsequently came up, and in fact he was already at Oates when Molyneux wrote to inquire further about his suitability as a tutor. Locke also may have recommended Coste to Richard Coote, first earl of Bellomont, who asked Locke in May of 1697 "to recommend me a good sort of French man to be Governour to my sons, I would have him Civill good humour'd and Learned both in Latin and greek." See Locke to William Molyneux, Oates, May 3, 1697 O.S.; Molyneux to Locke, Dublin, March 16, 1697 O.S., May 27, 1697 O.S., July 20, 1697 O.S., and Oct. 4, 1697 O.S., and Richard Coote, first earl of Bellomont to Locke, London, May 25[?], 1697 O.S., in De Beer, ed., *Correspondence of Locke* VI, pp. 106, 39–40, 133–4, 165–6, 220, 131.

32 Locke to Lady Masham, London, July 3, 1697 O.S., and R. de la Treille to Locke, [July 17, 1697 O.S.], in De Beer, ed., *Correspondence of Locke* VI, pp. 147–8, 157–8.

33 Coste, who was ill with "un rheumatisme opiniastre" (Guenellon to Locke, Aug. 13, 1697 N.S., in De Beer, ed., *Correspondence of Locke* VI, p. 170), was still in Amsterdam on August 25. Le Clerc to Locke, Amsterdam, Aug. 25, 1697 N.S., in De Beer VI, pp. 177–8.

34 Locke to Molyneux, Oates, Jan. 10, 1698 O.S., in De Beer, ed., *Correspondence of Locke* VI, p. 294.

35 Locke became involved in Le Clerc's social circle in Amsterdam through Guenellon, whom he had known in Paris. In January 1684 Guenellon undertook to dissect a lioness, and Locke attended the dissection, where he met several other doctors. Through Guenellon, a Remonstrant, he also met and befriended the Remonstrant ministers Philip van Limborch and Le Clerc. Locke was in exile in the Netherlands in association with Monmouth's rebellion; Guenellon hid Locke at his father-in-law's in Amsterdam during the summer of 1685, while Limborch transmitted Locke's letters and kept his will. Locke also lodged at Guenellon's house at the end of 1685 and in 1686. He returned to England in February 1689. See Jean Le Clerc, *The Life and Character of Mr. John Locke, Author of the Essay*

Concerning Humane Understanding, trans. F.T.P. (London: John Clark, 1706), pp. 11–15; and De Beer, *Correspondence of Locke* II, p. 648.

36 See Coste to Locke, [July/Aug. 1698]; June 29, 1699; *c*. Aug. 12, 1699; and Oates, July 12, 1700; in De Beer, *Correspondence of Locke* VI, pp. 445–7, 648–52, 666–9, and VII, pp. 107–9. De Beer's headnote for the letter of July/August 1698 (VI, p. 456) suggests that the information in it probably came from a letter from De la Motte; most of the information appears, however, to be from Le Clerc rather than De la Motte.

37 John Locke to Peter King, Oates, Feb. 27, 1701, in De Beer, ed., *Correspondence of Locke* VII, pp. 257–8. See also Awnsham Churchill to Locke, London, Mar. 1, 1700, in De Beer VII, p. 259.

38 Locke to Limborch, Oct. 29, 1697 O.S.; Oates, Feb. 21, 1698, O.S. and ff., in De Beer, ed., *Correspondence of Locke* VI, pp. 243, 321ff. The section in French is generally the part concerning business or philosophy; the other section, in Latin, is the friendlier part of the letter.

39 Coste to Locke, June 29, 1699, in De Beer, ed., *Correspondence of Locke* VI, pp. 648–9.

40 Ibid.

41 Pierre Coste in John Locke, *Essai philosophique concernant l'entendement humain*, 1st French ed., trans. Coste from the 4th English ed. (Amsterdam: Henri Schelte, 1700), "Avertissement du Traducteur."

42 In Locke, *Essai concernant l'entendement* (1700 ed.), "Monsieur Locke au Libraire." In French.

43 Coste in Locke, *Essai concernant l'entendement* (1700 ed.), "Avertissement du Traducteur."

44 BL Add. Ms. 4286, f. 253, De la Motte to Des Maizeaux, Amsterdam, Dec. 7, 1723.

45 BL Add. Ms. 4286, f. 11, De la Motte to Des Maizeaux, Amsterdam, Jan. 6, 1705.

46 BL Add. Ms. 4287, f. 47, De la Motte to Des Maizeaux, Amsterdam, Dec. 31, 1728.

47 Bibl SHPF Ms. 295, no. 68, Barbeyrac to De la Motte, Groningen, Feb. 18, 1730; BL Add. Ms. 4287, f. 88, De la Motte to Des Maizeaux, Amsterdam, Feb. 7, 1730. De la Motte had expected this treatment of Des Maizeaux; his main reaction to news of Collins' death was an eloquent discourse on his cheapness. "Je serai fort aise d'aprendre qu'il vous a legué quelque chose qui en vaille la peine. J'en doute pourtant, car la liberalité n'étoit pas son vice non plus que de la plupart des Anglois que j'ai connu. Je lui avois excroqué ici quelques charitez, que le point d'honneur lui avoit arraché presque malgré lui, & assez chichement, pour un homme de ses revenus. Il envoya d'ici en divers tems à Toland environ dix pieces. Il vouloit regaler Mr. le Cl. & sa famille & quelques autres personnes dans un Yacht, mais comme je connoissois son oeconomie, je lui dis qu'il lui en couteroit pour le moins dix pieces, il voulut bien les depenser, & il fut fort content de moi parce qu'il en couta un peu moins, & que je ne mis pas sur le compte quelques assietes de porcelaine ou copes qui se casserent & qui m'apartenoit. Il cassa lui-même une assiete, il ne me fit pas même compliment sur cela. Il est vrai qu'étant quelque tems après ensemble chez un Anglois où il y avoit un Bureau d'Angleterre, il dit que je devois avoir un tel meuble & qu'il vouloit m'en envoyer & à la Demoiselle qui demeure avec moi un habit. Nous les attendons encore, aussi bien que des pommes d'Angleterre. Il vous estimoit & aimoit beaucoup. Je souhaite qu'il en ait donné des preuves réelles." BL Add. Ms. 4287, ff. 86ᵛ–87, De la Motte to Des Maizeaux, Amsterdam, Jan. 24, 1730.

48 *Nouvelles de la République des Lettres* (February 1705), Art. II, pp. 154–

77. This article was reprinted as "The Character of Mr. Locke: in a Letter to the Author of the Nouvelles de la République des Lettres" in Pierre Des Maizeaux, ed., *A Collection of Several Pieces of Mr. John Locke, Never before printed, or not extant in his Works* (London: R. Francklin, 1720). The quotations here are from the English edition.

49 Coste, "Character of Locke," pp. iv–v, xxiv.

50 Ibid., pp. v–vi.

51 Ibid., pp. vi, ix–x, vii–viii, vi–vii, xxiv.

52 This is the volume edited by Des Maizeaux, cited above. The volume contains "The Fundamental Constitutions of Carolina," "Letter from a person of Quality to his Friend in the Country" on the debates in Lords in 1675 concerning the bill "to prevent the dangers which may arise from persons disaffected to the government," "Remarks upon some of Mr. Norris's Books," "Elements of Natural Philosophy," "Some Thoughts Concerning Reading and Study for a Gentleman," Rules of a Society, which met once a week, for their improvement in useful Knowledge, and for the promoting of Truth and Christian Charity," and letters to Henry Oldenburg, Lady Calverley, Rev. Richard King, and especially Antony Collins.

53 "A Letter to Mr. ***," in Des Maizeaux, ed., *Collection of Several Pieces of Locke*, pp. ii–iii.

54 *DNB* XII, p. 275.

55 Collins' tone in his letters to Des Maizeaux on this issue suggests that Des Maizeaux was only acting under his orders (or under his tutelage), a conclusion that may be too strong but probably bears some resemblance to reality. Collins, for example, wrote in 1719: "Mr Churchill would have no body to print any of Mr Lockes works but himself; and yet would have them for nothing: I beleive he is not to be dealt with: and therefore I leave the matter to you, who may therein wholly follow your own judgment and interest. By all means get the First Editions of Mr Norriss *Reason & Religion*, of his *Reflections on the conduct of human Life*, and of his Cursory Remarks or Reflections *on Mr Lockes Essay on HU* printed at the end of his *Discourses on the beatitudes*, in order to find out & verify the citations of Mr Locke. These are the only books of Mr Norris that M^r L could refer to, and the only editions he could have when he wrote." BL Add. Ms. 4282, ff. 168–168^v, Collins to Des Maizeaux, Baddow Hall, Oct. 25, 1719. In English.

56 BL Add. Ms. 4282, f. 125, Collins to Des Maizeaux, Hatfield Peverel, Feb. 28, 1716. In English.

57 BL Add. Ms. 4282, ff. 174–175^v; BL Add. Ms. 4289, f. 160, Des Maizeaux's hand, March 8, [1719]. Des Maizeaux wrote that he could not say who the author was but that he had the original in the author's hand in his possession (evidently Add. Ms. 4282 ff. 174–5^v). See also BL Add. Ms. 4288, ff. 16^v–17, Henri du Sauzet to Des Maizeaux, Amsterdam, Nov. 22, 1718; f. 18, same to same, Jan. 13, 1719. De la Motte warned Des Maizeaux that Collins had had a falling out with Coste the second time he had travelled to Holland, so that Collins' word about Coste might not be reliable. BL Add. Ms. 4286, f. 255^v, De la Motte to Des Maizeaux, Amsterdam, April 18, 1724.

58 BL Add. Ms. 4286, f. 242, De la Motte to Des Maizeaux, July 16, 1720. Letter damaged. De la Motte wrote in protest of this piece, "Il ne sert de rien de dire qu[e c]e n'est pas vous qui publiez ces choses injurieuses à M. Coste, que vous ne faites que les [imprime]r telles qu'on vous les a données."

59 BL Add. Ms. 4282, f. 125, Collins to Des Maizeaux, Hatfield Peverel, Feb. 28, 1716. In English.

60 This edition was based on the fifth

English edition.

61 Pierre Coste in John Locke, *De l'Education des Enfans*, trans. Coste (Amsterdam: Henri Schelte, 1708), xxviii–xxix, "Préface du Traducteur."

62 Ibid., p. xxix.

63 Ibid., pp. xxiv–xxv.

64 Ibid., p. 347, n. 1. Other places Coste corrected Locke were on p. 47, n. 1; p. 360, n. 1; and p. 402, n. 2.

65 He first published editions of La Bruyère's *Caractères* in 1720 and of Montaigne's *Essais* in 1724; in 1710 he had added critical remarks to a translation of Horace by the Père Tarteron.

66 Coste in Locke, *Education* (1708 ed.), pp. xxix–xxx, "Préface du Traducteur." Coste cites Montaigne in the following places: pp. 14, n. 1; 34, n. 1; 38, n. 1; 45–6, n. 1; 59, n. 1; 61–2, n. 1; 68–9, n. 1; 70, n. 1; 126, n. 1; 176, n. 1; 177, n. 1; 202–3, n. 1; 315, n. 1; 413, n. 1. He cites Horace on pp. 137, n. 1, and 341, n. 1; Suetonius on pp. 229–30, n. 1; and La Bruyère on pp. 272–3, n. 1; 366–7, n. 1.

67 Ibid., p. 14, n. 1.

68 Ibid., p. 38, n. 1.

69 Pierre Coste in John Locke, *Le Christianisme raisonnable, tel qu'il nous est representé dans l'Ecriture Sainte*, trans. Coste (Amsterdam: L'Honoré & Chatelain, 1715) I, pp. iii–iv, "Avertissement du Traducteur."

70 Ibid., II, pp. 317–18.

71 Ibid., I, pp. 320–2. Coste's note is asterisked.

72 Ibid., I, pp. 326–7.

73 Tantalizingly, Jean Barbeyrac suggested in a letter of 1715 his admiration for Coste's new notes in the 1714 edition, "sur tout celles où il critique son Auteur." BL Add. Ms. 4281, f. 28ᵛ, Barbeyrac to Des Maizeaux, Lausanne, Feb. 15, 1715. However, I have not been able to locate such notes in this edition.

74 Coste in John Locke, *Essai philosophique concernant l'entendement hu-*

main, trans. Coste, 3rd French ed. (Amsterdam: Pierre Mortier, 1735), p. xvi, "Avertissment du Traducteur."

75 Ibid., p. xix, "Avis sur cette troisième édition."

76 Ibid., pp. 110, n. 1; 111, n. 1; 112–13, n. 1 and 2.

77 Ibid., p. 73, n. 1.

78 Coste in Locke, *Essai philosophique concernant l'entendement*, trans. Coste, 4th French ed. (Amsterdam: Pierre Mortier, 1742), p. xx, "Avis sur cette quatrième édition."

79 Ibid., pp. 445–7.

80 Ibid., pp. 445n., 446n.

81 Ibid., p. 447n.

82 Coste, in trans. of Locke, *De l'Education* (Amsterdam: Uytwerf, 1744) II, pp. 464–5, n. 1.

83 Bibl SHPF, Ms. 295, no. 18, Coste to De la Motte, Mar. 22, 1739.

84 See this dedication, e.g., in John Locke, *De l'Education des Enfans*, trans. Pierre Coste, 5th ed. (Amsterdam: Maynard Uytwerf, 1744), pp. iii–iv; BL Add. Ms. 4286, f. 275, De la Motte to Des Maizeaux, Amsterdam, Sept. 11, 1725. De la Motte said in this letter that "L'Epit. dedicatoire de M. Coste m'avoit été envoyée pour la mettre au devant de l'Ed. de 1708 mais je la suprimai, & si je l'ai laissée à la derniere Ed. c'est pour des raisons particulieres." Coste must have updated the dedication, which is dated April 4, 1721.

85 Coste in Locke, *Essai concernant l'entendement humain*, (1735 ed.).

86 In similar fashion Coste showed himself willing to argue with Shaftesbury in their correspondence. See Barrell in *Shaftesbury Correspondence*, p. 105.

87 BL Add. Ms. 4286, f. 252, De la Motte to Des Maizeaux, Amsterdam, Dec. 7, 1723. De la Motte said that "Je ne saurois même me persuader encore que ce soit là le motif de votre inimité, Mais comme je ne demeure point à Londres, je ne saurois en deviner le sujet. Dans le tems M.C. m'écrivit qu'il ne le

comprenoit pas. J'ai soupçonné quelquefois que cela venoit de M. Coll. qui pourroit vous avoir fait quelque faux raport. Mais comme cela est injurieux à un homme que je crois honnête homme plus que ses sentimens ne comportent, je n'y saurois insister."

88 BL Add. Ms. 4286, f. 242, De la Motte to Des Maizeaux, July 16, 1720.

89 BL Add. Ms. 4286, f. 248, De la Motte to Des Maizeaux, "à une campagne de 4 lieues d'Amst.," Sept. 2, 1723.

90 BL Add. Ms. 4286, f. 253, De la Motte to Des Maizeaux, Amsterdam, Dec. 7, 1723.

91 Ibid.

92 Ibid., f. 252^v.

93 BL Add. Ms. 4286, f. 242^v, De la Motte to Des Maizeaux, July 16, 1720.

94 BL Add. Ms. 4286, f. 249, De la Motte to Des Maizeaux, Sept. 2, 1723, postscript.

95 Accounts of this controversy, which, however, do not draw broad conclusions from it, appear in Christiane Berkvens-Stevelinck, "La Cabale de l'Edition 1720 du *Dictionnaire* de Bayle, in *Prosper Marchand et l'histoire du livre*, pp. 79–133; Elisabeth Labrousse, *Inventaire critique de la correspondance de Pierre Bayle* (Paris: Librairie Philosophique J. Vrin, 1961), pp. 14–21; Joseph Almagor, *Pierre des Maizeaux*, pp. 81–101.

96 Almagor, *Pierre des Maizeaux*, pp. 1–8; J.H. Broome, "An Agent in Anglo-French Relationships," pp. 1–14; Sgard, *Dictionnaire des journalistes*, pp. 119–20; Haag, *La France protestante*, 2nd ed., V, pp. 315–18. Des Maizeaux's parents pressed him repeatedly to become ordained, his father pointing out that "vostre mere et moy vous avons consacré a Dieu . . . pour l'avancement de son regne," and insisted on the importance of his not becoming distracted from his theological studies. (See BL Add. Ms. 4289, ff. 29–30, Louis Des

Maizeaux to Pierre Des Maizeaux, Avenches, Dec. 2, 1699; f. 31, same to same, Aug. 8, 1700; and ff. 35–6, same to same, July 9, 1701.) Indeed, this was his father's final concern for his son when on his deathbed. Des Maizeaux's mother, writing to announce the death, said that "Il prioit Incessamment Dieu quil Vous fisse la grace dentrer dans le Sainct Ministaire Vous devies suivre ses bons conseils et vous faire Recevoir a geneve Comme il vous lavoit Ecrit diverses fois et ne Vous pas tant Eloigner de Nous pour nostre Consolation quelque Jour avant qu'il perdit la parolle il nous donna à tous sa sainte Benedition et me dit ainsi quand Vous écrives a mon fils Mandes luy qu'il demande bien pardon a Dieu de bon Coeur de ce qu'il ne ma pas Voulu Croire et suivre mes Sainctes Ezortations." BL Add. Ms. 4289, f. 37, Madeleine Dumonteil Des Maizeaux to Pierre Des Maizeaux, Avenches, Jan. 1, 1702. For various certificates of his theological education, see BL Add. Ms. 4289, ff. 80, 83, 87.

97 Le Clerc to Locke, Amsterdam, June 18, 1699, in De Beer, ed., *Correspondence of Locke* VI, p. 636; Coste to Locke, June 29, 1699, in *Correspondence of Locke* VI, p. 649.

98 Broome, "An Agent in Anglo-French Relationships," pp. 11–15, 20.

99 Ibid., p. 348.

100 Ibid., p. 20.

101 Elisabeth Labrousse, *Pierre Bayle* (The Hague: Martinus Nijhoff, 1963) I, pp. 1–3.

102 Broome, "An Agent in Anglo-French Relationships," p. 45. For examples of Shaftesbury using Des Maizeaux as intermediary with Bayle, see BL Add. Ms. 4288, ff. 95–95^v, Shaftesbury to Des Maizeaux, St. Giles's, Dorset, 17 Feb., no year; ff. 98^v–99, same to same, Aug. 5, 1701.

103 One of these works, the *Mélange curieux des meilleures pieces attribués à*

Mr. de Saint-Evremond, et de plusieurs autres ouvrages rares ou nouveaux (Amsterdam: Pierre Mortier, 1706), was quite open in its admission that the works it contained were not by St.-Evremond.

104 Des Maizeaux, "Vie de M^r. de Saint-Evremond," in ibid., I, pp. 84–7.

105 Broome, "An Agent in Anglo-French Relationships," pp. 39–40.

106 BL Add. Ms. 4288, f. 100, Shaftesbury to Des Maizeaux, Rotterdam, Nov. 2, 1708.

107 BL Add. Ms. 4281, f. 42, Jacques Basnage to Des Maizeaux, Aug. 19, 1707. Letter damaged.

108 BL Add. Ms. 4281, f. 41^v, Basnage to Des Maizeaux, Aug. 19, 1707.

109 BL Add. Ms. 4285, f. 68^v, Mathieu Marais to Des Maizeaux, Paris, Dec. 16, 1710. See also BL Add. Ms. 4281, f. 49^v, Basnage to Des Maizeaux, June 11, 1709; BL Add. Ms. 4281, f. 57, Basnage to Des Maizeaux, 1709. The first version of the biography was *The Life of Mr. Bayle. In a Letter to a Peer of Great Britain* (London: no publisher, 1708).

110 "Lettre de Mr. Des Maizeaux à Monsieur Coste," in De la Monnoye [pseud.], ed., *Histoire de Mr. Bayle et de ses Ouvrages*, 3rd ed. (Amsterdam: Jaques Desbordes, 1716), p. 468. The first two editions of this book were published in Geneva by Fabri and Barrillot. Christiane Berkvens-Stevelinck attributes this book to Des Maizeaux, but Fabri and Barrillot's correspondence with him suggests to me that although he contributed to the book, he was not the editor of it. The Genevan *libraires*, for example, insisted to Des Maizeaux that the first article *was* by La Monnoye, which they surely would not have bothered to do if Des Maizeaux himself had written it. See Berkvens-Stevelinck, "Cabale," p. 108; BL Add. Ms. 4283, f. 229, Fabri and Barrillot to Des Maizeaux, Geneva, Sept. 9, 1715, and ff. 232–232^v, Fabri and Barrillot to Des Maizeaux, Geneva, Sept. 1716.

111 BL Add. Ms. 4289, f. 125^v, Des Maizeaux to [du Rendel], May 24 [1711; dated by Birch], draft.

112 BL Add. Ms. 4283, f. 284, Fritsch and Böhm to Des Maizeaux, Rotterdam, Sept. 20, 1712. Aspects of the negotiations appear in BL Add. Ms. 4286, f. 106, De la Motte to Des Maizeaux, Amsterdam, April 22, [1710]; BL Add. Ms. 4286, ff. 148–148^v, De la Motte to Des Maizeaux, Sept. 1, 1711; BL Add. Ms. 4283, ff. 282–282^v, Fritsch and Böhm to Des Maizeaux, Rotterdam, Sept. 19, 1711; BL Add. Ms. 4286, f. 169, De la Motte de Des Maizeaux, Amsterdam, Mar. 15, 1712; BL Add. Ms. 4286, f. 180, De la Motte to Des Maizeaux, Amsterdam, July 22, 1712; BL Add. Ms. 4286, f. 184^v, De la Motte to Des Maizeaux, Aug. 26, 1712.

113 BL Add. Ms. 4226, ff. 317–18, incomplete draft of article by Des Maizeaux, dated July 22, 1729.

114 UBL, March. 5:2, Des Maizeaux to Marchand, London, Mar. 20, 1713.

115 BL Add. Ms. 4283, ff. 286–286^v, Anon. to Des Maizeaux, "Aix-la-Chapelle," May 14, 1713.

116 Ibid., f. 286.

117 BL Add. Ms. 4283, f. 287, Böhm to Des Maizeaux, Rotterdam, May 30, 1713.

118 UBL March. 5:2, Des Maizeaux to Marchand, London, Dec. 11, 1713 O.S.

119 Ibid.

120 BL Add. Ms. 4283, f. 288, Fritsch and Böhm to Des Maizeaux, Rotterdam, April 13, 1714. The *libraires* said Des Maizeaux had done the same thing with the *Vie de Boileau*: "vous avez rendu [the book] à un Libraire anglois & à un Libraire de ce paici en même tems."

121 BL Add. Ms. 4226, f. 315, Incomplete draft of pamphlet headed "Lettre à Mr. . . ." by Des Maizeaux, dated London, July 22, 1729.

122 UBL March. 2, Fritsch to Marchand, Frankfurt, Nov. 4, 1713.

123 BL Add. Ms. 4283, ff. 288^v–289,

Fritsch and Böhm to Des Maizeaux, April 13, 1714. Des Maizeaux said later that his concern was not the money, but Marchand's impertinence toward "personnes d'un grand Merite," and the fact that in the first place Fritsch and Böhm had "consenti que leur Correcteur d'Imprimerie s'apropriât l'edition." BL Add. Ms. 4289, f. 163ᵛ, Des Maizeaux to Covens and Mortier, London, Dec. 30, 1720, draft.

124 E.g. *Lettres choisies de Mʳ. Bayle, avec des Remarques* (Rotterdam: Fritsch and Böhm, 1714), II, p. 606, n. 1.

125 Marchand in ibid., II, p. 391, n. 22; p. 494, n. 2.

126 Ibid. I, p. 73, n. 1, and pp. 280–1, n. 1.

127 Marchand in ibid., I, vii. Preface. Marchand made a similar statement of his ideas about editing in his note about a collection of Vossius' correspondence, which had "laissé bien des choses, qui ne sont gueres dignes, ni de l'*Impression*, ni de la *Curiosité des Personnes de Lettres*. C'est ce qui arrive presque toujours à ces sortes de *Collections d'Ouvrages Posthumes*, dans lesquelles on ramasse, à tort & à travers, toutes les *Bagatelles* qu'un Homme peut avoir faites, & dans lesquelles on donne au Public, sans aucun égard, ni pour lui, ni pour des *Ecrivains* d'ailleurs *Illustres*, & d'un *Nom* fort célébre, mille choses, qu'ils n'ont jamais faites pour être imprimées; qui leur feroient honte, s'ils vivoient encore; & la *Publication* desquelles ils s'opposeroient, sans doute, de toutes leurs forces; puisqu'il n'y a guere d'*Injustice* plus criante que celle-là." Marchand in Bayle, *Lettres choisies* (1714) I, pp. 268–9, note (1).

128 It would, of course, be untrue to suggest that everyone supported Des Maizeaux in this dispute. He was of little more importance than Marchand in the Republic of Letters, and some, such as Bayle's passionate defender Mathieu Marais, whose goodwill Des Maizeaux thought he

had, were simply annoyed with his own pursuit of the Bayle industry. In 1710 Marais wrote that Des Maizeaux "me paroît un petit esprit, occupé de fadaises, et un auteur pauvre qui court après le libraire pour gagner" (Mathieu Marais to Mme de Mérigniac, August, 1710, in Mathieu Marais, *Journal et mémoires de Mathieu Marais, avocat au parlement de Paris, sur la Régence et le Règne de Louis XV (1715–1737)*, ed. de Lescure, [Paris: Firmin Didot Frères, Fils et Cie, 1863], I, p. 125), and his later correspondence with Marchand suggests that he was on his side. See UBL March. 2, Mathieu Marais to Marchand, Paris, April 18, 1720, and Marchand to Marais, n.d., draft. La Croze told Marchand that "les honnêtes gens de ce pais-ci sont pour vous, & blâment unanimement vos adversaires," although admittedly he had said the opposite to Des Maizeaux a year earlier: "Je sai que cet homme-là [Marchand] en a mal usé avec vous." La Croze did say that "en cela je crois qu'il y a eu plus d'imprudence que de malice," suggesting that his erudition did have merit. UBL March. 2, M.V. La Croze to Marchand, Berlin, Jan. 27, 1717; BL Add. Ms. 4283, ff. 33–33ᵛ, La Croze to Des Maizeaux, Berlin, Mar. 4, 1716.

129 Gen BPU, Ms. Court 50, f. 53ᵛ, Elie Benoît notebook, "Suite de l'Histoire de l'Edit de Nantes."

130 Marchand in Bayle, *Lettres choisies* (1714) II, p. 513, n. 6.

131 Ibid., II, pp. 694–5, n. 1.

132 *Journal litéraire* IV, pt. 2 (July–Aug. 1714), Art. VI, p. 364.

133 UBL March. 2, Ougier to Marchand, April 4, 1716.

134 "Factum des Amis de Mr. Bayle," in De la Monnoye [pseud.] ed., *Histoire de Mr. Bayle et de ses ouvrages*, p. 536. Although Fabri and Barrillot were undoubtedly deeply involved in this dispute, private letters between scholars indicate that the upset over Marchand's edition was not, as

Marchand claimed in the *Journal littéraire* (VIII, pt. 1, [1716], 113), simply a publicity stunt for the Genevan *librairie* and its edition of Bayle's *Dictionary*. Barbeyrac, for example, wrote to Turrettini in May 1714 that Marchand "a retranché les Lettres qu'il a voulu, & fait dans le Texte des autres plusieurs retranchemens de sa propre autorité" (Gen. BPU, Ms. fr. 484, f. 164ᵛ, Barbeyrac to Turrettini, Lausanne, May 15, 1714), and his correspondence with Des Maizeaux (e.g. BL Add. Ms. 4281, ff. 27, 28ᵛ, 32) indicates his displeasure at this. Basnage told Des Maizeaux in July that many people were unhappy with the letters, and that some, such as Le Clerc, were offended. He added in August that Fontenelle had complained to him about the edition (BL Add. Ms. 4281, ff. 62–62ᵛ, Basnage to Des Maizeaux, July 13 [1714], and ff. 64–5, Basnage to Des Maizeaux, Aug. 3(?) [1714]).

135 E.J. Kenney, *The Classical Texts: Aspects of Editing in the Age of the Printed Book* (Berkeley: University of California Press, 1974), p. 71. However, as Anthony Grafton points out, the great textual critics of the late seventeenth and early eighteenth centuries were consciously dependent on the established tradition of sixteenth-century critics like Scaliger and Casaubon. See Anthony Grafton, *Forgers and Critics: Creativity and Duplicity in Western Scholarship* (Princeton: Princeton University Press, 1990), pp. 73–5; also Grafton, *Defenders of the Text: The Traditions of Scholarship in an Age of Science, 1450–1800* (Cambridge, Mass.: Harvard University Press, 1991). On the debate on the ancients and moderns, see Richard Foster Jones, *Ancients and Moderns: A Study of the Background of the Battle of the Books* (St. Louis: Washington University, 1936), and especially Joseph M. Levine, *The Battle of the Books: History and Literature in the Augustan Age* (Ithaca:

Cornell University Press, 1991).

136 Quoted in R.C. Jebb, *Bentley* (London: Macmillan, 1882), p. 34. See also R.F. Jones, *Lewis Theobald: His Contribution to English Scholarship* (New York: Columbia University Press, 1919), p. 39.

137 Shaftesbury to Le Clerc, Reigate, July 19, 1710 O.S., printed in Barrell, *Shaftesbury Correspondence*, pp. 98–9. Bentley was famously satirized in the *Dunciad* as

> Thy mighty Scholiast, whose unweary'd pains
> Made Horace dull, and humbled Milton's strains.
> Turn what they will to Verse, their toil is vain,
> Critics like me shall make it Prose again.

Alexander Pope, *The Dunciad* IV, lines 211–14. In James Sutherland, ed., *The Dunciad*, 3rd ed.(London: Methuen, 1963), Twickenham edition of Pope, V.

138 [Thomas Edwards], *A Supplement to Mr. Warburton's Edition of Shakespear. Being the Canons of Criticism, and Glossary, collected from the Notes in that celebrated Work, and proper to be bound up with it* (London: M. Cooper, 1748), pp. 12, 13, 22–3.

139 Anne Dacier, *Des Causes de la corruption du goust* (Paris: Imprimerie Royale, 1714), p. 353; *Journal littéraire* VI, pt. 2 (1715), Art. XXV, p. 383.

140 *History of Learning* (1691), Art. IV, p. 21.

141 Anne Dacier, *Les Oeuvres d'Homère, traduites en françois* (Amsterdam: Wetstein and Smith, 1731), I, p. xlvii, preface.

142 According to Dacier, *Causes de la corruption du goust*, p. 4.

143 Ibid., pp. 392–3.

144 Baillet, *Jugemens des savans* I, pp. 97–8.

145 R.F. Jones, *Lewis Theobald*, p. 172.

146 Lewis Theobald, *Shakespeare restored: Or, a Specimen of the Many Errors, as well Committed as Unamended, by Mr. Pope in his Late Edition of this Poet*

(London: R. Francklin, T. Woodman, Charles Davis, and S. Chapman, 1726).

147 Francis Hare, *Epistola Critica . . .* (1726), p. 4, quoted and trans. in R.F. Jones, *Lewis Theobald*, p. 42. Richard Jebb characterizes Bentley's writings thus: "The tone is often as if the ancient author was reading his composition aloud to Bentley, but making stupid mistakes through drowsiness or inattention. Bentley pulls him up short; remonstrates with him in a vein of good-humoured sarcasm; points out to him that he can scarcely mean *this*, but—as his own words elsewhere prove—must, no doubt, have meant *that*; and recommends him to think more of logic. Sometimes it is the modern reader whom Bentley addresses as if begging him to be calm in the face of some tremendous blunder just committed by the ancient author, who is intended to overhear the 'aside:'—'Do not mind him; he does not really mean it. He is like this sometimes, and makes us anxious; but he has plenty of good sense, if one can only get at it. Let us see what we can do for him.'" Jebb, *Bentley*, pp. 16–17.

148 Theobald, *Shakespeare Restored*, p. iv, introduction.

149 *Journal littéraire* VI, pt. 2 (1715), Art. XXV, p. 382. The journal was generally favorable to La Motte's translation because "il a substitué aux idées qui plaisoient du tems d'*Homére*, des idées qui nous plaisent aujourd'hui." *Journal littéraire* IV, pt. 1 (May–June 1714), Art. VI, p. 146.

150 Pope, *Dunciad* IV, lines 119–129.

151 "Lettre à Messieurs Le Clerc & Bernard," in *Mémoires de littérature* II, pt. 2 (1717), 244.

152 Ibid., 258.

153 "Factum des Amis de Mr. Bayle," p. 546.

154 Bayle, "Preface de la Premiere Edition," reprinted in *Dictionnaire historique et critique*, 5th ed. in French (Amsterdam: P. Brunel, P. Humbert,

J. Wetstein & G. Smith, et al., 1740) I, p. viii.

155 *Journal littéraire* VIII, pt. 1 (1716), 108–9. Sallengre mentions Marchand's defense in *Mémoires de littérature* II, pt. 2 (1717), 258–9, pointing out that some of the changes—such as turning "Auteurs" into "Personnes" and adding the word "certainement"—were too large to be mere copyist's mistakes.

156 *Journal littéraire* VIII, pt. 1 (1716), 111.

157 Ibid., 110.

158 Of course, Bayle's reputation was not necessarily to be preserved by an exact rendition of his text, as we will see below.

159 Pierre Bayle [et al.], *A General Dictionary, Historical and Critical . . . with the Corrections and Observations printed in the late Edition at Paris . . . and . . . several thousand Lives never before published* [by John Peter Bernard, Thomas Birch, John Lockman, et al.], (London: G. Strahan et al., 1734–41), I, dedication to the Royal Society. The articles not by Bayle were marked with a pointing hand.

160 Bibl SHPF, Ms. 295, #18, Coste to De la Motte, [England], Mar. 22, 1739.

161 UBL March 2, Jean de Beyer to Marchand, Letter 45, Nijmegen, Dec. 19, 1742.

162 *Journal littéraire* VI, pt. 1 (1715; in 1732 Gosse and Neaulme ed.), Art. XIII, 202. Colletet, translator of Sainte-Marthe's *Eloges*, expressed a similar opinion. "Certes on peut dire que la vie particuliere des grands Hommes est une des principales pieces de l'Histoire generale, puisqu'ils en composent eux-mesmes la plus noble partie; & par consequent que la cognoissance que nous en acquerons nous en descouvre les secrets, & nous en esclaircit les obscuritez. Leurs moindres actions sont comme ces précieux restes de la table des Dieux, dont toute l'antiquité faisoit tant de cas. Il y a du plaisir a les voir par tout, aussi bien dans leur Cabinet, que dans les

Chaires publiques." G. Colletet in Scévole de Sainte-Marthe, *Eloges des hommes illustres, qui depuis un siecle ont fleury en France dans la profession des lettres,* trans. from Latin by Colletet (Paris: Antoine de Sommaville, Augustin Courbé, François Langlois, 1644), "Avis au Lecteur."

163 BL Add. Ms. 4286, f. 10ᵛ, De la Motte to Des Maizeaux, Amsterdam, Oct. 31, 1704; UBA, C 108 e, Nicaise to Le Clerc, Dijon, Jan. 1, 1694. (It is possible that Nicaise used *drogue* in its colloquial sense, "trash," as he said that "l'on nous promet incessamment *Harlequiniana* qui sera asseuremᵗ meilleur." The *Arlequiniana* was published in 1694.) Des Maizeaux quotes the editor of the *Naudaeana* in 1701: "Tout le monde sait . . . avec quelle avidité les *Ana* sont à présent reçus." Des Maizeaux, "Vie de Bayle," in Bayle, *Dictionnaire* (5th French ed., 1740) I, p. lxxxvi.

164 Pierre Des Maizeaux, ed., *Scaligerana, Thuana, Perroniana, Pithoeana, et Colomesiana, ou Remarques historiques, critiques, morales, & littéraires de Jos. Scaliger, J.A. de Thou, le cardinal du Perron, Fr. Pithou, & P. Colomiés* (Amsterdam: Covens and Mortier, 1740) I, dedication to Richard Mead.

165 *Naudaeana et Patiniana, ou singularitez Remarquables, prises des conversations de Mess. Naudé & Patin* (Paris: Chez Florentin & Pierre Delaulne, 1701); *Pithoeana,* in Des Maizeaux, ed., *Scaligerana . . .* I, p. 489; *Furetieriana ou les bons mots, et les remarques d'histoire, de morale, de critique, de plaisanterie, & d'erudition, de Mr. Furetiere, Abbé de Chalivoy, de l'Academie Françoise* (Brussels: François Foppens, 1696).

166 *Addisoniana* (London: Richard Phillips, 1803), I, p. iv, preface (in English); *Elite des bons mots et des pensées choisies, recüeillies avec soin des plus celebres auteurs, & principalement des livres en Ana* (Amsterdam: Jaques Desbordes, 1704).

167 DSB, Nachlass Formey, Jacques de

Pérard to Formey, f. 74ᵛ, Stettin, Sept. 5, 1742, postscript.

168 Prosper Marchand in *Lettres choisies de Bayle* (1714) I, pp. v–vi.

169 BL Add. Ms. 4289, f. 125, Des Maizeaux to [du Rendel], London, May 24 [1711; dated by Birch], draft. Des Maizeaux asked La Croze for any letters from Bayle "qui Vous paroitront dignes d'être données au Public." BJK Ms. Berol. Gall. Qu. 26, f. 487, Des Maizeaux to La Croze, London, Dec. 19/30, 1710.

170 Des Maizeaux in *Scaligerana, etc.,* dedicatory epistle to Mead.

171 [Gilles Ménage], *Menagiana, ou bons mots, rencontres agréables, pensées judicieuses, et observations curieuses, de M. Ménage, de l'Académie Françoise* (Amsterdam: Adrian Braakman, 1693), "Avertissement." "On ne trouvera rien de semblable dans le Ménagiana," this passage continues: unsurprising, as Ménage himself edited the collection.

172 BL Add. Ms. 4284, f. 112, Théodore Huet to Des Maizeaux, The Hague, May 12, 1711; BL Add. Ms. 4285, f. 57, Mathieu Marais to [Jacques Basnage], Paris, Sept. 27, 1709; BL Add. Ms. 4285, f. 76, Marais to Des Maizeaux, Paris, Sept. 23, 1711; BL Add. Ms. 4288, f. 192, Jean-Alphonse Turrettini to Des Maizeaux, Geneva, July 1, 1717 (writing of letters he sent for Des Maizeaux's 1729 edition).

173 Lenfant gave a two-page account of how Bayle fell into a canal in Rotterdam in BL Add. Ms. 4284, ff. 241–2, Lenfant to Des Maizeaux, July 8, no year.

174 Marais to Mme de Mérigniac, April 1711, in Marais, *Journal et mémoires* I, p. 140.

175 Elisabeth Labrousse presents the arguments for and against attributing the piece to Bayle in *Pierre Bayle* I, pp. 219–21. Labrousse believes that Daniel Larroque was probably the author of the book, but that Bayle made some additions and changes; and "quant au fond de l'ouvrage, il

est tout à fait indubitable qu'on doit en tenir Bayle pour entièrement responsable" (p. 221). At the time, as Pierre Rétat says, "personne ne doute, parmi ses adversaires, qu'il en soit l'auteur." See Rétat, *Le Dictionnaire de Bayle et la lutte philosophique au XVIIIe siècle* (Paris: Société d'Edition "les Belles Lettres," 1971), p. 45.

176 For summaries of Bayle's arguments and the response of the refugee community, see Guy Howard Dodge, *The Political Theory of the Huguenots of the Dispersion: With Special Reference to the Thought and Influence of Pierre Jurieu* (Morningside Heights, NY: Columbia University Press, 1947), pp. 94–138, and Walter Rex, *Essays on Pierre Bayle and Religious Controversy* (The Hague: Martinus Nijhoff, 1965), pp. 225ff.

177 Marchand, ed., *Lettres choisies de Bayle* I, p. 255, n. 3; I, pp. 287–8, n. 6; II, p. 487, n. 5; Table des Matières in III, under "Avis aux Réfugiés."

178 See Almagor, *Pierre des Maizeaux*, pp. 96–100.

179 Des Maizeaux, "Life of Bayle," in *The Dictionary Historical and Critical of Mr Peter Bayle*, 2nd ed., trans. Des Maizeaux (London: J.J. and P. Knapton et al., 1734) I, p. lxiii. For his inquiries, see BL Add. Mss. 4286–7, letters from Charles de la Motte, *passim*.

180 BL Add. Ms. 4281, f. 59, Basnage to Des Maizeaux, Feb. 23, 1714.

181 Even Des Maizeaux was not circumspect enough for the fanatically proBayle Marais, who did not want the subject discussed at all: "il me semble que c'est une matiere quil faudroit Laisser dans l'oubli." (BL Add. Ms. 4285, f. 90ᵛ, Marais to Des Maizeaux, Paris, Mar. 10, 1716). Others wanted more information, and Des Maizeaux reported in 1730 that "Quelques uns de Mes Amis ici & en Hollande m'ont blamé de n'avoir pas été assez affirmatif." (BL Add. Ms. 4289, f. 232, Des Maizeaux to ?, May 12, 1730, draft.)

182 Richard Popkin, "Serendipity at the Clark: Spinoza and the Prince of Condé," *The Clark Newsletter* No. 10 (Spring 1986), pp. 4–7.

183 BL Add. Ms. 4284, f. 77, Marais to Des Maizeaux, Paris, Sept. 23, 1711.

184 BL Add. Ms. 4284, ff. 123ᵛ–4, Théodore Huet to Des Maizeaux, The Hague, Aug. 7, 1714.

185 Des Maizeaux in *Lettres de Mʳ. Bayle, publiées sur les originaux: avec des remarques* (Amsterdam: Aux dépens de la Compagnie, 1729) I, p. xxiii.

186 BL Add. Ms. 4313, f. 15, Macclesfield to Peter Daval, Shirburn, July 4, 1755. It is notable that Macclesfield used the word "Eloge" to describe the piece he wanted written; this usage testifies the influence of the French in academic circles. For similar requests for information, see BL Add. Ms. 4307, ff. 129–130, "Questions à faire pour l'éloge de Mʳ Sloane," in hand of de Fouchy, *sécretaire perpetuel* of the Académie Royale des Sciences, Paris; and BL Add. Ms. 4303, f. 32, P. Collinson to Thomas Birch, London, May 20, 1763.

187 Jean-Pierre Niceron, *Mémoires pour servir à l'histoire des hommes illustres dans la République des Lettres* I (Paris: Briasson, 1729), preface.

188 Camusat, *Histoire critique des journaux* II, p. 50.

189 *Bibliothèque britannique* I, pt. 1 (April–June 1733), "Avertissement."

190 Niceron, *Mémoires* I, preface.

191 Georg Simmel's work on the nobility provides a useful perspective here. In most groups, he says, "the value of what is really common to all members, lies very close to the lowliest among them because, as a rule, the top can sink to the bottom, but the bottom cannot rise to the top. . . . With the nobility, however, the presumption is the opposite. In a noble group . . . , each constituent personality has in its value a share in the glory attained by the most outstanding members of it." The Republic of Letters, which maintained

an image of its own aristocracy (see Chap. 5 below), fits this picture very well; hence the eagerness to preserve any illusions about the greatness of its famous scholars. See Georg Simmel, "The Nobility," in *On Individuality and Social Forms*, ed. Donald N. Levine (Chicago: University of Chicago Press, 1971), p. 206.

192 See, for example, Donald A. Stauffer, *English Biography before 1700* (Cambridge, Mass.: Harvard University Press, 1930), pp. 233–4, 238–9; Richard D. Altick, *Lives and Letters: A History of Literary Biography in England and America* (New York: Alfred A. Knopf, 1966), p. 6; Vivian de Sola Pinto, *English Biography in the Seventeenth Century* (London: George G. Harrap, 1951), pp. 16–17; J. Paul Hunter, "Biography and the Novel," *Modern Language Studies* IX (Fall 1979), 74; Peter Millard, introduction to Roger North, *General Preface & Life of Dr. John North*, ed. Millard (Toronto: University of Toronto Press, 1984), p. 16. John McManamon makes this point about the eulogies delivered by humanist orators in Renaissance Italy, saying that "they celebrated virtue to render honor to the deceased, but also to inflame those listening to imitation." See John McManamon, *Funeral Oratory and the Cultural Ideals of Italian Humanism* (Chapel Hill: University of North Carolina Press, 1989), p. 32.

193 Charles B. Paul, *Science and Immortality: The Eloges of the Paris Academy of Sciences (1699–1791)* (Berkeley: University of California Press, 1980), p. 86.

194 Diderot, art. "Encyclopédie" in *Encyclopédie* V, p. 6464 (1), quoted in Georges G. Perla, "La controverse sur les 'Vies' dans l'*Encyclopédie*," *Revue française d'histoire du livre* n.s. no. 34 (Jan.–Mar. 1982), 55–6. According to Perla, the majority of the lives in the *Encyclopédie* (which were mainly written by the Chevalier de Jaucourt) were intended to illustrate

a larger point rather than actually commemorate the people concerned. See pp. 57–8, 60.

195 In Bayle et al., *A General Dictionary* I, dedication by Bernard, Birch, and Lockman to Sloane and the Royal Society. Orest Ranum observed the same motivation in seventeenth-century biographies of sixteenth-century humanists, which were mainly for the purpose of inspiring emulation. See Orest Ranum, *Artisans of Glory: Writers and Historical Thought in Seventeenth-Century France* (Chapel Hill: University of North Carolina Press, 1980), p. 37.

196 Charles Ancillon, *Mémoires concernant les vies et les ouvrages de plusieurs modernes célèbres dans la République des Lettres* (Amsterdam: The Wetsteins, 1709), p. xviii, preface; François Bruys, *Mémoires historiques, critiques, et littéraires*, ed. the Abbé L. Ph. Joly (Paris: Jean-Thomas Hérissant, 1751), I, p. 326.

197 Des Maizeaux in *Lettres de Mʳ. Bayle* (1729) I, p. xxiii.

198 McManamon, discussing humanist funeral orations, points out the constant stress on communal service in these eulogies. The humanist orators implied that Cicero's ideal of public service was in harmony with Jesus' lessons on altruism. (McManamon, *Funeral Oratory*, p. 19.) John W. O'Malley also writes of the oratorical emphasis on public service at the papal court in his *Praise and Blame in Renaissance Rome: Rhetoric, Doctrine, and Reform in the Sacred Orators of the Papal Court, c. 1450–1521* (Durham, NC: Duke University Press, 1979), pp. 168–72; see also O.B. Hardison, Jr., *The Enduring Monument: A Study of the Idea of Praise in Renaissance Literary Theory and Practice* (Chapel Hill: University of North Carolina Press, 1962). In the case of the Republic of Letters and its own eulogies, the community to be served was nearly always the scholarly one. Although some savants were praised in *éloges* for charity to the poor, these

articles much more commonly highlighted their services to fellow scholars. In the case of Bayle, Des Maizeaux made a point of emphasizing his character even more than his talents. His 1708 *Life of Mr. Bayle*, addressed to an anonymous Shaftesbury, compliments Bayle on his "Uprightness and Simplicity of . . . Heart," his "extreme Modesty and Sweetness of Temper," and his obliging manners, regular conduct, and moderation. Shaftesbury, he said, "admired the Beauty of his Wit, and the Justness of his Judgment; but you were still more charm'd with his Modesty, his Disinterestedness, and his Integrity of Heart. 'Twas by this part of him that he had the Happiness of pleasing you." [Pierre Des Maizeaux, *The Life of Mr. Bayle. In a Letter to a Peer of Great Britain* (London: no publisher, 1708), pp. 19–20, 4.

199 See Robert Darnton, "The High Enlightenment and the Low-Life of Literature," in *The Literary Underground of the Old Regime*, pp. 20–1; and Darnton, *Mesmerism and the End of the Enlightenment in France* (Cambridge, Mass.: Harvard University Press, 1968), pp. 83–5, 91–4, 97–100. The unequal status yet egalitarian aspirations of Enlightenment figures are discussed by Dena Goodman in her "Pigalle's *Voltaire nu*: The Republic of Letters Represents Itself to the World," *Representations* 16 (Fall 1986), 86–109. In his presentation of the world of England's Grub Street writers under Walpole, Pat Rogers describes a group with similar backgrounds and attitudes to Darnton's French hacks, a group longing to be distinguished writers but in fact characterized by a "notorious and fatal jealousy" because of their self-perception as outsiders. See Pat Rogers, *Grub Street: Studies in a Subculture* (London: Methuen, 1972), pp. 277–82. It should be noted that although Rogers characterizes this group as

the "Dunces" and elsewhere in his book includes such scholars as Bentley in his group, when discussing the Grub Street "subculture" he abandons the scholarly element of that society for the more purely literary and political. Although it is evident that the Republic of Letters was made up of an entire gradation of "savants" and "demi-savants," as they were described, I still do not see this sort of bitterness against a perceived scholarly "establishment" among the authors I have studied.

200 Vigneul-Marville, *Mélanges* I, p. 20.

201 G. Colletet in Scévole de Sainte-Marthe, *Eloges des hommes illustres, qui depuis un siecle ont fleury en France dans la profession des lettres*, trans. from Latin by Colletet (Paris: Antoine de Sommaville, Augustin Courbé, François Langlois, 1644), "Advis au Lecteur."

202 *Bibliothèque italique* VIII (May–Aug. 1730), 153–4, n. 22.

203 KB, 72 H 19/I, #9, La Croze to Cuper, Berlin, April 18, 1711. Baillet said that "quoique la Republique des Lettres ne reconnoisse point d'autre qualité ni d'autre dignité dans les jugemens qu'elle porte des Ecrivains que celle d'Auteur, & qu'elle fasse profession de ne point considerer davantage les tétes couronnées ni les autres personnes les plus qualifiées, que celles qui passent pour les derniers & les plus basses sur les rangs établis dans le monde: il faut reconnoître neanmoins qu'on n'y est pas entierement libre de préjugé sur ce point. . . . il n'y a presque personne qui ne se sente porté à distinguer les ouvrages des Grands d'avec les autres." However, he also said that this was only the case in the lifetime of the authors, and that afterwards noble authors were "traitez comme les autres" because "on n'a plus rien à esperer ni rien à craindre de leur part dans le monde." Baillet, *Jugemens des savans* I, pp. 166–8. This final statement suggests that Baillet is referring more to the fuss made over

certain authors' books than actual opinions of them.

204 BN Ms. fr. 12933, f. 49, César de Missy to Voltaire, London, Sept. 11, 1741.

205 *Bibliothèque germanique* I (July–Sept. 1720), Art. I, p. 23; Niceron III, p. 111. Other examples of this in early volumes of Niceron include Jacques Le Long ("Pendant toute sa vie il a partagé son temps entre la prière & l'étude, en donnant très-peu à la table & au sommeil."), Rapin, who studied whenever possible despite the disapproval of his aristocratic employer, and J.L. Le Cerf, whose "ardeur pour l'étude, & l'assiduité avec laquelle il s'y livroit, ont ruiné son temperament délicat de lui-même, & abrégé ses jours." See Niceron I, pp. 157, 291; II, p. 50.

206 Des Maizeaux, *Vie de Boileau*, dedication to Addison, p. 2.

207 *Nouvelles de la République des Lettres* II (1684), 429.

208 Niceron I, preface.

209 BCUL, Archives de Crousaz XII/ 162–3, Paul-Emile de Mauclerc to Jean-Pierre de Crousaz, Stettin, Feb. 9, 1731.

210 DSB, Nachlass Formey, Mathieu Maty to Formey, f. 1, London, Aug. 20, 1751; Gisbert Cuper to Bernard to Montfaucon, n.d. [end 1709 or beginning 1710], in Beyer, *Lettres de Cuper*, p. 52.

211 *Mémoires de Trévoux* I (Jan.–Feb. 1701), Preface.

212 *Journal littéraire* VI, pt. 2 (1715), Art. XV, p. 255.

213 *Bibliothèque italique* VIII (May– August 1730), 153–4, n. 22. The last sentence is "Il sembloit s'être borné à s'éclairer sans relache, où à éclairer les autres de la façon la moins brillante pour lui." Rémy Saisselin makes a similar point about Bernard de la Monnoye, who made a great name "without ever writing a book. . . . Above all he was praised for his modesty, disinterestedness, love of study, vast knowledge, and avoidance of cabals." See Saisselin,

The Literary Enterprise in Eighteenth-Century France (Detroit: Wayne State University Press, 1979), p. 31.

214 *Bibliothèque angloise* I (1716; 2nd ed. 1729), Art. XII, p. 275; *Histoire critique de la République des Lettres* IX (1715), Art. XVI, p. 412.

215 *Bibliothèque italique* XII (Sept.–Dec. 1731), Art. V, p. 107.

216 SPK, Sammlung Darmstaedter 2 m 1757 (1), Johann Joachim Ewald to Formey, Halle, Dec. 29, 1748.

217 Des Maizeaux, in *Lettres de Bayle* (1729) I, xviii, preface.

218 *Journal littéraire* VIII, pt. 2 (1716), 489.

219 Mencke, *Charlatanerie des savans*, pp. 87–90. Cuper wrote to La Croze in 1716, "Vous ditez tresbien, Mr, que Mr. Gronovius sera toujours Mr. Gronovius; et je me fache, qu'il a si mal traité Mr. Fabricius, qui est sans doute très savant et labourieux, et dont je ferois conscience de parler mal. Il merite plustost des louanges, et je ne les refuserai jamais." KB, 72 H 19/II, #20, Cuper to Maturin Veyssière La Croze, Deventer, June 1, 1716, draft.

220 DSB, Nachlass Formey, Cartier de St. Philippe to Formey, f. 2, June 2, 1750. Jurieu's death did prompt some satiric verse, such as the Dutch pamphlet containing "Uitvaert van P★★★ J★★★" and "Op de Afbeelding van P★★★ J★★★." It is unclear, however, who was responsible for these pieces.

221 BL Sloane Ms. 4041, ff. 338–338v, Bignon to Sloane, Paris, July 1, 1709.

222 UBA, Ms. C 3, Barbeyrac to Le Clerc, Berlin, April 10, 1706; BJK, Ms. Berol. Gall. Qu. 26, f. 502, Reboulet to Mirmand, Basle, Oct. 2, 1696, copy. See also, e.g., "un caractère d'honnête-homme, . . . un fonds de Christianisme, que j'estime plus que votre savoir, que tout votre habileté." (UBA Ms. A 158 C, César de Missy to Jean-Jacques Wetstein, Marylebone, March 10, 1752 O.S.); "La douceur de leurs moeurs les rend encore plus estimable que leur esprit

223 & leur science" (La Croze, quoted in Jordan, *Vie de La Croze*, p. 34).

223 *Bibliothèque italique* XI (May–Aug. 1731), Art. V, pp. 236–7, 246. For this controversy, see *Bibliothèque françoise* XIV, pt. 1, 106ff.; *Lettres sérieuses & badines* IV, 129ff.; *Bibliothèque françoise* XV, 144ff.; *Lettres sérieuses & badines* IV, 443ff.; *Bibliothèque françoise* XV, 312ff.; and *Bibliothèque italique* XI, 192ff. Ménage made a similar point to Garcin's when he attacked Baillet, who, he said, was unqualified to make judgments of scholars in part because he was "un nouveau venu sur le Parnasse qui n'avoit jamais conversé avec les gens de lettres." See Gilles Ménage, *Anti-Baillet ou critique du livre de Mr. Baillet, intitulé Jugemens des Savans* (The Hague: Estienne Foulque & Louis van Dole, 1688), preface.

224 *Bibliothèque italique* IX (May–Aug. 1731), 228.

225 DSB, Nachlass Formey, Pérard to Formey, f. 83, Stettin, Dec. 21, 1742. Janet Altman notes the way letters and *commerces* after the publication of Pasquier's correspondence in 1623 became economic and social commodities because they demonstrated membership in the Republic of Letters. Some people wrote letters to the famous purely for the status gained by the response. See Janet Gurkin Altman, "The Letter Book as a Literary Institution 1539–1789: Toward a Cultural History of Published Correspondence in France," *Yale French Studies* 71 (1986), 40.

226 *Bibliothèque italique* VI (Sept.–Dec. 1729), Art. V, 167–8.

227 Niceron I, p. 194; *Histoire critique de la République des Lettres* III (1713), 262.

228 Niceron I, pp. 246–7.

229 UBA, N 24 ae, Jean Le Clerc to Robert Chouet, 1685, copy or draft; UBA, G 67 c, Pierre-Daniel Huet to Etienne Morin, Paris, Nov. 9, 1686; Mencke, *Charlatanerie*, p. 124.

230 Abbé du Pons, "Dénonciation faite à

Monseigneur le Chancelier . . .", in *Journal littéraire* VI, pt. 2 (1715), Art. XXIX, 458–9.

231 Neu BPU, Ms. 1266/6, ff. 9–9v, Barnaud to Louis Bourguet, Geneva, Feb. 8, 1724.

232 *Works of the Learned* (Oct. 1691), Art. XXVIII, 101.

233 KB 72 H 19/II, #22+, M.V. La Croze to G. Cuper, Berlin, June 16, 1716.

234 Ibid.

235 BN Ms. fr. 19211, f. 154, Jacques Bernard to Delaissement, The Hague, July 7, 1701.

236 Mencke, *Charlatanerie*, pp. 24–30.

237 *Histoire critique de la République des Lettres* IX (1715), Art. I, 2.

238 *Histoire critique de la République des Lettres* I (1712), 262.

239 *Bibliothèque raisonnée* II, pt. 1 (Jan.–Mar. 1729), 6.

240 *Lettres sérieuses et badines* I, pt. 1 (1729; 2nd ed. 1740), xxv, preface.

241 Haag, *La France protestante*, ed. Henri Bordier, 2nd ed., vol. I (Paris: Librairie Sandoz & Fischbacher, 1877), pp. 784–5; Philippe Meylan, *Jean Barbeyrac (1674–1744) et les débuts de l'enseignement du droit dans l'ancienne Académie de Lausanne* (Lausanne: F. Rouge et Cie, 1937).

242 Jean Barbeyrac to Locke, [May/June 1702], in De Beer, ed., *Correspondence of Locke* VII, pp. 620–1, 619–20.

243 Ibid., p. 620.

244 BL Add. Ms. 4282, f. 37ᵛ, Pierre Daval to Des Maizeaux, London, June 8, 1706.

245 Ibid., p. 621.

246 Ibid., p. 622.

247 Barbeyrac to Locke, Berlin, Jan. 6, 1703, in De Beer, *Correspondence of Locke* VII, p. 727.

248 Ibid., p. 728.

249 Barbeyrac to Locke, [May/June 1702], in De Beer, ed., *Correspondence of Locke* VII, p. 622.

250 KB 72 H 26/I, f. 81, Samuel Masson to Gisbert Cuper, Dordrecht, Oct. 5, 1713.

251 *Histoire critique de la République des Lettres* II (1713), 165.

252 UBA, J 17 c, signed statement by the bishop of London; dated and received by John Chamberlayne, May 7, 1708. In English.

253 Jacques Bernard wrote to Desmaizeaux in 1700 that "Le Pr Gabillon de qui vous me demandez des Nouvelles ne mérite pas trop qu'on parle de lui: Vous saurez cependant, qu'il n'est pas encore jugé, on a reçu de France assez de piéces contre lui, pour en composer un Volume *in folio*, cependant il a de puissans amis, & il espére toujours de triompher, il y a huit ou dix jours, qu'il paroit un petit écrit anonyme de 2. feuilles, où l'on entreprend de le justifier, c'est une piéce où Mess. Jaquelot, de Bauval, & Huet, sont fort maltraitez; mais dans le fonds, il n'y a que de la malignité, sans raison. On prétend dans cette piéce que quand tout ce dont on l'accuse seroit vrai, ce ne seroient que des pecadilles, qui ne mériteroient point tout la vacarme que l'on fait. Il y est traité dès la premiere ligne, de *Jeune homme bien découplé*, jugez de la piéce par cet échantillon." BL Add. Ms. 4281, f. 82, Jacques Bernard to Desmaizeaux, The Hague, April 6, 1700.

254 *Lettre à Mr. Bernard sur l'Apologie de Frideric Auguste Gabillon, Moine défroqué* (Amsterdam: Henri Schelte, 1708), p. 12.

255 Frédéric-Auguste de Gabillon, *La Défense de la divinité de Jésus-Christ, et de la Grace intérieure, par l'Ecriture Sainte contre les paradoxes impies & extravagans de M. Le Clerc et de ses adherans, avec la réfutation de ses notes sur le Nouveau Testament* (The Hague: Printed for the author, 1707). Earlier he had published *La Vérité de la Réligion Réformée prouvé par l'Ecriture Sainte, & par l'antiquité* (The Hague: Abraham Troyel, 1701).

256 UBA, J 17 a, John Chamberlayne to Jean Le Clerc, Westminster, Nov. 25, 1707. In English.

257 UBA, J 17 c, signed statement by the bishop of London, May 7, 1708. In English.

258 UBA, J 17 a, John Chamberlayne to Jean Le Clerc, Westminster, Nov. 25, 1707. In English.

259 Ellipsis in text.

260 UBA, C 112, d'Origny Delaloge to Des Maizeaux, London, May 3, 1708.

261 Ibid.

262 UBA J 17 a, Chamberlayne to Le Clerc, Westminster, Nov. 25, 1707. In English.

263 *Lettre à Mr. Bernard*, p. 5.

264 Chamberlayne was particularly active in this, and the Universiteitsbibliotheek in Amsterdam contains a number of sworn statements and letters about the case. See, in addition to those cited above, UBA, J 17 b, a signed statement by Chamberlayne, dated Westminster, April 20, 1708, stating that Chamberlayne certified the truth of the information Le Clerc had given him "touching the Rogueries & Imposture of one Gabillon, formerly a Monk of the Theatin Order at Paris, now a Pretended Proselyte in Holland." See also UBA, J 17 d, copy of letter from Gabillon to Chamberlayne (The Hague, June 5, 1708), J 17 e, copy of letter from Chamberlayne to Gabillon (Westminster, May 31, 1708), and J 17 e, copy of letter from Chamberlayne to Gabillon (Westminster, June 25, 1708). These documents comprise a nasty correspondence between the two, in which Gabillon protested his innocence of impersonating Le Clerc, while Chamberlayne said the charge was virtually undeniable. Chamberlayne also placed advertisements in the *Post-Boy* (4–6 and 6–7 Oct. 1707) warning of Gabillon's impostures; and Bernard reported on him in the *Nouvelles de la République des Lettres*, Nov. 1707, pp. 579–80, and April 1708, pp. 478–9. Gabillon defended himself weakly in *Apologia, Seu Defensio Frederici Augusti de Gabillon, nefariis Jacobi Bernardi opposita calumniis, quas in suis Litter-*

ariae Reipublicae nuntiis Mensis Novembris 1707. inseruit, Paginâ 579. & 580. (no publ., no date [1708])

265 Le Clerc's propaganda noted that "S'il repassoit la mer, il trouveroit les gens, très disposez à lui donner des coups de bâtons, en place des honneurs, qu'il dit y avoir reçus." *Lettre à Mr. Bernard*, p. 12.

266 Charles Perrault, *Les hommes illustres qui ont paru en France pendant ce siecle* (Paris: Antoine Dezallier, 1697) I, preface.

267 Baillet, *Jugemens des savans* I, pp. 112–13.

268 "Avertissement de l'Editeur" in Pierre Coste, *Histoire de Louis de Bourbon* (3rd ed. 1748).

269 BL Add. Ms. 4287, f. 56, De la Motte to Des Maizeaux, Amsterdam, April 12, 1729.

270 Des Maizeaux, dedication to Robert Walpole, in Bayle, *The Dictionary Historical and Critical of Mr Peter Bayle*, trans. Des Maizeaux, 2nd ed. (London: for J.J. and P. Knapton et al., 1734–8) I.

271 BL Eg. Ms. 2429, f. 37ᵛ, Charles-Louis de Beausobre to [a minister in London], Berlin, Feb. 1, 1742.

272 Camusat, *Histoire critique des journaux* I, pp. 69–70.

273 Ibid.

274 BL Add. Ms. 4281, f. 22, Barbeyrac to Des Maizeaux, Berlin, May 7, 1707.

275 *Journal littéraire* XI, pt. 1 (1720), Art. XII, 164.

276 *Lettres sérieuses et badines*, I, pt. 1 (1729; 2nd ed. 1740), 21.

277 KB, 72 H 18, #30. Maturin Veyssière La Croze to Gisbert Cuper, Berlin, Aug. 23, 1709.

278 He was elected a member in 1701 and remained on the printed list until 1711. See ZAAWD I-III-2, ff. 10, 13. On May 9, 1709, he was ordered to appear before the Society to be told not to publish any more satirical writings (ZAAWD, I-IV-3, Régître général, f. 112, "Cabinet de Sa Majesté," May 9, 1709), and on July 27 his article on the medal and letter from Bignon were censured by the academy (ZAAWD, I-IV-44, ff. 34, 44–5).

279 Charles-Etienne Jordan, *Histoire de la vie et des ouvrages de Mr. La Croze, Avec des remarques de cet auteur sur divers sujets* (Amsterdam: François Changuion, 1741), p. 99. Jordan gives an account of Oelven on pp. 98–102.

280 This was printed by Oelven along with a letter from Bignon in *Lettre Tres-savante & tres-honorable de La Societé Royale des sciences de Paris à Mr. d'Oelven, Capitaine de Cavallerie de Sa Majesté le Roy de Prusse, Illustre de la Societé Royale de Berlin, Auteur des Presens, par son Excellence Mons. L'Abbé Bignon, President, &c.&c. Ecrite à Paris le 4 de Juillet 1709* (Cologne: Ulric Liebpert, 1709). In the copy in the Koninklijke Bibliotheek in The Hague (located at KB 72 H 18, #31), La Croze has underlined Oelven's mistakes in Greek and the laughable "Hymnus de Chiv." The article on the medal was scorned by, among others, Spanheim, who called it "bien absurde" (KB 72 H 18, #57, Schott to La Croze, Nov. 29, 1710). Oelven had actually asked La Croze for help with this work, despite his previous published insults. "Mais cela vient de ce qu'il voudroit que je lui dise qui est Hymnus de chiv . . . Il ne sait pas un mot de Grec & n'a aucune litterature. Je ne puis m'empêcher de rire quand je vois que ni lui ni ses amis n'ont pû déterrer leur prétendu Hymnus de Chiv." (KB, 72 H 18, #30, La Croze to Cuper, Berlin, Aug. 23, 1709.) Cuper responded that "Le *hymnus de Chiv* m'a fait bien rire; et je desire de savoir passionément, si c'est une faute de Mʳ. Oelven, ou si les Academiciens ayent ainsi exprimé, par megarde, ce que je crois difficilement, le nom de *Scymnus Chius*." (KB, 72 H 18, #32, Cuper to La Croze, Oxen, Sept. 7, 1709, draft.)

281 KB, 72 H 18, #30, La Croze to

Cuper, Berlin, Aug. 23, 1709.

282 Neu BPU, Ms. 1274/4, f. 13, Charles-Etienne Jordan to Louis Bourguet, Prenzlau, July 1, 1730.

283 KB, 72 H 18 #57, La Croze to Cuper, Nov. 26, 1710. La Croze learned this from a letter from Spanheim to his colleague at the Bibliothèque du Roy in Berlin, Schott.

284 KB, 72 H 18, #43, La Croze to Cuper, Berlin, May 12, 1710.

285 BL Add. Ms. 4286, ff. 210–11, De la Motte to Des Maizeaux, Amsterdam, June 30, 1716. This letter is about the collection *Histoire de Mr. Bayle et de ses ouvrages* and indicates that Des Maizeaux was not the author of the whole collection, as some have claimed.

286 BL Add. Ms. 4226, f. 315, incomplete draft of pamphlet headed "Lettre à Mr. . . ." dated London, July 22, 1729.

287 As we noted earlier, De la Motte made the same judgment of Des Maizeaux for having the poor grace to attack anonymously one of his own friends, Pierre Coste; Coste behaved properly in ignoring these attacks. BL Add. Ms. 4286, f. 249, De la Motte to Des Maizeaux, Sept. 2, 1723, postscript.

288 Ibid., f. 317. Des Maizeaux deleted this passage in his draft.

289 *Mémoires de littérature* II, pt. 2 (1717), 287–8, "Lettre à Messieurs Le Clerc & Bernard."

290 This point was made about Marchand in Berkvens-Stevelinck, "Cabale," p. 104, and about Des Maizeaux by Broome in his dissertation, pp. 12–13.

291 Recounted in Prosper Marchand, *Dictionnaire historique, ou Memoires critiques et litteraires, concernant la vie et les ouvrages de divers personnages distingués, particulierement dans la République des Lettres,* ed. J.-N.-S. Allamand (The Hague: Pierre De Hondt, 1758) I, "Avertissement de l'Editeur." Marchand mentions his collection of biographies in DSB,

Nachlass Formey, Marchand to Formey, f. 4, Feb. 6, 1741.

292 UBL, March. 2, Marchand to Mathieu Marais, n.d., draft.

293 BL Add. Ms. 4281, f. 25, Barbeyrac to Des Maizeaux, Lausanne, May 25, 1714.

294 "Remarques Critiques sur l'Edition des LETTRES DE MR. BAYLE, faite à Rotterdam en 1714. Où l'on donne un Enchantillon des faussetez, des bévûës, & des impertinences, qui se trouvent dans les Notes du Sieur MARCHAND," in *Histoire de Mr. Bayle & de ses ouvrages,* p. 387.

295 BL Add. Ms. 4281, f. 28ᵛ, Barbeyrac to Des Maizeaux, Lausanne, Feb. 15, 1715.

296 *Mémoires de littérature* II, pt. 2 (1717), 248–9, "Lettre à Messieurs Le Clerc & Bernard."

297 "Factum des Amis de Mr. Bayle" in *Histoire de Mr. Bayle et de ses ouvrages,* p. 552.

298 "Remarques critiques sur l'Edition des Lettres . . ." in *Histoire de Mr. Bayle et de ses ouvrages,* p. 421.

299 "Factum des Amis de Mr. Bayle," in *Histoire de Mr. Bayle et de ses ouvrages,* p. 576.

300 BL Add. Ms. 4282, f. 110, Le Clerc to Des Maizeaux, Amsterdam, Dec. 31, 1714.

301 Gen. BPU, Ms. fr. 484, f. 166, Barbeyrac to Turrettini, Lausanne, Oct. 4, 1714. He made similar remarks in discussing the possibility of a collection of the letters of Baux. "Je suis bien aise que Mʳ. Lenfant pense à ramasser tout ce qu'il pourra trouver des Ecrits de Mʳ. Baux, pour en faire un volume d'Oeuvres posthumes. C'étoit assûrement un très-beau génie. Mais à l'égard de ses lettres, il y aura beaucoup de choix à faire, si l'on ne veut pas chagriner bien des personnes vivantes qui s'y trouveront intéressées. Mʳ. Lenfant s'est déja brouillé avec Mʳ. Le Clerc, au sujet des Lettres de Mʳ. Bayle, qu'il a fournies. Il ne servira pas de beaucoup, d'effacer les noms: les choses mêmes feront assez connoître

les personnes dont il s'agira, dans les lieux où l'on sera instruit des faits dont il sera parlé. Et il se trouvera des gens, qui, comme *Marchand*, se feront un plaisir de tirer le rideau." Gen. BPU, Ms. fr. 484, ff. 182^v–183, Barbeyrac to Turrettini, Lausanne, July 21, 1715.

302　Bibl SHPF, Ms. 295, #85, Barbeyrac to De la Motte, Groningen, Aug. 19, 1740.

4　Of Two Minds

1　Jacques Bernard had conducted a dispute with Aymon over an astronomical point in 1701. He found Aymon's response to him "pitoiable," but planned to answer it with the help of the French scholar Delaissement. BN Ms. fr. 19211, f. 163, Jacques Bernard to Delaissement, The Hague, Nov. 4, 1701. Copy.

2　BN Ms. fr. nouv. acq. 1216, f. 60, Jacques Basnage to the Chevalier de Croissy, Sept. 12, 1707.

3　See Haag, *La France protestante*, 2nd ed. I (1877), col. 617. The Haags' account of Aymon's life is deficient at its end; they state (col. 622) that he died in about 1720 "sans qu'on ait aucun renseignement sur la manière dont se termina cette carrière véreuse." Actually Aymon was still alive and writing in 1730 at least; he contributed to the *Bibliothèque raisonnée* (participating in the fracas over Jacques Saurin's *Discours sur le mensonge officieux*) and was one of the many people insulted by François Bruys in his journal the *Critique désintéressée* (I [Jan.–March 1730], 143–5, and II [April–June 1730], iv) and *Mémoires historiques, critiques, et littéraires*, ed. L.P. Joly (Paris: Jean-Thomas Hérissant, 1751), I, pp. 168–9.

4　BN Ms. fr. nouv. acq. 1216, f. 115^v, Hennequin, burgermeester of Rotterdam, to ? [Colbert de Torcy?], Rotterdam, Oct. 10, 1707. This information came from the Grand

Pensionary, Anthonie Heinsius, who gave it to the Abbé de Louvois.

5　According the *libraire* Reinier Leers, Aymon had actually bought the book without having the money to pay for it, evidently expecting to make a sale to the Bibliothèque. "Depuis ma derniere, le Ministre de la Haye a dit à un de mes amis qu'il vous a ecrit sur le sujet de l'Herbarius vivus, il s'en trouve embarrassé, ne sacchant où trouver de l'argent, je croi qu'on le rachetteroit à tres bon marché." Reinier Leers to Nicolas Clément, Rotterdam, Dec. 17, 1705, printed in Lankhorst, *Leers*, p. 253.

6　BN Ms. fr. nouv. acq. 1216, ff. 2–3, Jean Aymon to Nicolas Clément, The Hague, Nov. 25, 1705.

7　BN Ms. fr. nouv. acq. 1216, f. 5^v, Aymon to Clément, The Hague, Nov. 30, 1705.

8　BN Ms. fr. nouv. acq. 1216, ff. 2–3, Aymon to Clément, The Hague, Nov. 25, 1705.

9　Ibid., f. 4.

10　Ibid.

11　BN Ms. fr. nouv. acq. 1216, ff. 15–16, "Mémoire du Sr Aymon," Paris, April 20, 1706.

12　BN Ms. fr. nouv. acq. 1216, f. 5^v, Aymon to Clément, The Hague, Nov. 30, 1705.

13　BN Ms. fr. nouv. acq. 1216, ff. 8–7^v, Aymon to Clément, The Hague, Dec. 31, 1705.

14　BN Ms. fr. nouv. acq. 1216, "Memoire du Sr Aymon . . ." Paris, April 20, 1706.

15　Antoine Arnauld, *La Perpetuité de la foy de l'Eglise Catholique touchant l'Eucharistie, défendue contre les Livres du Sieur Claude, Ministre de Charenton*, new ed., 4 vols. (Paris: La Veuve Charles Saureux, 1704).

16　BN Ms. fr. nouv. acq. 1216, f. 7^v, Aymon to Clément, The Hague, Dec. 31, 1705.

17　Ibid., ff. 7–8.

18　BN Ms. fr. nouv. acq. 1216, f. 9, Aymon to Clément, The Hague, Feb. 4, 1706.

19 BN Ms. fr. nouv. acq. 1216, f. 12, Aymon to Clément, The Hague, Feb. 11, 1706.

20 BN Ms. fr. nouv. acq. 1216, f. 9ᵛ, Aymon to Clément, The Hague, Feb. 4, 1706.

21 BN Ms. fr. nouv. acq. 1216, f. 10, Aymon to Clément, The Hague, Feb. 25, 1706.

22 BN Ms. fr. nouv. acq. 1216, f. 86ᵛ, "Lettre de M. Clement Garde de la Bibliotheque du Roy à un de ses Amis à la Haye . . ."

23 Barthélemy Hauréau, *Singularités historiques et littéraires* (Paris: Michel Lévy Frères, 1861), pp. 294–6. As Hauréau does not cite any sources for his rather detailed account of these interviews, I cannot be sure of its authenticity. However, he is perfectly accurate in other aspects of his account for which I have seen the manuscript sources.

24 BN Ms. fr. nouv. acq. 1216, f. 49, "Réponse à la lettre du Sʳ Aymon au sujet des vols qu'il a faits à Paris en l'année 1706," Sept. 12, 1707; ibid., f. 56, "Certificat de Mʳˢ. les Superieurs du Seminaire des missions etrangeres," Oct. 19, 1707.

25 BN Ms. fr. nouv. acq. 1216, f. 56, "Certificat de Mʳˢ. les Superieurs du Seminaire des missions etrangeres."

26 BN Ms. fr. nouv. acq. 1216, f. 16ᵛ, "Mémoire du Sʳ Aymon," Paris, April 20, 1706.

27 BN Ms. fr. nouv. acq. 1216, ff. 13–14, Aymon to the Abbé Renaudot, Seminaire des Missions étrangères, Sept. 11, 1706.

28 BN Ms. fr. nouv. acq. 1216, f. 16, "Mémoire du Sʳ Aymon . . ." Paris, April 20, 1706.

29 BN Ms. fr. nouv. acq. 1216, f. 87, "Lettre du M. Clement Garde de la Bibliotheque du Roy à un de ses Amis à la Haye . . ."

30 BN Ms. fr. nouv. acq. 1216, ff. 19–20, "Mémoire du Sʳ Aymon, touchant diverses affaires politiques, et militaires . . ." Paris, April 20, 1706.

31 BN Ms. fr. nouv. acq. 1216, f. 86ᵛ, "Lettre de M. Clement Garde de la Bibliotheque du Roy à un de ses Amis à la Haye . . ."

32 Ibid., f. 88.

33 Ibid., f. 86ᵛ.

34 He managed to leave France by addressing himself to Chamillard, Secretary of State, for a passport; see BN Ms. fr. nouv. acq. 1216, f. 49ᵛ, "Réponse à la lettre du Sʳ Aymon," Sept. 12, 1707. Aymon reappeared in The Hague eight months after his disappearance, according to Jacques Basnage: BN Ms. fr. nouv. acq. 1216, f. 60, Basnage to the Chevalier de Croissy, Sept. 12, 1707, copy.

35 UBL, March. 2, "Lettre de M.C. Directeur de la Bibliotheque du Roy, à un des ses Amis à la Haye," Nov. 16, 1707, copy; BN Ms. fr. nouv. acq. 1216, f. 115ᵛ, Hennequin to ? [Colbert de Torcy?], Rotterdam, Oct. 10, 1707.

36 The other manuscripts Aymon stole were a volume of the Epistles of St. Paul on vellum, a Latin Gospels on vellum, another Latin Gospels on vellum in Saxon characters, the letters of Visconti, papal nuncio at the council of Trent, the letters of Prospero Santa Croce, papal nuncio in France from 1561, a register of taxes of the Roman chancellery, "Dialogo politico sopra i tumulti di Francia dell'anno 1632 e altri discorsi," and two Chinese manuscripts. The sixteenth-century materials were useful to the Huguenots because they could be employed in the historical arguments with Catholics about the conduct of the Protestant party during the religious wars. Because of the disorder of the Bibliothèque du Roi, the theft of the manuscripts was not realized until after Aymon had begun bragging about it in The Hague. Clément also discovered that someone (who later turned out to be Aymon as well) had torn or cut pages out of several valuable manuscripts, most notably 35 pages from a Greek and Latin version of Paul's Epistles written in golden

letters and thought to be from the first centuries of the Christian era. See Léopold Delisle, *Le Cabinet des manuscrits de la Bibliothèque Impériale* (Paris: Imprimerie Impériale, 1868), pp. 329–32; Hauréau, pp. 299–300, 313–14; and BN Ms. fr. nouv. acq. 1216, f. 34ᵛ. Aymon was also said to have stolen an Arabic manuscript of the Koran from a *libraire* in the Hague on his departure (BN Ms. fr. nouv. acq. 1216, f. 31, "Memoire pour s'informer," [Netherlands], Mar. 10, 1707, and BN Ms. fr. nouv. acq. 1216, f. 32, Guillaume de Voys to Nicolas Clément, The Hague, July 20, 1707), which he later sold to the same person who bought one page of the Epistles of Paul and one page from the bible of Charles the Bold (Delisle, pp. 331–2).

37 BN Ms. fr. nouv. acq. 1216, ff. 50ᵛ–51, "Extrait des Registres de la Bibliothèque du Roy."

38 BN Ms. fr. nouv. acq. 1216, f. 58, Reinier Leers to Clément, Rotterdam, Sept. 13, 1707.

39 Jean Aymon, *Lettre du Sieur Aymon, Ministre du Saint Evangile, & Docteur aux Droits, à Monsieur N***. Professeur en Théologie, dans l'Université Réformée de N**** (The Hague: Charles Delo, 1707), pp. 3–4.

40 BN Ms. fr. nouv. acq. 1216, f. 73, copy of a certificate signed by Fr. Arnoul de Loo, Prieur de l'Abbaye de St.-Germain-des-Prés, Oct. 6, 1707.

41 Delisle, I, 330, n. 1; BN Ms. fr. nouv. acq. 1216, ff. 50ᵛ–51, "Extrait des Registres de la Bibliothèque du Roi." Several of the other stolen manuscripts *were* stamped with the library's seal.

42 UBL, March. 2, Clément to Leers, Paris, Oct. 3, 1707.

43 UBL, March. 2, Clément to Leers, Paris, Oct. 17, 1707.

44 BN Ms. fr. nouv. acq. 1216, f. 84, "Lettre de M. Clément Garde de la Bibliotheque du Roy à un de ses Amis à la Haye . . ."

45 BN Ms. fr. nouv. acq. 1216, f. 171,

Clément to Leers, March 8, 1708, copy; ibid., f. 50, "Réponse à la lettre du Sʳ Aymon au sujet des vols qu'il a faits à Paris en l'année 1706"; ibid., f. 158ᵛ, "Lettre de M.C. Directeur de la Bibliotheque du Roy, à un de ses Amis à la Haye . . ."

46 UBL, March. 2, Clément to Leers, Paris, Nov. 7, 1707.

47 BN Ms. fr. nouv. acq. 1216, f. 171, Clément to Leers, Mar. 8, 1708, copy.

48 BN Ms. fr. nouv. acq. 1216, f. 31, "Memoire pour s'informer," Mar. 10, 1707.

49 *Nouvelles de la République des Lettres*, August 1708, Art. V, 217, *extrait* of Aymon, *Monumens authentiques de la Religion des Grecs, et de la fausseté de plusieurs Confessions de Foi des Chrétiens Orientaux; produites contre les Théologiens Réformez, par les Prélats de France & les Docteurs de Port-Roial, dans leur fameux Ouvrage de la Perpetuité de la Foi de l'Eglise Catholique* (The Hague: Charles Delo, 1708); *Journal littéraire* VIII, pt. 1 (1716), 238, Art. XV, entry in "Livres nouveaux" about Aymon, *Maximes politiques du Pape Paul III*.

50 BN Ms. fr. nouv. acq. 1216, f. 46, Leers to Clément, Sept. 12, 1707.

51 Jean-Louis de Lorme to the Abbé Bignon, Dec. 15, 1707, printed in van Eeghen, *De Amsterdamse Boekhandel* I, p. 233. Leers also had a special relationship with Clément, who used his *librairie* as a major source of books for the Bibliothèque du Roi. See Marianne Grivel, "Le Cabinet du Roi," *Revue de la Bibliothèque Nationale* no. 18 (Winter 1985), 53; Leers to Clément, Rotterdam, Dec. 30, 1697, printed in Lankhorst, *Leers*, p. 245; UBL, March. 2, Clément to Leers, Paris, Nov. 24, 1707. Perhaps just as important, Leers had a business connection with Antoine Arnauld; see Lankhorst, *Leers*, pp. 58–9.

52 Charles Le Vier, "Eloge historique," in Jacques Basnage, *Annales des Prov-*

inces-Unies, depuis les Negociations pour la Paix de Munster (The Hague: Charles Le Vier, 1719) II, p. vii.

53 BN Ms. fr. nouv. acq. 1216, f. 145, Jacques Basnage to Clément, Nov. 7, [1707].

54 BN Ms. fr. nouv. acq. 1216, f. 148, Basnage to the Abbé de Beaumont, quoted in Beaumont to Clément, Rouen, Nov. 13, 1707; ibid., f. 166ᵛ, Basnage to Clément, Nov. 24, 1707, copy.

55 BN Ms. fr. nouv. acq. 1216, f. 148ᵛ, Beaumont to Clément, Rouen, Nov. 13, 1707.

56 KB, 72 H D 58, f. 88ᵛ, Basnage to Cuper, Oct. 8, 1707.

57 KB, 72 D 58, ff. 143ᵛ–144, Cuper to Basnage, Deventer, Nov. 26, 1707; KB, 72 H 18, #35, Cuper to Maturin Veyssière La Croze, Deventer, Nov. 1, 1709.

58 KB 72 D 58, f. 164, Cuper to Basnage, Deventer, April 20, 1708, draft.

59 KB, 72 H 18, #38, Cuper to La Croze, Deventer, Jan. 14, 1710; KB, 72 H 18, #19, Cuper to La Croze, Deventer, June 1, 1709.

60 BN Ms. fr. nouv. acq. 1216, f. 172, Basnage to Clément, March 22, [1708].

61 BL Add. Ms. 4281, f. 54, Basnage to Des Maizeaux, Oct. 28, 1709.

62 BW, A 63, nineteenth-century copy of a resolution of the Gecommitteerde Raden van Holland en West-Friesland, March 28, 1709.

63 Delisle, I, p. 332; BN Ms. fr. nouv. acq. 1216, ff. 187–8, "Memoire sur la restitution de 35 feuilles enlevées par Aymon du MS. des Epitres de Sᵗ Paul cotté n°. 2245 faite en 1729 a la Bibliotheque du Roy par Mylord Oxford et Mortimer," Sept. 1729. On the purchase of manuscripts from Aymon, see C.E. Wright and Ruth C. Wright, eds., *The Diary of Humfrey Wanley 1715–1726* (London: The Bibliographical Society, 1966), I, pp. 2, 6; 2 and 21 March 1715.

64 KB, 72 H 18, #13, Cuper to La Croze, Deventer, Nov. 19, 1708, draft.

65 Aymon, *Lettre à Monsieur N***, p. 5.

66 BN Ms. fr. nouv. acq. 1216, f. 48, "Réponse à la lettre du Sʳ Aymon au sujet des vols qu'il a faits à Paris en l'année 1706," Sept. 12, 1707.

67 BN Ms. fr. nouv. acq. 1216, f. 171, Clément to Leers, Mar. 8, 1708, copy; BN Ms. fr. nouv. acq. 1216, f. 158ᵛ, "Lettre de M.C. Directeur de la Bibliotheque du Roy, à un de ses Amis à la Haye . . ."

68 BN Ms. fr. nouv. acq. 1216, f. 139, Basnage to de Courson, intendant of Normandy, copied in a letter from Beaumont to Clément, Rouen, Oct. 21, 1707.

69 KB, 72 H 18, #39, La Croze to Cuper, Berlin, Jan. 28, 1710.

70 KB, 72 H 18, #26, La Croze to Cuper, Berlin, Aug. 14, 1709.

71 *Journal littéraire* VI, pt. 1 (1715; 1732 Gosse & Neaulme edition), Art. IX, 164, extrait of *Temoignage de la Verité dans l'Eglise* (1714).

72 *Bibliothèque raisonnée* I (1728), viii, "Avertissment des Libraires."

73 BL Eg. Ms. 2127, f. 6, Henri Justel to Sir Robert Southwell, July 7, 1684.

74 Des Maizeaux, *Life of Mr. Bayle* (1708), p. 215.

75 *Nouvelles de la République des Lettres* I (March 1684), preface.

76 *Histoire critique de la République des Lettres* VIII (1715), Art. VI, 217–18n. The *Histoire critique* had reacted similarly in 1714 to an article it published defending Boileau against Le Clerc. An "Eclaircissement" following the article addressed its author: "Vous blâmez Mr. *le Clerc* d'avoir trouvé mauvais qu'on l'ait représenté comme *un homme fort décrié sur la Religion*, parce, dites-vous, que c'est *un fait connu de tout le Monde*. Mais si cela est, quel besoin y avoit-il d'en grossir vôtre *Memoire?*" (*Histoire critique* VI [1714], 96.).

77 UBL, March. 1, Sallengre to the other authors of the *Journal littéraire*, Paris, April 16, 1714.

78 *Works of the Learned* (Oct. 1691), preface.

79 *Bibliothèque angloise* I (1716; 2nd ed. 1729), "Avertissement"; *Bibliothèque britannique* I, pt. 1 (April–June 1733), "Avertissement."

80 *Bibliothèque italique* I (Jan.–April 1728), xix–xx, "Preface."

81 *Journal de Trévoux* I (Jan.–Feb. 1710), Preface. It is true that the *Journal des sçavans*, after initially promising neutrality under Denis de Sallo, became more partisan under the editorship of the Abbé de la Rocque in 1675. He wrote of the *Nouvelles de la République des Lettres*, "L'Autheur de ces Nouvelles ne trouvera mauvais que nous soyions un peu plus severes sur tout ce qui regardera la Religion. Il croit faire son devoir en parlant, comme il fait, sur ces matieres, & nous manquerions au nostre si nous les laissions passer de la sorte. Les libertins & les profanes qui se mettent en peine de la Religion, y trouveront à redire: mais les gens sages loüeront nostre procedé." *Journal des sçavans* (new ed. 1724), "Au Lecteur." Camusat wrote of De la Roque that "on ne doit pas être surpris du zèle amer de cet Abbé; c'étoit alors la saison de crier contre le Protestantisme; c'étoit la meilleure maniere de faire sa cour." (Camusat, *Histoire critique des journaux* II, p. 6). But the *Journal des sçavans* was never known as fiercely partisan in the way the *Journal de Trévoux* was.

82 UBL, March. 2, Passionei to Basnage, Lucerne, June 23, 1723; Bibl SHPF, Ms. 192/2, f. 19, Basnage to the Chevalier de Frenelles, The Hague, Dec. 22, 1717, copy; Bibl SHPF, Ms. 192/2, ff. 22–3, Basnage to the Chevalier de Frenelles, The Hague, Dec. 30, 1717, copy; Bibl SHPF, Ms. 784¹, information about David Durand by his nephew, David Henri Durand, 1804. (The younger Durand reported that the manuscripts of this correspondence were burned when the nephew's house was burned, with sixty others, in "le grand incendie de Corn-hill" of November 1765.)

83 Emile G. Léonard, *Histoire générale du Protestantisme* II (Paris: Presses Universitaires de France, 1961), pp. 333–5.

84 Haag, *La France protestante*, 1st ed. VI (Paris: Joël Cherbuliez, 1856), pp. 115–16; Toinard to Locke, Paris, Oct. 4, 1681, in De Beer, *Correspondence of Locke* II, p. 440–1. According to Damaris Cudworth, Justel's home in Paris had been "the general Rendezvous of men of Letters" (UBA J 57 a, Damaris Cudworth, Lady Masham, to Jean Le Clerc, Oates, Jan. 12, 1704; letter in English).

85 BL Eg. Ms. 2127, f. 19ᵛ, Henri Justel to Sir Robert Southwell, Dec. 16, 1684. Justel said something similar in 1682: Bibl SHPF, Ms. 811, #56, Justel to Findekeller, London, fall 1682.

86 UBA, G 67 a, Pierre-Daniel Huet to Etienne Morin, Paris, Dec. 27, 1685.

87 KB, 72 H 19/I, #15, La Croze to Cuper, Berlin, Oct. 26, 1711: "Pendant que j'étois à Paris je lui [the Père Nourri] ai corrigé dans son *Apparat* je ne sai combien de fautes . . . & il rampoit devant moi, pour m'engager à passer la lime sur tout ce qu'il donnoit au public; quoique pendant le tems que je lui rendois ces services-là, il travaillât à me nuire. Je vous dira, Monsieur, mais en secret, qu'il est une des principales causes de ma sortie de France; car je ne suis point sorti pour la Religion; mais me trouvant à Basle d'où je voulois passer en Italie, un fort honnête homme me gagna. Je suis bien éloigné de m'en repentir, quoique selon les hommes j'y aie tout perdu. J'espere que selon Dieu j'y aurai gagné la vie éternelle."

88 KB 72 H 18, #1, La Croze to Cuper, Berlin, Mar. 30, 1708; KB 72

89 UBA, G 67 d, Pierre-Daniel Huet to Etienne Morin, Paris, Feb. 13, 1692.

H 18, #43, La Croze to Cuper, May 12, 1710. La Croze made a similar remark in KB 72 H 18, #39, La Croze to Cuper, Berlin, Jan. 28, 1710, and Leibniz adopted a "mauvaise opinion" of a book simply because it criticized Montfaucon (ZAAWD, Nachlass Leibniz Nr. 3, f. 65ᵛ, Leibniz to La Croze, Hanover, Feb. 18, 1708).

89 UBA, G 67 d, Pierre-Daniel Huet to Etienne Morin, Paris, Feb. 13, 1692.

90 Jordan, *Voyage littéraire*, p. 33.

91 KB, 72 H 13/I, series of letters from Godefroy Clermont to Cuper and Cuper to Clermont, spring/summer 1714.

92 BL Add. Ms. 4282, f. 270, Coste to Des Maizeaux, Paris, April 30, 1713.

93 BL Add. Ms. 4286, f. 194, De la Motte to Des Maizeaux, Amsterdam, Dec. 19, 1713; Gen BPU, Ms. fr. 484, f. 159, Barbeyrac to Turrettini, Lausanne, Dec. 26, 1713.

94 Bibl SHPF, Ms. 295, #34, Coste to De la Motte, n.d. [after 1736].

95 Gen BPU, Ms. fr. 484, f. 159, Barbeyrac to Turrettini, Lausanne, Dec. 26, 1713.

96 BL Add. Ms. 4286, f. 147, De la Motte to Des Maizeaux, Amsterdam, July 28, 1711.

97 Lorraine Daston, "The Ideal and Reality of the Republic of Letters in the Enlightenment," *Science in Context* 4, no. 2 (1991), 377–8.

98 The *nouvelles littéraires* from Paris in the Protestant-run *Journal littéraire* III, pt. 1 (Jan.–Feb. 1714), 232, brag about Ludolph Kuster's conversion to Catholicism: "M. *Kuster*, dont notre Parti a fait aquisition depuis peu . . ."

99 BL Add. Ms. 4281, f. 363, Claude Buffier to Des Maizeaux, Paris, May 10, 1710; UBL March. 2, Thierry Ruinart to Guillaume Bessin, Jan. 13, 1709; UBL March. 2, *mémoire* on Basnage's prospectus, in folder "Anonyme ad J. Basnage." See also (in same folder) "remarques du P Lamy de L'oratoire"; anonymous let-

ter of May 29, 1693, from Paris; anonymous letter of Dec. 11, 1709; see also UBL March. 2, Passionei to Basnage, Oct. 7, 1722.

100 Maarten Ultee, "Res publica litteraria and War, 1680–1715," in Sebastian Neumeister and Conrad Wiedemann, eds., *Res Publica Litteraria: Die Institutionen der Gelehrsamkeit in die frühen Neuzeit* (Wiesbaden: Otto Harrassowitz, 1987) II, pp. 539–41, and Ultee, "Learned Correspondence," 107.

101 Cuper, for example, complained to Nicaise that the Dutch were not receiving French books in wartime (Cuper to Nicaise, May 28, 1694, in Beyer, *Lettres de Cuper*, p. 434), and Bayle reported that the *Bibliothèque universelle*, reduced to a small size, was only continuing "dans l'esperance d'un meilleur tems" (BN Ms. fr. 9359, f. 370, Bayle to Nicaise, Rotterdam, April 21, 1692). Jean Cornand de la Crose made similar complaints in *Works of the Learned* (Aug. 1691), "To the Reader."

102 *Journal littéraire* VI, pt. 1 (1715; 1732 Gosse and Neaulme ed.), 251, nouvelles littéraires, The Hague.

103 Cuper to Nicaise, July 26, 1695, in Beyer, *Lettres de Cuper*, p. 438.

104 BL Sloane Ms. 4041, f. 315ᵛ, Geoffroy to Sloane, Paris, April 18, 1709.

105 UBA, C 108 f, Nicaise to Le Clerc, Dijon, June 23, no year.

106 BN Ms. fr. 19211, f. 179, Bernard to Delaissement, The Hague, Feb. 8, 1703; BL Add. Ms. 4281, ff. 161–2, Bignon to Des Maizeaux, April 27, 1708.

107 BL Add. Ms. 4281, f. 164ᵛ, Bignon to Des Maizeaux, Paris, June 11, 1708.

108 Such cabinets were first formed in the late Middle Ages and the Renaissance, but the seventeenth century was the time of their greatest glory. Tradescant's Ark in Lambeth later became the core of the Ashmolean Museum, while Hans Sloane's cabi-

net, which (according to a later trustee, Horace Walpole), contained "hippopotamuses, sharks with one ear, and spiders as big as geese," was the initial foundation of the British Museum. J. Mordaunt Crook, *The British Museum* (London: Allen Lane, The Penguin Press, 1972), pp. 21–3, 42–4, 46, 48; Edward Miller, *That Noble Cabinet: A History of the British Museum* (Athens, Ohio: Ohio University Press, 1974), pp. 24, 37–8. On museums, see particularly Krzysztof Pomian, *Collectors and Curiosities: Paris and Venice, 1500–1800*, trans. Elizabeth Wiles-Portier (Cambridge: Polity Press, 1990); Paula Findlen, "The Museum: Its Classical Etymology and Renaissance Genealogy," *Journal of the History of Collections* I, no. 1 (1989) 59–78.

109   KB 69 B 8, "Description de la Chambre des Raretez de Nicolas Chevalier avec les noms des amateurs qui mont honnore de leur presence qui ont souscrit chaqu'nt un dictont ou devise a la gloire de la curiositez amsterdam 1694." An abbreviated printed description of the chamber appears in Nicolas Chevalier, *Remarques sur la pièce antique de bronze, trouvée depuis quelques années aux environs de Rome, & proposée ensuite aux Curieux de l'Antiquité, pour tâcher d'en découvrir l'usage: Avec une Description de la Chambre des Raretez de l'Auteur* (Amsterdam: Abraham Wolfgang, 1694), pp. 104–28. See also G. van Klaveren, "Nicolaas Chevalier en zijn 'Chambre de Raretez,'" *Jaarboekje van "Oud-Utrecht"* (1940), 141–57.

110   On Chevalier, see Haag, *La France protestante*, 2nd ed. IV (Paris: Librairie Fischbacher, 1884), cols. 315–16. Chevalier mentions being a student in Sedan in KB 75 J 52, "Les Voyages de Nicolas Chevalier faitz en Hollande Angleterre, et France," 1685.

111   KB 72 G 19, Nicolas Chevalier to Cuper, Amsterdam, Feb. 18, 1695; KB 72 G 19, Cuper to Chevalier, Deventer, Sept. 24, 1694, draft; KB 72 G 19, Cuper to Chevalier, Deventer, July 13, 1708.

112   KB 72 G 19, Cuper to Chevalier, Deventer, Sept. 24, 1694, draft; KB 72 G 19, Chevalier to Cuper, Utrecht, Oct. 11, 1707; BL Sloane Ms. 4053, f. 191, Bruzen La Martinière to Sloane, The Hague, April 1, 1734.

113   KB 69 B 8, "Description de la Chambre des Raretez," ff. 41ff. The visitors' book included engraved portraits and devices, as well as remarks, of some of the visitors. Another indication that such chambers were considered scholarly is Leibniz' project from 1675 to put together an exhibition which, in his words, "would include Magic Lanterns, . . . flights, artificial meteors, all sorts of optical wonders, . . . fireworks, water fountains, strangely shaped boats; Mandragoras and other rare plants. Unusual and rare animals. A Royal Circle. Figures of animals. Royal Machine with races between artificial horses. Prize for Archery. Exhibitions of battle scenes. . . . Extraordinary rope-dancer. Perilous leap. Show how a child can raise a heavy weight with a thread," and so on. Despite its circus-like nature, Leibniz called this a project for "a New Sort of Exhibition (or rather, an Academy of Sciences . . .)." See Philip P. Wiener, "Leibniz's Project of a Public Exhibition of Scientific Inventions," *Journal of the History of Ideas* I (1940), 232–40.

114   Ibid., f. 59ᵛ, P. D'arennsy [?], Sept. 4, 1694.

115   Ibid., f. 53, Langey, July 7, 1694.

116   Ibid., f. 53ᵛ, entry of D'Uzy [?], Amsterdam, Aug. 9, 1694.

117   KB 75 J 52, "Les Voyages de Nicolas Chevalier," 1685, ff. 37ᵛ–40.

118   KB 69 B 8, "Description," ff. 12, 12ᵛ, 13, 14, 16ᵛ, 20, 20ᵛ, 21.

119   Van Klaveren makes the same observation in "Nicolaas Chevalier," 150, although he seems not to have known about the manuscript de-

scription now in the Koninklijke Bibliotheek.

120 KB 69 B 8, ff. 22ᵛ–23.

121 Ibid., f. 25ᵛ. The book was the *Histoire de Guillaume III. Roy d'Angleterre, d'Ecosse, de France, d'Irlande, Prince d'Orange.*

122 KB 69 B 8, f. 25ᵛ.

123 Ibid., ff. 25ᵛ–26ᵛ.

124 Ibid., f. 26ᵛ.

125 On this subject see also Bots, *Republiek der Letteren*, pp. 18–20.

126 Baillet, *Jugemens des savans* I, pp. 122–3. Baillet criticizes Aristotle's view that people from cold countries are naturally courageous and robust, but not very intellectual or able in the arts: "où est la solidité de cette pensée?" (p. 123)

127 Ibid., pp. 136ff.

128 "Il faut du moins que vous confessiez, dit Ariste, que le bel esprit est de tous les païs & de toutes les nations; c'est-à-dire, que comme il y a eû autrefois de beaux esprits Grecs & Romains, il y en a maintenant de François, d'Italiens, d'Espagnols, d'Anglois, d'Allemands mesme & de Moscovites. C'est une chose singuliere qu'un bel esprit Allemand ou Moscovite, reprit Eugene; & s'il y en a quelques-uns au monde, ils sont de la nature de ces esprits qui n'apparoissent jamais sans causer de l'étonnement. Le Cardinal du Perron disoit un jour, en parlant du Jesuite Gretser: *Il a bien de l'esprit pour un Allemand*; comme si c'eust esté un prodige qu'un Allemand fort spirituel. . . . [L]e bel esprit tel que vous l'avez défini, ne s'accommode point du tout avec les temperaments grossiers & les corps massifs des peuples du Nord. . . . [E]nfin on n'y connoist point nostre bel esprit, ni cette belle science dont la politesse fait la principale partie." Dominique Bouhours, *Les Entretiens d'Ariste et d'Eugene*, new ed. (Paris: Gabriel Huart, 1691), pp. 321–2, "Le Bel Esprit."

129 Ibid., pp. 145–8.

130 See, e.g., *Bibliothèque italique* III

(Sept.–Dec. 1728), 215–18, and *Bibliothèque raisonnée* I (1728), ix–x, "Avertissement des Libraires."

131 *Chevraeana* II, p. 12, quoted in Sallengre, *Mémoires de Littérature* I, pt. 1 (1715), 185. Lorraine Daston points out that Leibniz' proposal for an academy in Moscow suggested that only eventually might the participation of "even the Russians themselves" be possible (Daston, "Ideal and Reality," p. 374).

132 In BL Add. Ms. 4287, f. 8, De la Motte to Des Maizeaux, Amsterdam, Oct. 14, 1727, the corrector says that "Je ne connois point de bons Ecrivains de cette Nation [Germany] par raport au style"; the *Histoire critique de la République des Lettres* VII (1714), 416, defends the Germans against "un préjugé autant injuste que mal fondé, on fait peu de cas des Livres imprimez en Allemagne, pour ne pas dire des Auteurs *Allemans*"; and the *Journal litéraire* I, pt. 2 (July–Aug. 1713, 2nd ed. 1716), 290, praises Heiss' *Histoire de l'Empire* by saying that, although Heiss was born German, "on ne le diroit pas à en juger par son stile." Bernard's comment is in BL Add. Ms. 4281, f. 102ᵛ, Bernard to Des Maizeaux, The Hague, April 5, 1701: "Vous étes surpris, que je ne dis rien des livres Flamands; c'est qu'outre qu'il s'en imprime très-peu je ne dirai pas de bons, mais de médiocres, je ne sai pas trop bien ce qui se passe sur ce sujet."

133 *Bibliothèque italique* IV (Jan.–April 1729), 294, Art. XV, "Nouvelles Littéraires." A number of articles in the *Bibliothèque italique* were defensive about Italy, such as pieces in vol. III (Sept.–Dec. 1728), Art. IX, and vol. IX (Sept.–Dec. 1730), Art. IV. The preface to volume I of the *Bibliothèque germanique* defended the contribution of printing to the learned world, and other journals tried similar tactics.

134 Bibl SHPF, Ms. 295, #106, Le Courayer to De la Motte, England,

n.d. [1731]. The *Journal littéraire*, though written mainly by French refugees, admitted to the prejudices of its nation in *Journal littéraire* III, pt. 1 (Jan.–Feb. 1714), 184, Art. XII, although it went on to say that "il est très-naturel que la Poësie Hollandoise soit inférieure à la Françoise" (186).

135 See, for example, BL Add. Ms. 4283, f. 36, Jean-Pierre de Crousaz to Des Maizeaux, Lausanne, July 20, 1717: "Je continue, Monsieur, à vous feliciter d'étre dans un Pays de Savans"; or UBL March. 2, De Valois to Marchand, Paris, June 26, 1725: "Les Anglois ont un grand fonds d'amour pour les Lettres." Cuper was delighted that La Croze, after losing his position as librarian to the King of Prussia, intended to go to England. "La Grande Bretagne est le meilleur sejour du monde pour les Sçavans; il y a des Grands qui aiment les études, ils y sont mêmes Sçavans, pour ne parler pas des Ecclesiastiques, dont il y a si grand nombre, célébrés par leur sçavoir, tant à l'égard de la pieté qu'à l'égard des Belles Lettres, le Grec, & le Latin, qu'on n'en peut faire presque le dénombrement; ils estiment avec cela les Sçavans étrangers, les aident, & les font jouïr des benefices." KB 71 H 18, #60, Cuper to La Croze, Oxen, Dec. 6, 1710; also printed in Beyer, *Lettres de Cuper*, pp. 81–2.

136 BL Add. Ms. 4286, f. 107, De la Motte to Des Maizeaux, Amsterdam, May 9, 1710; *History of Learning* (1691), 1.

137 KB 120 B 21, Isaac de Larrey to d'Ausson, Marquis de Villarnoux, Berlin, Mar. 4, 1710; Le Clerc to Locke, Amsterdam, May 30, 1701, in De Beer, ed., *Correspondence of Locke* VII, p. 324.

138 UBL March. 2, Jordan to Marchand, Berlin, Dec. 12, 1734.

139 Henri Justel to Locke, *c.* June 28/July 8, 1679, in De Beer, ed., *Correspondence of Locke* II, p. 40; Neu BPU, Ms. 1262, Bourguet to Seigneux de Correvon, Oct. 10,

1730, copy.

140 Cuper to David Martin, Oct. 7, 1706, in Beyer, *Lettres de Cuper*, pp. 459–60.

141 Largely because of the tercentenary of the Revocation of the Edict of Nantes in 1985, considerable scholarly attention has been devoted to the Huguenot refuge in recent years. Among the useful works on the subject are Michelle Magdelaine and Rudolph von Thadden, eds., *Le Refuge huguenot* (Paris: Armand Colin, 1985); Elisabeth Labrousse, *La Révocation de l'Edit de Nantes* (Geneva: Labor et Fides, 1985); Janine Garrisson, *L'Edit de Nantes et sa Révocation: Histoire d'une intolérance* (Paris: Editions du Seuil, 1985); Robin Gwynn, *Huguenot Heritage: The History and Contribution of the Huguenots in Britain* (London: Routledge and Kegan Paul, 1985).

142 Jean Masson in *Histoire critique de la République des Lettres* VIII (1715), Art. VI, 216–17.

143 Neu BPU Ms. 1262, Bourguet to Seigneux de Correvon, Neuchâtel, Jan. 12, 1732.

144 On this subject see especially Guy Howard Dodge, *The Political Theory of the Huguenots of the Dispersion: With Special Reference to the Thought and Influence of Pierre Jurieu* (Morningside Heights, NY: Columbia University Press, 1947); Elisabeth Israels Perry, *From Theology to History: French Religious Controversy and the Revocation of the Edict of Nantes* (The Hague: Martinus Nijhoff, 1973); Gerald Cerny, *Theology, Politics and Letters at the Crossroads of European Civilization: Jacques Basnage and the Baylean Huguenot Refugees in the Dutch Republic* (Dordrecht: Martinus Nijhoff, 1987).

145 In one synod of 1695, for example, the Walloon church celebrated the surrender of Namur: "la Compagnie, aprés en avoir rendu à Dieu de tres-humbles actions de graces, & l'avoir prié ardemment de continuer de benir les Armes de cét Etat, & de ses

Hauts Alliez, pour nous conduire enfin à une bonne & solide Paix, a crû devoir députer des personnes de son Corps, pour feliciter du glorieux succés de ce siége important Sa Majesté le Roi de la Grande Brétagne" (Synod of Leeuwarden, Sept. 1695, Art. XXXIII). The consistory records of the French church in Amsterdam record numerous instances of prayers for the state, ordered by the burgermeesters of Amsterdam and the States of Holland, as well as orders to present a proper picture of events to the congregation. In January of 1689, the burgermeesters told Nicolas Colvius, one of the pastors, that the States of Holland had said "Que Le Roy de France faisant tout ce qu'il peut pour donner cette impression au monde que cette guerre qui se fait à present est une guerre offensive de Religion, Mrs Les Estats veulent qu'on croye le contraire, comme ainsi il est vray, cette affaire estant de grande consequence, nos dits venerables Bourgemaistres, ont trouvé bon que tous les Pasteurs menagent avec prudence, en leurs predications et en leurs prieres conformément à l'intention de M^rs les Estats." (GA Amst Part. Arch. [Waalse Gemeente] 201/1e, Actes du Consistoire, Jan. 23, 1689, in Double Consistoire). See also GA Amst Part. Arch. 201/e, July 5, 1693, in consistory; July 2, 1694, in Double Consistoire; July 2, 1702, in consistory; Sept. 7, 1704, in consistory.

146   Bibl SHPF, Ms. 784[1], David Henri Durand to Barbier, 1804; the younger Durand was attempting to remember what he could from a burned *mémoire* of his uncle's life. See also Durand's requests for a pension from Sunderland: BL Add. Ms. 61, 648, ff. 79–80, 81–2, Durand to Sunderland, Sept. 25 and Sept. 29, 1715. On Huguenot contributions to the defeat of Louis XIV, see Robin Gwynn, *Huguenot Heritage*, chap. 9. On Huguenot troops in the English

army, see David C.A. Agnew, *Henri de Ruvigny, Earl of Galway* (Edinburgh: William Paterson, 1864), pp. 81, 85, n. 1, 86–7, who states that in 1698 French regiments in the English army totaled 4,288 men.

147   For examples of such projects received by the English, see BL Add. Ms. 61337, ff. 203ff., "Projet pour une descente en France," Nov. 1 and Dec. 10, 1703 (a project apparently by Leers); BL Add. Ms. 61339, ff. 105ff., "Projet pour une descente sur les cotes de France," April 1707; BL Add. Ms. 61337, f. 247, letter[?] from a Huguenot to Marlborough[?] proposing an attack on France [1703?]; BL Add. Ms. 61648, which contains letters concerning spying, proposals for military operations, and ideas for fomenting trouble in the Cévennes.

148   Joseph Dedieu, *Le rôle politique des Protestants français (1685–1715)* (Paris: Bloud & Gay, 1920), p. 198.

149   See ibid., chaps. 8–11; P. Lemonnier, "Espionnage et contre-espionnage à Rochefort en 1696," *Bulletin de la Société des Archives Historiques de la Saintonge et d'Aunis* 41, no. 1 (1924), 1–20, which includes transcriptions of letters of Pontchartrain located in the Archives du Port du Rochefort, I E 38, Dépêches de la Cour 1696; ARA, Archief Heinsius 2117, copy of letter from ? to Jurieu, The Hague, Nov. 9, 1696; BL Add. Ms. 61548, ff. 1–24, 26–26^v, 28–30^v, letters of Jurieu and/or Caillaud to Sunderland, Aug. 9, 1704, Jan. 27, 1705, Dec. 24, 1706, Mar. 1, 1707, Mar. 18. 1707, Mar. 22, 1707, Mar. 25, 1707, April 1, 1707, May 6, 1707, Aug. 30, 1707; ibid., ff. 33–5, Caillaud de Charles Delafaye, Oct. 10, 1707; ibid., ff. 38–9, Caillaud to Thomas Hopkins, Nov. 22, 1707; ibid., ff. 70–1, Caillaud to Sunderland, Aug. 19, 1721. See also F.R.J. Knetsch, *Pierre Jurieu, Theoloog en Politicus der Refuge* (Kampen, 1967).

150   Synod of Goes, August 1694, Art.

XXXII.

151 In the Synod of Gorcum, April 1709, Arts. XXX and XXXI, the Walloon church urged its members again to press the issue with their sovereigns, which the consistory of the French church in Amsterdam, for example, resolved to do on June 23 (GA Amst Part. Arch. 201/1e, June 23, 1709).

152 Jurieu, Basnage, and Superville wrote to Marlborough in March of 1709 imploring his country's help and asking specifically that Queen Anne put an article about the Huguenots in the preliminaries of the peace (BL Add. Ms. 61366, ff. 163–6, March 22, 1709), and Basnage reiterated these points in a letter to Marlborough the next week (BL Add. Ms. 61366, ff. 167–8, April 2, 1709). In this they joined other Protestant leaders, such as Jean de Barjac, Marquis de Rochegude, who in an extended letter campaign to Sunderland in 1708–9 also requested the inclusion of protection for the Hugenots in the peace treaty. See BL Add. Mss. 61648, ff. 63–4 (Rochegude to Sunderland, The Hague, Oct. 26, 1708), f. 65 (same to same, London, before Oct. 28, 1708), f. 66 (same to same, Geneva, Mar. 19, 1709), ff. 70–1 (same to same, Frankfurt, May 19, 1709), ff. 72–3 (same to same, The Hague, May 28, 1709), ff. 74–5 (same to same, The Hague, June 14, 1709), and ff. 76–7, Rochegude, "Memoire et requete pour etre presentés avec un tres profond respect a la reyne." Benoît, Martin, Basnage and Superville wrote letters and made several journeys to Utrecht in 1712 and 1713 for the same purpose (Synod of Rotterdam, Sept. 1712, Art. XXI, and Synod of Bois-le-Duc, May 1713, Art. XXII); Basnage reported in 1709 that he had to make "frequens voyages a la Haye ou la negotiation de paix piquoit ma curiosite et ou je faisois des efforts asses inutiles pour obliger les puissances et les envoies de penser a nous" (BL Add. Ms. 4281, f. 49, Basnage to Des Maizeaux, June 11, 1709); in 1713 he said that he had travelled to Utrecht eight times during the negotiations (KB 72 D 58, ff. 107–8, Basnage to Cuper, Oct. 6, [1713]) On Basnage's particular involvement in the negotiations, see Cerny, *Theology*, pp. 172–7. For a general account, see Dedieu, *Rôle*, pp. 83–94, 251ff.

153 In a volume of letters and papers concerning the negotiations of 1705–9 located in the ARA, the issue of French Protestants appears to have been considered very little; a list of *galériens* is the only sign it was on anyone's mind (ARA, 1e Afdeling, French legation XIV-A). The preliminary articles, from May 28, 1709, signed by Eugene of Savoy, the Count of Zinzendorf, Marlborough, Townshend, Heinsius, and others from the United Provinces, contained nothing on this subject (ARA, Archief Heinsius 2230, "Articles praeliminaires pour servir aux Traittez de la Paix generale. Secreet," printed). In the end, Basnage, Martin, Benoît, and Superville had to tell the Synod of Bois-le-Duc that "ils ont eu la douleur de voir que les fréquentes & pressantes sollicitations qu'ils ont faites, n'ont pas produit jusqu'ici l'effet que nous en attendions, & que la paix a été concluë, sans que nos pauvres freres, qui gémissent dans l'oppression, en aient reçû de soulagement" (Synod of Bois-le-Duc, May 1713, Art. XXII).

154 BL Add. Ms. 61648, ff. 79–80, Durand to Sunderland, London, Sept. 25, 1715.

155 *Histoire des ouvrages des savans* (Sept. 1687), preface; Synod of Leiden, May 1691, Art. VIII. This work was "un Recueil de plusieurs pieces tres-considerables sur les affaires de nos Eglises de France, composé par feu Monsieur Tessereau, Ancien de l'Eglise de Charanton."

156 Gibbs, "Some Intellectual and Political Influences," pp. 279–82.

157 On Rapin, see Hugh Trevor-Roper, "A Huguenot Historian: Paul Rapin," in Irene Scouloudi, ed., *Huguenots in Britain and their French Background, 1550–1800: Contributions to the Historical Conference of the Huguenot Society of London, 24–25 September 1985* (Totowa, NJ: Barnes & Noble Books, 1987), pp. 3–19.

158 Graham Gibbs, "The Contribution of Abel Boyer to Contemporary History in England in the Early Eighteenth Century," in A.C. Duke and C.A. Tamse, eds., *Clio's Mirror: Historiography in Britain and the Netherlands*, Britain and the Netherlands series, vol. 8 (Zutphen: De Walburg Pers, 1985), pp. 93–4. According to Gibbs, this partisanship came out much more clearly in Boyer's *History of King William the Third* than in his *History of the Reign of Queen Anne digested into Annals*, but he says that Boyer's writings during Anne's reign and later constantly reaffirmed his commitment to the Revolution Settlement.

159 Jacques Basnage, *Annales des Provinces-Unies* I (The Hague: Charles Le Vier, 1719), dedicatory epistle; Cerny, *Theology*, pp. 269–90.

160 See his correspondence with Heinsius in ARA, Archief Heinsius 1945, 1987, 2013, 2118, 2043.

161 ARA, Archief Heinsius 2196, Mémoire of Jean Du Mont to Heinsius, The Hague, Feb. 1, 1700; see also his other request for this position, Archief Heinsius 2196, "Pour Memoire a Monsieur le Conseiller Pensionnaire," n.d. [1700]. On Du Mont, see Haag, *La France protestante*, 2nd ed., V, cols. 769–72, and Gibbs, "Some Intellectual and Political Influences," 281–2. This particular incident in his life seems up to now to have escaped notice.

162 ARA, Archief Heinsius 2196, Du Mont to Heinsius, Nov. 18, 1700, Nov. 19, 1700, Nov. 24, 1700, Nov. 26, 1700, Dec. 8, 1700, Dec. 17, 1700, Feb. 1, [1701], Feb. 6, [1701], and several undated letters and translations of Spanish documents.

163 See, e.g., Du Mont, *Batailles gagnées par le Serenissime Prince Fr. Eugene de Savoye sur les Ennemis de la Foi, et sur ceux de l'Empereur & de l'Empire, en Hongrie, en Italie, en Allemagne & aux Pais Bas* (The Hague: Pierre Gosse, Rutgert Ch. Alberts, 1725), whose preface exclaims, "Heureuse *Allemagne*! heureuse *Italie*! & vous *Hongrie* plus heureuse encore, ne doutez point que le Ciel ne vous protege. Vous voyez en quelles mains, il à fait tomber le Commandement des Armées qui vous servent de Rempart. Portez vos yeux plus haut, & voyez aussi quel Empereur il vous a donné. Car c'est à lui que tout est dû, & ces grands Coups d'Etat & de Guerre qui asseurent vôtre bonheur, ne sont enfin que les effets de sa haute *Sagesse*, de sa *Force* invincible, & de sa *Constance* inebranlable . . . Qu'il vive, & que toujours aimé de Dieu, revaré des Nations & adoré de ses Peuples." Du Mont also wrote at least one political pamphlet which objected to Britain's separate peace negotiations with France in 1713: translated as *Les Soupirs de l'Europe &c. Or, the Groans of Europe at the Prospect of the Present Posture of Affairs. In a Letter from a Gentleman at the Hague to a Member of Parliament* (1713).

164 Perry, *From Theology to History*, p. 17.

165 To cite only one example, Charles Le Vier dedicated volume II of the late Basnage's *Annales des Provinces-Unies* to George I. Le Vier praised the English for their opposition to an "ennemi secret de la Réligion, aussibien que de la liberté de ses sujets," and their close alliance to the Dutch. See Jacques Basnage, *Annales des Provinces-Unies, depuis les Negociations pour la Paix de Munster* II (The Hague: Charles Le Vier, 1726), dedication, and a manuscript version of this dedication in BL Add. Ms.

38503, ff. 217–18.

166   Elisabeth Labrousse makes the point that "a kind of 'Calvinist International' . . . bolstered Huguenot morale" in "Great Britain as Envisaged by the Huguenots of the Seventeenth Century" in Scouloudi, ed., *Huguenots in Britain and their French Background 1550–1800*, p. 143.

167   BL Add. Ms. 4281, f. 35, Barbeyrac to Des Maizeaux, Groningen, Aug. 24, 1719.

168   BL Add. Ms. 4283, f. 167, Le Duchat to Des Maizeaux, Sept. 27, 1720.

169   KB 72 H 19/I, #34, La Croze to Cuper, Berlin, June 1713.

170   Synod of Leiden, May 1719, Letter to the Synod of Zuid-Holland, Art. XLVII.

171   *Histoire critique de la République des Lettres* IV (1713), 343–4, nouvelles littéraires, London.

172   Synod of Zierikzee, May 1722, Art. XLVIII.

173   Synod of Rotterdam, Sept. 1700.

174   SMHR, Archives Tronchin, vol. 42, ff. 91–91^v, Jacques Lenfant to Louis Tronchin, Berlin, July 26, 1701.

175   See the Synod of Rotterdam, Sept. 1700, Art. XXXVIII; Synod of The Hague, May 1715, Art. XXIX; Synod of Utrecht, Sept. 1715, Art. XLV; Synod of Heusden, May 1716, Art. XLI; Synod of Kampen, May 1716, Art. XLI. The Walloon synod finally agreed to adopt Conrart's edition at the Synod of Bergen-op-Zoom, May 1717, Art. XXIII, but in the Synod of Zutphen, Sept. 1717, Art. XXXVII, they decided it was necessary to solicit the approval of the States-General. The issue continued to reappear at synods until the Synod of Maastricht, April 1720, Art. XLIV, when the slowness of the States-General made the synod look for a quicker method: having the church of each locality ask its magistrates. After further delays, the psalms were finally declared approved at the Synod of Nijmegen in September

1722. Even so, the consistory of the French church in Amsterdam was still uncertain in 1729 about whether the burgermeesters would approve such an introduction and went to inquire; on July 6, 1729, it was finally agreed to use the psalms there. (GA Amst Part. Arch. 201/1f, July 3 and July 6, 1729, in Double Consistoire). Bodel Bienfait reports that the psalms were not sung in Utrecht until April 23, 1730 (P.E.H. Bodel Bienfait, "L'Eglise Wallonne d'Utrecht," chap. 2, *Bulletin de la Commission pour l'Histoire des Eglises Wallonnes* III [1888], 265).

176   Gen BPU, Ms. fr. 485, f. 205, Gilbert Burnet to Turrettini, St. James's, Jan. 2, 1701, letter in English; SMHR, Archives Tronchin, vol. 42, ff. 88–88^v, Jacques Lenfant to Louis Tronchin, Berlin, Oct. 26, 1700.

177   SMHR, Archives Tronchin, vol. 42, ff. 86–7, Lenfant to Tronchin, Berlin, Oct. 3, 1700.

178   J.-F. Osterwald to Turrettini, Sept. 21, 1700, in De Budé, *Lettres à Turrettini* II, pp. 385–6.

179   *Nouvelles de la République des Lettres* I (March 1684), preface.

180   See Anne Goldgar, "The Absolutism of Taste: Journalists as Censors in 18th-century Paris," in Robin Myers and Michael Harris, eds., *Censorship and the Control of Print in England and France, 1600–1910* (Winchester: St. Paul's Bibliographies, 1992), pp. 87–110.

181   For an account of how scholars and scientists came to view certainty as unattainable, see Barbara J. Shapiro, *Probability and Certainty in Seventeenth-Century England: A Study of the Relationships between Natural Science, Religion, History, Law, and Literature* (Princeton: Princeton University Press, 1983).

182   *Journal littéraire* III, pt. 2 (Mar.–April 1714), Art. VIII, 438.

183   BL Add. Ms. 4281, f. 86, Bernard to Des Maizeaux, The Hague, May 20, 1700.

184 *Nouvelles de la République des Lettres* I (August 1684; 2nd ed.), 586; BCUL, Archives de Crousaz IX/229–30, W.J. 'sGravesande to Crousaz, Leiden, Feb. 9, 1726. The *Histoire critique de la République des Lettres* made the same point: VII (1714), 181.

185 UBA, C 19 c, Bignon to Le Clerc, Paris, Feb. 25, 1709.

186 See, e.g., Synod of Breda, Sept. 1692, Arts. LIII–LIV; Synod of Gouda, April 1694, Art. XIX; Synod of Heusden, Aug. 1703, Art. XVI.

187 Synod of Leeuwarden, Sept. 1695, Art. XLI.

188 "Extrait des Resolutions de Seigneurs les Etats de Hollande, & de West-Frise, prises en l'Assemblée de leurs Nobles & Grandes Puissances. Le Samedy 18 Decembre 1694." Printed after the Articles of the Synod of Goes, Aug. 1694.

189 Synod of Nijmegen, August 1707, Art. XLVIII. In another example, a minister and an elder of the French church in Amsterdam went in September 1703 "remercier messieurs nos Venerables Bourgemaitres du soin qu'ils ont pris de maintenir l'orthodoxie dans nôtre Eglise, et La paix entre les freres" (GA Amst Part. Arch. 201/1e, Sept. 30, 1703, in consistoire ordinaire).

190 On this issue see especially Dodge, *Political Theory*, chap. 6; W.J. Stankiewicz, *Politics and Religion in Seventeenth-Century France: A Study of Political Ideas from the Monarchomachs to Bayle, as Reflected in the Toleration Controversy* (Berkeley and Los Angeles: University of California Press, 1960); Henry Kamen, *The Rise of Toleration* (New York: World University Library, 1967), chaps. 8, 9. Kamen states (p. 236) that the Huguenots were forced by the end of the seventeenth century to disavow all persecution in the interests of their own position. It is true that theological disputes abated, especially after the old age and death of Jurieu; as Simon Pelloutier pointed out in

1741, "les Disputes qui regardent le Socinianisme et l'Arminianisme sont tombées depuis longtems." (UBL, March 2, Pelloutier to Marchand, Berlin, July 11, 1741.) But they did remain a feature of Protestant life, as the case of Jacques Saurin and the emphasis on orthodoxy show.

191 Jacques Saurin to Turrettini, The Hague, Dec. 13, 1727, in De Budé, *Lettres à Turrettini* III, pp. 300–2. Saurin called this "une chose déplorable." Barbeyrac had similar comments in 1713: "C'est une chose etrange que dans un païs où il y a tant de liberté pour les Sectes, il y aît tant de tyrannie dans la dominante" (Gen BPU, Ms. fr. 484, f. 156, Barbeyrac to Turrettini, Dec. 14, 1713). He earlier called this fact "facheux" (Gen BPU, Ms. fr. 484, f. 122, Barbeyrac to Turrettini, Lausanne, Jan. 5, 1712). For actions of the Walloon synod against heterodoxy, see, for example, the long deliberations about the orthodoxy of Joncourt's views, ending in August 1707, the censuring of Samuel Masson's "Dissertation sur le Pseaume CX.," which appeared in the *Histoire critique de la République des Lettres* in 1713, or such routine examinations of ministers' sentiments as the judgment on David Durand, Synod of Brill, May 1711, Art. XXXIX.

192 Samuel Turrettini to Jean-Alphonse Turrettini, Leiden, June 19, 1711, in De Budé, *Lettres à Turrettini* III, pp. 362–3.

193 Bibl SHPF, Ms. 295, unfoliated (last page), "Histoire de la Conduite du Consistoire à mon égard"; Barbeyrac's hand. César de Missy left Berlin for the Netherlands (from whence he went to London) because of his refusal to sign the act of orthodoxy; he wrote a very long piece concerning his reasons for refusing to sign. See Bibl SHPF, Ms. 154, César de Missy, "Lettres écrites à un ami au sujet de l'*Acte* que l'on fit signer aux Ministres et aux *Candidats* des Eglises

Françoises qui sont dans les Etats de S.M. le Roy de Prusse" (1719?). However, Missy did sign the Synod of Dordrecht and the Walloon church's *confession de foi* in Delft in 1727 (Synod of Brill, Sept. 1727, Art. LX). In addition, Jean Le Clerc left Geneva because he did not want to sign the *consensus.*

194 Haag, *La France protestante,* 2nd ed. I, col. 784, states that Barbeyrac left Lausanne for Groningen in 1717 because he was not willing to sign the *consensus,* but manuscript sources indicate that he left because of the isolation of Lausanne and his low pay. See his letter of resignation to the curators of the Academy of Lausanne, KB 121 E 3, draft, 1717; his letter to the secretary of the curators of the University of Groningen, KB, 121 E 3, Lausanne, Mar. 16, 1717, draft; the second life of Barbeyrac in Bibl SHPF, Ms. 295, unfoliated (Barbeyrac's hand). According to Barbeyrac, the *consensus* controversy was on a good footing during his time at Lausanne. "La chose alloit le mieux du monde, & sans bruit, sans éclat, sans aucun mouvement sujet à des inconveniens, les Consciences demeuroient libres, & le *Consensus* ne conservoit de pouvoir qu'exteriorement, & à l'égard de ceux qui vouloient bien s'y soumettre. Qui vouloit le signer absolument le signoit: d'autres ne le faisoient qu'avec cette clause, la plus juste & la plus raisonnable du monde, *Quat. script. s. consentit.* Pour moi, je reçûs sans hésiter cette signature, pendant que j'étois Recteur; & presque tous ceux qui reçûrent alors l'Imp. des mains, n'en firent point d'autre" (BCUL, Archives de Crousaz XIV/7, Barbeyrac to Jean-Jacques Sinner, quoted by Barbeyrac in letter to Crousaz, Groningen, Jan. 15, 1718).

195 BCUL, Archives de Crousaz XIV/ 12, Barbeyrac to Crousaz, Groningen, May 11, 1722; BCUL, Archives de Crousaz XIV/7, Barbeyrac

to Sinner, quoted in Barbeyrac to Crousaz, Groningen, Jan. 15, 1718; Gen BPU, Ms. fr. 484, f. 216, Barbeyrac to Turrettini, Groningen, Sept. 20, 1718.

196 BCUL, Archives de Crousaz XIV/ 12, Barbeyrac to Crousaz, Groningen, May 11, 1722.

197 Charles Le Vier, "Eloge historique de Mr. Basnage," in Basnage, *Annales des Provinces-Unies* II, p. vii. Le Vier noted that the synod "le choisissoient souvent pour Président ou pour Sécrétaire.... Chargé du soin des Eglises Françoises du dedans, & de celles du dehors, aussi bien que d'une infinité d'autres Affaires.... Quoique M. Jurieu ne l'aimât point, il ne pouvoit cependant s'empécher de le regarder comme celui de tous les Ministres Réfugiez qui étoit le plus capable de défendre la cause des Protestans."

198 Synod of Kampen, Sept. 1716, Art. XVI.

199 Jacques Saurin to Turrettini, The Hague, Dec. 13, 1727, in De Budé, *Lettres à Turrettini* III, p. 301. Saurin had good reason to be displeased with the behavior of his colleagues in The Hague, who, apparently from motives of jealousy over his talent for preaching and his consequent large salary (see GA 's-Gravenhage, Waalse Gemeente #3, consistory records, ff. 95, 98, 121, 123, 130–1, 133, 135), hounded him even to his deathbed over supposed blasphemies in a "Dissertation sur le mensonge officieux" which he published in 1729. The discourse was examined by the synod, with unfavorable results (BW Ms. 22, #7, "Rapport des Commissaires nommez pour examiner le Discours XXXI, & la Dissertation sur le mensonge, de M^r. Saurin," presented to the Synod of The Hague, Sept. 5, 1730). The case caused a considerable stir in the Republic of Letters, including lengthy debates over Saurin's ideas in such journals as the *Bibliothèque raisonnée* (which attacked Saurin fiercely in an

extrait written by one of his colleagues, Armand Boisbeleau de la Chapelle), the *Lettres sérieuses et badines*, and the *Critique désintéressée des journaux*, which resulted in prosections of some of those connected with these journals supporting Saurin (ARA, 3e Afdeling, Hof van Holland 5661 [Register van de Criminele Sententien 7/8/1729–10/5/1731], ff. 94ᵛ-101; BW Ms. A 337, f. 25, copy of condemnation of François Bruys). See *inter alia* Coenraad Busken Huet, *Jacques Saurin en Théodore Huet: Proeve van Kerkgeschiedkundige Kritiek* (Haarlem: A.C. Kruseman, 1855), and J. Gaverel and E. Des Hours-Farel, *Jaques Saurin: Sa Vie et sa Correspondance* (Geneva: J. Cherbuliez, 1864), although neither of these sources mentions the money-oriented motives which are evident from the consistory records in GA 's-Gravenhage; *Lettres sérieuses et badines* I, pt. 2, and supplement to IV, letter 31; *Bibliothèque raisonnée* II, pt. 1 (Jan.–Mar. 1729), 177–219; *Critique désintéressée* I, Art. XI, and II, Art. VI; François Bruys, *Mémoires historiques* I, pp. 221ff.; Jérémie Frescarode, *Apologie pour les Synodes, et pour Mʳ. Saurin* (Rotterdam: Jean Daniel Beman, 1731); BW Ms. 337, "Extrait du Regitre des Resolutions de la Cour de Hollande, prise le Vendredi 27 Juillet 1731," printed; BW Ms. A 337, ff. 19ff, Hof van Holland, "Deliberatien oover de Stellinge van de Mensonge officieux"; BW Ms. 337, ff. 15ff., "Rapport van de Heeren de Mauregnault en Vander Mieden"; BL Add. Ms. 4281, letters of François Bruys to Pierre Des Maizeaux, and numerous other sources. The debate continued long after Saurin's death, as Armand de la Chapelle was accused in 1736 of defaming Saurin and two women of his own parish in additions to his French translations of the *Tatler*, the *Babillard*. See especially BW Ms. 24,

Synodal papers, and, for a brief account of the controversy, Donald F. Bond, "Armand de la Chapelle and the First French Version of the *Tatler*," in Carroll Camden, ed., *Restoration and Eighteenth-Century Literature: Essays in Honor of Alan Dugald McKillop* (Chicago: University of Chicago Press, 1963), pp. 161–84.

200 BCUL, Archives de Crousaz I/5, De la Motte to Crousaz, Amsterdam, Sept. 25, 1711, copy.

201 BL Add. Ms. 4281, f. 92ᵛ, Bernard to Des Maizeaux, The Hague, Sept. 11, 1700.

202 Synod of Amsterdam, May 1704, Art. XXXVIII.

203 Letter from Synod of Zuid-Holland, July 14, 1719, printed in Articles of Synod of Vlissingen, August 1719. The Walloon synod had already passed the boundaries of its own authority by suggesting the investigation of Le Clerc's bible, although as a Remonstrant Le Clerc did not fall within their purview. Since they could not forbid its printing, they would have to write against it and attempt to get the government to stop the book instead. See Synod of Heusen, Aug. 1703, Art. XXXVIII.

204 *Bibliothèque italique* IV (Jan.–April 1729), Art. V, 122. The *Histoire critique* said in 1714 that the "passion de ces Ecclesiastiques" (the Walloon synod) must be opposed, for otherwise "les Lettres retomberont bien vite dans cette affreuse barbarie, d'où elles furent tirées il y a environ 250. ans". *Histoire critique de la République des Lettres* VI (1714), 432.

205 DSB, Nachlass Formey, Luzac to Formey, f. 10ᵛ, n.d. [Leiden, 1749], postscript. Luzac, a *libraire*, disagreed, saying that "Tout comme un Marchand de vin n'est pas tenu de le refuser à un ÿvrogne tant que celui-ci peut se satisfaire ailleurs, ainsi un imprimeur n'est pas obligé de refuser un Mss que son refus n'empêcheroit pas de voir le jour. D'ailleurs il faut une liaison nécessaire de l'effet à sa cause, & l'on ne peut dire qu'il ÿ a

206 cette liaison entre la production d'un livre & l'usage que le public en fait; car cet usage depend de ses caprices."

206 Neu BPU, Ms. 1262, Bourguet to Seigneux de Correvon, [Neuchâtel], Mar. 16, 1735.

207 KB 72 G 33, Cuper to Jurieu, July 14, 1705; KB 72 G 33, Cuper to Jurieu, June 7, 1704. Also printed in Beyer, *Lettres de Cuper*, pp. 469–70, 467.

208 J.-F. Osterwald to Turrettini, May 13, 1714, in De Budé, *Lettres à Turrettini* III, pp. 124–5.

209 BL Add. Ms. 4281, f. 86ᵛ, Bernard to Des Maizeaux, The Hague, May 20, 1700. Bernard was another Huguenot put into a bind by the *consensus*. In 1685 he reported to Jean Le Clerc that French ministers in Switzerland had to sign "La Confession Helvetique, le Catechisme d'Heidelberg & la formule du Consensus." Protests had few results. Bernard complained that "pauvres miserables qui ayant été chassez de France & méme condamnez à la mort pour la verité, sont encore pour cette méme verité persecutez par ceux qu'ils regardoient comme leurs freres." UBA, C 16, Bernard to Le Clerc, Lausanne, Nov. 9, 1685.

210 BL Add. Ms. 4281, f. 97, Bernard to Des Maizeaux, The Hague, Dec. 14, 1700. Bernard was explaining to Des Maizeaux why he could not print a *mémoire* Des Maizeaux had submitted in the form he had written it.

211 BCUL, Arch. de Crousaz I/5, De la Motte to Crousaz, Amsterdam, Sept. 25, 1711.

212 Barbara J. Shapiro, "Latitudinarianism and Science in Seventeenth-Century England," *Past and Present* 40 (July 1968) 22–3, 27–8; see also her *Probability and Certainty*, pp. 104ff. Michael Hunter makes the same argument in *Science and Society*, p. 27. They focus on a passage from Thomas Sprat which concerns the first meetings of the scientific group at Wadham College, Oxford, in the Interregnum: "Their first purpose was no more, then onely the satisfaction of breathing a freer air, and of conversing in quiet with one another, without being ingag'd in the passions, and madness of that dismal Age. . . . For such a candid, and unpassionate company, as that was, and for such a gloomy season, what could have been a fitter Subject to pitch upon, then *Natural Philosophy*? To have been always tossing about some *Theological question*, would have been, to have made that their private diversion, the excess of which they themselves dislik'd in the publick: To have been eternally musing on *Civil business*, and the distresses of their Country, was too melancholy a reflexion: It was *Nature* alone, which could pleasantly entertain them, in that estate. The contemplation of that, draws our minds off from past, or present misfortunes, and makes them conquerors over things, in the greatest publick unhappiness: while the consideration of *Men*, and *humane affairs*, may affect us, with a thousand various disquiets; *that* never separates us into mortal Factions; *that* gives us room to differ, without animosity; and permits us, to raise contrary imaginations upon it, without any danger of a *Civil War*" (Thomas Sprat, *History of the Royal Society*, ed. Jackson I. Cope and Harold Whitmore Jones [St. Louis: Washington University Press, 1958; 1st publ. 1667], pp. 53, 55–6).

213 See, for example, the *Journal littéraire* III, pt. 1 (Jan.–Feb. 1714), 205, which stated that the Dutch poet Vondel "étoit fort ignorant en matiére de Religion & par conséquent fort passioné."

214 Nicolas Lenglet du Fresnoy, *Méthode pour étudier l'histoire*, new ed. (Paris: Pierre Gandouin, 1735), I, xvi.

215 Baillet, *Jugemens des savans* I, "Avertissement au Lecteur."

216 UBL, March. 1, Abbé de St.-Pierre to the Baron d'Els, Paris, July 8, 1714: the message was to be delivered to the authors of the journal;

BL Add. Ms. 4281, f. 239ᵛ, Bignon to Des Maizeaux, Paris, Nov. 25, 1712.

217   See also Daston, "Ideal and Reality," p. 12.

218   'Nouvelles de la République des Lettres I (April 1684), 107–8; BN Ms. fr. 19211, f. 164, Bernard to Delaissement, The Hague, Oct. 8, 1701, copy; note that Bernard was writing this letter to a Catholic. On this subject see also Ultee, "Learned Correspondence," pp. 99, 106.

219   Neu BPU, Ms. 1262, Bourguet to Seigneux de Correvon, Neuchâtel, March 19, 1732.

220   Neu BPU, Ms. 1262, Bourguet to Seigneux de Correvon, Neuchâtel, Jan. 12, 1732. In this passage Bourguet was discussing the publication of his life, but it is evident that he himself applied the same arguments to private dealings with scholars.

221   Nouvelles de la République des Lettres I (March 1684), preface.

222   BN Ms. fr. 22230, f. 328, Lenfant to Bignon, Berlin, Feb. 24, 1728.

223   UBA, C 19 h, Bignon to Le Clerc, Paris, July 9, 1723.

224   See Anne Goldgar, "The Absolutism of Taste."

225   UBA, C 19 c, Bignon to Le Clerc, Paris, Feb. 25, 1709.

226   Histoire critique de la République des Lettres IX (1715), 327, nouvelles littéraires, Paris.

227   ZAAWD, I-I-5, f. 93, project to combine old and new Sociétés royales des sciences, n.d. [1743]. This had been a rule in the pre-existent literary society: see ZAAWD I-I-5, f. 80, "Reglement conventionel de la societé literaire de Berlin," n.d., draft, point 10.

228   Journal littéraire VI, pt. 2 (1730), Art. I, pp. 273–4.

229   Histoire critique de la République des Lettres VIII (1715), Art. VI, 217–18n.

230   Journal de Trévoux III (May–June 1701), "Avertissement."

231   Ibid.

232   Bibliothèque italique I (1728) xxi, preface.

233   BN Ms. fr. nouv. acq. 1216, f. 148, Basnage to Beaumont, quoted in Beaumont to Clément, Rouen, Nov. 13, 1707.

5   TALKING ABOUT NOTHING

1   For an introduction to Jordan, see Prologue above.

2   Neu BPU, Ms. 1274/4, f. 4, Charles-Etienne Jordan to Louis Bourguet, Prenzlau, Jan. 14, 1729.

3   Neu BPU Ms. 1274/4, f. 6, Jordan to Bourguet, Prenzlau, Mar. 30, 1729.

4   Neu BPU, Ms. 1274/2, f. 3, Jordan to Bourguet, Prenzlau, Jan. 14, 1729.

5   Neu BPU, Ms. 1274/4, f. 9ᵛ, Jordan to Bourguet, Prenzlau, Nov. 10, 1729.

6   Neu BPU, Ms. 1274/4, f. 4, Jordan to Bourguet, Prenzlau, Jan. 14, 1729; Neu BPU, Ms. 1274/4, f. 18, Jordan to Bourguet, Prenzlau, Nov. 1, 1730.

7   Charles-Etienne Jordan, Recueil de littérature, de philosophie, et d'histoire (Amsterdam: François L'Honoré, 1730), p. 137.

8   Ibid., p. 25.

9   Ibid. pp. 119–20, 22, 33.

10   Ibid., pp. 43, 46ff., 62–5, 66, 125, 136.

11   UBL, March. 2, La Croze to Marchand, Berlin, Oct. 18, 1730.

12   Neu BPU, Ms. 1274/4, f. 23, Jordan to Bourguet, Strasbourg, May 15, 1733.

13   BL Add. Ms. 4283, f. 34, La Croze to Des Maizeaux, Berlin, June 27, 1733; Neu BPU, Ms. 4281, ff. 305–305ᵛ, Bourguet to Des Maizeaux, Neuchâtel, June 19, 1733.

14   Jordan, Voyage, 147. Carolus Rali Dadichi was in fact a fraudulent Orientalist, a "Schwindler," as his biographer called him, who claimed to be a learned Syrian but was in fact "ein frecher Französer . . . der es etliche Jahre verstanden hatte, die

deutsche Gelehrentwelt zu mystifizieren." See Wolfram Suchier, *C.R. Dadichi, oder wie sich deutsche Orientalisten von einem Schwindler düpieren liessen* (Halle: Ehrhardt Karras, 1919), p. 16.

15 Jordan, *Voyage littéraire*, p. 151.

16 Ibid., pp. 17–18.

17 *Bibliothèque raisonnée* XV, pt. 2 (Oct.–Dec. 1735), 309.

18 *Bibliothèque germanique* XXXII (1735), 108.

19 *Voyage littéraire*, pp. 20, 149.

20 Ibid., p. 52.

21 Ibid., pp. 181–2.

22 Ibid., pp. 85–6.

23 Ibid., pp. 68–9, 114, 27.

24 Jean de La Bruyère, *Les Caracteres de Théophraste traduits du Grec: avec les caractères ou les moeurs de ce siècle*. 2nd ed. (Paris: Estienne Michallet, 1688), p. 123, "Du Mérite personnel."

25 Francis Bacon, *The Advancement of Learning*, ed. Arthur Johnston (Oxford: Clarendon Press, 1974), III.2, p. 18.

26 DSB, Nachlass Formey, Georges Guillaume Mousson to Formey, f. 3ᵛ, Danzig, Sept. 11, 1737.

27 Shapiro, *Probability and Uncertainty*.

28 See Rosalie Colie, *Light and Enlightenment: A Study of the Cambridge Platonists and the Dutch Arminians* (Cambridge: Cambridge University Press, 1957); Shapiro, "Latitudinarianism and Science." Leibniz, Burnet, Turrettini, Jaquelot, Le Clerc, and other scholars we have discussed were interested in Protestant reunion; see, for example, letters to Turrettini on the subject in De Budé, *Lettres à Turrettini*, II, pp. 112–13, 113–14, 116–19, 120–1, 131, 150–2, 156–7, 158–9, 161–2, and III, pp. 395–7, as well as manuscript letters at Gen BPU in (*inter alia*) Mss. fr. 484, 485, 487, 493, and at SMHR, Archives Tronchin, vols. 42, 50.

29 UBL, March. 2, Pelloutier to Marchand, Berlin, May 1, 1745.

30 UBL, March. 2, Michel Mattaire to Marchand, London, July 28, 1746.

Letter in English.

31 *Critique désintéressée* I (1730), preface.

32 Theodore Parrhase [Jean Le Clerc] *Parrhasiana, ou pensées diverses sur des matières de critique, d'histoire, de morale et de politique avec la défense de divers ouvrages de Mr. L.C.* (Amsterdam: Henri Schelte, 1701) I, pp. 225–6.

33 UBA, G 67 c, Pierre-Daniel Huet to Etienne Morin, Paris, Nov. 9, 1686. It could also be argued that this perception of decline was based in part on the difficulties being experienced by most European universities in the late seventeenth century. Except for the German universities and classical studies in France, it has been argued, the university was in a peculiarly transitional phase which manifested itself in an intellectual stagnation and lack of interest. Certainly many of the scholars we have considered here were not associated with universities, and much of the central business of the community—such as the writing of literary journals—took place outside of that setting. L.G. Mitchell, taking his cue from Lucy Sutherland, defends eighteenth-century Oxford against the traditional charge of stagnation, but he appears on the defensive: "On the central questions of teaching and examining, continuity between periods of excellence, if nothing more, was maintained. . . . Eighteenth-century Oxford was . . . not the moribund institution that its critics depicted, even if it still fell short of the high standards claimed by its apologists." Introduction, L.S. Sutherland and L.G. Mitchell, eds., *The History of the University of Oxford* V: The Eighteenth Century (Oxford: Clarendon Press, 1986), pp. 5, 7–8.

34 KB, 72 H 18, #61, Cuper to La Croze, Deventer, Dec. 8, 1710. Also printed in Beyer, *Lettres de Cuper*, p. 83.

35 See, for example, Mencke, *Charlatanerie*, pp. 45–7, who complains of the desire of second-rate authors to write as much as possible.

He quotes Lilienthal to this effect: "'Ils se hâtent, & bornent leur Ambition à remplir les Boutiques de leurs Barbouillages, & les Catalogues de leurs Noms infortunez.'"

36 Obadiah Oddy to Thomas Hearne, Jan. 12, 1709, printed in *Remarks and Collections of Thomas Hearne* (Oxford: Clarendon Press, 1885–1921) II, p. 163.

37 See, e.g., *Nouvelles de la République des Lettres* I (June 1684), 347; Bénédict Pictet to Turrettini, n.d. [1692?], in De Budé, *Lettres à Turrettini* III, p. 237.

38 BL Add. Ms. 4284, f. 42ᵛ, Camusat to Des Maizeaux, Amsterdam, Feb. 20, 1732.

39 KB, 72 H 13/I, Clermont to Cuper, Amsterdam, Aug. 7, 1716.

40 DSB, Nachlass Formey, Marchand to Formey, f. 22ᵛ, The Hague, April 19, 1743.

41 DSB, Nachlass Formey, Luzac to Formey (film), [1756], postscript; BL Add. Ms. 4288, ff. 27–27v, Henri de Sauzet to Des Maizeaux, Amsterdam, June 16, 1719; BL Add. Ms. 4288, f. 25v, same to same, Amsterdam, May 30, 1719; BL Add. Ms. 4288, f. 42, same to same, Amsterdam, Dec. 12, 1719.

42 UBL, March. 2, La Croze to Marchand, Berlin, Oct. 18, 1730.

43 The rise in demand for books in general appears not to have improved the lot of authors; publishers, rather than authors, seem to have benefited from the trend. See Darnton, "The High Enlightenment and the Low Life of Literature" in *The Literary Underground*, p. 16.

44 See Eric Walter, "Les auteurs," in Martin, *Histoire de l'édition française* II, p. 388; Viala, *Naissance*, pp. 75–8.

45 Paul Korshin, "Types of Eighteenth-Century Literary Patronage," *Eighteenth-Century Studies* VII, no. 4 (Summer 1974), 473. Korshin is anxious to point out the availability of other types of support from such sources as audiences, governments, and universities; see "Types," 454,

and Korshin's review of Michael Foss' *The Age of Patronage* in *Eighteenth-Century Studies* VII, no. 1 (Fall 1973), 102. It should be remembered, however, that government support itself was limited and that the taste of audiences appeared to be running counter to that of many scholars.

46 BL Sloane Ms. 4055, f. 22ᵛ, Bourguet to Sloane, Neuchâtel, Dec. 14, 1736.

47 Browne Willis to Thomas Hearne, July 26, 1715, printed in Hearne, *Remarks and Collections* V, p. 81.

48 *Journal des sçavans* (1675; new ed. 1724), "Au Lecteur," signed De la Roque.

49 H.J. Reesink, *L'Angleterre et la littérature anglaise dans les trois plus anciens périodiques français de Hollande de 1684 à 1709* (Paris: Librairie Ancienne Honoré Champion, 1931), pp. 86–7; Viala, *Naissance*, p. 293. For a different view, see Roger Zuber, "L'Humanisme et les savants: de Peiresc aux Perrault," *Revue française d'histoire du livre*, new ser. 38 (Jan.–Mar. 1983), 33–4. Mordechai Feingold points to a supplantation of scholarly literature by science ("or at least its pleasing, entertaining aspects such as clocks and mechanical gadgets") and later by art and music, which led to a decline in aristocratic patronage around the beginning of the eighteenth century. He attributes this to a slacking-off of aristocratic intellectual pretensions, an increase in foreign travel and exposure to foreign art and music, and the increasing "commonness" of science, which led to a switch to the arts as "the defining feature of elite culture." See Feingold, "Philanthropy, Pomp, and Patronage: Historical Reflections upon the Endowment of Culture," *Daedalus* 116, no. 1 (Winter 1987), 171.

50 Quoted in Darnton, "High Enlightenment," pp. 12–13.

51 DSB, Nachlass Formey, Jean Deschamps to Formey, f. 22, Lon-

don, Aug. 6, 1763.

52 BCUL, Archives de Crousaz XIII/
    K/44–5, Crousaz to Formey,
    Lausanne, Jan. 7, 1745, copy; SPK,
    Sammlung Darmstaedter 2a 1733 (1),
    f. 10, Crousaz to Formey, Lausanne,
    Jan. 8, 1745. Crousaz was speaking
    of Frederick the Great.

53 *Bibliothèque italique* XV (Sept.–Dec.
    1732), Art. I, p. 11.

54 *Journal littéraire* I, pt. 1 (May–June
    1713; 2nd ed. Johnson 1715), 197–8.
    For other praise of French govern-
    mental patronage by Huguenot refu-
    gees, see *Nouvelles de la République des
    Lettres* III (Jan. 1685), 5, and *Histoire
    critique de la République des Lettres* X
    (1715), 390, nouvelles littéraires,
    Paris.

55 Viala, *Naissance*, pp. 81–3. According
    to Eric Walter, the French govern-
    ment gave out about 95,000 livres a
    year from 1663 to 1673, but this
    declined to 60,000 a year in 1674 to
    1683, and to 11,900 in 1690; the
    number of beneficiaries also fell from
    90 to 30. Walter, "Les auteurs," in
    Martin, *Histoire de l'édition française* II,
    p. 388. On declining patronage for
    academicians in the Académie
    Royale des Sciences, see Alice
    Stroup, *A Company of Scientists:
    Botany, Patronage, and Community at
    the Seventeenth-Century Parisian Royal
    Academy of Sciences* (Berkeley: Uni-
    versity of California Press, 1990), pp.
    36–7.

56 Korshin, "Types," 473.

57 BL Sloane Ms. 4068, ff. 333–333ᵛ,
    Sloane to Bignon, 1737, draft.

58 Gen BPU, Ms. fr. 484, f. 147ᵛ,
    Barbeyrac to Turrettini, Lausanne,
    July 23, 1713; KB, 72 H 19/I, #30,
    La Croze to Cuper, Berlin, May 20,
    1713; KB, 72 H 19/II, #1, La Croze
    to Cuper, Berlin, Jan. 14, 1714; KB,
    72 H 19/II, #11, La Croze to
    Cuper, Berlin, Nov. 13, 1714; KB,
    72 H 19/I, #36, Cuper to La Croze,
    Deventer, Nov. 22, 1713, draft; KB,
    72 D 58, Gabriel d'Artis to Cuper, f.
    5ᵛ, Amsterdam, Mar. 17, 1714; KB,
    72 H 19/II, #5, La Croze to Cuper,

Berlin, May 22, 1714; KB, 72 H 19/
II, #17, La Croze to Cuper, Berlin,
Nov. 22, 1715. La Croze lost his
salary as librarian again in 1723:
UBL, March. 2, La Croze to
Marchand, Berlin, July 26, 1723.

59 Gen BPU, Ms. fr. 484, f. 145ᵛ,
    Barbeyrac to Turrettini, Lausanne,
    June 16, 1713; *Histoire critique de la
    République des Lettres* III (1713), 310,
    nouvelles littéraires, Berlin.

60 Feingold, "Philanthropy," 176.

61 d'Argenson, "Discours sur la
    nécessité d'admettre des étrangers
    dans les sociétés littéraires," printed
    in Jean-Henri-Samuel Formey,
    *Choix des mémoires et abrégé de
    l'histoire de l'Académie de Berlin* (Ber-
    lin: Haude, 1761), I, 62ff.

62 Hahn, *Anatomy of a Scientific Institu-
    tion*, pp. 11–14.

63 ZAAWD I-I-5, f. 91, project to
    combine the old and new Sociétés
    royales des Sciences, n.d. [1743];
    ZAAWD I-I-5, f. 125, [Philippe de
    Jariges], plan of the new academy,
    n.d. [1743/4].

64 Hahn, *The Anatomy of a Scientific
    Institution*, p. 10.

65 ZAAWD, I-I-5, f. 56ᵛ (Schmettau to
    Frederick the Great, draft [1743]), f.
    191 ([Schmettau] to Frederick, draft
    [1744]), ff. 278ff. ("Reglement pour
    l'Academie des Sciences et
    des belles lettres"), f. 269 (Frederick
    to Maupertuis, Berlin, May 12,
    1746). The king and Schmettau did
    consult various scholars of the old
    academy and a new literary society
    (which were to be combined) about
    the academy's reformulation, and
    Charles-Etienne Jordan, for one,
    protested the plan for the king to
    choose the new members. See
    ZAAWD, I-I-5, ff. 131–131ᵛ, com-
    ments on plans for a new academy
    [1743–4]. It should be remembered,
    of course, that Jordan was not only
    an academician but a councillor of
    state.

66 ZAAWD I-III-9, f. 76ᵛ, Schmettau
    to another member of the directorate
    of the academy, Mar. 18, 1746.

67 *Die Registres der Berliner Akademie der Wissenschaften 1746–1766,* ed. Eduard Winter (Berlin: Akademie Verlag, 1957), p. 143 (Order of the King read by Maupertuis, Oct. 30, 1749). This book is a printed version of ZAAWD I-IV-31.

68 Stroup, *Company,* p. 37.

69 Priscilla P. Clark and Terry Nichols Clark, "Patrons, Publishers, and Prizes: The Writer's Estate in France," in Joseph Ben-David and Terry Nichols Clark, *Culture and its Creators: Essays in Honor of Edward Shils* (Chicago: University of Chicago Press, 1977), pp. 202–3.

70 Pearl Kibre, *Scholarly Privileges in the Middle Ages: The Rights, Privileges, and Immunities, of Scholars and Universities at Bologna, Padua, Paris, and Oxford* (Cambridge, Mass.: Mediaeval Academy of America, 1962), pp. 327–30.

71 Gunter E. Grimm, "Vom Schulfuchs zum Menschheitslehrer. Zum Wandel des Gelehrtums zwischen Barock und Aufklärung," in Hans Erich Bödeker and Ulrich Herrmann, eds., *Über den Prozess der Aufklärung in Deutschland im 18. Jahrhundert: Personen, Institutionen und Medien* (Göttingen: Vandenhoeck & Ruprecht, 1987), pp. 17–18.

72 UBA C 117 b, Le Clerc, quoted in Bots, *Republiek der Letteren,* p. 10.

73 Viala, *Naissance,* p. 57.

74 *Journal littéraire* VI, pt. 2 (1715), Art. XXIX (by the Abbé du Pons), 453.

75 Bibl SHPF Ms. 295, #110, Jordan to De la Motte, Charlottenburg, Sept. 26, 1740.

76 [Charles Sorel], *De la Connoissance des bons livres, ou examen de plusieurs autheurs* (Paris: Andre Pralard, 1671), pp. 33–4.

77 Gen. BPU, Ms. fr. 484, f. 137, Barbeyrac to Turrettini, Lausanne, Feb. 28, 1713; Bibl SHPF, Ms. 295, #69, Barbeyrac to De la Motte, Groningen, May 6, 1730.

78 Bibl SHPF, Ms. 295, #58, La Chapelle to De la Motte, Sept. 24, 1738; Bibl SHPF, Ms. 295, #74, Barbeyrac to De la Motte, Groningen, April 6, 1737; Bibl SHPF, Ms. 295, #75, Barbeyrac to De la Motte, Groningen, May 28, 1737; Bibl SHPF, Ms. 295, #76, Barbeyrac to De la Motte, Groningen, June 25, 1737; Bibl SHPF, Ms. 295, #98, Barbeyrac to De la Motte, Groningen, April 15, 1738; Bibl SHPF, Ms. 295, #84, Barbeyrac to De la Motte, Groningen, May 10, 1740. Barbeyrac told De la Motte about his experiences with the prince and princess in much greater detail than anything else in his correspondence.

79 Mencke, *Charlatanerie,* p. 49.

80 UBL, March. 2, Marchand to d'Argens, draft, n.d.

81 UBL, March. 2, Pérard to Marchand, Stettin, May 5, 1738. See also DSB, Nachlass Formey, Pérard to Formey, f. 11ᵛ, Grambzow, April 20, 1738, and Barbeyrac's tirade against the court in BCUL, Arch. de Crousaz XIV/11, Barbeyrac to Crousaz, Groningen, Mar. 14, 1721.

82 See Simon Pelloutier's complaint that Pérard "entretient . . . avec plusieurs grands une correspondance, qui lui fait negliger plusieurs de ses anciens amis, mais qui ne le dedommage peutetre pas de ce qu'il y a à gagner dans un commerce litteraire. J'auray l'occasion de lui écrire un de ces jours, et je ne manquerai pas de lui faire part des reproches obligeans que son silence lui attire justement de vôtre part." UBL March. 2, Pelloutier to Marchand, Berlin, Aug. 8, 1746.

83 Gibbs, "Huguenot Contributions to the Intellectual Life of England," p. 196.

84 My emphasis. The Abbé Bignon was described in this way in the *Histoire critique de la République des Lettres* III (1713), 302, note (a), and in Des Maizeaux, *Vie de Boileau,* p. 152. The *Histoire critique* also used this phrase of the Emperor's librarian: *Histoire critique* IV (1713), 352. On the concept of *nobilitatis litteraria,* see

also Bots, *Republiek der Letteren*, p. 5.

85 Daniel Roche, "Literarische und geheime Gesellschaftsbildung im vorrevolutionären Frankreich: Akademien und Logen," in Otto Dann, ed., *Lesegesellschaften und bürgerliche Emanzipation: Ein europäischer Vergleich* (Munich: Verlag C.H. Beck, 1981), p. 186; Roche, *Le Siècle des lumières en province* I, pp. 254–5; Roche, *Les Républicains des Lettres*, pp. 167–8. Roche points out in *Siècle*, p. 223, that the nobility itself had been shorn of power and consequently took part in eighteenth-century provincial academies in a similar effort at self-affirmation.

86 Jacques Revel, "The Uses of Civility," in Roger Chartier, ed., *The Passions of the Renaissance*, vol. III of *The History of Private Life*, trans. Arthur Goldhammer (Cambridge, Mass.: Belknap Press, 1989), pp. 195–6.

87 *Journal littéraire* VI, pt. 2 (1715), Art. XXIX, p. 455; BL Add. Ms. 4286, f. 100ᵛ, De la Motte to Des Maizeaux, Amsterdam, Jan. 17, 1710, postscript. The *Bibliothèque angloise* paraphrases Richard Johnson's view that nothing is more "honteux" or "indigne" of a man of letters than to be insulting in scholarly debate. *Bibliothèque angloise* I, pt. 2 (1716; 2nd ed. 1729), Art. I, 285.

88 Des Maizeaux, "Histoire des Scaligerana. A Monsieur Morehead, in *Scaligerana* II, xix.

89 Revel, "Uses of Civility," in Chartier, *Passions*, p. 194.

90 Nicolas Faret, *L'Honeste Homme; ou, l'Art de plaire à la cour* (Paris: Mathurin Henault, 1637; orig. publ. 1632), pp. 54–8, 63–7, 71, 76, 80–2.

91 Maurice Magendie, *La Politesse mondaine et les théories de l'honnêteté en France au XVIIᵉ siècle, de 1600 à 1660* (Paris: Presses Universitaires de France, 1925), pp. 896–7, 892. See also Jean-Pierre Dens, *L'Honnête homme et la critique du goût: esthétique et société au XVIIe siècle* (Lexington, KY: French Forum, 1981), p. 17;

Christoph Strosetzki, *Rhétorique de la conversation: sa dimension littéraire et linguistique dans la société française du XVIIe siècle*, trans. into French by Sabine Seubert (Paris, Seattle, Tübingen: Biblio 17, 1984), pp. 120–1. There is some disagreement about the issue of morality in relation to the *honnête*. Strosetzki suggests (p. 121) that the nobility returned toward the end of the seventeenth century to a moral, Christianized view of *honnêteté*. Domna Stanton holds instead that the seventeenth-century *honnête homme* was merely captivating, and that it was not until Voltaire that virtue and morality become associated with the *honnête*. See Domna Stanton, *The Aristocrat as Art: A Study of the Honnête Homme and the Dandy in Seventeenth and Nineteenth-Century French Literature* (New York: Columbia University Press, 1980), p. 9. Carolyn Lougee, meanwhile, opts for the moral element of the *honnête* but insists that the main divide over the issue was that of feminists and anti-feminists, not bourgeois and aristocratic. See Carolyn C. Lougee, *Le Paradis des Femmes: Women, Salons, and Social Stratification in Seventeenth-Century France* (Princeton: Princeton University Press, 1976), pp. 28, 107–8. My own reading of the sources suggests the interpretation endorsed by Magendie and Dens. For recent discussions of eighteenth-century conversation in England and France, see Lawrence E. Klein, *Shaftesbury and the Culture of Politeness: Moral Discourse and Cultural Politics in Early Eighteenth-Century England* (Cambridge: Cambridge University Press, 1994), and Michèle B. Cohen, "A Genealogy of Conversation: Gender Subjectivation and Learning French in England" (PhD dissertation, University of London, 1993; forthcoming, Routledge).

92 See Antoine Gombaud, Chevalier de Méré, *De la conversation* (Paris: Denys Thierry and Claude Barbin, 1677).

This analysis is that of Elizabeth C. Goldsmith, *"Exclusive Conversations": The Art of Interaction in Seventeenth-Century France* (Philadelphia: University of Pennsylvania Press, 1988), pp. 9–10. Goldsmith bases her view of the primacy of social process over content on Georg Simmel's analysis of the aristocracy of the *ancien régime*. See Georg Simmel, *On Individuality and Social Forms*, ed. Donald N. Levine (Chicago: University of Chicago Press, 1971); Simmel's essay on the nobility was originally published in 1908.

93 Méré, *Conversation*, p. 79.
94 For a recent application of this argument in relation to seventeenth-century English science, see Steven Shapin, " 'A Scholar and a Gentleman': The Problematic Identity of the Scientific Practitioner in Early Modern England," *History of Science* 29, part 3, no. 85 (Sept. 1991), 279–327, and Shapin's book, *A Social History of Truth: Civility and Science in Seventeenth-Century England* (Chicago: University of Chicago Press, 1994). Emilio Bonfatti also discusses the problems of combining aristocratic manners and learning in "Vir Aulicus, Vir Eruditus," in Sebastian Neumeister and Conrad Wiedemann, eds., *Res Publica Litteraria: Die Institutionen der Gelehrsamkeit in die frühen Neuzeit* (Wiesbaden: Otto Harrassowitz, 1987) I, pp. 175–87.
95 Bouhours, *Entretiens*, pp. 306–7.
96 *Mémoires de littérature* I, pt. 2 (1716), 220.
97 Charles Le Vier, "Eloge historique de Mr. Basnage," in Basnage, *Annales des Provinces-Unies* II, v.
98 Magendie, *La Politesse mondaine*, pp. 725–8.
99 Méré, *Conversation*, pp. 25, 66–7.
100 Norman Hampson, "The Enlightenment in France," in Roy Porter and Mikuláš Teich, *The Enlightenment in National Context* (Cambridge: Cambridge University Press, 1981), pp. 44–5.

101 René Saisselin, *The Literary Enterprise in Eighteenth-Century France* (Detroit: Wayne State University Press, 1979), pp. 133–4; Thomas J. Schlereth, *The Cosmopolitan Ideal in Enlightenment Thought: Its Form and Function in the Ideas of Franklin, Hume, and Voltaire, 1694–1790* (South Bend, Ind.: University of Notre Dame Press, 1977), p. 12.
102 Charles Pineau-Duclos, *Considérations sur les moeurs de ce siècle* (Berlin: Etienne de Bourdeaux, 1751), p. 133.
103 Jean-Jacques Garnier, *L'Homme de lettres* (Paris: Pancoucke, 1764), pp. 171–2.
104 Ibid., p. 175.
105 *Encyclopédie* (Faulche ed.) V, p. 917, art. "Erudition."
106 See Edward Gibbon, *Essai sur l'etude de la littérature* (London: T. Becket and P.A. De Hondt, 1761), p. 8; Lionel Gossman, *Medievalism and the Ideologies of the Enlightenment: The World and Work of La Curne de Sainte-Palaye* (Baltimore: Johns Hopkins Press, 1968), p. 114; Joseph Levine, "The Antiquarian Enterprise," in Levine, *Humanism and History: Origins of Modern English Historiography* (Ithaca, NY: Cornell University Press, 1987), pp. 100–1; Krzysztof Pomian, *Collectors and Curiosities: Paris and Venice, 1500–1800*, trans. Elizabeth Wiles-Portier (Cambridge: Polity Press, 1990).
107 Garnier, p. 199.
108 Mercier, *De la litterature* (1778), pp. 40–1, 9. See also Schlereth, pp. xxiii–xxiv, 42, 47, 90–6; Saisselin, pp. 126, 144–5, 152.
109 *Lettres sérieuses & badines* I, pt. 1 (1729; 2nd ed. 1740), 45; ibid., pt. 2, 168, note.
110 UBA, J 60 c, Needham to Le Clerc, St. John's College, Cambridge, Nov. 9, 1710 O.S. Letter in English.
111 Le Clerc, *Parrhasiana* I, pp. 251, 255.
112 Ibid., pp. 253–4.
113 BL Add Ms. 4289, f. 184, Des Maizeaux to [De la Motte], draft, [London, Sept. 14, 1725?].

114 Charles Paul makes the point that these *éloges* were for the sake of publicity in *Science and Immortality*, p. 86.

115 Jean Barbeyrac, *Discours sur l'utilité des lettres et des sciences, par rapport au bien de l'Etat. Prononcé aux Promotions publiques du Collège de Lausanne, le 2. de Mai M.DCC.XIV* (Amsterdam: Pierre Humbert, 1715).

116 Neu BPU, Ms. 1274/4, f. 26, Jordan to Bourguet, [London, 1733].

117 Best. D634, textual note.

118 Jordan, *Voyage littéraire*, 63.

119 Uta Janssens-Knorsch, ed., *The Life and 'Mémoires Secrets' of Jean Des Champs (1707–1767): Journalist, Minister, and Man of Feeling*, Huguenot Society New Series, no. 1 (Huguenot Society of Great Britain and Ireland, 1990), p. 151.

120 "Epître" from Frederick II to Jordan, in Frederick, *Oeuvres complettes* (1790), XVI, p. 13.

121 Frederick II to Jordan, Potsdam, Sept. 24, 1740, in ibid., XVI, p. 35.

122 Frederick II (as Prince Royal) to Jordan, Harac de Prusse, Aug. 10, 1739, in Frederick, *Oeuvres complettes* (1790), XVI, p. 29.

123 Frederick to Jordan, Potsdam, Aug. 26, 1743, in ibid., XVI, p. 267.

124 Frederick to Duhan de Jandan, Camp of Staudenz, Sept. 24, 1745, in *Oeuvres de Frédéric le Grand*, ed. Preuss, XVII, p. 288; Frederick to Madame de Camas, Camp of Semonitz, Aug. 30, 1745, in ibid., XVIII, pp. 141–2.

125 Free translation of Voltaire, *Le Temple du Goût*, pp. 4–6.

126 UBL March. 2, Simon Pelloutier to Marchand, Berlin, Feb. 7, 1741; UBL March. 2, same to same, Berlin, July 11, 1741.

127 DSB, Nachlass Formey, Pérard to Formey, f. 54ᵛ, Dresden, Jan. 30, 1741.

128 UBL, March. 2, Jean de Beyer to Marchand, letter 81, Nijmegen, Feb. 3, 1745.

129 DSB, Nachlass Formey, Marchand to Formey, f. 19ᵛ, March 5, 1743.

130 DSB, Nachlass Formey, Elie Luzac to Formey, f. 38, Leiden, Mar. 3, 1750.

131 UBL, March. 2, Marchand to the Marquis d'Argens, letter 12, undated.

132 UBL March. 2, Pelloutier to Marchand, Sept. 26, 1750.

133 DSB, Nachlass Formey, Jean Causse to Formey, f. 6, Frankfurt on the Oder, March 7, 1738.

134 Frederick to Jordan, Postdam, May 12, 1743, in Frederick, *Oeuvres complettes* (1790), XVI, 260–1. "Jordanomanie" is intended to echo the title of the *Voltaromanie*.

135 Frederick to Jordan, Postdam, Nov. 20, 1743, in ibid., XVI, 271.

136 Frederick to Jordan, Potsdam, Nov. 17, 1743, in ibid., XVI, 271.

137 "Eloge de Jordan," in Preuss, ed., *Oeuvres de Frédéric le Grand* VII, 7.

138 Ibid.

139 Ibid., p. 6.

140 UBL March. 2, Pérard to Marchand, Stettin, Feb. 2, 1742.

141 UBL March. 2, Jean de Beyer to Marchand, letter 18, Hulse, July 1, 1741.

142 UBL March. 2, Pelloutier to Marchand, Berlin, Aug. 11, 1740.

143 BJK, Ms. Berol. Gall. Qu. 26, quoting *Eclogues* I.6.

144 For this episode, see Janssens-Knorsch, ed., *Life and 'Mémoires Secrets' of Jean Des Champs*, and Janssens-Knorsch, "Jean Deschamps (1709–67) and the French Colony in Berlin," *Proceedings of the Huguenot Society of London* XXXIII no. 4 (1980), 227–39.

BIBLIOGRAPHY

PRIMARY SOURCES

Manuscripts

AN:
ARCHIVES NATIONALES, PARIS

O¹ 43. Registre du Secretariat, 1699.

M 767. Portfolios of the Père Léonard de St.-Catherine de Sienne. "Troisième volume du recueil de quelques *Nouvelles journalières de la République des Lettres* venues à ma connaissance depuis le commencement de l'année 1698."

TT 439. Documents concerning French Protestants 1735–1775.

ARA:
ALGEMEEN RIJKSARCHIEF, THE HAGUE

ARCHIEF HEINSIUS:

1379, 1945, 1987, 2013, 2043, 2075. Letters from Jacques Basnage to Anthonie Heinsius.

2117. Papers concerning dispute among Elie Saurin, Pierre Jurieu, and Samuel Basnage de Flottemanville.

2118. Papers of Jacques Basnage and letters from him to Heinsius.

2196. Papers of Jean Du Mont and letters from him to Heinsius.

2230. Papers concerning peace negotiations 1705–12.

2245. Papers concerning peace negotiations 1709–12.

2244. Papers concerning peace negotiations 1709.

2276. Papers concerning quadruple alliance.

HOF VAN HOLLAND:

5661. Register of criminal sentences, 1729–1731.

5422, 15. Documents concerning trials relating to the Saurin affair.

STATEN VAN HOLLAND EN WEST-FRIESLAND:

291. Index to registers of resolutions, 1701–13.

1888, 1890. Incoming articles laid before the States, 1707, 1708.

FRENCH LEGATION:

XIV-A. Concerning peace negotiations, 1705–9.

COLLECTIE CUPERUS:

10, 15.

STATEN-GENERAAL:

11247, 11251. Incoming letters, 1708–9.

BCUL:
BIBLIOTHÈQUE CANTONALE ET UNIVERSITAIRE, LAUSANNE

Archives Jean-Pierre de Crousaz, vols. I–VI, VIII–XIV. Correspondence.

TH 983. Includes documents concerning Armand de la Chapelle's *Nécessité du culte public*.

Bibl SHPF:
BIBLIOTHÈQUE DE LA SOCIÉTÉ DE L'HISTOIRE DU PROTESTANTISME FRANÇAIS, PARIS

Ms. 154. César de Missy. "Lettres écrites à un ami au sujet de l'Acte que l'on fait signer depuis quelques années aux ministres et aux candidats des Eglises françoises que sont dans les Etats de S.M. le roy de Prusse." 1725.

Ms. 192. Copies of letters from Jacques Basnage and members of his family; documents about Basnage family.

Ms. 295. Correspondence of Charles de la Motte, documents concerning Barbeyrac.

Ms. 784¹. Papers concerning David Durand.

Ms. 843. Dossier Elie Benoît.

Ms. 811. Letters of Henri Justel to Findekeller, 1669–82.

Ms. 871¹. Copies of papers concerning Pierre Jurieu's spy ring.

BJK:
BIBLIOTEKA JAGIELLÓNSKA, KRAKÓW

Mss. Berol. Gall. Qu. 25, 26. Letters to Maturin Veyssière La Croze.

BL:
BRITISH LIBRARY, LONDON

Add. Ms. 4226. Letters of Pierre Bayle and papers about their publication.

Add. Mss. 4254–5. Literary papers and correspondence of Thomas Birch.

Add. Ms. 4280. Pell papers.

Add. Mss. 4281–4289. Correspondence of Pierre Des Maizeaux.

Add. Ms. 4299. Miscellaneous collected letters and papers on foreign affairs.

Add. Ms. 4295. Toland papers.

Add. Mss. 4301–4314. Correspondence of Thomas Birch.

Add. Ms. 4370. Papers of Samuel Clarke and Benjamin de Daillon.

Add. Mss. 4433, 4444. Papers of the Royal Society.

Add. Ms. 4465. Toland Papers.

Add. Ms. 4476. Birch Miscellanea.

Add. Ms. 28536. Correspondence of Emmanuel Mendez da Costa.

Add. Ms. 28889. Miscellaneous official correspondence of John Ellis, undersecretary of state.

Add. Ms. 28911. Foreign correspondence of John Ellis.

Add. Ms. 28926. Letters to John Ellis from officers on active service abroad.

Add. Ms. 28899. Official correspondence of John Ellis.

Add. Ms. 32418. Correspondence of Caspar Wetstein 1711–1760.

Add. Ms. 32725. Newcastle papers: correspondence 1751.

Add. Mss. 38503–4. Townshend papers.

Add. Ms. 38730. Collection of assignments of copyright of English authors and publishers, 1704–1828.

Add. Mss. 61337, 61338. Proposals for military operations against France 1703–7.

Add. Ms. 61366. Correspondence of Marlborough.

Add. Mss. 61648, 61652. Correspondence of and about Lord Sunderland.

Add. Ms. 61548. Letters from Jurieu to Sunderland and from Etienne Caillaud to various.

Add. Ms. 61652, Sunderland letter-book.

Add. Ms. 61637B. Diary of Charles Delafaye, 1713–14.

Add. Ms. 61607. Memorials relating to Abel Boyer, 1707.

Add. Ms. 61655. Includes drafts of political pamphlets by Pierre Des Maizeaux.

Add. Ch. 76124. Appointment of Miremont as negotiator at Utrecht, 1711.

Eg. Ms. 1728. Letters of Charles Bentinck to his brother, William, Count Bentinck.

Eg. Mss. 1745–6, 1749. Correspondence of William, Count Bentinck.

Eg. Ms. 2127, #2. Henri Justel letters to Sir Robert Southwell, 1683–8.

Eg. Mss. 2429, 2623. Miscellaneous letters and papers.

Harleian Ms. 3780. Correspondence of Michel Mattaire.

Sloane Mss. 4036, 4037, 4038, 4041, 4043, 4045, 4051, 4052, 4053, 4055, 4056, 4057, 4058, 4059, 4064, 4066, 4067, 4068. Correspondence of Hans Sloane.

Stowe Mss. 228–230. Hanover papers.

Stowe Ms. 242. State papers and correspondence 1688–1744.

BN:
BIBLIOTHÈQUE NATIONALE, PARIS

Ms. fr. 9359. Correspondence of the Abbé Nicaise.

Ms. fr. 12933. Correspondence of Voltaire with César de Missy.

Ms. fr. 15161. Concerning Joseph Saurin.

Ms. fr. 15189. Letters and papers of Pierre-Daniel Huet, bishop of Avranches.

Ms. fr. 17707. Correspondence of Dom Bernard de Montfaucon.

Ms. fr. 19211. Correspondence of the Père Léonard de Ste-Cathérine de Sienne.

Ms. fr. 22230. Letters and papers of the Abbé Jean-Paul Bignon.

Ms. fr. 24410. Correspondence of Jean Bouhier.

Ms. fr. 14469. Correspondence of Jean Bouhier.

Ms. fr. nouv. acq. 1216. Papers concerning the thefts of manuscripts by Jean Aymon from the Bibliothèque du Roi.

Ms. fr. nouv. acq. 3543. Miscellaneous letters, mostly addressed to Bignon and de Boze.

Ms. fr. nouv. acq. 14898. Miscellaneous papers.

BVBBB:
BIBLIOTHEEK VAN DE VEREENIGING TOT DE BEVORDERING VAN DE BELANGEN DES BOEKHANDELS, AMSTERDAM

Amsterdam Boekverkopers Gilde, Ms. 52. "Memoriaal van 't Comptoir van het Boek-Kunst-verkoopers en Boek-druckers Gildt." 1661–1804.

Amsterdam Boekverkopers Gilde, Ms. 57. Copies of requests to and of the guild, ordinances, clarifications of guild affairs, etc. 1700–1782.

Personalia #7. Account book of Samuel and Jean Luchtmans, 1753–1772.

Personalia, Luchtmans IV. Written contracts.

BW:
BIBLIOTHÈQUE WALLONNE, AMSTERDAM

In A 16. "Acte copié de la Declara[ti]on de N.N.S.S. Gecomiteerde Raaden du 16 May 1736 en réponse à la Requete presentée par le Consistoire de la Haye."

A 21. Letters between Gisbert Cuper and Louis Bourguet and from Bourguet to Leibniz.

A 37. Includes documents concerning Jean Royer.

A 63. Copy of some resolutions of the Gecommitteerde Raden of Holland and West Friesland; copy of request of Jean Aymon to the States-General for a pension, Jan. 11, 1707.

A 337. Pieces concerning Saurin affair. 1731.

B 4. Correspondence of Jean Royer.

9. "Repertoire du Synode des Eglises Wallonnes des Provinces Unies des Pays-Bas."

10. "Table des Titres du Repertoire."

18. Acts and papers of the Walloon synod, 1708–1722.

19. Acts and papers of the Walloon synod, 1721–4.

20. Acts and papers of the Walloon synod, 1724–7.

21. Acts and papers of the Walloon synod, 1727–9.

22. Acts and papers of the Walloon synod, 1730–2.

23. Acts and papers of the Walloon synod, 1733–5.

24. Acts and papers of the Walloon synod, 1736–8.

25. Acts and papers of the Walloon synod, 1739–41.

26. Acts and papers of the Walloon synod, 1742–44.

DSB:
FORMER DEUTSCHE STAATSBIBLIOTHEK, EAST BERLIN

(Now Staatsbibliothek Preussischer Kulturbesitz, Haus 1)

NACHLASS FORMEY:
Correspondence of Jean-Henri-Samuel Formey.

GA Amst:
GEMEENTEARCHIEF, AMSTERDAM

PA 201 (WAALSE GEMEENTE):

1e. Acts of the consistory, 1670–1725.

1f. Acts of the consistory, 1725–55.

4b. Register of copies of incoming and outgoing letters, 1715–1797.

62. Pieces concerning Gregorio Leti.

65. Concerning Samuel Pastre.

66. "Livre rouge": register of those appearing before the consistory for not showing sufficient respect. 1733–1789.

108d–i. Articles of the Walloon Synod, 1670–66.

114. Protest against Synod of Gorkum, Art. XXXIV, concerning Bernard. 1724.

GUILD RECORDS:

PA 366, #75. Accounts, Boekverkopers, drukkers & kunstverkopersgilde. 1728–86.

NOTARIAL ARCHIVES:

N.A. 8299, 5830. Contracts between authors and *libraires*.

GA Den Haag:
GEMEENTEARCHIEF, 'S-GRAVENHAGE

BEHEERSNUMMER 241 (WAALS-HERVORMDE GEMEENTE):
  2. Register of deliberations of consistory 1709–21.
  3. Register of deliberations of consistory 1722–1747.
  4. Register of deliberations of consistory beginning 1748.
 31. Incoming and outgoing letters, 1608–1758.
 43. Incoming synodal pieces, 18th century.
 78. Register of instructions for deputies to synods, 1726–1826.

GL:
GUILDHALL LIBRARY, LONDON

Ms. 994. Church minute book, French Protestant Church at St. Martin Orgar, Martin's Lane, 1701–30.

Ms. 1161. Miscellaneous receipts and letters relating to the French Protestant Church at St. Martin Orgar, 1708–75.

Ms. 7412. Minutes of the consistory of the French Protestant Church and of the consistory of the Dutch Church at Austin Friars (i.e. minutes of the Coetus). 1649–1820.

Gen BPU:
BIBLIOTHÈQUE PUBLIQUE ET UNIVERSITAIRE, GENEVA

Mss. Bonnet 24–25. Correspondence of Charles Bonnet, 1740–58.

Ms. 2463. Miscellaneous correspondence.

Mss. Court, vols. 2–15. Miscellaneous correspondence and papers of Antoine Court and Huguenot refugees.

Ms. Court 50. Notebook of Elie Benoît and manuscript of *Suite de l'Histoire de l'Edit de Nantes*.

Mss. fr. 435–440. Ecclesiastical correspondence, 1673–1760.

Ms. fr. 468. Papers concerning 17th-century controversies.

Ms. fr. 481. Letters from Jean-Alphonse Turrettini.

Mss. fr. 484–493. Correspondence of J.-A. Turrettini.

Ms. fr. 851. Miscellaneous correspondence.

Ms. fr. 1001.

Inv. 1562. Miscellaneous correspondence.

KB:
KONINKLIJKE BIBLIOTHEEK, THE HAGUE

68 B 10, 72 C 3, 72 C 27, 72 D 58, 72 G 9, 72 G 10, 72 G 16, 72 G 17, 72 G 19, 72 G 33, 72 H 7, 72 H 13, 72 H 18, 72 H 19, 72 H 25, 72 H 26. Correspondence of Gisbert Cuper.

69 B 8. "Description de la chambre des raretez de Nic. Chevalier avec les noms des amateurs qui mont honnore de leur precence, qui ont souscrit chaqu'nt on dictont ou devise à la gloire de la curiositez," 1694.

72 C 27 z. Pierre Bayle to Gilles Ménage.

72 D 37/12. Albert–Henri de Sallengre to ?

73 B 34. Letters to Bruzen de la Martinière.

73 B 36/6. Rousset de Missy to a secretary of William IV.

73 B 37. Henri Basnage de Beauval to Reinier Leers, Letters to Bruzen de la Martinière.

72 H 26. Philippe Masson to La Croze.

74 H 47. Album amicorum of J.C. Ihring.

75 J 52. Account of Nicolas Chevalier's trip through Holland and France.

120 B 21–22. Correspondence of d'Ausson, Marquis de Villarnoux.

121 E 3. Papers of Jean Barbeyrac.

129 J 19, 130 H 1. Papers concerning Jacques Saurin.

134 B 1. Album amicorum of Nicolas Chevalier.

135 B 184. Justus van Effen to ? Claude.

NLSB:
NIEDERSACHSISCHE LANDESBIBLIOTHEK, HANNOVER

LEIBNIZ PAPERS:

Bodemann I: 12, 18, 42, 153, 445, 517, 537, 956. Correspondence of Leibniz with Ancillon, d'Artis, Beausobre, Chauvin, Jaquelot, La Croze, Le Duchat, Des Vignoles, Humbert.

Neu BPU:
BIBLIOTHÈQUE PUBLIQUE ET UNIVERSITAIRE, NEUCHÂTEL

Mss. 1249–63, 1265–70, 1272–85. Correspondence of Louis Bourguet.

Ms. 1257. Catalogus librorum quibus usus est. L[ouis]. B[ourguet].

SMHR:
SOCIÉTÉ DU MUSÉE HISTORIQUE DE LA RÉFORMATION, GENEVA

Archives Tronchin, vols. 42, 44, 45, 49, 50, 51, 55, 57, 60, 62, 71, 210, 291. Papers of Louis Tronchin, Louis II Tronchin and other miscellaneous correspondence and papers.

SPK:
STAATSBIBLIOTHEK PREUSSISCHER KULTURBESITZ,
HAUS 2, BERLIN

SAMMLUNG DARMSTAEDTER:

H 1711 (1). Letters from Johann·Wilhelm Wagner to Formey.

H 1730 (1). Letters from Giulio Carlo Fagnano to Formey.

H 1737 (1). Letters from Andreas Mayer to Formey.

H 1741 (1). Letters from Jens Kraft to Formey.

H 1741 (2). Letters from Jens Kraft to Formey.

H 1745 (2). Letters from François Achard to Jean-Henri-Samuel Formey.

2a 1733 (1). Letters from Jean-Pierre de Crousaz to Formey.

2a 1736 (1). Letters from Büttner to Formey.

2a 1745 (1). Letters from Johann Philipp Heinius to Formey.

2a 1754 (1). Letters from André Pierre de Prémontval to Formey.

2d 1750 (5). Letters from Christian K.H. van der Aa to Formey.

2d 1758 (5). Letters from Theremin to Formey.

2f 1690 (1). Letters from Charles Ancillon to Formey.

2f 1710 (1). Letters from Maturin Veyssière La Croze to Formey.

2f 1727 (1). Letters from Jacques Lenfant to Formey.

2f 1747 (1). Letters from Simon Pelloutier to Formey.

2f 1750 (1). Letters from Formey's son to Formey and other papers by Formey.

2f 1751 (1). Letters from Hanselmann to Formey.

2g 1740 (1). Letters from Theodor Sproegel to Formey.

2h 1710 (1). Letters from Jean Barbeyrac to Formey.

2h 1743 (2). Letters from Emmerich de Vattel to Formey.

2h 1744 (2). Letters from Ludwig Martin Kahle to Formey.

2h 1750 (2). Letters from Philippe Joseph de Jariges to Formey.

2h 1751 (2). Letters from Elie Luzac to Formey.

2i 1745 (1). Letters from Francheville to Formey.

2l 1756 (2). Letters from von Schlabrendorf to Formey.

2l 1730 (2). Letters from Johann Klefeker to Formey.

2m 1757 (1). Letters from Johann Joachim Ewald to Formey.

SAMMLUNG ADAM:
Nachl. 141. Petition of Etienne Chauvin.

UBA:
UNIVERSITEITSBIBLIOTHEEK, AMSTERDAM

B 36, B 37, C 2, C 3, C 11, C 14, C 16, C 19, C 23, C 36, C 37, C 38, C 39, C 40, C 41, C 45, C 46, C 48, C 50, C 51, C 53, C 57, C 65, C 69,

C 71, C 73, C 77, C 78, C 81, C 82, C 83, C 89, C 91, C 108, C 115, C 116, C 124, C 126, C 130, C 134, C 135, C 136, J 1, J 3, J 6, J 12, J 13, J 17, J 18, J 20, J 22, J 23, J 25, J 33, J 39, J 40, J 41, J 42, J 45, J 53, J 54, J 57, J 58, J 60, J 70, J 73, J 76, J 81, J 82, J 96, K 3, K 13, K 14, K 17, K 25, K 43, K 53, K 87, K 89, K 90, N 24, S 10, E.p. 88, III D 17, III D 24, E.p. 89. Correspondence of Jean Le Clerc.

A 20. Letters from Jean Claude to François Turrettini.

A 21. Letters from François Turrettini to Jean Claude.

A 92. Letters from David Martin to F. Hesselius.

A 158, Q 97 a–b. Letters from César de Missy to Jean-Jacques Wetstein.

A 169. Letters from Jacques Wetstein to Jean-Jacques Wetstein.

C 38. Letters from Jean Claude to Jean Le Clerc.

C 112. Letter from d'Origny Delaloge to Pierre Des Maizeaux.

E 138, III E 10. Letters from Henri Justel to Isaac Vossius.

G 1 27. Letter from Prosper Marchand to Pierre Mortier.

G 1 87, G m 8. Letters from Johan Hendrik Wetstein to Gilles Ménage.

G 67. Letters from Pierre-Daniel Huet to Etienne Morin.

J 2, M 16. Letters from Pierre Allix to Philipp van Limborch.

K 127. Prosper Marchand.

M 16. Letters from Pierre Allix to Philipp van Limborch.

M 19. Letters from Gilbert Burnet to Philipp van Limborch.

M 20. Letters from Pierre Coste to Philipp van Limborch.

M 29. Letters from Charles Le Cène to Philipp van Limborch.

M 33. Letters from Jean Masson to Philipp van Limborch.

N 24. Letters from Pierre Bayle to Jacques Lenfant.

N 100. Correspondence of Henri Wetstein and J. Goethals.

2 T 1. Letters from Jean Barbeyrac to J. Suderman.

258. Letters from John Locke to Philipp van Limborch.

III D 16, 17. Philipp van Limborch correspondence.

III D 24, "Epistolae ad Anglos."

III E 9 #236. Letters from Etienne Le Moyne to Isaac Vossius.

III E 10. Letters from Henri Justel to Isaac Vossius, Etienne Le Moyne to Vossius.

IV Ag^2 y. Letter from G. van Doeveren to Mathieu Maty.

UBL:
UNIVERSITEITSBIBLIOTHEEK, LEIDEN

March. 1. Papers of the literary society associated with the *Journal litéraire*.

March. 2. Correspondence of Prosper Marchand.

Correspondence of Jacques Basnage.

Letters to Charles Le Vier.

Letters to Reinier Leers.

Letters of Bernard de la Monnoye to Du Homel.

March. 4:1. Letters from, to, and about Pierre Bayle 1672–1706.

March. 5:2. Letters from Des Maizeaux to Marchand.

March. 5:4. Letters concerning 1714 ed. of Bayle's *Letters*.

March. 29. Papers concerning *libraires'* quarrels.

March. 44:3, f. 1★. Contract between Charles de la Motte (acting on behalf of Pierre Coste) and Charles Le Vier, Aug. 14, 1716.

March. 45. Life of Pierre Coste and collection of documents about him.

March. 49. Documents concerning Jacques Saurin.

March. 50. Documents concerning Jacques Saurin.

March. 59. Satiric songs and poems, 1727–1756.

March. 62. Michel Mattaire, observations on Toland's *Pantheisticon*.

March. 65. Varia theologica.

Pap. 15. Letters to Etienne Morin

Letters to Pierre Bayle

BPL 246, BPL 2L/6, XVIII.246, Letters to Reinier Leers.

ZAAWD:
FORMER ZENTRALES-ARCHIV DER AKADEMIE DER
WISSENSCHAFTEN DER DDR, BERLIN

I-I-2. Leibniz papers about organization of academy.

I-I-4. Affairs, 1714–1723.

I-I-5. Founding and organization of academy 1743–6.

I-I-7. Acts concerning reform of the society, 1744.

I-III-1. Appointment of officers and pensions.

I-III-2. Acts of members and officers, 1701–37.

I-III-9. Acts of members and officers.

I-IV-3. "Registre général de l'Académie contenant tout ce qui concerne les affaires publiques 1700–68."

I-IV-5. "Registre général contenant la partie littéraire."

I-IV-6. Protocollum concilii Societatis, 1700–1726.

I-IV-13. Extracts of registers, with all deliberations under Maupertuis, 1740–54.

I-IV-39. Register of literary-orientalist class, 1711–42.

I-IV-44. "Actes pour la censure des livres, 1708–69."

I-V-1. Scientific discussions, 1699–1737.

I-V-2. Scientific discussions, 1708–26.

I–V–3. Scientific discussions, 1705–34.

I–V–4. Scientific discussions, 1723–31.

I–V–5. Scientific discussions, 1710–1748.

I–V–5a. Literary correspondence or writings of various savants at the Academy, 1700–50.

I–VII–1. Names of contributors to the *Miscellanea* up to 1786.

I–VIII–18. Concerning almanacs; and academy affairs around 1744.

I–XII–1. Papers of the library.

I–XII–2. Papers of the library, 1726–77.

I–XVI–66. Accounts, 1701.

I–XVI–219. Pension receipts.

NACHLASS LEIBNIZ:

Nr. 3. Correspondence of Leibniz with Maturin Veyssière La Croze.

Printed

Ablabew, Timorowitz [pseud.]. *Voltariana ou Eloges Amphigouriques de Fr. Marie Arrouet.* Paris: no publisher, 1748.

Addisoniana. 2 vols. London: Richard Phillips, 1803.

Alembert, Jean-Le-Rond d'. "Essai sur la Société des Gens de Lettres et des Grands, sur la Réputation, sur les Mécènes, et sur les Récompenses Littéraires." In *Mélanges de littérature, d'histoire, et de philosophie*, vol. II. Berlin: no publisher, 1753.

Ancillon, Charles. *Mémoires concernant les vies et les ouvrages de plusieurs Modernes célèbres dans la République des Lettres.* Amsterdam: Wetsteins, 1709.

Agrippa, Henry Cornelius. *The Vanity of Arts and Sciences.* London: R.B., 1684.

Ana, ou Choix de bons mots; Contes et anecdotes des homme célèbres depuis la naissance des lettres jusqu'à nos jours; suivis d'un choix de propos joyeux, mots plaisans, réparties fines et contes à rire tirés de différens recueils. 10 vols. Amsterdam: no publisher, 1789.

Anti-Menagiana, où l'on cherche ces bons mots, cette morale, ces pensees judicieuses, & tout ce que l'affiche du Menagiana nous a promis. Paris: Laurent d'Houry, Simon Langronne, Charles Osmont, 1693.

Arnauld, Antoine. *La Perpetuité de la foy de l'Eglise Catholique touchant l'Eucharistie, défendue contre les livres du Sieur Claude, Ministre de Charenton.* New ed. 4 vols. Paris: La Veuve Charles Saurex, 1704.

Articles résolus au synode des Eglises Wallonnnes des Provinces Unies des Païs-Bas. Printed after each Synod. Bound copies of those for 1688–1725 and 1720–1760 are in KB, shelf marks 534 B 1–2 and 427 E 25–6.

Artis, Gabriel d'. "Requeste portant plainte contre l'Article XLII. des Résolutions du Synode Wallon tenu à Maestricht le 3. de Mai 1714. & jours suivans. A tres Hauts et tres Puissans Seigneurs, nos Seigneurs les Etats Generaux des Provinces-Unies." N.d. or publisher [1714].

Aubrey, John. *Brief Lives*. Ed. Oliver Lawson Dick. Harmondsworth, Middlesex: Penguin Books, 1962.

Aymon, Jean. *Lettre du Sieur Aymon, Ministre du Saint Evangile, & Docteur aux Droits, a Monsieur N★★★. Professeur en Théologie, dans l'Université Réformée de N★★★*. The Hague: Chez Charles Delo, 1707.

——. *Monumens authentiques de la religion des Grecs, et de la fausseté de plusieurs confessions de foi des chrétiens orientaux; produites contre les théologiens réformez, par les prélats de France & les docteurs de Port-Roial, dans leur fameux ouvrage de la Perpetuité de la foi de l'Eglise Catholique*. The Hague: Charles Delo, 1708.

Bacon, Francis. *The Advancement of Learning and New Atlantis*. Ed. Arthur Johnston. Oxford: Clarendon Press, 1974.

——. *The New Organon and Related Writings*. Ed. Fulton H. Anderson. New York: Liberal Arts Press, 1960.

Baillet, Adrien. *Jugemens des savans sur les principaux ouvrages des auteurs*. Ed. and continued by La Monnoye. 7 vols. Paris: Charles Moette et al., 1722.

Barbeyrac, Jean. *Discours sur l'utilité des lettres et des sciences, par rapport au bien de l'Etat. Prononcé aux Promotions publiques du Collége de Lausanne, le 2. de Mai M.DCC.XIV*. Amsterdam: Pierre Humbert, 1715.

Bardin, Pierre. *Le Lycée du Sr Bardin, ou en plusieurs promenades il est traité des connoissances, des actions, & des plaisirs d'un honneste homme*. Paris: Jean Camusat, 1632.

Barrell, Rex A., ed. *Anthony Ashley Cooper, Earl of Shaftesbury (1671–1713) and "Le Refuge Français"—Correspondence*. Lewiston: Edwin Mellen Press, 1989.

Basnage, Jacques. *Annales des Provinces-Unies, depuis les negotiations pour la Paix de Munster. Avec la description historique de leur gouvernement*. 2 vols. The Hague: Charles Le Vier, 1719 and 1726.

[Baston, Thomas]. *Thoughts on Trade, and a Publick Spirit*. London: Printed for the Author, 1716.

Bayle, Pierre. *Dictionaire historique et critique*. 3rd French ed. 4 vols. Rotterdam: Michel Böhm, 1720.

——. *Dictionnaire historique et critique*. 5th French ed. Amsterdam: P. Brunel, P. Humbert, J. Wetstein & G. Smith, F. l'Honoré et Fils, Z. Chatelain, Covens & Mortier, Pierre Mortier, F. Changuion, J. Catuffe & H. Uytwerf; Leiden: Samuel Luchtmans; The Hague: P. Gosse, J. Neaulme, A. Moetjens, G. Blocke, A. van Dale; Utrecht: Etienne Neaulme, 1740.

——. *The Dictionary Historical and Critical of Mr Peter Bayle*. Trans. Pierre Des Maizeaux. 2nd ed. 5 vols. London: For J.J. & P. Knapton et al., 1734–8.

——, John Peter Bernard, Thomas Birch, George Sale, John Lockman, et al. *A General Dictionary, Historical and Critical . . . with the Corrections and Observations printed in the late Edition at Paris . . . and . . . several thousand Lives never before published*. 10 vols. London: G. Strahan et al., 1734–41.

———. See also Des Maizeaux, Pierre, and Marchand, Prosper.

Bellegarde, Jean-Baptiste Morvan de. *Réfléxions sur ce qui peut plaire ou déplaire dans le commerce du monde.* Paris: Arnoul Seneuze, 1690.

———. *Réfléxions sur le ridicule, et sur les moyens de l'éviter.* Paris: Jean Guignard, 1696.

Bergerac, Cyrano de. "Le Pédant joué." In *Les Contemporains de Molière*, vol. III. Ed. Victor Fournel. Paris: Firmin-Didot, 1875.

Bernard, Jacques. *Actes et mémoires des négociations de la Paix de Ryswick.* 4 vols. The Hague: Adrian Moetjens, 1699.

Beyer, Jean de. *Journaal van Mr. Justinus de Beyer, Heer van Hulzen, over de jaren 1743–1767.* Ed. H.D.J. van Schevichaven. Werken uitgegeven door Gelre, Vereeniging tot Beoefening van Geldersche Geschiedenis, Oudheidkunde en Recht, no. 6. Arnhem: P. Gouda Quint, 1906.

[Beyer, Jean de], ed. *Lettres de critique, d'histoire, de littérature, &c. écrites à divers savans de l'Europe par feu Monsieur Gisbert Cuper.* Amsterdam: Henri du Sauzet & Guillaume Smith, 1742.

Bouhours, Dominique. *Les Entretiens d'Ariste et d'Eugene.* New ed. Paris: Gabriel Huart, 1691.

Boyer, Abel. *The Correspondence of Abel Boyer, Huguenot Refugee 1667–1729.* Ed. Rex A. Barrell. Lewiston: Edwin Mellen Press, 1992.

Bruys, François. *Mémoires historiques, critiques, et littéraires.* Ed. and intro. L. Ph. Joly. Paris: Jean-Thomas Hérissant, 1751.

Bruzen de la Martinière, Antoine Augustin, ed. *Lettres choisies de M. Simon.* 4 vols. New ed. Amsterdam: Pierre Mortier, 1730.

Budé, E. de, ed. *Lettres inédites adressées de 1680 à 1737 à J.-A. Turrettini, Théologien genevois.* 3 vols. Geneva: Imprimerie-Librairie Jules Carey, 1887.

Burman, Peter. *Le Gazettier menteur, ou Mr. le Clerc convaincu de Mensonge & de Calomnie.* Utrecht: Guillaume van de Water, 1710.

Burnet, Gilbert. *The History of the Reformation of the Church of England. The Third Part.* London: For J. Churchill, 1715.

———. *A Letter to Mr. Thevenot. Containing a Censure of Mr. Le Grand's History of King Henry the Eighth's Divorce.* London: For John Starkey and Richard Chiswell, 1689.

———, trans. *A Relation of the Death of the Primitive Persecutors.* By Lucius Coelieus Firmianus Lactantius. 2nd ed. London: A. Baldwin, 1713.

———. *Some Letters Containing, An account of what seemed most remarkable in Switzerland, Italy, &c.* Rotterdam: Abraham Acher, 1686.

Camden, William. *The History of the Most Renowned and Victorious Princess Elizabeth, Late Queen of England.* Ed. Wallace T. MacCaffrey. Chicago: University of Chicago Press, 1970.

[Camusat, Denis-François]. *Histoire critique des journaux.* 2 vols. Ed. Jean-Frédéric Bernard. Amsterdam: J.-F. Bernard, 1734.

Chambers, E. *Cyclopaedia: or, an Universal Dictionary of Arts and Sciences*. 2 vols. London: D. Midwinter et al., 1741.

Chauffepié, Jacques-Georges de. *Nouveau dictionnaire historique et critique, pour servir de supplement ou de continuation au Dictionaire historique et critique, de Mr. Pierre Bayle*. 4 vols. Amsterdam: Z. Chatelain et Fils, H. Uytwerf, J. Wetstein, Arkstee & Merkus, M. Uytwerf, M.M. Rey; The Hague: Pierre de Hondt; Leiden: E. Luzac le jeune, 1750–6.

[Chatelain, J. Samuel, et al.]. "Declaration justificative donnée par le consistoire de l'Eglise Walonne de Rotterdam, à M^r. Frescarode, l'un de ses pasteurs; Contre les bruits diffamans & injurieux, qui ont été repandu *faussement* sur son sujet dans le public." No place, date, publisher [1730].

Chevalier, Nicolas. *Remarques sur la pièce antique de bronze, trouvée depuis quelques années aux environs de Rome, & proposée ensuite aux curieux de l'antiquité, pour tâcher d'en découvrir l'usage: Avec une description de la Chambre de Raretez de l'auteur*. Amsterdam: Abraham Wolfgang, 1694.

Contat, Nicolas, dit Le Brun. *Anecdotes typographiques. Où l'on voit la description des coutumes, moeurs et usages singuliers des compagnons imprimeurs*. Ed. Giles Barber. Oxford: Oxford Bibliographical Society, 1980. (Written in 1762.)

Coste, Pierre. "The Character of Mr. Locke: in a Letter to the Author of the Nouvelles de la République des Lettres." Printed in *A Collection of several Pieces of Mr. John Locke*. Ed. Pierre Des Maizeaux. London: R. Francklin, 1720, pp. iv–xxiv.

——, trans. *Le Christianisme raisonnable, tel qu'il nous est represené dans l'Ecriture Sainte*. By John Locke. 2 vols. 2nd ed. Amsterdam: l'Honoré & Chatelain, 1715.

——, trans. *Le Christianisme raisonnable, tel qu'il nous est represené dans l'Ecriture Sainte*. By John Locke. 2 vols. 3rd ed. Amsterdam: Zacharie Chatelain, 1731.

——, trans. *De l'Education des Enfans*. By John Locke. Amsterdam: Henri Schelte, 1708.

——, trans. *De l'Education des Enfans*. 2 vols. 5th ed. Amsterdam: Maynard Uytwerf, 1744.

——, trans. *Essai philosophique concernant l'entendement humain*. By John Locke. Amsterdam: Henri Schelte, 1700.

——, trans. *Essai philosophique concernant l'entendement humain*. 2nd ed. The Hague: Pierre Husson, 1714.

——, trans. *Essai philosophique concernant l'entendement humain*. 3rd ed. Amsterdam: Pierre Mortier, 1735.

——, trans. *Essai philosophique concernant l'entendement humain*. 4th ed. Amsterdam: Pierre Mortier, 1742.

——. *Histoire de Louis de Bourbon, second du nom, Prince de Condé, et premier Prince du Sang. Contenant ce qui s'est passé en Europe depuis 1640, jusques en 1686. inclusivement*. 2 vols. 3rd ed. The Hague: Jean Neaulme, 1748.

Cuper, Gisbert. See Beyer, Jean de, and Veenendaal, A.J.

Dacier, André. *Nouveaux Eclaircissmens sur les oeuvres d'Horace, avec la réponse à la critique de M. Masson, Ministre refugié en Angleterre.* Paris: Pierre Cot, 1708.

Dacier, Anne. *Des Causes de la corruption du goust.* Paris: Aux dépens de Rigaud directeur de l'Imprimerie Royal, 1714.

——, trans. *Les Oeuvres d'Homère, traduites en françois.* I: *l'Iliade.* Amsterdam: Wetsteins & Smith, 1731.

De Beer, E.S., ed. *The Correspondence of John Locke.* 8 vols. Oxford: Clarendon Press, 1976–82.

"Deductie, Beweerende het Recht der Besluyten, gemomen by 't Walsche Synodus tot laste van D. Armand de la Chapelle Predikant van de Walsche Kerk in s'Hage, overgelevert by de Gecommitteerden van 't gemelde Synodus in name ende van megen 't selve aan Haar Edele Mogende de Heeren Commissarissen tot onderzoek van die zaak aangestelt by Resolutie van Haar Edele Groot Mogende de Heeren Staten van Holland en West Friesland." No place, date, publisher. In BW A 61.

[Des Maizeaux, Pierre], ed. *A Collection of several pieces of M^r. John Locke, Never before printed, or not extant in his Works.* London: R. Francklin, 1720.

——, ed. *Lettres de M^r. Bayle, publiées sur les originaux: avec des remarques.* 3 vols. Amsterdam: Compagnie des Libraires, 1729.

[——]. *The Life of Mr. Bayle. In a Letter to a Peer of Great Britain.* London: no publisher, 1708.

——, ed. *Mélange curieux des meilleurs pieces attribués à Mr. de Saint-Evremond, et de plusieurs autres ouvrages rares ou nouveaux.* 2 vols. Amsterdam: Pierre Mortier, 1706.

——, ed. *Recueil de diverses pieces sur la philosophie, la religion naturelle, l'histoire, les mathematiques, &c. par Mrs. Leibniz, Clarke, Newton, & autres autheurs célèbres.* 2 vols. Amsterdam: H. du Sauzet, 1720.

——, ed. *Scaligerana, Thuana, Perroniana, Pithoeana, et Colomesiana, ou Remarques historiques, critiques, morales, & littéraires de Jos. Scaliger, J.A. de Thou, le cardinal du Perron, Fr. Pithou, & P. Colomiés.* Amsterdam: Covens and Mortier, 1740. 2 vols.

——. *La Vie de Monsieur Boileau Despreaux.* Amsterdam: Henri Schelte, 1712.

Diderot, Denis, et al. *Encyclopédie, ou dictionnaire raisonnée des sciences, des arts et des métiers.* Neuchâtel: Samuel Faulche & Cie, 1765.

Dodsley, Robert. *The Correspondence of Robert Dodsley 1733–1764.* Ed. James E. Tierney. Cambridge: Cambridge University Press, 1988.

Du Mont, Jean. *Batailles gagnées par le Serenissime Prince Fr. Eugene de Savoye sur les ennemis de la Foi, et sur ceux de l'Empereur & de l'Empire, en Hongrie, en Italie, en Allemagne, & aux Pais-Bas.* The Hague: Pierre Gosse, Rutgert Ch. Alberts, 1725.

——. *Les Soupirs de l'Europe &c. Or, the Groans of Europe at the Prospect of the Present Posture of Affairs. In a Letter from a Gentleman at the Hague to a Member of Parliament.* No place or publisher, 1713.

——. *Mémoires politiques pour servir à la parfaite intelligence de l'histoire de la Paix de Ryswick*. 4 vols. The Hague: François l'Honoré & Etienne Foulque, 1698–9.

[Du Refuge, Eustache]. *Traicté de la Court*. [Antwerp?: 1615?]

[Edwards, Thomas]. *A Supplement to Mr. Warburton's Edition of Shakespear. Being the Canons of Criticism, and Glossary, collected from the Notes in that celebrated Work, and proper to be bound up with it*. London: M. Cooper, 1748.

Elite des bons mots et des pensées choisies, recüeillies avec soin des plus celebres auteurs, & principalement des livres en Ana. Amsterdam: Jaques Desbordes, 1704.

Erman, J.P., and P.C.F. Reclam. *Mémoires pour servir à l'histoire des réfugiés françois dans les états du Roi*. 9 vols. Berlin: Jean Jasperd (vols. I–VII), 1782–90; Frédéric Barbiez (VIII and IX), 1794–9.

"Extrait des Articles du Synode des Eglises Wallonnes des Provinces Unies des Païs-Bas, assemblé à Flessingue le Jeudi 31 May [1736] & jours suivans, concernant Mr. de la Chapelle." No place, publisher, date [1736].

Faret, Nicolas. *L'Honneste homme ou, l'art de plaire à la court*. Paris: Toussaincts du Bray, 1632.

——. *L'Honeste Homme; ou, l'Art de plaire à la cour*. Paris: Mathurin Henault, 1637.

Fertel, Martin Dominique. *La Science pratique de l'imprimerie*. Saint Omer: Martin Dominique Fertel, 1723.

[Formey, Jean-Henri-Samuel]. *Choix de mémoires et abrégé de l'histoire de l'Académie de Berlin*. 2 vols. Berlin: Haude, 1761.

——, ed. *Ducatiana, ou Remarques de feu M. Le Duchat, sur divers sujets d'histoire et de litterature, recueillies dans ses MSS. & mises en ordre par M.F.* 2 vols. Amsterdam: Pierre Humbert, 1738.

——. *Eloges des académiciens de Berlin, et de divers autres savans*. 2 vols. Berlin: Etienne de Bourdeaux, 1757.

——. *Histoire de l'Academie Royale des Sciences et Belles Lettres, depuis son origine jusqu'à présent*. Berlin: Haude & Spener, 1750.

——. *Histoire de l'Academie Royale des Sciences et Belles Lettres, depuis son origine jusqu'à présent*. Berlin: Haude & Spener, 1752.

Frederick II. *Oeuvres posthumes de Frederic II, Roi de Prusse*. Berlin: Voss & fils and Decker & fils, 1788.

Frescarode, Jérémie. *Apologie pour les Synodes, et pour Mr. Saurin, dans laquelle, sans toucher à la question du mensonge officieux, on justifie les procedures de ces assemblées, et on démontre que cet auteur a pleinement rectifié l'explication qu'il avoit proposée, comme la plus naturelle, sur I Sam. XVI. vs. 2*. Rotterdam: Jean Daniel Beman, 1731.

Furetieriana ou les bons mots, et les remarques d'histoire, de morale, de critique, de plaisanterie, & d'érudition, de Mr. Furetiere, Abbé de Chalivoy, de l'Academie Françoise. Brussels: François Foppens, 1696.

Gabillon, Frédéric Auguste. *Apologia, Seu Defensio Frederici Augusti de Gabillon, nefariis Jacobi Bernardi opposita calumniis, quas in suis Litterariae Reipublicae nuntiis*

Mensis Novembris 1707. inseruit, Paginâ 579. & 580. No publisher or date [1708]

———. *La Défense de la divinité de Jésus-Christ, et de la Grace intérieure, par l'Ecriture Sainte contre les paradoxes impies & extravagans de M. Le Clerc et de ses adherans, avec la réfutation de ses notes sur le Nouveau Testament.* The Hague: Printed for the author, 1707.

———. *Oraison funebre de tres haut, tres puissant, tres excellent, & tres pieux monarque, Guillaume III . . . prononcée à Leyde le jeudi 18 Mai 1702 dans l'Eglise Françoise.* 2nd ed. London: Paul Vaillant, 1707.

———. *La Vérité de la Réligion Réformée prouvé par l'Ecriture Sainte, & par l'antiquité.* The Hague: Abraham Troyel, 1701.

Garnier, Jean-Jacques. *L'Homme de lettres.* Paris: Panckoucke, 1764.

Gerretson, C., and P. Geyl, eds. *Briefwisseling en Aanteekeningen van Willem Bentinck, Heer van Rhoon (tot aan de Dood van Willem IV 22 October 1751).* Vol. I. Werken Uitgegeven door het Historisch Genootschap, 3rd ser., no. 62. Utrecht: Keminck en Zoon, 1934.

Gibbon, Edward. *Essai sur l'étude de la littérature.* London: T. Becket and P.A. De Hondt, 1761.

Grenaille, François de. *Le Bon Esprit.* Paris: André Soubron, 1641.

Hearne, Thomas. *Remarks and Collections of Thomas Hearne.* 11 vols. Ed. C.E. Doble (vols. I–III); D.W. Rannie (IV–V); Committee of the Oxford Historical Society (VI–VIII); H.E. Salter (IX–XI). Oxford: Clarendon Press for the Oxford Historical Society, 1885–1921.

Heinsius, Anthonie. See Veenendaal, A.J., Jr.

Heumann, Christoph August. *Conspectus Reipublicae Literariae sive Via ad Historia Literarium.* 4th ed. Hanover: Foerster and Sons, 1735.

L'Histoire des imaginations extravagantes de Monsieur Oufle causées par la lecture des livres qui traitent de la magie . . . 2 vols. Amsterdam: Estienne Roger, Pierre Humbert, Pierre de Coup, & les Frères Chatelain, 1710.

Hodgson, Norma, and Cyprian Blagden, eds. *The Notebook of Thomas Bennet and Henry Clements (1686–1719) with some aspects of Book Trade Practice.* Oxford Bibliographical Society Publications n.s. VI, 1953.

Huet, Pierre-Daniel. *Huetiana, ou pensées diverses de M. Huet, Evesque d'Avranches.* Paris: Jacques Estienne, 1722.

Janssens-Knorsch, Uta, ed. *The Life and 'Mémoires Secrets' of Jean Des Champs (1707–1767).* Huguenot Society of Great Britain and Ireland, Quarto Series, n.s. no. 1, 1989.

Jordan, Charles-Etienne. *Disquisitio Historico-Literaria, de Jordano Bruno, Nolano.* St. Primkenau: Ragoczy, 1725.

———. *Histoire d'un voyage litteraire, fait en M.DCC.XXXIII. en France, en Angleterre, et en Hollande.* The Hague: Adrien Moetjens, 1735.

———. *Histoire d'un voyage litteraire, fait en M.DCC.XXXIII. en France, en Angleterre, et en Hollande.* 2nd ed. The Hague: Adrien Moetjens, 1736.

———. *Histoire de la vie et des ouvrages de Mr. La Croze, avec des remarques de cet auteur sur divers sujets.* Amsterdam: François Changuion, 1741.

[———]. *Recueil de littérature, de philosophie, et d'histoire.* Amsterdam: François L'Honoré, 1730.

Knuttel, W.P.C., ed. *Acta der Particuliere Synoden van Zuid-Holland.* Vols. V and VI. Rijks Geschiedkundige Publicatiën, Kleine Serie 15 and 16. The Hague: Martinus Nijhoff, 1915–16.

La Bruyère, Jean de. *Les Caracteres de Theophraste traduits du Grec: avec les caracteres ou les moeurs de ce siècle.* 2nd ed. Paris: Estienne Michallet, 1688.

[La Croze, Maturin Veyssière]. *Entretiens sur divers sujets d'histoire et de religion, entre Mylord Bolingbroke et Isaac d'Orobio, Rabin des Juifs Portugais à Amsterdam.* London: no publisher, 1770.

La Monnoye, Mr. de, pseud. *Histoire de M^r. Bayle et de ses ouvrages.* Amsterdam: Jaques Desbordes, 1716.

La Pillonnière, François de. *An Answer to the Reverend Dr. Snape's Accusation.* London: James Knapton and Timothy Childe, n.d. [1717].

Larkin, Steve, ed. *Correspondance entre Prosper Marchand et le marquis d'Argens.* Studies on Voltaire and the Eighteenth Century, no. 222. 1984.

[Le Clerc, Jean]. *An Account of the Life and Writings of Mr. John Le Clerc (Philosophy and Hebrew Professor in the College of the Arminians at Amsterdam) To this present Year MDCCXI.* London: For E. Curll and E. Sanger, 1712.

———. *The Life and Character of Mr. John Locke, Author of the Essay concerning Humane Understanding.* Trans. T.F.P. London: John Clark, 1706.

[———]. *Parrhasiana, ou pensées diverses sur des matières de critique, d'histoire, de morale et de politique avec la défense de divers ouvrages de Mr. L.C.* Amsterdam: Henri Schelte, 1701.

Leibniz, Gottfried Wilhelm. *Philosophische Schriften.* Vol. VI: *Nouveaux Essais.* Berlin: Akademie-Verlag, 1962.

Lenglet du Fresnoy, Nicolas. *Méthode pour étudier l'histoire.* New ed. 4 vols. Paris: Pierre Gandouin, 1735.

Lettre à Mr Bernard, Pasteur de Leide, & Lecteur en Philosophie, dans l'Académie de la même ville, sur l'Apologie de Frideric Auguste Gabillon, moine défroqué. Amsterdam: Henri Schelte, 1708.

"Lettre circulaire du consistoire de l'eglise walonne de Leyden aux églises walonnes des Provinces Unies, au sujet de l'affaire de Mr. Saurin." [Untitled: title is from catalogue of KB; shelf mark is 358 E 101 9.] No place or publisher, 1730.

"Lettre circulaire de l'Eglise de Leyden au sujet de la Déclaration justificative donnée par le Consistoire de Rotterdam à M^r. Frescarode touchant des ratures faittes dans les Articles du Synode de la Haye dont il êtoit le Secretaire." [Untitled: title is from contemporary table of contents in front of collection of pamphlets, KB shelf mark 358 E 101 11.] No place or publisher, 1731.

"Lettre circulaire de l'Eglise de Rotterdam, pour justifier sa Déclaration donnée

à M^r. Frescarode et pour combattre les raisonnemens de M^rs. de Leyden."
[Untitled: title from contemporary table of contents in front of collection of pamphlets, KB shelf mark 358 E 101 12.] No place or publisher, 1732.

Lilienthal, Michael. *De Machiavelismo literario, sive De perversis quorundam in Republica Literaria inclarescendi artibus Dissertatio Historico-Moralis.* Königsberg & Leipzig: Henricus Boye, 1713.

Livre synodal contentant les articles résolus dans des Synodes des Eglises Wallonnes des Pays-Bas. 2 vols. The Hague: Martinus Nijhoff, 1896–1904.

Locke, John. *An Essay Concerning Human Understanding.* Ed. Alexander Campbell Fraser. 2 vols. New York: Dover Publications Reprint. (Edition first published in 1894.)

———. "The Reasonableness of Christianity, as Delivered in the Scriptures." In *The Works of John Locke.* Vol. VII, pp. 3–158. London: Thomas Tegg et al., 1823.

———. *Familiar Letters between Mr. John Locke, and Several of his Friends.* London: F. Noble, T. Wright, and J. Duncan, 1742.

———. See also Coste, Pierre; Axtell, James, L.; and De Beer, E.S.

McKenzie, D.F., and J.C. Ross. *A Ledger of Charles Ackers, Printer of "The London Magazine."* Oxford Bibliographical Society Publications, n.s. XV, 1968.

Marais, Mathieu. *Journal et mémoires de Mathieu Marais, avocat au Parlement de Paris, sur la Régence et le règne de Louis XV (1715–1737).* Ed. de Lescure. 4 vols. Paris: Firmin Didot Frères, Fils et Cie, 1863.

Marchand, Prosper. *Dictionnaire historique, ou mémoires critiques et littéraires, concernant la vie et les ouvrages de divers personnages distingués, particulierement dans la Republique des Lettres.* Ed. J.-N.-S. Allamand. The Hague: Pierre de Hondt, 1758.

———, ed. *Lettres choisies de M^r. Bayle, avec des remarques.* 3 vols. Rotterdam: Fritsch and Böhm, 1714.

Maslen, Keith, and John Lancaster. *The Bowyer Ledgers.* London: Bibliographical Society, 1991.

Maty, Paul. *Protestation du Sr Paul Maty, Ministre du St. Evangile, & Docteur en Philosophie, contre ce qui s'est passé dans le Synode Wallon, assemblé à Campen en Mai 1730. sur le sujet de la "Lettre d'un théologien à un autre théologien sur le Mystére de la Trinité."* The Hague: Corneille van Zanten, 1730.

Ménage, Gilles. *Anti-Baillet ou Critique du livre de M^r. Baillet, intitulé Jugemens des Savans.* The Hague: Estienne Foulque and Louis van Dole, 1688.

———. *Menagiana, ou bons mots, rencontres agréables, pensées judicieuses, et observations curieuses, de M. Menage, de l'Academie Françoise.* Amsterdam: Adrian Braakman, 1693.

Mencke, Johann Burchard. *De la charlatanerie des savans; par Monsieur Menken: avec des remarques critiques de differens auteurs.* Trans. from Latin by David Durand. The Hague: Jean van Duren, 1721.

[Mercier, Louis-Sébastien]. *De la littérature et des littérateurs.* Yverdon: no publisher, 1778.

Méré, Antoine Gombaud, Chevalier de. *De l'esprit*. Paris: Denys Thierry and Claude Barbin, 1677.

———. *De la conversation*. Paris: Denys Thierry and Claude Barbin, 1677.

"The Minute Book of the Partners in the *Grub Street Journal*." [Ms. 450, Queen's College Library, Oxford.] Printed in *Publishing History* IV (1978), 49–94.

Molhuysen, P.C., ed. *Bronnen tot de Geschiedenis der Leidsche Universiteit: Vierde deel, 18 Febr. 1682–8 Febr. 1725*. Rijks Geschiedkundige Publicatiën, Grote Serie 45. The Hague: Martinus Nijhoff, 1920.

Molière, J.-B.P. "Les Femmes savantes." In *Le Bourgeois gentilhomme, Les Femmes savantes, Le Malade imaginaire*. Ed. Georges Couton. Paris: Gallimard, 1971.

Motteux, Pierre, ed. *The History of the Renowned Don Quixote de la Manch*. By Miguel de Cervantes Saavedra. 4 vols. London: Samuel Buckley, 1705–6.

Moxon, Joseph. *Mechanick Exercises on the Whole Art of Printing*. Ed. Herbert Davis and Harry Carter. London: Oxford University Press, 1958.

Naudaeana et Patiniana, ou singularitez remarquables, prises des conversations de Mess. Naudé & Patin. Paris: Chez Florentin & Pierre Delaulne, 1701.

Naudé, Gabriel. *Instruction à la France sur la verité de l'histoire des Freres de la Rose-Croix*. Paris: François Iulliot, 1623.

Newton, Isaac. *The Correspondence of Isaac Newton*. 7 vols. Ed. H.W. Turnbull, J.F. Scott, A. Rupert Hall and Laura Tilling. Cambridge: Cambridge University Press, 1959–77.

Niceron, Jean-Pierre. *Memoires pour servir à l'histoire des hommes illustres dans la République des Lettres*. 43 vols. Paris: Briasson, 1729–45.

North, Roger. *General Preface and Life of Dr. John North*. Ed. Peter Millard. Toronto: University of Toronto Press, 1984.

[Oelven, Christoph Heinrich.] "Lettre tres-savante & tres honorable de La Societé Royale des sciences de Paris à Mr. d'Oelven, Capitaine de Cavallerie de Sa Majesté le Roy de Prusse, Illustre de la Societé Royale de Berlin, Auteur des presens, par son Excellence Mons. L'Abbé Bignon, President, &c&c. Ecrite à Paris le 4 de Juillet 1709." Cologne: Ulric Liebpert, Imprimeur du Roy, 1709.

[Ortigue de Vaumorière, P. d'.] *L'Art de plaire dans la conversation, par feu Mr. l'Abbé de Bellegarde*. The Hague: Antoine van Dole, 1743.

Perrault, Charles. *Les Hommes illustres qui ont paru en France pendant ce siecle*. 2 vols. Paris: Antoine Dezallier, 1697.

Pineau-Duclos, Charles. *Considérations sur les moeurs de ce siècle*. Berlin: Etienne de Bourdeaux, 1751.

Pope, Alexander. "The Dunciad." Ed. James Sutherland. Twickenham edition. Vol. V. 3rd ed. London: Methuen, 1963.

Réfléxions sur les Jugemens des Sçavans, envoyées à l'Auteur. The Hague: Arnout Leers, 1691.

Romanus, Carolus Fridericus. *Dissertatio Academica de Republica Litteraria*. Leipzig: Gozianis, 1698.

Russell, Rachel. *Letters of Rachel Lady Russell*. Ed. Berry and Martin. 2 vols. London: Longman, Brown, Green, and Longmans, 1853.

[St. Hyacinthe, Thémiseul de.] *Le Chef d'Oeuvre d'un Inconu. Poëme heureusement découvert & mis au jour, avec des remarques savantes & recherchées. Par M. le Docteur Chrisostome Matanasius*. 4th ed. Revûë, corrigée, augmentée, & diminuée. The Hague: Pierre Husson, 1716.

Sainte-Marthe, Scévole de. *Eloges des homme illustres, qui depuis un siecle ont fleury en France dans la profession des lettres*. Trans. from Latin by G. Colletet. Paris: Antoine de Sommaville, Augustin Courbé, François Langlois, 1644.

Saurin, Jacques. *Dissertation sur le mensonge*. 2nd ed. The Hague: Pierre de Hondt, 1730.

Savary des Brusons, Jacques. *Dictionnaire universel de commerce*. Ed. and contd. by Philemon-Louis Savary. 3 vols. Paris: Jacques Estiennes, 1723–30.

———. *Le Parfait négociant ou instruction generale pour ce qui regarde le commerce des marchandises de France, & des pays etrangers*. Ed. Philemon-Louis Savary. Paris: La veuve Estienne, 1736.

"Seconde lettre circulaire de l'Eglise de Leyden pour justifier son procédé et se deffendre des attaques de Mrs de Rotterdam." [No title: this title is the description in a collection of pamphlets, KB, shelf mark 358 E 101 12.] N.p., no publisher, April 6, 1732.

Shadwell, Thomas. *The Virtuoso*. London: Henry Herringman, 1676.

Six Letters from A—d B—r to Father Sheldon, provincial of the Jesuits in England. London: J. Morgan, 1756.

Sorel, Charles. *La Bibliotheque françoise, de M.C. Sorel, Ou le Choix et l'Examen des Livres François . . .* Paris: Compagnie des Libraires du Palais, 1664.

———. *De la Connoissance des bons livres, ou examen de plusieurs autheurs*. Paris: André Pralard, 1671.

Sprat, Thomas. *History of the Royal Society*. Ed. Jackson I. Cope and Harold Whitmore Jones. St. Louis: Washington University Press, 1958.

Subligny, Adrien Perdou de. "La Folle querelle ou la critique d'Andromaque." In *Les Contemporains de Molière*. Ed. Victor Fournel. Vol. III. Paris: Firmin-Didot, 1875.

Tablettes de l'homme du monde, ou analise de sept qualitez essentielles à former le beau caractére d'homme du monde accompli. "Cosmopoli: chez Auguste le Catholique, à l'Enseigne de l'Orthodoxie," 1715.

Theobald, Lewis. *Shakespeare restored: Or, a Specimen of the Many Errors, as well Committed, as Unamended, by Mr. Pope in his Late Edition of this Poet*. London: R. Franklin, T. Woodman, Charles Davis, and S. Chapman, 1726.

Trembley, Maurice, ed. *Correspondance inédite entre Réaumur et Abraham Trembley*. Geneva: Georg & Cie, 1943.

Turner, Winifred, ed. *The Aufrère Papers: Calendar and Selections*. Huguenot Society of London, Quarto Series XL (1940).

Tyrwhitt, Thomas. *Observations and Conjectures upon some Passages of Shakespeare*. Oxford: Clarendon Press, 1766.

"Uitvaert van P★★★ J★★★." Printed with "Op de Afbeelding van P★★★ J★★★." [No place, publisher, date: KB copy lacking title page. 1713?]

Veenendaal, A.J., ed. *Het Dagboek van Gisbert Cuper Gedeputeerde te Velde Gehouden in de Zuidelijke Nederlanden in 1706*. Rijks Geschiedkundige Publicatiën, Kleine Serie, 30. The Hague: Martinus Nijhoff, 1950.

Veenendaal, A.J., Jr., ed. *De Briefwisseling van Anthonie Heinsius 1702–1720*. 8 vols. Rijks Geschiedkundige Publicatien, Grote Serie, vols. 158, 163, 169, 177, 183, 189, 194, 198. The Hague: Martinus Nijhoff, 1976–86.

"A View of the True Interest of the Several States of Europe since the Accession of their Present Majesties to the Imperial Crown of Great Britain. Also Shewing the many Advantages of a Strict Union in Opposition to the Unjust Usurpations and False Pretensions of the French King." London: Thomas Newborough & John Bullord, 1689.

Vigneul-Marville [i.e. Noël Bonaventure d'Argonne]. *Mélanges d'histoire et de littérature*. 2 vols. Rouen: Antoine Maurry, 1700.

"Le Vrai interêt des princes chretiens, opposé aux faux interêts, qui ont été depuis peu mis en lumiére." "Cologne: Pierre Marteau," [i.e. the Netherlands], 1686.

Wanley, Humfrey. *The Diary of Humfrey Wanley 1715–1726*. Ed. C.E. Wright and Ruth C. Wright. 2 vols. London: Bibliographical Society, 1966.

The Weekly Oracle: Or, Universal Library, By a Society of Gentlemen. Dec. 1734– 1736.

Winter, Eduard, ed. *Die Registres der Berliner Akademie der Wissenschaften 1746– 1766*. Berlin: Akademie Verlag, 1957.

Wolff, Johann Christoph. *Casauboniana, sive Isaaci Casauboni varia Scriptoribus Librisque judicia, Observationes sacrae in utriusque Foederis loca, Philologicae item & Ecclesiasticae, Ut & Animadversiones in Annales Baronii Ecclesiasticos ineditae, Ex varii Casauboni MSS. In Bibliotheca Bodlejana reconditis*. Hamburg: Christian Libezeit, 1710.

Periodicals

Bibliothèque angloise, ou Histoire littéraire de la Grande Bretagne. 1717–27.

Bibliothèque britannique, ou Histoire des ouvrages des savans de la Grande-Bretagne. 1733–47.

Bibliothèque choisie, pour servir de suite à la Bibliothèque universelle. 1703–18.

Bibliothèque germanique ou Histoire littéraire de l'Allemagne et des pays du Nord. 1720– 41.

Bibliothèque italique ou Histoire littéraire de l'Italie. 1728–34.

Bibliothèque raisonnée des ouvrages des savans de l'Europe. 1728–53.

Critique désintéressée des journaux littéraires et des ouvrages des savans. 1730.

Histoire critique de la République des Lettres, tant ancienne que moderne. 1712–18.

Histoire des ouvrages des sçavans. 1687–1709.

The History of Learning: or, an Abstract of several Books Lately Published, as well abroad, as at home. 1691.

Journal des sçavans. 1665–1828.

Journal littéraire. 1713–22, 1729–39.

Journal littéraire d'Allemagne, de Suisse et du Nort. 1741–6.

Lettres historiques; contenant ce qui se passe de plus important en Europe; et les réfléxions nécessaires sur ce sujet. 1692–1736.

Lettres sérieuses et badines sur les ouvrages des savans, et sur d'autres matières. 1729–33.

Memoirs for the Ingenious. Containing Several Curious Observations in Philosophy, Mathematicks, Physick, Philology, and other Arts and Sciences. In Miscellaneous Letters. 1693.

Memoirs of Literature. 1710–14.

Mémoires pour l'histoire des sciences & des beaux arts. 1701–69.

Memoires de littérature. 1715–17.

Mercure sçavant. 1684.

Nouvelles de la République des Lettres. 1684–89, 1699–1710, 1716–18.

The Spectator. Ed. Donald F. Bond. 5 vols. Oxford: Clarendon Press, 1965.

Universal Historical Bibliotheque: or an Account of most of the Considerable Books printed in all Languages . . . 1687.

Useful Transactions in Philosophy, And other sorts of Learning. 1709.

Works of the Learned, or an Historical Account and Impartial Judgment of Books newly Printed, both Foreign and Domestick. 1691–2.

SECONDARY SOURCES

Books

Acomb, Frances. *Mallet du Pan (1749–1800): A Career in Political Journalism.* Durham, NC: Duke University Press, 1973.

Adams, Geoffrey. *The Huguenots and French Opinion 1688–1787: The Enlightenment Debate on Toleration.* Waterloo, Ontario: Canadian Corporation for Studies in Religion, 1991.

Agnew, David C.A. *Henri de Ruvigny, Earl of Galway. A Filial Memoir, with a Prefatory Life of his Father, Le Marquis de Ruvigny.* Edinburgh: William Paterson, 1864.

Aiton, E.J. *Leibniz: A Biography.* Bristol: Adam Hilger, 1985.

Almagor, Joseph. *Pierre des Maizeaux (1673–1745): Journalist and English Correspondent for Franco-Dutch Periodicals 1700–1720*. Amsterdam and Maarssen: Holland University Press, 1989.

Altick, Richard D. *Lives and Letters: A History of Literary Biography in England and America*. New York: Alfred A. Knopf, 1966.

Anderson, Judith H. *Biographical Truth: The Representation of Historical Persons in Tudor-Stuart Writing*. New Haven: Yale University Press, 1984.

Axtell, James L., ed. and intro. *The Educational Writings of John Locke*. Cambridge: Cambridge University Press, 1968.

Baal, Jan van. *Reciprocity and the Position of Women*. Assen: Koninklijke Van Gorcum, 1975.

Bachman, Albert. *Censorship in France from 1715 to 1750: Voltaire's Opposition*. New York: Publications of the Institute of French Studies, 1934.

Badstübner-Gröger, Sibylle, et al. *Hugenotten in Berlin*. Berlin: Nicolaische Verlagsbuchhandlung, 1988.

Baker, Keith Michael, ed. *The Political Culture of the Old Régime*. Oxford: Pergamon Press, 1987.

Bakker, G. *De Guerilla der Camisards: Een episode uit de Hugenotenstrijd, 1702–1710*. Zutphen: De Walburg Pers, 1981.

Bakker, M., et al. *Hugenoten in Groningen: Franse Vluchtelingen tussen 1680 en 1720*. Groningen: Wolters-Noordhoff/Bouma's Boekhuis, 1985.

Baldwin, John, and Richard A. Goldthwaite, eds. *Universities in Politics*. Baltimore: Johns Hopkins Press, 1972.

Barnes, Annie. *Jean Le Clerc (1657–1736) et la République des Lettres*. Paris: Librairie E. Droz, 1938.

Basker, James G. *Tobias Smollett: Critic and Journalist*. Newark, Del.: University of Delaware Press, 1988.

Baxter, Stephen B. *William III and the Defense of European Liberty 1650–1702*. New York: Harcourt, Brace & World, 1966.

Behrens, C.B.A. *Society, Government and the Enlightenment: The Experiences of Eighteenth-Century France and Prussia*. New York: Harper & Row, 1985.

Belin, J.-P. *Le Commerce des livres prohibés à Paris de 1750 à 1789*. Paris: Belin frères, 1913.

Beljame, Alexandre. *Men of Letters and the English Public in the Eighteenth Century, 1660–1744*. Ed. Bonamy Dobrée, trans. E.O. Lorimer. London: Kegan Paul, Trench, Trubner, 1948. (First published in French, 1881.)

Ben-David, Joseph, and Terry Nichols Clark. eds. *Culture and its Creators: Essays in Honor of Edward Shils*. Chicago: University of Chicago Press, 1977.

Berkvens-Stevelinck, Christiane M.G. *Prosper Marchand et l'histoire du livre: quelques aspects de l'érudition bibliographique dans la première moitié du XVIIIᵉ siècle, particulièrement en Hollande*. Proefschrift, University of Amsterdam. Bruges: Drukkerij Sinte Catharina, 1978.

——. *Prosper Marchand: La vie et l'oeuvre (1678–1756)*. Studies over de Geschiedenis van de Leidse Universiteit, vol. 4. Leiden: E.J. Brill, 1987.

——, Hans Bots, P.G. Hoftijzer, and Otto S. Lankhorst. *Le Magasin de l'Univers: The Dutch Republic as the Centre of the European Book Trade*. Leiden: E.J. Brill, 1992.

Black, Jeremy. *The Rise of the European Powers 1679–1793*. London: Edward Arnold, 1990.

Biagioli, Mario. *Galileo, Courtier: The Practice of Science in the Culture of Absolutism*. Chicago: University of Chicago Press, 1993.

Blagden, Cyprian. *The Stationers' Company: A History, 1403–1959*. London: George Allen & Unwin, 1960.

Blanning, T.C.W. *Reform and Revolution in Mainz 1743–1803*. Cambridge: Cambridge University Press, 1974.

Blau, Peter M. *Exchange and Power in Social Life*. New York: John Wiley, 1964.

Bond, Donovan H., and W. Reynolds McLeod, eds. *Newsletters to Newspapers: Eighteenth-Century Journalism*. Morgantown: School of Journalism, West Virginia University, 1977.

Bond, Richmond P., ed. *Studies in the Early English Periodical*. Chapel Hill: University of North Carolina Press, 1957.

Bonno, Gabriel. *Les Relations Intellectuelles de Locke avec la France*. University of California Publications in Modern Philology, vol. 38, no. 2. Berkeley and Los Angeles: University of California Press, 1955.

Bots, Hans, ed. *Henri Basnage de Beauval en de Histoire des Ouvrages des Savans, 1689–1709: Verkenningen binnen de Republiek der Letteren aan de Vooravond van de Verlichting*. Studies van het Instituut voor Intellectuele Betrekkingen tussen de Westeuropese Landen in de Zeventiende Eeuw, 4. 2 vols. Amsterdam: Holland Universiteits Pers, 1976, 1984.

——, ed. *Pieter Rabus en de Boekzaal van Europe 1692–1702: Verkenningen binnen de Republiek der Letteren in het laatste kwart van de zeventiende eeuw*. Studies van het Instituut voor Intellectuele Betrekkingen tussen de Westeuropese Landen in de Zeventiende Eeuw, 2. Amsterdam: Holland Universiteits Pers, 1974.

——. *Republiek der Letteren: Ideaal en Werkelijkheid*. Amsterdam: APA-Holland Universiteits Pers, 1977.

——, H. Hillenaar, J. Janssen, J. van der Korst, and L. van Lieshout. *De "Bibliothèque Universelle et Historique" (1686–1693): Een Periodiek als Trefpunt van Geletterd Europa*. Studies van het Instituut voor Intellectuele Betrekkingen tussen de Westeuropese Landen in de Zeventiende Eeuw, 7. Amsterdam and Maarssen: APA-Holland Universiteits Pers, 1981.

——, G.H.M. Posthumus Meyjes, eds. *La Révocation de l'Edit de Nantes et les Provinces-Unies 1685*. Colloque international du Tricentenaire, Leiden, April 1–3, 1985. Amsterdam and Maarssen: APA-Holland University Press, 1986.

——, G.H.M. Posthumus Meyjes, and Frouke Wieringa. *Vlucht naar de Vrijheid: De Hugenoten en de Nederlanden.* Amsterdam/Dieren: De Bataafsche Leeuw, 1985.

Bourdieu, Pierre. *Homo Academicus.* Trans. Peter Collier. Cambridge: Polity Press, 1988.

——. *Outline of a Theory of Practice.* Trans. Richard Nice. Cambridge: Cambridge University Press, 1977.

Boyce, George, James Curran, and Pauline Wingate. *Newspaper History from the Seventeenth Century to the Present Day.* London: Constable, 1978.

Braudel, Fernand. *The Wheels of Commerce.* Civilization and Capitalism 15th–18th Century, vol. 2. New York: Harper & Row, 1982. (First published in French, 1979.)

Braudy, Leo. *Narrative Form in History and Fiction: Hume, Fielding, and Gibbon.* Princeton: Princeton University Press, 1970.

Brewer, John. *Party Ideology and Popular Politics at the Accession of George III.* Cambridge: Cambridge University Press, 1976.

Brockliss, L.W.B. *French Higher Education in the Seventeenth and Eighteenth Centuries: A Cultural History.* Oxford: Clarendon Press, 1987.

Brockmeier, Peter, Roland Desné, and Jürgen Voss, eds. *Voltaire und Deutschland: Quellen und Untersuchungen zur Rezeption der Französischen Aufklärung.* Stuttgart: J.B. Metzlersche Verlagsbuchhandlung, 1979.

Brown, Harcourt. *Scientific Organizations in Seventeenth Century France (1620–1680).* New York: Russell and Russell, 1967. (First published in 1934.)

Browning, J.D., ed. *Biography in the 18th Century.* New York: Garland Publishing, 1980.

Burke, Peter. *The Renaissance Sense of the Past.* London: Edward Arnold, 1969.

Busken Huet, Coenraad. *Jacques Saurin en Théodore Huet: Proeve van Kerkgeschiedkundige Kritiek.* Haarlem: A.C. Kruseman, 1855.

Butler, Jon. *The Huguenots in America: A Refugee People in the New World Society.* Cambridge, Mass.: Harvard University Press, 1983.

Caldicott, C.E.J., H. Gough, and J.-P. Pittion, eds. *The Huguenots and Ireland: Anatomy of an Emigration.* Dun Laoghaire, Ireland: Glendale Press, 1987.

Calhoun, Craig, ed. *Habermas and the Public Sphere.* Cambridge, Mass.: MIT Press, 1992.

Carpenter, Kenneth E., ed. *Books and Society in History.* New York: R.R. Bowker, 1983.

Carrière, Charles. *Négociants Marseillais au XVIIIᵉ siècle.* 2 vols. Marseille: Institut Historique de Provence, 1973.

Cassirer, Ernst. *The Philosophy of the Enlightenment.* Trans. Fritz C.A. Koelln and James P. Pettegrove. Princeton: Princeton University Press, 1951. (First publish in German, 1951.)

La Catégorie de l'Honneste dans la culture du XVIe siècle. Actes du Colloque international de Sommières II, 1983. Saint-Etienne: Institut d'études de la Renaissance et de l'Age Classique, 1985.

Censer, Jack R., and Jeremy D. Popkin, eds. *Press and Politics in Pre-Revolutionary France*. Berkeley and Los Angeles: University of California Press, 1987.

Cerny, Gerald. *Theology, Politics and Letters at the Crossroads of European Civilization: Jacques Basnage and the Baylean Huguenot Refugees in the Dutch Republic.* Dordrecht: Martinus Nijhoff, 1987.

Chartier, Roger. *Cultural History: Between Practices and Representations*. Trans. Lydia Cochrane. Cambridge: Polity Press, 1987.

——. *The Cultural Origins of the French Revolution*. Trans. Lydia G. Cochrane. Durham and London: Duke University Press, 1991.

——. *The Cultural Uses of Print in Early Modern France*. Trans. Lydia G. Cochrane. Princeton: Princeton University Press, 1987.

——, ed. *Les Usages de l'imprimé (XVᵉ–XIXᵉ siècle)*. Paris: Librairie Arthème Fayard, 1987.

——, ed. *Passions of the Renaissance*. A History of Private Life, vol. III. Trans. Arthur Goldhammer. Cambridge, Mass.: Belknap Press, 1989.

Chaussinand-Nogaret, Guy. *The French Nobility in the Eighteenth Century: From Feudalism to the Enlightenment*. Trans. William Doyle. Cambridge: Cambridge University Press, 1985.

Chauvet, Paul. *Les Ouvriers du livre en France des origines à la Révolution de 1789*. Paris: Presses Universitaires de France, 1959.

Colie, Rosalie L. *Light and Enlightenment: A Study of the Cambridge Platonists and the Dutch Arminians*. Cambridge: Cambridge University Press, 1957.

Collingwood, R.G. *The Idea of History*. Oxford: Clarendon Press, 1946.

Couperus, Marianne, ed. *L'Etude des périodiques anciens: Colloque d'Utrecht*. Paris: Editions A.-G. Nizet, 1972.

——. *Un Périodique français en Hollande: Le Glaneur historique (1731–1733)*. Proefschrift, Rijksuniversiteit te Utrecht. The Hague: Mouton, 1971.

Cranston, Maurice. *John Locke: A Biography*. London: Longmans, Green, 1957.

Cressy, David. *Literacy and the Social Order: Reading and Writing in Tudor and Stuart England*. Cambridge: Cambridge University Press, 1980.

Cristin, Claude. *Aux origines de l'histoire littéraire*. Grenoble: Presses Universitaires de Grenoble, 1973.

Crook, J. Mordaunt. *The British Museum*. London: Allen Lane, The Penguin Press, 1972.

Crucitti Ullrich, Francesca Bianca. *La "Bibliothèque italique": Cultura "italianisante" e giornalismo letterario*. Milan: Riccardo Ricciardi Editore, 1974.

Dann, Otto, ed. *Lesegesellschaften und bürgerliche Emanzipation: Ein europäischer Vergleich*. Munich: Verlag C.H. Beck, 1981.

Darnton, Robert. *The Business of Enlightenment: A Publishing History of the*

Encyclopédie 1775–1800. Cambridge, Mass.: Belknap Press of Harvard University Press, 1979.

——. *The Great Cat Massacre and Other Episodes in French Cultural History*. New York: Basic Books, 1984.

——. *The Kiss of Lamourette*. London: Faber and Faber, 1990.

——. *The Literary Underground of the Old Régime*. Cambridge, Mass.: Harvard University Press, 1982.

——, and Daniel Roche, eds. *Revolution in Print: The Press in France 1775–1800*. Berkeley and Los Angeles: University of California Press, 1989.

Dedieu, Joseph. *Le Rôle politique des Protestants français (1685–1715)*. Paris: Bloud & Gay, 1920.

Delisle, Léopold. *Le Cabinet des Manuscrits de la Bibliothèque Impériale*. Vol. I. Paris: Imprimerie Impériale, 1868.

Dens, Jean-Pierre. *L'Honnête homme et la critique du goût: esthétique et société au XVIIe siècle*. Lexington, KY: French Forum, 1991.

Desautels, Alfred R. *Les Mémoires de Trévoux et le mouvement des idées au XVIIIe siècle 1701–1734*. Rome: Institutum Historicum S.I., 1956.

Dewald, Jonathan. *Aristocratic Experience and the Origins of Modern Culture: France, 1570–1715*. Berkeley: University of California Press, 1993.

Dibon, Paul, ed. *Pierre Bayle: Le philosophe de Rotterdam*. Amsterdam: Elsevier, 1959.

——, and Françoise Waquet. *Johannes Fredericus Gronovius: pèlerin de la République des Lettres: recherches sur le voyage savant au XVIIe siècle*. Geneva: Librairie Droz, 1984.

La Diffusion et la lecture des journaux de langue française sous l'Ancien Régime. Actes du Colloque International, Nijmegen, 3–5 June 1987. Amsterdam and Maarssen: APA-Holland University Press, 1988.

D'Israeli, Isaac. *The Calamities and Quarrels of Authors*. 2nd ed. London: Frederick Warne, 1867.

——. *Curiosities of Literature*. 3 vols. Boston: Lilly, Wait, Colman, and Holden, 1833.

——. *A Second Series of Curiosities of Literature*. 3 vols. London: John Murray, 1824.

Dock, Marie-Claude. *Etude sur le droit d'auteur*. Paris: R. Pichon & R. Durand-Auzias, 1963.

Dodge, Guy Howard. *The Political Theory of the Huguenots of the Dispersion*. Morningside Heights, NY: Columbia University Press, 1947.

Douglas, David. *English Scholars 1660–1730*. 2nd ed. London: Eyre & Spottiswoode, 1951. (First published in 1939.)

Dubois, Claude-Gilbert. *La Conception de l'histoire en France au XVIe siècle (1560–1610)*. Paris: A.-G. Nizet, 1977.

Dülmen, Richard van. *Die Gesellschaft der Aufklärer: Zur bürgerlichen Emanzipation und aufklärischen Kultur in Deutschland.* Frankfurt: Fischer Taschenbuch Verlag, 1986.

——. *The Society of the Enlightenment: The Rise of the Middle Class and Enlightenment Culture in Germany.* Trans. Anthony Williams. Cambridge: Polity Press, 1992.

Eastman, Carol M. *Aspects of Language and Culture.* San Francisco: Chandler & Sharp, 1975.

Eeghen, I.H. van. *De Amsterdamse Boekhandel 1680–1725.* 5 vols. Amsterdam: Scheltema & Holkema, 1961–7 (vols. I–IV); N. Israel, 1978 (vols. V^1 and V^2).

——. *Inventarissen der Archieven van de Gilden en van het Brouwerscollege, Archief der Gemeente Amsterdam.* Amsterdam: 1951.

Eisenstein, Elizabeth L. *Grub Street Abroad: Aspects of the French Cosmopolitan Press from the Age of Louis XIV to the French Revolution.* Oxford: Clarendon Press, 1992.

——. *Print Culture and Enlightenment Thought.* The Sixth Hanes Lecture, presented by the Hanes Foundation for the Study of the Origin and Development of the Book. Chapel Hill: University of North Carolina Press, 1986.

——. *The Printing Press as an Agent of Change.* Cambridge: Cambridge University Press, 1979.

Ekkart, R.E.O. *Haagse drukkers van de 16ᵉ tot en met de 19ᵉ eeuw.* N.p.: Sijthoff Pers, n.d.

Elias, Norbert. *The Court Society.* Trans. Edmund Jephcott. New York: Pantheon Books, 1983. (First published in 1969.)

——. *The History of Manners.* Trans. Edmund Jephcott. New York: Pantheon Books, 1978. (First published in 1939.)

Ellis, Aytoun. *The Penny Universities: A History of the Coffee-Houses.* London: Secker and Warburg, 1956.

Enno van Gelder, H.A. *Getemperde vrijheid.* Groningen: Wolters-Noordhoff, 1972.

Escarpit, Robert, ed. *Le Littéraire et le social: Eléments pour une sociologie de la littérature.* Paris: Flammarion, 1970.

——. *Sociology of Literature.* Trans. Ernest Pick. 2nd ed. London: Frank Cass, 1971.

Estivals, Robert. *La Statistique bibliographique de la France sous la monarchie au XVIIIe siècle.* The Hague and Paris: Mouton, 1965.

Farnham, Fern. *Madame Dacier: Scholar and Humanist.* 2nd ed. Monterey, CA: Angel Press, 1980.

Febvre, Lucien, and Henri-Jean Martin. *The Coming of the Book: The Impact of Printing 1450–1800.* Trans. David Gerard. London: Verso Editions, 1984. (First published in 1958.)

Ferguson, Arthur B. *Clio Unbound: Perception of the Social and Cultural Past in Renaissance England.* Durham, NC: Duke University Press, 1979.

Feyel, Gilles. *La "Gazette" en province à travers ses réimpressions, 1631–1751.* Amsterdam: APA-Holland University Press, 1982.

Field, Arthur. *The Origins of the Platonic Academy of Florence.* Princeton: Princeton University Press, 1988.

Firth, Raymond. *Essays on Social Organization and Values.* London School of Economics Monographs on Social Anthropology. London: Athlone Press, 1969. (First published in 1964.)

———. *Symbols Public and Private.* London: George Allen & Unwin, 1973.

———, ed. *Themes in Economic Anthropology.* London: Tavistock Publications, 1967.

Foss, Michael. *Man of Wit to Man of Business: The Arts and Changing Patronage 1660–1750.* Bristol: Bristol Classical Press, 1988. (First published in 1971.)

Fox, Levi, ed. *English Historical Scholarship in the Sixteenth and Seventeenth Centuries.* London: Oxford University Press, 1956.

Funck-Brentano, Frantz. *Les Nouvellistes.* Paris: Librairie Hachette, 1905.

Furet, François, et al. *Livre et société dans la France du XVIIIᵉ siècle.* 2 vols. Paris: Mouton, 1965, 1970.

———, and Jacques Ozouf. *Reading and Writing: Literacy in France from Calvin to Jules Ferry.* Cambridge: Cambridge University Press, 1982.

Fussner, F. Smith. *The Historical Revolution: English Historical Writing and Thought 1580–1640.* London: Routledge and Kegan Paul, 1962.

Gaberel, J., and E. Des Hours-Farel. *Jaques Saurin: Sa vie et sa correspondance.* Geneva: J. Cherbuliez, 1864.

Gardair, Jean-Michel. *Le "Giornale de' Letterati" de Rome (1668–1681).* Florence: Leo S. Olschki, 1984.

Garin, Eugenio. *Italian Humanism: Philosophy and Civic Life in the Renaissance.* Trans. Peter Munz. New York: Harper and Row, 1965.

Garraty, John A. *The Nature of Biography.* London: Jonathan Cape, 1958.

Garrisson, Janine. *L'Edit de Nantes et sa Révocation: Histoire d'une intolérance.* Paris: Editions du Seuil, 1985.

Gaskell, Philip. *A New Introduction to Bibliography.* 2nd ed. Oxford: Clarendon Press, 1974.

Gay, Peter. *The Enlightenment: An Interpretation.* 2 vols. New York: Alfred A. Knopf, 1967.

———. *The Party of Humanity.* New York: Norton, 1971.

Geertz, Clifford. *The Interpretation of Cultures.* New York: Basic Books, 1973.

Gilbert, Felix. *Machiavelli and Guicciardini: Politics and History in Sixteenth-Century Florence.* Princeton: Princeton University Press, 1973. (First published in 1965.)

Gilmore, Myron P. *Humanists and Jurists: Six Studies in the Renaissance.* Cambridge, Mass.: Belknap Press, 1963.

Goldsmith, Elizabeth C. *"Exclusive Conversations": The Art of Interaction in Seventeenth-Century France.* Philadelphia: University of Pennsylvania Press, 1988.

Golinski, Jan. *Science as Public Culture: Chemistry and Enlightenment in Britain, 1760–1820*. Cambridge: Cambridge University Press, 1992.

Gooding, David, Trevor Pinch, and Simon Schaffer. *The Uses of Experiment: Studies in the Natural Sciences*. Cambridge: Cambridge University Press, 1989.

Gossman, Lionel. *Medievalism and the Ideologies of the Enlightenment: The World and Work of La Curne de Sainte-Palaye*. Baltimore: Johns Hopkins Press, 1968.

Graff, Harvey J., ed. *Literacy and Social Development in the West*. Cambridge: Cambridge University Press, 1981.

Grafton, Anthony. *Defenders of the Text: The Traditions of Scholarship in an Age of Science, 1450–1800*. Cambridge, Mass.: Harvard University Press, 1991.

———. *Forgers and Critics: Creativity and Duplicity in Western Scholarship*. Princeton: Princeton University Press, 1990.

———, and Lisa Jardine. *From Humanism to the Humanities*. Cambridge, Mass.: Harvard University Press, 1986.

Graham, Walter. *The Beginnings of English Literary Periodicals: A Study of Periodical Literature 1665–1715*. New York: Oxford University Press, 1926.

———. *English Literary Periodicals*. New York: Thomas Nelson, 1930.

Greenblatt, Stephen. *Renaissance Self-Fashioning: From More to Shakespeare*. Chicago: University of Chicago Press, 1980.

Gundersheimer, Werner L., ed. *French Humanism 1470–1600*. New York: Harper and Row, 1969.

Gwynn, Robin D. *Huguenot Heritage: The History and Contribution of the Huguenots in Britain*. London: Routledge & Kegan Paul, 1985.

Haag, Eugène, and Emile Haag. *La France protestante*. 1st ed. 9 vols. Paris: Joël Cherbuliez, 1846–59.

———. *La France protestante*. Ed. Henri Bordier. 2nd ed. 6 vols. Paris: Librairie Sandoz & Fischbacher, 1877–88.

Haase, Erich. *Einführung in die Literatur des Refuge: Der Beitrag der französischen Protestanten zur Entwicklung analytischer Denkformen am Ende des 17. Jahrhunderts*. Berlin: Duncker & Humblot, 1959.

Habermas, Jürgen. *The Structural Transformation of the Public Sphere: An Inquiry into a Category of Bourgeois Society*. Trans. Thomas Burger and Frederick Lawrence. Cambridge, Mass.: MIT Press, 1989.

Hahn, Roger. *The Anatomy of a Scientific Institution: The Paris Academy of Sciences, 1666–1803*. Berkeley and Los Angeles: University of California Press, 1971.

Hampson, Norman. *A Cultural History of the Enlightenment*. New York: Pantheon Books, 1968.

Hardison, O.B., Jr. *The Enduring Monument: A Study of the Idea of Praise in Renaissance Theory and Practice*. Chapel Hill: University of North Carolina Press, 1962.

Harris, Michael. *London Newspapers in the Age of Walpole: A Study of the Origins of the Modern English Press*. London: Associated University Presses, 1987.

——, and Alan Lee, eds. *The Press in English Society from the Seventeenth to Nineteenth Centuries*. London: Associated University Presses, 1986.

Hatin, Eugène. *Les Gazettes de Hollande et la presse clandestine aux XVIIᵉ et XVIIIᵉ siècles*. Paris: Librairie Richelieu, 1845.

——. *Histoire du Journal en France 1631–1853*. 2nd ed. Paris: P. Jannet, 1853.

Hauréau, Barthélemy. *Singularités historiques et littéraires*. Paris: Michel Lévy Frères, 1861.

Hazard, Paul. *The European Mind 1680–1715*. Trans. J. Lewis May. Cleveland: Meridian Books, 1968. (First published in 1935.)

——. *European Thought in the Eighteenth Century from Montesquieu to Lessing*. Trans. J. Lewis May. New Haven: Yale University Press, 1954.

Hellinga, Wytze Gs. *Copy and Print in the Netherlands: An Atlas of Historical Bibliography*. Amsterdam: North-Holland Publishing Company, 1962.

Hemprich, Paul. *Le Journal littéraire de La Haye*. Diss. Friedrich-Wilhelms-Universität, Berlin. Berlin: Fritz Hermann, 1915.

Hepburn, James. *The Author's Empty Purse and the Rise of the Literary Agent*. London: Oxford University Press, 1968.

Hesse, Carla. *Publishing and Cultural Politics in Revolutionary Paris, 1789–1810*. Berkeley: University of California Press, 1991.

Hofstadter, Albert. *Locke and Scepticism*. New York: Albee Press, 1935.

Holmes, Geoffrey, ed. *Britain after the Glorious Revolution, 1689–1714*. London: Macmillan, 1969.

Homans, George Caspar. *Social Behaviour: Its Elementary Forms*. London: Routledge & Kegan Paul, 1973. (First published in 1961.)

Hull, William I. *Benjamin Furly and Quakerism in Rotterdam*. Swarthmore College Monographs on Quaker History, 5. Lancaster, PA: Lancaster Press, 1941.

Hunt, Lynn, ed. *The French Revolution in Culture*. Special issue of *Eighteenth-Century Studies* 22 (Spring 1989).

Hunter, Michael. *Establishing the New Science: The Experience of the Early Royal Society*. Woodbridge, Suffolk: Boydell Press, 1989.

——. *Science and Society in Restoration England*. Cambridge: Cambridge University Press, 1981.

Huppert, George. *Les Bourgeois Gentilshommes: An Essay on the Definition of Elites in Renaissance France*. Chicago: University of Chicago Press, 1977.

——. *The Idea of Perfect History: Historical Erudition and Historical Philosophy in Renaissance France*. Urbana, IL: University of Illinois Press, 1970.

Jacob, Margaret C. *The Newtonians and the English Revolution 1689–1720*. Ithaca, NY: Cornell University Press, 1976.

——. *Living the Enlightenment: Freemasonry and Politics in Eighteenth-Century Europe*. New York: Oxford University Press, 1991.

——. *The Radical Enlightenment: Pantheists, Freemasons and Republicans*. London: George Allen and Unwin, 1981.

Janssens-Knorsch, Uta. *Matthieu Maty and the Journal Britannique 1750–55.* Proefschrift Katholieke Universiteit te Nijmegen. Amsterdam: Holland University Press, 1975.

Jebb, Richard C. *Bentley.* London: Macmillan, 1882.

Johnson, Hubert C. *Frederick the Great and his Officials.* New Haven: Yale University Press, 1975.

Jolley, Nicholas. *Leibniz and Locke: A Study of the "New Essays on Human Understanding."* Oxford: Clarendon Press, 1984.

Jones, Richard Foster. *Ancients and Moderns: A Study of the Background of the "Battle of the Books."* St. Louis: Washington University, 1936.

———. *Lewis Theobald: His Contribution to English Scholarship.* New York: Columbia University Press, 1919.

Jordan, W.K. *The Development of Religious Toleration in England from the Beginning of the English Reformation to the Death of Queen Elizabeth.* London: George Allen and Unwin, 1932.

Kamen, Henry. *The Rise of Toleration.* New York: World University Library, 1967.

———. *The War of Succession in Spain 1700–15.* Bloomington IN: Indiana University Press, 1969.

Kämmerer, Jürgen. *Russland und die Hugenotten im 18. Jahrhundert (1689–1789).* Wiesbaden: Otto Harrassowitz, 1978.

Kaufman, Paul. *Libraries and their Users.* London: Library Association, 1969.

Kelley, Donald R. *The Beginning of Ideology: Consciousness and Society in the French Reformation.* Cambridge: Cambridge University Press, 1981.

———. *Foundations of Modern Historical Scholarship: Language, Law, and History in the French Renaissance.* New York: Columbia University Press, 1970.

Kenney, E.J. *The Classical Text: Aspects of Editing in the Age of the Printed Book.* Berkeley and Los Angeles: University of California Press, 1974.

Keohane, Nannerl O. *Philosophy and the State in France: The Renaissance to the Enlightenment.* Princeton: Princeton University Press, 1980.

Kernan, Alvin. *Printing Technology, Letters and Samuel Johnson.* Princeton: Princeton University Press, 1987.

Kettering, Sharon. *Patrons, Brokers and Clients in Seventeenth-Century France.* New York: Oxford University Press, 1986.

Kibre, Pearl. *Scholarly Privileges in the Middle Ages: The Rights, Privileges, and Immunities, of Scholars and Universities at Bologna, Padua, Paris, and Oxford.* Cambridge, Mass.: Mediaeval Academy of America, 1962.

Klaits, Joseph. *Printed Propaganda under Louis XIV: Absolute Monarchy and Public Opinion.* Princeton: Princeton University Press, 1976.

Kleerkooper, M.M., and W.P. van Stockum. *De Boekhandel te Amsterdam voornamelijk in de 17ᵉ Eeuw: Biographische en Geschiedkundige Aanteekeningen.* 2 vols. 's-Gravenhage: Martinus Nijhoff, 1914–16.

Klein, Lawrence E. *Shaftesbury and the Culture of Politeness: Moral Discourse and Cultural Politics in Early Eighteenth-Century England*. Cambridge: Cambridge University Press, 1994.

Knetsch, F.R.J. *Pierre Jurieu: Theoloog en Politicus der Refuge*. Kampen: 1967.

Koenen, H.J. *Geschiedenis van de Vestiging en den Invloed der Fransche Vluchtelingen in Nederland*. Leiden: S. & J. Luchtmans, 1846.

Kors, Alan Charles. *D'Holbach's Coterie: An Enlightenment in Paris*. Princeton: Princeton University Press, 1976.

——, and Paul Korshin, eds. *Anticipations of the Enlightenment in England, France, and Germany*. Philadelphia: University of Pennsylvania Press, 1987.

Korshin, Paul J., ed. *The Widening Circle: Essays on the Circulation of Literature in 18th-Century Europe*. Philadelphia: University of Pennsylvania Press, 1976.

Koselleck, Reinhart. *Critique and Crisis: Enlightenment and the Pathogenesis of Modern Society*. Oxford: Berg, 1988.

Kossmann, E.F. *De Boekhandel te 's-Gravenhage tot het eind de 18de eeuw*. 's-Gravenhage: Martinus Nijhoff, 1937.

Krieg, Walter. *Materialen zu einer Entwicklungsgeschichte der Bücher-Preise und des Autoren-Honorars vom 15. bis zum 20. Jahrhundert*. Vienna: Herbert Stubenrauch Verlagsbuchhandlung, 1953.

Kroll, Richard, Richard Ashcraft, and Perez Zagorin, eds. *Philosophy, Science, and Religion in England 1640–1700*. Cambridge: Cambridge University Press, 1992.

Kronick, David A. *A History of Scientific and Technical Periodicals: The Origins and Development of the Scientific and Technical Press 1665–1790*. 2nd ed. Metuchen, NJ: Scarecrow Press, 1976.

Kuper, Adam. *Anthropology and Anthropologists: The Modern British School*. 2nd ed. London: Routledge & Kegan Paul, 1983.

Labrosse, Claude, and Pierre Rétat. *L'Instrument périodique: la fonction de la presse au XVIIIᵉ siècle*. Lyon: Presses Universitaires de Lyon, 1985.

Labrousse, Elisabeth. *Inventaire critique de la correspondance de Pierre Bayle*. Paris: Librairie Philosophique J. Vrin, 1961.

——. *Pierre Bayle*. 2 vols. The Hague: Martinus Nijhoff, 1963, 1964.

——. *"Une foi, une loi, un roi?": La Révocation de l'Edit de Nantes*. Geneva: Labor et Fides, 1985.

Labrousse, Ernest, et al. *Histoire économique et sociale de la France*. Vol. 2. Paris: Presses Universitaires de France: 1970.

Laeven, A.H. *De 'Acta Eruditorum' onder Redactie van Otto Mencke (1644–1707): De Geschiedenis van een Internationaal Geleerdenperiodiek tussen 1682 en 1707*. Amsterdam and Maarssen: APA-Holland University Press, 1986.

Lankhorst, Otto S. *Reinier Leers (1654–1714) Uitgever & Boekverkoper te Rotterdam: Een Europees "Libraire" en zijn Fonds*. Amsterdam and Maarssen: APA-Holland Universiteits Pers, 1983.

Laplanche, François. *L'Ecriture, le sacré et l'histoire: Erudits et politiques protestants devant la Bible en France au XVIIe siècle.* Amsterdam and Maarssen: APA-Holland University Press, 1986.

Le Goff, Jacques, and René Rémond, eds. *Histoire de la France religieuse.* Vol. II: *Du christianisme flamboyant à l'aube des Lumières (XIVᵉ–XVIIIᵉ siècle).* Paris: Editions du Seuil, 1988.

Leiner, Wolfgang, ed. *Horizons européens de la littérature française au XVIIᵉ siècle. L'Europe: lieu d'échanges culturels? La Circulation des oeuvres et des jugements au XVIIᵉ siècle.* Actes du 17ᵉ Colloque du CMR 17, 30 Jan.–1 Feb. 1987, Tübingen. Tübingen: Gunter Narr Verlag, 1988.

Léonard, Emile G. *Histoire générale du protestantisme.* 2 vols. Paris: Presses Universitaires de France, 1961, 1964.

Levasseur, E. *Histoire du commerce de la France.* Vol. I. Paris: Arthur Rousseau, 1911.

Lévi-Strauss, Claude. *The Elementary Structures of Kinship.* Trans. James Harle Bell, John Richard von Sturmer, and Rodney Needham. Boston: Beacon Press, 1969. (First published in 1949.)

——. *Structural Anthropology.* Trans. Claire Jacobson and Brooke Grundfest Schoepf. New York: Basic Books, 1963. (First published in 1958.)

Levine, Joseph M. *The Battle of the Books: History and Literature in the Augustan Age.* Ithaca, NY: Cornell University Press, 1991.

——. *Dr. Woodward's Shield: History, Science, and Satire in Augustan England.* Berkeley and Los Angeles: University of California Press, 1977.

——. *Humanism and History: Origins of Modern English Historiography.* Ithaca: Cornell University Press, 1987.

Levy, Darline Gay. *The Ideas and Careers of Simon-Nicolas-Henri Linguet: A Study in Eighteenth-Century French Politics.* Urbana, Ill.: University of Illinois Press, 1980.

Levy, F.J. *Tudor Historical Thought.* San Marino: Huntington Library, 1967.

Lévy, Robert. *Le Mécénat et l'organisation du crédit intellectuel.* Paris: Presses Universitaires de France, 1924.

Lougee, Carolyn C. *Le Paradis des Femmes: Women, Salons, and Social Stratification in Seventeenth-Century France.* Princeton: Princeton University Press, 1976.

Lough, John. *Writer and Public in France from the Middle Ages to the Present Day.* Oxford: Clarendon Press, 1978.

Lunsingh Scheurleer, T.H., and G.H.M. Posthumus Meyjes, eds. *Leiden University in the Seventeenth Century: An Exchange of Learning.* Leiden: Universitaire Pers Leiden/E.J. Brill, 1975.

McAdoo, Henry R. *The Spirit of Anglicanism: A Survey of Anglican Theological Method in the Seventeenth Century.* New York: Charles Scribner's Sons, 1965.

McClellan, James E. III. *Science Reorganized: Scientific Societies in the Eighteenth Century.* New York: Columbia University Press, 1985.

Mack, Phyllis, and Margaret C. Jacob, eds. *Politics and Culture in Early Modern Europe*. Cambridge: Cambridge University Press, 1987.

McKenzie, D.F. *The Cambridge University Press 1696–1712: A Bibliographical Study*. 2 vols. Cambridge: Cambridge University Press, 1966.

McKerrow, Ronald B. *Introduction to Bibliography for Literary Students*. 2nd ed. Oxford: Clarendon Press, 1967. (First published in 1927.)

McLachlan, H. John. *Socinianism in Seventeenth-Century England*. London: Oxford University Press, 1951.

McManamon, John M. *Funeral Oratory and the Cultural Ideals of Italian Humanism*. Chapel Hill: University of North Carolina Press, 1989.

Magdelaine, Michelle, and Rudolf von Thadden, eds. *Le Refuge huguenot*. Paris: Armand Colin, 1985.

Magendie, Maurice. *La Politesse mondaine et les théories de l'honnêteté en France au XVIIᵉ siècle, de 1600 à 1660*. Paris: Presses Universitaires de France, 1925.

Magne, Emile. *Voiture et l'Hôtel de Rambouillet: Les Origines 1597–1635*. 6th ed. Paris: Editions Emile-Paul Frères, 1929.

Malinowski, Bronislaw. *Argonauts of the Western Pacific*. New York: E.P. Dutton, 1950.

Martin, Henri-Jean. *Le Livre français sous l'Ancien Régime*. Paris: Promodis, 1987.

——. *Livre pouvoirs et société à Paris au XVIIᵉ siècle (1598–1701)*. 2 vols. Geneva: Librairie Droz, 1969.

——, and Roger Chartier, eds. *Histoire de l'édition française*. Vol. II: *Le Livre triomphant 1660–1830*. Paris: Promodis, 1984.

Martines, Lauro. *The Social World of the Florentine Humanists 1390–1460*. Princeton: Princeton University Press, 1963.

Mauss, Marcel. *The Gift: Forms and Functions of Exchange in Archaic Societies*. Trans. Ian Cunnison. New York: W.W. Norton, 1967.

Mélèse, Pierre. *Un Homme de lettres au temps du grand roi: Donneau de Visé, fondateur du Mercure galant*. Paris: Librairie E. Droz, 1936.

Meylan, Philippe. *Jean Barbeyrac (1674–1744) et les débuts de l'enseignement du droit dans l'ancienne Académie de Lausanne*. Lausanne: F. Rouge, 1937.

Miller, Edward. *That Noble Cabinet: A History of the British Museum*. Athens, Ohio: Ohio University Press, 1974.

Moerikofer, J.-C. *Histoire des réfugiés de la Réforme en Suisse*. Paris: Librairie Sandoz & Fischbacher, 1978.

Moran, Bruce T., ed. *Science, Technology, and Medicine at the European Court 1500–1750*. Woodbridge, Suffolk: Boydell Press, 1991.

Morgan, Betty Trebelle. *Histoire du Journal des Sçavans depuis 1665 jusqu'en 1701*. Paris: Presses Universitaires de France, 1928.

Mortimer, Ruth. *A Portrait of the Author in Sixteenth Century France*. Chapel Hill: Hanes Foundation, 1980.

Mousnier, Roland. *Les Institutions de la France sous la monarchie absolue.* 2 vols. Paris: Presses Universitaires de France, 1974, 1980.

——, and Jean Mesnard, eds. *L'Age d'or du Mécénat (1598–1661).* Actes du colloque international CNRS (March 1983): Le Mécénat en Europe, et particulièrement en France avant Colbert. Paris: Editions du Centre National de la Recherche Scientifique, 1985.

Murdoch, Tessa, et al. *The Quiet Conquest: The Huguenots 1685 to 1985.* Exhibition catalogue. London: Museum of London in association with A.H. Jolly, 1985.

Musée Historique de l'Ancien-Evêché, Lausanne. *Le Refuge Huguenot en Suisse/ Die Hugenotten in der Schweiz.* Exhibition catalogue. Geneva: Editions du Tricorne, 1985.

Myers, Robin, and Michael Harris, eds. *Author/Publisher Relations during the Eighteenth and Nineteenth Centuries.* Oxford: Oxford Polytechnic Press, 1983.

Neumeister, Sebastian, and Conrad Wiedemann, eds. *Res Publica Litteraria: Die Institutionen der Gelehrsamkeit in die frühen Neuzeit.* 2 vols. Wiesbaden: Otto Harrassowitz, 1987.

O'Keefe, Cyril B. *Contemporary Reactions to the Enlightenment (1728–1762): A Study of Three Critical Journals: the Jesuit "Journal de Trévoux," the Jansenist "Nouvelles ecclésiastiques," and the secular "Journal des Savants."* Paris: Librairie Honoré Champion, 1974.

Olby, R.C., G.N. Cantor, J.R.R. Christie and M.J.S. Hodge, *Companion to the History of Modern Science.* London: Routledge, 1990.

O'Malley, John W. *Praise and Blame in Renaissance Rome: Rhetoric, Doctrine, and Reform in the Sacred Orators of the Papal Court, c. 1450–1521.* Durham, NC: Duke University Press, 1979.

Ousby, Ian. *The Englishman's England: Taste, Travel and the Rise of Tourism.* Cambridge: Cambridge University Press, 1990.

Parent, Annie. *Les Métiers du livre à Paris au XVIe siècle (1535–1560).* Geneva: Librairie Droz, 1974.

Paul, Charles, B. *Science and Immortality: The Eloges of the Paris Academy of Sciences (1699–1791).* Berkeley and Los Angeles: University of California Press, 1980.

Pellisson, Maurice. *Les Hommes de lettres au XVIIIe siècle.* Paris: Librairie Armand Colin, 1911.

Perry, Elisabeth Israels. *From Theology to History: French Religious Controversy and the Revocation of the Edict of Nantes.* The Hague: Martinus Nijhoff, 1973.

Picard, Roger. *Les Salons littéraires et la société française 1610–1789.* New York: Brentano's, 1943.

Pickering, Andrew, ed. *Science as Practice and Culture.* Chicago: University of Chicago Press, 1992.

Pienaar, W.J.B. *English Influences in Dutch Literature and Justus van Effen as Intermediary.* Cambridge: Cambridge University Press, 1929.

Pinto, Vivian de Sola. *English Biography in the Seventeenth Century*. London: George G. Harrap, 1951.

Plant, Marjorie. *The English Book Trade: An Economic History of the Making and Sale of Books*. London: George Allen and Unwin, 1939.

Pocock, J.G.A. *The Ancient Constitution and the Feudal Law: English Historical Thought in the Seventeenth Century*. New York: W.W. Norton, 1967. (First published in 1957.)

———. *Politics, Language and Time*. New York: Atheneum, 1973.

Pomian, Krzysztof. *Collectors and Curiosities: Paris and Venice, 1500–1800*. Trans. Elizabeth Wiles-Portier. Cambridge: Polity Press, 1990.

Popkin, Jeremy. *News and Politics in the Age of Revolution: Jean Luzac's Gazette de Leyde*. Ithaca: Cornell University Press, 1989.

———. *The Right-Wing Press in France, 1792–1800*. Chapel Hill: University of North Carolina Press, 1980.

Porter, Roy. *The Enlightenment*. London: Macmillan, 1990.

———, and Mikuláš Teich, eds. *The Enlightenment in National Context*. Cambridge: Cambridge University Press, 1981.

———, and Mikuláš Teich, eds. *The Scientific Revolution in National Context*. Cambridge: Cambridge University Press, 1992.

Pottinger, David T. *The French Book Trade in the Ancien Regime 1500–1791*. Cambridge, Mass.: Harvard University Press, 1958.

Prestwich, Menna, ed. *International Calvinism 1541–1715*. Oxford: Clarendon Press, 1985.

Quéniart, Jean. *Culture et société urbaines dans la France de l'Ouest au XVIIIe siècle*. Paris: Librairie C. Klincksieck, 1978.

———. *La Révocation de l'Edit de Nantes: Protestants et catholiques en France de 1598 à 1685*. Paris: Desclée de Brouwer, 1985.

Radcliffe-Brown, A.R. *Structure and Function in Primitive Society*. London: Free Press, 1965. (First published in 1952.)

Radiguer, Louis. *Maîtres imprimeurs et ouvriers typographes (1470–1903)*. Paris: Société Nouvelle de Librairie et d'Edition, 1903.

Ranum, Orest. *Artisans of Glory: Writers and Historical Thought in Seventeenth-Century France*. Chapel Hill: University of North Carolina Press, 1980.

Reed, Gervais E. *Claude Barbin, Libraire de Paris sous le règne de Louis XIV*. Geneva: Librairie Droz, 1974.

Reesink, H.J. *L'Angleterre et la littérature anglaise dans les trois plus anciens périodiques français de Hollande de 1684 à 1709*. Paris: Librairie Ancienne Honoré Champion, 1931.

Le Refuge Huguenot en Suisse/Die Hugenotten in der Schweiz. Exhibition Catalogue. Lausanne: Editions du Tricorne/Musée Historique de l'Ancien-Evêché, 1985.

Rétat, Pierre. *Le Dictionnaire de Bayle et la lutte philosophique au XVIIIe siècle*. Paris: Société d'Edition "Les Belles Lettres," 1971.

——. *Le Journalisme d'ancien régime: questions et propositions.* Table ronde CNRS, 12–13 June 1981. Lyon: Presses Universitaires de Lyon, 1982.

——, and Jean Sgard, eds. *Presse et histoire au XVIIIe siècle: l'année 1734.* Paris: Centre National de la Recherche Scientifique, 1978.

Reverdin, Olivier, et al. *Genève au temps de la Révocation de l'Edit de Nantes.* Geneva: Editions Société d'histoire et d'archéologie de Genève. 1985.

Rex, Walter. *Essays on Pierre Bayle and Religious Controversy.* The Hague: Martinus Nijhoff, 1965.

Reynolds, L.D., and N.G. Wilson. *Scribes and Scholars: A Guide to the Transmission of Greek and Latin Literature.* London: Oxford University Press, 1968.

Roche, Daniel. *Les Républicains des lettres: Gens de culture et lumières au XVIIIe siècle.* Paris: Librairie Arthème Fayard, 1988.

——. *Le Siècle des lumières en province: Académies et académiciens provinciaux, 1680–1789.* 2 vols. Paris: Mouton, 1978.

Rogers, Pat. *Grub Street: Studies in a Subculture.* London: Methuen, 1972.

Rosenberg, Hans. *Bureaucracy, Aristocracy and Autocracy: The Prussian Experience 1660–1815.* Cambridge, Mass.: Harvard University Press, 1958.

Rothrock, George A. *The Huguenots: A Biography of a Minority.* Chicago: Nelson-Hall, 1979.

Rudwick, Martin J.S. *The Great Devonian Controversy: The Shaping of Scientific Knowledge among Gentlemanly Specialists.* Chicago: University of Chicago Press, 1985.

Sahlins, Marshall. *Stone Age Economics.* Chicago: Aldine Atherton, 1972.

Saisselin, Rémy G. *The Enlightenment against the Baroque: Economics and Aesthetics in the Eighteenth Century.* Berkeley: University of California Press, 1992.

——. *The Literary Enterprise in Eighteenth-Century France.* Detroit: Wayne State University Press, 1979.

Saunders, John Whiteside. *The Profession of English Letters.* London: Routledge and Kegan Paul, 1964.

Sautijn Kluit, W.P. *Nagelaten Geschriften.* Bijdragen tot de Geschiedenis van den Nederlandschen Boekhandel, VII. Amsterdam: P.N. van Kampen & Zoon, 1896.

Sauvy, Anne. *Livres saisis à Paris entre 1678 et 1701.* The Hague: Martinus Nijhoff, 1972.

Sawyer, Jeffrey K. *Printed Poison: Pamphlet Propaganda, Faction Politics, and the Public Sphere in Early Seventeenth-Century France.* Berkeley: University of California Press, 1990.

Sayce, R.A. *Compositorial Practices and the Localization of Printed Books.* Oxford: Oxford Bibliographical Society, 1979.

Schalk, Ellery. *From Valor to Pedigree: Ideas of Nobility in France in the Sixteenth and Seventeenth Centuries.* Princeton: Princeton University Press, 1986.

Schiebinger, Londa. *The Mind has no Sex?: Women in the Origins of Modern Science.* Cambridge, Mass.: Harvard University Press, 1989.

Schlereth, Thomas J. *The Cosmopolitan Ideal in Enlightenment Thought: Its Form and Function in the Ideas of Franklin, Hume, and Voltaire, 1694–1790.* Notre Dame: University of Notre Dame Press, 1977.

Schneiders, Werner, ed. *Christian Thomasius 1655–1728: Interpretationen zu Werk und Wirkung.* Hamburg: Feliz Meiner Verlag, 1989.

Schumann, Herwart, Christa Kirsten, and Eva Beck. *Hugenotten in der Berliner Akademie: Dokumente ihres Wirkens im 18. Jahrhundert.* East Berlin: Akademie-Verlag, 1986.

Scouloudi, Irene, ed. *Huguenots in Britain and their French Background 1550–1800.* Totowa, NJ: Barnes and Noble Books, 1987.

Scoville, Warren C. *The Persecution of Huguenots and French Economic Development 1680–1720.* Berkeley and Los Angeles: University of California Press, 1960.

Sgard, Jean. *Prévost Romancier.* Paris: Librairie José Corti, 1968.

——, ed. *Dictionnaire des journaux 1600–1789.* Paris: Universitas, and Oxford: Voltaire Foundation, 1991.

——, with Michel Gilot and Françoise Weil. *Dictionnaire des journalistes (1600–1789).* Grenoble: Presses Universitaires de Grenoble, 1976.

Shapin, Steven. *A Social History of Truth: Civility and Science in Seventeenth-Century England.* Chicago: University of Chicago Press, 1994.

——, and Simon Schaffer. *Leviathan and the Air-Pump: Hobbes, Boyle, and the Experimental Life.* Princeton: Princeton University Press, 1985.

Shapiro, Barbara J. *Probability and Certainty in Seventeenth-Century England: A Study of the Relationships between Natural Science, Religion, History, Law, and Literature.* Princeton: Princeton University Press, 1983.

Simmel, Georg. *On Individuality and Social Forms.* Ed. Donald N. Levine. Chicago: University of Chicago Press, 1971.

Simpson, Percy. *Proof-Reading in the Sixteenth, Seventeenth, and Eighteenth Centuries.* London: Oxford University Press, 1935.

Sir Thomas Browne Institute. *Refugees and Emigrants in the Dutch Republic and England.* Leiden: Werkgroep Engels-Nederlandse Betrekkingen/Sir Thomas Browne Institute, 1986.

——. *The Role of Periodicals in the Eighteenth Century.* Leiden: Werkgroep Engels-Nederlandse Betrekkingen/Sir Thomas Browne Institute, 1984.

Smith, David Nichol. *Shakespeare in the Eighteenth Century.* Oxford: Clarendon Press, 1928.

Smith, Raymond. *The Archives of the French Protestant Church of London.* Huguenot Society of London Quarto Series, L. London: Huguenot Society of London, 1972.

Solomon, Howard M. *Public Welfare, Science, and Propaganda in Seventeenth Century France: The Innovations of Théophraste Renaudot.* Princeton: Princeton University Press, 1972.

Stankiewicz, W.J. *Politics and Religion in Seventeenth Century France: A Study of Political Ideas from the Monarchomachs to Bayle, as Reflected in the Toleration Controversy.* Berkeley and Los Angeles: University of California Press, 1960.

Stanton, Domna C. *The Aristocrat as Art: A Study of the Honnête Homme and the Dandy in Seventeenth and Nineteenth-Century French Literature.* New York: Columbia University Press, 1980.

Stauffer, Donald A. *The Art of Biography in Eighteenth Century England.* Princeton: Princeton University Press, 1941.

——. *English Biography before 1700.* Cambridge, Mass.: Harvard University Press, 1930.

Stewart, Larry. *The Rise of Public Science: Rhetoric, Technology, and Natural Philosophy in Newtonian Britain, 1660–1750.* Cambridge: Cambridge University Press, 1992.

Strosetzki, Christoph. *Rhétorique de la conversation: Sa dimension littéraire et linguistique dans la société française du XVIIe siècle.* Trans. into French by Sabine Seubert. Paris, Seattle, Tübingen: Biblio 17, 1984.

Suchier, Wolfram. *C.R. Dadichi, oder wie sich deutsche Orientalisten von einem Schwindler düpieren liessen.* Halle: Ehrhardt Karras, 1919.

Stroup, Alice. *A Company of Scientists: Botany, Patronage and Community at the Seventeenth-Century Parisian Royal Academy of Sciences.* Berkeley: University of California Press, 1990.

Sullivan, Alvin, ed. *British Literary Magazines: The Augustan Age and the Age of Johnson, 1698–1788.* Westport, CT: Greenwood Press, 1983.

Sutherland, L.S., and L.G. Mitchell, eds. *The History of the University of Oxford.* Vol. V: *The Eighteenth Century.* Oxford: Clarendon Press, 1986.

Sutherland, Nicola M. *The Huguenot Struggle for Recognition.* New Haven: Yale University Press, 1980.

Tave, Stuart M. *The Amiable Humorist.* Chicago: University of Chicago Press, 1960.

Tucoo-Chala, Suzanne. *Charles-Joseph Panckoucke et la librairie française 1736–1798.* Pau: Editions Marrimpovey Jeune, 1977.

Turner, Victor. *The Ritual Process: Structure and Anti Structure.* Ithaca: Cornell University Press, 1969.

Ultee, Maarten, ed. *Adapting to Conditions: War and Society in the Eighteenth Century.* University, Ala.: University of Alabama Press, 1986.

Van Kley, Dale. *The Jansenists and the Expulsion of the Jesuits from France 1757–1765.* New Haven: Yale University Press, 1975.

Veyrin-Forrer, Jeanne. *La Lettre et le texte: Trente années de recherches sur l'histoire du livre.* Paris: Ecole Normale Supérieure de Jeunes Filles, 1987.

Viala, Alain. *Naissance de l'écrivain: Sociologie de la littérature à l'âge classique.* Paris: Editions de Minuit, 1985.

Voet, Léon. *The Golden Compasses.* Trans. Raymond H. Kaye. 2 vols. Amsterdam: Vangendt, 1972.

Wade, Ira O. *The Clandestine Organization and Diffusion of Philosophic Ideas in France from 1700 to 1750.* Princeton: Princeton University Press, 1938.

——. *The Intellectual Origins of the French Enlightenment.* Princeton: Princeton University Press, 1971.

Wagner, Jacques. *Marmontel journaliste et le Mercure de France (1725–1761).* Grenoble: Presses Universitaires de Grenoble, 1975.

Waquet, Françoise. *Le Modèle français et l'Italie savante: Conscience de soi et perception de l'autre dans la République des Lettres (1660–1750).* Rome: Ecole française de Rome, 1989.

Webster, Charles. *The Great Instauration: Science, Medicine and Reform 1626–1660.* London: Duckworth, 1975.

Weill, Georges. *Le Journal: Origines, évolution, et rôle de la presse périodique.* Paris: La Renaissance du Livre, 1934.

Weiss, Charles. *Histoire des réfugiés protestants de France depuis la Révocation de l'Edit de Nantes jusqu'à nos jours.* 2 vols. Paris: Charpentier, 1853.

Westerfield, Ray Bert. *Middlemen in English Business Particularly Between 1660 and 1760.* (Transactions of the Connecticut Academy of Arts and Sciences, XIX, no. 2, May 1915.) New Haven: Yale University Press, 1915.

Westfall, Richard S. *Science and Religion in Seventeenth Century England.* Ann Arbor: University of Michigan Press, 1973. (First published in 1958.)

Whigham, Frank. *Ambition and Privilege: The Social Tropes of Elizabethan Courtesy Theory.* Berkeley: University of California Press, 1984.

Wolf, John B. *Louis XIV.* New York: W.W. Norton, 1968.

Wuthnow, Robert. *Communities of Discourse: Ideology and Social Structure in the Reformation, the Enlightenment, and European Socialism.* Cambridge, Mass.: Harvard University Press, 1989.

Wijngaards, Guus N.M. *De "Bibliothèque choisie" van Jean Le Clerc: Een Amsterdams geleerdentijdschrift uit de jaren 1703 tot 1713.* Amsterdam and Maarssen: APA-Holland Press, 1986.

Yates, Frances A. *The French Academies of the Sixteenth Century.* London: Routledge, 1988. (First published 1947.)

Yolton, John W. *Locke and the Compass of Human Understanding.* Cambridge: Cambridge University Press, 1970.

Ziechmann, Jürgen. *Panorama der Fridericianischen Zeit: Friedrich der Grosse und seine Epoche: Ein Handbuch.* Bremen: Edition Ziechmann, 1985.

Articles

Aarsleff, Hans. "Leibniz on Locke on Language." *American Philosophical Quarterly* I, no. 3 (1964), 165–88.

Allard, A. "Quelques réflexions sur le 'Rôle politique des Protestants Français,' de 1685 à 1715, et sur 'l'Histoire Politique des Protestants Français,' de 1715 à 1794, par l'abbé Joseph Dedieu." *Bulletin de la Commission de l'Histoire des Eglises Wallonnes* 3ᵉ ser., 12ᵉ livraison (1926), 21–35.

Altman, Janet Gurkin. "The Letter Book as a Literary Institution 1539–1789: Toward a Cultural History of Published Correspondences in France." *Yale French Studies* 71 (1986) 17–62.

Arnal, J. "Le Comité Vaudois." *Bulletin de la Commission pour l'Histoire des Eglises Wallonnes.* 4ᵉ ser., 8ᵉ livraison (1936), 5–40.

Baker, Keith. "Politics and Public Opinion under the Old Régime: Some Reflections." In Jack R. Censer and Jeremy Popkin, eds., *Press and Politics in Pre-Revolutionary France* (Berkeley: University of California Press, 1987).

Bax, W. "Sedan." *Bulletin de la Commission de l'Histoire des Eglises Wallonnes.* 4ᵉ ser., 8ᵉ livraison (1936), 41–104.

Berkvens-Stevelinck, Christiane M.G. "Les *Chevaliers de la Jubilation*: Maçonnerie ou libertinage?" *Quaerendo* XIII, pt. 1 (Winter 1983), 50–73, and XIII, pt. 2 (Spring 1983), 124–48.

———. "Prosper Marchand, 'trait d'union' entre auteur et éditeur." *De Gulden Passer* 56 (1978), 65–99.

———. Review of Margaret Jacob, *The Radical Enlightenment.* In *LIAS* IX, no. 1 (1982), 129–35.

Biagioli, Mario. "The Anthropology of Incommensurability." *Studies in History and Philosophy of Science* 21 (1990) 183–209.

———. "Galileo the Emblem Maker." *Isis* 81 (1990) 230–58.

———. "Galileo's System of Patronage." *History of Science* 28 (1990) 1–62.

———. "Scientific Revolution, Social Bricolage, and Etiquette." In Roy Porter and Mikuláš Teich, eds., *The Scientific Revolution in National Context.* Cambridge: Cambridge University Press, 1992.

———. "The Social Status of Italian Mathematicians, 1450–1600." *History of Science* 27 (1989) 69–95.

Birn, Raymond. "Le Journal des Savants sous l'Ancien Régime." *Journal des Savants* (Jan.–Mar. 1965), 15–35.

———. "*Livre et société* after ten years: Formation of a discipline." *Studies on Voltaire and the Eighteenth Century* CLI, no. 1 (1976), 287–312.

Bodel Bienfait, P.E.H. "L'Eglise Wallonne d'Utrecht." Part 2. *Bulletin de la Commission pour l'Histoire des Eglises Wallonnes* III (1888), 240–92.

Bond, Donald F. "Armand de la Chapelle and the first French Version of the Tatler." In Carroll Camden, ed., *Restoration and Eighteenth-Century Literature: Essays in Honor of Alan Dugald McKillop.* Chicago: University of Chicago Press, 1963, pp. 161–84.

Bonno, Gabriel. "Locke et son traducteur français Pierre Coste." *Revue de littérature comparée* XXXIII, no. 2 (1959) 161–79.

Botein, S., J. Censer, and H. Ritvo. "La Presse périodique et la société anglaise et française au XVIIIᵉ siècle: une approche comparative." *Revue d'histoire moderne et contemporaine* XXXII (April–June 1985), 209–36.

Bots, Hans. "L'Esprit de la République des Lettres et la tolérance dans les trois premiers périodiques savants hollandais." *XVIIᵉ siècle* CXVI (1977), 43–57.

Bresson, L. "L'Eglise Wallonne de Rotterdam: sa vie intérieure, son développement, et son influence." *Bulletin de la Commission pour l'Histoire des Eglises Wallonnes.* 2ᵉ ser. IV (1909), 355–98.

Briggs, Robin. "The Académie Royale des Sciences and the Pursuit of Utility." *Past and Present* 131 (1990) 38–88.

Broome, J.H. "Bayle's Biographer: Pierre Des Maizeaux." *French Studies* IX, no. 1 (Jan. 1955), 1–17.

———. "Pierre Desmaizeaux, journaliste. Les nouvelles littéraires de Londres entre 1700 et 1740." *Revue de littérature comparée* XXIX, no. 2 (April–June 1955), 184–205.

Brown, Harcourt. "History and the Learned Journal." *Journal of the History of Ideas* XXXIII, no. 3 (July–Sept. 1972), 365–78.

Chartier, Roger. "Espace social et imaginaire social: Les intellectuels frustrés au XVIIᵉ siècle." *Annales E.S.C.* XXXVII, no. 2 (March–April 1982), 389–400.

———, and Daniel Roche. "L'Histoire quantitative du livre." *Revue français d'histoire du livre* n.s. XVI (1977) 477–501.

———. "Le Livre: Un changement de perspective." In Jacques Le Goff and Pierre Nora, eds., *Faire de l'histoire: Nouveaux objets.* Paris: Gallimard, 1974. III, pp. 115–36.

Cler, S. "La Bourse des Etudes et le Recrutement du Corps Pastoral Wallon." *Bulletin de la Commission pour l'Histoire des Eglises Wallonnes* 3ᵉ ser., 1ᵉ livraison (1911), 7–45.

———. "Les Versions Bibliques dans les Eglises Wallonnes des Pays-Bas." *Bulletin de la Commission pour l'Histoire des Eglises Wallonnes.* 3ᵉ ser., 10ᵉ livraison (1924), 1–30.

Clifford, James L. "How Much Should a Biographer Tell? Some Eighteenth-Century Views." In Philip B. Daghlian, ed., *Essays in Eighteenth-Century Biography.* Bloomington: Indiana University Press, 1968.

Cranston, Maurice. "John Locke's Correspondence with Esther Masham." *Newberry Library Bulletin* ser. 2, no. 4 (July 1950), 121–35.

Darnton, Robert. "A Police Inspector Sorts his Files: The Anatomy of the Republic of Letters." In *The Great Cat Massacre and Other Episodes in French Cultural History.* New York: Basic Books, 1984.

———. "Sounding the Literary Market in Prerevolutionary France." *Eighteenth-Century Studies* 17, no. 4 (Summer 1984), 477–92.

Daston, Lorraine. "The Ideal and Reality of the Republic of Letters in the Enlightenment." *Science in Context* 4, no. 2 (1991), 367–86.

Davis, Natalie Zemon. "Beyond the Market: Books as Gifts in Sixteenth-Century France." *Transactions of the Royal Historical Society* 5th ser., 33 (1983), 69–88.

———. "A Renaissance Text to the Historian's Eye: The Gifts of Montaigne." *Journal of Medieval and Renaissance Studies* 15, no. 1 (Spring 1985) 47–56.

Dear, Peter. "*Totius in verba*: Rhetoric and Authority in the Early Royal Society." *Isis* 76 (1985) 145–61.

De Beer, E.S. "The Huguenots and the Enlightenment." *Huguenot Society of London Proceedings* XXI, no. 3 (1968), 179–85.

Dens, Jean-Pierre. "L'Art de la conversation au dix-septième siècle." *Les Lettres Romanes* 27, no. 3 (Aug. 1973) 215–24.

Dibon, Paul. "Communication in the Respublica literaria of the 17th century." *Res Publica Litterarum* I (1978), 43–55.

———. "Les échanges épistolaires dans l'Europe savante du XVIIᵉ siècle." *Revue de synthèse* 3rd ser., 81–2 (Jan.–June 1976), 31–50.

———. "L'Université de Leyde et la République des Lettres au 17ᵉ siècle." *Quaerendo* V, no. 1 (Jan. 1975), 4–38.

Du Bois-Reymond, Emil. "Die Berliner Französische Kolonie in der Akademie der Wissenschaften." In *Reden von Emil Du Bois-Reymond*. Vol. II. 2nd ed. Leipzig: Veit, 1912, pp. 301–20.

Duchêne, Roger. "Lettres et gazettes au XVIIᵉᵐᵉ siècle." *Revue d'histoire moderne et contemporaine* XVIII (Oct.–Dec. 1971), 489–502.

Du Rieu, W.N. "Essai bibliographique concernant tout ce qui a paru dans les Pays-Bas au sujet des Vaudois et en leur faveur." *Bulletin de la Commission pour l'Histoire des Eglises Wallonnes* IV (1890), 105–38.

Dijk, Willibrord-Christian van. "Remarques sur les 'Epîtres dédicatoires' des XVIIᵉ et XVIIIᵉ siècles." *Revue française d'histoire du livre* n.s. no. 40 (July–Sept. 1983), 191–209.

Eeghen, I.H. van. "Newspaper Management in the 18th Century: from the Commercial Books of the Amsterdamse Courant, 1767–1795." *Gazette: International Journal of the Science of the Press* I, no. 1 (Jan. 1955), 5–16.

Enschedé, J.-W. "Quelques mots sur Etienne Roger, marchand libraire à Amsterdam." *Bulletin de la Commission pour l'Histoire des Eglises Wallonnes* 2nd ser. I (1896), 208–15.

Enschedé, M.A.J. "Résolutions prises par les Etats Généraux, les Etats de Hollande et de West-Frise, la Commission Permanente de ces Etats, ainsi que par le Conseil-d'Etat en faveur des Réfugiés." *Bulletin de la Commission pour l'Histoire des Eglises Wallonnes* IV (1890), 313–36.

Feather, John. "The Commerce of Letters: The Study of the Eighteenth-Century Book Trade." *Eighteenth-Century Studies* XVII, no. 4 (Summer 1984), 405–24.

Findlen, Paula. "The Economy of Scientific Exchange in Early Modern Italy." In Bruce T. Moran, *Patronage and Institutions: Science, Technology and Medicine at the European Court 1500–1700*. Woodbridge, Suffolk: Boydell Press, 1991.

——. "Science as a Career in Enlightenment Italy: The Strategies of Laura Bassi." *Isis* 84 (1993), 441–69.

Feingold, Mordechai. "Philanthropy, Pomp, and Patronage: Historical Reflections upon the Endowment of Culture." *Daedalus* CXVI, no. 1 (Winter 1987), 155–78.

Fuchs, James L. "Borrowed Criticism and Bayle Criticism." *Nouvelles de la République des Lettres* I (1985), 97–110.

Fumaroli, Marc. "La Conversation." In Pierre Nora, ed., *Les Lieux de mémoire* vol. III, no. 2. Paris: Gallimard, 1992.

——. "The Republic of Letters." *Diogenes* 143 (Fall 1988), 134–9.

Gagnebin, F.H. "Liste des Eglises Wallonnes des Pays-Bas et des Pasteurs qui les ont desservies." *Bulletin de la Commission pour l'Histoire des Eglises Wallonnes* III (1888), 25–64, 97–120, 209–40, 313–45.

——. "Pasteurs de France réfugiés en Hollande." *Bulletin de la Commission pour l'Histoire des Eglises Wallonnes* I (1885), 97–151.

Gelbart, Nina R. "'Frondeur' Journalism in the 1770s: Theater Criticism and Radical Politics in the Prerevolutionary French Press." *Eighteenth-Century Studies* 17 (1984) 493–514.

Gibbs, Graham C. "Huguenot Contributions to the Intellectual Life of England, c. 1680–c. 1720, with some Asides on the Process of Assimilation." In *La Révocation de l'Edit de Nantes et les Provinces-Unies*, 1685. Colloque International du Tricentaire, Leiden, 1–3 April 1985. Amsterdam and Maarssen: APA, Holland University Press, 1986.

——. "Some Intellectual and Political Influences of the Huguenot Emigrés in the United Provinces, c. 1680–1730." *Bijdragen en Mededelingen betreffende de Geschiedenis der Nederlanden* XC, afl. 2 (1975), 255–87.

——. Review of Margaret Jacob, *The Radical Enlightenment*. In *British Journal for the History of Science* XVIII (1984), 67–79.

——. "The Role of the Dutch Republic as the Intellectual Entrepôt of Europe in the Seventeenth and Eighteenth Centuries." *Bijdragen en Mededelingen betreffende de Geschiedenis der Nederlanden* LXXXVI, afl. 3 (1971), 323–49.

Gigas, Emile. "La Première ébauche d'un ouvrage célèbre." *Bulletin de la Commission pour l'histoire des Eglises Wallonnnes*, 2nd ser. II (1899), 65–74.

Goldgar, Anne. "The Absolutism of Taste: Journalists as Censors in Eighteenth-Century Paris." In Robin Myers and Michael Harris, eds., *Censorship and the Control of Print in England and France, 1600–1910*. Winchester: St. Paul's Bibliographies, 1992.

Goldgar, Bertrand A. "Pope and the Grub-street Journal." *Modern Philology* LXXIV, no. 4 (May 1977), 366–80.

Golinski, Jan. "A Noble Spectacle: Phosphorus and the Public Cultures of Science in the early Royal Society." *Isis* 80 (1989) 11–39.

——. "The Secret Life of an Alchemist." In John Fauvel, Raymond Flood,

Michael Shortland, and Robin Wilson, eds. *Let Newton Be!* Oxford: Oxford University Press, 1988.

——. "The Theory of Practice and the Practice of Theory: Sociological Approaches in the History of Science." *Isis* 81 (1990) 492–505.

Goodman, Dena. "Enlightenment Salons: The Convergence of Female and Philosophic Ambitions." *Eighteenth-Century Studies* 22, no. 3 (Spring 1989) 329–50.

——. "The Hume-Rousseau Affair: From Private *Querelle* to Public *Procès*." *Eighteenth-Century Studies* 25, no. 2 (Winter 1991–2) 171–201.

——. "Pigalle's *Voltaire nu*: The Republic of Letters Represents Itself to the World." *Representations* XVI (Fall 1986) 86–109.

——. "Public Sphere and Private Life: Toward a Synthesis of Current Historiographical Approaches to the Old Régime." *History and Theory* 31, no. 1 (1992) 1–20.

——. "Seriousness of Purpose: Salonnières, Philosophes, and the Shaping of the Eighteenth-Century Salon." *Proceedings of the Annual Meeting of the Western Society for French History* 15 (1988) 111–18.

——. "Story-Telling in the Republic of Letters: The Rhetorical Context of Diderot's *La Réligieuse*." *Nouvelles de la République des Lettres* no. 1 (1986), 51–70.

Gordon, Daniel. " 'Public Opinion' and the Civilizing Process in France: The Example of Morellet." *Eighteenth-Century Studies* 22, no. 3 (Spring 1989) 302–28.

Goujard, Philippe. " 'Féodalité' et Lumières au XVIIIe siècle. L'exemple de la noblesse." *Annales historiques de la Révolution Française* 49 (1977) 103–18.

Grimm, Gunter E. "Vom Schulfuchs zum Menschheitslehrer. Zum Wandel des Gelehrtums zwischen Barock und Aufklärung." In Hans Erich Bödeker and Ulrich Herrmann, eds., *Über den Prozess der Aufklärung in Deutschland im 18. Jahrhundert: Personen, Institutionen und Medien*. Göttingen: Vandenhoeck und Ruprecht, 1987, pp. 14–38.

Grivel, Marianne. "Le Cabinet du Roi." *Revue de la Bibliothèque Nationale* XVIII (winter 1985), 36–57.

Gwynn, Robin D. "The Arrival of Huguenot Refugees in England 1680–1705." *Proceedings of the Huguenot Society of London* XXI, no. 4 (1968), 366–73.

——. "The Distribution of Huguenot Refugees in England." *Proceedings of the Huguenot Society of London* XXI, no. 5 (1969), 404–35.

Hahn, Roger. "The Age of Academies." Nobel Symposium, "Salomon's House Revisited," Stockholm, Aug. 14, 1989.

Hanley, William. "The Policing of Thought: Censorship in Eighteenth-Century France." *Studies on Voltaire and the Eighteenth Century* CLXXXIII (1980), 265–95.

Harris, Michael. "The Management of the London Newspaper Press during the Eighteenth Century." *Publishing History* IV (1978), 95–112.

——. "Newspaper distribution during Queen Anne's Reign" Charles Delafaye and the Secretary of State's Office." In R.W. Hunt et al., eds., *Studies in the Book Trade in Honour of Graham Pollard*. Oxford: Oxford Bibliographical Society, 1975, pp. 139–51.

Hunter, J. Paul. "Biography and the Novel." *Modern Language Studies* IX (Fall 1979), 68–84.

Iliffe, Rob. "'In the Warehouse': Privacy, Property and Priority in the Early Royal Society." *History of Science* 30 (1992) 29–68.

Jacob, James R. "Restoration, Reformation and the Origins of the Royal Society." *History of Science* XIII (1975), 155–76.

Jacob, Margaret C. "The Crisis of the European Mind: Hazard Revisited." In Phyllis Mack and Margaret C. Jacob, eds., *Politics and Culture in Early Modern Europe: Essays in Honor of H.G. Koenigsberger*. Cambridge: Cambridge University Press, 1987.

——. "The Knights of Jubilation—Masonic and Libertine—A Reply." *Quaerendo* XIV, pt. 1 (Winter 1984), 63–75.

Janssens, Uta. "Jean Deschamps (1709–67) and the French Colony in Berlin." *Proceedings of the Huguenot Society of London* XXXIII, no. 4 (1980), 227–39.

Kan, J.B. "Bayle et Jurieu." *Bulletin de la Commission pour l'Histoire des Eglises Wallonnes* IV (1890), 139–99.

Kettering, Sharon. "Gift-giving and Patronage in Early Modern France." *French History* 2, no. 2 (June 1988) 131–51.

King, George V. "Michel de La Roche et ses *Mémoires Littéraires de la Grande-Bretagne*," *Revue de littérature comparée* XV, no. 2 (April–June 1935), 298–300.

Klaveren, G. van. "Nicolaas Chevalier en zijn 'Chambre de Raretez.'" *Jaarboekje van "Oud-Utrecht"* (1940), 141–57.

Klein, Lawrence. "Liberty, Manners, and Politeness in early Eighteenth-Century England." *Historical Journal* 32, no. 3 (1989), 583–605.

——. "The Third Earl of Shaftesbury and the Progress of Politeness." *Eighteenth-Century Studies* 18, no. 2 (Winter 1984–5) 186–214.

Knight, Charles A. "Bibliography and the Shape of the Literary Periodical in the Early Eighteenth Century." *The Library*, 6th ser. VIII, no. 3 (Sept. 1986), 232–48.

Knox, Dilwyn. "*Disciplina*: The Monastic and Clerical Origins of European Civility." In John Monfasani and Ronald G. Musto, eds., *Renaissance Society and Culture: Essays in Honor of Eugene F. Rice, Jr*. New York: Italica Press, 1991.

Korshin, Paul J. "Types of Eighteenth-Century Literary Patronage." *Eighteenth-Century Studies* VII, no. 4 (Summer 1974), 453–73.

——. Review of Michael Foss, *The Age of Patronage: The Arts in England 1660–1750*. In *Eighteenth-Century Studies* VII, no. 1 (Fall 1973), 101–5.

Krauss, Werner. "La Correspondance de Formey." *Revue d'histoire littéraire de la France* LXIII (1963), 207–16.

Lemonnier, P. "Espionnage et contre-espionnage à Rochefort en 1696." *Bulletin de la Société des Archives Historiques de la Saintonge et d'Aunis* XLI no. 1 (1924), 1–20.

Lévi-Strauss, Claude. "Introduction à l'oeuvre de Marcel Mauss." In Mauss, *Sociologie et Anthropologie*. 3rd ed. Paris: Presses Universitaires de France, 1966.

Levine, Joseph M. "Ancients, Moderns, and History: The Continuity of English Historical Writing in the Later Seventeenth Century." In Paul J. Korshin, ed., *Studies in Change and Revolution: Aspects of English Intellectual History 1640–1800*. London: Scolar Press, 1972.

Lougee, Carolyn. "Salons and Conversation: Comment." *Proceedings of the Annual Meeting of the Western Society for French History* 15 (1988) 119–21.

McKenzie, D.F. "Printers of the Mind: Some Notes on Bibliographical Theories and Printing-House Practices." *Studies in Bibliography* XXII (1969), 1–75.

Malinowski, Bronislaw. "The Primitive Economics of the Trobriand Islanders." *Economic Journal* XXXI (1921), 1–16.

Marx, Jacques. "Une revue oubliée du XVIIIᵉ siècle: *La Bibliothèque impartiale*." *Romanische Forschungen* LXXX, no. 2–3 (1968), 281–91.

Masson, Gustave. "Des Maizeaux et ses Correspondants." *Bulletin de la Société de l'Histoire du Protestantisme Français* XV (1866), no. 5, 237–47; no. 6, 284–92; no. 7, 332–9.

Mauss, Marcel. "Essai sur le don: Forme et raison de l'échange dans les sociétés archaïques." *L'Année sociologique* n.s. I (1923–4), 30–186.

Mayo, Ronald. "The British Huguenots 1681–1791." *Proceedings of the Huguenot Society of London* XXI, no. 5 (1969), 437–54.

Maza, Sara. "Le Tribunal de la nation: les mémoires judiciaires et l'opinion publique à la fin de l'Ancien Régime." *Annales ESC* (Jan.–Feb. 1987), 73–90.

Merton, Robert K. "Science, Technology and Society in Seventeenth Century England." *Osiris* IV (1938) 360–632.

Mesnard, Pierre. "Le Commerce épistolaire, comme expression sociale de l'individualisme humaniste." In *Individu et société à la Renaissance*. Colloque international, April 1965. Brussels: Presses Universitaires de Bruxelles, 1967.

Mirandolle, R.-N.-L. "A propos d'une lettre de Pierre Jurieu." *Bulletin de la Commission pour l'Histoire des Eglises Wallonnes* 2nd ser. II (1899) 237–70.

Mornet, Daniel. "Comment étudier les écrivains ou les ouvrages de troisième ou quatrième ordre (Le Mercure galant de 1672 à 1700)." *Romanic Review* XXVIII, no. 3 (Oct. 1937), 204–17.

———. "Les enseignements des bibliothèques privées (1750–1780)." *Revue d'histoire littéraire de la France* XVII (1910), 449–98.

Mounier, P.J.J. "Les Eglises Wallonnes des Pays-Bas, lien entre l'Eglise Réformée du Pays et les Eglises soeurs de l'Etranger." *Bulletin de la Commission pour l'Histoire des Eglises Wallonnes* 2nd ser. IV (1909), 51–83.

Oosterzee, Jan Jacob van. "Nog iets over Jacques Saurin." *Jaarboeken voor Wetenschappelijke Theologie* XVIII (1856), 469–78.

Outram, Dorinda. "Cosmopolitan Correspondence: A Calendar of the Letters of Georges Cuvier (1769–1832)." *Archives* XVI no. 69 (April 1983) 47–53.

——. "The Language of Natural Power: The 'Eloges' of Georges Cuvier and the Public Language of Nineteenth-Century Science." *History of Science* 16 (1978) 153–78.

Ozouf, Mona. "'Public Opinion' and the End of the Old Régime." *Journal of Modern History* 60 (Sept. 1988), 1–21.

Panoff, Michael. "Marcel Mauss's *The Gift* Revisited." *Man: The Journal of the Royal Anthropological Institute* n.s. V, no. 1 (March 1970), 60–70.

Perk, M.A. "La Révocation de l'Edit de Nantes et ses conséquences pour les Eglises Wallonnes des Pays-Bas." *Bulletin de la Commission pour l'Histoire des Eglises Wallonnes* II (1867), 2–45.

Perla, Georges G. "La Controverse sur les 'Vies' dans l'*Encyclopédie*." *Revue française d'histoire du livre* n.s., XXXIV (Jan.–Mar. 1982), 41–61.

Phillipson, Nicholas. "Intuitions and Interactions." *Times Literary Supplement*, Jan. 24, 1975, p. 90.

Pinto, Louis. "Une science des intellectuels est-elle possible?" *Revue de synthèse* 4th ser. IV (Oct.–Dec. 1986), 345–60.

Popkin, Richard H. "Serendipity at the Clark: Spinoza and the Prince of Condé." *Clark Newsletter* no. 10 (Spring 1986), 4–7.

Pottle, Frederick A. "Printer's Copy in the Eighteenth Century." *Papers of the Bibliographical Society of America* XXVII, pt. 2 (1933), 65–73.

Preston, Joseph H. "Was there an Historical Revolution?" *Journal of the History of Ideas* XXXVIII, no. 2 (April–June 1977), 353–64.

Radcliffe-Brown, A.R. "The Interpretation of Andaman Island Ceremonies." In *The Social Anthropology of Radcliffe-Brown*. London: Routledge and Kegan Paul, 1977.

Reynolds, Beatrice. "Shifting Currents in Historical Criticism." *Journal of the History of Ideas* XIV, no. 4 (Oct. 1953), 471–92.

Rychner, Jacques. "Running a Printing House in Eighteenth Century Switzerland: The Workshop of the Société Typographique de Neuchâtel." *The Library* 6th ser. I, no. 1 (March 1979), 1–24.

Sahlins, Marshall. "The Spirit of the Gift: *Une explication de Texte*." In Jean Pouillon and Pierre Maranda, eds., *Echanges et communications: Mélanges offerts à Claude Lévi-Strauss à l'occasion de son 60ème anniversaire*. The Hague: Mouton, 1970.

Sarasohn, Lisa T. "Nicolas-Claude Fabri de Peiresc and the Patronage of the New Science in the Seventeenth Century." *Isis* 84 (1992), 70–90.

Schaffer, Simon. "The Consuming Flame: Electrical Showmen and Tory Mystics in the World of Goods." In John Brewer and Roy Porter, eds., *Consumption and the World of Goods*. London: Routledge, 1993.

——. "Making Certain." *Social Studies of Science* 14 (1984) 137–52.

——. "Natural Philosophy and Public Spectacle in the Eighteenth Century." *History of Science* 21 (1983) 1–43.

Sgard, Jean. "Journalistes français en Suisse (1685–1789)." In Jean-Daniel Candaux and Bernard Lescaze, eds., *Cinq siècles d'imprimerie genevoise*. Geneva: Société d'Histoire et d'Archéologie, 1981.

Shapin, Steven. "Homo Phrenologicus: Anthropological Perspectives on an Historical Problem." In Barry Barnes and Steven Shapin, eds., *Natural Order: Historical Studies of Scientific Culture*. Beverley Hills, CA: Sage Publications, 1979.

——. "The House of Experiment in Seventeenth-Century England." *Isis* 79 (1988) 373–404.

——. " 'The Mind is its Own Place': Science and Solitude in Seventeenth-Century England." *Science in Context* 4, no. 1 (1990), 191–218.

——. "O Henry." *Isis* 78 (1987) 417–24.

——. "Pump and Circumstance: Robert Boyle's Literary Technology." *Social Studies of Science* 14 (1984) 481–520.

——. "Social Uses of Science." In G.S. Rousseau and Roy Porter, eds., *The Ferment of Knowledge: Studies in the Historiography of Eighteenth-Century Science*. Cambridge: Cambridge University Press, 1980.

——. " 'A Scholar and a Gentleman': The Problematic Identity of the Scientific Practitioner in Early Modern England." *History of Science* 29, part 3, no. 85 (Sept. 1991) 279–327.

Shapiro, Barbara J. "Latitudinarianism and Science in Seventeenth-Century England." *Past and Present* 40 (July 1968), 18–41.

Slee, J.C. van. "De Waalsche Gemeente te Deventer." *Bulletin de la Commission de l'Histoire des Eglises Wallonnes* 3rd ser., 9th livraison (1921), 47–142.

Stewart, Larry. "The Selling of Newton: Science and Technology in Early Eighteenth-Century England." *Journal of British Studies* 25 (April 1986), 178–92.

Stone, Lawrence. "The Educational Revolution in England 1560–1640." *Past and Present* 28 (1964), 41–80.

Sypher, George Wylie. "Popelinière's *Histoire de France*: A Case of Historical Objectivity and Religious Censorship." *Journal of the History of Ideas* XXIV (1963), 41–54.

——. "Similarities between the Scientific and the Historical Revolutions at the End of the Renaissance." *Journal of the History of Ideas* XXVI, no. 3 (July–Sept. 1965), 353–68.

Taton, René. "Le Role et l'importance des correspondances scientifiques aux XVIIᵉ et XVIIIᵉ siècles." *Revue de synthèse*, 3rd ser., 81–2 (Jan.–June 1976), 7–22.

Treadwell, Michael. "London Trade Publishers 1675–1750." *The Library*, 6th ser. VI, no. 2 (June 1982), 99–134.

Tribby, Jay. "Cooking (with) Clio and Cleo: Eloquence and Experiment in Seventeenth-Century Florence." *Journal of the History of Ideas* 52, no. 3 (July–Sept. 1991), 417–39.

Ultee, Maarten. "The Republic of Letters: Learned Correspondence 1680–1720." *Seventeenth Century* II, no. 1 (Jan. 1987), 95–112.

Waquet, Françoise. "De la lettre érudite au périodique savant: les faux semblants d'une mutation intellectuelle." *XVIIe siècle* XXXV, no. 3 (July–Sept. 1983), 347–59.

———. "Qu'est-ce que la République des Lettres? Essai de sémantique historique." *Bibliothèque de l'Ecole des chartes* 147 (1989), 473–502.

———, and Jean-Claude Waquet. "Presse et société: le public des 'Novelle Letterarie' de Florence (1749–1769). *Revue française d'histoire du livre* n.s. XXII (Jan.–Mar. 1979), 39–60.

Westerfield, Ray Bert. "Middlemen in English Business, Particularly between 1660 and 1760." *Transactions of the Connecticut Academy of Arts and Sciences* XIX, no. 2 (May 1915), 345–61.

Wiener, Philip P. "Leibniz's Project of a Public Exhibition of Scientific Inventions." *Journal of the History of Ideas* I (1940), 232–40.

Woodmansee, Martha. "The Genius and the Copyright: Economic and Legal Conditions of the Emergence of the 'Author.'" *Eighteenth-Century Studies* XVII, no. 4 (Summer 1984), 425–48.

Yardeni, Myriam. "Journalisme et histoire contemporaine à l'époque de Bayle." *History and Theory* XII, no. 2 (1973), 208–29.

Zuber, Roger. "L'Humanisme et les savants: de Peiresc aux Perrault." *Revue française d'histoire du livre* n.s. no. 38 (Jan.–Mar. 1983), 33–51.

Theses

Broome, J.H. "An Agent in Anglo-French Relationships: Pierre Des Maizeaux, 1673–1745." PhD thesis, University of London, 1949.

Cohen, Michèle B. "A Genealogy of Conversation: Gender Subjectivation and Learning French in England." PhD thesis, University of London, 1993.

Deyk, Frank van. "De Spiegel van Clio: Een Beschouwing van de Politieke en Historiografische Activiteiten van Elie Benoist (1640–1728)." Doctoraal scriptie, Rijksuniversiteit te Leiden, 1988.

Gordon, Daniel. "The Idea of Sociability in Pre-Revolutionary France." PhD thesis, University of Chicago, 1990.

Johns, Adrian. "Wisdom in the Concourse: Natural Philosophy and the History of the Book in Early Modern England." PhD thesis, Cambridge University, 1992.

INDEX

DATE DUE
